LANDMARK CASES IN SUCCESSION LAW

The *Landmark Cases* series highlights the historical antecedents of what are widely considered to be the leading cases in a discipline, and seeks to provide contexts in which to better understand how and why certain cases came to be regarded as the 'landmark' cases in any given field. Succession law's long pedigree, near-universal application, immense capacity for human interest stories, somewhat uncertain future in England and Wales, and close connection to demographics make it an ideal candidate for a *Landmark Cases* volume. The distinguished contributors to this collection consider cases ranging in decision date from 1720 to 2017, covering issues such as will-making and interpretation, the position of beneficiaries and personal representatives, testamentary promises, and the extent of testamentary freedom in England and Wales and beyond. The cases are relevant not only to scholars and students of succession law per se, but also those working in fields such as tax, trusts, tort and land law. They raise issues as diverse as class, colonialism, familial dynamics, expectations and obligations, mental health, and the proper roles of the legal profession and the welfare state. The collection will provoke much discussion on what makes a 'landmark' case, as well as on the peculiarities and limitations of the case law method.

Landmark Cases in Succession Law

Edited by
Brian Sloan

•HART•
OXFORD • LONDON • NEW YORK • NEW DELHI • SYDNEY

HART PUBLISHING
Bloomsbury Publishing Plc
Kemp House, Chawley Park, Cumnor Hill, Oxford, OX2 9PH, UK
1385 Broadway, New York, NY 10018, USA
29 Earlsfort Terrace, Dublin 2, Ireland

HART PUBLISHING, the Hart/Stag logo, BLOOMSBURY and the Diana logo are trademarks of Bloomsbury Publishing Plc
First published in Great Britain 2019

First published in hardback, 2019
Paperback edition, 2021

A catalogue record for this book is available from the British Library.

Library of Congress Cataloging-in-Publication Data

Names: Sloan, Brian, 1984- editor.

Title: Landmark cases in succession law / edited by Brian Sloan.

Description: Oxford ; New York Hart, 2019. | Series: Landmark cases | Includes bibliographical references and index.

Identifiers: LCCN 2019029558 (print) | LCCN 2019029559 (ebook) | ISBN 9781509919000 (hardback) | ISBN 9781509919017 (EPub)

Subjects: LCSH: Inheritance and succession—England—Cases. | LCGFT: Textbooks.

Classification: LCC KD1500 .L36 2019 (print) | LCC KD1500 (ebook) | DDC 346.4205/2—dc23

LC record available at https://lccn.loc.gov/2019029558

LC ebook record available at https://lccn.loc.gov/2019029559

ISBN: HB: 978-1-50991-900-0
PB: 978-1-50995-210-6
ePDF: 978-1-50991-902-4
ePub: 978-1-50991-901-7

Typeset by Compuscript Ltd, Shannon

Preface

I AM DELIGHTED to have been allowed to subject succession law to the *Landmark Cases* treatment. While it would be both a cliché and a gross exaggeration to claim that this book breathes life into the crucial discipline, I do hope that it will be of both interest and utility to those working inside the field and in the wider legal world. Since there is more on the nature of, and the thinking behind, the volume in my introduction, I will use this preface to express some well-deserved thanks.

First and foremost, I am very grateful to Paul Mitchell, the series editor, for trusting me to edit this volume when I suggested the prospect. My eternal gratitude must also extend to the distinguished and talented authors who have contributed chapters. It has been a pleasure (and often a humbling one) to commission, read and (lightly) edit their efforts. I hope they have survived the experience unscathed!

The papers in this volume were presented in draft form at a small conference held at Robinson College, Cambridge in September 2018. I would venture to suggest that the conference made the enterprise less solitary and even more enjoyable than it might otherwise have been, and possibly even that it made this volume more coherent. This immediately leads to more thanks: David Foster, Jamie Glister, Anthony Good, Siôn Hudson (who is owed gratitude for many more reasons besides), Ruth Hughes, Janet O'Sullivan and Penelope Reed QC kindly attended as discussants and provided immensely valuable insights from their diverse perspectives. I must acknowledge the support of the Cambridge Humanities Research Grant Scheme for their generous funding of the conference, as well as the invaluable assistance of Rosie Šnajdr in applying for and managing the grant. My colleagues Rosalind Marsh and other members of the conference and catering teams at Robinson were immensely helpful in making sure that the event ran smoothly.

At the conference dinner, we were looked after with typical efficiency and style by Glenys Denton. Glenys has achieved a semi-divine status amongst generations of Robinson students, Fellows and visitors for her kindness, sympathy, effectiveness, humour and occasional well-directed sternness in ensuring that things in College run as they should. Personally, I have benefited from her sterling work more than most. At the time of writing, her retirement is imminent. While of course I wish her every happiness, and particularly in her inevitably exotic travels, I do so with sadness as well as affection as I struggle to imagine Robinson without her (albeit that her successor will be excellent).

The team at Hart Publishing have been typically brilliant in guiding this volume through the production process, from vague proposal to printing. There are risks in naming individuals, but I have worked directly with Bill Asquith (who has now moved to pastures new), Rosamund Jubber, Sinead Moloney, Linda Staniford and Kate Whetter, and am extremely grateful for their efforts.

I should also record sincere gratitude to my colleagues at the Cambridge Family Law Centre, under whose auspices the project was undertaken. Jens Scherpe, Jo Miles,

Claire Fenton-Glynn, Mark Elliott and Lionel Bently have been very supportive. The same is true of my academic colleagues at Robinson, particularly those of a legal persuasion: Christopher Forsyth, Elaine Freer, Jamie Glister (again), David Yates and Alison Young. I offer them, my students, my family and friends, and Siôn both my gratitude and my apologies for the times when I have prioritised this book when I arguably should have been doing something else. I hope they think that was at least partly worthwhile!

Brian Sloan
Robinson College, Cambridge
February 2019

Table of Contents

List of Contributors

Juliet Brook is a Senior Lecturer at Portsmouth Law School, University of Portsmouth.

Daniel Carr is a Senior Lecturer in Private Law and Director of Undergraduate Studies at the School of Law, University of Edinburgh.

Heather Conway is a Professor of Law at the School of Law, Queen's University Belfast.

Simon Cooper is a Professor of Law and Research Convenor at Aston Law School.

Dominic de Cogan is University Senior Lecturer in Tax Law at the University of Cambridge and a Fellow of Christ's College.

Martin Dixon is Professor of the Law of Real Property at the University of Cambridge and a Fellow of Queens' College.

Elizabeth Drummond is a Stipendiary Lecturer in Law at Mansfield College, Oxford.

Birke Häcker is the Professor of Comparative Law and Director of the Institute of European and Comparative Law at the University of Oxford and a Fellow of Brasenose College.

Neil Jones is Reader in English Legal History at the University of Cambridge and a Fellow of Magdalene College.

Roger Kerridge is an Emeritus Professor of Law at the University of Bristol.

James Lee is Reader in English Law at the Dickson Poon School of Law, King's College London and Associate Academic Fellow of the Honourable Society of the Inner Temple.

Ying Liew is a Senior Lecturer in Law at the University of Melbourne.

John Mee is a Professor of Law at University College, Cork.

Charles Mitchell QC (*hc*) is a Professor of Law at University College, London.

Nicola Peart is a Professor of Law at the University of Otago.

Barbara Rich is a Barrister at 5 Stone Buildings.

Walter Pintens is an Emeritus Professor of Law at the Catholic University of Leuven.

Judith Skillen is a Teaching Fellow at the Dickson Poon School of Law, King's College London.

Brian Sloan is a College Lecturer and Fellow in Law at Robinson College, Cambridge.

Prue Vines is Professor and Director of First Year Studies at UNSW Law, University of New South Wales.

Table of Cases

United Kingdom

Australia

Canada

France

Germany

Ireland

New Zealand

Spain

United States

REGIONAL

European Court of Human Rights

European Union

Table of Legislation

United Kingdom

Statutes

Statutory Instruments

Australia

Austria

Bahamas

Belgium

Bermuda

Canada

Cayman Islands

Czech Republic

Denmark

France

Germany

Greece

Hungary

Ireland

Italy

Lithuania

New Zealand

Norway

Poland

Portugal

Spain

Sweden

Switzerland

United States

European Union

International

Roman Law

1

Introduction

BRIAN SLOAN

SUCCESSION LAW'S LONG pedigree, near-universal application, immense capacity for human interest stories and somewhat uncertain future in England and Wales[1] make it an ideal candidate for a *Landmark Cases* volume. This is particularly true as the field faces challenges such as the ageing population and varying family structures and expectations.[2] For the purposes of this volume, 'succession law' mostly encompasses the destination of a person's property after his or her death, although Heather Conway's chapter on *Williams v Williams* is an important reminder of the importance of the destination of one's earthly remains.[3] The aim of the series, edited by Paul Mitchell, is 'to highlight the historical antecedents of what are widely considered to be the leading cases in the common law … and … to provide a context, or contexts, in which to better understand how and why certain cases came to be regarded as the "Landmark" cases in any given field'.[4] The contributors to this collection have considered diverse cases with this objective in mind, ranging in decision date from 1720 to 2017. While some of the cases considered in earlier volumes inevitably have relevance to succession law,[5] care has been taken to ensure that the cases at the centre of this volume do not duplicate those earlier targets.

In this short introduction, I have the opportunity to explain the somewhat unorthodox structure of the book and provide an overview of its content, to highlight some themes that emerge from the chapters and to consider the nature of a 'landmark case in succession law'. I must recognise the immense contributions not only of the contributors, but also of the discussants at the conference in Cambridge[6] to the content of this chapter, and to the volume as a whole.

[1] Law Commission, *Making A Will* (Law Commission Consultation Paper 231, 2017).

[2] See, eg B Sloan, *Borkowski's Law of Succession*, 3rd edn (Oxford, Oxford University Press, 2017) 8–12.

[3] Chapter 14.

[4] Hart Publishing, 'Landmark Cases' www.bloomsburyprofessional.com/uk/series/landmark-cases/.

[5] See, eg W Pintens and J Scherpe, 'The Marckx Case: A "Whole Code of Family Law"?' in S Gilmore, J Herring and R Probert (eds), *Landmark Cases in Family Law* (Oxford, Hart Publishing, 2011).

[6] David Foster, Jamie Glister, Anthony Good, Siôn Hudson, Ruth Hughes, Janet O'Sullivan and Penelope Reed QC.

I. AN OVERVIEW OF THE BOOK'S STRUCTURE AND CONTENT

The vast majority of the volumes in Hart's *Landmark Cases* series arrange the chapters according to the date of the case. In formulating my proposal, I had the thought that arrangement according to subject matter might more easily allow common themes to emerge. It seemed a shame, for example, for Nicola Peart[7] and John Mee's chapters,[8] addressing testamentary promises in New Zealand and England and Wales respectively, to be separated by Judith Skillen and James Lee's on the liability of will drafters to would-be beneficiaries[9] because of the order of events. Discussion at the Cambridge conference revealed opinion to be sharply divided on the question. After much thought, I decided to retain a thematic structure, notwithstanding the risk that the cases might be robbed of their historical context, the necessity of attempting to justify the order of chapters (a task undertaken later in this section) and the inevitable provocation of disagreement that a non-chronological order involves. In any event, it goes without saying that the chapters are self-contained and that the reader is entirely free to read them in any order desired!

With Hart's forbearance, I have also broken with convention both by including several chapters on cases that are not directly relevant to English law (Walter Pintens's on *S and S*,[10] Nicola Peart's on *Re Welch*,[11] Daniel Carr's on *Lashley v Hog*,[12] Prue Vines's on *Re Estate Wilson, deceased*[13] and to a lesser extent Ying Liew's on *Birmingham v Renfrew*)[14] and by commissioning two on cases decided just around two years before submission of the manuscript (Prue Vines's again[15] and my own on *Ilott v The Blue Cross*).[16] I hope the reader will agree that there were good reasons for these decisions: the former allows the English cases to be set in their comparative context (even extending beyond the common law that is generally the hallmark of the series), and while the latter inevitably limits the extent to which the cases can be reflected upon in the light of subsequent developments, in my view this is outweighed by the very significance of the judgments. On a related note, contributors to this collection may have experienced less of the 'free choice of case, and complete freedom of method in how to approach their material' that has characterised previous books in the series.[17] While I dread to think what this says about my approach to editing and my personality more generally, I do at least hope that I have aided the coherence of the volume.

The volume opens with two older cases on construction. Birke Häcker tells the fascinating story of *All Souls v Codrington*, involving how a bequest of a 'library' contributed to the establishment of the rule that a will speaks from death.[18] *Jesson v Wright* is the

[7] Chapter 12.
[8] Chapter 11.
[9] Chapter 7.
[10] Chapter 18.
[11] Chapter 12.
[12] Chapter 19.
[13] Chapter 20.
[14] Chapter 9.
[15] Chapter 20.
[16] Chapter 19.
[17] C Mitchell and P Mitchell, 'Preface' in C Mitchell and P Mitchell (eds), *Landmark Cases in the Law of Contract* (Oxford, Hart Publishing, 2008).
[18] Chapter 2.

focus of Neil Jones's contribution, the case being the leading one on the ill-fated rule of construction known as the rule in *Shelley's Case*.[19]

We then move to attributes that a testator must have to make a valid will, specifically capacity (both retrospective and prospective), knowledge and approval. Juliet Brook analyses the highly cited case of *Banks v Goodfellow* on testamentary capacity, inter alia highlighting its ambitious theorising of the mind, nuance and emphasis on testamentary freedom, but also its role in facilitating submissions to the effect that the testator failed to make the 'right' will.[20] Barbara Rich then considers a leading case on statutory wills for living persons judged incapable of making a will, *Re D(J)*. She highlights the fact that although the case pre-dates the significant change from a 'substituted judgment'- to a 'best interests'-oriented approach heralded by the Mental Capacity Act 2005, it may yet have an influential afterlife as a landmark case in succession law.[21] Roger Kerridge emphasises the background to and role of *Hastilow v Stobie* in first permitting the plea of want of knowledge and approval, before analysing the difficult subsequent history that in his view has encouraged dishonest pleading until the present day.[22]

The contributions of other fields to succession law, namely tort, land (whatever the actual facts of the chosen case) and trusts law, form the subject of the next informal section of the volume. Judith Skillen and James Lee continue the theme of will drafting by analysing *White v Jones*, the seminal decision establishing that a professional drafter who fails to draft a will expeditiously can be liable in negligence to would-be estate beneficiaries.[23] They highlight the significance of the case for the laws of tort and contract more generally (on assumption of responsibility and pure economic loss) as well as for succession law, albeit that on their analysis it is less significant in retrospect than some expected. Martin Dixon considers the key decision in *Williams v Hensman* on severing a joint tenancy, a vital succession-related device that can change the posthumous destination of property without the need to amend a will per se.[24] Dixon describes severance as 'Janus personified' because it both relieves people from the restrictive effects of a joint tenancy and frustrates the once-clear intentions of purchasers or donors. He highlights the number of vital questions that *Williams* left unanswered. *Birmingham v Renfrew*, an Australian case on mutual wills with much international influence, is then discussed by Ying Liew.[25] He brings attention to the case's impact in sowing seeds of doctrinal difficulty that still persists.

The volume then moves to consider formalities (albeit that they are also relevant to mutual wills) and how they may be circumvented. Simon Cooper's chosen case is the extraordinary one of *Sugden v Lord St Leonards*, involving probate of a missing will,[26] which Cooper uses as a springboard to consider the broader rationales of formality requirements and how they are arguably undermined by *Sugden*, rather than merely

[19] Chapter 3.
[20] Chapter 4.
[21] Chapter 5.
[22] Chapter 6.
[23] Chapter 7.
[24] Chapter 8.
[25] Chapter 9.
[26] Chapter 10.

focusing on the rules of evidence, procedure and revocation more directly raised by the case.[27] There are then two chapters on the enforcement of testamentary promises. The leading English proprietary estoppel case, *Thorner v Major*, receives a comprehensive critique from John Mee, who highlights its role in disrupting the strict application of succession rules. Nicola Peart then considers a very prominent case under the Law Reform (Testamentary Promises) Act 1949 (New Zealand), *Re Welch*.[28] She highlights (with considerable reference to the legislative history) that while the difficulties with testamentary promise enforcement do not disappear simply because it is achieved via statute rather than judicial innovation, *Re Welch* in fact managed to introduce some clear principles into the jurisdiction.

The position of personal representatives and will beneficiaries are analysed next. The rule in *Strong v Bird* is assessed via the case that bears its name, with Elizabeth Drummond accepting that there is reason to be sympathetic to the executor on the facts of the case but querying whether the rule thus developed is sufficiently coherent to be justifiable.[29] Heather Conway then takes us beyond property law to *Williams v Williams*, and the status of directions to personal representatives and others on funerals and on related expenses claims.[30] She considers the case for funeral directions being binding, with reference to modern technologies with the potential to be just as controversial as cremation was at the time of *Williams*. Moving to beneficiaries, Charles Mitchell considers the Privy Council decision in *Commissioner of Stamp Duties (Queensland) v Livingston* on the nature of a beneficiary's interest in an unadministered estate, engaging in the process in a very useful comparative study of the nature of such rights as compared to those of a trust beneficiary.[31] On a related matter, Dominic de Cogan then argues that *Gartside v IRC*, concerning the nature of an interest in a testamentary discretionary trust, has had its significance overestimated as a general authority on property law but underestimated in the context of tax and succession law.[32]

The vital issue of limitations on testamentary freedom, both in England and Wales and abroad, comes next. In my own chapter, I trace the history of claims under the Inheritance (Provision for Family and Dependants) Act 1975 leading up to the recent Supreme Court decision in *Ilott v The Blue Cross*, highlighting the importance of the case in confirming key principles but also the clarification still needed on some fundamental principles.[33] Walter Pintens considers the very different starting point of compulsory portions present in civil law jurisdictions, before analysing the German case of *S and S* and the circumstances in which that expectation can be departed from.[34] He analyses the vital issue of the impact of compulsory portions in cross-border cases. Daniel Carr then analyses compulsory portions (mainly 'legitim') closer to England via the Scots law case of *Lashley v Hog*, which also raised thorny issues relating to the conflict of

[27] Chapter 11.
[28] Chapter 12.
[29] Chapter 13.
[30] Chapter 14.
[31] Chapter 15.
[32] Chapter 16.
[33] Chapter 17.
[34] Chapter 18.

laws and domicile.[35] Finally, Prue Vines rounds off the volume by continuing the theme of 'alternative' views on succession. Her chosen case is the fascinating one of *Re Estate Wilson, deceased*, which was the first to apply the provisions inserted into the Succession Act 2006 (New South Wales) to allow the recognition of Aboriginal traditions and customary laws in the context of intestacy.[36] While Vines makes clear the significance of both the case and the legislation applied, she cannot conceal her disappointment about some of the conclusions reached.

II. EMERGING THEMES

In such a lengthy and diverse collection, readers will no doubt decide for themselves what the implications of the chapters are. That said, it might be helpful to highlight some common themes, and particularly to attempt to give readers the benefit of the fruitful Cambridge discussion.

One discussant expressed the view in email correspondence that the cases in this volume could often be described as 'very English', and it is certainly true that many of them reflect the concerns of the Caucasian, privileged classes existing at a particular time. Nevertheless, there is a sense in which familial disputes about succession are both timeless and classless, and chapters such as Rich's,[37] Conway's[38] and mine[39] illustrate the potential for succession law to deal with what might be termed 'ordinary' people. The chapters by Pintens and Carr take us beyond England,[40] and Vines's chosen case could plausibly be described as 'anti-English' in light of the legislation applied in it.[41] It is interesting how colonialism features in the collection at opposite ends of the book, of the historical spectrum and of the possible responses to it. While the property in dispute in *All Souls v Codrington* is, as Häcker puts it, 'inextricably linked to both the glory and the unspeakable abominations of England's colonial past' even today,[42] the legislation at issue in *Re Estate Wilson* arguably facilitates limited relief from the effects of colonialism by permitting the application of Aboriginal custom and law in the light of 'pillow births', forced adoption and the stolen generations.[43]

Issues of culture are also significant in many cases, with culture-related assumptions being made about what a person means by his or her sheep, horses, library (see Häcker's chapter) or farm (see Mee's chapter).[44] Culture may help to explain the civilian approach to compulsory portions in Germany (analysed by Pintens), given the solidarity more generally present in German law.[45] Succession legislation and cases also make assumptions

[35] Chapter 19.
[36] Chapter 20.
[37] Chapter 5.
[38] Chapter 14.
[39] Chapter 17.
[40] Chapters 18 and 19, respectively.
[41] Chapter 20.
[42] Chapter 2.
[43] Chapter 20.
[44] Chapter 11.
[45] Chapter 18.

about the nature of family, with Vines's chapter perfectly demonstrating the enormous possible range of views on the question.[46]

On a point strongly related to culture, whether or not a testator is doing the 'expected' thing is key to the reality of almost any succession system. Brook highlights the paradox (despite the nuanced approach taken in *Banks*) that the more a testator does what is expected, the more alleged 'freedom' he or she will apparently be given not to do so,[47] and Mee considers behaviour within or outside accepted norms to be crucial to the outcome in estoppel cases.[48] In Peart's chapter, however, it is made clear that what is expected by way of benefits conferred *on* a testator by a claimant can limit a testamentary promises claim.[49] The vast majority of the cases in this book involve a challenge to a will or enactment by someone disappointed and/or surprised by the result, often in the context of some familial turmoil, and it is inevitable that most such litigants will care much more about achieving the 'correct' result (based on a particular version of events: see Mee's chapter)[50] than the precise legal basis on which the original one was 'wrong'. This approach is often perfectly understandable behaviour for litigants, but can cause doctrinal difficulty (as demonstrated by Kerridge and Liew's contributions, for example).[51] The issue of whether the state (sometimes via the imputation of a reasonableness standard) or the individual knows best as to the fate of one's property becomes key not only in obvious cases on family provision and compulsory portions (see the chapters by Pintens, Carr and myself),[52] but also in the context of a 'best interests' decision surrounding a statutory will (see Rich's contribution).[53]

On a related note, different forms of intention (and the significance we choose to attach to them) form a key aspect of cases on succession law, even if intentions and wishes (see Conway's chapter in addition to those considered above)[54] can be overridden. While the formality requirements (analysed by Cooper)[55] are ostensibly given primacy, the chapters of Mee, Peart and, to some extent, Drummond highlight that informal promises can sometimes supplant intentions expressed using those requirements.[56] The courts' willingness to create exceptions to such formal rules (inherently deciding that those exceptions are 'fair') may suggest a level of discomfort with the rules.

Moreover, while in general the courts are anxious to establish the 'last wishes' validly expressed (the mutual wills doctrine considered by Liew being one exception to that),[57] in the context of allegedly doubtful capacity (see Brook's and Rich's chapters),[58] there can be real issues as to what those 'last wishes' are, and courts and relatives may struggle to accept that they have changed dramatically even in a context where wills are ostensibly

[46] Chapter 20.
[47] Chapter 4.
[48] Chapter 11.
[49] Chapter 12.
[50] Chapter 11.
[51] Chapters 6 and 9, respectively.
[52] Chapters 18, 19 and 16, respectively.
[53] Chapter 5.
[54] Chapter 14.
[55] Chapter 10.
[56] Chapters 11, 12 and 13, respectively.
[57] Chapter 9.
[58] Chapters 4 and 5, respectively.

ambulatory by nature. On the other hand, cases on construction, such as *Jesson v Wright* (considered by Jones),[59] suggest that we are not always looking for what the testator meant in any event, but the 'true' meaning of the words used. In addition, where cases involve documents containing considerable complexity, it is arguable that it is unreal to think about what the testator meant and the draughtsperson's intentions will be more influential, which relates to the point about legal practice made below.

The activities of the legal profession and their importance in succession law come under scrutiny in several chapters (though thankfully the academic and practitioner participants left the Cambridge conference on speaking terms). This is perhaps most obvious in the context of Skillen and Lee's chapter on *White v Jones*,[60] but the point is pervasive (see, for example, Dixon's chapter),[61] albeit that in the case of *Jesson v Wright* (the subject of Jones' chapter) it is not clear whether the profession were involved in drafting the will.[62] On a related point, pleadings and conduct of litigation (including court structure) have considerable influence: Häcker detects problems with pleadings in *All Souls v Codrington*,[63] while Kerridge blames practice for the development of want of knowledge and approval, and the confusion surrounding it up to the present day.[64] This is also linked to the point about the strategy of pursing multiple claims made above. As for the structure of legislation and almost inevitably therefore litigation, Nicola Peart and I both find ourselves wondering whether the outcomes we are discussing would have been fundamentally different if more of the dispute had been open to our higher courts when they had heard our respective cases.[65]

Finally, in the context of a subject that affects essentially everyone, it is remarkable that the contribution of individuals to it can sometimes be very considerable, even if not always intentionally. For example, although the associated cases were by no means chosen for this reason, we encounter Lord St Leonards as renowned counsel (*sub nom* Edward Sugden) in *Jesson v Wright* (considered by Jones),[66] as an influential Lord Chancellor on the issue of reform of and practice in Kerridge's contribution[67] and eventually as the testator of the 'missing will' in Cooper's chapter on *Sugden v Lord St Leonards*.[68] This is a clear reflection of the absence of diversity, highlighted by the corresponding discussant, characterising the practice of succession law at one particular time that is thankfully less present today.[69] More positively, Skillen and Lee highlight the considerable jurisprudential contribution of Lord Goff on practical justice leading up to the decision in *White*.[70]

It now remains to consider the nature of a 'landmark' case in this field, a task undertaken in the next section.

[59] Chapter 3.
[60] Chapter 7.
[61] Chapter 8.
[62] Chapter 3.
[63] Chapter 2.
[64] Chapter 6.
[65] Chapters 12 and 17, respectively.
[66] Chapter 3.
[67] Chapter 6.
[68] Chapter 10.
[69] That said, while we were very fortunate to have three female members of the chancery bar participating in our Cambridge conference, it is telling that one of them asked me to draw attention to an event aimed at encouraging more women to consider joining it.
[70] Chapter 7.

III. THE NATURE OF A 'LANDMARK CASE IN SUCCESSION LAW'

I make absolutely no claims that the chapters chosen for this volume represent a definitive collection of landmark cases in succession law. Moreover, while it was clear that some broad areas very much had to be included, no doubt some of the contributors would be similarly diffident about whether their chosen case is the best example of a landmark within that particular sub-field, and in some instances there was some debate before the relevant case was finally settled. Nevertheless, it might be helpful to reflect on what the chapters in this volume tell us about what makes such a landmark case.

It will become clear to the reader that the cases in this book are landmarks for different reasons. *Strong v Bird*, for example, gives its very name to a doctrine, even if that doctrine is rarely invoked and arguably difficult to justify.[71] Similarly, the '*Banks v Goodfellow* test'[72] and the '*Williams v Hensman* methods'[73] have become part of the core language of property law, even if Dixon describes *Williams*' status as a leading authority as 'a combination of chance, time and opportunity'.[74] *Hastilow v Stobie* did established a doctrine, namely want of knowledge and approval, even if it is not widely known for having done so.[75] *White v Jones* established a key principle on tortious liability whose potential reach extends well beyond succession law, even if Skillen and Lee argue that it was more of a 'high-water mark' that was 'temporal[ly] contingent' and whose implications seem more limited in retrospect.[76] *Williams v Williams* 'establishes core principles' outside the purely proprietary context.[77] Similarly, Carr heralds *Lashley v Hog* as a landmark case because of the legal principles relating to the conflict of laws and avoidance of obligations that can be derived from it.[78]

Some cases represent important firsts: *Re Estate Wilson* was the first case to consider New South Wales provisions allowing the recognition of Aboriginal traditions and customary law in intestacy (and thus represents a turning point);[79] *Ilott v The Blue Cross* was the first House of Lords/Supreme Court case concerning the Inheritance (Provision for Family and Dependants) Act 1975;[80] and *Re Welch* was the first (and only) time that the Privy Council applied the Law Reform (Testamentary Promises) Act 1949 (NZ).[81] Some, such as *Thorner v Major* on proprietary estoppel,[82] *S and S* on German compulsory portions,[83] *Sugden v Lord St Leonards* on presumed revocation and relevant rules of procedure and evidence,[84] arguably *Commissioner of Stamp Duties (Queensland) v Livingston*

[71] Chapter 13.
[72] Chapter 4.
[73] Chapter 8.
[74] Chapter 8.
[75] Chapter 6.
[76] Chapter 7.
[77] Chapter 14.
[78] Chapter 19.
[79] Chapter 20.
[80] Chapter 17.
[81] Chapter 12.
[82] Chapter 11.
[83] Chapter 18.
[84] Chapter 10.

on the nature of beneficiary rights[85] and *Birmingham v Renfrew* on mutual wills,[86] *Ilott* on family provision[87] and perhaps even *Banks* on testamentary capacity[88] and *White* on drafters' liability to beneficiaries,[89] had a vital role in confirming fundamental principles, often in the face of doubts. Substantive influence is also given as a reason for regarding a case as a landmark, internationally in the cases of *Birmingham* (even if it has been relatively infrequently cited in a formal sense in England and its influence has been gradual)[90] and *Thorner*,[91] and within New Zealand in the case of *Re Welch*.[92]

In some instances, the reasons for 'landmark' status are less obvious but still valid. Some of the cases in the volume have been chosen for their narrative value, and some (such as *Thorner*)[93] have such value even if their status can be justified for other reasons. The story is Häcker's justification for choosing *All Souls v Codrington*,[94] and the same reason must surely have influenced Cooper's selection of *Sugden v Lord St Leonards*.[95] It is interesting, conversely, that however compelling the series of events leading to the decision in *Hastilow v Stobie* are, the facts of the case itself are unknown,[96] while Dixon finds 'nothing unusual about the trials and tribulations of the moderately comfortable … family' at the centre of *Williams v Hensman*.[97] Jones draws inspiration from Brian Simpson's *Leading Cases in the Common Law*[98] in justifying *Jesson v Wright* as a landmark case.[99] Others, such as *Gartside v IRC*[100] and arguably *White v Jones*,[101] may even have had their 'landmark' status overestimated in some respects, but remain key because of the extent to which they are still discussed. Even if the reader disagrees about the 'landmark' status of some of the cases, the discussion that may thus ensue, as well as the analysis of the cases' background and implications, still has value.

In closing, I wish to point out an irony. It is that, as this collection is published, some of the cases considered in it are at risk of having their influence considerably reduced as the Law Commission (perfectly reasonably) suggests that they be replaced by statutory principles, even if this occurs after more than a century of influence. This is particularly noteworthy in the case of *Banks v Goodfellow*, which sits uneasily with the approach to statutory wills in the Mental Capacity Act 2005 and uses language that is out of step with modern times.[102] Moreover, *Hastilow v Stobie*'s doctrine of 'want of knowledge and

[85] Chapter 15.
[86] Chapter 9.
[87] Chapter 17.
[88] Chapter 4.
[89] Chapter 8.
[90] Chapter 9.
[91] Chapter 11.
[92] Chapter 12.
[93] Chapter 11.
[94] Chapter 2.
[95] Chapter 10.
[96] Chapter 6.
[97] Chapter 8.
[98] AWB Simpson, *Leading Cases in the Common Law* (Oxford, Oxford University Press, 1995).
[99] Chapter 3.
[100] Chapter 16.
[101] Chapter 7.
[102] Law Commission (n 1) ch 2.

approval' has caused much uncertainty, grief and (on Kerridge's analysis) subterfuge.[103] There may be a tendency at times to fetishise the case and the case law method in the common law realm, with the result that venerable authorities are allowed to outlive their usefulness until a body such as the Commission is able to suggest reform. That said, even if some of the cases in this volume are 'formally' replaced by statute in the future (as, for example, *All Souls v Codrington* and to some extent the broader principle in *White v Jones* already have been),[104] they will still represent landmarks on succession law's endless journey.

[103] ibid ch 7.
[104] Chapters 2 and 7, respectively.

2

All Souls College v Codrington (1720): Money, Books and the Interpretation of Wills – A Testamentary Drama in Three Acts

BIRKE HÄCKER*

I. A LONG PROLOGUE: HOW THE 'AMBULATORY' QUALITY OF WILLS CAME TO BE ESTABLISHED

Scene 1 – London, AD 1611

HENRY SWINBURNE (C 1551–1624), arguably England's most significant ecclesiastical lawyer and scholar, has just completed the second edition of his *Briefe Treatise of Testaments and Last Willes*.[1] This seminal compilation will be the first port of call for generations of probate and succession lawyers over the following two centuries. Written in the technical style of contemporary legal scholarship, but in English rather than Latin, and intended as an accessible manual for students and interested lay people, it blends Continental learning with English canon law practice. Within the 'newly corrected and augmented' edition, Swinburne has inserted an addendum into the chapter dealing with 'vncertaintie in reſpect of the time or date of the Teſtament':

> It is a famous queſtion amongſt the Ciuilians, whether the time of the making of the teſtament, or of the death of the teſtator, is to be reſpected? and conſequently, whether the teſtator be

* This chapter draws and builds on an earlier contribution entitled 'A Case Note on *All Souls College* v. *Cod[d]rington* (1720)', published in (2012) 76 *Rabels Zeitschrift für ausländisches und internationales Privatrecht* (*RabelsZ*) 1051–77. I am grateful for the opportunity to follow up some of the issues discussed there, to take account of additional material which has appeared or come to my attention since the article was published, and to correct a few errors. For a fuller picture of the story, especially of the civilian historical and comparative perspective, the reader may wish to consult both pieces side-by-side. Any reader with a specific interest in the South African Roman-Dutch tradition will additionally like to look at AJ McGregor, 'From What Point of Time Does a Will (*Testamentum*) Speak?' (1937) 54 *South African Law Journal* 146, an article which I regret to have missed when compiling the contribution for the *RabelsZ*.

[1] H Swinburne, *A Briefe Treatise of Testaments and Last Willes* (London, Companie of Stationers, 1611). Unless otherwise stated, all references are to this edition. The first edition had been published (by John Windet, London) in 1590–91.

preſumed to bequeath thoſe things onely which hee had at the time of the making of his Will, or of his death: for the determining of which queſtion, diuers doe vſe ſundry diſtinctions, whereof ſome ſeeme to make the matter more intricate, wherefore pretermitting thoſe diſtinctions I haue choſen a plaine and eaſie courſe of deciding the controuerſie, by propounding a rule with extenſions and limitations. The rule is this. *That the time of the teſtament, and not of the teſtators death is to be regarded.* And ſo thoſe goods which the teſtator had at the time when hee made his will, are bequeathed vnto, and recouerable by the legatarie, but not thoſe goods which hee got afterwards.[2]

Scene 2 – London, in the Late 1830s

On 1 January 1838, the Wills Act 1837 (1 Vict c 26) enters into force. Under the heading 'A will shall be construed to speak from the death of the testator', it provides in section 24:

> Every will shall be construed, with reference to the real estate and personal estate comprised in it,[3] to speak and take effect *as if it had been executed immediately before the death of the testator*, unless a contrary intention shall appear by the will. [Emphasis added.]

James Wigram, Chancery barrister and author of the authoritative guidance on the interpretation of wills,[4] is at this time in the process of updating his popular treatise. The third edition, published in 1840, repeats *verbatim* a passage already contained in the second edition of 1835 – interestingly without any reference to the new statute:

> [E]vidence of the amount of a testator's personal estate, at the time of making his will … is, in general, inadmissible. The reason is obvious. The will, *quoad* the personal estate, speaks from the death of the testator, and consequently, its amount at the time of making the will, although it might bias the judgment, could not, in general, form a just ground of inference as to the meaning of the testator's words.[5]

How did English law get from Swinburne's position to that ultimately espoused by section 24, with its radical evidentiary endorsement in the so-called 'Wigram rules'? When and why, in other words, did wills stop speaking from the time of their execution and start speaking from the testator's death? And what does the case of *All Souls College v Codrington* (1720) have to do with it?

In order to broach these questions, it is necessary to distinguish between personal and real property. Until the Land Transfer Act 1897, these devolved separately upon a person's

[2] Swinburne (n 1) pt VII, § XI, starting at p 315r, here 316r (italics in the original, all references omitted).

[3] I would like to thank Professor John Mee for pointing out that the corresponding provision in the Irish legislation, s 89 of the Succession Act 1965, goes beyond s 24 of the Wills Act 1837 and speaks of 'all estate comprised in the will *and every devise or bequest contained in it*' (emphasis added). A marginal note to s 89 explains that the provision was deliberately extended by the Irish legislator so as to abolish the rule in *Wild's Case* (1599) 6 Co Rep 16b, 77 ER 277 (concerning the meaning of a devise of the format 'to A and his children', where A had no issue at the time the will was made). See also the comment in n 126 below on the respective scope of application of the two sections.

[4] J Wigram, *An Examination of the Rules of Law, Respecting the Admission of Extrinsic Evidence in Aid of the Interpretation of Wills* (London, Charles Hunter, 1831), 2nd edn (London, Charles Hunter, 1835), 3rd edn (London, Maxwell, 1840).

[5] See, respectively, ibid 81 (3rd edn) and 63–64 (2nd edn).

death (personal property to the deceased's personal representative, ie his executor or administrator; real property directly to his devisee or heir-at-law), and the two separate parts of the estate were – historically speaking – subject to radically different rules and procedures.[6]

Section 24 of the Wills Act 1837 was primarily an attempt to get to grips with a problem besetting realty. Since realty first became devisable at common law through the Statute of Wills 1540, it had been held that the devise could only take effect if the testator was already entitled to the relevant property at the moment when he made his will *and* subsequently remained entitled to it until his death.[7] Various explanations were offered[8] for why wills relating to land were not 'ambulatory' (in the relevant sense),[9] but none of them persuaded the Royal Commission charged with looking into the law and suggesting reforms.[10] Reporting in 1833, the Commission found:

> The rule, that Freehold and Copyhold Estates acquired after the date of the Will cannot pass by it, is attended with several inconveniences. It renders it necessary for a Testator to republish his Will, or to make a new one as often as he acquires other property. It prevents (except in a few cases in Equity) a devise from taking effect, if a Testator makes any alteration in his estate, or does any act which prevents the interest in it, to which he was entitled at the date of his Will, from continuing unaltered until his death. It creates many nice and unnecessary questions in the Laws relating to the revocation of Wills; it frequently defeats the intention of the Testator, and

[6] Until the Court of Probate Act 1857, for instance, the exclusive jurisdiction for granting probate or letters of administration concerning a deceased's personal estate lay with the ecclesiastical courts (with a short interruption during the Commonwealth, 1649–60), while the ordinary common law courts were in charge of succession to realty. From about the seventeenth century onwards, the Court of Chancery obtained a concurrent jurisdiction (alongside the courts spiritual) in respect of determining and enforcing bequests of personalty, probably because the executor was seen as akin to a trustee. This explains why the case of *All Souls College v Codrington* (1720) was heard in Chancery. See generally TE Atkinson, 'Brief History of English Testamentary Jurisdiction' (1943) 8 *Missouri Law Review* 107.

[7] F Pollock and FW Maitland, *The History of English Law Before the Time of Edward I*, vol 2 (Cambridge, Cambridge University Press, 1895) 313 suggest that the courts were 'apparently … but following a rule which had long been applied [prior to 1540] to those wills of land that were sanctioned by local custom'. A similar observation is made by Lord Mansfield in *Harwood v Goodright* (1774) 1 Cowp 87, 90; 98 ER 981, 982–83.

[8] Outlined in B Häcker, 'A Case Note on *All Souls College v. Cod[d]rington* (1720)' (2012) 76 *RabelsZ* 1051, 1067–68.

[9] The word 'ambulatory' can be used with several different shades of meaning. According to Pollock and Maitland (n 7) 313, an 'ambulatory' instrument in the present sense is one 'capable of bestowing … property which does not belong to the testator when he makes his will, but which does belong to him at the moment of his death'. In the civilian tradition, by contrast, 'ambulatory' is usually equated with 'revocable': *voluntas testatoris ambulatoria est usque ad mortem*, it is said, and what is meant is that the testator can change his mind right up to the point of death. Literally, however, 'ambulatory' means 'relating to or adapted for walking'. In the context of succession law, it could thus be understood as signifying that the instrument, while afloat during the testator's lifetime, is capable of 'walking' alongside him and (subject to being revoked) of adapting its dispositive effect in accordance with his changing circumstances. See further below, text accompanying n 19.

[10] The so-called 'Real Property Commission' was instituted in 1828 to examine thoroughly the law of real property. It reported to Parliament on various aspects in 1829, 1830, 1832 and 1833. The fourth and last report covers the whole of the law of wills, including personal property: Real Property Commission, 'Fourth Report Made to His Majesty by the Commissioners Appointed to Inquire into the Law of England Respecting Real Property' (1833). It explains (at 4): 'Although it is not within the object of our Commission to recommend any alteration in the law, except so far as it affects Real Property, yet we think that we cannot make a just or comprehensive view of the subject of Wills, with respect to Real Property, without considering the rules which relate to Wills generally. The mischiefs we hope to remedy, and the reasons for the amendments we propose, extend to Wills of every description.'

has been disapproved by eminent Judges.[11] The usual intention of the Testator is to dispose, not of the property which he has when he makes his Will, but of the property which he may have at his death; and if Wills were to be construed[12] with reference to the property comprised in them, both real and personal, as speaking at the Testator's death, unless a contrary intention appears, the rule would get rid of the greatest part of the intricate laws relating to revocation and republication.

We therefore propose that a Will shall pass property of any description comprised in its terms, which a testator may be entitled to at the time of his death, unless an intention to the contrary shall appear upon the Will. If this recommendation be adopted, the Law respecting the time from which a devise of Freehold or Copyhold Estates is to be considered to take effect, will be precisely similar to that which is at present in force as to Personal Estate; and there will be one uniform rule in this respect applicable to Wills of property of every description.[13]

The Wills Act 1837 implemented the Commission's various recommendations. In addition to section 24, it contains a second provision targeting the inconvenient old rule regarding realty. Insofar as is relevant here, section 3 reads:

It shall be lawful for every person to devise, bequeath, or dispose of, by his will executed in manner herein-after required, all real estate and all personal estate which he shall be entitled to, either at law or in equity, at the time of his death …; and the power hereby given shall extend … to all contingent, executory or other future interests in any real or personal estate …; and also to all rights of entry for conditions broken, and other rights of entry; and also to such of the same estates, interests, and rights respectively, and other real and personal estate, as the testator may be entitled to at the time of his death, notwithstanding that he may become entitled to the same subsequently to the execution of his will.

Although the two provisions are closely related by genesis, it has rightly been observed that their ultimate remit differs: while section 3 is a *rule of law* outlining what property the testator *can* dispose of by will, section 24 contains a *rule of construction* and gives guidance on how his dispositions are to be *understood* in a concrete case.[14]

As regards personalty, it was always beyond doubt that the testator had in principle the legal power to make dispositions concerning after-acquired property. The question was whether and when the instructions in his will were intended and effective to do so. It is not entirely clear how much of an impact section 24 actually had on the interpretation of testamentary instruments regarding a testator's personal property. According to some contemporary authors, including the Real Property Commissioners drafting the 1833 Report and James Wigram (who – it will be recalled – does not even mention the statute), wills of personalty were to be interpreted in exactly the same way, whether they were made before or on/after 1 January 1838.[15] Underlying this view is the assumption

[11] Reference to Lord Mansfield's observation in *Roe v Griffits* (1766) 4 Burr 1952, 1960; 98 ER 17, 21: 'one would wish that no such rule had ever been established, and lament that such nice subtilties should have been admitted as the ground of it'.

[12] Note that the Commissioners had previously professed that they 'did not propose to enter' more widely upon the 'general subject of the construction of legal Instruments': Real Property Commission, 'Fourth Report' (n 10) 3.

[13] Real Property Commission, 'Fourth Report' (n 10) 24.

[14] R Kerridge, assisted by AHR Brierley, *Parry and Kerridge: The Law of Succession*, 13th edn (London, Sweet & Maxwell, 2016) [12-02]. It is worth emphasising, however, that the Real Property Commissions themselves apparently regarded the proposed 'rule of construction' as a viable solution to the 'rule of law' issue.

[15] This is the relevant cut-off date according to s 34 of the Wills Act 1837.

that such wills (properly called 'testaments')[16] literally already 'spoke from death' in the 1830s. Yet according to other writers, section 24 is what essentially propelled English law from Swinburne's basic position into the modern era.[17]

The truth is likely to lie somewhere in between the two extreme positions, as is so often the case. From Swinburne's time and, indeed, before, the interpretation of testaments underwent a constant evolution – an evolution which did not end with the enactment of the Wills Act 1837, but has continued since.[18] Caught between the strict grammatical and the intention-orientated approaches to construction, English law had, by the early nineteenth century, already edged its way towards the recognition that testaments were 'ambulatory' in the interpretative sense:[19] not only were they capable of dealing with after-acquired property; one actually expected them to do so.[20] The testator would, after all, draft his wishes with a view to dying sometime in the future, and – pending his demise – the unrevoked 'last will' had to amble along as best it could and adapt its meaning to the changing circumstances of the testator's life. Nonetheless, section 24 entailed a substantive reorientation. By stipulating that every will was to be interpreted with respect to the property comprised therein, prima facie, 'as if it had been executed immediately before the death of the testator', it introduced a fiction and thereby over-enshrined the ambulatory principle (a theme to which we will have to return).[21]

All Souls College v Codrington, decided at the beginning of 1720, but reported under '*All Souls College versus Coddrington, & e contra*' as case number 173 at the Rolls in Hilary Term '1719',[22] was one of the stepping stones along the way. It lies on the path between wills speaking from the time of their execution and testaments speaking from death. And though the case may not even have been a particularly big stepping stone, it

[16] Historically, the word 'will' referred to dispositions over real estate, while a 'testament' was the instrument that concerned a testator's personal estate.

[17] Most notably T Jarman, *A Treatise on Wills*, vol 1 (London, Sweet, 1844) 277–92, who writes at 277–78 (all references omitted, emphasis added): 'For some purposes a will is considered to speak from its date or execution, and for others from the death of the testator: the former being the period of the inception, and the latter that of the consummation of the instrument. *In determining to which of these the language points, it is necessary to distinguish between wills that are subject to the recent act, and those which are regulated by the pre-existing law.* It may be stated, as a general rule, in regard to wills made before the year 1838, that wherever a testator refers to an actually existing state of things, his language is referential to the date of the will, and not his death, as this is then a prospective event.'

[18] For an assessment of the current position, see B Häcker, 'What's in a Will? – Examining the Modern Approach Towards the Interpretation and Rectification of Testamentary Instruments' in B Häcker and C Mitchell (eds), *Current Issues in Succession Law* (Oxford, Hart Publishing, 2016) 131, esp 133–39.

[19] See the third possible meaning outlined in n 9 above.

[20] See, eg, W Roberts, *Supplement to the Treatise on Wills and Codicils (Third Edition, 1826)* (London, Saunders and Benning, 1837) 63: 'As the law has stood hitherto, a will has been considered as speaking as to the general personal estate from the death of the testator: and with respect to real estate, and specific bequests of chattels real or personal, from the time of the making of it.'

[21] Häcker (n 8) 1073, 1076. See already Jarman (n 17) 287–92, esp 289, writing in 1844: 'The new rule of construction … will, according to the general terms in which the enactment is framed, apply to many cases in which its effect will be less decidedly salutary, nay, where it will, in all probability, defeat the intention'. The matter is discussed further below, in the text accompanying and following n 123.

[22] *All Souls College v Coddrington* (1720) 1 P Wms 597; 24 ER 533. In Peere Williams's Report, *All Souls v Codrington* is listed as the first case decided in 'Term. S. Hillary 1719', immediately following the last case of 'Term. S. Michaelis 1719'. The explanation lies in the fact that, until the middle of the eighteenth century, when the Gregorian calendar was adopted, the new 'civil' or 'legal' year in England did not start until 25 March.

can be seen as representative of the gradually evolving attitudes towards interpretation. In short, the *Codrington* litigation did not mark a seismic shift on its own, but is a good illustration of steady drops eventually hollowing the stone. This, and the fact that the case comes with a riveting background story which we can reconstruct with reasonable precision from various sources,[23] was deemed sufficient to warrant its inclusion in the present volume.

II. ACT ONE: THE LIFE OF THE TESTATOR, CHRISTOPHER CODRINGTON THE YOUNGER[24]

Scene 1 – Oxford, 1690

The College of All Souls of the Faithful Departed elects Christopher Codrington, who has for the past year already been there as a scholar on 'probationary' terms, to a full fellowship. This is no mean feat. Since the practice of effectively 'auctioning off' vacant fellowships to the highest bidder has been suppressed,[25] the election is based on merit. Christopher Codrington, previously a gentleman-commoner at Christ Church,[26] is known for his erudition, wit and learning.[27] A close student friendship links him with some of the up-and-coming intellectuals of his day, such as Joseph Addison and Charles Boyle.

Codrington comes from an old family of Gloucestershire gentry. He is the third Codrington by the name of Christopher. His grandfather, as a younger son, had no prospect of succeeding to the family estate at Dodington and therefore emigrated to the West Indies in around 1640. His father, known as 'Christopher Codrington the Elder', managed to acquire[28] several lucrative sugar plantations in Barbados and Antigua, and so built up a great fortune. In due course, he became Governor-General of the Leeward Islands. Our Christopher, 'the Younger', was born in Bridgetown, Barbados, during the heyday of pirate activity in the Caribbean in 1668, the year in which a dreadful fire ravaged the busy merchant seaport. A remarkably intelligent child, he was at the age of 12 sent to England for private schooling at Enfield, and thence he progressed to Oxford.

[23] The present account of the litigation and its background summarises and expands that given in Häcker (n 8) 1053–61.

[24] General biographical information which is not specifically referenced may be found in the various accounts of Christopher Codrington's life, esp M Burrows, *Worthies of All Souls: Four Centuries of English History* (London, Macmillan & Co, 1874) 324–46; VT Harlow, *Christopher Codrington* (Oxford, Clarendon Press, 1928); S Mandelbrote, 'The Vision of Christopher Codrington' in SJD Green and P Horden (eds), *All Souls under the Ancien Régime* (Oxford, Oxford University Press, 2007) 132; M Parker, *The Sugar Barons* (London, Hutchinson, 2011) 186–89, 197–216; GC Simmons, 'Towards a Biography of Christopher Codrington the Younger' (1972) 12 *Caribbean Studies* 32.

[25] In the early 1680s under Warden Jeames: see Burrows (n 24) 256–86; S Mandelbrote, 'All Souls from Civil War to Glorious Revolution' in Green and Horden (n 24) 55, 71–74.

[26] Codrington matriculated in 1685.

[27] He was also an able poet, of both cheeky and romantic verse: see, eg, the satirical poem against Richard Blackmore attributed to Codrington in R Anderson (ed), *The Works of the British Poets, with Prefaces, Biographical and Critical* (London, John & Arthur Arch and others, 1795) 581; JAV Chapple, 'Christopher Codrington's Verses to Elizabeth Cromwell' (1961) 60 *Journal of English and Germanic Philology* 75.

[28] Some of the acquisitions are shrouded in controversy: Parker (n 24) 163–66.

Scene 2 – Namur and Oxford, 1695

King William III (William of Orange) has been waging war against the Catholic King Louis XIV of France for seven years.[29] As part of the European 'Grand Alliance', he is trying to recapture Namur from the French. Among his men is an officer who has in 1693 already served him on the North American leg of his campaign[30] and who now catches his eye.[31] Christopher Codrington has sought leave from the College to fight for king and country.[32] He is rewarded by being promoted to lieutenant-colonel and returns to Oxford '*[t]am Marti quam Mercurio*'[33] – as distinguished in war as in business.

When King William visits Oxford in November 1695, the Public Orator falls ill. In his stead, 'Mr Codrington of All Souls, in a very elegant oration, express'd the publick joy of ye University to see his Majesty'.[34] A more entertaining account is later provided by the German traveller and book collector Zacharias Conrad von Uffenbach:

> [A]mongst all the members of the University (the scandal of it!) no one could be found who could really make a speech. So Codrington dressed himself up as a professor and in the name of the University delivered a brilliant address in Latin, which greatly pleased the King, who did not recognize him.[35]

[29] The so-called 'Nine Years' War' was to continue until 1697.

[30] Commonly known as 'King William's War'.

[31] Codrington's involvement in the siege is remembered within a 1695 poem by Thomas Yalden called *On the Conquest of Namur*:

> Indulge one grateful Labour more, my Muse,
> A Subject Friendship bids thee chuse:
> Let *Codrington's* lov'd Name inspire thy thought,
> With such a Warmth and Vigour as he fought:
> In vain thou dost of Arms and Triumphs sing,
> Unless he crowns thy Verse, and tunes thy sounding String.
> Victorious youth! your *Charwell's* greatest pride,
> Whom glorious Arms, and learned Arts divide:
> Whilst imitating great *NASSAU* [ie William III] you fight,
> His Person guard, and conquer in his sight:
> Too swift for Fame your early Triumphs grow,
> And Groves of Laurel shade your youthful Brow.
> In you the Muses and the Graces join,
> The glorious Palm, and deathless Laurels thine:
> Like *Phoebus* self your charming Muse hath sung,
> Like his your warlike Bow and tuneful Lyre is strung.

[32] Interestingly, Codrington had previously been a fervent supporter of King James II, writing a scathing poem against the 'pretender' William of Orange (published in Harlow (n 24) 46–47); but he changed his allegiance when James fled to France in the wake of the Glorious Revolution.

[33] Letter by Thomas Burnett of Kemnay to Gottfried Wilhelm Leibniz of 20 October 1700, published as letter no 132 in Leibniz-Archiv Hannover (ed), *Gottfried Wilhelm Leibniz: Allgemeiner politischer und historischer Briefwechsel*, vol 19 (Berlin, Akademie-Verlag, 2005) 277.

[34] Account by Dr [Edmund] Gibson of 9 November 1695: Oxford, Bodleian Library, MSS Ballard, vol 5, letter no 53, fol 89v, also published in *Oxoniana*, vol 1 (Oxford, Slatter and Munday, 1806) 142; Burrows (n 24) 330–31; Harlow (n 24) 82–84.

[35] ZC von Uffenbach, *Merkwürdige Reisen durch Niedersachsen, Holland und Engelland*, vol 3 (Ulm, Gaum, 1754) 172. English translation: WH Quarrell and WJC Quarrell (tr), *Oxford in 1710: From the Travels of Zacharias Conrad von Uffenbach* (Oxford, Blackwell, 1928) 61. Uffenbach visited Oxford only in 1710, so his is a second-hand account. It seems unlikely that the King would not have recognised Codrington, given that the latter appears in his oration to have 'narrated the noble deeds of war with the same courage as he had shown in their performance': Burrows (n 24) 331, citing – in translation – a dedication to Codrington by Bodley's Librarian, Dr [John] Hudson, in his *Dionysius of Halicarnassus*: see *Dionysii Halicarnassensis quae extant rhetorica et critica*, vol 2 (London, Bennet, 1704) p 2 of the *Dedicatio*.

Scene 3 – Oxford, 1700

Codrington's life is about to change dramatically. For the past five years, he has been busy as Captain of the First Foot Guards, travelling between England and the Continent, and after the end of the war as a socialite in London, Paris and (occasionally) Oxford. He has made the acquaintance of Alexander Cunningham, scholar of Roman law and well-connected book agent,[36] and has engaged Cunningham to help augment his growing collection of scholarly works. In June 1700, he writes that 'Mr Cunningham is going into France and from thence into Italy, and will mis[s] nothing y^{t} is curious',[37] and soon afterwards it is reported that Codrington's library comprises 'a rare and vast Collection'[38] which is 'increased dayly by [Cunningham] buying for him the most valuable books in Europe at any pryce'.[39] When Uffenbach later inspects the collection, his expert eye will estimate the library to consist of around 8,000 volumes of mainly 'new and costly' French, Spanish and Italian publications.[40]

Codrington is wealthy enough to indulge his collector's passion. He inherited his father's large fortune when the latter passed away in 1698. These funds now enable him to buy the family estate at Dodington Park in Gloucestershire from the less well-to-do senior branch of the family. The King has not forgotten his services and has appointed him to the position of Governor-General of the Leeward Islands. But, just as Codrington is getting his affairs in order to leave for the Caribbean, a tragic suicide gives rise to public scandal. Codrington's friend and protégé, the respected translator of classical texts Thomas Creech, is found hanging from his belt in his Oxford lodgings.[41] It appears that he has recently been expelled from All Souls[42] and has since rented rooms from a local apothecary, William Ives, opposite the College on the High Street. Codrington is a

[36] See JW Cairns, 'Alexander Cunningham's proposed edition of the Digest' (2001) 69 *Tijdschrift voor Rechtsgeschiedenis* 81 and 307; idem, 'Alexander Cunningham, Book Dealer: Scholarship, Patronage, and Politics' (2010) 5 *Journal of the Edinburgh Bibliographical Society* 11.

[37] Letter by Codrington to Dr [Arthur] Charlett of 25 June 1700, Bodleian Library, Oxford, MSS Ballard, vol 20, letter no 33, fol 57v.

[38] Burnett (n 33) 277.

[39] ibid 276.

[40] Uffenbach (n 35) 183 (p 69 of the English edition). This casts some doubt on Thomas Hearne's assertion in 1706 that the library (Codrington's 'study') consisted of around 12,000 volumes 'of wch some scarce, but ye greatest part Riff- Raff': CE Doble (ed), *Remarks and Collections of Thomas Hearne*, vol 1 (Oxford, Clarendon Press, 1885) 303. E Craster, *The History of All Souls College Library* (ed by EF Jacob, London, Faber and Faber, 1971) 69 writes that the collection was 'extensive but … of disappointing quality'. However, Craster bases this assessment solely on Hearne's recollection (not the most reliable of sources by any means) together with a note in the College's records which was deliberately aimed at downplaying the value of the after-acquired books for reasons of litigation tactics (see n 92 and the accompanying text). By the contemporary estimate of Richard Rawlinson, a renowned collector of books and manuscripts, the library Codrington eventually bequeathed to All Souls was in fact a 'most notable collection' worth around £6,000: Oxford, Bodleian Library, MSS Rawlinson, J 4to, II, entry no 270 on 'Christopher Codrington', fol 77r. Before Uffenbach saw the books himself in 1710 (but after he had met Thomas Hearne), he described Codrington's library as 'a fine collection of books worth three thousand pounds': Uffenbach (n 35) 172 (p 61 of the English edition).

[41] This happened in mid-June 1700. Thomas Hearne later recollects that the discovery was made on 19 July: HE Salter (ed), *Remarks and Collections of Thomas Hearne*, vol 9 (Oxford, Clarendon Press, 1914) 80. Yet there are various reports of Creech's death by late June, including in one of Codrington's own letters: see n 48 below.

[42] Uffenbach (n 35) 183–84 (p 69 of the English edition).

longstanding financial backer.[43] As part of this arrangement, Creech has been looking after Codrington's books.[44] Speculation is rife over what caused the suicide.[45] One garrulous pamphlet suggests unrequited love;[46] others implicate Codrington by putting Creech's despair down to a refusal of more money,[47] such that Codrington feels compelled to vindicate his conduct.[48] The coroner's inquest finds Creech to have been 'non compos mentis'.[49] A form of mental disorder or a severe bout of depression is indeed the most plausible explanation for his self-inflicted death.[50]

Before setting sail for the West Indies in mid-August 1700, Codrington entrusts his books to another friend, John Caswell, a scholar who is later to become Oxford's Savilian Professor of Astronomy. He leaves behind a newly made will,[51] and thus much guessing and gossiping about where the collection is eventually destined to go.[52] A small hand library at least accompanies him on his journey across the Atlantic.[53]

Scene 4 – Barbados, Easter 1710

It is 7 April, Good Friday, and Christopher Codrington is on his deathbed. In retrospect, the last 10 years have been a disappointment. His governorship was short-lived and rocked

[43] Creech's 1694 translation of Lucretius was dedicated to Codrington: Harlow (n 24) 225–27.

[44] Burnett (n 33) 276–77. My speculation in Häcker (n 8) 1056–57, at fn 30, that the books were only brought across the road from the College after Creech's death cannot be sustained in light of the fact that Creech already lodged with William Ives when he killed himself. According to Uffenbach's account (n 42), Codrington's books were stored in three chambers on the floor below Creech's garret room.

[45] See AL Baker, 'Investigating the Rumours and the Cause of Thomas Creech's Suicide' (2009) 56 *Notes & Queries* 236.

[46] *A Step to Oxford: Or a Mad Essay on the Reverend Mr Tho Creech's Hanging himself (as 'tis said) for Love* (London, 1700). But *cf* Burnett's report to Leibniz in late November 1700 that the lady in question was as much in love with Creech as he with her: letter no 133 in *Allgemeiner politischer und historischer Briefwechsel* (n 33) 288.

[47] Arthur Charlett may have been referring to Codrington when he alleged that 'there was a fellow-collegian of whom Creech frequently borrowed money; but that repeating his application too often, he met one day a cold reception, and in a fit of gloomy disgust retired, and in three days was found hanging in his study': Baker (n 45) 237.

[48] Codrington's long letter to Charlett of 25 June 1700 (n 37) begins thus (fol 55r): 'The same good natured People Who would represent Us unkind to Mr Creech since His death very probably are some of those who w[oul]^{d} have had Us believed too partial in His favour whilst alive … I never sayd or did any thing to Mr Creech, w[hi]^{ch} I wisht unsaid or undone … I used ye liberty and did ye duty of a Friend; but my Sincerity was ill tim'd …'

[49] Hearne, vol 9 (n 41) 216.

[50] See the evidence collected by Baker (n 45) 238–39 as well as Codrington's letter of 25 June 1700 (n 37) fol 57r, which states that certain 'new difficultys came upon [Creech] at a time when He was not fit to encounter [th]em[,] encreast His disorder and ended His life'.

[51] This will, dated 15 August 1700, is later superseded and (apparently) left unopened at Codrington's death: C Trice Martin, *Catalogue of the Archives in the Muniment Rooms of All Souls College* (London, Spottiswoode, 1877) 351, no 317; Mandelbrote (n 24) 142, text between fn 30 and 31, with further references.

[52] In June 1700, Codrington (n 37) fol 57v writes that 'tis possible, considering my circumstances I may make very little use of [the books] myself, and am not yet resolved w[ha]^{t} to doe wth them at my death, tho I am very fully determined I will not dispose of them as I at first intended'. Thomas Tanner, in a letter to Dr [Arthur] Charlett on 4 July 1700 (Oxford, Bodleian Library, MSS Ballard, vol 4, letter no 22, fol 43), was evidently concerned: 'I hope the unwelcome Resolution of Col Codrington's is not, to remove his Books from Oxford'. Yet already in October 1700, Burnett (n 33) 277 reports to Leibniz that the books were intended for All Souls.

[53] Burnett (n 33) 277: 'Colonell Codrington heth bought ane portable library of above 1000 £ Sterl to take to the Indies with him, the tyme he is absent from that rare and vast Collection Monsieur Cuningham heth got together for him and which he heth set up in England.'

by allegations of power abuse in handling a dispute between a wealthy landowner and a poor planter (Codrington was later exonerated).[54] The economic, social and judicial reforms he started with the aim of combating illegal trade and corruption,[55] and generally improving the administration and living conditions on the islands, were slow to bear fruit. When war with France broke out again on Queen Anne's accession to the throne in 1702,[56] Codrington was ill and wished for nothing more than to see England again, 'to pas[s] my life in my Library and be buryed in my garden'.[57] Instead, he had to raise a force which he led first (successfully) against St Kitts, driving out the French, and then (unsuccessfully) against Guadeloupe. Still unwell, he was replaced as Governor and failed to get reinstated when his immediate successor succumbed to tropical disease after only a few months in office. The man thereafter appointed, Daniel Parke, became a bitter foe. The governorship was his reward for bringing Queen Anne the good news of the Duke of Marlborough's victory at the battle of *Blindheim* [Blenheim]. Parke turned out to be 'one of the worst abusers of the existing system'.[58] Codrington, too weak for the journey to England, eventually retreated to his family home in Bridgetown, Barbados, where he 'led a very Private Retired Life, and spent most of his Time in Contemplation and Study'.[59] His burial takes place in Bridgetown on Holy Saturday, the day after his death at the age of just 42.

A few weeks, later, Daniel Parke will gleefully report to the Council of Trade and Plantations:

> Codrington (that Machivall) that was the author and contriver of all this villanny against me, is now answering for it, and a Vollpony[60] will he made takes place so that the most of his estate goes to those he mortally hated, before he died he was in great perplexity before he died [sic!] to alter his will and accordingly sent six times for one to do it, but those about him prevented the messengers going.[61]

If Parke's account is to be trusted, and if it is referring to the will that is subsequently proved,[62] then Codrington must have fallen out with some of those standing to benefit, for the will in question was already made in 1703, just before the attack on Guadeloupe.[63]

[54] A full account of *Herbert v Meade* and Codrington's involvement in it is given by Harlow (n 24) 130–46.

[55] See the Report on 'The Present State of Justice in the American Plantations, and Particularly in Barbadoes' of 4 September 1700, published (as no 751) in C Headlam (ed), *Calendar of State Papers Colonial, America and West Indies, 1700*, vol 18 (London, HM Stationery Office, 1910) 512: 'It is grown a proverb with the English merchants that, if a man goes over never so honest to the Plantations, yet the very air does change him in a short time. But it is not the air; it is the universal corruption of justice.'

[56] The so-called 'War of the Spanish Succession'.

[57] Letter to William Popple(?) on 30 November 1702, published (as no 125) in C Headlam (ed), *Calendar of State Papers Colonial, America and West Indies*, vol 21 (London, HM Stationery Office, 1913) 90. The letter continues by requesting: 'let one of your under gardiners plant me some fruit-trees and vines at Doddington'.

[58] Mandelbrote (n 24) 147.

[59] W Gordon, *A Sermon Preach'd at the Funeral of the Honourable Colonel Christopher Codrington* (London, Strahan, 1710) 21.

[60] A reference to Ben Jonson's play *Volpone*, in which a rich man pretends to be on his deathbed so as to trick those who hope to inherit his fortune.

[61] Letter of 11 May 1710, published (as no 228) in C Headlam (ed), *Calendar of State Papers Colonial, America and West Indies*, vol 25 (London, HM Stationery Office, 1924) 93. Little did he know it, but Parke himself was headed for a bad end, being violently murdered by rioting planters before the year was out.

[62] On 8 February 1711 by the Prerogative Court of Canterbury. The will is set out in Harlow (n 24) 217–20. A copy is available in the National Archives (ref: Prob 11/519).

[63] The will itself bears the date of 22 February 1702, but this must be read as 1703: see n 22 above.

It contains a great number of generous bequests, among them to John Caswell and Alexander Cunningham,[64] and it provides for a young man who is (probably) either Codrington's half-brother or an illegitimate son by a certain 'Maudline Morange'.[65] The three main beneficiaries, however, are Christopher's cousin and heir-at-law William Codrington, All Souls College, and the recently founded Society for the Propagation of the Gospel in Foreign Parts. The latter is to receive land in Barbuda as well as two plantations on Barbados in order to erect a college there.[66] Cousin William, 'a slippery character' at whom Daniel Parke's comments may well be targeted,[67] is appointed recipient of Codrington's Antiguan plantation 'Betty's Hope', residuary legatee and also the will's (principal)[68] executor. More importantly for present purposes:

> I give my nearest kinsman Leiuetenent Collonell William Codrington all my Estate in and about Doddington aforesaid provided and upon condition that he pay to all Souls Colledge in Oxford ten thousand pounds Sterling in manner Following vizt two thousand pounds within one yeare after my decease and the sume of two thousand pounds yearly afterwards untill the said Sume of ten thousand pounds be paid I doe appointe that Six thousand pounds thereof be Expended in the Building of a Library For the Use of the said Colledge and that the remaining Four thousand pounds be Laid out in bookes to Furnish the same[.]
>
> Item I give and bequeath unto the said Colledge my Library now in the Custody of Mr John Caswell in Oxford[.]

III. ACT TWO: EVOLUTION OF THE LEGAL DISPUTE BETWEEN ALL SOULS AND WILLIAM CODRINGTON[69]

Scene 1 – The Dispute Commences (1710–12)

News of Christopher Codrington's death reaches England in the summer of 1710, and by the end of August the Warden and Fellows of All Souls have decided that a catalogue

[64] Caswell was to receive 100 guineas. As to Cunningham: 'I bequeath to my very good Frind Mr Alexander Cuningham one hundred guineas besides what I have already given him by a Deed of Gift the due and constant payment whereof I most earnestly and particularly recommend to my Cozin Leiuetenent Collonell William Codrington not only For the great respect and Friendshipp I have for that worthy Gentleman but by reason the Annuity provided by the said deed of Gift will be an assistance to him in the great and usefull Labours in which he Employes himselfe for the publick benefitt'.

[65] 'Five hundred pounds sterling unto William the son of Maudline Morange when he shall arrive at the age of one and twenty yeares and that they in the mean time allow him Forty pounds Sterling per annum For his education and it's my desire that he should be bred up in the Sea Service.' A similar bequest had already been contained in the will of Codrington's father, Christopher Codrington the Elder.

[66] On the history of this bequest, see Mandelbrote (n 24) 151–63; JA Schutz, 'Christopher Codrington's Will: Launching the S.P.G. into the Barbadian Sugar Business' (1946) 15 *Pacific Historical Review* 192.

[67] Parker (n 24) 214.

[68] The will provided as follows: 'I desire Appointe and Impower my Friends Archibald Hutchinson Esquire Mr Richard Cary and Mr Richard Bates to be my Executors For the payment of my [aforementioned] Legacies out of the moneys which I now have in England and which shall be raised out of the Cropp which I have directed to be sent home which Legacies being paid I doe appointe my Cozen Leiuetenent Collonell William Codrington to be my sole Executor ...'

[69] Reconstructed, unless otherwise indicated, from the archival material held at All Souls (*Acta in Capitulis* 1707–53 and the memoranda and account books relating to Codrington's legacy mentioned in Trice Martin's *Catalogue* (n 51) 291–92, 416), as well as from the parties' pleadings available in the National Archives (ref: C 11/11/8, bill and two answers). For detailed references, quotes and numbers see Häcker (n 8) 1056–61.

of his books should be compiled. As it happens, they are already in the process of setting their existing library 'in order'.[70] But they cannot have got very far, for in mid-September, when Zacharias Conrad von Uffenbach first asks to see the College's collection, he finds that no one is able or willing to show him around.[71] Coming back a week later, Uffenbach is disappointed to find the All Souls 'library' very sparse and in a 'small poor room'.[72] He is all the more excited about Codrington's generous bequest (of which he deems 'these lazy Fellows, as they mostly are' unworthy)[73] and particularly the deceased's collection of books and manuscripts, still stored across the road in William Ives's house.[74]

In April 1711, the executor's year having expired, the College sends its 'Law Bursar',[75] Edward Kinaston [or Kynaston], to 'demand Mr Codrington's Legacy & books on behalf of ye Coll[ege]'.[76] In the autumn, William Codrington transmits a payment order for £2,000, 'being the first payment of Coll. Codrington's legacy', to be 'receive[d] of Mr Cary',[77] yet nothing eventuates. This is probably because Richard Cary, whom Christopher Codrington has charged in his will with paying some of the legacies (such as that to John Caswell and Alexander Cunningham),[78] is already in a legal dispute with William Codrington and his English representatives over the grant of probate and the proceeds of sale of some sugar crop.[79]

As far as Codrington's books are concerned, All Souls soon runs into a different problem. John Caswell, who has been looking after them, dies in April 1712. William Ives, the apothecary, is refusing to hand them over unless and until all the outstanding rent (of over £200) is paid for the rooms in which they have been kept. In legal terms, he is asserting his landlord's lien over the personal property of his tenant. Though the College protests that it is for William Codrington to discharge Christopher's debts, the Warden and Fellows agree in August 1712 to grant William Ives an interest-free loan of £200, to be repaid in due course,[80] and 'in consideration of ye sayd money, Coll. Codrington's books should be

An exciting newly discovered primary source that adds to the picture is the Chancery decree of 29 January 1720, which concluded the *Codrington* litigation. It was never enrolled and thus hard to find. I am deeply indebted to Dr David Foster for locating it in the 'Entry Books of Decrees and Orders' at the National Archives under the unlikely heading 'Guard of All Souls College v Codrington' (ref: C33/333/256v). 'Guard' is probably a reference to the Warden of the College (Latin: *custos*), who at the time happened to be a man by the name of Gardiner. I am also extremely grateful to Dr Robin Darwall-Smith for transcribing the decree.

[70] *Acta in Capitulis* (n 69) fol 6v.

[71] Uffenbach (n 35) 159 (p 52 of the English edition).

[72] ibid 172 (p 61 of the English edition): 'inconsiderable number of books', with the manuscripts 'scattered about'.

[73] ibid.

[74] According to Uffenbach's account, he visited the (old) College library on 26 September and saw Codrington's collection on 7 October 1710: ibid 173, 183 (pp 61–62, 69 of the English edition).

[75] Trice Martin (n 51) 335, no 126.

[76] *Acta in Capitulis* (n 69) fol 14r.

[77] ibid fol 17r.

[78] See n 68 above.

[79] *Cary v Prissick, Carpenter, and Codrington*. Bill and answer available in the National Archives (ref: C 6/393/48). Probate of the will having initially been granted to Christopher Prissick and Nathaniel Carpenter acting as William Codrington's attorneys in February 1711, a further grant is subsequently made in April 1716, this time including Richard Cary, Archibald Hutchinson and Richard Bates (*cf* n 68).

[80] In 1719, William Codrington will indeed agree to pay precisely this sum to William Ives: *Acta in Capitulis* (n 69) fol 51r. However, it is unclear whether this payment eventuated as promised. The Chancery decree of 29 January 1720 (n 69) contains an order that the College should pay Mr Ives the room rent due to him and should itself 'be reimbursed the same out of the assetts of the sd Testators personall estate'.

delivered into ye Coll. hands, and plac'd in ye Butler's chamber …, till a more convenient station shall be provided for them'.[81]

At this point, patience with William Codrington has already run out. His excuses for failing to pay up are becoming ever more spurious. At times, he flatly refuses to acknowledge the existence of the will and/or the bequest to All Souls;[82] at others, he denies that the Dodington Estate charged with the £10,000 legacy is of sufficient value to meet the obligation; and finally, he insinuates that the College would not put the money to the intended use. In March 1712, the Warden and Fellows have therefore agreed 'that a bill in Chancery should be prefer'd against ye Executor of Col. Codrington for not paying ye legacy left us by the sayd Coll.'[83] In early August, the College's legal counsel, a barrister by the Dickensian name of Scroggs Goad, files the relevant paperwork.[84] Thus begins the case of *All Souls College v Cod[d]rington.*

Scene 2 – Christopher Codrington's Reinterment and Fresh Controversy (1716–17)

It is June 1716, and Christopher Codrington's remains are about to be reinterred at All Souls, in accordance with instructions in his will.[85] Members of the Codrington family, including William, are present for the ceremony. The University marks the occasion by bestowing a DCL upon William,[86] and All Souls has made sufficient progress with its plans for the new library to allow for its foundation stone to be officially laid on 21 June.[87] Relations appear relatively cordial. Since 1713, William has been paying sums of between £270 and £1,000 in irregular instalments. By his own reckoning, he now still owes the College £2,871/18s/3d. In the autumn, he commissions the manager of the Dodington Estate to relay to All Souls an offer to make up the full £10,000.

The College, however, expects to be paid with interest and refuses to settle. Instead, it decides in late November to 'revive ye bill in Chancery against Col. Codrington for ye remainder of Coll. Codringtons Legacy'.[88] William Codrington's response is swift. In his answer to the bill of 1712, dated 8 February 1717, he admits that he has proved the will and 'by vertue thereof Entered upon the s^d Estate at Dodington and hath received

[81] *Acta in Capitulis* (n 69) fol 19r. The decree of 29 January 1720 (n 69) makes no mention of where the books were at the time (probably in College), but only recites William Ives's original answer to the College's bill.

[82] This allegation in the College's bill is later described in William Codrington's answer (which concedes the existence of the will and the bequest) as being 'unjustly charg'd upon him'.

[83] *Acta in Capitulis* (n 69) fol 18r.

[84] The bill lists William Ives as a second defendant, but the dispute with him is at this point only a week from being effectively resolved.

[85] 'I desire that my owne body may be Enterr'd in all Souls Chappell in Oxford and a plaine black Marble of twenty pounds price Laid thereon.' (This slab still lies in the Chapel today.)

[86] Thomas Hearne reports that William Codrington was created Master of Arts (MA) on 21 June 1716: DW Rannie (ed), *Remarks and Collections of Thomas Hearne*, vol 5 (Oxford, Clarendon Press, 1901) 239. However, according to the University's own *Catalogue of All Graduates in Divinity, Law, and Medicine, 1659–1800* (Oxford, Clarendon Press, 1801) 97, William Codrington had already received an MA on 27 June 1711 and was on 21 June 1716 made a Doctor of Civil Law (DCL).

[87] The date and William's presence are attested by an inscription above the library door (Catte Street entrance).

[88] *Acta in Capitulis* (n 69) fol 40v.

and still doth receive the Rents and profits thereof and hath possessed himself of a considerable personal Estate'; yet William claims that all of this is insufficient to pay the debts Christopher owed in the West Indies and in England and to satisfy the various other legacies bequeathed by his will. He insists that none of the testator's assets, either real or personal, are

> charged or chargeable with the s^d^ Ten thousand pounds other than his Estate at Dodington which at his death ... was not worth or let[89] for more than four hundred and fifteen pounds. And nor is now above four hundred and thirty nine pounds.[90]

He suggests that Christopher, having been resident abroad for so long and 'having never seen nor had any Account of the Estate at Dodington', grossly overestimated the estate's annual value, assuming it to cover the five £2,000 instalments of the All Souls bequest. Moreover, he argues that the College is not entitled to interest as a matter of law, and in any event he suspects that the Warden and Fellows have 'employ^d^' the money they have already received 'at Interest or otherwise to their own private profit'.

Knowing that a good offensive is sometimes the best form of defence, William Codrington then launches an outright counter-attack in connection with the books. He is unhappy that the College has possessed itself of Christopher's library 'without [his] privity or Assent'. Quite apart from the 'Library of books' (which he impliedly confines to the collection as it stood in 1703), he knows that the Warden and Fellows of All Souls have also taken into their keeping 'a great quantity of other valuable books and Manuscripts bought for the Testat[or's] use after he made his s^d^ Will of the value of many hundred pounds'. Of these, he wants an inventory and account, so that an 'allowance' can be calculated which may then be deducted from the £4,000 earmarked for the purchase of further books. The College's answer to William Codrington's cross-bill is not preserved, but its content is revealed by some internal documents.[91] The books in dispute, All Souls argues, are 'of small value',[92] and Codrington will moreover have to 'prove which they are':

> His Pretence is, That some Bookes were bought after ye date of ye Will, and woud not therefore pass by ye Will to ye College, 'tho now in our Custody.
>
> Wee say; if they were then bought wee doubt not but ye Law will give 'em to us: and wee know not of them; only have reason to suppose 'em to be of inconsiderable value.[93]

[89] William's reference to what Dodington was 'worth' must thus be understood as referring to the estate's annual income rather than as a statement of its absolute value.

[90] The tentative suggestion in Häcker (n 8) 1059 that William Codrington treated the bequest to All Souls as a so-called 'demonstrative legacy', while arguably the most plausible legal analysis of the gift, would not have enabled Codrington to escape payment on the ground that the fund from which the money was to be taken had been exhausted.

[91] Trice Martin (n 51) 292, nos 14, 15. The Chancery decree of 29 January 1720 (n 69) simply notes that the College's answer to the cross-bill was to the same effect as the College's original bill.

[92] It was even suggested that, for some years before Codrington's death, John Caswell had not received any books from Alexander Cunningham, 'saying that what he sent were not worth Carriage' (emphasis removed). A puzzling aspect of the report in Trice Martin (n 51) 292, no 15, is that the document claims John Caswell died in March '1708' (ie, probably 1709), when in fact he lived until 1712. In early 1709, he succeeded David Gregory († October 1708) as Professor of Astronomy.

[93] Underlining as in the original.

Scene 3 – Conclusion of the Dispute (1719–21)

By 1719, William Codrington is evidently tiring of the dispute. He is now involved in so many legal cases connected, in one way or another, with his inheritance[94] that he offers All Souls a total of £4,000, including £1,128 worth of interest,[95] in full and final settlement of the claim.[96] By the College's calculation, the interest due at this point already amounts to £1,623. As to the difference, the Warden and Fellows reckon that '£495 Abatement is more than wee can expend in ye suit, tho' wee shoud be forc'd to Appeal to the H. of Lords'.[97]

Luckily for All Souls, an appeal to the House of Lords proves unnecessary. The main source of disagreement remaining between the parties at this point concerns the after-acquired books,[98] and early in 1720, Sir Joseph Jekyll finds in the College's favour on this count.[99] Since no allowance therefore needs to be made for the books, the identification problem becomes irrelevant. After several more rounds of negotiations and further waiting, the remaining money is (it appears)[100] eventually received in July 1721.[101] It may have helped that William Codrington has just – on 21 April of the same year – been created the first Baronet of Dodington Park and is intending to stand for election as a Member of Parliament representing Banbury in 1722.[102]

[94] See esp *Codrington v Broderick* (National Archives, ref: C 11/847/53, bill dated 1716); *Courthope v Codrington* (National Archives, ref: C 11/1392/8, bill dated 1716); *Society for the Propagation of the Gospel v Codrington, Prissick, Chester and others* (National Archives, ref: C 11/1980/16, bill dated 1717); *Codrington v Orme* (Mr Byam's award on Chris. Codrington Esq's will, January 1718, Gloucestershire Archives, ref: D1610/F30a – Robert Orme was acting for his wife Elizabeth, the widow of John Caswell, and obtained £350 for Caswell's services and expenditure in looking after the books, and possibly also including the testamentary bequest of 100 guineas); *Codrington v Prissick* (National Archives, ref: C 11/25/10, bill dated October 1718 – William Codrington thus appears to have turned against his own agent).

[95] If, in line with the College's argument, one made no allowance for the after-acquired books.

[96] A previous attempt to settle having failed in mid-1718: *Acta in Capitulis* (n 69) fols 47r, 47v.

[97] Trice Martin (n 51) 292, no 15.

[98] In June 1719, the College noted that William Codrington 'has long since had a Copy of our Method of Computing ye Interest, to wch he has never signified any exception: nor given any reason for any Abatement, but That of ye Books': Trice Martin (n 51) 292, no 14.

[99] The Chancery decree of 29 January 1720 (n 69) shows that the court nevertheless ruled on the money issue as well: 'This Court doth think fitt and so order & Decree That it be referred to Master Lightbourne & to take an Acc[oun]t and see what part of the sd Legacy of £10000 devised to All Souls Coll hath been pd & to see when such summes as have been pd became payable & to Compute Interest for the same … from the time such Summes became payable & the said Master is to ascertaine when such part of the said Legacy as is remaining unpaid ought to have been paid by the sd Testators Will & to Compute Interest for the same & from the respective times of the same ought to have been pd by the testators Will & what shall appear to be due for Interest of the said Legacy of £10000 is to be deducted out of the said moneys already paid & the remainder is to be applyed to … the principall as mony so paid exceeded the Interest & when the said Master hath setled how much is due & unpaid of the said Legacy he is to carry on Interest or the same to such time as he shall appoint for the payment thereof … [there follows an order concerning the cost of the litigation].'

[100] Though query the significance of the Chancery suit against William Codrington mentioned in March 1723: *Acta in Capitulis* (n 69) fol 73r.

[101] A sum of almost £5,000 was received from William Codrington on 18 July 1721: Trice Martin (n 51) 292, no 20. The total amount of interest for late payment came to £2,123/19s/7d: Trice Martin (n 51) 291, no 7.

[102] He was unsuccessful, in Banbury and elsewhere, but eventually managed to win a by-election at Minehead in 1737, just a year before his death.

IV. ACT THREE: SIR JOSEPH JEKYLL'S JUDGMENT AND ITS AFTERMATH

London, Rolls House, Hilary Term 1719 (ie, 1720)

The case of *All Souls College v Codrington* comes before Sir Joseph Jekyll, who has been Master of the Rolls since 1717.[103] The decision is not reported until 1740, and then in fairly brief terms, such that it can be set out in full:[104]

> Colonel *Coddrington* deviſed to *All Souls College* in *Oxford* in theſe Words, *I deviſe my Library of Books now in the Cuſtody of Mr.* Carſwell, to All Souls College *in* Oxford; and in the ſame Will he deviſed to the ſaid College 4000 *l.* more to augment their Library. After which the Teſtator bought ſeveral Books of Value which were placed in the ſaid Library.
>
> Objected, That the Books purchaſed afterwards ſhould not paſs; becauſe the Gift is of his Library of Books *now* in the Cuſtody of *Carſwell*, which Word [now] muſt be relative to the Time of making the Will, otherwiſe muſt be rejected; but it was ſaid to be againſt an eſtabliſhed Rule in the Conſtruction of Wills, to reject any Word that can be made to take Effect; it was admitted that without the Word [now] the Will, as to the perſonal Eſtate, would relate to the Time of the Death of the Testator; *ſecus* where that Word was inſerted; that if I ſhould deviſe all the Leaſes which I now have, or all the Horſes which I now have in my Stable, and afterwards purchaſe more of each, theſe new Leaſes or Horſes would not paſs.
>
> *Master of the Rolls:* Where I deviſe all the Corn *now* in my Barn, if that Corn be afterwards ſpent, and new Corn put in, ſuch new Corn will not paſs: But if I deviſe all my Flock of Sheep *now on ſuch a Hill, or in ſuch a Paſture*; in that Caſe, becauſe Sheep are in their Nature fluctuating, ſome must die, ſome be killed, and ſome Lambs be produced which will afterwards breed, and it being the Caſe of a collective Body, the Sheep produced afterwards ſhall paſs; and this is within the Reaſon of a Deviſe of Perſonal Eſtate, which, because always fluctuating, ſhall therefore relate to the Time of the Teſtator's Death; beſides the Will, as to Perſonals, does not ſpeak till after the Teſtator's Death.
>
> It is natural to think that the Teſtator did not in the Principal Caſe intend his Executor ſhould be garbling the Library after his Death, by picking out the Books bought ſince the making of the Will, which appears more plainly from the ſubsequent Deviſe of 4000 *l.* to the College to buy Books, ſo that his Deſign manifeſtly was to *increaſe* rather than *diminiſh*.
>
> As to the Caſes that have been put of a Deviſe of all the Leaſes which I now have, or of all the Horſes now in my Stable, and afterwards I purchaſse more of each, the new Leaſes or Horſes will not paſs; the Reason is becauſe theſe are particular Chattels, and not Part of a collective Body as a Flock of Sheep, or a Library of Books. Indeed a Flock of Sheep differs ſomewhat from a Library of Books; for the former muſt of Neceſſity fluctuate as above; but there is no Neceſſity that Books ſhould be changed.

[103] Interestingly, it was Joseph Jekyll, on becoming Master of the Rolls, who had caused the old Rolls House to be pulled down and rebuilt according to a design by Colen Campbell. The new and expensive building was 'a Royal Gift from our most Gracious Sovereign King George to Sir Joseph Jekyll': HE Stutchbury, *The Architecture of Colen Campbell* (Manchester, Manchester University Press, 1967) 47. See further E Edwards, *Libraries and Founders of Libraries* (London, Trübner and Co, 1865) 267–68, who also discusses Joseph Jekyll's remarkable bequest in his own will to pay off the national debt, giving rise to litigation and even the passing of an Act of Parliament.

[104] Spelling and italics as in the original Report by Peere Williams (n 22).

> However in this Cafe it was decreed that the Books afterwards bought by the Teftator, and put into his Library, fhould pafs to the College by the Will: the Court being of Opinion that the Word *Now* did not relate to the Books which were in the Library at the Time of making the Will, but, on Conftruction of the whole Sentence, denoted where the faid Library was, and might be intended to diftinguish it from any other Library of the Teftator's.[105]

The first thing to note is that Christopher Codrington actually bequeathed to All Souls his '<u>Library</u> now in the Custody of Mr John Caswell' and not, as the report suggests, his '<u>Library of Books</u> now in the Custody of Mr. Carswell [name mis-spelt]',[106] but this discrepancy is probably explicable by the way the case was pleaded and an apparent change of legal counsel on the College's side before the hearing.[107]

Yet words matter, especially at the time when *All Souls College v Codrington* came to be heard. According to Henry Swinburne's treatise of 1611, the case of 'books' would usually be captured by the general rule that 'the time of the testament, and not of the testator's death is to be regarded'.[108] By contrast, a 'library' might well count as a 'collective' or 'universal' thing with respect to which it was recognised that – exceptionally – the will spoke from death.[109] The same distinction can be found in John Godolphin's book known as *The Orphan's Legacy*, of which the fourth and last edition appeared in 1701:[110]

> To find out the Teftators mind and meaning, which is the very Index of the Teftament, the time of making thereof is regularly more confiderable in point of Legacies, than the time of the Teftators death, becaufe the prefumption of Law is, That the mind is not altered, unlefs it may otherwife appear by fufficient Evidence. Therefore the Teftators words are fpecifically to be referred to the time when the Teftament was made, and more efpecially if the Teftators words be general words. So if a Father bequeath to his Son, who is a Student, all his Books, and after buy other Books, thofe other pafs not by that Legacy [...]
>
> And yet notwithftanding alfo all this which hath been faid, that the time of the making of the Teftament is chiefly and fpecially to be referred to in the due Conftruction of Legacies, yet this is to be underftood only when the words of the Teftator speak of the time paft or prefent; Not when he fpeaks of the time to come by words of the Future Tenfe ... Also when the Legacy is Univerfal under fome name Appellative, and in its Nature Collective, as Herd, Flock, and the like; fuch a Legacy admitting of increafe and decreafe, the time (in that cafe) of the Teftator's death is more to be infpected and confidered than the time when he made the Teftament.

[105] The corresponding passage in the decree of 29 January 1720 (n 69) reads: 'this Court declared That all the Books of the sd Testator that were in the Custody of Mr Caswell of Oxford at the time of the Death of the sd Testator belong to the Plts the Word /Then/ in the Will not relateing to the Books that were in the Library at the time of the making the Will but upon the Construction of the whole Sentence only denoting the place where the Library was & dothe therefore order That the Cross Bill do stand dismissed'. The reference to 'then' rather than 'now' is probably explicable by the account earlier in the decree of the fact that Christopher Codrington 'gave the Coll' his Library *then* in the Custody of Jno Caswell in Oxford' (emphasis added).

[106] Emphasis by underlining added. The decree of 29 January 1720 (n 69) contains the correct spelling of Caswell's name, so that this particular error appears to be the reporter's.

[107] Häcker (n 8) 1062. Just like the College's bill of complaint and William Codrington's answer to it, the Chancery decree of 29 January 1720 (n 69) also contains several references to the testator's 'Library of Books'.

[108] See the quote accompanying n 2 above.

[109] See Swinburne (n 2) 316v–317r (third 'extenfion or ampliation' of the basic rule) as well as 317v–318r (first and second 'limitations' of the rule).

[110] J Godolphin, *The Orphan's Legacy or, A Testamentary Abridgement*, 4th edn (London, Vincent, 1701) 272–74 (pt III, ch 1, § 3). All references omitted.

Swinburne's and Godolphin's commentaries, with which Sir Joseph Jekyll would have been well-acquainted, may go some way towards explaining the Master of the Rolls' charming comparison between a library and a flock of sheep, and also his perceptive remark that books do not fluctuate in the same way as cattle.[111]

However, it is clear from the judgment that the main focus of debate surrounding the construction of Christopher Codrington's will was on the word 'now'. This is not something we find discussed in either Swinburne or Godolphin. While Swinburne expressly points out that use of the possessive pronoun 'my' (eg 'my plate' or 'my books') normally 'hath the force of the preſent time',[112] we must assume that 'now' merited no mention since it would only reinforce the basic rule. Yet by 1720, there has been an actual case deciding that the word 'now' refers to the time when a will was made,[113] so who can blame William Codrington for trying his luck? From our modern perspective, he rightly lost the litigation with All Souls; but at the time, he was perhaps unfortunate to have come up before Sir Joseph Jekyll – a man who made no secret of preferring the intention-based approach to construction over giving words their strict grammatical meaning,[114] and who, just two years previously, had held (directly contrary to Swinburne)[115] that '[t]he deviſe of all one's Houſhold Goods will paſs all Houſhold Goods that the Teſtator has at the Time of his Death'.[116]

As already mentioned, *All Souls v Codrington* can be seen as part of a more general trend, starting in earnest around a decade and a half earlier,[117] which will eventually

[111] There is an interesting anthropological question about why horses are perceived differently from more generic cattle such as sheep, particularly in early modern times (*cf* Sir Joseph Jekyll's example of 'all the horses in my stable' as well as Sir William Page Wood VC's express reference to horses discussed in n 112 immediately below). Their identity tends to be established individually rather than collectively, probably on account of the close relationship between a man and his horse. Contrast classical Roman law, where horses are often visible in legal texts as part of a larger entity, a 'collective thing' such as an *equitium* (stud of horses) or a *quadriga* (a yoke of four horses pulling a chariot).

[112] Swinburne (n 2) 319v, though note that this remark is already made in connection with an intention-orientated exception. For the civilian background, see Häcker (n 8) 1070–71. As regards the English position prior to the Wills Act 1837, see *Miller v Little* (1840) 2 Beav 259; 48 ER 1180. Concerning the position afterwards, there is a statement by Sir William Page Wood VC in *Goodland v Burnett* (1855) 1 K & J 341, 348–49; 69 ER 489, 492–93: 'When I refer to a particular thing, such as a ring or a horse, and bequeath it as "my ring" or "my horse," it seems to me there might be considerable difficulty in saying that the "contrary intention" to which the Act, in its 24th section refers, does not appear on the face of the will; but when a bequest is of that which is generic – of that which may be increased or diminished, then, I apprehend, the Wills Act requires something more on the face of the will for the purpose of indicating such "contrary intention" than the mere circumstance that the subject of the bequest is designated by the pronoun "my".'

[113] *Attorney General v Bury* (1701) 1 Eq Cas Abr 201; 21 ER 989: 'A man devised all the Arrears now due, and unjustly detained from me by the Dean and Chapter of *York*, to be employed in a certain Charity; and the Question was, whether the Arrears incurred after the making of the Will, and a small Time before the Death of the Testator, and which were never demanded by the Testator, should pass; and *per* Ld K not; for though a general Devise of all a Man's Goods will carry all he had at his Death, though purchased after the making his Will; yet here it is confined to the Arrears due at the making the Will.'

[114] *Cowper v Earl Cowper* (1734) 2 P Wms 720, 741; 24 ER 930, 937: 'I am sensible there is a diversity of opinions among the learned judges of the present time, whether the legal operation of words in a will, or the intent of a testator, shall govern? for my part, I shall always contend for the intention where it is plain.'

[115] Swinburne (n 2) 317r–318r ('householdstuffe').

[116] *Masters v Masters* (1718) 1 P Wms 421, 424–25; 24 ER 454, 455. He explained: '[H]ouſhold Goods are always changing, and periſhing; and therefore the Will, as to Perſonal Eſtate, ſhall relate to the Time of the Teſtator's Death; otherwiſe it would be very inconvenient; for then a Man muſt make a new Will every Day'.

[117] See *Gayre* v *Gayre* (1706) 2 Vern 538; 23 ER 949 (pictures); *Sayer v Sayer* (1715) Prec Chan 392; 24 ER 176; Gilb 87; 25 ER 60 (personal estate in a particular place); and *cf* already *Roberts v Bennet* (1690) 2 Vern 136; 23 ER 695 (release of debts) – all contrary to Swinburne (n 2) 316v–318r.

merge into the enactment of section 24 of the Wills Act 1837. Before the century was out, it had helped English law get to a position where it mattered not so much whether something was *generally* regarded as being of a 'universal' or 'collective' nature, but whether the *testator* might reasonably have expected its constitution to change over time when making the will. If so, then a bequest of 'all my pictures, prints, and drawings' included after-acquired art,[118] and a gift of '£50 to every child [AB] *hath* by his wife' extended to children born between the date of the will and the testator's death.[119] If not,[120] then the time of the will continued to count: 'A will is ambulatory; but a specific bequest is fixed as much as a devise of land';[121] however, 'no legacy is to be held specific, unless demonstrably so intended'.[122]

The reason why the Wills Act 1837 can be said to have 'over-enshrined' the ambulatory principle[123] is that is has (apparently inadvertently) created a situation where the testator's very intention with respect to the nature and extent of a bequest has to be established by reference to a time other than that when the will was made. The repercussions and potential problems of 'making [the will] operate by construction, as if it had been executed immediately before the death of the testator'[124] were already evident when the statute was passed. In a special supplement to his *Treatise on Wills and Codicils*, William Roberts commented with respect to section 24:[125]

> As it has been the plain design of the Legislature in this clause to put an end to the distinctions existing between real and personal property, and general and specific bequests in this respect, by making a will act upon the testator's property of every kind as it exists at his death, unless the expressions or context of the instrument, without reference to extrinsic circumstances, should manifest an intention inconsistent with such a construction; it may be doubted whether Courts of Justice, in administering the law under this statute, will suffer any words indicating grammatically the present time, as 'now' or 'to the children which he hath,'[[126]] or the 'property which I am possessed of,' or such like words or phrases, to limit the effect of a devise or bequest to the date of the instrument; for if a will is to be construed to speak and take effect as if it had been executed immediately before the death of the testator, that juncture becomes the time to which words of present import have their proper relation.

[118] *Dean and Chapter of Christchurch v Barrow* (1767) Amb 641; 27 ER 415.

[119] *Ringrose v Bramham* (1794) 2 Cox 384, 30 ER 177 – again contrary to Swinburne (n 2) 316r–316v.

[120] As, eg, in *Wilde v Holtzmeyer* (1801) 5 Ves Jun 811; 31 ER 871, where the testator was 'a man ignorant of the English language' who had used the words 'all I am possessed of' non-technically in his will. (As a matter of 'legal construction', these words meant all interest which the testator had in personal estate at his death.)

[121] *Baugh v Read* (1790) 1 Ves Jun 257, 260; 30 ER 330, 332 (Thurlow LC). He said: 'The difficulty of the case is, that here [the] testator has described this stock as being his property then existing as such a fund; it turns out, that, if this is not added, the testator has no such property; and therefore creates, what the law calls, a latent ambiguity; and induces a right of proving, what he did mean by a description, insensible without that proof … Where a testator uses certain words, which *prima facie* give a clear account, the same fact that enables you to prove, that there is a latent ambiguity, enables you to prove, what was his intention.'

[122] *Kirby v Potter* (1799) 4 Ves Jun 748, 753; 31 ER 387, 389.

[123] See n 21 above and text thereto.

[124] Roberts (n 20) 64.

[125] ibid.

[126] *cf* n 3 above concerning the intention behind and effect of s 89 of the Irish Succession Act 1965. It thus appears that the limitation built into s 24 of the Wills Act 1837 (namely, that the new rule of construction applied only 'with reference to the real estate and personal estate comprised in [the will]') was not initially taken very seriously by contemporaries. Yet in *Bullock v Bennett* (1855) 7 De G M & G 283; 44 ER 111 it was held that under s 24 the will does not speak from death with respect to the 'objects of the testator's bounty', ie the beneficiaries under the will. This is also the understanding of Kerridge (n 14) [12-15], who explains cases such as *Ringrose v Bramham* (n 119) on the basis that they involve a gift to beneficiaries answering a 'class' description: ibid [12-16], [11-12]. One is tempted to conclude that s 24 of the Wills Act 1837, while inadvertently

Thomas Jarman warned of automatically construing the word 'now' (eg 'the house in which I now reside') as if it signified the time of the testator's death, expressing the hope 'that the principle will not be carried such a length, and that this would be considered as a case in which "a contrary intention appears by the will."'[127] Luckily, the courts have for the most part heeded his advice. As Lindley LJ once observed in characteristically robust manner, section 24 'does not say that we are to construe whatever a man says in his will as if it were made on the day of his death',[128] and Lord Chancellor Cottenham in *Cole v Scott* specifically held that the testator's reference to 'now' normally indicated the time when the will was made.[129] In the case of *Re Whitby*, concerning a bequest of 'all articles of jewellery and other chattels and effects belonging to me … which are now deposited for safe custody at the Manchester Safe Deposit Co', a unanimous Court of Appeal reached the same conclusion.[130] Lord Greene MR said:

> Reading this simply as a piece of straightforward English I should have thought that the reference to time is just as essential a part of the description as the reference to place. The contrary view involves, in effect, striking out of this codicil the word 'now.' … However rightly it may have been held in other cases, where 'now' appeared in quite different contexts, that the word was not an essential part of the description, the question we have to decide is whether in this codicil and in this context it is an essential part of the description. Speaking for myself I find it impossible to construe these words in any other sense. It seems to me that the testator was thinking of a particular time, namely, the date of his codicil, just as he was thinking of a particular place. In the result, therefore, I am of opinion that s. 24 does not apply …[131]

Yet, as Lord Greene's statement indicates, none of this calls into question the possibility that the testator may have used the word 'now' in a different sense on an overall (and especially on a modern 'contextual')[132] interpretation of the will.[133] From today's perspective, Sir Joseph Jekyll in the *All Souls* case hit the nail right on the head in observing that Christopher Codrington's intention was to leave his continuously increasing book collection to the College and that

over-enshrining the ambulatory principle with respect to the property comprised in the will, may at the same time inadvertently have undone progress already made by the courts with respect to the intended beneficiaries of the testator's bounty.

[127] Jarman (n 17) 291.

[128] *Re Portal v Lamb* (1885) 30 ChD 50 (CA) 55, prefacing this by saying: 'I am always unwilling to strain this Act or any other Act in such a way as to defeat a man's plain intention. The object of this section was not to defeat, but to give effect to the testator's intention.' Lindley LJ continued: 'The question is, are we bound by this section to defeat this intention? I think not, and for this reason [:] … [Section 24] refers to the real and personal estate comprised in the will, and nothing else … When there is a puzzle as to which clause of the will carries a particular property, the statute does not say which clause is to outweigh the other, but only that the property is to be comprised in the will. Be it so. The question still remains which clause carries the property, the residuary or the specific devise?'

[129] *Cole v Scott* (1849) 1 Mac & G 518; 41 ER 1366; 1 Ha & Tw 477; 47 ER 1498, followed by *Hutchinson v Barrow* (1861) 6 Hurl & N 583, 593; 158 ER 240, 246: 'In our opinion a contrary intention does appear by this will. We think it was the intention of the testator, as expressed in this devise, to state his will to be, that the lands to be taken by his wife were as described by the then existing state of circumstances, and that the word "now" merely expresses the date as if he had said, "On the 10th of April, 1854."' Note that the strong disapproval of *Cole v Scott* expressed by Sir Richard Malins VC in *Castle v Fox* (1871) LR 11 Eq 542 (Ct Ch), esp 553–54, may be at least partly explained by the fact that he was counsel for the unsuccessful defendant in *Cole*.

[130] *Re Whitby* [1944] Ch 210 (CA).

[131] ibid 215.

[132] *Marley v Rawlings* [2014] UKSC 2, [2015] 1 AC 129, [17]–[26]; but *cf* the comments in Häcker (n 18) 135–38; Kerridge (n 14) [10-67].

[133] See, eg, *Re Champion* [1893] 1 Ch 101 (CA); *Re Willis* [1911] 2 Ch 563 (ChD). More questionable is the case of *Wagstaff v Wagstaff* (1869) LR 8 Eq 229, where Lord Romilly MR reasoned as follows: 'If the testator

the Word *Now* did not relate to the Books which were in the Library at the Time of making the Will, but, on Conſtruction of the whole Sentence, denoted where the ſaid Library was, and might be intended to diſtinguish it from any other Library of the Teſtator's.

V. A SHORT EPILOGUE: THE LEGACY'S COLONIAL LEGACY

Scene 1 – Oxford, 1751

Thirty-five years after its foundation stone was laid, the 'Codrington Library' is finally completed and opened.[134] It is a grand edifice, with a gothic exterior and light-flooded classical interior, framing the northern side of the College's new 'Great Quad'. Its architect is the celebrated Nicholas Hawksmoor,[135] in accordance with whose designs the whole of the new quadrangle has been built. William Blackstone, a Fellow of the College who is in due course to become the first Vinerian Professor of English Law and the first person ever to give a university lecture on the common law of England, is actively involved in putting the final touches to the building project, setting the books in order and (probably) drafting the library rules.[136] A sculpture of Christopher Codrington, the benefactor whose munificence has made all of this possible, has been commissioned from Henry Cheere and graces the library's central recess.

Scene 2 – Oxford, 2018

Codrington's statue still stands on its plinth, but perspectives on the man and his bequest have changed or have at any rate becomes more diverse. In the wake of the 'Rhodes Must Fall' movement, a spotlight has been shone on the transatlantic sugar and slave trade: a triangular system involving the kidnapping and enslavement of native Africans, their trafficking under atrocious conditions across the sea to spend their life toiling on the Caribbean sugar plantations so that the European hunger for sugar as a luxury good may be satiated, and then transport of English goods (such as weapons and cloth) back to Africa, there to be used for the purchase of even more slaves.[137] The Codrington family wealth was built on just this triangular trading system. And while Christopher Codrington

had said, "I give all my real and personal estate," there can be no doubt that after-acquired property would have passed. So again, if he had said, "I give all the real and personal estate I possess." Does it make any difference when he puts in the word "now"? The words "I possess" mean the same thing as "I now possess."'

[134] A detailed account of the lengthy building process may be found in Craster (n 40) 71–80.

[135] Hawksmoor originally wanted the entire building to be in the neo-Gothic style, but this could not persuade George Clarke, Fellow of the College and architectural enthusiast: EL Daniel, 'English Baroque Libraries' (1998) 72 *Yale University Library Gazette* 116, 130–31.

[136] W Prest, *William Blackstone: Law and Letters in the Eighteenth Century* (Oxford, Oxford University Press, 2008) 75–81; Craster (n 40) 79–80; N Aubertin-Potter, '"A Mighty Consumption of Ale": Blackstone, Buckler and All Souls College, Oxford' in W Prest (ed), *Blackstone and his Commentaries: Biography, Law, History* (Oxford, Hart Publishing, 2009) 35, 37–39; *Acta in Capitulis* (n 69) fols 192v–194v.

[137] See generally RB Sheridan, *Sugar and Slavery: An Economic History of the British West Indies, 1623–1775* (Baltimore, Johns Hopkins University Press, 1974); RA Austen and WD Smith, 'Private Tooth Decay as Public Economic Virtue: The Slave–Sugar Triangle, Consumerism, and European Industrialization' (1990) 14 *Social Science History* 95; PR Emert (ed), *Colonial Triangular Trade: An Economy Based on Human Misery* (Carlisle, MA, Discovery Enterprises, 1995); K Morgan, *Slavery, Atlantic Trade and the British Economy* (Cambridge,

the Younger may – by the standards of his time – have been a relatively enlightened Governor of the Leeward Islands, and while he may actually have been opposed to the very worst excesses of slave exploitation and maltreatment,[138] there is no doubt that he never questioned the institution of slavery or forced labour per se.[139]

By the terms of his will, of course, the library bequest was to be funded primarily from the Dodington Estate (no doubt using rents there extracted from poor Gloucestershire peasant farmers!); yet even if its payment was not 'topped up' directly with sugar and blood money, Christopher the Younger could not have acquired the Gloucestershire land without the wealth left to him by his father, Christopher the Elder, whose West Indian fortune was made rather more ruthlessly.[140] The Codrington Library thus shares the heritage of so many public buildings and stately homes, which are in one way or another inextricably linked to both the glory and the unspeakable abominations of England's colonial past. To mark this heritage, visitors to All Souls College will today find the following inscription set in stone at the Catte Street entrance to the Codrington Library:

IN MEMORY
OF THOSE
WHO WORKED
IN SLAVERY
ON THE
CODRINGTON
PLANTATIONS
IN THE
WEST INDIES

Cambridge University Press, 2001); K Harley, 'Slavery, the British Atlantic Economy, and the Industrial Revolution' in AB Leonard and D Pretel (eds), *The Caribbean and the Atlantic World Economy* (Basingstoke, Palgrave Macmillan, 2015) 161.

[138] See, eg, Mandelbrote (n 24) 142–47, 152–59; 171; Simmons (n 24) 40, 42–43; Parker (n 24) 197–201.

[139] On 10 July 1699, for instance, Codrington wrote in a letter to the Council of Trade and Plantations that 'the negroes are as much our property as our cattle', published (as no 628) in C Headlam (ed), *Calendar of State Papers Colonial, America and West Indies*, vol 17 (London, HM Stationery Office, 1908) 337. For a recent assessment of how slave conversion fitted with British imperial politics and Codrington's role in all of this, see K Gerbner, *Christian Slavery: Conversion and Race in the Protestant Atlantic World* (Philadelphia, University of Pennsylvania Press, 2018) 100–10. On the public perception of Christopher Codrington with respect to slavery, see S Gikandi, *Slavery and the Culture of Taste* (Princeton, Princeton University Press, 2011) 119–25.

[140] Parker (n 24) 163–65. Even authors who are generally well disposed towards the historical Codrington family are very critical of Christopher the Elder: see, eg, Harlow (n 24) 11–37, esp 11: 'the pursuit of riches and power became an obsession which gradually dominated his outlook, so that the last years of his life were marred by arrogance, injustice and self-seeking'. Gikandi (n 139) 121, in his critical assessment of the 'two sides of the narrative of [the younger] Codrington's life', bemoans that '[a]ny references to West Indian fortunes – the control of slaves and the production of sugar – are attributed to the father, and the moral responsibility of slavery is transferred from successors to progenitors', but he appears to overlook the Dodington link of the library bequest.

3

Jesson v Wright (1820): Wills, Coal and the Rule in *Shelley's Case*

N G JONES

I. INTRODUCTION

THE MODERN HISTORIOGRAPHY of English leading cases began in 1995, with AWB Simpson's *Leading Cases in the Common Law*,[1] the first chapter of which concerned *Shelley's Case* (1581).[2] It seems fitting, therefore, that this volume include *Jesson v Wright* – heard, as *Doe d Jesson v Wright*, in 1816 in the King's Bench, and on writ of error in the House of Lords in 1820[3] – described by *Theobald on Wills* as leading on the 'rules of construction with reference to cases coming within the operation of the rule in *Shelley's Case*'.[4]

II. EZEKIEL PERSEHOUSE AND HIS WILL

Jesson v Wright arose from the will, dated 24 April 1773, of Ezekiel Persehouse 'of the parish of Tipton ... in the County of Stafford Gentleman',[5] who died on that day,[6] perhaps the Ezekiel Persehouse described in 1771 as a maltster.[7] Tipton lies north-west of Birmingham, north and a little east from Dudley, close to the heart of the Black Country.

[1] AWB Simpson, *Leading Cases in the Common Law* (Oxford, Oxford University Press, 1995).

[2] 'Politics and Law in Elizabethan England, *Shelley's Case* (1581)', ibid, 13–44. *Wolfe v Shelley* (1581) 1 Co Rep 88b; 1 And 69; Moo KB 136; 3 Dyer 373b.

[3] *Doe d Wright and others v Jesson and others* (1816) 5 M & S 95; *Jesson and others v Doe d Wright and others* (1820) 2 Bli 1.

[4] J Ross Martyn *et al*, *Theobald on Wills*, 18th edn (London, Sweet & Maxwell, 2016) [26-158]. For the rule see below, text to n 44.

[5] The National Archives (TNA) PROB 11/1002/246.

[6] This is stated in the special verdict, 2 Bli 1, 5.

[7] Dudley Archives DE/1/6/114, mortgage deed, 17 August 1771. The land devised included a 'malthouse': TNA PROB 11/1002/246. Persehouse seems to have left neither widow nor children. He has not been identified more precisely. The Ezekiel, son of Abraham and Bettey Persehouse, baptised in St Martin's, Tipton, on 17 August 1755 was probably too young to have been the testator: Staffordshire Parish Registers Society, *Tipton, St Martin Parish Registers*, pt 2 (Staffordshire Parish Registers Society, 2011) 41.

After provision for debts and expenses, the will made bequests to a total of £3,700 to nieces and nephews. Turning to realty, it began with a devise to 'William one of the sons of my said sister Ann Wright before marriage',[8] of 'all that messuage tenement or dwelling house malthouse stable buildings garden hereditaments and premises with their and every of their appurtenances' in the parish of Tipton in the testator's possession, with 'all those two dwelling houses barn shops buildings gardens hereditaments and premises' in the same parish now in the occupation of John Law and one Timmins,[9] and also 'all those seven closes pieces or parcels of land or ground to the said two dwelling houses and buildings adjoining or nearly adjoining and belonging with their and every of their appurtenances' now in the testator's possession,

> to hold the same premises unto the said William son of my said sister Ann Wright for and during the term of his natural life … and from and after his decease I give and devise all the said dwelling houses or tenements buildings gardens lands hereditaments and premises with their and every of their appurtenances unto the heirs of the body of the said William son of my said sister Ann Wright lawfully issuing in such shares and proportions as he the said William in and by any deed or writing deeds or writings or in and by his last will and testament in writing … shall give direct limit or appoint the same and for want of such gift direction limitation or appointment then to the heirs of the body of the said William son of my said sister Ann Wright lawfully issuing share and share alike as tenants in common and if but one child the whole to such only child and for want of such issue I give and devise all the said dwelling houses buildings lands hereditaments and premises to my own right heirs for ever.[10]

There followed a bequest of £100 to Elizabeth Wall, daughter of Ezekiel's sister Elizabeth Persehouse, and of the residuary personal estate to William, son of Ann Wright. William, Daniel and Ann, children of the testator's sister Ann Wright, were appointed executors.

The events that followed appear from the special verdict in *Doe d Wright v Jesson* (1816).[11] On Ezekiel's death, his co-heirs were his nephew Thomas Stokes (son of Ezekiel's deceased sister Martha[12]) and Ezekiel's sisters Ann Wright and Elizabeth Persehouse. Ann and Elizabeth were succeeded by Daniel Wright (Ann's son) and Elizabeth Mosley (Elizabeth's daughter). Thomas Stokes, Daniel Wright and Elizabeth Mosley were plaintiffs in the King's Bench. On Ezekiel's death, William Wright entered the land and on 13 December 1774 married Mary Jones,[13] with whom he had seven sons and three daughters. One daughter, Elizabeth, died without issue in 1798. Of the surviving children, eight – Ezekiel, John, Thomas, George, Isaac, William, Lucy and Mary (the ninth being Edward, the eldest son) – were also plaintiffs in the King's Bench.[14]

[8] William Wright was perhaps the William, son of Edward and Ann Wright, baptised at Tipton on 25 September 1748: Staffordshire Parish Registers Society (ibid) 28.

[9] The registered copy of the will lacks Timmins's first name.

[10] There was also a devise to Thomas Fereday of a 'small piece or parcel of land or ground' in Tipton.

[11] The special verdict is included in the printed case prepared for the House of Lords. The copy used here is in Lincoln's Inn Library (LI), in a volume entitled *Cases on Appeals to the House of Lords*, vol 18, May–July 1820. A summary appears in 2 Bli 1, 2–6.

[12] Martha was perhaps the Martha Pershouse who married Joseph Stocks on 24 March 1742/3: Staffordshire Parish Registers Society (n 7) 18.

[13] Staffordshire Parish Registers Society, *Tipton, St Martin Parish Registers*, pt 3 (Staffordshire Parish Registers Society, 2012) 20 (the correct date may be 18 December 1774: the entry dated 13 December appears in the register immediately following an entry for 18 December).

[14] LI, *Cases on Appeals* (n 12) 94 (handwritten), 3 (printed).

In January 1800, assuming that William Wright was a tenant in fee tail, William, Mary and Edward Wright initiated a common recovery of the land to one Joseph Marston 'for docking, barring and extinguishing all Estates Tail, and all Remainders and Reversions expectant thereupon'.[15] Marston was put in seisin on 10 Feburary 1800.[16] By 1814 the land had come into the hands of the defendants in the King's Bench, Richard Jesson, Joseph Hately, William Whitehouse, Joseph Watton, and Edward and Thomas Dangerfield.

III. THE STRUCTURE OF THE LITIGATION

The action was in ejectment,[17] and the essential question was whether William Wright had taken an estate for life, with remainder to his children for life, or an estate in fee tail. The plaintiffs contended that William had taken an estate for life. If so, the common recovery could not convey valid title to the defendants, and had caused the forfeiture of William and Edward's life estates. The defendants maintained that William had taken an estate in fee tail, which had been barred by the common recovery, creating an estate in fee simple now in their hands.

The action was tried at Stafford assizes on 16 March 1815 before Dallas JCP. A special verdict, returned by agreement, was argued in the King's Bench on 10 May 1816, before Lord Ellenborough CJKB and Bayley JKB, Abbott and Holroyd JJ having 'declined to give any opinion, as they had been engaged in the case while at the Bar'.[18] Judgment was for the plaintiffs.

The defendants brought a writ of error in the House of Lords, arguing that 'the Court by their Judgment have decided that the said *William Wright* took only a Life Estate under the said Will of the said *Ezekiel Pershouse*, with Remainder to his Children for Life', whereas 'the Testator intended to embrace all the issue of the said *William Wright*, which Intention can only be effected by giving the said *William Wright* an Estate Tail, and the Words of the Will are fully sufficient for that Purpose'.[19]

The writ of error reached the House of Lords on 18 March 1817,[20] and on 29 March was ordered to be heard on the first vacant day.[21] On 18 May the defendants in error (plaintiffs in the King's Bench) petitioned for an early day for consideration of the cause, alleging that the plaintiffs in error 'had declared that they should keep the Matter unsettled as long as they could', and that they (the defendants in error) – noting that Richard Jesson

[15] ibid. A common recovery was a collusive real action by force of judgment, in which an entail could be barred and converted into a fee simple. See Sir John Baker, *An Introduction to English Legal History*, 5th edn (Oxford, Oxford University Press, 2019) 300–05.

[16] LI, *Cases on Appeals* (n 12) 95 (handwritten), 4 (printed).

[17] The action of ejectment, which began to be used to try freehold title in the later sixteenth century was the precursor of the modern action to recover possession. See Baker (n 15) 320–22.

[18] 5 M & S 95, 102. Holroyd and Abbott were appointed to the King's Bench in 1816, on 20 February and 2 May, respectively: Sir John Sainty, *The Judges of England 1272–1900*, Selden Society supplementary series 10 (London, Selden Society, 1993) 38.

[19] LI, *Cases on Appeals* (n 12) 96 (handwritten), 5 (printed) (italics in the original).

[20] *Journal of the House of Lords*, vol 51, 116.

[21] ibid 144.

and Joseph Hateley, two of the plaintiffs in error, were attorneys – believed that 'the present Writ of Error has been brought only for the Purpose of delaying and harassing' them, 'and thereby compelling them to accede to Terms injurious to their Interests', and that in any event, they were 'indigent', the ligitation having cost more than £600 which they were 'wholly unable to afford'.[22] The petition was repeated on 14 December 1819,[23] and again on 1 May 1820.[24] On 18 May 1820 the Committee for considering causes in which prints of the cases had not been delivered were of the opinion that the cause should be heard on 29 May 1820.[25] Counsel were heard on 7,[26] 12 and 14 June,[27] the plaintiffs in error being represented, as in the King's Bench, by Edward Sugden, with Thomas Jervis,[28] and the defendants in error by William Taunton (as in the King's Bench), with Philip Dauncy.[29] The House considered the matter on 16 June,[30] and on 19 June made order and judgment reversing the King's Bench decision.[31]

IV. THE CONTEXT OF THE CLAIM

A number of prominent barristers were involved in the case. Two of the four justices of the King's Bench in 1816 had been engaged in it: Charles Abbott, later Baron Tenterden, who succeeded Ellenborough in 1818 as chief justice of the King's Bench,[32] and George Holroyd, who, while destined only for a puisne justiceship, was regarded by Lord Brougham as 'one of the most able, most learned, and most virtuous men that ever … adorned the profession of the law'.[33] Of those appearing as counsel, Edward Sudgen, subsequently lord chancellor as Lord St Leonards, had published in 1805 his great work *Vendors and Purchasers of Legal Estates*,[34] and it had come to be said that 'no abstract of title could be sure unless Sugden had perused in it chambers'.[35] William Taunton was appointed to the King's Bench in 1830, with a reputation as a black-letter lawyer.[36] It may be no surprise that Lord Eldon observed that 'no case was ever better argued at this bar'.[37]

[22] *Journal of the House of Lords*, vol 52, 587–88.

[23] ibid, 956–57.

[24] *Journal of the House of Lords*, vol 53, 44–45.

[25] ibid 78–79.

[26] ibid 112.

[27] ibid 122, 130.

[28] Both Sugden and Jervis signed the printed case prepared for the House of Lords, but only Sugden is reported as having argued it.

[29] Both Taunton and Dauncy signed the printed case, but only Taunton is reported as having argued it.

[30] *Journal of the House of Lords*, vol 53, 133.

[31] ibid 137–38. The date 15 June 1820 in the report at 2 Bli 1 appears to be an error.

[32] M Lobban, 'Abbott, Charles, first Baron Tenterden (1762–1832)' in *Oxford Dictionary of National Biography* (Oxford, Oxford University Press, 2004).

[33] Quoted in WR Cornish, 'Holroyd, Sir George Sowley (1758–1831)' in *Oxford Dictionary of National Biography* (ibid).

[34] EB Sugden, *A Practical Treatise of the Law of Vendors and Purchasers of Estates* (London, Brooke and Clarke, 1805).

[35] J Getzler, 'Sugden, Edward Burtenshaw, Baron St Leonards (1781–1875)' in *Oxford Dictinonary of National Biography* (n 32).

[36] W Carr, rev E Metcalfe, 'Taunton, Sir William Elias (1773–1835)' in *Oxford Dictionary of National Biography* (n 32).

[37] 2 Bli 1, 53.

The first-named defendant was Richard Jesson, of a prominent West Bromwich family,[38] 'many of whom since the 17th century had been iron merchants'.[39] *Jesson v Wright* itself was closely related to coal: in 1837 a partnership was dissolved between Richard Jesson and Joseph Hateley, both of Walsall, formerly colliery owners,[40] probably the first-named plaintiffs in error.[41] Coal's role is confirmed by the House of Lords petitions of the defendants in error, alleging that 'Two of the … Plaintiffs in Error, have sunk a Coal Mine, from which they have, for Eighteen Years past, raised Coals and Iron Stone to the Amount of several Thousand Pounds a Year',[42] having purchased the land from the father of the defendants in error 'for the comparatively inconsiderable Sum of Four thousand Pounds'. The plaintiffs in error, it was alleged, had 'continued to work the said Coal Mine' from the time of judgment against them in the King's Bench until a bill of injunction was filed. They then ceased to work the mine, 'though it is suspected that they have since worked it surreptitiously, by means of a Pit or Shaft sunk in the adjoining Field'. The defendants in error were 'now experiencing a very great Loss, in consequence of their being prevented from working the Coal Mine in the said Premises'.[43]

V. THE RULE IN *SHELLEY'S CASE*

While not referred to by name in the reports of *Doe d Wright v Jesson* or *Jesson v Wright*, the rule in *Shelley's Case* was central to the dispute, providing that where a life estate was given, and by the same instrument the remainder was limited to the heir – or the heirs of the body – of the tenant for life, whether immediately or subject to other estates, the life estate and the remainder would unite, the intended life tenant receiving instead an estate in fee simple or fee tail (without prejudice to any intervening interests).[44] Given the structure of Ezekiel Persehouse's will, the potential relevance of the rule is clearly apparent.

With the printing of Coke's report of *Shelley's Case* in 1600, the rule had become 'part of the received legal culture'.[45] But before the time of *Jesson v Wright* '[t]hings were not going well with the rule'.[46] In the seventeenth century it had been accepted as a rule of law:[47] 'a positive law, of which there can no reason be given, but [which] is a land-mark by which other cases are bounded'.[48] However, during the eighteenth century

[38] See generally M Willett, *A History of West Bromwich* (West Bromwich, 1882).

[39] *A History of the County of Stafford, vol 17, Offlow Hundred (Part)* (London, University of London Institute of Historical Research, 1976), 38. For the Jesson family's involvement in iron manufacture see A Birch, *The Economic History of the British Iron and Steel Industry 1784–1879* (London, Cass, 1967) 31; WKV Gale, *The Black Country Iron Industry: A Technical History* (London, Iron and Steel Institute, 1966) 26–27.

[40] Deed of dissolution, Walsall Local History Centre, 35/23/12a–b.

[41] They are described as being 'Parties principally interested' in the petitions in the House of Lords of the defendants in error, *Journal of the House of Lords*, vol 53, 44 (the earlier petitions, referred to above, were in the same terms).

[42] Suggesting that Jesson and others had purchased the land shortly after the common recovery in 1800.

[43] ibid.

[44] For a contemporary statement of the rule, see J Tyrrell, *Suggestions Sent to the Commissioners Appointed to Inquire into the Laws of Real Property, with Minutes of the Evidence Given Before Them* (London, printed for the author, 1829), 334, quoted in Simpson (n 2) 2.

[45] Simpson (n 2) 39.

[46] *Van Grutten v Foxwell* [1897] AC 658, 669 (Lord Macnaghten).

[47] WS Holdsworth, *A History of English Law*, vol 3, 3rd edn (Boston, MA, Little Brown, 1923) 109.

[48] *Lisle v Gray* (1679) Sir T Raym 315, 319.

questions arose, and in *Perrin v Blake* (1770) Lord Mansfield CJ, leading a majority of the King's Bench,[49] treated the rule as one of construction only: 'This rule is clear law, but is not a general proposition, subject to no controul, as where a testator's intention was manifestly on the other side, and where the objections might be answered'.[50] As Charles Fearne noted in 1772 – responding to Mansfield's heresy, as he saw it, in *Perrin v Blake* – 'the unprecedented judgment given in that case has since been reversed in the Exchequer Chamber',[51] but the controversy[52] to which the case gave rise left the rule's position uncertain.

VI. THE CASE LAW IN *JESSON* v *WRIGHT*

The value of authority in this area might be doubted. In *Doe d Wright v Jesson* Lord Ellenborough is not reported as referring to case law. He had 'looked into' the cases cited, but 'we are not ... to draw the sources of our judgment from the mere language or construction of other wills differently compounded, but from the language and intention of the testator in the will before us'.[53] And there was the difficulty that 'it was hardly to be expected that judges should agree in the decision of all these cases; for the mind is overpowered by their multitude, and the subtlety of the distinctions between them'.[54] That said, counsel in *Jesson v Wright* cited 41 cases in the House of Lords, 24 from the King's Bench,[55] 10 from the Common Pleas,[56] six from Chancery and one from the Exchequer. Most were from the nineteenth (16) or eighteenth century (16), though five were from the seventeenth century and four from the sixteenth. Insofar as they shared factual similarities, the predominant pattern was a devise of real property to a first taker for life, with provisions over, and an ultimate remainder to a stranger or to the testator's right heirs, thereby raising the question of whether the first taker had taken an estate for life or in fee tail.

A. The Rationale of the Rule in *Shelley's Case*

The rule in *Shelley's Case* had medieval roots, linked perhaps to the common law's reluctance to accept contingent remainders. By the 1580s, however, the validity of contingent

[49] Mansfield CJ, Willes and Aston JJ, Yates J dissenting, 1 Black W 672; 4 Burr 2579; F Hargrave (ed), *A Collection of Tracts Relative to the Law of England*, vol 1 (London, printed by T Wright, 1787), 490.

[50] F Hargrave, *Collectanea Juridica, Consisting of Tracts Relative to the Law and Constitution of England*, vol 1 (London, E and R Brooke, 1791) 283, 319.

[51] C Fearne, *An Essay on the Learning of Contingent Remainders and Executory Devises* (London, printed by Strahan and Woodfall, 1772) 18. The King's Bench was reversed by majority in the Exchequer Chamber (4 Burr 2579, 2582; 1 Black W 671, 673). An appeal to the House of Lords was compromised.

[52] See Lord Macnaghten in *Van Grutten v Foxwell* [1897] AC 650, 670. Macnaghten suggested that much of the debate was 'little more than verbal controversy', ibid 675.

[53] 5 M & S 95, 97.

[54] 2 Bli 1, 50 (Lord Eldon).

[55] One was subsequently heard in Exchequer Chamber, one in the House of Lords.

[56] Some in the common law courts had come through a request for an opinion in cases commenced in Chancery.

remainders was accepted,[57] and this rationale had lapsed. In 1986 Simpson suggested other possible rationales, applicable in the time of Elizabeth: ensuring freedom of alienation and preventing evasion of the incidents of tenure.[58] Subsequent work led to a further suggestion that, while the successful claimant in *Shelley's Case* had conformed to the new religion, the other was from the recusant branch of the family, and the judges had favoured 'the politically correct branch of the Shelley family against a dangerous papist'.[59]

Some attention was paid to the rule's history in the cases cited in *Jesson v Wright*. In *Doe d Long v Laming* (1760) Lord Mansfield CJKB suggested that the rule 'was originally introduced in favour of the lord, to prevent his being deprived of the fruits of the tenure; and likewise for the sake of specialty creditors'. But, if this were so,

> [t]he reason for this maxim has long ceased; because tenures are now abolished, and contingent remainders may be preserved from being defeated before they come in esse; yet, having become a rule of property, it is adhered to in all cases literally within it. But where there are circumstances which take the case out of the letter of this rule, it is departed from, in favour of intention; because the reason of the rule has ceased.[60]

B. The Role of Intention

Intention looms large in the cases cited in *Jesson v Wright*. It was clear that this was the intention of the testator or testatrix:[61] as Grose JKB said in *Goodtitle d Sweet v Herring* (1801), the court was to consider 'what the intent of the testatrix was, and whether such intent can be effectuated within settled rules of law'.[62] If such effectuation were possible, then, as Lord Mansfield put it in *Doe d Long v Laming* (1760), courts both of law and of equity were 'bound to construe and effectuate the will according to [the] intention of the testator'.[63] This was not invariably a straightforward exercise.

One aspect of the difficulty was that the courts were seeking to 'interpret the dispositions of the unlearned part of mankind'.[64] It was possible that a testator had 'expressed no opinion at all' on a given point, 'which point perhaps never entered into his contemplation';[65] or that his contemplation had not extended to 'the absurdities that will follow' from the dispositions made;[66] or that he had not known 'the legal consequences of all the words which he had used';[67] or that, given 'much obscurity' in a will, a court

[57] *Colthirst v Bejushin* (1550), Plowd 21. On contingent remainders see Sir John Baker, *Oxford History of the Laws of England, vol 6, 1483–1558* (Oxford, Oxford University Press, 2003) 701–05.

[58] AWB Simpson, *A History of the Land Law*, 2nd edn (Oxford, Oxford University Press, 1986) 99–100. The incidents of tenure were financial benefits accruing in certain circumstances to feudal lords by reason of their lordship. See Baker, *Introduction to English Legal History* (n 15) 258–62.

[59] ibid 40.

[60] 2 Burr 1000, 1106–07. See also Mansfield's suggestion as counsel in *Jones v Morgan* (1778) that 'The rule is laid down upon the construction of a deed; and that at a time when it was material to third persons, whether the person should take as a purchaser, or as heir' (seemingly a reference to the position of creditors): 1 Bro CC 206, 215.

[61] Or what the testator 'meant' (Lord Kenyon CJ in *Doe d Candler v Smith* (1798) 7 TR 531, 533) or his 'plan' (*arguendo* in *Mogg v Mogg* (1811) 1 Mer 654, 671 and 682).

[62] 1 East 264, 274.

[63] 2 Burr 1101, 1108–09.

[64] M Nolan, note to *Coulson v Coulson* (1740), 93 ER 1074, 1076.

[65] *Doe d Strong v Goff* (1809) 11 East 668, 673 (Lord Ellenborough).

[66] Willes CJCP in *Goodtitle d Cross v Wodhull* (1745) Willes 592, 595.

[67] Alvanley CJCP in *Seale v Barter* (1801) 2 Bos & Pul 486, 494–95.

'compelled to conjecture what the testator meant, possibly [would] not wholly succeed'.[68] It seems likely that many, if not most, of the wills in the cases cited in *Jesson v Wright* had been drawn without competent legal advice: plaintiff's counsel in *Denn d Briddon v Page* (1783) thought it worth observing that the will had 'evidently [been] drawn by a conveyancer, and is technical throughout'.[69]

A second aspect of the difficulty was the extent to which testators might be permitted to give their own meaning to words – to 'translate' them, as Sugden put it in *Jesson v Wright*.[70] In a grant 'to A and the heirs of his body', the words 'heirs of his body' would normally take effect, under the rule in *Shelley's Case*, as words of limitation defining the grant as conferring an estate in fee tail upon A, rather than words of purchase, conferring an interest upon the heirs of the body. But could a testator be taken to have used the phrase in another sense?

This had been firmly denied in the King's Bench in *Lisle v Grey* (1678) in response to argument that the devise was 'to the heirs male, that is, to his (issues) male, and so as much as (sons)'. 'True it is, in Scripture [the] phrase 'tis sometimes so taken, as, *This is the heir, let us kill him* ... But in our law 'tis never taken so, no, not in a will.'[71] But others took a more flexible approach. In *Doe d Long v Laming* (1760) Lord Mansfield CJKB referred to Lord Hardwicke C's view in Chancery in *Bagshaw v Spencer* (1748)[72] '"that heirs of the body", (after an estate for life to the father,) should be construed as words of purchase', holding that it was 'not disagreeable to or inconsistent with the rules of law, that "heirs of the body" should, in some cases, be construed as designatio personae'.[73] This view persisted after *Perrin v Blake*. Thus, in *Goodtitle d Sweet v Herring* (1801) Lord Kenyon CJKB, reviewing the authorities, took the view that while Lord Holt was said to have opined that 'the words "heirs of the body" were so positive to give an estate-tail to the first taker that they could not be gotten rid of by subsequent words', that was 'certainly too straight-laced a construction'.[74] The case law leading up to *Jesson v Wright* thus permitted 'the words "heirs lawfully to be begotten" [to] be explained by the subsequent words to mean heirs of a certain description', as by provision that 'by heirs lawfully to be begotten I mean the first and other sons successively'.[75]

[68] Gibbs CJCP in *Doe d Cole v Goldsmith* (1816) 7 Taunt 209, 212–13. Perhaps for this reason, it had been said by Lords Mansfield and Kenyon CJJKB that conjecture by the court beyond the terms of the will was impermissible. See *Denn d Briddon v Page* (1783) 3 Dougl 294, at 297 (Lord Mansfield); *Hay v Earl of Coventry* (1789) 3 TR 83, 84 (Lord Kenyon).

[69] 3 Dougl 294, 295. Compare Buller J's observation in *Burnsall v Davy* (1798) that 'There is a circumstance attending this will which might give reason to suppose that the testator had something of a legal understanding. Suppose that he knew for how long a time he could tie up his property?', 1 Bos & Pul 215, 221.

[70] 2 Bli 1, 8.

[71] Raym Sir T 315, 318 (emphasis in the original) (referring to Matthew 21:33–43, Mark 12:2–12 and Luke 20:9–19).

[72] The case came before Hardwicke on appeal from a decree at the Rolls. His opinion is reported at 2 Atk 577, 1 Ves Sen 142, 1 Wils KB 238.

[73] 2 Burr 1100, 1107 and 1111. Fearne suggested that in *Bagshaw* Lord Hardwicke had 'open[ed] the way for an equitable construction of a testator's will, deviating from the legal import of the words', which 'supposes that testator a lawyer', C Fearne, *An Essay on the Learning of Contingent Remainders and Executory Devises*, 10th edn, vol 1 (London, Saunders and Benning, 1844) 141. For a discussion of *Bagshaw*'s relevance at common law, see Lord Thurlow C's judgment in *Jones v Morgan* (1778) 1 Bro CC 206, 215ff.

[74] 1 East 264, 273. Holt was chief justice of the King's Bench 1689–1710. See, similarly, *Gretton v Haward* (1816) 6 Taunt 94.

[75] Lord Kenyon CJKB in *Goodtitle d Sweet* (ibid) 272.

Whether such explanation had occurred turned upon the wording of the will, which in this period was construed within the purposive doctrine of general and particular intent,[76] the origin of which has been traced[77] to the King's Bench decision in *Robinson v Robinson* (1756).[78] In the cases cited in *Jesson v Wright* the doctrine appeared most frequently in the guise of a conclusion that the testator's general intent had been that the estate not pass to the ultimate remainderman until all the heirs of the body or issue of an earlier taker were extinct, so that the first taker, having been expressly devised an estate for life, must nevertheless take an estate in fee tail. As Lord Kenyon CJKB put it in *Doe d Cock v Cooper* (1801),

> [p]erhaps we should best fulfil the particular intent of the testator in this case by giving Richd. Cock only an estate for life; but the general intent was that all his issue should inherit the entire estate before it went over; and that intent can only be answered by giving him an estate-tail by implication from the subsequent words 'in default of his leaving issue'.[79]

Thus, in *Doe d Cole v Goldsmith* (1816) a devise had been made to Francis Goldsmith and his assigns for his life, immediately after Francis's death to the heirs of his body, as Francis should appoint, and in default of such heirs of the body to John Goldsmith in fee. It was held in the Common Pleas that this gave Francis an estate in fee tail, it being 'the testator's general intent, that the estate should never go over to John Goldsmith, till all the heirs of the body of F Goldsmith were extinct'.[80]

The application of the doctrine of general and particular intent, and the meaning of 'heirs of the body', depended upon the wording of each will, two aspects of which played a prominent part in the cases cited in *Jesson v Wright*: provisions for tenancy in common, and use of the word 'such' in phrases such as 'such issue'.

In relation to provisions for tenancy in common, it was clear that those taking as tenants in common must take as purchasers, not by descent. How far did provision for a tenancy in common therefore require the will to be construed so as to give the first taker only an estate for life? In *Pierson v Vickers* (1804) land had been devised to Ann Vickers 'and to the heirs of her body lawfully to be begotten, whether sons or daughters, as tenants in common and not as joint-tenants', with provisions over to the testator's sisters 'in default of such issue'.[81] It was argued that Ann took only for life, followed by a fee in her children as purchasers, because

> the limitation to the heirs of the body of Ann Vickers, which in itself would have given her an estate tail, was controlled by the subsequent words 'sons and daughters,' which are words of

[76] On the doctrine, and its various applications, see generally S Anderson, 'Succession, Inheritance, and the Family' in WR Cornish *et al*, *Oxford History of the Laws of England*, vol 12 (Oxford, Oxford University Press, 2010) 26–31.

[77] JC Gray, *The Rule Against Perpetuities*, 4th edn, vol 2 (Boston, MA, Little Brown, 1942) [881]. For a discussion of the history of the rule after *Robinson v Robinson*, see Lord Kenyon CJKB's judgment in *Doe d Cock v Cooper* (1801), 1 East 229, 234–36.

[78] 1 Burr 38.

[79] 1 East 229, 235–36.

[80] 7 Taunt 209, 213 (Gibbs CJCP). His lordship noted that the testator appeared not to have had a clear understanding of the meaning of 'heirs of his body', but regarded it as nevertheless clear that he did not mean the estate to go over until the heirs of Francis's body were extinct.

[81] 5 East 547, 548.

> purchase … and by the limitation to such sons and daughters as tenants in common; for, as such, they can only take by purchase and not by descent.[82]

Against this it was argued that Ann must take an estate tail, inter alia because

> there are no words of limitation superadded to the devise to her children … so that unless Ann Vickers takes an estate tail, it does not appear that her issue can have a greater estate than for life; and there being no cross remainders the share of each dying would go over, which would be manifestly contrary to the general intent of the testastor to prefer his daughter's issue to his sisters.[83]

It was held that Ann took an estate in fee tail.

Provision for tenancy in common could, however, have the opposite effect, as in *Doe d Strong v Goff* (1811). Land had been devised to Mary Goff

> and to the heirs of her body lawfully begotten or to be begotten, as tenants in common, and not as joint tenants. But if such issue should depart this life before he, she, or they, shall respectively attain their age or ages of 21 years, then … unto … Joseph Matthews, his heirs and assigns for ever.

The King's Bench held that Mary Goff took an estate for life, and her children estates in common by purchase, Lord Ellenborough CJKB observing that the

> words 'heirs of the body' are undoubtedly primâ facie words of limitation, but they may be construed to be words of purchase where it is clearly so intended; and we think that in this case such intention is clear. The provision, that they should take as tenants in common, and not as joint tenants, shews very distinctly that the testator was contemplating something very different from an estate tail.[84]

In relation to the word 'such', in *Doe d Strong v Goff* Lord Ellenborough reinforced his conclusion as follows:

> And the words which follow [the provision for tenancy in common] put it past all doubt that the testator used the words, 'heirs of the body,' not as words of limitation … but as equivalent to children or issue of her body, to give such children a distinct and independent interest. The words are, 'But if such issue should depart this life before he, she, or they should respectively attain 21, then he devised to his son in fee.' What does he mean then by 'such issue' but the persons to whom he had before referred, by the description of 'heirs of his daughter's body?' And when he is contemplating the possibility that he, she or they may depart this life before 21, to whom can he be referring but the immediate children of his daughter?[85]

Here the word 'such' tended in favour of an estate for life in the first taker, but this was not invariably so. Thus, in *Doe d Cole v Goldsmith* (1816), as has been seen, the devise was to Francis Goldsmith and his assigns for his life, immediately after Francis's death to the heirs of his body, in such parts and shares as Francis should appoint, and 'in default of

[82] ibid 552.

[83] ibid 553. Implication of cross-remainders arose in several of the cases cited in *Jesson v Wright*. They would prevent the fractional share of a dead tenant in common passing to the ultimate remainderman while the other or others were still living.

[84] 11 East 668, 671. Albeit this would mean, for example, that if Mary Goff had 10 children, one of whom died under the age of 21, that child's one-tenth share would pass to Joseph Goff, leaving the surviving children as tenants in common of nine-tenths.

[85] ibid 671–72.

such heirs' of Francis's body to John Goldsmith in fee. Gibbs CJCP observed that counsel for the plaintiff (arguing for an estate tail) relied on the words 'and in default of such heirs of the body of F Goldsmith, then, immediately after his decease, over to J Goldsmith', contending that they meant that the estate was to go over upon indefinite failure of issue. To this, counsel for the defendant responded that 'heirs of the body' meant children of Francis, since appointment could only be made among those in being, and that 'the default of such issue must therefore be a default of such persons, who can only be the children', and not the heirs of the body in the 'ordinary legal sense'. Despite this, the court held for the plaintiff on the basis of the general intent. In giving the first taker in such cases more than an estate for life it was 'very doubtful', as Lord Ellenborough observed in *Pierson v Vickers* (1804),[86] 'whether we do not act contrary to the real intention of the testator': despite the courts' emphasis upon the testator's intention, his 'real' meaning might well be defeated by the doctrine of particular and general intent.

VII. THE KING'S BENCH JUDGMENTS

Judgment in the King's Bench in *Doe d Wright v Jesson* was given by Ellenborough CJ and Bayley J, Abbott and Holroyd JJ having recused themselves. Lord Ellenborough began by observing that the question was whether the recovery was well suffered, which turned upon the effect of the words 'heirs of the body'. Feeling it needless to discuss the authorities, his lordship immediately stated his view that 'the words "heirs of the body," which, in their ordinary and natural sense, import an estate tail, mean in this instance, children only', which he supported by a number of arguments.

William had been given a power of appointment among the heirs of his body, who, absent appointment, were to take as tenants in common, which was 'certainly incompatible with an estate tail in W Wright'. Moreover, a sole child was to take the whole. It followed that the testator had supposed that were there more than one child 'it would go, not the whole to one, but divisim, to each a share', and therefore must be regarded as having 'put his own construction upon the term "heirs of the body"', words which could 'only be satisfied by construing them to mean children'. Admittedly, for want of such issue the testator had devised to his own right heirs, 'which limitation generally denotes an estate tail', but the words were '"for want of such issue;" and "such" is a word of reference, throwing us back upon the antecedent words, which are explained by the context to mean, child or children': the estate was to go over not on a 'general and indefinite failure of issue', but on failure of William's children.

> It appears to me clearly, therefore, that this will gives an estate for life, no words of limitation being added to the devise [to the heirs of the body], and the devise over not being a giving over after an indefinite failure of issue.

This, Ellenborough asserted, 'clashes with none of the cases', 'because they do not apply to a will constructed as this is: we determine this case by the canons of construction, which the testator himself has furnished'.[87]

[86] 5 East 548, 553.
[87] 5 M & S, 95, 997–99.

Bayley J was 'entirely of the same opinion'. Admittedly, 'where there is a limitation to the heirs of the body of a person who has an estate for life given him by the same will, these are primâ facie words of limitation and enlarge the prior estate'. But

> if it is plainly seen that the testator used them in a different sense, then we are not at liberty to treat them as words of limitation. Where the same words occur in different parts of the same will, the rule is, that you are to give them the same meaning in the different parts;[88] and if it turns out that they are used in one place where it is impossible that they can be used as words of limitation, this affords ground for concluding, that when the testator uses them again, he is using them in the sense as before.[89]

Had William Wright exercised the power, those taking under it must have taken as purchasers, so in that clause 'heirs of the body' cannot have been used as words of limitation. The following clause provided that in default of appointment the heirs of the body should take as tenants in common. Had there been no mention of tenancy in common, the presumption would have been that the words 'heirs of the body' were likewise meant as words of purchase, but such presumption was not required, since the provision for tenancy in common 'could never be if these words were intended as words of limitation'. Furthermore, a sole child was to take the whole, which provision would have been unnecessary had 'heirs of the body' been intended as words of limitation, since the sole child would then have taken without need of any special direction. Admittedly, the general intention rule would require words expressing a particular intention inconsistent with a general intention to be rejected,[90] but here the testator did not express any intention inconsistent with the intention that the children should take as tenants in common, and a decision that William took only for life would 'break in upon no case, and no precedent'.[91] Bayley J added that *Burnsall v Davy* (1798) 'comes very near the question', but that he was 'glad that the question is on the record, so that if we have taken an erroneous view of this case, it will be open to the consideration of wiser and abler men'.[92]

VIII. THE OPINIONS IN THE HOUSE OF LORDS

In *Burnsall v Davy* land had been devised to Mary Owstwick and the issue of her body 'as tenants in common, but in default of such issue, or being such, if they should all die under twenty-one and without leaving issue', then over. Should the words 'if they should all die under twenty-one and without leaving issue' be rejected? If they were, then, as Eyre CJCP put it,

> I should be of the opinion that this must be construed to be an estate for life to M.O. remainder in tail to her issue as purchasers, with cross remainders to every one of that family, and then over to the next branch. But I am at a loss to know what to do with these words.[93]

[88] For this Bayley J cited no authority. In *King v Burchall* (1759), cited in *Jesson v Wright*, Henley LK said in Chancery that if a provision in a will 'be a word of limitation in one part of the clause, it must have the same signification in another', note to *Doe d Cooper v Collis*, 100 ER 1028, 1030.

[89] 5 M & S 95, 99.

[90] Referring here to *Doe d Blandford and Dymock v Applin* (1790) 4 TR 82; *Doe d Candler v Smith* (1798) 7 TR 531; *Doe d Cock v Cooper* (1801) 1 East 229; and *Pierson v Vickers* (1804) 5 East 548.

[91] 5 M & S 95, 103.

[92] ibid 99–103.

[93] 1 Bos & Pul 215, 221.

In Buller JCP's view, 'it will be impossible to reject the words "if they shall all die under the age of twenty-one years"',[94] and Eyre and Buller certified their opinion that Mary Owstwick took an estate for life, with contingent remainders to her children in tail. At the heart of *Jesson v Wright* was a similar question as to whether a court construing a will might reject some of its provisions.

At close of argument in the House of Lords, Lord Eldon observed that it

> is a general rule of law ... that a particular intent expressed in a will, must give way to a general intent. It is surprising that so much pains should have been taken to establish such a rule, the effect of which is, usually, to enable the first taker to destroy both general and particular intent.[95]

It was also true that the words 'heirs of the body'

> prima facie, mean all descendants; and it is likewise a rule of law, that all descendants should take under these words, unless they are clearly qualified and restricted by other words so as to give them a more limited sense.

The difficulty arose 'in the application of these rules to the words of each will'. The court would take advice before judgment was moved.[96]

Upon moving judgment, Lord Eldon referred to the general intent rule, again doubting its wisdom, but concluding that 'it has been acted upon so long, that it would be to remove the landmarks of the law, if we should dispute the propriety of applying it to all cases to which it is applicable'. Turning to the clauses of the will, he observed that 'it is absurd to suppose that the testator could have such intention as the rules of law compel us to ascribe to this will'. The initial devise to William Wright 'for and during the term of his natural life', taken alone, expressed an intention to give William an interest for life only. But there followed the provision that after William's death the estate pass to the heirs of his body. Stopping there, notwithstanding the reference to William's life,

> it is clear that, by the effect of these following words, he would be tenant in tail; and in order to cut down this estate tail, it is absolutely necessary that a particular intent should be found to control and alter it as clear as the general intent here expressed.

The words 'heirs of the body'

> will indeed yield, to a clear particular intent, that the estate should be only for life, and that may be from the effect of superadded words, or any expressions showing the particular intent of the testator; but that must be clearly intelligible and unequivocal.

There then followed the provisions for William to appoint among the heirs of his body and, for default of such appointment, for the heirs of the body to take 'share and share alike as tenants in common'.

As 'heirs of the body' comprehended 'all the posterity of the donee in succession', William 'could not strictly and technically appoint to heirs of the body', and the descendants for all time to come could not be tenants in common. It had therefore been argued that 'heirs of the body' must mean 'some particular class of persons within the general

[94] ibid.

[95] That is, application of the general intent frequently gave the first taker an estate tail, which could be barred by common recovery, destroying the provision for heirs of the body and similar.

[96] 2 Bli 1, 49–50.

description of heirs of the body', which must be children, since a sole 'child' was to take the whole estate upon default of appointment. This would give William an estate for life, and his children an estate for life as tenants in common. But 'it does not follow that heirs of the body must mean children, where you can find upon the will a more general intent comprehending more objects'.

It had then been argued that the words 'for want of issue' in the final provision over must mean for want of children, since the previous provision referred to a child. Against this it had been argued that 'heirs of the body' was the general description of those who were to take. It being 'difficult to put any reasonable construction' on the reference to taking as tenants in common, 'children would be merely objects included in the description, and so would an only child'. Eldon observed that if

> the words children and child are so to be considered as merely within the meaning of the words *heirs of the body*, which words comprehend them and other objects of the testator's bounty, (and I do not see what right I have to restrict the meaning of the word 'issue') there is an end of the question.

His lordship did, however, advert to *Doe d Strong v Goff* (1809),[97] where, as has been seen, it had been held that reference to tenancy in common indicated that the devisor had not intended an estate tail. The case was said by the defendants in error to be 'applicable generally in language and in principle, if not in precise circumstances'.[98] *Doe v Goff* was, in Eldon's view, 'difficult to reconcile with this case – I do not say impossible; but that case is as difficult to be reconciled with other cases'. Therefore '[u]pon the whole, I think it is clear that the testator intended that all the issue of William should fail before the estate should go over according to the final limitation'. Such a decision would enable the first taker to destroy both the general and particular intent.[99] 'But it is more important to maintain the rules of law, than to provide against the hardships of particular cases.'[100]

Lord Redesdale began by observing that such was the variety of combination in words that it

> has the effect of puzzling those who are to decide upon the construction of wills. It is therefore necessary to establish rules, and important to uphold them, that those who have to advise may be able to give opinions on titles with safety.[101]

There followed two key propositions. Firstly,

> it cannot at this day be argued, that, because the testator uses in one part of his will words having a clear meaning in law, and in another part words inconsistent with the former, that the first words are to be cancelled or overthrown.[102]

[97] 11 East 668.
[98] 2 Bli 1, 49.
[99] As had happened through the common recovery.
[100] For this, and the other quotations from Eldon's opinion, see 2 Bli 1, 50–55. The need for rules had been noted by Lord Mansfield CJKB, opining in *Doe d Long v Laming* (1760) that the best way to settle questions in this area was 'to reduce the matter, if possible, to some certain rules', 2 Burr 1100, 1106.
[101] 2 Bli 1, 56.
[102] ibid.

And, secondly, '[i]t is dangerous, where words have a fixed legal effect, to suffer them to be controlled without some clear expression, or necessary implication'.[103] In the present case, it had been argued that the testator had not intended the words 'heirs of the body' in their ordinary legal sense because inconsistent words had also been used,

> but it only follows that he was ignorant of the effect of one or the other. All the cases but *Doe* v *Goff* decide that the latter words, unless they contain a clear expression, or a necessary implication of some intent, contrary to the legal import of the former, are to be rejected. That the general intent should over-rule the particular, is not the most accurate expression of the principle of decision. The rule is, that technical words shall have their legal effect, unless, from subsequent inconsistent words, it is very clear that the testator meant otherwise.[104]

His lordship then turned to the cases, opining that in all except *Doe v Goff*, it had been held that the words 'tenants in common' did not overrule the legal sense of words of settled meaning, and that the same was true of powers of appointment such as that in Ezekiel Persehouse's will. It had been argued that heirs of the body could not take as tenants in common, but it did not follow that the testator did not intend that heirs of the body should take; it simply meant that the 'words of modification are to be rejected'.[105] Likewise, the words 'for want of *such* issue' were far from sufficient to overrule the words 'heirs of the body'.[106] Indeed, they had almost constantly been construed to mean indefinite failure of issue, and frequently held to give a fee tail, and his lordship saw 'no ground to restrict the words "heirs of the body" to mean children in this will'.

Before concluding, Lord Redesdale considered *Doe v Goff*. In several cases cited it had been established that a devise to A for life, and then to the heirs of his body, created an estate tail, which subsequent words did not prevent. In *Doe v Goff* there were no subsequent words except the provision for issue dying under 21, which introduced the gift over. These words were very far from a declaration that the testator did not mean 'heirs of the body' in the technical sense. Indeed, the age of 21 would be irrelevant absent an estate tail: it related to a power of alienation, which made sense only in the context of an estate tail. And even had the general intent been that William take an estate for life, nevertheless absurdities would follow: with merely an estate for life William might nevertheless destroy the settlement by agreement with the heir. And if he had several children, of whom some died, the after-born children would not come in to take the shares of the deceased.

> These are absurdities arising out of the construction proposed. If the testator had considered the effect of the words he used, and the rules of law operating upon them, he probably would have used none of the words in the will.[107]

Agreement in the House of Lords was not quite perfect, Lord Redesdale preferring to avoid reliance upon the doctrine of general intent and more clearly disapproving *Doe v Goff* than had Lord Eldon. But the thrust was the same: the King's Bench judgment

[103] ibid.
[104] ibid 56–57.
[105] ibid 57.
[106] ibid (emphasis in the original).
[107] ibid 59.

should be reversed; William Wright took an estate tail, not an estate for life; the common recovery had been well suffered; and the plaintiffs in error were entitled to judgment.

IX. A NEW DEPARTURE?

In assessing the significance of *Jesson v Wright*, it may be instructive to compare two judicial statements:

> Where there is a limitation to the heirs of the body of a person who has an estate for life given him by the same will, these are primâ facie words of limitation … and … in order to come to a contrary conclusion, it must be seen plainly that the testator used these words in a different sense.[108]

> The rule is, that technical words shall have their legal effect, unless, from subsequent inconsistent words, it is very clear that the testator meant otherwise.[109]

The first is by Bayley J in the King's Bench, the second by Lord Redesdale in the House of Lords. Stuart Anderson has said that it was decided in *Jesson v Wright* that 'The rule in *Shelley's* case (and indeed any other rule) was … to be reinforced by a rule of construction that technical words used in a will were to be given their technical meaning'.[110] It might be preferable to say that it remained the case, as it had long been,[111] that technical words were to be given their technical meaning, unless the testator showed a contrary intention, and that the difference between the courts lay in their approaches to how such contrary intent could be shown, with particular emphasis upon a willingness, manifest in the House of Lords, to disregard later provisions inconsistent with the technical meaning of earlier words: as Lord Redesdale put it,

> It cannot at this day be argued, that, because the testator uses in one part of his will words having a clear meaning in law, and in another part words inconsistent with the former, that the first words are to be cancelled or overthrown.[112]

Admittedly, either approach might produce odd results, and neither might effectuate the real intentions of the testator, but Lords Eldon and Redesdale claimed for their approach the merit of certainty. It had been said in the King's Bench in 1541 that 'it is better to suffer a mischief to one man than an inconvenience to many, which would subvert the law';[113] it was now Lord Eldon C, reversing the King's Bench, who took the view that 'it is more important to maintain the rules of law, than to provide against the hardships of particular cases'.[114]

[108] 5 M & S 95, 99.

[109] 2 Bli 1, 57.

[110] Anderson (n 76) 31.

[111] See, eg Wilmot J's observation in *Doe d Long v Lamy* (1760) that the 'question therefore, in the present case, comes to this: "whether it be absolutely necessary, that the words heirs, or heirs males, or heirs of the body, must be in all cases, and under all circumstances, words of limitation" … They are not to be construed as words of limitation, either upon a will or upon a deed, when the manifest intention of the testator or of the parties is declared to be, or clearly appears to be, "that they shall not be so construed"', 2 Burr 1100, 1112–13.

[112] 2 Bli 1, 56.

[113] 1 Dyer 51a.

[114] 2 Bli 1, 55. *Jesson v Wright* was not in Chancery, and the questions in it arose largely at law, but it is perhaps possible that Eldon C was sensitive to delay and expense arising from uncertainty, parliamentary agitation

X. THE AFTERMATH

The reception of *Jesson v Wright* has been traced by Lord Macnaghten:[115] 'For a time [it] was loyally followed',[116] but 'very soon cases occurred, such as *Right v Creber*,[117] in which proper effect does not seem to have been given to the authority of *Jesson v Wright*'.[118] In 1845, in *Montgomery v Montgomery*,[119] Sugden himself, now Lord Chancellor of Ireland, sought to 'clear up the doubts on this branch of the law'.[120] The result 'was unfortunate. No difficulties were cleared up – no doubtful points explained.'[121] Worst of all, perhaps, Sudgen suggested that '*Doe v Goff* was not really overruled, and that "a similar case would be open to consideration"'.[122]

The authority of *Jesson v Wright* was 'restored, and its supremacy finally established in *Roddy v Fitzgerald*' in 1858. As Lord Wensleydale put it in the House of Lords, having taken the advice of the English judges,

> Your lordships are placed in the very singular position of having to decide this case upon the argument of which, in the Irish Court of Exchequer Chamber, the ten Judges present were equally divided, and the eight English Judges who heard the argument at your Lordships' Bar, and have delivered their opinions would, I believe, have been equally divided also, if Baron Martin had not been prevented ... from giving his opinion.[123]

Referring to *Jesson v Wright* as 'the great leading case',[124] Lord Wensleydale had no hesitation. The rules were perfectly clear and plain: the court's first duty was to ascertain the meaning of the words used by the testator; technical terms or words of known legal import 'must have their proper legal effect attributed to them'; to deprive technical words of their appropriate sense 'there must be sufficient to satisfy a judicial mind that they were meant ... to be used in some other sense, and to show what that sense is'; and reference to general and particular intent, disapproved by Lord Redesdale in *Jesson v Wright*, 'had better be discontinued'.[125] Lord Wensleydale was satisfied, following *Jesson v Wright*, that the devise was to be construed as to the first taker for life, and to the heirs of his body, 'and that the rule in Shelley's case must be applied'.[126] The same inevitably followed in 1897 in *Van Grutten v Foxwell*.

for reform of the Chancery having 'resurfaced' in March 1819, little more than a year before *Jesson v Wright*: RA Melikan, *John Scott, Lord Eldon, 1751–1838: The Duty of Loyalty* (Cambridge, Cambridge University Press, 1999) 299.

[115] *Van Grutten v Foxwell* [1897] AC 658, 672–77.

[116] ibid 673. See, eg *Doe d Bosnall v Harvey* (1825) 4 B & C 610.

[117] 5 B & C 866.

[118] [1897] AC 658, 673.

[119] 3 J & Lat 47.

[120] ibid 60.

[121] [1897] AC 658, 673.

[122] ibid 673–74.

[123] 6 HLC 823, 876. Martin B had recused himself, being a plaintiff in another case in which a writ of error would almost certainly be brought were the judgment in *Roddy v Fitzgerald* reversed, 6 HLC 823, 861.

[124] ibid 879.

[125] ibid 876–78. Lord Wensleydale noted that the terms had been used by Lord Eldon in *Jesson v Wright*, but that Lord Redesdale had disapproved them. For the rule's eventual demise see Anderson (n 76) 26–31.

[126] 6 HLC, 823, 883.

XI. CONCLUSION

Of the 40 or so cases cited in argument in *Jesson v Wright*, only one had reached the House of Lords.[127] That *Jesson v Wright* itself did so may have owed at least as much to the value of coal – and perhaps to the fact that the leading protagonists on one side were attorneys – as it did to the legal questions raised, not in themselves dissimilar to those in a large number of comparable cases in the decades following *Perrin v Blake*. In the years before *Jesson v Wright*, chancellors and masters of the rolls had referred questions on the construction of wills to the judges for advice.[128] In *Jesson v Wright* two equity judges – and lifelong friends[129] – had the final word. The King's Bench had sought a construction reflecting the full wording of Ezekiel Persehouse's will. Lords Eldon and Redesdale, emphasising certainty, were prepared to reject provisions inconsistent with the technical meaning of 'heirs of the body'. But the distinctions were fine, the degree to which the testator's 'real' intention had been effectuated doubtful, and it was difficult to make *Jesson v Wright* stick. Sudgen himself, victorious in *Jesson v Wright*, proved to be no true believer, and in *Roddy v Fitzgerald* both the Irish Court of Exchequer and the English judges were equally divided, Lord Wensleydale observing that,

> in the application of established rules for the construction of wills, and all other written instruments, even where these rules are correctly and properly applied, the forms of language are so various, and strike the mind of each reader so differently, that it is not surprising that uniformity of opinion should not prevail.[130]

Roddy v Fitzgerald and *Van Grutten v Foxwell* formally settled the matter in favour of *Jesson v Wright*. But when *Van Grutten v Foxwell* was decided, the rule in *Shelley's Case*, reborn in the time of Elizabeth and by the nineteenth century lacking any clearly explicable rationale, had less than 30 years to live.[131]

[127] *Robinson v Robinson*, 1 Burr 38, 52.
[128] *Robinson v Robinson* itself provides an example.
[129] See DS Greer, 'Mitford, John Freeman, first Baron Redesdale (1748–1830)' in *Oxford Dictionary of National Biography* (n 32); Melikan (n 114) 309: 'the noble lord's old and tried friend'.
[130] 6 HLC, 823, 876.
[131] It was abolished (under that name) by s 131 of the Law of Property Act 1925.

4

Banks v Goodfellow (1870): Defining Testamentary Capacity

JULIET BROOK

I. INTRODUCTION

DESCRIBED AS THE 'classic' statement of the degree of mental competence required to make a will,[1] *Banks* is so well known that the core dicta has travelled across the Atlantic and the Pacific, and has also made the legal jump from the law of succession into the *inter vivos* context.[2] The facts are not complex: the deceased made a will, which left his entire estate to his closest living relative. The sole question was whether the deceased had the requisite mental capacity to make a valid will, but to answer this required analysis of the main theories of the mind at the time.

The principle of testamentary freedom was an important one for Victorian property owners;[3] the ability to leave your property as you wish on death 'stimulates industry and encourages accumulation', and allows property to be 'moulded according to the circumstances of every family'.[4] Testamentary freedom had existed since the sixteenth century,[5] and the few remaining limitations on that freedom would be removed completely in 1891.[6] However, this freedom had never been given to certain people, notably minors,[7] 'feme covert'[8] and those who were of unsound mind.[9] Whilst the members of these first two categories were clearly identifiable, the confines within which an individual would be classified as lacking mental capacity were less clear.

[1] R Kerridge, *Parry and Kerridge: The Law of Succession*, 13th edn (London, Sweet & Maxwell, 2016) 68; B Sloan, *Borkowski's Law of Succession*, 3rd edn (Oxford, Oxford University Press, 2017) 71.

[2] *Kicks v Leigh* [2014] EWHC 3926 (Ch), [2015] 4 All ER 329.

[3] S Anderson, 'Succession, Inheritance and the Family' in W Cornish et al, *The Oxford History of the Laws of England*, vol XII (Oxford, Oxford University Press, 2010) 6.

[4] First Report of the Commission on the Law of Real Property (1829), *Parliamentary Papers* 1829 (263) 7. This report was considering real property only.

[5] Kerridge (n 1) 183.

[6] With the enactment of the Mortmain and Charitable Uses Act 1891.

[7] Wills Act 1837, s 7.

[8] ibid s 8.

[9] Whilst the Statute of Wills 1540 had not excluded these categories of people from the ability to make a will, s 14 of the 1542 Act for the Explanation of the Statute of Wills had specified that the wills made by 'idiots' and those 'de non sane memory' were ineffective at law.

Unusually for a landmark case, for the most part *Banks* was merely restating the test for capacity that had already been used for almost 300 years[10] – in this regard it was not so much a landmark as another stepping stone. However, it enhanced and expanded the test, focusing on the minimum needed to preserve legal competence. In so doing it helped to develop the notion that the provisions of intestacy are a fallback, not a default, and that it is preferable for an individual's intentions to be upheld if possible, especially when the intestacy provisions could lead to 'perverse results far removed from what the deceased would have liked'.[11] Furthermore the judgment displays an eloquence and an appreciation of the subtle nuances of capacity that has led to passages being quoted and requoted in courts around the world even today.[12]

II. FACTUAL BACKGROUND

John Banks died, unmarried, in July 1865. He was predeceased by both his sister and his half-brother, but was survived by his niece (his sister's daughter) Margaret Goodfellow, who had lived with him, and by his half-brother's children – a son (also called John Banks) and 'several daughters'.[13] In December 1863, John Banks had made a simple will by which he appointed two friends to be his executors and left all of his real and personal property to Margaret Goodfellow. The will was the logical updating of a prior will that John Banks had made in 1838 in favour of his sister, and was described by the Chief Justice Lord Cockburn as 'idle', as 'the object of his bounty was his heir at law'.[14] This was, though, an oversimplification; if it was true, then there would have been no point in challenging the validity of the will. The difference lay in what would happen to Margaret Goodfellow's estate should she die intestate. If Margaret Goodfellow was devised the real property by will, then on her death the subsequent descent would be determined by reference to *her* family relationships. In contrast, if Margaret Goodfellow inherited the real property by the laws of intestacy, the heir-at-law of that property would be determined by her uncle's surviving family members, as he was the last 'purchaser'.[15]

The will was proved in August 1865; there was no initial challenge to its validity. However, Margaret then died in 1867, 'under age and unmarried',[16] with her closest relatives being half-siblings. On her death intestate, all of her real and personal property (including that inherited from John Banks) therefore passed to her younger half-brother Edward Goodfellow as her heir-at-law.[17] Edward was related to Margaret through their

[10] *James v James* [2018] EWHC 43 (Ch), [2018] COPLR 147 [86].

[11] F Burns, 'Property of the Mentally Incapacitated: Statutory Wills in England and Australia' in W Barr (ed), *Modern Studies in Property Law*, vol 8 (Oxford, Hart Publishing, 2015) 135.

[12] See, eg *Dougherty v Rubenstein* 914 A2d 184 (Md Ct Spec App 2007); *DJ Singh v DH Singh and Others* [2018] NSWCA 30.

[13] *Banks v Goodfellow* (1870) LR 5 QB 549, 550. The daughters were irrelevant to the litigation because, under the intestacy rules at the time, males inherited real property in priority to females of equal degree – W Holdsworth, *The Law of Succession* (Oxford, BH Blackwell, 1899) 107.

[14] *Banks v Goodfellow* (ibid) 571.

[15] Inheritance Act 1833, ss 1 and 2.

[16] *Banks v Goodfellow* (n 13) 553. Margaret was aged 18 at the death of her uncle and died aged 20.

[17] Inheritance Act 1833, s 6; C Sanger, *The Rules of Law and Administration Relating to Wills and Intestacies*, 2nd edn (London, Sweet & Maxwell, 1925) 150.

father; he was not a blood relative of John Banks[18] and it is this turn of events that led Margaret's half-cousin to commence proceedings.

If the 1863 will could be successfully challenged, then, as the sole heir under his 1838 will had predeceased, Margaret Goodfellow would have inherited all of John Banks's real property (15 rental properties in Keswick) by intestacy. Under the Inheritance Act 1833[19] the descent of this real property on Margaret's death would therefore be traced from John Banks senior as the last purchaser,[20] and John Banks junior would be the heir.[21] Unfortunately the potential for Margaret to die as a minor (and therefore intestate) 'does not … appear to have presented itself to the mind of any of the parties at the time of making the will'.[22] As is so often the case in disputes about the validity of a will, the background to the most well-known case about testamentary capacity was the realisation that 'family' money would pass to someone outside of the family.

On one view, the challenge should have been easy. John Banks had a violent aversion to a man by the name of Featherstone Alexander, and any mention of this gentleman's name would put him in a state of 'violent excitement',[23] even after the death of Alexander. Banks also believed that he was being pursued by evil spirits, and there was a further body of evidence presented to the court to support a case of general insanity; he had previously been confined in a lunatic asylum and his delusions continued for the rest of his life. From our modern understanding of mental disorders it would appear that he was a paranoid schizophrenic. On the other hand, the will reflected John Banks's affections towards his closest living relative.

III. LEGAL BACKGROUND

It had long been established that those who were not of sound mind could not make a will.[24] Although there is no capacity requirement in the Wills Act 1837, a will could be challenged on the basis that the testator was not of 'sound mind, memory and understanding'.[25] This phrase does not explain the 'degree of mental disturbance which will amount to a want of disposing mind and memory',[26] so this required judicial elucidation. In the sixteenth century, in the *Marquess of Winchester's Case*, the capacity test was expressed as follows:

> By law it is not sufficient that the testator be of memory when he makes his will, to answer familiar and usual questions, but he ought to have a disposing memory, so that he is able to make a disposition of his lands with understanding and reason.[27]

[18] *Banks v Goodfellow* (n 13) 554. Note that the intestacy laws at the time favoured the paternal line over the maternal one – Inheritance Act 1833, s 7.

[19] ss 1 and 2.

[20] Inheritance Tax Act 1833, s 1.

[21] ibid s 9; Holdsworth (n 13) 111.

[22] *Banks v Goodfellow* (n 13) 554.

[23] ibid 551.

[24] See n 9 above.

[25] Contentious Probate Rules 1862 (amended 1865), r 40a, para 2.

[26] *Banks v Goodfellow* (n 13) 556.

[27] *Marquess of Winchester's Case* (1598) 6 Co Rep 23, in *Banks v Goodfellow* (n 13) 557.

By the mid-nineteenth century it had been expanded as follows:

> I take it a mind and memory competent to dispose of property, when it is a little explained, perhaps may stand thus:- having that degree of recollection about him that would enable him to look about the property he had to dispose of, and the persons to whom he wished to dispose of it. If he had a power of summoning up his mind, so as to know what his property was, and who those persons were that then were the objects of his bounty, then he was competent to make his will.[28]

The legal test for capacity was therefore relatively settled at the time insofar as there was a requirement that the testator know their property and the potential objects of his bounty. In addition, the principle of 'lucid intervals' had been used to good effect in cases such as *Cartwright v Cartwright*,[29] to enable someone with fluctuating capacity to make a valid will. Swinburne, the principal textbook of the time, explained this principle as operating such that if someone had occasional periods of incapacity but the terms of the will did not suggest of any 'frenzy or folly', then the presumption was that the will was made during an intermission.[30]

However, none of the authorities prior to *Banks* had dealt specifically with the question of partial insanity. This was described as 'monomania', when the deceased might have delusions that impacted upon one aspect of his life whilst other mental functions appeared unaffected. Swinburne had tentatively addressed this type of difficulty, noting that

> although it cannot be proved that the testator useth to have any clear and quiet intermissions at all, yea nevertheless I suppose that if the testament be wisely and orderly framed the same ought to be accepted for a lawful testament.[31]

However, no case had yet been heard on this point.

The closest that the courts had come was in *Dew v Clark*,[32] which was an almost mirror image of *Banks*. In *Dew v Clark*, an apparently competent and independent testator had left his only daughter relatively little under his will (an annuity of £100 per year, out of an estate of £40,000), with the residue passing to his nephews, who were 'nearly utterly strangers'.[33] In a lengthy judgment, the court analysed the testator's relationship with his daughter and found that his dislike of her was wholly irrational, concluding that 'the deceased's whole conduct towards and in respect to his daughter, as it stands in the evidence, is irreconcilable with the notion of his having been of sound mind *in this particular*'.[34]

However, as well as considering the deceased's behaviour towards his daughter, the court also identified other evidence of insanity in the deceased's life.[35] Whilst this analysis helped to support the court's finding that the deceased lacked capacity on the facts, it also supported the notion that eccentricities and partial insanity tended to be symptoms of

[28] *Greenwood v Greenwood* (1844) 3 Curt App 1.

[29] *Cartwright v Cartwright* (1793) 1 Phillim 90.

[30] Swinburne, *A Treatise of Testaments and Last Wills*, 7th edn (London, 1793) pt II, s III, para 14. Quoted in *Cartwright* (n 29) 101 and requoted in *Banks v Goodfellow* (n 13) 558.

[31] Swinburne (ibid) [15].

[32] *Dew v Clark* (1826) 3 Add 79, (1826) 162 ER 410.

[33] *Dew v Clark* (n 32) 454.

[34] ibid 446 (emphasis added).

[35] ibid 453.

a more pervasive general insanity. Although Sir John Nicholl had approved the principle that someone could be partially insane and yet *sui juris* in other matters,[36] it was in the context of *depriving* someone of testamentary capacity.[37] As the belief at the time was that mental states persisted,[38] the effect of *Dew* was therefore to make it very difficult to prove that anyone who had exhibited symptoms of insanity was in fact capable of making a will.

Following on from *Dew v Clark*, two subsequent cases (*Waring v Waring*[39] and *Smith v Tebbitt*[40]) had gone further by adopting the doctrine of the indivisibility of the mind. This doctrine held that, as the mind is indivisible, any degree of mental incapacity affected the whole of the testator's capacity. In both of these cases the testator was capable of handling his or her own affairs and therefore appeared to have legal capacity, but it was also acknowledged that they had delusions. In *Waring* the Privy Council had held that:

> But we *never* can rely on the act, however rational in appearance, done by the [partially insane], because we have no security that the lurking delusion, the real unsoundness, does not mingle itself with, or occasion, the act. We are wrong in speaking of partial unsoundness; we are less incorrect in speaking of occasional unsoundness; we should say that the unsoundness always exists, but it requires a reference to the peculiar topic, else it lurks and appears not.[41]

Lord Brougham made it clear that, in his opinion, no will could 'be so framed as to rebut all presumptions of insanity arising from proved facts'.[42] In other words, someone with a known mental impairment would lack testamentary capacity even in the absence of any causal link between the impairment and their action, and this reasoning was followed by Sir JP Wilde in *Smith v Tebbitt*.[43] In neither *Waring* nor *Smith v Tebbitt* had this principle been necessary for the decision,[44] but this line of reasoning, whereby even the slightest unsound mind would affect the testator's capacity, would have deprived a number of people of testamentary freedom if it had been permitted to flourish.

IV. DECISION AT FIRST INSTANCE AND GROUNDS FOR APPEAL

The case was heard at the Cumberland spring assizes in 1869 before Brett J, where it was admitted that there were times at which the testator was incapable of making a will.[45] The jury were directed as follows:

> The question is whether … the testator was capable of having such a knowledge and appreciation of facts, and was so far master of his intentions, free from delusions, as would enable him to have a will of his own in the disposition of his property, and act upon it.[46]

[36] ibid.
[37] ibid 416.
[38] Swinburne (n 30) [7].
[39] *Waring v Waring* (1848) 6 Moo PCC 341.
[40] *Smith v Tebbitt* (1867) LR 1 P & D 398.
[41] *Waring v Waring* (n 39) 351–352 (emphasis added).
[42] ibid 358.
[43] *Smith v Tebbitt* (n 40) 401.
[44] In *Waring* there was strong evidence that the delusion had influenced the terms of the will: *Waring v Waring* (n 39) 369.
[45] *Banks v Goodfellow* (n 13) 550.
[46] ibid.

The burden of showing that the testator had capacity was on the defendant (Edward Goodfellow)[47] but despite John Banks's proven delusions, together with further evidence of a more general insanity,[48] the jury upheld the will.

John Banks the Younger appealed to the Court of Queen's Bench on two grounds, first of all that the judge had misdirected the jury, and secondly that the verdict was against the weight of the evidence.[49] The allegation was that even if the deceased's delusions had not been foremost in his mind at the time of making the will, they remained latent at all times. It was argued that this meant that the deceased could not be said to be 'free from delusions' and was therefore not of sound mind, and the jury should have been directed to this effect. In effect, the claim was that any insane delusion so permeated the testator that it deprived them of all testamentary capacity. The appeal was heard by a panel comprising the Chief Justice, Sir Alexander Cockburn, together with Blackburn, Mellor and Hannen JJ, although the sole judgment was given by Cockburn CJ.

V. APPEAL TO THE COURT OF QUEEN'S BENCH

Cockburn was well equipped to counter the theory of the unity of the mind, having previously been a key member of the defence team of David M'Naghten, in a case which considered how partial insanity affected criminal responsibility.[50] It has been suggested that he may have been waiting for a suitable case on testamentary capacity to come up for appeal.[51] Despite the acknowledgement that John Banks had periods of insanity, Cockburn CJ's judgment starts from the premise that he had capacity at the time of making the will as he was able to manage his own affairs and there was no manifest delusion,[52] which contrasts sharply with the judgments in *Waring* and *Smith v Tebbitt*. Cockburn CJ phased the crucial question as being 'whether partial unsoundness, not affecting the general faculties, and not operating on the mind of a testator in regard to the particular testamentary disposition, will be sufficient to deprive a person of the power of disposing of his property'.[53]

Although the lucid intervals principle was of no direct assistance for the will of John Banks (a lucid interval required the complete absence of delusions, whereas John Banks's delusions were permanently present), Cockburn CJ noted that *Cartwright* had shown 'a more indulgent view of insanity as affecting testamentary incapacity was then taken than has latterly prevailed'[54] and that he was 'unable to concur' with the theory of the unity of the mind.[55]

[47] ibid.
[48] ibid 552.
[49] ibid 554.
[50] *Daniel M'Naughten's Case* (1843) 10 Cl & F 200, (1843) 8 ER 718; A transcript of the trial can be found at https://www.oldbaileyonline.org/browse.jsp?div=t18430227-874.
[51] M Frost, *A Victorian Tragedy* (London, Wildy, Simmonds & Hill, 2018) 133.
[52] *Banks v Goodfellow* (n 13) 554–55.
[53] ibid 556.
[54] ibid 559.
[55] ibid 559.

The problem was that, in *Cartwright*, the capacity of the testator was evidenced solely by the rationality of the will.[56] This was the best way to uphold a will that reflected the testator's affections,[57] but if rationality determines validity, then one's conception of rationality becomes pivotal. It would have enabled a jury to declare a will to be invalid simply because it did not match with their familial or societal expectations of what the testator ought to do. Had Cockburn CJ simply repeated the rationality/capacity link from *Cartwright*, this would have reinforced the argument that an 'inofficious'[58] will is, itself, proof of insanity. He therefore emphasised that he was not 'adopting to its full extent' the dicta from *Cartwright* but that the rationality of the will was 'evidence of the sanity of the testator',[59] reflecting earlier comments in *Dew v Clark*.[60]

This is the start of a remarkable exposition of his own theory of the mind. He noted that 'every one must be conscious that the faculties and functions of the mind are various and distinct, as are the powers and functions of our physical organization',[61] and, whilst acknowledging that those who suffer from delusions have an unsound mind, the question instead became:

> [W]hether such partial unsoundness of the mind, if it leaves the affections, the moral sense, and the general power of the understanding unaffected, and is wholly unconnected with the testamentary disposition, should have the effect of taking away the testamentary capacity.[62]

Specifying this causal link enabled Cockburn CJ to distinguish between the delusions in cases such as *Dew* and *Waring* and the 'innocuous' delusions of John Banks, which 'must be taken neither to have had any influence on the provisions of the will, nor to have been capable of having any'.[63] However, this question opens up more profound issues of the boundaries of testamentary freedom as the reference to 'the moral sense' immediately brings to mind theories of natural law.

To solve this problem, in true Victorian style, Cockburn CJ took the question of testamentary capacity back to first principles, emphasising the need for a causal connection between insanity and incapacity by declaring that 'the ground on which insanity should *cause* incapacity appears to have been overlooked in the reasoning on which it is founded. It is important to recall it.'[64] There follows an eloquent and wide-ranging discussion of the justifications for testamentary freedom in England and Wales, in contrast to the fixed inheritance rules found on the continent. Emphasising that 'the power of disposing of property in anticipation of death has ever been regarded as one of the most valuable of the rights incidental to property',[65] Cockburn CJ concluded:

> The English law leaves everything to the unfettered discretion of the testator, on the assumption that, though in some instances, caprice, or passion, or the power of new ties, or artful

[56] *Cartwright v Cartwright* (n 29) 100.
[57] ibid 93.
[58] *Banks v Goodfellow* (n 13) 570.
[59] ibid 559.
[60] *Dew v Clark* (n 32) 454.
[61] *Banks v Goodfellow* (n 13) 560.
[62] ibid 560.
[63] ibid 561.
[64] ibid 563 (emphasis added).
[65] ibid 564.

> contrivance, or sinister influence, may lead to the neglect of claims that ought to be attended to, yet, the instincts, affections, and common sentiments of mankind may be safely trusted to secure, on the whole, a better disposition of the property of the dead, and one more accurately adjusted to the requirements of each particular case, than could be obtained through a distribution prescribed by the stereotyped and inflexible rules of a general law.[66]

In other words, we have testamentary freedom in order that we can make a choice, instead of only having freedom if we make the right choice. Whilst the philosophical theories of property at the time were broadly in agreement that property could not be taken from individuals during their lifetime without just cause,[67] there were competing viewpoints as to who should receive it on death. The Lockian notion of natural entitlement included a familial inheritance right,[68] whilst the utilitarian principles espoused by Bentham prioritised personal freedom.[69] Cockburn CJ's comments clearly reflect this debate and are reminiscent of the words of Bentham, who had observed that 'the law cannot know individuals ... The power of making a will, is an instrument placed in the hands of individuals for the prevention of private calamity.'[70] Bentham had justified complete testamentary freedom on the basis that it enables the testator to 'recompense the cares' of those to whom he is most attached.[71] Likewise, after noting that a testator 'would naturally distribute among his children or nearest relatives the property which he possessed',[72] Cockburn CJ observed that some of those 'may be better provided for than others; some may be more deserving than others; some from age, or sex, or physical infirmity, may stand in greater need of assistance'; and furthermore that '[f]riendship and tried attachment, or faithful service, may have claims that ought not to be disregarded'.[73]

John Stuart Mill's 'On Liberty', which had been published only 11 years prior to the *Banks* judgment, had emphasised our inability to judge the appropriateness of purely personal conduct due to the subjectivity of our own opinion and preferences.[74] Cockburn CJ's comments used this notion to explain why the testator's decision should be respected; similar views had previously been seen in the United States, where it had been held that to set aside a will due to the eccentricities of the testator would be the 'tyranny of a general opinion'.[75]

Having set out all of the competing scientific and philosophical arguments, Cockburn CJ finally explained the test for capacity as follows:

> It is essential to the exercise of such a power that a testator shall understand the nature of the act and its effects; shall understand the extent of the property of which he is disposing; shall be able to comprehend and appreciate the claims to which he ought to give effect; and with a view

[66] ibid 564.

[67] J Frecknall Hughes, 'The Concept of Taxation and the Age of Enlightenment' in J Tiley (ed), *Studies in the History of Tax Law*, vol 2 (Oxford, Hart Publishing, 2007).

[68] J Locke, *The First Treatise of Government Ch VIII* (London, Whitmore and Fenn, 1821) [88].

[69] J Bentham, *Principles of the Civil Code Part II Ch IV* (Edinburgh, William Tait, 1843) 336–37.

[70] ibid.

[71] ibid 338.

[72] *Banks v Goodfellow* (n 13) 563.

[73] ibid 564.

[74] JS Mill, *On Liberty* (London, Penguin Classics, 1985) ch 4, 151.

[75] *McMasters v Blair* 29 Pa 298, 304 (1857), cited in SL Blumenthal, 'The Deviance of the Will: Policing the Bounds of Testamentary Freedom in Nineteenth-Century America' (2006) *Harvard Law Review* 959, 1016.

> to the latter object that no disorder of the mind shall poison his affections, pervert his sense of right, or prevent the exercise of his natural faculties; that no insane delusion shall influence his will on disposing of his property, and bring about a disposal of it which, if the mind had been sound, would not have been made.[76]

At first glance, this is not ground-breaking. It borrows heavily on the earlier case law, echoing the requirements that the testator know the nature of his act (that he is making a will which will take effect on death – the essence of testamentary intention), the extent of his property and the claims of those to which the testator ought to give effect. The only significant difference between the two is the addition of the fourth limb – that no disorder of the mind has influenced the writing of the will; it is this fourth limb that aimed to protect testamentary freedom as far as possible.

In *Smith*, Sir JP Wilde's judgment focused on restricting testamentary freedom to those testators whose minds are 'not unduly impaired by old age, enfeebled by illness or tainted by morbid influence'.[77] In contrast, *Banks* emphasises that we need a rational ground for depriving someone of freedoms that are 'universally felt and acknowledged'.[78] Partial insanity and general declines in cognitive abilities that are unconnected to the exercise of the faculties should not be impediments to testamentary freedom. Such an emphasis is far more akin to our modern perceptions; instead of asking what the testator has lost, the focus is on what capacity remains.

Although *Banks* was a case about delusions, Cockburn CJ also took the opportunity to discuss the relevant capacity test for unsoundness of mind resulting from 'supervening physical infirmity or the decay of advancing age'.[79] He stated that, although there may be a reduction in mental power, 'yet if there be sufficient intelligence to understand and appreciate the testamentary act in its different bearings, the power to make a will remains'.[80] In support of this assertion he called upon numerous cases from the United States which had focused more on the capacity that was left than that which was lost; the question in each case was whether the testator had, despite a serious decline in his or her faculties, retained sufficient capacity to make a will.[81] Although these cases were on age-related incapacity, as opposed to mental disease, Cockburn CJ noted that any difference between the two

> becomes immaterial on the hypothesis that the disorder of the mind has left the faculties, on which the proper exercise of the testamentary power depends, unaffected, and that a rational will, uninfluenced by the mental disorder, has been the result.[82]

Having espoused all of these principles, Cockburn CJ's conclusion was simple. John Banks's delusion was 'quite unconnected' to the terms of the will, so any omission by the trial judge to draw attention to this issue specifically cannot have affected the verdict.[83]

[76] *Banks v Goodfellow* (n 13) 565.
[77] *Smith v Tebbitt* (n 40) 400.
[78] *Banks v Goodfellow* (n 13) 566.
[79] ibid 566.
[80] ibid 566.
[81] ibid 564–68.
[82] ibid 570.
[83] *Banks v Goodfellow* (n 13) 571–72.

There had therefore been no misdirection to the jury, their verdict was not against the weight of evidence and the will was upheld.

VI. IDENTIFYING INCAPACITY

At a time when there was no ability for the court to make a statutory will, the *Banks* test gave testamentary freedom to many who had a diagnosed mental impairment.[84] In the United States it had been noted that tougher tests for capacity might operate 'to exclude females, ignorant persons, and persons laboring under violent and painful disease, from the power of testamentary disposition'.[85] Prohibiting those who had some degree of legal competency from making a will would have resulted in

> the curious spectacle of a person debarred from having any voice in the final disposition of his property – in an act which really comes within the reach of his understanding – while in the continued management of his property, a judicious committee is paying all the deference to his wishes and suggestions which their reasonableness deserves.[86]

However, if the '*only* legitimate or rational ground for denying testamentary capacity to persons of unsound mind' was an 'inability to take into account and give due effect to the considerations which ought to be present to the mind of a testator in making his will',[87] then the ways in which this inability would be presented needed further analysis. Cockburn CJ explained that these occur when 'reason and judgment are lost'[88] and when 'the mind becomes a prey to insane delusions calculated to interfere with and disturb its functions'.[89] This suggests two different manifestations of incapacity. The first is when the thought process is itself irrational, reflecting earlier dicta in *Harwood v Baker* that had focused on the ability of the testator to 'deliberately form[] an intelligent purpose'.[90] The second is when mental unsoundness 'is capable of influencing the result',[91] ie when what appears to be a rational thought process is premised on an insane delusion.

This raises three further questions. First, what amounts to a rational thought process? Secondly, how do you identify an insane delusion? Thirdly, what degree of influence (if any) is permissible between the delusion and the terms of the will?

A. The Rationality of the Thought Process

The fourth limb of *Banks* directs that the terms of the will (often the only contemporaneous evidence of the testator's capacity) be compared with the terms of a notional will that the testator would have made had it not been for the delusion. This requires

[84] Burns (n 11) 136–37.

[85] *Stewart's Executor v Lispenard*, 26 Wend 255, 303 (NY 1841), cited in SL Blumenthal, 'The Default Legal Person' (2007) 54 *UCLA Law Review* 1135, 1208.

[86] I Ray, *A Treatise on the Medical Jurisprudence of Insanity* (Boston, Charles C Little and James Brown, 1838) 130.

[87] *Banks v Goodfellow* (n 13) 566 (emphasis added).

[88] ibid 565.

[89] ibid.

[90] *Harwood v Baker* (1840) 13 ER 117, (1840) 3 Moo PC 282, 291, cited in *Banks v Goodfellow* (n 13) 569.

[91] *Banks v Goodfellow* (n 13) 566.

consideration of whether the testator was acting in accordance with long-held values and wishes; what we would now regard as higher level, 'best desire' autonomous actions.[92] In many cases this can provide a relatively straightforward objective standard, especially if the testator had voiced his or her testamentary wishes consistently prior to losing capacity; it is akin to a substituted judgment exercise.[93] In earlier lucid intervals cases the fact that the will reflected the deceased's particular family attachments (*Cartwright v Cartwright*[94]) or the testamentary intentions of the deceased before he lost capacity (*Coghlan v Coghlan*[95]) provided evidence for the lucid interval. As Sir William Wynne had expressed it, 'the strongest and best proof … is that which arises from the act itself';[96] a will was rational if it was consistent with the testator's authentic self.

In contrast, a marked departure from previously stated intentions undermined a will's validity. In *Harwood v Baker* the fact that the will 'was not in accordance with any purpose deliberately formed before his mind became enfeebled by disease'[97] had supported the contention of lack of capacity. Cockburn CJ was also aware of the vulnerability of testators to 'artful contrivance, or sinister influence';[98] an inexplicable change in the terms of a will could indicate not just lack of capacity but also undue influence, as in *Marsh v Tyrell and Harding*.[99]

Extrinsic evidence of the testator's wishes can provide the objectivity needed for the court's assessment of rationality, justifying their intervention with what appears to be testamentary freedom as the effect is to uphold the testator's deeper autonomy. Unfortunately it also involves a presumption that the testator's wishes will have remained relatively constant over time; many testators with diminishing capacity change their mind,[100] and these are the often most difficult cases for the application of *Banks* as the courts strive to assess the cause of such alterations.

B. Delusional Beliefs

The more we acknowledge individuality, the harder it is to distinguish between merely eccentric or mean-spirited beliefs (which do not invalidate a will) and delusions, where 'insane suspicion, or aversion [have taken] the place of natural affection'.[101] It is 'vacuous'[102] to stipulate that a delusion must have no basis in fact; in *Dew v Clark*

[92] J Coggon, 'Varied and Principled Understandings of Autonomy in English Law: Justifiable Inconsistency or Blinkered Moralism?' (2007) 15 *Health Care Analysis* 235.

[93] *Re D(J)* [1982] 1 Ch 237, 243–44. See also Barbara Rich's chapter in this volume, as well as Burns (n 11) 141 for a criticism of the substituted judgment approach.

[94] *Cartwright v Cartwright* (n 29).

[95] *Coghlan v Coghlan* (1790) 1 Phillim 120.

[96] *Cartwright v Cartwright* (n 29) 100.

[97] *Harwood v Baker* (n 90) 297.

[98] *Banks v Goodfellow* (n 13) 564.

[99] *Marsh v Tyrell and Harding* (1832) 2 Hag 84, 87.

[100] See, eg *Parker v Litchfield* [2014] EWHC 1799 (Ch), in which the testator made six wills in 13 years, and *Re Dharamshi* [2013] EWHC 3917 (Ch), in which the testator made three wills in three months. These can be contrasted with *Vaughan v Vaughan* [2002] EWHC 699 (Ch), in which a last-minute change of testamentary wishes supported a finding of undue influence.

[101] *Banks v Goodfellow* (n 13) 565.

[102] BES Fogel, 'The Completely Insane Law of Partial Insanity: The Impact of Monomania on Testamentary Capacity' (2007) 42 *Real Property, Probate and Trust Journal* 67, 87.

it was stated that most delusions are based on a fact, which is then magnified 'beyond all reasonable bounds'.[103] Sir John Nicholl had cited medical opinion that an idea was delusional if the testator had a 'pertinacious adhesion' to it despite evidence to the contrary,[104] and had further elucidated that a delusion had to be the sort of belief that 'no rational person would have believed',[105] although this test is clearly tautological.[106]

Cockburn CJ was lucky; John Banks's beliefs were obviously delusional as they were both false and irrational, at least once Featherstone Alexander had died. The facts of most insane delusion cases are not so straightforward; where family members are involved, it can be almost impossible for a third party to differentiate between an insane delusion and a justifiable aversion, especially as the third party cannot know all that has passed between the testator and the potential beneficiaries. This assessment is at its most difficult when the alleged delusions are beliefs that the testator had about the worth of his children, whose right to inherit is at the heart of the notion of natural justice.

In 1872, only two years after *Banks*, Sir James Hannen (who had been on the bench in *Banks*) heard the case of *Boughton v Knight*.[107] The facts of this case were more akin to those of *Dew v Clark*; the testator was eccentric, but there was no actual diagnosis of a mental disorder. His will left various small pecuniary legacies and life interests to his children, but the primary beneficiary was a friend and neighbour. The testator's views of the worth of his children were long-held (as had been the case in *Dew v Clark*), but was his aversion to them evidence of lack of capacity?

Banks was cited frequently in the arguments put to the court,[108] and Sir James Hannen emphasised the ability of a testator to be capricious[109] and the need for objectivity in determining whether a belief was delusional.[110] Furthermore, Sir James Hannen reiterated Cockburn CJ's comments on the purpose of testamentary freedom in England[111] and the need to make allowance 'for the difference of individual character', especially amongst those with less common family arrangements.[112] He also noted that the court's duty was limited to ensuring that 'the true expression of a man's real mind shall have effect given to it as his will'.[113] However, despite this focus on the reasoning process, Sir James Hannen then declared that:

> It is so contrary to the whole current of human nature that a man should not only form a harsh judgment of his children, but that he should put that into practice so as to do them injury or deprive them of advantages which most men desire above all things to confer upon their children. I say there is a point at which such repulsion and aversion are themselves evidence of unsoundness of mind.[114]

[103] *Dew v Clark* (n 32) 445.
[104] ibid 414.
[105] Cited in *Waring v Waring* (n 39) 353.
[106] *Boughton v Knight* (1873) LR 3 P & D 64, 68.
[107] *Boughton v Knight* (n 106).
[108] ibid 73.
[109] ibid 66.
[110] ibid 68.
[111] ibid 66.
[112] ibid 67.
[113] ibid 66.
[114] ibid 69.

This comment potentially undermined the whole of his previous discussion; the reports of *Boughton* do not set out the details of the testator's delusions, but this suggests that the testator's beliefs were identified as delusional not because they did not reflect the deceased's 'real mind', but by comparison with societal norms and expectations. The consequentialist reasoning employed here opens the door to assessments of what the testator *should* have put in their will, especially when certain people are seen to 'be fitting objects of the testator's bounty'.[115]

A similar debate was raging in the United States during the latter half of the nineteenth century. As the century went on, there was an increased tolerance towards eccentricities in the United States, with the courts focusing on respecting the autonomy of the individual instead of ensuring their conformity to more general perceptions of morality.[116] It had been emphasised that the 'power of disposition belongs equally to the good and to the bad, and wills cannot be set aside merely because unequal or unjust',[117] and unworthy or spiteful motives were permitted as long as they did not amount to 'mental perversion'.[118] However, *Boughton* illustrates the difficult legacy of *Banks*; an assessment of whether the will disregards 'natural affection and the claims of near relationship'[119] depends on our perceptions of natural affection.

Of course, at the time there was no family provision legislation,[120] so it is easy to see the motivation for Sir James Hannen's comments; Bentham had noted that, whilst giving testamentary freedom, it was also 'proper to guard against making [the testator] a tyrant'[121] and perhaps this was what Sir James Hannen had in mind. He had commented that the testator in *Dew v Clark* had left his daughter 'a sum of money which would have been sufficient … to save her from actual want'[122] and noted that it was 'right' that John Banks should have taken care of his niece on his death,[123] demonstrating his strong opinions on familial obligations.

The relationship between capacity, rationality and autonomy has always been a difficult one for the testamentary sphere. Testamentary freedom entitles the testator to be capricious, but such acts can be symptomatic of a deeper lack of capacity. There is now a greater acceptance that parents are not morally obliged to leave their property to independent adult children,[124] which decreases the risk of the *Banks* test being used to impose normative standards onto testators. Instead, the courts strive to identify whether the deceased 'reach[ed] conclusions which no reasonable person could have reached'[125] by examining whether a belief is justifiable in light of the underlying commitments and convictions of the individual.

[115] ibid 65–66.
[116] Blumenthal (n 75) 1017.
[117] *Trumbull v Gibbons* 22 NJL 117 (NJ 1849) 153, in Blumenthal (n 75) 1002.
[118] *Potter v Jones* 25 P 769 (Or 1891) 774–75, in Blumenthal (n 85) 1214.
[119] *Banks v Goodfellow* (n 13) 570.
[120] The Inheritance (Family Provision) Act 1938 came into force on 13 July 1939.
[121] Bentham (n 69) 337.
[122] *Boughton v Knight* (n 106) 70.
[123] *Boughton v Knight* (n 106) 73.
[124] *Ilott v The Blue Cross & Others* [2017] UKSC 17, [2018] AC 545 [51]–[59]; see also Brian Sloan's chapter in this volume.
[125] *Walters v Smee* [2008] EWHC 2902 (Ch) [123].

For example, in *Carr v Beaven*[126] a will excluding the testator's children in favour of his second wife and grandchildren was upheld because there was 'nothing irrational' in the exclusions,[127] and in the United States *Banks* was cited with approval in a judgment that upheld a will excluding the testator's only son.[128] Although the testator in that case had a false belief about his son, the belief was not a product of mental disease because it was not 'inexplicable'[129] but was 'a reasonable interpretation of the evidence'.[130] Similarly, in *Perpetual Trustee Co Ltd v Baker*[131] the New South Wales Court of Appeal applied the *Banks* test to uphold the will of a testator who had given 'three sensible, logical and rational views' as to why the claimant family members were excluded from her will in favour of charities.[132]

In contrast, in *Re Ritchie*[133] the testator suffered from a number of delusions that were unconnected with the will, but she also claimed that her children had done little to help her and so excluded them from her will. The key point for consideration was whether the testator was expressing her 'authentic self'.[134] The evidence presented convinced the court that the testator's beliefs about her children were untrue and, as she did not recognise them as untrue, they were delusions that had poisoned her mind.[135]

It will always be difficult to avoid suggestions that the court is evaluating who is the 'right' recipient of the testator's property, especially where legacies to the testator's children are concerned. It is noteworthy that in *Sharp v Adam*[136] the opposing counsel each cited passages from *Boughton v Knight*,[137] leading May LJ to stress that, although the court must enquire why children have been disinherited when there is a possibility of mental disease, that inquiry 'is directed to the testator's soundness of mind, and not to general questions of perceived morality'.[138]

This potential for moral approbation is all the more pertinent when the capacity of the testator is to be determined by the jury, as was usually the case in England in the nineteenth century.[139] There is a greater potential for a jury to see a case through their own moral compass, so the directions that are given to the jury by the judge before they begin their deliberation are fundamental if this problem is to be avoided.

The jury at the Cumberland assizes in *Banks* had upheld the validity of the will, not least because they had been directed that the question was whether the testator was 'so far master of his intentions, free from delusions' that he could have 'a will of his own

[126] *Carr v Beaven* [2008] EWHC 2582 (Ch).
[127] ibid [86].
[128] *Dougherty v Rubenstein* 914 A2d 184 (Md 2007).
[129] ibid 198.
[130] ibid 199.
[131] *Perpetual Trustee v Baker* [1999] NSWCA 244.
[132] ibid [30].
[133] *Re Ritchie* [2009] EWHC 709 (Ch).
[134] ibid [5].
[135] ibid [174]–[191].
[136] *Sharp v Adam* [2006] EWCA Civ 449.
[137] ibid [78]. Counsel for the appellants relied on page 66 and counsel for the defendants relied on page 69.
[138] *Sharp v Adam* (n 136) [79].
[139] The use of juries in civil trials decreased over the course of the latter half of the nineteenth century until they were effectively abolished for most civil cases by the enactment of the Administration of Justice (Miscellaneous Provisions) Act 1933, s 6 – see *Ward v James* [1965] 1 All ER 563, 568.

in the disposition of his property'.[140] As John Banks was able to manage his financial affairs, this direction made it hard for the jury to reach the conclusion that he lacked testamentary capacity.

In contrast, Sir James Hannen's summing up in *Boughton v Knight*[141] directs the jury to consider the fact that the testator had left his real estate and residue to someone 'who had no natural claims upon him, of whom he knew little, and to whom he was under no such obligations as are usually recognized as the foundation of such gifts'.[142] These directions give a clear indication of what he thought the 'right' conclusion should be.

Similar issues can be seen in the mid-nineteenth century in the United States. Both trial and appellate judges emphasised that the will could be unreasonable, provided that it was the result of the testator's free exercise of his own judgement,[143] and noting that if this were not the case it would be better to prohibit wills from being made at all.[144] However, the appellate courts in the United States were frequently required to overturn jury decisions that found against 'unequal' or 'unnatural' dispositions, and as they did so they made similar pronouncements to those seen in *Banks* about the subjective knowledge to which only the testator had been privy.[145]

Interestingly, the majority of capacity determinations in the United States are still made by a jury, and it has been shown that they are more likely to determine the validity of a will based on their own sense of equity.[146] It has been argued that this jury bias leads to a greater probability of an 'abhorrent' will being deemed to be the result of incapacity,[147] whereas the capacity requirements have been interpreted extremely liberally when the testamentary disposition reflects public presumptions in favour of the family.[148] Overall, juries can focus on deciding 'which party appears most entitled to the property, not whether the instrument accurately represents the will of the testator'.[149]

The only way to avoid the possibility of personal prejudices would be if there was an objective test for the identification of delusions, but all of the current medical assessments of cognitive abilities have been described as 'blunt instruments' that are not 'nuanced enough nor accurate enough' to determine testamentary capacity.[150] The *Banks* test is not without its difficulties, which Cockburn CJ acknowledged,[151] but at least it enables each case to be dealt with on its own merits.

[140] *Banks v Goodfellow* (n 13) 550.

[141] *Boughton v Knight* (n 106).

[142] ibid 76.

[143] Blumenthal (n 85) 1211–15.

[144] *Boardman* 47 NH 120 (1866), 139, cited in Blumenthal (n 75) 1018.

[145] Blumenthal (n 85) 1210–12.

[146] EG Spitko, 'Gone but Not Conforming: Protecting the Abhorrent Testator from Majoritarian Cultural Norms through Minority-Culture Arbitration' (1999) 49 *Case Western Reserve Law Review* 275, 286.

[147] ibid 282; Fogel (n 102) 70 and 100.

[148] M Fellows, 'In Search of Donative Intent' (1988) *Iowa Law Review* 611, 621–22.

[149] J Athanas, 'The Pros and Cons of Jury Trials in Will Contests' (1990) *University of Chicago Legal Forum* 529.

[150] Law Commission, *Making A Will* (Law Com No 231, 2017) [2.61].

[151] *Banks v Goodfellow* (n 13) 571.

C. The Connection between Delusions and the Terms of the Will

Even when there is little doubt as to their nature, it remains unclear what degree of connection between the delusions and the potential beneficiaries will invalidate a will. In *Banks* Cockburn CJ was faced with a delusion that 'neither exercise[d] nor [was] calculated to exercise any influence on the particular disposition'.[152] Most cases of testamentary capacity are much less clear cut, as the subsequent case of *Smee v Smee*[153] (again heard by Sir James Hannen) demonstrated. It was conceded that the testator in *Smee* had certain delusions concerning his brothers. He had left a first will entirely in favour of his wife, and a later will by which his wife was given a life interest, with remainder to the City of Brighton. The jury was directed that the deceased had capacity to make a will only if 'the delusions could not reasonably be conceived to have had anything to do with the deceased's power of considering the claims of his relations upon him'.[154] Sir James Hannen stated the question to be whether the testator made his will '*entirely free* from the delusions under which he suffered'.[155] As the delusions concerned close relatives who might be expected to receive some benefit under his will,[156] he was found to lack capacity.

One year later, in the case of *Jenkins v Morris*,[157] Vice-Chancellor Hall rejected the notion that the delusions must be 'wholly unconnected with the subject-matter of the disposition'.[158] However, he acknowledged that any connection between the delusion and the terms of the disposition might have 'much weight in determining the point', although it would not be 'in itself conclusive against testamentary capacity' as there may be trivial delusions that did not affect the disposition.[159]

The distinction between the potential and actual impact of delusions is a subtle but important one, though it does not appear to have received much attention in England since *Smee*.[160] In the 1938 case of *In the Estate of Bohrmann*[161] Langton J summarised *Banks* as only permitting those delusions that have 'no relation to any testamentary capacity'.[162] More recently, in *Kostic v Chaplin*[163] it was identified as a question of some interest, and Henderson J stated that it would be a 'rare case indeed'[164] in which a court would be satisfied that a delusion was likely to influence a disposition but did not, in fact, do so.

There has been much more explicit discussion of the linkage between the delusion and the will in the United States, where insane delusions forms a stand-alone doctrine

152 ibid 565.
153 *Smee v Smee* (1879) 5 PD 84.
154 ibid 91.
155 ibid 93 (emphasis added).
156 ibid 93. Sir James Hannen emphasised the lack of any contingency in favour of the testator's brothers, when this might have been expected.
157 *Jenkins v Morris* (1880) 14 ChD 674.
158 ibid 680.
159 ibid.
160 *Kostic v Chaplin* [2007] EWHC 2298 (Ch) [233].
161 *In the Estate of Bohrmann* [1938] 1 All ER 271.
162 ibid 278.
163 *Kostic v Chaplin* (n 160).
164 ibid [233].

within the law of capacity.[165] The Official Code of Georgia Annotated expressly provides that a 'monomaniac' can make a valid will as long as the will 'is in no way connected with the monomania'.[166] In other states the insane delusion doctrine comes from common law; in *Johnson v Johnson*[167] it was stated that to invalidate a will on the grounds of insane delusion the will must be 'the *product* of that delusion',[168] but what amounts to 'a product' is less clear. The 1865 case of *American Seamen's Friend Society v Hopper*[169] held that a will was invalid if its provisions 'were or might have been caused or affected by the delusion',[170] and this was approved by the Court of Appeals of New York in 1960. However, the subsequent New York case of *In the Matter of Zielinski*[171] required the much more direct linkage of whether the delusion 'directly affected' the testator's decision.[172]

The dicta in *Banks* tend to accord with the wider requirement that the delusions must not have been capable of influencing the disposition.[173] This, coupled with Sir James Hannen's dicta in *Smee*, implies that any delusion concerning close relatives may be sufficient to support a finding that the testator lacks capacity, even if the will itself followed both common dispositional patterns[174] and the testator's long-held views. The likelihood of a link between the subject of the delusion and the terms of the will is especially high in dementia cases and, notwithstanding the comments in *Kostic*, this could become a more pertinent question in future.

VII. THE SIGNIFICANCE OF THE FOURTH LIMB

It has been shown that the reason *Banks* is a landmark case is the introduction of the fourth limb, which enabled individual, act-specific assessments of capacity. Most of the recent capacity cases in England focus on the first three elements of the *Banks* test,[175] and there is ongoing debate about the role and scope of the fourth limb. In *Hawes v Burgess* the fourth limb was subsumed into the third limb[176] (that the testator shall be able to comprehend and appreciate the claims to which he ought to give effect) and, possibly because of this demotion, the Court of Appeal was unable to express a concluded view on the issue of capacity in this case. In contrast, the fourth limb was central to the decisions in *Walters v Smee*[177] and *Sharp v Adam*,[178] in the latter of which the Court of

[165] Fogel (n 102) 85.

[166] Georgia Code Ann, Art 2, s 53-4-11 (2017). Identical wording has been in place in Georgia since at least 1933 – see *Morgan v Bell* 189 Ga 432, 436 (1939).

[167] *Johnson v Johnson* 105 Md 81 (1907).

[168] ibid 85 (emphasis in original).

[169] *American Seamen's Friend Society v Hopper* 33 NY 619 (1865) (emphasis added).

[170] *Honigman* 168 NE2d 676, 679 (NY 1960), citing *American Seamen's Friend Society v Hopper* (n 169) 625.

[171] *In the Matter of Zielinski* 208 AD 2d 275 (NY App Div 1995).

[172] ibid 279.

[173] See especially *Banks v Goodfellow* (n 13) 561, 566, 570 and 571, which all emphasise that the delusions were not capable of having any influence on the will.

[174] J Finch and J Mason, *Passing On: Kinship and Inheritance in England* (Routledge, 2000) 77.

[175] *Sharp v Adam* [2005] EWHC 1806 (Ch) [138].

[176] *Hawes v Burgess* [2013] EWCA Civ 9 [11] and [55].

[177] *Walters v Smee* (n 125) [7].

[178] *Sharp v Adam* (n 136).

Appeal rejected the claim that the judge at first instance had given 'a new meaning or prominence'[179] to the fourth limb. May LJ made extensive use of *Banks* to put the fourth limb into its proper context, noting that modern neurology enabled a distinction between the cognitive requirements themselves (covered by the first three aspects of the *Banks* test) and the affections of mood, concluding that the fourth limb was 'concerned as much with mood as with cognition'.[180] On the facts of the case it was only the fourth limb that the testator had not satisfied.[181]

Since then, the Law Commission has commented that the fourth limb might be necessary 'to account for illnesses affecting a testator's personality rather than his or her cognitive ability'.[182] This, surely, was what Cockburn CJ was attempting to describe when he referred to the human instincts and affections being perverted by mental disease.[183] The fourth limb of *Banks* attempts to provide an element of objectivity; the question is whether the will is the product of the testator's authentic self or a self that has been affected by mental impairment. However, it has been shown that there is always the potential for subjective notions of entitlement to impinge on the identification of delusional beliefs, and the academic literature from the United States indicates that this question is not an appropriate one for jury determination.

There have been suggestions in the United States that the insane delusions doctrine is fatally flawed and should be abandoned, leaving just the general testamentary capacity test to determine the validity of wills, to avoid arbitrary results.[184] However, removal of this doctrine could create a void that is not adequately dealt with by other areas within the law of succession.[185] The fourth limb of the *Banks* capacity test enables courts to go beyond a purely functional test; consideration of the testator's known desires and emotional attachments is essential if we are to uphold the testator's autonomous wishes. It would be impossible to assess testamentary capacity retrospectively without this detailed consideration.

VIII. CONCLUSION

Banks's initial importance was limited to cases of partial insanity – Holdsworth's 1899 textbook uses Sir James Hannen's dicta from *Boughton v Knight* to elucidate the general requirement that the testator be of 'sound mind, memory and understanding'.[186] *Banks* is not mentioned in Holdsworth's discussion of the principles that are used to distinguish between mere eccentricity and sanity, nor does *Banks* form part of the discussion of lucid intervals. The only reference to *Banks* appears on the fourth and last page of the

179 ibid [80].
180 ibid [93].
181 ibid [69], citing the first instance decision that was subsequently upheld.
182 Law Commission (n 150) [2.39].
183 *Banks v Goodfellow* (n 13) 565.
184 Fogel (n 102) 111.
185 British Columbia Law Institute, 'Report on Common-Law Tests of Capacity', BCLI Report no 73 (2013) 39.
186 Holdsworth (n 13) 64.

testamentary capacity section and is in the context of partial insanity, ie those cases where 'a man is insane only on certain points'.[187] *Banks* therefore tended to be relied on when a testator appeared in other respects to be *sui juris*, but where there are specific facts that indicate lack of capacity.[188]

The majority of capacity cases today concern dementia patients and testators with other age-related mental disorders[189] and, as those who are suffering from dementia can have distorted views of the worth of the potential claimants,[190] the assimilation of delusions within the broader context of capacity explains why the relevance of *Banks* has grown. Cockburn CJ's acknowledgement that delusions would be more likely to result in an 'inofficious will'[191] but that they could be discounted as long as the faculties that exercise testamentary power remain unaffected[192] attempted a still-unresolved balancing act. How do you keep the threshold low enough to preserve capacity for as long as possible, to protect 'the will and preferences of the person', yet also ensure that the exercise of legal capacity is 'free of conflict of interest and undue influence'?[193]

In the absence of precise indicators of testamentary capacity[194] we will continue to struggle to pinpoint when a dementia sufferer has crossed the 'imprecise divide'.[195] Cockburn CJ did a remarkable job in elucidating the determining factors, which is why *Banks* remains at the heart of the law of testamentary capacity today. By emphasising the rationale behind testamentary freedom, the *Banks* judgment provides only limited circumstances in which this freedom can be curtailed. Cockburn CJ's focus on the effect of the ailment carefully separated the medical diagnosis from legal capacity, ensuring that mental incapacity did not necessarily deprive someone of all legal competence.

The resulting test is complex; the Law Commission of England and Wales has noted concerns that the *Banks* test is 'archaic'[196] and 'unclear',[197] and have suggested that reform is needed to produce 'a simple, clear and effective test that reflects modern understandings of capacity'.[198] However, whilst the Law Commission's proposal to adopt the Mental Capacity Act 2005 test for testamentary capacity might provide the desired 'more modern approach to capacity',[199] it is doubtful whether any capacity test could be both

[187] ibid 67.
[188] See, eg *Battan Singh v Amirchand* [1948] AC 161, in which the testator did not know who his family were.
[189] There are estimated to be 850,000 dementia sufferers in the UK: see https://www.dementiastatistics.org/statistics/numbers-of-people-in-the-uk/.
[190] N O'Neill and C Pesiah, *Capacity and the Law* (Sydney, Sydney University Press, 2012) ch 2; https://www.alz.org/care/alzheimers-dementia-suspicion-delusions.asp. See, eg *Walters v Smee* (n 125) [23].
[191] *Banks v Goodfellow* (n 13) 570.
[192] ibid.
[193] Committee on the Rights of People with Disabilities (2014) General Comment No 1 on Article 12: Equal recognition before the law CRPD/C/GC/1 [22].
[194] Kenneth Shulman et al, 'Psychiatric Issues in Retrospective Challenges of Testamentary Capacity' (2005) 20 *International Journal of Geriatric Psychiatry* 63.
[195] *Sharp v Adam* (n 136) [94].
[196] Law Commission (n 150) [2.35].
[197] ibid [2.42].
[198] ibid [2.42].
[199] ibid [2.66].

simple and accurate. Whatever reforms are made, it will not be surprising if the dicta of Cockburn CJ continue to be used to elucidate the various factors whenever a court is asked to determine testamentary capacity.

POSTSCRIPT

John Banks junior returned to court the following year, to determine who should bear the costs of the litigation.[200] He lost this case, too, and was required to pay the executor's costs.[201]

[200] *Banks v Goodfellow* (1871) LR 11 Eq 472.
[201] ibid 473.

5

Re D(J) (1981): Statutory Wills

BARBARA RICH

I. INTRODUCTION

RE D(J)[1] WAS the first published decision in England to fully articulate some guiding principles for the Court of Protection in the exercise of its power to direct the making of a 'statutory will' for a person who lacks testamentary capacity. A statutory will makes possible what would otherwise be impossible, by providing a judicial process to replicate the outcome of one of the most significant decision-making processes that people who do not lack capacity can undertake for themselves. Once a statutory will is executed in accordance with required legal formalities, it is admissible to probate and has precisely the same status and effect as any other valid will, although the judicial process by which a statutory will is made means that its validity will never be questioned on the ground that the person making it lacked testamentary capacity,[2] did not know or approve his will, or was the victim of undue influence.[3]

II. THE POWER TO DIRECT A STATUTORY WILL: INTRODUCTION

The power to direct a statutory will was only introduced in English law in 1970, by an amendment to Part VIII of the Mental Health Act 1959,[4] which governed the jurisdiction of the then Court of Protection to make decisions about the property and affairs of 'patients': people who were incapable, by reason of mental disorder, of managing and administering [their] property and affairs. The amendment to the law which added the power to authorise a statutory will was an addition to a list of powers

[1] *Re D(J)* [1982] Ch 237.

[2] See Juliet Brook's chapter in this volume.

[3] See Roger Kerridge's chapter in this volume.

[4] Part III of the Administration of Justice Act 1969 (1969 c58), headed Power to make Wills and Codicils for Mentally Disordered Persons, added s 103(1)(dd) to the Mental Health Act 1959 (1959 c72) and some supplementary provisions, all re-enacted in the Mental Health Act 1983 (1983 c20).

which a nominated judge[5] or the Master or Deputy Master of the Court of Protection[6] could exercise over a patient's property and affairs, and was in these terms:

> the execution for the patient of a will making any provision (whether by way of disposing of property or exercising a power or otherwise) which could be made by a will executed by the patient if he were not mentally disordered.

There was no specific guidance as to how this significant power was to be exercised, other than the pre-existing general statutory framework which enabled the nominated judge or the Master or Deputy Master of the Court of Protection to do whatever was necessary or expedient:

> (a) for the maintenance or other benefit of the patient,
> (b) for the maintenance or other benefit of members of the patient's family,
> (c) for making provision for other persons or purposes for whom or which the patient might be expected to provide if he were not mentally disordered, or
> (d) otherwise for administering the patient's affairs.[7]

Prior to the addition of subsection 103(1)(dd), the Court of Protection had had power since 1926 to direct settlements of the property of people who lacked capacity to manage their property and affairs. Before then, the judges who exercised the delegated royal prerogative in lunacy had on occasions directed payments out of the estates of those found to be lunatics as an incident of that prerogative power but had neither directed settlements nor wills on their behalf. The 1969 provisions were re-enacted without any change in Part VII of the Mental Health Act 1983, and remained in force unchanged until that legislation was replaced by the Mental Capacity Act 2005.

The Mental Capacity Act 2005 came into force on 1 October 2007, and Part VII of the Mental Health Act 1983 was repealed. The Mental Capacity Act 2005 re-enacted the judicial power to make a statutory will on behalf of a person who lacked testamentary capacity, within an entirely new legal framework of 'best interests' for decision making about both the personal welfare and the property and affairs of people who lack capacity, by a completely reconstituted Court of Protection. The concept of 'best interests' decision making had its roots in the non-statutory jurisdiction of the High Court to make decisions about welfare and medical treatment on behalf of people who lacked capacity to do so, and was also well-established in the law relating to children. However, neither the welfare jurisdiction nor that relating to children had significantly extended to acts of altruism towards others,[8] such as making a will, so the Mental Capacity Act 2005 provisions were entirely new in this respect.

Re D(J) is a decision which has been influential in English law, and in other jurisdictions where similar powers exist. The case established an approach to statutory wills

[5] A judge of the High Court or Court of Appeal nominated by the Lord Chancellor under the Mental Health Act 1959, s 100(1).

[6] As constituted by the Mental Health Act 1959, s 100(2).

[7] Mental Health Act 1959, s 102(1).

[8] In *Re Y (Mental Patient: Bone Marrow Donation)* [1997] Fam 110 the court authorised blood tests and bone marrow harvesting from Y, who did not have capacity to consent, but who offered the best donor match for her older sister, holding that it was in Y's best interests to do so in order to prolong her positive relationship with her mother.

which subsisted until the Mental Capacity Act 2005 came into force, and continues to be relevant to the present and future of the statutory wills jurisdiction. Despite the fundamental change of approach embodied in the Mental Capacity Act 2005, the question at the heart of *Re D(J)*, and which remains at the heart of any statutory will jurisdiction, is what is the right intellectual framework for the task? The dispositive contents of an English will made by a person who has testamentary capacity are idiosyncratic and, apart from the possibility that a failure to make reasonable provision for certain individuals will give rise to claims under the Inheritance (Provision for Family and Dependants) Act 1975[9] or claims arising from alleged testamentary promises binding in equity, are limited only by technical rules (eg those relating to perpetuities or to purpose trusts) about the validity of gifts and testamentary trusts. How can a judicial process, in which the 'testator' may not be able to participate at all, properly replace the decision making of an individual with sufficient mental capacity to undertake the task?

III. THE HISTORICAL BACKGROUND TO THE STATUTORY WILL JURISDICTION

Under the Crown's ancient prerogative jurisdiction in lunacy, the judges who, from the mid-seventeenth century onwards, exercised the prerogative on behalf of the Lord Chancellor, sometimes directed voluntary payments for some person or purpose other than the maintenance of the lunatic himself without any particularly clearly articulated rationale for doing so. For example, in 1816, in *Re Hinde, ex parte Whitbread*,[10] Lord Eldon spoke in the same sentence of 'considering what the Lunatic would probably do, and what it would be beneficial to him should be done', when directing an allowance from a lunatic's inherited estate for brothers and sisters

> slenderly or not at all provided for … upon the principle that it would naturally be more agreeable to the lunatic, and more for his advantage, that they should receive an education and maintenance suitable to his condition, than that they should be sent into the world to disgrace him as beggars.[11]

There is nothing in the case report, however, to suggest that the court considered any evidence as to 'what the Lunatic would probably do', rather than making highly generalised assumptions as to how a person in such circumstances might act. As Cross J commented in *Re L*[12] in 1965, speaking generally of this historic approach:

> the cases show clearly that in those days the court would never direct a payment simply because it was the sort of payment which the patient might well have made but only if it was a payment which he would undoubtedly have made unless he was a very oddly constituted person.

In *Re L*, the court had to consider a proposed settlement to be made for a man in his late 60s – in other words, a man born at the end of the nineteenth century – who was described as 'in an advanced state of mental deterioration', and whose mind had been

[9] See Brian Sloan's chapter in this volume.
[10] *Re Hinde, ex parte Whitbread* (1816) 2 Mer 99.
[11] ibid 102.
[12] *Re L (WJG)* [1966] Ch 135, 142.

affected since he was 17. At the date of the application, he had been living in a mental hospital since his mother's death in 1941 and had an estate of about £130,000. L was accumulating surplus income from his estate, as his care was paid for by the NHS.[13] Apart from a fund of £20,000 to pay costs and tax and to preserve the balance for L during his life, the intended beneficiaries of the proposed settlement were individuals who were not members of L's 'family' for whom he might provide maintenance or some other benefit within the narrow meaning of section 103(1)(b) of the 1959 Act. The proposed settlement was to be irrevocable, and a large part of its motivation was to save tax on L's intestate estate at death. The court approved this settlement (subject to some increase of the fund to be retained for L himself), which had the effect of both accelerating the transfer of the majority of L's estate to the chosen beneficiaries and altering the distribution of it which would otherwise have taken effect on his intestacy. The judgment is significant because the authorisation of an irrevocable settlement (following his death) of the entirety of L's estate was a large step towards the enactment of a statutory wills jurisdiction, and because of its formative influence on the reasoning in *Re D(J)*. The court considered how the words 'making provision for other persons or purposes for whom or which the patient might be expected to provide if her were not mentally disordered' should be interpreted. As the judge, Cross J, said:

> Obviously, all bachelor uncles of 68 with a fortune of £130,000 would not react in exactly the same way to a suggestion that they should settle the greater part of it in their lifetime irrevocably on their nephews and niece and their families. Some would regard the possibility that they might themselves marry and have children as a matter to be taken into account; others would, for one reason or another, be sure that they would have no issue. Some would be spending the whole of their income – and even perhaps some of their capital – either on themselves or on causes which interested them. Others would be living well within their income. Some would feel an impartial affection for all their relatives; others an impartial dislike for all of them; others again would like some and dislike others.[14]

He rejected the idea that the court should only approve the settlement 'if any normally constituted person in the position of [L] would make it', and concluded that he had to 'assume that the patient becomes a sane man for a sufficient time to review the situation but knows that after a brief interval of sanity he will once more be as he was before' and that, making those 'very curious assumptions', he had no doubt that L would execute an irrevocable settlement of a substantial part of his property.[15]

The judgment in *Re L* is also a useful exposition of the history of the lunacy and early Court of Protection jurisdiction to authorise acts of financial altruism on the part of individuals who lacked mental capacity. One aspect of this history, which appears very clearly from *Re L* itself, is that it was entirely rooted in the financial circumstances of wealthy landowners: the aristocracy and landed gentry. L was entitled to some entailed property,

[13] Although 'best interests' did not form any part of the court's consideration of whether or not the settlement of L's property should be authorised, it did use the phrase in connection with his welfare: 'He could well afford the fees payable at a private mental hospital, but the evidence shows that to move him to one would be against his best interests' (ibid 137–8).

[14] ibid 141.

[15] ibid.

and the court approved the execution of documents to effect a disentailing to enable him to deal with the property as an absolute owner. The judgment refers to L's mother caring for him 'with the aid of her domestic staff and, in particular, of the family chauffeur',[16] the chauffeur being one of the intended beneficiaries of the proposed settlement. The judge's historical survey sweeps across '[y]our rich man in Victorian, Edwardian and early Georgian days', before reaching the post-Second World War world, in which such a man faced a choice between giving his children financial independence in his lifetime or having his estate substantially taxed on his death.[17]

One respect in which *Re D(J)* marks a conspicuous difference from this background was that Mrs D's financial circumstances were far more typical of ordinary property-owning families of her generation and of succeeding generations. The decision in *Re D(J)*, in the autumn of 1981, reflects some of the social change which had taken place since 1965, and also coincided with the first term of a Conservative administration under Margaret Thatcher which encouraged the acquisition of assets by a new property-owning class, through creation of the right to buy property from a local authority landlord and the democratisation of share ownership through the privatisations of formerly nationalised industries in the 1980s. This was a different world from that envisaged by the legislature when the original power to direct a statutory will first came into force. As it was no more than one of a number of miscellaneous provisions in the Administration of Justice Act 1969, it was not preceded by any significant consultation or legislative debate. When the Administration of Justice Bill was introduced for its second reading in the House of Commons by the Attorney-General, all that he said about the statutory will provisions was:[18]

> Although the existing law is intended to safeguard the position of the mental patient and those for whom he might have been expected to provide, its practical effect is to place him at a disadvantage. For instance, a patient might, on marriage, have made a will in favour of her husband; subsequently, he may leave her, obtain a divorce abroad which is not recognised by the English courts, and re-marry. Meanwhile, the wife becomes mentally ill and is no longer of testamentary capacity.
>
> The only way to prevent the will from taking effect is by means of a settlement, but it would be much simpler and cheaper if a new will could be made for the patient; and, furthermore, to make provision for the patient's family or for a servant by a legacy or an annuity in a will would be far less complicated and less expensive than by using the process of a settlement.
>
> There is another reason in this somewhat complex field why the patient is at a disadvantage. This is because a settlement of property is a disposal of assets for Capital Gains Tax purposes. In addition, stamp duty is payable. If the patient was of sound mind and had testamentary capacity, his legal advisers would undoubtedly recommend that he should make a will under which there would be no immediate Capital Gains Tax liability or stamp duty payable rather than effect a settlement.
>
> The Treasury has been consulted and agrees that, just because a person is unfortunate enough to be mentally ill or incapable of managing his affairs, there is no reason why those affairs should not be administered with the same regard to tax considerations as in other cases.

[16] ibid 137.
[17] ibid 143.
[18] *Hansard*, HC Vol 477, cols 416–17 (5 February 1969).

This brief analysis does not articulate either the approach to the statutory wills jurisdiction of *Re D(J)* or of the modern best-interests test: and, as one commentator has observed:

> One startling aspect of this parliamentary discourse is the extent to which the imaginary 'mental patient' is both classed and gendered: she is a wife who succumbs to mental illness (while her husband illicitly divorces her in order to remarry); she would want to change her will to ensure that her biological family and servants benefit on her death, rather than her deserting husband.[19]

IV. FACTS AND HISTORY OF *RE D(J)*

Mrs D was born around the turn of the twentieth century, married and had five adult children. In the case that bears her anonymised name, by the date of the statutory will application which commenced in the spring of 1979, her children were divided, two on one side and three on another, as to their prospective inheritance from their mother's estate. Mrs D had made a will in 1962, but there had been many changes in her and her family's lives between then and 1979. One of those changes was that she was suffering from age-related dementia and no longer had the mental capacity to review her 1962 will or make a new one.

As her family's identities are also anonymised, it is impossible to discover any more about Mrs D's life history or family relationships, or her wishes about what should happen to her estate after her death, than is disclosed in the facts narrated in the Law Reports. The narrative commences when Mrs D and her husband were living in Cornwall in the mid-1950s. Mrs D's husband was dying of cancer. Mrs D wrote to her daughter, Mrs A, in October 1955, to tell her of her husband's illness. Mrs A was then living and working in Manchester. She was married, but separated from her husband. She took leave from her work and went to her parents' home in Cornwall, where she stayed until after her father's death in April 1956. As the judge, Mr Justice Megarry, explained, there then followed an unsettled period in both Mrs D's and her daughter A's lives:

> After the funeral Mrs A continued to live with [Mrs D] in Cornwall as she was very upset by her husband's death; and she left most business matters, including winding up the father's estate, to Mrs A. In September 1957 the house in Cornwall was sold, and for a few months [Mrs D] and Mrs A went to live with Mrs W, another daughter of [Mrs D]'s, and then in lodgings. Early in 1958 [Mrs D] and Mrs A moved into a house in Hampshire which [Mrs D] had bought.[20]

The spare judicial prose gives a glimpse of a Home Counties King Lear – a parent moving from the home and care of one adult child to another, and becoming increasingly or

[19] R Harding, 'The Rise of Statutory Wills and the Limits of Best Interests Decision-Making in Inheritance' (2015) 78 *MLR* 945, 951.

[20] *Re D(J)* (n 1) 240.

remaining consistently dependent on one of them. This is not an uncommon background for cases which the Court of Protection has to decide.

In 1962, when she would have been around 60, Mrs D made a will, in which she left the house she had bought in Hampshire a few years earlier, her furniture and personal possessions to her daughter Mrs A, who was then still living with her. She then divided the residue of her estate between all five of her children. At the date of the will, Mrs A was still separated from her husband, from whom she eventually divorced in 1965. Mrs A had commenced a relationship with another man, who was himself separated from his wife, but intended to marry Mrs A when he was free to do so, and Mrs A's mother, Mrs D, knew this. In 1972, he and Mrs A married and set up home elsewhere. Mrs D visited A and her husband shortly afterwards, and refused to return to her home but insisted on staying with them after her originally projected visit of one month came to an end. In April 1973 Mrs D sold her own home in Hampshire for £13,500 and bought a smaller one only a few doors away from A and her husband's home for £10,800. The original intention appears to have been that Mrs D would keep her own independence in her own home, with her daughter and son-in-law close at hand, but in fact she only slept at her new home for a few nights before moving in with A and her husband, spending no more than an hour or two a day in her own home. The judge commented that Mrs D's refusal to return to her own home was at about the time that the first signs of her dementia began to be apparent. It is not difficult to imagine how this would have added to her sense of dependency on her daughter to help her in her daily life.

As the first signs of Mrs D's dementia appeared, A and her husband took on most of the burden of caring for Mrs D, and A's sister R was appointed as her mother's receiver. In May 1979 A and R applied to the Court of Protection for a direction to execute a codicil to Mrs D's will so as to compensate A for the ademption of the gift of her mother's house to her in the 1962 will and for what she had done in caring for her mother. Mrs D's house was sold in October 1979 for £22,000. As her entire estate constituted about £50,000, the proceeds of sale of the house accounted for about 44% of the net estate. Making due adjustment for inflation in asset values since the late 1970s, this was, and would today be, an entirely typical story of later life in the middle of the affluence scale of middle Britain. The Court of Protection directed that the will should contain a legacy of £10,000 to A and the residue should be divided equally among the five children. A and R appealed against this, and the judgment of Megarry J, published on 14 October 1981, is the judgment on their appeal.

Table 5.1 shows the financial effect for Mrs D's daughters of her 1962 will, the sale of her house in 1973 and the subsequent sale in 1979, the original Court of Protection order and the order on appeal. The last four rows of the table are based on an estate value of £50,000 at the date of the statutory will, of which the 1979 proceeds of sale accounted for £22,000, leaving £28,000 accounted for by other assets. A was significantly better off under both Court of Protection orders than she would have been under her mother's 1962 will, following the sale in 1973 of the house which was the subject of the specific gift to her in the 1962 will and the consequent ademption of the gift.

However, the outcome has been less important to legal posterity than the process of reasoning by which the court reached this result.

Table 5.1

	A	R	B	C	D
1962 will before any sale of house	House + 1/5 residue House sold £13,500[21] in 1973 Value of residue unknown	1/5 residue	1/5 residue	1/5 residue	1/5 residue
1962 will after ademption following sale of house in 1973	10,000	10,000	10,000	10,000	10,000
1962 will after further sale of house in 1979	10,000	10,000	10,000	10,000	10,000
Original Court of Protection order	10,000 + 8,000 = 18,000	8,000	8,000	8,000	8,000
Court of Protection order on appeal	15,000 + 7,000 = 22,000	7,000	7,000	7,000	7,000

V. PRINCIPLES IN *RE D(J)*

The fundamental problem in exercising any statutory will jurisdiction is that it attempts to do something which a person does not have the mental capacity to do for himself, but which a person who did have capacity could do in almost limitless ways. The guidance set out in *Re D(J)* is essentially guidance for the exercise of substituted judgment, in other words, following *Re L*, for assuming that the person does briefly have capacity to make a will and then deciding what decisions that person would make. In summary, these five guiding principles are:

1. The patient should be assumed to have a brief lucid interval at the time when the will is made.
2. During the lucid interval the patient has full knowledge of the past, and a full realisation that as soon as the will is executed he will relapse into the actual mental state that previously existed, with the prognosis as it actually is.
3. It is the actual patient who has to be considered and not a hypothetical patient.
4. The patient is to be envisaged as being advised by competent solicitors.
5. In all normal cases the patient is to be envisaged as taking a broad brush to the claims on his bounty, rather than an accountant's pen.

In practice, the application of these principles in *Re D(J)* involved reviewing all of the evidence about the patient's life and family, and any previous wills he had made or views

[21] If Mrs D had retained her Hampshire house unsold in 1973, Land Registry data suggests that it would have approximately trebled in value by the date of the hearing, with significant inflation from 1978 onwards, but of course the value of residue would have been smaller, as she downsized to a cheaper property in 1973.

he had expressed, and using that evidence to decide on what the will should contain, having regard to the technical advice that a solicitor would give a testator who did have capacity about the structure, contents and drafting of a will. It became a similar exercise for a professional to drafting a will as instructed by a private client, but with the court substituting itself as far as possible for the private client giving instructions: 'the will is being made by the court, and so by an impartial entity skilled in the law, rather than the actual patient, whose views while still of a sound disposing mind might be idiosyncratic and far from impartial'.[22]

It was also an exercise which could give rise to some tension between what might subjectively have been the wishes of the patient and the assumption that the patient would act in an objectively reasonable way. In his judgment in *Re D(J)*, Megarry J recognised this, observing that:

> Before losing testamentary capacity the patient may have been a person with strong antipathies or deep affections for particular persons or causes, or with vigorous religious or political views; and of course the patient was then able to give effect to those views when making a will. I think that the court must take the patient as he or she was before losing testamentary capacity. No doubt allowance may be made for the passage of years since the patient was last of full capacity, for sometimes strong feelings mellow into indifference, and even family feuds evaporate. Furthermore, I do not think that the court should give effect to antipathies or affections of the patient which are beyond reason. But subject to all due allowances, I think that the court must seek to make the will which the actual patient, acting reasonably, would have made if notionally restored to full mental capacity, memory and foresight.[23]

VI. STATUTORY WILLS BETWEEN *RE D(J)* AND THE MENTAL CAPACITY ACT 2005

The few published cases decided subsequently to *Re D(J)* illustrated some of the different circumstances in which the court had to consider and apply its guidelines.

Re D(J) itself was an example of a case of an adult who had previously had testamentary capacity and led a full life before losing capacity as a consequence of dementia in old age, and whose full life had included making a previous will. In this and similar cases, there was generally a significant amount of evidence for the court to consider and draw inferences from. This evidence might be exactly the same sort of evidence as would influence a person of full capacity when reviewing and making changes to their existing will: the birth or death of a close family member; some change in relationships or interests in charitable causes; and/or changes in the value and structure of a person's estate. Taking a previous will as a starting point and deciding on how far to depart from it (or not) in the light of evidence of changed circumstances since the previous will was made is a structured exercise in which decisions can be justified by findings on the evidence.

[22] ibid 243F.

[23] Compare *Re S (Gifts by Mental Patient)* [1997] 1 FLR 96, 99, where Ferris J said that a judge should have 'a reasonable degree of confidence' that changes to the status quo made by a statutory will were 'not only … objectively reasonable but … something which the patient herself would have wished to be done if she were of full capacity and aware of the circumstances'.

Where the validity of the previous will was itself doubtful, because evidence suggested it might have been made at a time when the testator lacked capacity or was susceptible to undue influence, the court had to take this into account. Under the Mental Capacity Act 2005, this remains the case: there is no presumption or general principle that the court should not consider making a statutory will in these circumstances.[24]

It is inevitably more difficult to decide on the contents of a will for an adult who has never had capacity but has been born with an impairment or disturbance in the functioning of their mind or brain, or who has acquired such an impairment or disturbance during childhood, and whose testamentary wishes have inevitably been a blank canvas. In such a case, 'there is no material on which to construct a subjective assessment of what the patient would have wanted to do' and

> the court must assume that [P] would have been a normal decent person, acting in accordance with contemporary standards of morality. In the absence of actual evidence to the contrary, no less should be assumed of any person and in this case there is nothing to displace such an assumption.[25]

In cases of this type it is difficult to draw a real distinction between assumed subjective wishes and objective reasonableness, yet inevitable that there will be patent judicial subjectivity in the outcome. In *Re C*, which involved both lifetime gifts and a will, C's estate was divided between the institutions in which she had lived and her family, with special provisions for a cousin with Down syndrome and for a volunteer who had befriended C. In *Re S*, however, which also involved a 'blank canvas' approach to the estate of an elderly spinster, the court directed that 75% of S's estate should go to her family and 25% to charity.[26]

VII. THE MENTAL CAPACITY ACT 2005

The new legal framework introduced by the Mental Capacity Act 2005 was preceded by consultation and consideration by the Law Commission, but this did not include any fresh specific consideration of the principles relevant to statutory wills.[27] The new approach, which applies to all decisions made for people who lack capacity, is articulated in the principles set out in section 1 of the Act, and the principle which has most directly

[24] See *Re D* [2010] EWHC 2159 (Ch), [2012] Ch 57, where the court was asked to rule on this question.

[25] *Re C (Spinster and Mental Patient)* [1992] 1 FLR 51 (Hoffmann J). The resort to assumptions about contemporary standards of morality has continued to be relevant under the Mental Capacity Act 2005, and not only in the context of statutory wills. In *Secretary of State for the Home Department v Skripal* [2018] EWCOP 6, [2018] COPLR 220, the court took a similar approach to the decision on behalf of Sergei and Yulia Skripal to authorise the taking of blood samples and complying with other requests from the Organisation for the Prohibition of Chemical Weapons, regarding them as 'reasonable citizens' who would 'believe that justice should be done'.

[26] *Re C* (n 25). In the post-Mental Capacity Act 2005 decision in *Re LM* [2015] EWCOP 91, the court decided that LM would wish to give 20% of an estate derived from a criminal injuries compensation award to charity, with the charity associated with the NHS trust funding LM's care being a principal object.

[27] The Law Commission's 1995 report, *Mental Incapacity* (Law Com No 231, 1995) [8.34]), simply recommended that the court's powers should extend to making a will, as they had done under the predecessor legislation.

affected the statutory will jurisdiction is section 1(5): 'an act done, or decision made, under this Act for or on behalf of a person who lacks capacity must be done, or made, in his best interests'.

The Act does not attempt to define or prescribe what best interests are, as that is a value judgement for the decision maker in every decision taken on behalf of a person who lacks capacity. Instead, section 4, headed 'Best interests', sets out a number of considerations for the decision maker. These function as a kind of compliance checklist for best-interests decisions.

Subsection 4(6) directs the decision maker to consider, 'so far as is reasonably ascertainable':

(a) the person's past and present wishes and feelings (and, in particular, any relevant written statement made by him when he had capacity),
(b) the beliefs and values that would be likely to influence his decision if he had capacity, and
(c) the other factors that he would be likely to consider if he were able to do so.

As the statutory wills jurisdiction under the 2005 Act has developed, these have generally been the most important subsections of section 4 in determining a person's best interests in the contents of a statutory will. As is apparent at a glance from the wording of subsections (b) and (c), they import into the best interests test an element of substituted judgement through the words 'would be likely', and require the decision maker to consider what influence beliefs, values and 'other factors' would have on the subjective decision making of the individual who lacks capacity to make a will for himself.

VIII. STATUTORY WILLS AFTER THE MENTAL CAPACITY ACT 2005

The application of the Mental Capacity Act 2005 to statutory wills was first considered in two cases decided in 2009: *Re P*[28] and *Re M*.[29] Both are decisions of High Court judges: Lewison J in the Chancery Division and Munby J in the Family Division – the latter with extensive experience of the best interests principle in the law relating to children. *Re P*, the earlier of the two decisions, is a case which cannot be read in the context of its full facts, as they are largely redacted from the judgment, although it is clear that (harking back to the landed classes who were the subject of pre-*Re D(J)* decisions) it involved making a decision about an entailed interest in property in England. *Re M*, like *Re D(J)*, tells a fuller story, but with anonymised protagonists. Again, like *Re D(J)*, the broad facts of *Re M* are far from unique in modern England. M was an elderly childless widow living in a London suburb, without any other close family members, who had become increasingly dependent on a neighbour, Z, to provide her with care and assist her with managing her property and affairs. At the date of the hearing, M had made previous wills, in the most recent of which she had left Z her entire estate, on the apparent understanding that he would provide her with care at home for the remainder of her life. On the application of the professional deputy, who had replaced Z as M's unsatisfactory property and affairs attorney, following litigation over Z's suitability to act in this role and at a time when M had been removed

[28] *Re P (Statutory Will)* [2009] EWHC 163 (Ch), [2010] Ch 33.
[29] *Re M (Statutory Will)* [2009] EWHC 2525 (Fam), [2011] 1 WLR 344.

from Z's unsatisfactory care by the local authority under an order of the court, the court directed a statutory will which entirely excluded Z from benefit.

As *Re P* and *Re M* make clear, the 2005 Act has made a radical change to the forensic approach to statutory wills. The court must make a value judgement about the contents of a statutory will, having complied with the principles in section 1 and considered all the relevant circumstances in accordance with section 4. This exercise no longer requires the court to make any counterfactual assumption about what P would do if he were not mentally incapacitated, nor is it necessary to hypothesise about the will that P would make in a notional lucid interval, having received, but not necessarily followed, competent advice. Instead, the court must consider P as he actually is, and recognise that his best interests may not be expressed simply in the form of a will which gives effect to his known and/or inferred wishes, whether with or without the further assumption of 'acting reasonably'. Lewison J held that:

> in my judgment, ... the guidance given under the Mental Health Acts 1959 and 1983 about the making of settlements or wills can no longer be directly applied to a decision being made under the 2005 Act. I say this for a number of reasons:
>
> i) The 2005 Act does not require the counter-factual assumption that P is not mentally disordered. The facts must be taken as they are. It is not therefore necessary to go through the mental gymnastics of imagining that P has a brief lucid interval and then relapses into his former state.
> ii) The goal of the enquiry is not what P 'might be expected' to have done; but what is in P's best interests. This is more akin to the 'balance sheet' approach than to the 'substituted judgment' approach. The code of practice[30] makes this clear in that it points out that the test of best interests was one that was worked out by the courts mainly in decisions relating to the provision of medical care (para 5.1).
> iii) The previous guidance was concerned with deciding what P would have wanted if he were not mentally disordered. But the 2005 Act requires the decision maker to consider P's *present* wishes and feelings, which *ex hypothesi* are wishes and feelings entertained by a person who lacks mental capacity in relation to the decision being made on his behalf.
> iv) The same structured decision making process applies to all decisions to be made on P's behalf, whether great or small, whereas the previous guidance was specific to the making of a will, gift or settlement. Moreover, it is a decision making process which must be followed, not only by the court, but by anyone who takes decisions on P's behalf.
> v) In making his decision the decision maker must consider 'all relevant circumstances'.
> vi) The Act expressly directs the decision maker to take a number of steps before reaching a decision. These include encouraging P to participate in the decision. He must also 'consider' P's past and present wishes, and his beliefs and values and must 'take into account' the views of third parties as to what would be in P's best interests.
>
> Having gone through these steps, the decision maker must then form a value judgment of his own giving effect to the paramount statutory instruction that any decision must be made in P's best interests. In my judgment this process is quite different to that which applied under the former Mental Health Acts.[31]

[30] Department for Constitutional Affairs, *Mental Capacity Act 2005: Code of Practice* (London, The Stationery Office, 2007).

[31] *Re P* (n 28) [38]–[39].

In *Re M*, Munby J described Lewison J's analysis in *Re P* as 'of compelling force', agreeing that:

> the 2005 Act marks a radical change in the treatment of persons lacking capacity, in particular (para [37]) by enacting the overarching principle that any decision made on behalf of P must be made in P's best interests. Thus it follows, as he says (para [38]), that the guidance given in the cases decided under the Mental Health Acts 1959 and 1983 about the making of settlements or wills can no longer be directly applied to a decision being made under the 2005 Act.
>
> …
>
> The starting point now must be what Lewison J aptly described (para [38]) as the 'structured decision making process' prescribed by the 2005 Act, a process which requires the decision maker – here the Court of Protection – to take a number of steps before reaching a decision, including, as Lewison J described it, encouraging P to participate in the decision, 'considering' P's past and present wishes, and her beliefs and values, and 'taking into account' the views of third parties as to what would be in P's best interests. And there is, in my judgment, no place in that process for any reference to – any harking back to – judicial decisions under the earlier and very different statutory scheme, decisions which, as Lewison J justly observed, required the judges to perform 'mental gymnastics' and which, as Palmer J equally justly observed in *Re Fenwick, Application of JR Fenwick & Re Charles* …[32] at para [87], reached the high water mark of artificiality in *In re C*.[33]

He went on to note that the process 'of applying structurally somewhat similar schemes' was a very familiar one to judges of the Family Division, and made three points deriving from that experience which he considered to be applicable to the statutory scheme under the MCA:

> i) The first is that the statute lays down no hierarchy as between the various factors which have to be borne in mind, beyond the overarching principle that what is determinative is the judicial evaluation of what is in P's 'best interests'.
>
> ii) The second is that the weight to be attached to the various factors will, inevitably, differ depending upon the individual circumstances of the particular case. A feature or factor which in one case may carry great, possibly even preponderant, weight may in another, superficially similar, case carry much less, or even very little, weight.
>
> iii) The third, following on from the others, is that there may, in the particular case, be one or more features or factors which, as Thorpe LJ has frequently put it, are of 'magnetic importance' in influencing or even determining the outcome: see, for example, *Crossley v Crossley* … [34], at para [15] (contrasting 'the peripheral factors in the case' with the 'factor of magnetic importance') and *White v White* … [35] where at page 314 he said 'Although there is no ranking of the criteria to be found in the statute, there is as it were a magnetism that draws the individual case to attach to one, two, or several factors as having decisive influence on its determination.' Now that was said in the context of section 25 of the

[32] In the New South Wales case of *Re Fenwick* [2009] NSWSC 530 [105], Palmer J reviewed the development of the English law from its origins to the enactment of the MCA in some depth, concluding that the English courts 'had for a long time been paying only the scantest lip service to the principles enunciated in *Re D(J)* … by 2005 courts were taking the realistic and pragmatic approach that whether a statutory will should be ordered was to be determined having regard to the best interests of the patient, ascertained objectively, and to the wishes of the patient, if known. That approach is now enshrined in legislation.'

[33] *Re M* (n 29) [28]–[29].

[34] *Crossley v Crossley* [2007] EWCA Civ 1491, [2008] 1 FLR 1467.

[35] *White v White* [1999] Fam 304 (CA), affirmed [2001] 1 AC 596 (HL).

> Matrimonial Causes Act 1973 but the principle, as it seems to me, is of more general application.[36]

In *Re G(TJ)*, Morgan J described these observations as 'valuable comments as to the way in which a court should identify and weigh relevant factors in assessing … overall best interests'.[37]

IX. STATUTORY WILLS SINCE *RE P* AND *RE M*

The most recently published cumulative tables of Family Court Statistics Quarterly, for July–September 2018,[38] show the number of Court of Protection orders made for wills, gifts and settlements, without further refining the data to each type of application. These numbers are very small: 79, 61 and 42 for the first three quarters of 2018 respectively. There have never been more than 1,000 orders in a year since the 2005 Act came into force. An even smaller percentage of the decided cases on statutory gifts and wills are published as judgments of the court, despite transparency guidance dating from 2014 to this effect, and Megarry J's observations in *Re D(J)* that:

> it is important that the public should be kept informed of the principles on which the Court of Protection acts, and this is best secured by making public (with, of course, suitable safeguards of anonymity) any judgments which deal with matters of principle.[39]

One reason for a lack of published reports is that many cases conclude in a negotiated compromise for the court to consider and approve. Quite apart from the reasoning and outcome of such cases remaining private, it is inevitable that such compromises will reflect pragmatism and negotiating strengths and weaknesses between the parties as to what can be justified as being in P's best interests.

Two particular and related themes have emerged in the decisions which have been reported. The first is the weight to be given to P's wishes, and in particular to P's assumed present wishes in cases where there has been a change of circumstances unforeseen when P last had testamentary capacity. In *Re G(TJ)* Morgan J said:

> the word 'interest' in the best interests test does not confine the court to considering the self interest of P. The actual wishes of P, which are altruistic and not in any way, directly or indirectly self-interested, can be a relevant factor. Further, the wishes which P would have formed, if P had capacity, which may be altruistic wishes, can be a relevant factor. It is not necessary to establish that P would have been aware of the fact that P's wishes were carried into effect. Respect for P's wishes, actual or putative, can be a relevant factor even where P has no awareness of, and no reaction to, the fact that such wishes are being respected.

[36] *Re M* (n 29) [31]–[32].

[37] *Re G(TJ)* [2010] EWHC 3005 (Ch), [2011] Med LR 89 [50]. This decision was an application to authorise gifts in the form of substantial maintenance for the adult daughter of the surviving widow of the couple whose property and affairs were considered in the pre-Mental Capacity Act 2005 case of *G v Official Solicitor* [2006] EWCA Civ 816, [2006] WTLR 1201, and which had to be reviewed in the light of supervening events. Although it conscientiously followed a best interests approach, it is difficult to envisage that an exercise of substituted judgement would have led to any different outcome.

[38] Ministry of Justice, *Family Court Statistics Quarterly, England and Wales, July to September 2018* (London, Ministry of Justice, 2018).

[39] *Re D(J)* (n 1) 239.

Since this decision, assumed present wishes have played a significant role in many statutory will applications, as it is frequently the case that P is incapable of forming or expressing wishes about the effect of changes which have taken place since losing testamentary capacity.

Secondly, what factors are capable of being of 'magnetic importance'? These include matters which arise from the wider 'relevant circumstances' to be considered, rather than being identifiable as a past or present wish, feeling, belief or value attributable to P. For example, in *Re JC*,[40] the factor of magnetic importance was the absence of any personal interaction between JC and the applicant, D, who was his daughter by birth but who had been adopted as an infant and had never had any contact with her father. In *NT v FS*,[41] an application was brought by a neutral professional deputy, and there were numerous respondents: FS's elderly mother, his adult siblings, his current cohabitee, his previous cohabitee and an adult son of that relationship. FS's siblings unsuccessfully argued that the contents of a manuscript document written and signed by FS probably between 1984 and 1986, described by him as his will and containing an attestation clause but not attested by any witnesses, were of magnetic importance in determining the content of a statutory will to be made many years later.

Other cases have illustrated the role of a statutory will as part of a jigsaw of remedies for misconduct by those responsible for P's property and affairs, as in *Re Meek*[42] and *Re Treadwell*.[43]

An aspect of the best interests test on which different judges have expressed a range of views – some dissenting from attaching any weight to it, others endorsing it – is Lewison J's observation in *Re P* that:

> what will live on after P's death is his memory; and for many people it is in their best interests that they be remembered with affection by their family and as having done 'the right thing' by their will. In my judgment the decision maker is entitled to take into account, in assessing what is in P's best interests, how he will be remembered after his death.[44]

To the extent that this forms part of the best-interests test for making a statutory will, how far does it differ from the assumption in *Re D(J)* that a patient in a lucid interval would be 'acting reasonably' and in reliance on competent advice? Arguably, not very far at all. In *Re Jones*[45] the court directed a statutory will which made some provision for P's adult daughter of a previous marriage, even though she had been excluded from the original proposed statutory will. The court considered the authorities on 'being remembered as having done the right thing' and concluded that

> they are not as incompatible as is sometimes implied … For many but not all people it is in their best interests that they be remembered with affection by their family as having done the right thing by their Will. This is something which the judge is 'entitled to take into account' – it is a relevant consideration – alongside the other factors specified in section 4, … [but] the onset of mental incapacity is not an opportunity for moral correction.

[40] *Re JC* [2012] WTLR 1211.
[41] *NT v FS* [2013] EWHC 684 (COP), [2013] WTLR 867.
[42] *Re Meek* [2014] EWCOP 1, [2014] COPLR 535.
[43] *Re Treadwell* [2013] EWHC 2409 (COP), [2013] WTLR 1445.
[44] *Re P* (n 28) [44].
[45] *Re Jones* [2014] EWCOP 59, [2016] WTLR 661 [60] and [66] (District Judge Eldergill).

X. STATUTORY WILLS IN THE FUTURE

As Professor Rosie Harding has argued, there are grounds for reconsidering the legal framework of the statutory wills jurisdiction.[46] The statutory best interests test in its present form was not designed specifically for decisions which are more altruistic than self-interested, and even when it is used as a compliance checklist for making a statutory will, there is inevitable convergence with the element of substituted decision making which is inherent in the wording of subsections 4(6)(b) and (c) of the Mental Capacity Act 2005. Further, Professor Harding and others have questioned whether a best-interests approach is compliant with Article 12 of the UN Convention on the Rights of Persons with Disabilities, which provides for equal recognition of persons with disabilities before the law and directs that states which are parties to the Convention:

> shall ensure that all measures that relate to the exercise of legal capacity provide for appropriate and effective safeguards to prevent abuse in accordance with international human rights law. Such safeguards shall ensure that measures relating to the exercise of legal capacity respect the rights, will and preferences of the person …

The UK has ratified the Convention, but has not yet adopted it into domestic law.

The Law Commission has also considered this issue in the context of statutory wills, and has published two relevant documents: a report, *Mental Capacity and Deprivation of Liberty*, published on 13 March 2017,[47] and a public consultation document, *Making a Will*, on every aspect of the law of wills, published on 13 July 2017.[48] This latter document does not propose any reform of the law of statutory wills other than as set out in the report on mental capacity and deprivation of liberty. This included a proposal to enhance the role of P's past and present wishes and feelings in best-interests decisions by providing that:

> Section 4(6) of the Mental Capacity Act should be amended to require that the individual making the best interests determination must ascertain, so far as is reasonably practicable: (1) the person's past and present wishes and feelings (and, in particular, whether there is any relevant written statement made by him or her when they had capacity); (2) the beliefs and values that would be likely to influence the person's decision if he or she had capacity; and (3) any other factors that the person would be likely to consider if he or she were able to do so; and in making the determination must give particular weight to any wishes or feelings ascertained.[49]

This proposal was reflected in clause 8 of a draft bill published with the report, but these proposed amendments do not form part of the Mental Capacity (Amendment) Bill currently before Parliament. The enactment of these proposals and their effect on the statutory will jurisdiction of the future therefore remain to be seen. But despite Munby J's view in *Re M* that 'such well-known authorities as *In re L (WJG)*, *In re D (J)*, *In re* C and *G v Official Solicitor*, are best consigned to history',[50] *Re D(J)* may yet continue to have an influential afterlife as a landmark case in the law of succession.

[46] Harding (n 19).
[47] Law Commission, *Mental Capacity and Deprivation of Liberty* (Law Com No 372, 2017).
[48] Law Commission, *Making A Will* (Law Com No 231, 2017).
[49] Law Commission (n 47) Recommendation 40.
[50] *Re M* (n 27) [29].

6

Hastilow v Stobie (1865): Lack of Knowledge and Approval

ROGER KERRIDGE

I. INTRODUCTION

Hastilow v Stobie appears, at first glance, an odd suggestion as a 'landmark case' on the law of succession. It is a case at first instance, it is not particularly well known and it will be suggested, in due course, that it has led in the wrong direction. But it has been followed, it has done significant harm and it is to be hoped that, one day, this harm can be undone. This can happen only if what was decided in the case is properly understood and seen in its historical setting.

Hastilow was decided in December 1865, less than eight years after the creation of the Court of Probate. To put the case in context, something needs to be said about how that court came into being.

II. CREATING THE COURT OF PROBATE

Before 1926, there were two sets of rules relating to succession in England and Wales – one applicable to realty – *the rules of inheritance* – and the other to personalty – *the rules of distribution*.

It had been established by the thirteenth century that realty could not be devised[1] by will. It came within the jurisdiction of the common law courts and, on death, it passed directly to the owner's heir. By contrast, personalty could be bequeathed by testament[2] and, if not so bequeathed, it would pass, via the deceased's personal representatives,[3] to his or her widow(er) and next of kin. Jurisdiction over the passing of personalty on death, whether it was by testament or on intestacy, belonged to the ecclesiastical courts. They would 'prove', ie they would authenticate, testaments of personalty and they would supervise the appointment and the conduct of personal representatives. Nobody had duties corresponding to those of the personal representatives in relation to the deceased's realty, which passed directly to the heir.

[1] To 'devise' is to leave realty by will. For personalty, the equivalent verb is 'bequeath'.
[2] A 'testament' was the term in general use for a will which bequeathed personalty.
[3] So called because they were concerned with the deceased's personalty.

In 1540, Henry VIII[4] permitted Parliament to pass the Statute of Wills, an act which allowed freeholders to devise their realty by will. So, from 1540 onwards, the freeholder was able to devise it to someone other than his heir, but, if he did so, it passed directly to such devisee[5] and not via representatives.[6]

What did not change in 1540 was that there remained two systems for dealing with the descent of property on death. The ecclesiastical courts administered the system which covered personalty, whereas the common law courts oversaw the rules relating to realty.[7]

A. Reform in the Nineteenth Century

The Court of Probate Act 1857[8] received the royal assent in August 1857 and came into force on 1 January 1858. It appeared to be radical. It took all probate work away from the ecclesiastical courts and vested contentious probate in a new Court of Probate. It went on to enact that appeals should go from the new court to the House of Lords. But the Act was based on political compromise. It may have seemed radical, but appearances can be deceptive.

To understand how this very limited reform had come about, it is necessary to go back to the final years of the reign of George III.

In 1828, Henry Brougham[9] made a six-hour speech to the Commons, which led, inter alia, to the creation of two royal commissions, one to look at the common law and the other to look at real property. The Real Property Commissioners produced their Fourth Report in April 1833. It was devoted entirely to wills and was divided into seven parts. The recommendations made in the first six parts[10] were, in due course, enacted in the Wills Act 1837.[11] The seventh part of the report (about 60 per cent of it)[12] was concerned with probate. The recommendations contained in this part were radical. Probate should be abolished, wills should, instead, be registered[13] and all contentious probate should be transferred to Chancery![14]

But the Real Property Commissioners were not the only ones looking at the possibility of reform in this area. In 1830 another Royal Commission had been established, to look

[4] There is insufficient space here to discuss the interrelationship between the Statute of Uses in 1535 and the Stature of Wills five years later. The Statute of Uses had been forced on Parliament by Henry; the Statute of Wills was, to some extent, a retreat by him.

[5] 'Devise' is a noun and a verb. A 'devisee' is someone who takes a devise.

[6] There were no real representatives, equivalent to personal representatives.

[7] There were other differences between testaments of personalty and wills of realty, the most important concerned formalities.

[8] 20 & 21 Vict c 77.

[9] Then an MP, later Lord Chancellor.

[10] I: Formalities; II: Incapacity on grounds of age and sex; III: Entails; IV: Date from which wills take effect; V: Revocation; VI: Republication.

[11] 7 Will 4 & 1 Vict c 20.

[12] Formalities, pt I, constituted about 25%, so the other five parts accounted only for about 15% between them.

[13] Prop 15.

[14] Props 24 and 34.

into the state of the ecclesiastical courts. The Ecclesiastical Commissioners produced a report in two parts. The first part – the Special Report – was completed in 1831 and recommended the abolition of the High Court of Delegates, the court which had, since the Reformation, been the final appeal court in England in matters of ecclesiastical law.[15] The composition and conduct of the High Court of Delegates were nothing short of scandalous and no one attempted to defend it.[16] The Special Report[17] was implemented quickly. The High Court of Delegates was abolished in 1832, and its functions were transferred to the Privy Council.[18]

The second part of the Ecclesiastical Commissioners' report – the General Report – was completed in 1832. It recommended the abolition of all ecclesiastical courts except the provincial courts,[19] which were to be reformed and were to deal only with succession and matrimonial causes.[20]

The ecclesiastical commissioners had begun their work after the real property commissioners, but finished ahead of them, so, by 1833, there were two sets of suggestions as to what should happen to contentious probate. Should it go to Chancery or remain with the (reformed) ecclesiastical courts?

The First Lord of the Admiralty (the minister for the navy), Sir James Graham, wanted to reform the Admiralty Court and any reform would be virtually impossible if probate were taken out of the hands of the civilians. So Sir James ensured that this did not happen. He organised a Commons Select Committee to examine the recommendations of the Ecclesiastical Commissioners on the one side and the Real Property Commissioners on the other. He weighted it towards the civilians and, as planned, it preferred the views of the Ecclesiastical Commissioners.[21] So the move towards reform of the probate jurisdiction stalled and nothing much happened for almost 20 years.

Early in 1852 Lord Derby became Prime Minister and Lord St Leonards, the self-educated barber's son, became Lord Chancellor.[22] Within a month of taking office, St Leonards had promoted the act which bore his name, amending section 9 of the 1837 Wills Act.[23] More significantly, in the present context, in November 1852 he increased the

[15] Final appeals, before the Reformation, had been to Rome.

[16] Its death knell had been sounded in 1826 in *Dew v Clarke* 1 Hagg Ecc 311, 162 ER 596.

[17] Completed in 1831.

[18] The Judicial Committee of the Privy Council was established a year later.

[19] The provincial courts were the courts of the archdioceses of Canterbury and York. Some members of the commission wanted to abolish the court at York. The court of the province of Canterbury was the Prerogative Court, the highest ecclesiastical court of first instance. Its testamentary jurisdiction included cases where the deceased had personalty in more than one diocese. There were also diocesan courts and the courts of peculiars.

[20] The commissioners divided the work of the ecclesiastical courts into (i) temporal (probate and matrimonial); (ii) spiritual (clergy discipline); and (iii) mixed (tithes and church rates).

[21] See RH Heimholz, *The Oxford History of the Laws of England, Volume 1, The Canon Law and Ecclesiastical Jurisdiction from 597 to the 1640s* (Oxford, Oxford University Press, 2004) 705. Brougham, whose speech in the Commons had led to the setting up of the Real Property Commission, was now Lord Chancellor, and it is surprising that he did not give more backing to the Commissioners' Report. But he was, by this stage, unpopular.

[22] St Leonards (he was then Edward Sugden) was counsel in *Jesson v Wright*, discussed in Neil Jones's chapter in this volume; and his will was at the centre of the dispute in *Sugden v Lord St Leonards*, discussed in Simon Cooper's chapter.

[23] The Wills Act Amendment Act 1852, commonly known as Lord St Leonards' Act, 15 & 16 Vict c 24.

number of the Commissioners, originally appointed in 1850, to examine the administration of Chancery, and then widened the scope of their enquiry to cover 'the working of the testamentary jurisdiction in the different courts of the country'. The idea of moving contentious probate to Chancery was back on the agenda.

The Derby ministry fell the following month and Lord Aberdeen became head of a coalition ministry, but the idea of transferring probate to Chancery was not abandoned. The new Solicitor General, Sir Richard Bethell,[24] was keen on the idea, as was the new Lord Chancellor, Lord Cranworth. Even before the Chancery Commissioners had completed their report, Bethell produced a Bill which would give probate jurisdiction to Chancery,[25] but the Bill met with opposition and was not proceeded with. The Chancery Commissioners produced their report in January 1854.[26] This time, the members of the Commission were not in agreement. The majority were now in favour of compromise, of creating a new Court of Probate.

B. Three Possible Ways of Proceeding

If one were to stand back at this point in history, halfway through the nineteenth century, and consider what might happen to probate work, there were three possibilities. First, the ecclesiastical courts could be reformed and could then be permitted to retain probate. Secondly, the work could be transferred to Chancery. Thirdly, it could be transferred to a newly established court, a new Court of Probate.[27] Looked at from the contentious probate viewpoint, it is submitted that the recommendations of the Real Property Commissioners, in their 1833 Fourth Report, were clearly to be preferred to those of the Ecclesiastical Commissioners in 1832 or the Chancery Commissioners in 1854. The Real Property Commissioners had noted that: (i) Chancery already dealt with the interpretation of wills; (ii) jurisdiction in respect of legacies had already been almost entirely transferred to the Courts of Equity;[28] (iii) the mode of trial, by written depositions, in the Spiritual Courts was unsuited to dealing with disputes concerning the validity of wills; and (iv) jurisdiction in relation to allegations of fraud belonged naturally to the Courts of Equity.

But, although Chancery had now been reformed and was in a better position to take on probate work than it had been 20 years earlier, there was now another misfortune for the pro-Chancery lobby: Charles Dickens's novel *Bleak House* appeared in serial form between March 1852 and September 1853. Given the picture it painted of the Court of Chancery (albeit in the 1830s), this was not a good moment to transfer work to it.

Undeterred, Bethell and Cranworth soldiered on. Early in 1854, Cranworth introduced a Testamentary Jurisdiction Bill which would transfer probate to Chancery. The Bill met

[24] Later Attorney General and then (as Lord Westbury) Lord Chancellor.

[25] Or to a separate court controlled by Chancery.

[26] It was their second report; 1731 HC (1854).

[27] A fourth possibility was to transfer it to the common law courts, but, though this was suggested from time to time, it was never taken seriously.

[28] Fourth Report, 61.

with sustained opposition from a number of quarters – particularly the proctors,[29] who were concerned about their future. The Crimean War, which had begun in the autumn of 1853,[30] also played a part in thwarting the transfer of the probate jurisdiction to Chancery because it raised the profile of the ecclesiastical lawyers.[31] The 1854 Bill was dropped. Bethell made further attempts in 1855, and again in 1856, but always with the same result.

C. The 1857 Compromise

Finally, early in 1857, Lord Cranworth introduced a new Bill. The main thrust now was to get the legislation through. The central compromise was to adopt the position taken by the Chancery Commissioners in 1854 and to accept that contentious probate should be transferred to a newly constituted court. Cranworth's original preference was that the judge of this new Court of Probate would be one of the Vice-Chancellors and that appeals from the new court should go to the Court of Appeal in Chancery, created in 1851, but neither of these suggestions proved palatable to those minded to ensure that the new court had no Chancery links.

There was an election in the spring of 1857 and Lord Palmerston, who had now replaced Aberdeen, was confirmed as prime minister. He was not a law reformer, but a political fixer. The 1857 Act followed, in general, the recommendations of the Chancery Commissioners' Report of 1854. In Dr Hutton's words, 'the Government produced a measure which purported to offer something to everyone'.[32] Or did it? It might be more accurate to say that it offered something to all the lawyers.

The 1857 Act provided that, although there would still be no grants of probate in relation to realty, challenges to wills of realty should (generally) be decided by the new court.[33] The first judges of the new court were to be common lawyers, not civilians,[34] and they were to make rules of practice to hear evidence viva voce under common law rules. But the new court was to follow the practice of the Prerogative Court and, although barristers could practise before the new court, the advocates who had practised before the Prerogative Court were also given rights of audience, and from the outset they came to dominate its proceedings. Furthermore, the judges of the new court doubled up as judges of the newly created Divorce Court, a court entirely dominated by civilians. The proctors lost the monopoly they had had over probate work, but were compensated for their loss, while attorneys and solicitors were permitted to take on the work which had been done by the proctors.

[29] The proctors were, in the ecclesiastical courts, the equivalent of attorneys in the common law courts and of solicitors in Chancery.

[30] The war began in the autumn of 1853, the British and French became involved early in 1854.

[31] They dealt with admiralty work and international law.

[32] Brian Hutton submitted his PhD thesis, 'The Reform of the Testamentary Jurisdiction of the Ecclesiastical Courts, 1830–1857', to Brunel University in 2002. It has been a helpful source for much of the information in this part of this chapter.

[33] This gave the new court jurisdiction which had belonged to the common law courts, see ss 60–63 of the 1857 Act.

[34] The judges who had sat in the Prerogative Court (and the Consistory Court) were former advocates, trained in the universities as civilians, not in the inns of court as barristers.

The 1857 Act gave limited jurisdiction to the recently created county courts over contentious probate and created district registries to deal with non-contentious probate in the place of the diocesan courts.

What had been created was, in substance, an amalgamation of the Prerogative Court with the Consistory Court, the court of the Bishop of London, a court chiefly concerned with matrimonial matters. The judge of the new court might be a common lawyer, but his main task was to come to terms with the new divorce law. A major factor in pushing through probate reform in 1857 was to tie it in with the major reforms to the law of divorce.

Who lost out? The litigants involved in contentious probate. They were the ones who would have benefited from a transfer of it to Chancery. They had to wait another 113 years for this to come about, by which time it was too late.

III. THE PREROGATIVE COURT

So, if it is true that the new Court of Probate was a relabelled version of the Prerogative Court combined with the Consistory Court, rather than a part of Chancery, why did it matter? For litigants, the compromise whereby contentious probate remained in the hands of the ecclesiastical lawyers and those who followed on in their tradition was a mini-disaster, one that has remained with us until today. To understand the problem, it is necessary to grasp what was wrong with the way in which contentious probate litigation was conducted in the ecclesiastical courts before 1858.

A. Beneficiary-Made Wills

When looking at the way in which the Prerogative Court had dealt with contentious probate before 1858, it is possible to discern a number of general patterns. To start with, most of the cases involved beneficiaries who had been involved in the will-making process. There were often allegations of incapacity, as well as beneficiary involvement, but beneficiary involvement was the central problem.[35]

B. Rules as to the Pleadings

In the Prerogative Court, there were rules as to the pleadings – the rules governing challenges to grants of probate – but these rules were never clear. It was agreed that a will could be attacked for lack of due execution, because the testator lacked capacity, or if it were shown that he or she had been subjected to undue influence (sometimes called 'imposition').[36] But, apart from these three agreed pleadings, other grounds of attack were

[35] One very rare case of incapacity, involving no suggestion of beneficiary involvement in the will-making process, was *Dew v Clark* (n 16).

[36] *Ingram v Wyatt* (1828/29) 1 Hagg Ecc 382, 162 ER 621; 3 Hagg Ecc 466, 162 ER 1228; *Constable v Tufnell* (1833) 4 Hagg Ecc 465, 162 ER 1516.

attempted. 'Importunity' was raised in *Lamkin v Babb*[37] and *Barry v Butlin*,[38] 'perjury' in *Constable v Tufnell*[39] and 'conspiracy' in *Constable v Tufnell* and *Barry v Butlin*.[40]

C. The Roman Law Rule

The civilians who practised in the Prerogative Court did not adopt the Roman law rule that a will in the preparation of which a beneficiary had played a part was automatically void. There was never any explanation for this; it was simply stated in the cases,[41] without discussion, that the Roman law rule did not apply. The Roman law rule was straightforward and strict. Not only was the will itself void,[42] but the beneficiary who took part in its preparation was automatically subject to the penalties for forgery,[43] ie the salt mines or crucifixion. So, why did those who practised in the ecclesiastical courts not apply the Roman law rule as to the will's being void? The law they practised was based on Roman law. The advocates in the Prerogative Court were doctors of civil law.[44] The obvious reason for failing to apply the Roman law rule in this instance was to maintain their workload.[45]

D. Presumptions

Given that they did not apply the Roman law rule, which would have automatically voided any will in the preparation of which a beneficiary had taken part, the next best thing would have been to have adopted clear presumptions designed to deter those involved in the will-making process from taking advantage of their position. Again, this did not happen. A presumption that any beneficiary who had been involved in the will-making process had subjected the testator to undue influence and/or fraud would have been easy to apply and would have saved huge amounts of time and effort.[46] That is the sort of presumption which Chancery would have introduced if it had had jurisdiction over contentious probate. What the Prerogative Court actually did was to create fudged presumptions, formulae whereby it was not clear whether anything was being presumed, and if it was, what it was. An early[47] example is *Billinghurst v Vickers* where there was the

[37] *Lamkin v Babb* (1752) 1 Lee 1, 161 ER 1.

[38] *Barry v Butlin* (1837/38) 1 Curt 614, 163 ER 215; 2 Moo PC 480, 12 ER 1089.

[39] *Constable v Tufnell* (1833) (n 36).

[40] ibid and n 38 above.

[41] See *Paske v Ollat* (1815) 2 Phill Ecc 323, 161 ER 1158; *Ingram v Wyatt* (1828–29) 1 Hagg Ecc 382, 162 ER 621; 3 Hagg Ecc 466, 162 ER 1228.

[42] Dig XXXIIII.8.1.

[43] Lex Cornelia de Falsis Dig XXXXVIII 10.6 pr, 15 pr.

[44] Civil Law at Oxford, or Law at Cambridge.

[45] The advocates, the judges, the court officials and the proctors all had an interest in maintaining the workload.

[46] Undue influence and fraud are different, though the distinction became clearer after 1858: see *White v White and Cato* (1862) 2 Sw & Tr 504. The confusion between them in the Prerogative Court was just another example of a lack of rigour.

[47] 'Early' in terms of the reported cases – there are few before 1800.

following sentence: 'Though the court will not presume fraud, it will require strong proof of intention.'[48] What did this mean? In *Billinghurst* a part of a will in the handwriting of the principal beneficiary was refused probate, but the formula did not achieve the same result in other cases. In *Paske v Ollat* a will prepared by a lawyer left most of the client's estate to the lawyer. This time, it was said that '[t]he presumption and onus probandi are against the instrument; but as the law does not render such an act invalid, the Court has only to require strict proof'.[49] So the lawyer won, as lawyers who prepared wills in their own favour almost invariably did.[50] The fudged presumptions allowed the judges of the Prerogative Court great flexibility.

E. Long Drawn-out Cases

The effect of the confusion over the pleading rules, combined with the decision not to apply the Roman law rule as to what was to happen when a beneficiary was involved in the will-making process, and not even to have any clear presumptions of misbehaviour when a beneficiary was so involved, was that the cases had a tendency to drag on interminably. Suggestions of lack of capacity were tacked on to allegations of undue influence, and once that happened, it became possible to organise an investigation into the testator's entire life story. *Barry v Butlin*[51] is a good example of this. Sir Herbert Jenner, the judge of the Prerogative Court, remarked that: 'this mass of evidence, unprecedented in this Court, and the accumulation of expense caused thereby, are utterly disproportionate to the question at stake between the parties'.[52]

That makes it sound as though the fault lay with the parties, but did it? The case involved a challenge to a will which had been drawn up by a solicitor substantially in his own favour and the challenge was by the testator's son. Had the Roman law rule applied, or had there been a clear presumption against a will drawn up by a beneficiary, the case could have been disposed of quickly, and in the son's favour. As it was, the case was not disposed of quickly and the son lost. A cynic might wonder whether Sir Herbert's concern at the 'accumulation of expense' was entirely genuine. After all, expense for the parties was profit for the lawyers. And the suggestion that the expense was 'utterly disproportionate to the question at stake' is especially interesting in the context of the parties' means. The dispute related only to the testator's personalty. The Prerogative Court would have had no jurisdiction over his realty, which was held in a strict settlement. The personalty was valued at less than £14,000 – a little more than £3 million in present-day terms. It would have been a shame for the lawyers if they had exhausted the estate and there had been a costs shortfall. But, no need to worry, Sir Herbert made an order that, apart from what was to be paid from the estate personalty, the son was himself to pay part of

[48] *Billinghurst v Vickers* (1810) I Phill Ecc 187, 194, 161 ER 956.

[49] *Paske v Ollat* (n 41).

[50] R Kerridge, 'Draftsmen and Suspicious Wills' in M Dixon (ed), *Modern Studies in Property Law*, vol 5 (Oxford, Hart Publishing, 2009) 162–63.

[51] *Barry v Butlin* (n 38).

[52] ibid. On appeal to the PC there was a reference to 'an immense mass of evidence, more or less material', 2 Moo PC 480, 486.

the costs – and he could, of course, afford it. He had the realty, valued at about £70,000 (nearly £17 million at today's rates), from which he could make a further contribution.

F. Costs

That brings us to the question of costs. There are three possible orders as to costs in contentious probate cases: (i) the loser pays his own costs and is ordered to pay the winner's; (ii) there may be no order as to costs, ie each party must pay his own; or (iii) costs may be ordered from the estate, ie the winner pays his own costs and pays the loser. Just as, before 1859, the presumptions were not clear, so the rules as to costs were not clear either. The judge seemed to have had more discretion than he would have had at common law. The standard common law rule, that costs follow the event, so the loser pays, was not necessarily followed.

G. Solicitor Beneficiaries

Two final points about the position before 1858: first, there were not a huge number of reported cases from the Prerogative Court, but the success rate for those challenging beneficiary-prepared wills was very close to 50 per cent; secondly, a very high proportion of the beneficiaries who prepared wills in their own favour, and who then succeeded in obtaining probate of the wills they had prepared, were solicitors.[53] But if, say, a doctor did the same thing, a challenge by the next of kin would generally succeed.

H. What Changed in 1858?

So what changed in 1858? The judges of the new court were common lawyers. Barristers were now permitted to appear as advocates, but few did so in the early years after the new court was set up; the civilian advocates went on appearing and continued to exercise huge influence over the conduct of litigation. What would have been an improvement would have been a clarification as to the presumptions of misbehaviour, such as they were, but this did not happen – though it certainly would have happened if the jurisdiction had gone to Chancery. Given that this did not happen, one change in the wrong direction was noted in *Summerell v Clements* in 1862, when Sir Cresswell Cresswell, the first Judge Ordinary of the new court, said 'I have gone a good deal beyond the Prerogative Court in condemning costs, where the opposition has been unsuccessful'.[54] In other words, he, the common lawyer, was moving more towards the common law rule that the loser pays. In the circumstances, given how hard it already was to challenge beneficiary prepared wills, this was unfortunate. If the Roman law rule were not to be applied and if beneficiaries were to continue to be permitted to take part in the will-making process, there would be

[53] See R Kerridge (n 50). If the overall success rate for beneficiaries who prepared wills in their own favour was 50% and the success rate for solicitor beneficiaries was high, this indicates that other claimants tended to fail.

[54] *Summerell v Clements* (1862) 3 Sw & Tr 35.

much to be said for having special costs rules which would make challenges easier. But, there is insufficient space in this chapter to discuss this in greater detail and this is the point at which we come to *Hastilow v Stobie* itself.

IV. *HASTILOW v STOBIE*

Sir Cresswell Cresswell, the first Judge Ordinary of the Court of Probate, was killed in a riding accident in July 1863. A successor had to be found, fast, and Sir JP Wilde was appointed in his place. Before he had taken his place in the Court of Probate, Cresswell had been a judge of the Court of Common Pleas, for 16 years. For the three years before he took Cresswell's place, Wilde had been a Baron of the Exchequer, and so was the second common law judge who needed to learn quickly about divorce and probate. Each of these men had a dual role, and it is reasonable to assume that getting to grips with the new divorce law would have been both more daunting and more urgent.

A. Lack of Knowledge and Approval

Hastilow v Stobie[55] came before Wilde in November 1865. The report of the case says nothing about the facts; the dispute, as reported, related to the pleadings. On what grounds could someone claim that a will should be refused probate? Those challenging the will wanted to do so on the grounds of: (i) lack of due execution; (ii) lack of capacity; (iii) lack of knowledge and approval of the contents; and (iv) undue influence. Those propounding the will claimed that the third of these pleas, ie lack of knowledge and approval of the contents, was bad in substance on the ground that a will might be valid even if the testator did not know and approve its contents, and they called into aid obiter dicta of Sir Cresswell Cresswell in *Middlehurst v Johnson*[56] and *Cunliffe v Cross*.[57]

Most of the discussion concerning the plea of lack of knowledge and approval in *Hastilow* centred on what would happen if a testator in full possession of his faculties allowed someone else to draft a will for him and then executed it without making any enquiry as to its contents. Wilde thought that, in such a case, a plea of 'lack of knowledge and approval' should be permitted, and that such a document ought to be refused probate. There is insufficient space at this point in this chapter to discuss in detail the question as to whether a testator may delegate his testamentary power. Since *Hastilow*, there have been dicta in *Chichester Diocesan Fund and Board of Finance v Simpson*[58] to the effect that a testator may not so delegate, but these dicta may be in conflict with the rules relating to testamentary powers of appointment, and a more nuanced approach was taken by Hoffman J in *Re Beatty*.[59]

[55] *Hastilow v Stobie* (1865–69) LR 1 P&D 64.
[56] *Middlehurst v Johnson* 30 LJ (PM & A) 14.
[57] *Cunliffe v Cross* 3 Sw & Tr 37.
[58] *Chichester Diocesan Fund and Board of Finance v Simpson* [1944] AC 341.
[59] *Re Beatty* [1990] 1 WLR 1503. See also *Re Park* [1932] 1 Ch 580; L Smith, 'What Is Left of the Non-delegation Principle?' in B Häcker and C Mitchell (eds), *Current Issues in Succession Law* (Oxford, Hart Publishing 2016); JD Davies, 'Flexible Wills' (1991) 107 *LQR* 211.

Actually, given that the facts in *Hastilow* were not set out in the report, it is not clear whether the question of delegation of testamentary powers had any direct relevance to whatever they were, but it seems probable that the discussion concerning delegation was effectively academic, or obiter.

What Wilde seems to have been attempting to do was to make it easier for those challenging wills made in dubious circumstances, particularly beneficiary-made wills, to launch successful challenges against them. He could not now introduce the Roman law rule that beneficiary-prepared wills were void, nor could he easily introduce a presumption of misbehaviour where a beneficiary had been involved in the will-making process and fraud and/or undue influence were pleaded. So, it seems that he was trying to permit a plea which might operate as a disguised allegation of misbehaviour. The problem is that, although his object was commendable, his means of achieving it were too convoluted to work without creating misunderstandings. It would have been much better had he had the courage to scrap the absurd rules that he had inherited from the Prerogative Court and had laid down that, whenever a beneficiary was in any way involved in the will-making process, there would be a clear presumption both of fraud and of undue influence.

At the end of the penultimate paragraph of his judgment, Wilde, in an attempt to justify his approach, said the following:

> [T]here is a whole class of cases, of which *Butlin v Barry* is the chief, in which wills have been set aside on the express ground that the testator did not know and approve of the contents of the instrument at the time when he executed it. I hold, therefore, that this plea to be good in law.

On a quick reading, this makes it sound as though Wilde was saying that there was a plea of lack of knowledge and approval in *Barry v Butlin*, but he had not said this. In fact, he had earlier said, in the course of listening to the arguments of counsel, that 'In the Ecclesiastical Court it was not requisite to specify by plea the precise ground of every objection that might be taken to a will'.[60]

Had he suggested that there had been a plea of lack of knowledge and approval in *Barry*, he would have been wrong. There was no mention anywhere in *Barry* of 'lack' or of 'approval'. What did appear, from time to time, were references to 'knowledge'. These references appeared when it was being suggested by the propounders of the will that the attacks on it were ill founded.[61] In effect, they were saying that the testator knew what was in his will and that there was no justification for the challenges to it.

In fact, it is not clear what the grounds on which the will in *Barry* had been challenged were. There was clearly an allegation of lack of capacity and another of undue influence. It was said[62] that 'the pleas were long' and there were probably five of them, but they were not spelled out clearly in the report. The case was a mess. There were 149 witnesses, and it was almost impossible to keep track of what was going on. This was the chaos which the lawyers of the ecclesiastical courts had managed to create. The other three pleas, apart from lack of capacity and undue influence, were probably lack of due execution, fraud and conspiracy. It is, in fact, clear that lack of knowledge and approval

[60] *Hastilow v Stobie* (n 55) 66.

[61] There is mention, both in the case and in the headnote, of 'knowledge of and assent to' but not to 'lack' of either.

[62] *Barry v Butlin* (n 38) 615.

could not have been a plea in *Barry*: Sir Cresswell Cresswell had refused, as a judge, to recognise it as a plea in *Middlehurst v Johnson*[63] and *Cunliffe v Cross*,[64] but he had, many years earlier, been counsel for the son when the son had appealed to the Privy Council in *Barry*.[65] Had the plea been adopted in *Barry*, it would have been at his instigation. Furthermore, at the start of *Hastilow*, counsel for the propounders of the will pointed out that *Williams on Executors* stated that there were three grounds only on which a will might be invalidated: lack of capacity, undue influence and criminal conduct of a party concerned in its preparation.[66]

B. What Pleas Would Be Permitted?

Wilde was not claiming that lack of knowledge and approval had been a plea in *Barry v Butlin*. What he was doing was introducing a new plea, though he wanted to disguise the novelty. But he then had a further problem. He did not want undue imprecision, if he could avoid it. Having said that '[i]n the Ecclesiastical Court it was not requisite to specify by plea the precise ground of every objection that might be taken to a will',[67] he had gone on to say, after hearing counsel but before he gave judgment: 'but in this court the various defences form the subject of separate pleas, and it may be a great saving of expense to divide the defence into separate pleas. I will consider the matter.'

That was in November. At the end of his judgment, on 12 December, he went on to say:

> The other matters urged in argument are proper for discussion only on an application … to disallow the plea, on account of its generality … And I hope shortly to devise some general rules which will make any such applications in each particular case unnecessary.

He was as good as his word, and on 29 December 1865 he amended the Contentious Probate Rules, which had been adopted in 1863, by inserting a new Rule 40a, which read as follows:

> The party or parties pleading to a declaration propounding a will or testamentary script shall be allowed to plead only the pleas hereunder set forth, unless by leave of the Judge …
>
> 1. That the paper writing … alleged by the plaintiff … to be the last will and testament … of *AB*, … *&c*, … was not duly executed …
> 2. That *AB* the deceased … was not of sound mind, memory, and understanding.
> 3. That the execution of the said alleged will … was obtained by the undue influence of *CD* …
> 4. That the execution of the said alleged will … was obtained by the fraud of *CD* …
> 5. That the deceased at the time of the execution of the alleged will … did not know and approve of the contents thereof.

[63] *Middlehurst v Johnson* (n 56).
[64] *Cunliffe v Cross* (n 57).
[65] *Barry* was appealed to the Privy Council shortly after appeals to the Delegates were abolished. A common law QC (such as Cresswell) could now take part in an appeal from the Prerogative Court.
[66] This last would include fraud.
[67] *Hastilow* (n 55) 66.

> Any party pleading the last of the above pleas shall therewith … deliver to the adverse parties … particulars in writing, stating shortly the substance of the case he intends to set up thereunder; and no defence shall be available thereunder which might have been raised under any other of the said pleas, unless such other plea be pleaded therewith.

So, now that he had allowed in the plea of lack of knowledge and approval and had then amended the Contentious Probate Rules, what was the effect? What had he intended to do? And what had he actually done? On the one hand, he had probably wanted to make it easier, for those minded to do so, to challenge wills, especially wills in the making of which beneficiaries had been involved. But at the same time, he had wanted to have clear separate pleas, to avoid vagueness and 'generality'. There was a conflict here. The straightforward way of effecting clarity would have been to have drafted a number of separate pleas, which would, of course, have included undue influence and fraud, and then to have introduced clear presumptions of misbehaviour to cover circumstances where beneficiaries had been involved in the will-making process. But he did not do this. He introduced the plea of lack of knowledge and approval, which was, in effect, an overarching plea, one which could cover almost all the others. But then, in his amendment to the Contentious Probate Rules, he restricted its scope. The latter part of the last paragraph of the new Rule 40a said that lack of knowledge and approval could not be pleaded by itself as a disguised way of alleging something which was covered by one of the other pleas. Or, put more simply, someone attacking a will and wanting to claim that there had been fraud or undue influence had to plead fraud or undue influence (with or without a plea of lack of knowledge and approval), and was not permitted to claim, or to hint, that there had been fraud or undue influence unless they were specifically pleaded (with all the disadvantages relating to burdens of proof and costs which such pleas carried). The net result, if the new Rule 40a were read straightforwardly, was that the new plea would hardly ever apply.

If the new Rule 40a were read straightforwardly, what did the new plea cover which was not covered by one of the other pleas set out in Rule 40a? The answer, it is suggested, is that the new plea of lack of knowledge and approval might cover cases where the testator had delegated his will-making power (the sorts of case discussed in *Hastilow*) and, more importantly, would cover cases of mistake. But that would be all. And if the new plea really covered only these two matters, would it not have been better to have set them out as separate new pleas, rather than to invent an overarching plea and then say that this overarching plea would not apply where it overlapped with two of the others?

The likelihood is that Wilde realised that there was something wrong with a system which made it so difficult to challenge wills drawn up in what may politely be called 'dubious circumstances'. So, when the challengers in *Hastilow* suggested having a new plea of lack of knowledge and approval, he went along with the suggestion. Lawyers do not want to appear to be introducing novelties, so he pretended that lack of knowledge and approval had been in existence for some time. But, at the same time as introducing this new plea, he wanted to have clear separate pleas to avoid vagueness and 'generality', so he drew up Rule 40a. Whether he was aware of the conflict of objectives is not clear. Had he wanted to give challengers a better chance of success when faced with dubious or suspicious wills, and had he not been able or willing to make changes to the rules concerning presumptions and to the rules concerning the onus of proof, which had been inherited from the ecclesiastical courts, his simplest course of action would have been to have introduced the new plea of lack of knowledge and approval and then to have permitted only one other plea, lack of due execution. In this way, lack of capacity, fraud, undue influence and mistake would all have fallen under the one new plea, and would not have continued to exist as separate pleas. This would then have meant that those alleging fraud and undue influence could much more easily have hinted at them, and the judges could have set wills aside without needing to feel too judgmental. But he had not done this, and the result was confusion. He had not created one overarching plea, nor had he created four or five clear separate pleas. He had created four clear separate pleas *and* one overarching plea, but had laid it down that the overarching plea could not apply where one of the other separate pleas applied (at least unless the separate plea was itself included, which would mean that the overarching plea would be otiose).

V. CASES IN THE LATE NINETEENTH CENTURY

So what happened after *Hastilow*? The following year, lack of knowledge and approval was pleaded in *Guardhouse v Blackburn*,[68] but that was a case where the plea was appropriate. It involved an alleged mistake, and there was no hint of misbehaviour, ie of fraud or of undue influence.[69] Then came *Cleare v Cleare*,[70] where Lord Penzance, as Sir JP Wilde had now become, made it clear that a plea of lack of knowledge and approval, allied with pleas of lack of due execution and lack of capacity but unaccompanied by pleas of undue influence or fraud, would give the challengers protection against an order for costs. The facts are not spelled out, so the case is not helpful. There was then a brief period when it seemed that the courts might take a more robust approach towards dubious wills.

A. The Chancery Lawyers' Approach

Fulton v Andrew,[71] in 1875, was one of the very few contentious probate cases to reach the House of Lords, and is especially important because Lord Cairns and Lord Hatherley both indicated in the course of their judgments that they were minded to presume misbehaviour when dealing with a case where a beneficiary had prepared a will in his own favour. Cairns and Hatherley were Chancery lawyers, and their approach is an indication of what might have been if contentious probate had, indeed, been transferred to Chancery in 1858. Then, in *Parker v Duncan*,[72] Sir James Hannen, the first President of the Probate Divorce and Admiralty Division of the High Court, referred to *Fulton v Andrew* and went on to tell a jury that they were entitled to presume undue influence

[68] *Guardhouse v Blackburn* (1866) LR 1 P&D 109.

[69] The plea was appropriate, but did not succeed. The mistake was the fault of the testatrix's solicitor: he had been negligent. Nowadays, the error could be cured by rectification and the solicitor would pay the costs of putting things right. *Collins v Ellstone* [1893] P 1 is a better known but similar case, though involving no lawyer.

[70] *Cleare v Cleare* (1869) LR 1 P&D 655.

[71] *Fulton v Andrew* (1875) LR 7 HL 448.

[72] *Parker v Duncan* (1890) 62 LT 642.

when looking at a case of a beneficiary-made will. This was quite different from the usual approach, but, sadly, Sir James's lead was not followed.

B. The Confusion

What did follow, four years later, was *Tyrell v Painton*,[73] and here can be seen the confusion which stemmed from *Hastilow v Stobie* combined with Rule 40a. In *Tyrell*, Mrs B, a childless widow, originally made two wills, each in favour of X. Then X did something which upset her, whereupon Mrs B instructed her solicitor – the same solicitor who had drafted her earlier wills in favour of X – to prepare for her a will in favour of her cousin, Y. The new will was executed by Mrs B in the presence of three witnesses: Mrs B's solicitor, her doctor and her vicar. This was a textbook exercise in will preparation and execution,[74] and this will may be regarded as the 'clean will'. Mrs B died shortly afterwards and X's son then produced another will, prepared by him and in his handwriting, the 'questionable will'. The questionable will was dated two days after the clean will. It appeared to have been signed by Mrs B and her signature was witnessed by the son and one of his friends. The questionable will had been shown to no one while Mrs B had been alive, and she had made statements just before her death which indicated that she believed that the clean will was operative. Y challenged the questionable will on the grounds of fraud and lack of knowledge and approval. The next stage looked like a rerun of a standard case from the Prerogative Court. The trial judge, Sir Francis Jeune P, examined X's son and his friend, accepted their evidence as to the execution of the questionable will, said that he could find no evidence of fraud and granted it probate. Sir Francis seems to have been ever so slightly gullible. What possible evidence of fraud did he expect to find? In probate, fraud occurs when the testator has been deceived, as opposed to undue influence, which occurs when he has been coerced.[75] Obtaining direct evidence of fraud, once the testator is dead, is almost impossible.[76] Y, having lost the case at first instance, now appealed to the Court of Appeal. That court obviously wanted to find a way of refusing probate to the questionable will. To have said, as should have been said, that there was a presumption of fraud in this case would have been to have departed from a century's case law from the Prerogative Court, and the Court of Appeal did not have the courage to take that step. So, what the court did instead was to call in aid the plea of lack of knowledge and approval and to link it in with the 'suspicious circumstances' rule. Sir Francis had not considered 'suspicious circumstances'. The Court of Appeal thought that they should be brought into play and, on this basis, the challenge to the questionable will succeeded. It is respectfully submitted that the result achieved by the Court of Appeal was the correct result, but the manner of getting there was wrong. The right way (the route the members of the Court of Appeal would not take) was to presume fraud. So what was wrong with

[73] *Tyrell v Painton* [1894] P 151.

[74] In ensuring that the doctor was present, the solicitor was anticipating 'the golden rule' which should be followed if there may be doubts as to the testator's capacity.

[75] *White v White and Cato* (1862) 2 Sw & Tr 504.

[76] It is not clear if there has ever been any case in an English court which has upheld a plea of fraud by itself (as contrasted with a plea of fraud mixed with other pleas – and even these latter cases are extremely rare).

linking lack of knowledge and approval with 'suspicious circumstances'? What was, and still is, wrong with this approach is that the 'suspicious circumstances' rule only makes sense if there is a suspicion of something, and that 'something' has to be misbehaviour, ie, in this context, fraud or undue influence.[77]

C. 'Suspicious Circumstances'

So where did this 'suspicious circumstances' rule come from? It came from a number of earlier cases, including, and in particular, *Barry v Butlin*. It made sense in *Barry v Butlin*, because that was a case where there was a plea of undue influence and 'suspicious circumstances' were considered in the light of that plea. By contrast, in *Tyrell*, once the allegation of fraud had been dismissed (as it had been, by Sir Francis), there was no allegation of misbehaviour left. If the propounders of the questionable will had asked 'what is it that someone is supposed to be suspicious of?', what answer could have been given to them? What the Court of Appeal did in *Tyrell* was to turn the plea of lack of knowledge and approval into a disguised plea of fraud, after having accepted the trial judge's finding that there had been no fraud. This was dishonest and confusing. That is the problem. Rule 40a said that lack of knowledge and approval should not be used as a way of disguising a plea of misbehaviour, ie a plea of fraud or of undue influence. But linking in 'suspicious circumstances' (thus indicating a suspicion of misbehaviour) with lack of knowledge and approval did exactly what was forbidden.

Given that the writer of this chapter believes that it should be made easier to challenge wills, why is he opposed to what has happened here? The answer is that he wants clear, straightforward rules which everyone can understand and apply. The problem with any form of half-disguised rules is that they are neither always understood nor always applied. This can be seen in what followed after *Tyrell*.

VI. TWENTIETH-CENTURY CASE LAW

In the 50 or more years after *Tyrell*, there were almost no reported English cases[78] concerned with the plea of lack of knowledge and approval. This may be because there

[77] In 'Burdens, Presumptions and Confusion in the Law on Want of Knowledge and Approval' [2017] *Conveyancer & Property Lawyer* 440, 451 Brian Sloan questions the idea (suggested elsewhere by the writer of this chapter) that the 'suspicious circumstances' rule only makes sense if there is a suspicion of something, and that that 'something' has to be misbehaviour. He claims that it might be sufficient simply to say that some facts raise a suspicion that the testator did not know and approve of the will's contents. There are two interlinked answers to this. First, there has to be a reason why 'some facts' might raise such a suspicion. It is not clear to the writer what sort of facts (or what 'circumstances') he is suggesting might be covered by this. Secondly, the expression 'suspicious circumstances' implies misbehaviour. There are various verbs, nouns and adjectives which have the same source, but which carry slightly different implications. The verb 'suspect' does not, by itself, indicate that misbehaviour is suspected, but the noun 'suspect' goes much further and implies that 'the suspect' is suspected of involvement in something criminal. 'Suspicious circumstances' is a phrase regularly used by the police to indicate a suspicion of criminal activity. It is suggested that the expression 'suspicious circumstances' used by someone other than a policeman does not go as far as to suggest crime, but *does* clearly suggest misbehaviour.

[78] *Farrelly v Corrigan* [1899] AC 563 is a Privy Council case on appeal from Queensland, Australia.

were no cases, or because such cases as there were may have been too convoluted to make sense of, and so may have been ignored. There were two cases on costs[79] in the first decade of the new century, and they did would-be challengers no favours.

In *Re R*, in 1951,[80] Willmer J took a strict line on the application of Rule 40a. An allegation of undue influence should be pleaded in plain and unambiguous terms and not under the cover of a plea of lack of knowledge and approval.

A. *Wintle* v *Nye*

The decision in *Re R* was clear and straightforward, but clarity and straightforwardness do not last long in this area of the law. The latter part of the 1950s was taken up with the well-known, but poorly understood, case of *Wintle v Nye*.[81] There is insufficient space in this chapter to go through the whole history of this case. For those not familiar with them, the writer's views on it are set out in an article in the *Cambridge Law Journal*.[82] In *Wintle* the only possible honest plea was fraud, but those challenging the will did not make any mention of it, choosing instead to plead lack of knowledge and approval as the sole plea. The challenge was ultimately successful and, 10 years later, in *Re Fuld*,[83] Scarman J said:

> It may well be that positive charges of fraud and undue influence will not feature as largely in the pleadings of probate cases, now that *Wintle v Nye* has been decided, as they have done in the past; clearly it would be preferable if they did not.

In years that have gone by since *Fuld*, this passage has been quoted on occasions too numerous to mention. It was actually quoted in the Law Commission's 2017 Consultation Paper *Making a Will*.[84] But not only was the plea in *Wintle* dishonest, the passage in *Fuld* is worse. Scarman was saying that pleading lack of knowledge and approval in *Wintle* was the correct way to proceed, and it is implicit in this that it led to a successful outcome. But it did not. At the start of the case, Col Wintle, the challenger, engaged a very expensive legal team and the team (not Wintle himself) chose the plea. They lost the case at first instance, left Wintle with an enormous bill for his costs and deserted him. One advantage of pleading lack of knowledge and approval would be that an unsuccessful challenger gets his costs from the estate. Wintle's legal team did not even manage that. And so, who was in Wintle's very expensive legal team, the team which lost the case, left him with an enormous bill for costs and then deserted him? Scarman was;[85] he drafted the pleadings.

[79] *Wilson v Bassil* [1903] P 239; *Spiers v English* [1907] P 122.

[80] *Re R* [1951] P 10.

[81] *Wintle v Nye* [1959] 1 WLR 284.

[82] R Kerridge, 'Wills Made in Suspicious Circumstances: The Problem of the Vulnerable Testator' (2000) 59 *CLJ* 310. For a briefer account, see R Kerridge, *Parry and Kerridge: The Law of Succession*, 13th edn (London, Sweet & Maxwell, 2016) [5.34]ff.

[83] *Re Fuld* [1968] P 675.

[84] Law Commission, *Making a Will* (Law Com No 231, 2017) [7.79].

[85] Scarman was originally the junior in the case, and would have drafted the pleadings. He took silk while the case was proceeding, so Wintle ended up with two silks and two juniors (in those days, a silk had to be accompanied by a junior). That explains, in part, the expense.

All further comment seems superfluous.[86] How could the person who drafted the pleadings and lost the case imply that this was the right way to proceed? It is true that Wintle went on, by himself, as a litigant in person, to succeed in the House of Lords, but he did not win because of the way the case was pleaded; he won in spite of the way the case was pleaded. He won because he had every newspaper in the country on his side and they were not going to permit the lawyers to get away with this travesty.

Wintle v Nye was a case of fraud – if there was no fraud, there was nothing wrong with the will.

Since *Wintle v Nye*, there have been a huge number of cases where lack of knowledge and approval has been pleaded, and the pattern is almost always the same. It has become a thinly disguised cloak for alleging fraud or undue influence. How it fits in with the other pleas is not now clear. In *Re Key*[87] Briggs J, having, quite appropriately, criticised a solicitor for the part he played in the making of a will, went on to say 'a conclusion that a testator lacks capacity necessarily compels a conclusion that he did not know and approve the contents of his will'.[88] It is submitted that this is self-evidently correct. No one who lacks capacity, who has been unduly influenced or who has been the object of fraud can be truly said to have both known and approved of the contents of a will he has executed. In each of these circumstances, either knowledge or approval, or both, must be missing. Having said this, Briggs J's view is not universally held. Some judges seem to think that lack of knowledge and approval can only be found if the testator did have capacity.[89]

Rule 40a was still in force, in its original 1865 form, when *Wintle v Nye* was decided. Nye, the propounder of the challenged will, should have called it into aid and should have argued that it was not clear what Wintle's team were really alleging. He could have based this approach on *Re R*.[90] In fact, he did not take the point until *Wintle* reached the House of Lords. By that time it was too late. Had the point been argued early in the case, it might have clarified things. The rule was slightly amended in 1962, when it became RSC Order 76, rule 9(3), but there was no change of substance.

B. Polite Fictions

In *Re Stott*,[91] in 1980, a will made by a patient in a 'nursing home' was challenged on the grounds of lack of capacity and lack of knowledge and approval. The propounder of the will attempted to strike out certain allegations on the ground that they amounted to allegations of undue influence and that, as it had not been pleaded, they could not stand.

[86] Which did not, of course, stop Wintle from commenting. What he said about his legal team is better not repeated, but he had a point.

[87] *Re Key* [2010] EWHC 408 (Ch), [2010] 1 WLR 2020.

[88] ibid [116].

[89] *Re Ashlettle* [2013] EWHC 2125 (Ch), [2013] WTLR 1331; *Markou v Goodwin* [2013] EWHC 4570 (Ch), [2014] WTLR 605.

[90] *Re R* (n 80).

[91] *Re Stott* [1980] 1 WLR 246.

Given the way in which Rule 40a (now RSC Order 76, rule 9(3)) was set out, this argument appeared to be sound, but Slade J did not accept it. This is an example of deliberate obfuscation. If the applicable rules had been drawn up sensibly and had operated logically, there would have been a clear presumption of fraud and undue influence in this case. But English law in this area does not operate sensibly and logically. There are too many polite fictions. In *Stott*, the 'nursing home' was not a nursing home at all; it was a flat in a mansion block in an upmarket part of London. And the 'nurse' from the 'nursing home' who purported to take instructions from the testatrix to a firm of solicitors who appear never to have had any direct contact with her was not a 'nurse'. That becomes apparent from a reading of another case the facts of which relate to the same 'nursing home' – *Re Davey*.[92] The 'nurse' in *Davey* married one of the patients (but he did *not* appear as a 'nurse' on the marriage certificate). What is odd about *Stott* and *Davey* is that there is no reference in either case to the other. They are only a year apart, they relate to the same 'nursing home' and they both involve, albeit in different roles, the same 'nurse'. They illustrate how reluctant the courts dealing with these kinds of case are to confront what is happening. To do so would appear to be in bad taste.

This is not the place to attempt to make a list of all the recent cases involving 'suspicious wills' in which lack of knowledge and approval has been pleaded as a cloak for an allegation of fraud or undue influence,[93] but two relatively recent ones give a flavour of what is wrong with the plea introduced in *Hastilow v Stobie*.

In *Fuller v Strum*,[94] a will written entirely in the handwriting of one of the beneficiaries, and the signature to which was said by a court-appointed handwriting expert to have been 'highly likely' to have been forged, was challenged on the grounds of forgery and lack of knowledge and approval. Despite the expert evidence, the trial judge held that the signature had not been forged, but he did refuse probate to most of the will on the ground of lack of knowledge and approval. The result was correct; the manner of getting there was not. But that was not the end. The beneficiary who had written out the entire will now appealed, and he succeeded. The Court of Appeal thought that a decision to the effect that most, but not all, of the will should be refused probate on the ground of lack of knowledge and approval could not be justified. Yet, if the Court of Appeal was unhappy about refusing probate to most, but not all, of the will, the better course would have been a retrial. But what is more seriously wrong in *Strum* is that both Peter Gibson LJ and Chadwick LJ criticised the trial judge for quoting from Lord Hatherley in *Fulton v Andrew* and for referring to what had happened as an 'unrighteous transaction'. This *was* an 'unrighteous transaction'. The expression is one with which any Chancery lawyer should feel at home. So, although contentious probate was transferred from the Probate Divorce and Admiralty Division to Chancery in 1971, the ecclesiastical lawyers' way of thinking, of polite but dishonest obfuscation, has survived the move.

92 *Re Davey* [1981] 1 WLR 164.
93 A number are listed in Parry and Kerridge (n 82) [5-40]–[5-45].
94 *Fuller v Strum* [2001] EWCA Civ 1879, [2002] 1 WLR 1097.

VII. A NEW CENTURY – MORE OF THE SAME

This account of the case law which descends from *Hastilow* ends with one last case, *Burgess v Hawes*.[95]

Mrs B died in May 2009, aged 80, leaving two daughters and a son. She was in poor health, suffering from hypertension, diabetes, dizzy spells and memory loss, and had probably had a series of minor strokes. In 1996 she made a clean will which divided her estate between her three children. But, in December 2006, Mrs B was taken by one of her daughters to a solicitor and this daughter gave instructions to the solicitor for the execution of another will which disinherited Mrs B's son.

A legal system with sensible rules would have dismissed, quickly and finally, any attempt to authenticate a document created as this will was. Much of the blame for permitting this situation to have arisen lay with the solicitor. He took instructions from a beneficiary. He knew that the testatrix had three children, but failed to ask about any previous will, or whether the son knew that he was being disinherited.

No doctor had been asked to examine Mrs B at the time she had made the disputed will, so the medical experts at the first instance hearing had to base their views on inferences from Mrs B's medical records and from listening to the evidence given by 26 lay witnesses. This was a bit like a rerun of *Barry v Butlin*.

At the end of a six-day trial HHJ Walden-Smith held that Mrs B lacked capacity, and then went on to hold that she did not know and approve the terms of the will. This is the classic way of hinting at misbehaviour. The judge did say[96] that the daughter who had taken Mrs B to see the solicitor was 'the controlling force in the instructions given for the drafting of this will' and that should, by itself, have led to a refusal of probate, without the need for anything more. The judge also gave the solicitor a mild ticking off: 'What I find surprising and concerning is the manner in which instructions were taken by [the solicitor].'[97] That should have been the end of the story, but this was England.

The daughter who had been 'the controlling force in the instructions given for the drafting of this will' now dared to appeal against what should have been an unappealable first instance decision, and the most surprising aspect of this case was the approach taken by the Court of Appeal. The fact that the solicitor had gone ahead with the making of this will was now seen as a reason for upholding it, rather than criticising him. This was just like the good old days in the Prerogative Court. In the end, the three Court of Appeal judges reluctantly upheld the trial judge on the issue of capacity, and then went on to uphold her on lack of knowledge and approval – without explaining what it meant or how it fitted in. So much for the legacy of *Hastilow v Stobie*.

But the most astonishing thing about this case is a passage in the leading judgment in the Court of Appeal, that of Mummery LJ. It reads as follows:

> The cost of contesting the 2007 Will is a calamity for this family in every way … the Deceased's estate is modest, less than £200,000 … A 6 day trial with 26 witnesses does not come cheap. Now there is this appeal. It may be recalled that the foggy family law suit in *Jarndyce v Jarndyce*

[95] *Burgess v Hawes* [2013] EWCA Civ 94, [2013] WTLR 453.
[96] [2012] WTLR 423 [120].
[97] ibid [105].

> dragged on before the Lord Chancellor for generations until nothing was left for the parties to take. The Civil Procedure Rules and the efforts of legal advisers have not dissuaded these parties from following a course leading to the dissipation of the whole of the Deceased's estate in costs and legal fees ...[98]

The reference to the *Jarndyce* case in *Bleak House* is incomprehensible. *Jarndyce* was supposed to illustrate the outrageous behaviour of lawyers in a Chancery suit in about 1830. It was an attack on lawyers for dragging out a case concerning a will; dragging it out until the entire estate was dissipated in legal costs. Dickens's message was that the lawyers were the villains, the litigants their victims. Mummery LJ implied that it was the other way round.

One last point: if the theme of this chapter is correct, *Bleak House* was, itself, a minor part of the problem. The plot of the book centred round a fictional case of a will in Chancery, in about 1830. In fact, Chancery did not deal with contentious probate. The case that is probably the model for *Jarndyce* is the Thellusson litigation, which started with *Thellusson v Woodford*[99] in 1799 and was not a really a will case at all; rather, it concerned a trust in a will. The tragedy is that the novel probably helped to prevent the transfer of contentious probate to Chancery in 1858. Of course, the Court of Chancery was not perfect, and we shall never know what would have happened if it had been given contentious probate 160 years ago, but it is inconceivable that, had it taken over, it would have kept so many remnants from the ecclesiastical courts and permitted such a hugely unsatisfactory situation to remain as it is. Chancery in 1830 may have had its failings, but, by 1858, it would have been infinitely better to have transferred contentious probate to it rather than to leave it with a remodelled Prerogative Court, which is what the Court of Probate was.

VIII. THE FUTURE

The writer of this chapter is not an optimist. Having said this, there may actually be a glimmer of light somewhere in the dark tunnel of contentious probate. After this chapter was originally commissioned, the Law Commission produced their Consultation Paper 231, *Making a Will*. The paper attempts to cover too much ground and it does not cover this area of the law in sufficient depth.[100] But it does at least begin to attempt to examine the relationship between undue influence and lack of knowledge and approval, and provisionally proposes that the 'requirement' of knowledge and approval should be 'confined'. How exactly this would operate would, of course, depend on what presumptions there would be concerning undue influence (and fraud). The writer maintains that the knowledge and approval rule should either be scrapped in its entirety and replaced by clear simple rules and clear simple presumptions relating to capacity, undue influence, fraud and mistake, or the rules relating to capacity, undue influence, fraud and mistake should

[98] *Burgess v Hawes* (n 95) [5].

[99] *Thellusson v Woodford* (1799) 4 Ves Jun 227, 31 ER 117.

[100] In Law Commission (n 84) [7.79] the CP quotes what Scarman J said in *Fuld*, without noting his part in *Wintle*. This should have been spotted.

go and the overarching plea of lack of knowledge and approval should take their place. Mixing up the limited pleas and the overarching plea is a recipe for confusion, but at least the Law Commission are considering the topic. The problem is that it requires not just one chapter in a Law Commission consultation paper and report, it requires a whole report to itself.

While this chapter was in the process of being written, work on the Law Commission's project on wills was delayed because it was decided that work on a 'weddings' project had become more urgent and is, by implication, more important.[101] In 1858, probate deferred to divorce; history is now repeating itself.

[101] This is likely to be a reflection of governmental priorities rather than merely those of the Law Commission.

7

White v Jones (1995): A Legacy of the Search for Principle

JUDITH SKILLEN AND JAMES LEE*

'If I were asked what is the most potent influence upon a court in formulating a statement of legal principle, I would answer that in the generality of instances it is the desired result in the particular case before the court …'[1]

I. INTRODUCTION

WHITE v JONES[2] sits at the juncture of succession, contract and tort law. The basic issue was framed well by Sir Donald Nicholls at the Court of Appeal stage:

> A solicitor accepts instructions to prepare a will for a client. In breach of his professional duty to his client he is dilatory, and the client dies before the will has been prepared or signed. Can the solicitor be liable in damages to the disappointed prospective beneficiary?[3]

The Court of Appeal, and then a majority of the House of Lords, held that the solicitor could be so liable. In what follows, we examine the background to and significance of *White*, situating the case in its context of the duty of care (especially pure economic loss) cases from the 1990s. We address the contemporary reaction to it and the shaping of the assumption of responsibility as a control mechanism for liability. We then move to the legacy of the case, and argue that it has not had as significant an impact as was anticipated at the time, at least in its direct area. This more limited impact is partly the result of the enactment of the Contracts (Rights of Third Parties) Act 1999, which addressed

* The authors would like to thank David Foster, Mark Lunney, Colm McGrath, Janet O'Sullivan and Brian Sloan for helpful comments in our preparation of this chapter. All views, and any errors, are ours alone.

[1] R Goff, 'The Search for Principle' (1984) 69 *Proceedings of the British Academy* 169, 183.

[2] *White v Jones* [1995] 2 AC 207.

[3] ibid, 216 (the Court of Appeal decision was previously reported in [1993] 3 WLR 730, but references in this chapter will be to the Law Report, which reports the Court of Appeal judgments alongside those of the House of Lords). We offer a fuller account of the facts in section III below.

some of the wider privity implications through statute, but it also attributable to judicial caution in the expansion of liability. Then we look at influence of the 'strong impulse to do practical justice'[4] in very different areas. Most recently, the Supreme Court has overseen something of a retrenchment on pure economic loss, having revisited and reaffirmed the assumption of responsibility device.[5]

We therefore argue that, with hindsight, the explosive potential of *White v Jones* has not been realised, but it marks the high point of the House of Lords' mid-1990s reorientation of the law in cases of pure economic loss: indeed, it is a key case in the (recent) legal history of the tort of negligence. It also stands as a landmark in terms of judicial creativity when faced with the 'strong impulse to do practical justice',[6] especially where legal categories intersect.

A further point relates to the contribution of the leading figure in *White*, Lord Goff.[7] We argue that *White v Jones* can be seen as a paradigm of Lord Goff's judicial methodology, as set out in his 1983 Maccabean Lecture in Jurisprudence, 'The Search for Principle'.[8] Immediately after the quotation which began this chapter, Robert Goff explained in more detail his view of the influence of the merits of a case:

> When we talk about the desired result, or the merits, of any particular case, we can do so at more than one level ... But there is a more sophisticated, lawyerly level, which consists of the perception of the just solution in legal terms, satisfying the gut and the intellect. It is in the formulation, if necessary the adaptation, of legal principle to embrace that just solution that we can see not only the beneficial influence of facts upon the law, but also the useful impact of practical experience upon the work of practising lawyers in the development of legal principles.[9]

Twelve years later, Lord Goff put this extra-curial approach into practice in *White*. We may therefore respectfully disagree with Weir, who, in a case note, wryly observed that 'We may ignore the precise facts. The House did so, except to say that they did not matter.'[10] Rather, it will be seen that both the views of the majority and the subsequent case law have emphasised the fact-specificity of the outcome in *White* itself and the duty which it recognised. The decision in *White* can be understood as what Lord Goff elsewhere described as 'an educated reflex to facts, though always within the framework of established legal principle'.[11]

[4] *White* (n 2) 259 (Lord Goff).

[5] See section VC below.

[6] *White* (n 2) 259.

[7] On Lord Goff's major contribution to the law of restitution and unjust enrichment, see eg G Jones, 'Lord Goff's Contribution to the Law of Restitution' and P Birks, 'The Role of Fault in the Law of Unjust Enrichment' in G Jones and W Swadling (eds), *The Search for Principle: Essays in Honour of Lord Goff of Chieveley* (Oxford, Oxford University Press, 1999); G Virgo, 'The Law of Unjust Enrichment in the House of Lords: Judging the Judges' in J Lee (ed), *From House of Lords to Supreme Court: Judges, Jurists and the Process of Judging* (Oxford, Hart Publishing, 2011).

[8] Goff (n 1).

[9] ibid 183. See similarly, Lord Goff, 'The Future of the Common Law' (1997) 46 *ICLQ* 745, 754. Compare Simon Whittaker, writing on exactly the issue in *White*: 'we need to be constantly watching to ensure that the legal concepts we employ are not simply manipulated in order to achieve a desirable result in a particular case': S Whittaker, 'Privity of Contract and the Tort of Negligence: Future Directions' (1996) 16 *OJLS* 191, 213.

[10] T Weir, 'A Damnosa Hereditas?' (1995) 111 *LQR* 357, 357.

[11] Rt Hon Lord Goff, 'Judge, Jurist and Legislature, The Child & Co Oxford Lecture 1986' (1987) 2 *Denning Law Journal* 79, 82.

II. THE LAW PRIOR TO *WHITE v JONES*

In this section, we place *White v Jones* in its appropriate context. First, we conduct a brief examination of general developments within duty of care, mainly in the House of Lords. We then move on to the particular: *Hedley Byrne v Heller* and its recognition that damages for pure economic loss may be recovered in negligence, and then the important precursor to *White v Jones* in the specific context of claims against solicitors, *Ross v Caunters*.

A. Duty of Care: General

The late twentieth century was a time of flux for duty of care, as the courts struggled with whether it was possible to articulate a general principle for establishing a duty of care in negligence. The source for an expansionist approach can be found in Lord Atkin's speech in *Donoghue v Stevenson* and his Lordship's neighbour principle:

> You must take reasonable care to avoid acts or omissions which you can reasonably foresee would be likely to injure your neighbour … persons who are so closely and directly affected by my act that I ought reasonably to have them in contemplation as being so affected when I am directing my mind to the acts or omissions which are called in question.[12]

Lord Wilberforce then sought to refine the neighbour principle in *Anns v Merton*.[13] In *Anns* a local authority was held liable for failing to inspect building work which had been conducted on the plaintiffs' properties, the poor execution of which had resulted in structural damage. For Lord Wilberforce, the question of duty of care had to be taken in two stages: first, asking whether there was sufficient proximity and foreseeability of harm to give rise to a 'prima facie duty of care'; secondly, asking whether there were considerations which ought to negative the recognition of the duty (or limit its scope).[14] In essence, under *Anns*, when imposing duty of care, a court was to ask 'why not?'

Anns marked the apex of a relatively expansionist approach to duty of care: the courts then began a retreat in the late 1980s and early 1990s through a series of appellate decisions, principally concerning pure economic loss. A restrictive approach to Lord Wilberforce's two-stage test was adopted in *D&F Estates v Church Commissioners for England*, in which *Anns* was not extended to introduce a duty of care for builders to inspect the work of subcontractors.[15] The House of Lords then departed from *Anns* in *Murphy v Brentwood*,[16] and *Caparo v Dickman*[17] gave the approach its quietus, as Lord Bridge was at pains to show 'the inability of any single general principle to provide a practical test which can be applied to every situation to determine whether a duty of care is owed and, if so, what is its scope'.[18] It was instead preferable for the law to develop

[12] *Donoghue v Stevenson* [1932] AC 562, 580.
[13] *Anns v Merton London Borough Council* [1978] AC 728.
[14] ibid 751–52.
[15] [1989] AC 177. See, eg 212–15 (Lord Oliver).
[16] *Murphy v Brentwood District Council* [1991] AC 398. See in particular 472–92 (Lord Oliver).
[17] *Caparo Industries plc v Dickman* [1990] 2 AC 605.
[18] ibid 617.

incrementally in accordance with established categories of duties of care.[19] In novel cases, where established principle does not indicate the outcome, a court could impose a duty of care if there were

> foreseeability of damage ... [and] that there should exist between the party owing the duty and the party to whom it is owed a relationship characterised by the law as one of 'proximity' or 'neighbourhood' and that the situation should be one in which the court considers it fair, just and reasonable that the law should impose a duty.[20]

The UK Supreme Court has more recently confirmed that, following *Caparo*, 'the characteristic approach of the common law [to finding a duty of care] is to develop incrementally and by analogy with established authority'.[21]

B. Negligent Misstatements and *Hedley Byrne*

Generally, there is no liability in English tort law for pure economic loss caused by negligence.[22] In *Hedley Byrne v Heller* the House of Lords recognised what has come to be interpreted as a wide-ranging exception to the general rule.[23] The law's reluctance towards recovery for negligently caused economic loss which is not directly consequential on some form of physical damage has been rationalised on a number of bases. One common explanation is that economic interests fall below other interests, such as physical safety and property rights, in our law's value system.[24] Policy concerns have also been offered as justification for the general rule against recovery, typically that an action for economic loss risks giving rise to indeterminate liability.[25] Liability for pure economic loss in negligence is positioned on the boundary between contract law and tort law, with damage caused to purely economic interests being viewed as within the traditional purview of the law of contract:[26] thus, the type of loss suffered by the plaintiffs in *White v Jones* is inherently controversial within tort law.

The development of liability for pure economic loss in negligence was through cases involving misstatements, which we mention here for context, although *White v Jones* itself

[19] ibid 618.

[20] ibid 617–18.

[21] *Robinson v Chief Constable of West Yorkshire Police* [2018] UKSC 4, [2018] AC 736 [27]; *Darnley v Croydon Health Services NHS Trust* [2018] UKSC 50, [2018] 3 WLR 1153 [15].

[22] A classic illustration of this general principle can be found in *Spartan Steel & Alloys Ltd v Martin & Co (Contractors) Ltd* [1973] QB 27. For an overview of the law relating to intentionally caused economic loss, see H Carty, *An Analysis of the Economic Torts*, 2nd edn (Oxford, Oxford University Press, 2010).

[23] *Hedley Byrne & Co Ltd v Heller & Partners Ltd* [1964] AC 465.

[24] See, eg C Witting, *Liability for Negligent Misstatements* (Oxford, Oxford University Press, 2004) 155; T Weir, *A Casebook on Tort*, 10th edn (London, Sweet & Maxwell, 2004) 6–7; R Stevens, *Torts and Rights* (Oxford, Oxford University Press, 2007) 329–40.

[25] *Spartan Steel* (n 22) 37–39 (Lord Denning MR); J Stapleton, 'Duty of Care and Economic Loss: A Wider Agenda' (1991) 107 *LQR* 249; T Weir, *Economic Torts* (Clarendon Press, 1997) 9. For a critique of such policy-based rationales, see Stevens (n 24) 20–42.

[26] A point acknowledged by Lord Goff in *White* (n 2) 260. Concern for the tort/contract boundary was raised by, inter alia, Weir in T Weir, 'Liability for Syntax' (1963) 21 *CLJ* 216, 219 ('The decision [in *Hedley Byrne v Heller*] has also gone far to destroy the distinction between breach of contract and tort'); B Hepple, 'Negligence: The Search for Coherence' (1997) 50 *Current Legal Problems* 69, 69–70 ('negligence has expanded its reach into what was once seen as the exclusive sphere of contract in respect of recovery for economic loss').

does not involve a misstatement.[27] *Derry v Peek*[28] had suggested that a defendant would only be liable for economic loss caused by fraudulent as opposed to negligent misstatements, ie through the tort of deceit as opposed to negligence.[29] This position was reaffirmed in *Le Lievre v Gould*:[30] relying on *Derry v Peek*, the Court of Appeal held that 'in the absence of contract, an action for negligence cannot be maintained when there is no fraud'.[31]

Nocton v Lord Asburton[32] was a significant early authority which cast doubt on the scope of *Derry v Peek*. A solicitor wrongly advised his client, a mortgagee, that it would be safe to release a part of the mortgage security. The client suffered loss when the mortgagor defaulted and successfully brought a claim against his solicitor. Though the House of Lords agreed with the trial judge that actual fraud could not be established, it declined to reverse the Court of Appeal's decision, which had provided relief to the plaintiff. Instead of basing its decision on the tort of deceit, the House of Lords found that a fiduciary relationship existed between solicitor and client, and in this context embraced a wider definition of fraud than Lord Herschell espoused in *Derry v Peek*:

> when fraud is referred to in the wider sense in which the books are full of the expression … it is a mistake to suppose that an actual intention to cheat must always be proved … What it really means in this connection is, not moral fraud in the ordinary sense, but *breach of the sort of obligation which is enforced by a Court* that from the beginning regarded itself as a Court of conscience.[33]

Moreover, their Lordships indicated that this wider notion of fraud was not limited to equitable actions but could apply at common law, leaving open the possibility that the plaintiff could have succeeded with a claim in negligence.[34] As such, '*Nocton v Lord Ashburton* constituted a serious challenge to the integrity, if not the actual authority, of *Derry v Peek*', with the 'door thus opened to the upholding of appropriate claims in negligence'.[35]

A further notable challenge to the scope of *Derry v Peek* came with Denning LJ's dissent in *Candler v Crane, Christmas & Co Ltd*.[36] The plaintiff sought to recover his losses from an investment from the defendants, who had negligently prepared accounts on which he had relied. In the Court of Appeal, the plaintiff was denied recovery. The majority (Cohen and Asquith LJJ) relied upon *Derry v Peek* and *Le Lievre* in holding that, outside of a contractual or fiduciary relationship, a plaintiff must prove actual fraud when claiming for loss caused by misstatements.[37]

[27] See Part III below for detailed discussion of the facts.

[28] *Derry v Peek* (1889) 14 App Cas 337.

[29] ibid 374.

[30] *Le Lievre v Gould* [1893] QB 491.

[31] ibid 498 (Lord Esher MR).

[32] [1914] AC 932, 947 (Viscount Haldane LC): 'the authorities subsequent to [*Derry v Peek*] shew a tendency to assume that it was intended to mean more than it did. In reality, the judgment covered only a part of the field in which liabilities may arise'. See further Witting (n 24) 156: 'the equity lawyers in the House of Lords sought to remedy the perceived errors in *Derry v Peek*'.

[33] ibid 954 (Viscount Herschell LC) (emphasis added).

[34] ibid 957 (Viscount Haldane LC): 'My Lords, since the Judicature Acts any branch of the Court may give both kinds of relief, and treat what is alleged either *as a case of negligence at common law* or as one of breach of fiduciary duty' (emphasis added).

[35] Witting (n 32) 157.

[36] *Candler v Crane, Christmas & Co* [1951] 2 KB 164.

[37] ibid 186–87, 195 (Asquith LJ) and 197–201 (Cohen LJ).

For Denning LJ, *Nocton* had 'exposed' the error that there can be no recovery in tort for negligent statements following *Derry v Peek*.[38] The combined effect of dicta in *Nocton* and the privity fallacy being put to rest in *Donoghue v Stevenson*[39] was sufficient for Denning LJ to feel able to re-examine the law's treatment of negligent statements 'afresh'.[40] For Denning LJ, the scope of such a duty is limited to the statement being used for purposes of which the defendants were aware.[41] In setting out these boundaries, there should not be any 'dangerous precedent' established 'when it is remembered that [the duty] is limited to in respect of the persons by whom and to whom it is owed and the transactions to which it applies'.[42]

Considerations of policy were also obviously influential for Denning LJ: 'the law would fail to serve the best interests of the community if it should hold that accountants and auditors owe a duty to no one but their client'[43] – in particular, that an 'accountants' certificate, which should be a safeguard, becomes a snare for those who rely on it'.[44] The factors highlighted by Denning LJ as pointing towards a duty of care proved to be extremely influential in the House of Lords' recognition that, under certain circumstances, there shall be liability for negligent misstatements in *Hedley Byrne v Heller*.[45]

Hedley Byrne saw the plaintiffs, who were advertising agents, bring a claim against the defendant bankers for misstatements contained in a credit reference (which had been offered with a disclaimer of responsibility): relying on the reference, the claimants suffered loss when their clients failed to pay. *Hedley Byrne v Heller* raised two novel issues in negligence: (i) whether there could be liability for loss caused by words as opposed to acts; and (ii) whether pure economic loss was recoverable. The first issue received more attention by their Lordships than the latter.[46] As Witting notes, 'their Lordships all but ignored the nature of the damage which had been pleaded'.[47] Both questions were answered in the affirmative, though liability was denied on the facts due to the disclaimer of responsibility inserted by the defendants.

The multiplicity of speeches by their Lordships has meant that the ratio of *Hedley Byrne* has not always emerged clearly.[48] However, each of their Lordships 'agreed that it was not a simple matter of applying the neighbour principle from *Donoghue v Stevenson*'.[49] Differing emphases can be found in the five speeches handed down by their Lordships, though the concepts of the assumption of responsibility on the part of the plaintiff and the defendant's reliance upon the plaintiff were a common theme throughout. Lord Reid made use of assumption of responsibility in reasoning that there can be

[38] *Candler* (n 36) 177.
[39] [1932] AC 562.
[40] ibid 178.
[41] ibid 182–83.
[42] ibid 184.
[43] ibid 184.
[44] ibid 185.
[45] *Hedley Byrne* (n 23) 484 (Lord Reid): 'It must now be taken that *Derry v Peek* did not establish any universal rule that in the absence of contract an innocent but negligent misrepresentation cannot give rise to an action.'
[46] See, eg 482–83, 486 (Lord Reid).
[47] Witting (n 7) 161.
[48] T Weir, 'Errare Humanum Est' in P Birks (ed), *The Frontiers of Liability*, vol 2 (Oxford, Oxford University Press, 1994) 104: 'Never has there been such a judicial jamboree as *Hedley Byrne*.'
[49] P Mitchell, '*Hedley Byrne & Co Ltd v Heller & Partners Ltd* (1963)' in C Mitchell and P Mitchell (eds), *Landmark Cases in the Law of Tort* (Oxford, Hart Publishing, 2010) 176.

liability for pecuniary loss in negligence, though was ambivalent as to whether this was an obligation undertaken or imposed by law.[50] Lord Morris also spoke of assumption of responsibility, and emphasised the voluntary nature of such an undertaking.[51] However, it was not clear from his Lordship's speech whether the requirement is to assume responsibility for liability if loss occurs or whether simply assuming responsibility for the task is sufficient.[52] Lord Devlin, more than any other Law Lord in *Hedley Byrne*, was emphatic in holding that assumption of responsibility must be voluntary and should not be imposed by law, and notably did not read the other speeches as saying anything different.[53] Lord Devlin drew particular attention to parallels with contractual liability by holding that 'wherever there is a relationship equivalent to contract, there is a duty of care'.[54]

The full force of *Hedley Byrne v Heller* was arguably not immediate. Whilst clearly being viewed as an important case for the law of misstatements,

> [o]utside of negligent misstatements, *Hedley Byrne* largely disappeared in England in the decade post *Anns v Merton London Borough*. In *Anns*, *Hedley Byrne* was, contrary to what was said there, treated as a direct descendant of *Donoghue v Stevenson*. As a result it was justified by Lord Wilberforce's two-stage test.[55]

A clear example of *Hedley Byrne* being misinterpreted and subsumed into the ambit of *Donoghue v Stevenson* is *Ross v Caunters*, which is discussed in detail below. Therefore, the idea of *Hedley Byrne* as providing a distinct method of establishing a duty of care is one which has cemented itself as an orthodox view in more recent years. As we argue in detail below, Lord Goff in a trilogy of pure economic loss cases in the mid-1990s (*Spring v Guardian Assurance plc*, *Henderson v Merrett Syndicates Ltd* and *White v Jones*) helped to usher in the new orthodoxy of viewing *Hedley Byrne*, and cases like *White* falling under the extended-*Hedley Byrne* principle, as distinct from established *Donoghue v Stevenson* principles whereby foreseeability, proximity and policy considerations form the basis of recognising a duty of care. As Lord Mustill put it in his dissent in *White*,

> at a time when the courts had for some years been wrestling with the problems of the general law of negligence exemplified by the line of cases … the speeches in the *Henderson* case brought back to prominence the *Hedley Byrne* case and *Nocton v Lord Ashburton*, and gave them new life as a growing point for the law of negligence.[56]

C. *Ross v Caunters* and Solicitors' Duties of Care Owed to Intended Beneficiaries

Ross v Caunters is an important precursor as it recognised the potential for a duty of care owed by solicitors towards intended beneficiaries when preparing a will.[57] The defendant

[50] *Hedley Byrne* (n 23) 483, 492.
[51] ibid 494–95.
[52] ibid 502–03.
[53] ibid 529–30.
[54] ibid 530.
[55] W Swain, '*Hedley Byrne v Heller* in Australia: "Never Has There Been Such a Judicial Jamboree"' in K Barker, R Grantham and W Swain (eds), *The Law of Misstatements: 50 Years on from* Hedley Byrne v Heller (Oxford, Hart Publishing, 2015) 49.
[56] *White* (n 2) 288.
[57] *Ross v Caunters* [1980] Ch 297.

solicitors prepared a will for the testator and then allowed it to be executed without warning the testator that the will should not be witnessed by the spouse of an intended beneficiary.[58] Two years after the witnessing of the will, the testator died and the defendants realised the error which had been made. The gift to the intended beneficiary was void and the plaintiff successfully brought a claim in negligence against the defendant solicitors for the financial loss she suffered.

Earlier authority which had indicated that solicitors would not owe a duty of care to intended beneficiaries to carefully prepare a will was cast off in light of more recent developments in the law of tort. In *Robertson v Fleming*, Lord Campbell LC stated that a duty between a solicitor and intended beneficiary could be established 'only by showing privity of contract between the parties', otherwise

> a disappointed legatee might sue the solicitor employed by a testator to make a will in favour of a stranger, whom the solicitor never saw or before heard of, if the will were void for not being properly signed and attested.[59]

However, Sir Robert Megarry VC was of the view that the law had moved on since *Robertson v Fleming*:

> *Robertson v Fleming* was, of course, decided nearly 120 years ago, and some 70 years before *Donoghue v Stevenson* ... it is difficult today to see the logic in the proposition that if A employs B to do an act for the benefit of C, the existence of B's contractual duty to A to do the act with proper care negates any possible duty of B towards C, since B has no contract with C. Why should the existence of a contractual duty to A preclude the existence of any non-contractual duty to others?[60]

Thus, Sir Robert reasoned that *Robertson v Fleming* was based on the prevailing but flawed logic of the 'privity fallacy'[61] which has emerged from the decision in *Winterbottom v Wright*.[62] In *Winterbottom v Wright*, the Court of Exchequer came to be interpreted as having 'laid down a general rule' that

> a plaintiff who was a third party to a contract could not make a claim in tort, that is a claim based on an *independent* tort duty, if the conduct of the defendant identified as tortious also happened to constitute a breach of contract.[63]

Since the 'privity fallacy' had been firmly rejected by the House of Lords in *Donoghue v Stevenson*,[64] *Robertson v Fleming* was no longer decisive on the question of duties owed by solicitors to intended beneficiaries.[65] Sir Robert was therefore able to find a duty of care owed by the defendant solicitor to the intended beneficiary.

[58] See s 15 of the Wills Act 1837.

[59] *Robertson v Fleming* (1861) 4 Macq 167 (HL) 177.

[60] *Ross v Caunters* (n 60) 305.

[61] To use the terminology of Jane Stapleton in 'Duty of Care and Economic Loss: A Wider Agenda' (n 25) 250–52.

[62] *Winterbottom v Wright* (1842) 10 M&W 109, (1842) 152 ER 402.

[63] J Stapleton (n 25) 250. The privity fallacy was described by Denning LJ in *Candler* (n 36) 176 as an 'error' which 'appears time and time again in nineteenth century thought'.

[64] *Donoghue v Stevenson* (n 39) 596–98 (Lord Atkin), 602–03 (Lord Thankerton) and 609–10 (Lord Macmillan). Though see D Ibbetson, '*George v Skivington* (1869)' in Mitchell and Mitchell (n 49) for analysis of the prior case of *George v Skivington* (1869) L R 5 Ex 1.

[65] *Ross v Caunters* (n 57) 308: 'With that ground of objection removed, the question is whether a solicitor owes a duty of care to a beneficiary under a will that he makes for a client, and, if so, on what basis that duty rests.'

In contrast to the House of Lords in *White v Jones*, a duty of care was imposed by Sir Robert Megarry VC based on principles articulated in *Donoghue v Stevenson* as opposed to being rationalised as a case which could be accommodated under *Hedley Byrne v Heller*. As noted above, in *Hedley Byrne* much emphasis was placed upon the manner in which the pure economic loss was caused, through negligent misstatement. This led to doubt over the proper scope of *Hedley Byrne*, namely whether the case should be confined to negligent misstatements or whether the decision could be more broadly conceived as establishing a more general exception to the rule against recovery for pure economic loss in negligence where the defendant exercises a special skill and the plaintiff acts in reliance upon the defendant exercising his special skill with proper care.[66] Though with some diffidence,[67] Sir Robert viewed *Hedley Byrne* as applying only to misstatements.[68] This left applying straightforward *Donoghue v Stevenson* principles to the case; at this time, the prevailing orthodoxy was Lord Wilberforce's two-stage test in *Anns v Merton LBC*,[69] under which a duty of care could be easily imposed on the defendant solicitors:

> If one approaches the present case in the manner indicated by Lord Wilberforce, I can see only one answer to the question … Prima facie a duty of care was owed by the defendants to the plaintiff because it was obvious that carelessness on their party would be likely to cause damage to her … I can see nothing in this case which suggests that the scope of the prima facile duty of care ought to be negatived or reduced or limited.[70]

The 'close degree of proximity' of the parties was brought into focus given that the 'plaintiff was named and identified in the will that the defendants drafted for the testator. [The defendants'] contemplation of the plaintiff was actual, nominate and direct.'[71] No countervailing policy issues to the imposition of the duty of care were of persuasion to the court, with Sir Robert Megarry VC being keen to emphasise that finding in favour of the intended beneficiaries would not open the floodgates to widespread or indeterminate liability for the defendants.[72] Sir Robert clarified the differences in the duty owed by a solicitor to his client and the duty owed by the same solicitor to an intended beneficiary:

> In broad terms, a solicitor's duty to his client is to do for him all that he properly can, with, of course, proper care and attention … The duty owed by a solicitor to a third party is entirely different. There is no trace of a wide and general duty to do all that properly can be done for him. Instead, in a case such as the present, there is merely a duty, owed to him as well as the client, to use proper care in carrying out the client's instructions for conferring the benefit on the third party.[73]

[66] ibid 313–18.

[67] ibid 316: 'The subject is one of great difficulty, especially for a mere Chancery judge adrift on the limitless seas of the common law.'

[68] ibid 313.

[69] *Anns v Merton London Borough Council* [1978] AC 728, 751–52.

[70] *Ross v Caunters* (n 57) 310.

[71] ibid 308.

[72] ibid 309: recognition of the duty 'would raise no spectre of imposing on the defendants an uncertain and unlimited liability. The liability would be to one person alone, the plaintiff. The amount would be limited to the value of the share of residue intended for the plaintiff. There would be no question of widespread or repeated liability.'

[73] ibid 322.

In summary, the significance of *Ross v Caunters* is that the courts recognised that solicitors may owe a duty of care in negligence towards intended beneficiaries when preparing a will, and there was some articulation of what that duty entailed. For Cane, the judgment adopted a 'most helpful and realistic approach',[74] as denying the relevance of *Hedley Byrne* avoided the need to explain the absence of reliance when seeking to establish liability for pure economic loss outside of misstatement cases.[75]

Why, then, did *White v Jones* reach the House of Lords, and why is it viewed as *the* landmark case on duties owed by solicitors to third parties in negligence? First, *White v Jones* could be distinguished on its facts: it involved an omission, with the defendant solicitors failing to execute the testator's instructions. Secondly, the authority of *Ross* was questionable given that it was decided under the auspices of *Anns v Merton*,[76] which had been roundly rejected by the House of Lords in *Murphy*.[77] It was time to re-examine the question in light of the House of Lords' changing jurisprudence towards duty of care in negligence in the early 1990s.

III. *WHITE v JONES*

A. Facts and First Instance Decision

A family quarrel led to the litigation. Mr Arthur Barratt and Mrs Barratt lived in Birmingham; they had two daughters, Carole White and Pauline Heath. Mrs Barratt died on 23 January 1986, and there was subsequently a row between Arthur and Pauline over the removal of Mrs Barratt's money box from the family home. We are told in the report that Carole 'sided with her sister' in the argument.[78] As a result, Arthur wrote a will disinheriting his two daughters; the will was prepared by the defendant firm of solicitors, for whom Mr Jones worked, and executed on 4 March. The estate in question consisted of a house worth £27,000, £1,000 in a building society account and insurances of around £1,000: the overall value was roughly £80,000 in today's money.[79] Mr Jones was also one of the executors of the will as appointed by Arthur. The quarrel was short-lived, with the family reconciled by mid-June 1986. Arthur grew concerned about having disinherited his daughters. He told his daughters about the terms of his first will, as well as his revised wishes for his legacy. By way of a telephone call, he informed Mr Jones that he wanted to change his will. Carole also spoke to Mr Jones on the telephone about her father's wishes. A letter containing new instructions for Arthur's will was received by the defendants on 17 July: £9,000 was to be given to each daughter.[80] The solicitors did nothing

[74] P Cane, 'Negligent Solicitors and Disappointed Beneficiaries' (1980) 96 *LQR* 182, 182.

[75] ibid, 183–5.

[76] Weir (n 10) 357: 'The general, almost abstract question was whether a person deprived of an intended legacy by the negligence of a testator's solicitor could sue the solicitor in tort. Megarry J [sic] had answered the question in the affirmative in *Ross v Caunters* …, but that was under the 13-year reign of Queen *Anns*, now dead.'

[77] *Murphy* (n 16).

[78] *White v Jones* (n 2) 217.

[79] Figure derived from The National Archives' currency converter: www.nationalarchives.gov.uk/currency-converter/#currency-result.

[80] ibid. Worth approximately £25,000 today.

for a month – Mr Jones missed three appointments to visit Arthur. Eventually, on 16 August, Mr Jones dictated a memorandum concerning the preparation of a new will, but again nothing was done with the memo. Mr Barratt died while on holiday on 14 September, without a new will having been prepared, let alone executed. The defendants did not act upon the instructions before Mr Barratt died of a heart attack on 14 September. Mr Barratt's letter, not having been witnessed, could not take effect as a will. As such, the executed will of March 1986 was admitted into probate and the daughters brought their claim in negligence against the defendants, claiming that Mr Jones's negligent delay caused them £18,000 of loss from their father's estate.

Turner J dismissed the daughters' claim. *Ross v Caunters* was distinguished on the basis that in negligently failing to ensure the proper execution of a will, as in *Ross v Caunters*, a solicitor will have 'actual, nominate and direct contemplation' of the intended beneficiary; such proximity was held not to be present in the *White v Jones* scenario of a solicitor failing to prepare a will: there was 'a great factual divide'[81] between the facts of *White* and *Ross*. Turner J also voiced concern that the loss was 'too speculative and uncertain to be recoverable'. We are told that '[h]e reached his conclusion with reluctance'.[82]

B. The Court of Appeal

The Court of Appeal unanimously allowed the appeal and held that the claim could succeed. A particular question was whether, in the light of the developments in *Caparo* and *Murphy*, *Ross v Caunters* stood as good law. Sir Donald Nicholls VC considered that the point remained open,[83] pointing particularly to the observations of Lord Oliver of Aylmerton in each case.[84] For the Vice-Chancellor, it was 'of the utmost importance' that if there was no liability 'the only person who has a valid claim against the solicitor has suffered no loss, and the only person who has suffered a loss has no valid claim': 'It would be a sorry reflection on English law if, indeed, that is the position today.'[85] Sir Donald Nicholls 'frankly recognised' that this involved 'fashioning an effective remedy for the solicitor's breach of his professional duty to his client'.[86] 'The resources of the law must be sufficient to fill what would otherwise be a serious lacuna.'[87] Both Sir Donald Nicholls and Steyn LJ referred to the undesirability of the solicitor getting away 'scot-free'.[88] Steyn LJ rejected the argument that the principle in *Ross v Caunters* was 'uncontrollable'[89]

[81] *White* (n 2) 231 (Farquharson LJ). No report of Turner J's first instance judgment has been identified – save for what is recounted or quoted by the judgments in the Court of Appeal and the House of Lords.

[82] ibid 218.

[83] ibid 220.

[84] *Caparo* (n 17) 636D–E; *Murphy* (n 16) 486B–C.

[85] *White* (n 2) 220–21.

[86] ibid 223.

[87] ibid 224.

[88] ibid 224 (Sir Donald Nicholls V-C) and 236 (Steyn LJ). Lord Mustill, dissenting in the Lords (278), took issue with this characterisation of the situation: 'The purpose of the courts when recognising tortious acts and their consequences is to compensate those plaintiffs who suffer actionable breaches of duty, not to act as second-line disciplinary tribunals imposing punishment in the shape of damages.'

[89] ibid 239.

and expressed confidence that special considerations in favour of a duty of care in such circumstances amounted to a limited exception that would not create wider difficulties.[90]

C. The House of Lords

The House of Lords dismissed the appeal by a majority of three to two: Lords Goff, Browne-Wilkinson and Nolan upheld the decision below, while Lords Keith of Kinkel and Mustill dissented.

Giving the leading judgment for the majority, Lord Goff framed the putative duty as 'exceptional',[91] and did not view 'the sweeping statements made in *Robertson v Fleming*'[92] as settling the matter. We explore Lord Goff's judgment and his wider development of assumption of responsibility in the next section, but for his Lordship, the most influential matter was

> the extraordinary fact that, if such a duty is not recognised, the only persons who might have a valid claim (ie, the testator and his estate) have suffered no loss, and the only person who has suffered a loss (ie, the disappointed beneficiary) has no claim … It can therefore be said that, if the solicitor owes no duty to the intended beneficiaries, there is a lacuna in the law which needs to be filled. This I regard as being a point of cardinal importance in the present case.[93]

Lord Browne-Wilkinson emphasised that 'assumption of responsibility' concerns 'the defendants' assumption of responsibility for the task, not the assumption of legal liability'.[94] The facts indicated a sufficiently 'special relationship' between solicitor and intended beneficiaries such as to give rise to a duty of care.[95] Lord Nolan took the view that the daughters' claim was 'simple justice', and that they should be entitled to 'the only remedy which the law can offer':[96] the facts were relevant to the 'pragmatic, case-by-case approach which the law now adopts towards negligence claims'.[97]

Of the dissentients, Lord Keith, then Senior Law Lord, thought the claim contrary to principle and beyond the bounds of incremental development,[98] facing as it did numerous 'formidable' conceptual difficulties.[99] The fuller dissent was from Lord Mustill, who elegantly and forcefully critiqued the majority's view. A key theme for Lord Mustill was that the apparently intuitive support for the beneficiaries' claim was not as obvious as the majority thought:

> I have felt it difficult to join company with those who, judges and commentators alike, have almost unanimously found it too plain to need elaboration that the plaintiffs' claims ought to succeed, if only an intellectually sustainable means can be found.[100]

[90] ibid 239–40.
[91] ibid 259.
[92] ibid.
[93] ibid 259–60. Lord Goff used the same language at 262.
[94] ibid 273.
[95] ibid 276.
[96] ibid 293.
[97] ibid 295.
[98] ibid 251.
[99] ibid 252.
[100] ibid 276.

His Lordship did not believe that denying a duty would 'leave a wholly unacceptable gap in the law'.[101] Lord Mustill also placed the issues in the context of the development of the law: 'it may be that Sir Robert Megarry VC would have reached the same conclusion in the very different legal climate of 1994, but I think it unprofitable to speculate. It is better to start again.'[102] *Henderson* had 'brought [*Hedley Byrne* and *Nocton*] back to prominence'.[103] Applying it to the facts of *White*, though, would not be 'an application of *Hedley Byrne* by enlargement … but the enunciation of something quite different'.[104] His Lordship could not identify a legitimate method of developing such a new principle, nor a way of placing appropriate limits on it:[105]

> it does not conduce to the orderly development of the law, or to the certainty which practical convenience demands, if duties are simply conjured up as a matter of positive law, to answer the apparent justice of an individual case.[106]

D. Lord Goff's Jurisprudence

One of enduring legacies of *White v Jones* is its contribution to establishing assumption of responsibility as a general principle for pure economic loss cases. This is particularly remarkable given the apparently slim basis on which to find an assumption of responsibility on the facts of *White v Jones*, which Stevens has described as an 'unfortunate descent into a fiction'[107] and 'of no explanatory force'.[108] Lord Goff even acknowledged in his speech that

> there is great difficulty in holding, on ordinary principles, that the solicitor has assumed any responsibility towards an intended beneficiary under a will which he has undertaken to prepare on behalf of his client but which, through his negligence, has failed to take effect in accordance with his client's instructions. The relevant work is plainly performed by the solicitor for his client; but, in the absence of special circumstances, it cannot be said to have been undertaken for the intended beneficiary.[109]

White's significance in the re-establishment of assumption of responsibility is emphasised by the fact that it was the third of three cases in which Lord Goff led the House of Lords in using the device to expand the reach of liability for pure economic loss, all decided within a year between 1994 and 1995.

In *Spring v Guardian Assurance*,[110] the House held that the defendant company could be liable for a negligently prepared reference for a former employer which caused him

[101] ibid 290.
[102] ibid 283.
[103] ibid 288.
[104] ibid 290.
[105] ibid 291.
[106] ibid 291.
[107] Robert Stevens, 'Torts' in Louis Blom-Cooper QC, Brice Dickson and Gavin Drewry (eds), *The Judicial House of Lords 1876–2009* (Oxford, Oxford University Press, 2009).
[108] Stevens (n 24) 35.
[109] *White* (n 2) 262.
[110] *Spring v Guardian Assurance* [1995] 2 AC 296.

loss when another company refused to appoint him on the basis of it. Lord Goff referred to the 'wide scope of the principle recognised in *Hedley Byrne*';[111] his Lordship stated, though, that the assumption of responsibility device limited the potential for liability for references beyond the facts of the instant case.[112] As in *White*, justice was invoked as a key consideration.[113] Lord Keith dissented, as he would later do in *White*.

Henderson v Merrett Syndicates Ltd[114] saw a unanimous House of Lords recognise that there could be concurrent liability in contract and tort, with Lord Goff reaffirming the value of the assumption of responsibility device, based on its endorsement in *Hedley Byrne*:[115]

> the concept provides its own explanation why there is no problem in cases of this kind about liability for pure economic loss; for if a person assumes responsibility to another in respect of certain services, there is no reason why he should not be liable in damages for that other in respect of economic loss which flows from the negligent performance of those services.[116]

His Lordship again stressed his view that assumption of responsibility operates as a control mechanism in limiting liability.[117] Recognising that a tortious duty of care could arise in the contractual context was, for Lord Goff, a question of 'develop[ing] the principle of assumption of responsibility as stated in *Hedley Byrne* to its logical conclusion'.[118] *Henderson* was heard immediately after the arguments in *White*, by the same panel of Law Lords, but decided six months earlier.[119] *White* thus represented the culmination of a series of assumption of responsibility decisions led by Lord Goff.

Following the trio of decisions ending in *White*, contemporary scholars questioned the utility of assumption of responsibility as a general test for imposing a duty of care in cases of pure economic loss. Lord Goff's treatment of assumption of responsibility has come under fire from academic commentators. Stanton observed 'that Lord Goff has, through his speeches [in *Spring*, *Henderson* and *White*,] attempted to put "assumption of responsibility" back at the centre of *Hedley Byrne* theory',[120] while Powell described his Lordship as 'the grand revisionist',[121] arguing that 'deemed assumption of responsibility (for that is what it amounts to) is not a reason for the conclusion of a duty of care but another way of expressing the same conclusion. It begs the question *why*.'[122]

A final noticeable feature of Lord Goff's judgment in *White* is his Lordship's use of comparative law. On appeal, each side added a leading comparative private law academic

[111] ibid 318.
[112] ibid 322.
[113] ibid 325: 'Justice, in my opinion, requires that this should be done; and I, for my part, cannot see any reason in policy why that justice should be denied.'
[114] *Henderson v Merrett Syndicates Ltd* [1995] 2 AC 145.
[115] ibid 181.
[116] ibid.
[117] ibid.
[118] ibid 193.
[119] *BP Plc v AON Ltd* [2006] EWHC 424 (Comm), [2006] 1 All ER (Comm) 789 [67] (Colman J). Lord Mustill noted in *White* at 288 that, given the timings of argument, their Lordships did not receive submissions on the relevance of *Henderson* to the issues in *White*.
[120] KM Stanton, 'Professional Negligence in Tort: The Search for a Theory' in P Birks (ed), *Wrongs and Remedies in the Twenty-First Century* (Oxford, Oxford University Press, 1996) 76.
[121] JL Powell, 'Professional and Client: The Duty of Care' in Birks (ibid) 58.
[122] ibid 62.

to their counsel: Professor JA Jolowicz appeared for the appellants,[123] while the respondents had instructed Professor Basil Markesinis.[124] Writing in 1997,[125] Lord Goff told of meeting a QC, in the wake of *White*, who said 'Hullo Lord Goff; I see that in future we have got to provide you with all the relevant German authorities as well as all the English authorities.'[126]

The trilogy marked a reassertion of the 'primacy' assumption of responsibility following what Jackson LJ has described as 'the heroic age of the law of negligence [the 1970s and 1980s] [when] other more expansive bases were developed for negligence liability'.[127] As we have argued, it is necessary to understand the jurisprudential context in which *White* was decided in order to appreciate why what may now be seen as a limited exception caused such controversy. At the time, the case seemed like the latest in a line of decisions deploying and developing the assumption of responsibility device, and thus expanding liability. With hindsight, it perhaps marked the end of an era.

IV. BOUNDARIES

As noted in our introduction, a key feature of *White v Jones* as a potential landmark case is the interplay between various areas of private law: succession, contract and tort law. The majority's (and in particular Lord Goff's) reasoning was concerned by the need to fill what would otherwise be a lacuna in the law:

> the real reason for concern in cases such as the present lies in the extraordinary fact that, if a duty owed by the testator's solicitor to the disappointed beneficiary is not recognised, the only person who may have a valid claim has suffered no loss, and the only person who has suffered a loss has no claim.[128]

In this section we shall consider whether the result in *White v Jones* could have been better reached through these other avenues of private law, or whether the law of tort was the appropriate vehicle for driving legal change. Ultimately, we conclude that tort law was, and remains, the path of least resistance for compensating the plaintiffs on the exceptional facts of *White*.

[123] Alongside Duncan Matheson QC and Teresa Peacocke, who had appeared for the defendants in the Court of Appeal. Ms Peacocke has written on post-*White* developments: TR Peacocke, 'The Remedy in *White v Jones* Cases: Smoothing the Analytical Wrinkles' (2008) 24 *Professional Negligence* 138.

[124] Alongside John Mitting QC and James Quirke, who had likewise appeared for the claimants in the court below.

[125] Rt Hon The Lord Goff of Chieveley, 'Comparative Law: The Challenge to the Judges' in B Markesinis (ed), *Law Making, Law Finding and Law Shaping* (Oxford, Oxford University Press, 1997).

[126] ibid 39. Lord Goff added the 'lawyers acting for the disappointed legatees instructed Basil as one of their Counsel, so that they were able to place all [the German] material before the Appellate Committee. It so happened that I knew it already; but this at least meant that counsel on the other side had the opportunity to comment on it.' For different comparative perspectives on the issues, on German and Roman law see D Johnston, 'Appointments and Disappointments: *White v Jones* in Rome and Today' (2000) 53 *Current Legal Problems* 283; looking primarily at French law, see S Whittaker (n 9); S Whittaker, 'Privity of Contract and the Law of Tort: The French Experience' (1995) 15 *OJLS* 327.

[127] *Robinson v PE Jones (Contractors) Ltd* [2011] EWCA Civ 9, [2012] QB 44 [72].

[128] *White* (n 2) 262 (Lord Goff).

A. Contract Law

Contract law struggles to accommodate cases such as *White v Jones* falling under the *Hedley Byrne* principle for a number of interrelated reasons, not least the doctrine of consideration as highlighted by Lord Devlin in *Hedley Byrne*.[129] In *White v Jones* a further barrier to the plaintiffs recovering through contract law was a lack of intention to create legal relations between the defendant solicitors and the intended beneficiaries of the will; the intended contractual arrangements were between the solicitors and their client, the testator. An additional challenge is the lack of privity between the plaintiffs and the defendants.

Since *White v Jones*, the Contracts (Rights of Third Parties) Act 1999 offers some aid for third parties seeking to enforce contractual terms. However, contract law appears to still be inapt to deal with the *White v Jones* paradigm. Section 1(1) provides that a third party 'may in his own right enforce a term of the contract' if, under section 1(1)(a), 'the contract expressly provides that he may', or under section 1(1)(b), 'the term purports to confer a benefit on him'. For the Law Commission, the language eventually used in the Act would not cover the facts of *White v Jones*:

> The crucial words are that the promise must be one to *confer a benefit on* the third party. The solicitor's express or implied promise to use reasonable care is not one by which the solicitor is to confer a benefit on the third party. Rather it is one by which the solicitor is to enable the client to confer a benefit on the third party.[130]

This is also the accepted interpretation of a similar provision[131] in the New Zealand Contracts (Privity) Act 1982.[132] The privity barrier to intended beneficiaries establishing a cause of action in contract therefore remains after the 1999 Act. Conversely, the potential for *White* to be developed in an expansive way to accommodate other challenges to privity (which we shall consider in the next section) has not been necessary because of the Act.

Commenting on *Hedley Byrne*, Weir drew attention to the potential implications for the law of contract in recognising that there can be liability for mere pecuniary loss caused by the defendant's negligence. It was suggested that careless advisors (and now, following *Henderson*, those whose careless acts cause loss) may be turned into 'unpaid and involuntary'[133] insurers for parties who did not go to the trouble of securing contractual arrangements to protect their financial interests.[134] However, Weir's general criticism of the law of negligence extending to compensate pure economic loss does not easily map onto the *White v Jones* scenario. Whilst one might accept that gratuitous recipients

[129] *Hedley Byrne* (n 23) 525–26.

[130] Law Commission, *Privity of Contract: Contracts for the Benefit of Third Parties* (Law Com No 242, 1996) [7.20] (original emphasis).

[131] Contracts (Privity) Act 1982, s 4: 'Where a promise contained in a deed or contract *confers, or purports to confer, a benefit* on a person, designated by name, description, or reference to a class, who is not a party to the deed or contract …' (emphasis added).

[132] *Gartside v Sheffield, Young & Ellis* [1983] NZLR 37.

[133] Weir (n 26) 220.

[134] ibid 218.

of professional advice or expertise ought to have been more proactive in protecting their own financial interests through contract, it is difficult to fault the plaintiffs in *White v Jones* for not having done so. There is generally no expectation of intended beneficiaries to make separate contractual arrangements with the solicitors in charge of preparing and executing the will in order to secure their position. In this sense, intended beneficiaries recovering through the law of tort should not pose an undue threat to the tort/contract boundary.

B. Succession

Whilst ultimately it was the law of tort which was expanded in order to accommodate disappointed beneficiaries under a will, there were some who argued that reform of the law of succession would be a more appropriate response to the *White v Jones* scenario. For example, Weir's preferred solution to the problem raised by the case would have been to extend statutory remedies from the law of succession under the Inheritance (Provision for Family and Dependants) Act 1975[135] in order to 'allow intended beneficiaries as well as deprived dependants to claim against the estate, notwithstanding the will'.[136] For Weir, a further benefit of amending the law of succession to cover the *White v Jones* scenario is to deprive the unintended beneficiaries of their gain, something which the law of tort cannot easily do.[137] Similarly, Smith has argued that problems such as those in *White v Jones* are products of the strict approach to formalities in succession law.[138] However, this call for statutory reform has come under criticism; a powerful rebuttal came from Stephen Cretney, who viewed the call to amend the 1975 Act as 'misconceived', because the aims of the legislation, mainly focused upon providing for maintenance for dependants, differ from the problem to which *White* is designed to respond.[139] A more limited, targeted extension of the tort of negligence to the facts in *White v Jones*, as opposed to reform of the 1975 Act, has the benefit of circumventing the difficulties highlighted by Cretney. When it comes to wills, there may be other options available, notably rectification under the Administration of Justice Act 1982, section 20, which permits for rectification where the will fails to carry out the testator's intentions 'in consequence of a clerical error; or (b) of a failure to understand his instructions'. But, of course, rectification would not help in *White*: the will did reflect the instructions of the testator at the time he made it; the problem was that the solicitors had not drawn up the new will to reflect the change in his intentions.

[135] Weir (n 10) 359–60: 'If the real problem is that our rules regarding the distribution of a decedent's estate may occasionally deprive a person of benefits he should have, the law of tort may not be the right place to solve it ... The question is not, as might appear from the speeches and certainly emerged from the submissions, "tort or contract?" but rather "obligations or succession?".'

[136] ibid 359.

[137] ibid 359: 'one of the features which arguably made this case "extraordinary" was not only that the right people were going to get the money, but that the wrong people were'.

[138] SA Smith, 'Contracts for the Benefit of Third Parties: in Defence of the Third-Party Rule' (1997) 17 *OJLS* 643, 627, esp fn 27.

[139] SM Cretney, 'Negligent Solicitors and Wills: A Footnote' (1996) 112 *LQR* 54, 55.

Overall, the alternative avenues for dealing with the *White* 'problem' reveal their own limitations; therefore, the law of tort was the most viable option, provided that any developed exception could be kept within reasonable bounds. As we argue in the following section, the *White* legacy suggests that the duty recognised in the case has indeed proved to be an exception.

V. LEGACY

The legacy of *White v Jones* is a mixed one, partly because the case has been cited in different contexts. It has been relied upon in pure economic loss cases, both against solicitors and more widely. '[The] judicial creativity has encouraged the testing of the limits of the principle of *White v Jones*.'[140] Although there have been incremental extensions, there have also been several cases where the courts have declined to recognise a duty. *White v Jones* has additionally been cited as a more general example of the 'strong impulse to do practical justice',[141] in wider contexts. We shall consider first the key cases considering *White* in the context of negligence and then the broader citation of *White* as support for judicial innovation.

A. Applications, Extensions and Distinctions

The testing of the boundaries of the principle in *White* can initially be seen in cases concerning wills and solicitors. In *Carr-Glynn v Frearsons*,[142] the testatrix had jointly owned a property with her nephew. She had intended to leave her share to her niece, and executed a will to that effect. The will had been drawn up by the defendants, who had failed to advise the testatrix of the need to sever the joint tenancy. When the testatrix died, without having severed the joint tenancy, her share vested in her nephew by survivorship. The niece sued the solicitors, alleging that they owed a duty under *White*, and the Court of Appeal found that there was such a duty. A difference from *White* was that the estate on such facts would have a remedy, because its assets were less than they would have been had the proper advice been given.[143] However, any such recovery would not benefit the claimant, as she was not the residuary beneficiary. Chadwick LJ held that the availability of a remedy for the estate did not preclude a duty being owed to the niece: precluding a duty 'ought properly be regarded as equally unacceptable and unjust', as in *White*. The respective duties to be owed to the testatrix and to the niece on the facts were 'complementary', as they both required care to be taken to give effect to testatrix's intentions.[144] Concurring, Thorpe LJ referred to the 'instinct to do justice [being] clearly aroused'[145] and viewed Chadwick LJ's approach as a 'permissible incremental extension' of *White*.[146]

140 *Worby v Rosser* [2000] PNLR 140, 150.
141 *White* (n 2) 259.
142 *Carr-Glynn v Frearsons* [1999] Ch 326.
143 Chadwick LJ accepted that 'at first sight' the present case fell outside the ambit of *White*: ibid 336.
144 ibid 337.
145 ibid 339.
146 ibid.

In *Chappell v Somers & Blake*[147] Neuberger J (as he then was) held that where solicitors had failed to obtain probate, with the result that the estate lost income from properties which were unable to be rented out in the interim, they could be sued by the executrix on behalf of the beneficiaries: there was no risk of double recovery because the damages would ultimately go to the beneficiary.[148] Indeed, Neuberger J thought that recognising a duty in such circumstances was not 'even to fall foul of the reasoning or conclusions' of the minority in *White*.[149] The Court of Appeal subsequently considered in *Daniels v Thompson*[150] a claim relating to negligent advice given to an elderly lady by the defendant solicitor concerning one of her properties: the result was an additional inheritance tax liability. The claimant was executor of his mother's estate and it was held that the duty could be owed to him as a personal representative, given that 'the damage would in the normal course of events only be suffered by those representing the testator after his or her death'.[151] A clear extension was made by the Court of Appeal in *Gorham v British Telecommunications*,[152] where negligent pensions advice had been given to a customer and had led to a loss of benefits to his wife and children after his death. Pill LJ regarded the case as 'in its structure, … identical to that in *White*',[153] and 'practical justice' required a remedy.[154] For Sir Murray Stuart-Smith, the case was 'even stronger than *White*' as, rather than losing a windfall, the widow had a reduced pension.[155]

There are, though, numerous instances of the courts distinguishing *White v Jones*. Shortly after *Carr-Glynn*, Chadwick LJ also led the court in *Worby v Rosser*,[156] in which a duty was rejected on the basis that there were alternative remedies available. The claimants were beneficiaries under a prior will who sued the defendant for costs which they had incurred in challenging probate of a subsequent will, which the defendant had prepared. The proper route was to recover costs from the estate, which could then, in turn, recover from the defendant. There was thus 'no lacuna to be filled'.[157] Further examples include attempts to extend a duty to family members alleged to have exerted undue influence on their relatives[158] and to a solicitor not directly involved in the wills;[159] to a solicitor

[147] *Chappell v Somers & Blake* [2003] EWHC 1644 (Ch), [2004] Ch 19.

[148] ibid [16]–[17].

[149] ibid [21]: *Chappell* was described by Lady Smith as reflecting 'the narrowness of the *White v Jones* principle' in *George Gordon, Marquess of Aberdeen & Temair v Messrs Turcan Connell* [2008] ScotCS CSOH 183 [50]. *White v Jones* has been accepted in Scotland, although the method of reaching a result may vary: *Steven v Hewats* [2013] ScotCS CSOH 61, [10] (Lord Tyre): 'It is noteworthy that in some of the English decisions that have followed *White v Jones*, the court has referred to "extending" the principle to the circumstances of the instant case. For my part I would respectfully prefer, according to Scots methodology, to seek to identify the principle and then to assess whether the facts averred by the pursuer are or are not capable of falling within its scope.'

[150] *Daniels v Thompson* [2004] EWCA Civ 307.

[151] ibid [56] (Dyson LJ).

[152] *Gorham v British Telecommunications* [2000] 1 WLR 2129.

[153] ibid 2140.

[154] ibid 2141–42.

[155] ibid 2146 (Sir Murray dissented in part in the appeal, but not on the existence of the duty).

[156] *Worby v Rosser* [2000] PNLR 140.

[157] ibid 149. See also 150–51 (Peter Gibson LJ).

[158] *Hart v Burbidge* [2013] EWHC 1628 (Ch), [2013] WTLR 1191 [136]: '*White v Jones* … related to a wholly different situation, provides no support for the existence of that duty.'

[159] *Herring v Shorts Financial Services LLP* [2016] EW Misc B12 (CC) [96(5)] (HHJ Behrens): '[This case] is plainly distinguishable from *White v Jones* … It would in my view involve a considerable extension to the principle in *White v Jones* to impose a duty of care in this case.'

dealing with *inter vivos* gifts under certain trusts.[160] The courts have been particularly astute where there could be a conflict between a *White*-like duty and the duty owed by the solicitor to their client.[161] In addition, in the specific case of solicitors, the caution of Lord Goff in fashioning the remedy has been described as 'very limited'.[162] Indeed, in *Walker v Geo H Medlicott & Son*,[163] that the claimant had not sought rectification of the will in question was viewed as a failure to mitigate his loss (if any). The existence of an adequate remedy will be a strong factor pointing against a duty by analogy with *White*,[164] albeit not necessarily conclusive.[165] Overall, the 'potential for the incremental development' of *White v Jones* has been said to be 'very limited'.[166]

B. The 'Strong Impulse to Do Practical Justice': Mind the Gap

As we have seen, Lord Goff was motivated by the 'strong impulse to do practical justice',[167] and concluded that 'the common law is not so sterile as to be incapable of supplying that remedy when it is required'.[168] WA Seavey noted in 1951, when commenting on Denning LJ's dissent in *Candler v Crane, Christmas & Co Ltd*, that

> to preserve archaic individual rules in a modern society, to fail to respond to changing ideals and needs, necessarily saps the vitality of the law … It is one of the glories of the common law that its capacity for change enables it to remain human and vital.[169]

Sedley LJ applauded the approach in *White*:

> It is thus from an objective appraisal of the actors' specific relationship with one another that the law will either deduce or decline to deduce the duty. Inevitably, since no two cases are alike, this gives rise to criticism that the law is being rendered uncertain. The criticism may wound when it is applied to cases such as *White v Jones* and *Gorham v British Telecommunications* so as to suggest that these are decisions driven as much by merits as by law. If so, the wounds are honourable, for they represent the constant endeavour to do justice according to law.[170]

[160] *Joseph v Farrer & Co LLP* [2017] EWHC 2072 (Ch) (HHJ Purle QC). See also *Hickland v Mckeone* [2018] NIQB 81 [54]–[55] (Colton J).

[161] *Joseph* (ibid) and *P&P Property Ltd v Owen White & Catlin LLP* [2018] EWCA Civ 1082, [2018] 3 WLR 1244 [80] (Patten LJ). See also more generally A Tettenborn, 'Professional negligence: Can You Owe a Duty to the Dead?' [2005] *Conveyancer and Property Lawyer* 288.

[162] *McLeod v Crawford* [2010] ScotCS CSOH 101 [23].

[163] *Walker v Geo H Medlicott & Son* [1999] 1 WLR 727; E O'Dell, 'Restitution, Rectification, and Mitigation: Negligent Solicitors and Wills, Again' (2002) 65 *MLR* 360; R Kerridge and AHR Brierley, 'Mistakes in Wills: Rectify and Be Damned' (2003) 62 *CLJ* 750.

[164] 'Given that Mr Raja has an adequate remedy against DFL and (on my view of the case) the receivers, I can see no reason why he should also have a remedy against the appellant valuers. I do not subscribe to the principle: "the more the merrier"': *Raja v Austin Gray (a firm)* [2002] EWCA Civ 1965 [43] (Clarke LJ).

[165] *Johnson v Gore Wood* [1999] Lloyds Rep PN 91, 99 (Ward LJ).

[166] *London Borough of Islington v University College London Hospital NHS Trust* [2005] EWCA Civ 596 [29] (Buxton LJ). See also *Kapfunde v Abbey National Plc* [1999] Lloyd's Rep Med 48.

[167] *White* (n 2) 259.

[168] ibid 269.

[169] WA Seavey, '*Candler v Crane, Christmas & Co*: Negligent Misrepresentation by Accountants' (1951) 67 *LQR* 466, 468.

[170] *Dean v Allin & Watts (A Firm)* [2001] EWCA Civ 758, [2001] 2 Lloyd's Rep 249 [48].

However, whilst recourse to practical justice can act as a positive force in spurring legal change, there are some obvious risks with this form of reasoning.

As Lord Mustill observed in his dissent, it can be dangerous to assume 'too readily that it so reflects the moral imperatives of the situation that the law of delict should be strained to bring it about'.[171] As we have seen, his Lordship was concerned that reliance on 'practical justice' can induce the courts to 'conjure' duties of care in new situations without a framework of principle. His Lordship continued that

> it does not conduce to the orderly development of the law, or to the certainty which practical convenience demands, if duties are simply conjured up as a matter of positive law, to answer the apparent justice of an individual case.[172]

The House of Lords returned to assumption of responsibility in *Williams v Natural Life Health Foods*.[173] Lord Steyn, who sat in the Court of Appeal in *White*, said that the case was decided on 'special facts' and defended it on the basis that 'the general criticism is overstated. Coherence must sometimes yield to practical justice.'[174] In that case, the House declined to find liability established. A little later, Lord Steyn relied on *White* when holding that the traitor George Blake should account for his profits made in breach of contract with the Crown: 'the enduring strength of the common law is that it has been developed on a case-by-case basis by judges for whom the attainment of practical justice was a major objective of their work'.[175]

An example of the wider use of the 'impulse' to justify recovery is *Shell v Total*.[176] The essential facts were very different from *White*: the defendant Total's negligence caused an explosion at an oil depot, causing extensive damage to pipelines. The pipes were owned by a vehicle company, which held them on trust for a number of oil companies, including the claimants, Shell. Total admitted liability for the physical damage to the pipes and to the oil that was in the pipes at the time. However, Shell suffered various wider losses as a result of the explosion, and sought to recover them. The difficulty was that, as a beneficiary, Shell had neither legal ownership of nor possessory title to the relevant property,[177] and thus had no entitlement to sue. Its losses were in principle purely economic. Drawing support from *White* via *Chappel*, the Court of Appeal held that Shell was entitled to recover, because otherwise the losses would fall. Their Lordships 'confess[ed] to being somewhat influenced … by what Lord Goff of Chieveley called "the impulse to do practical justice"'.[178]

With respect, this reasoning is unconvincing: there is a difference between a 'lacuna' showing that there must be a deficiency in the law and a gap caused by legal policy limiting recovery of certain losses.[179] The mere fact that a claimant is left out of pocket does

[171] *White* (n 2) 278.
[172] ibid 291.
[173] *Williams v Natural Life Health Foods* [1998] 1 WLR 830.
[174] ibid 837.
[175] *Attorney General v Blake* [2001] 1 AC 268, 292.
[176] *Shell UK Ltd v Total UK Ltd* [2010] EWCA Civ 180, [2011] QB 86.
[177] *Leigh and Sillavan Ltd v Aliakmon Shipping Co. Ltd* [1986] AC 785, 809F (Lord Brandon).
[178] *Shell* (n 176) [143].
[179] J Lee, '*Yearworth v North Bristol NHS Trust*: Instrumentalism and Fictions in Property Law' in E Waring, S Douglas and R Hickey (eds), *Landmark Cases in Property Law* (Oxford, Hart Publishing, 2015). See also Lord Hodge in *Realstone Ltd v Messrs J & E Shepherd* [2008] ScotCS CSOH 31 [19]: 'It is important to recall that

not in itself justify a remedy. As Lord Rodger put it in *JD v East Berkshire*, 'Harm which constitutes a "wrong" in the contemplation of the law must, of course, be remedied. But the world is full of harm for which the law furnishes no remedy.'[180] Lord Mustill made the point as follows:

> Even under the most supportive of legal regimes there must be many situations in which the well founded expectations of a potential beneficiary are defeated by an untoward turn of events and yet he or she is left without recourse. Nobody suggests otherwise.[181]

Sometimes the inability to make a successful claim (as where a potential defendant is of limited means) will be 'a weakness of the facts not a lacuna in the law'.[182]

In the abstract, 'Justice is extremely hard to pin down'.[183] Therefore, where the requirements of 'practical justice' are thought to be determinative, they should be interrogated, so that they can be seen to be more than merely the personal judgement of the judge(s) in question.[184] One such example is the judgment of Eder J in *Sebry v Companies House*,[185] recognising a limited duty on Companies House for losses. The need for development by 'analogy and incrementalism'[186] was emphasised: a key factor, in addition to carelessness going without a remedy, was that imposing a duty was 'likely to improve the accuracy of the Register[,] which is plainly in the public interest'.[187]

In *CGL Group Ltd v The Royal Bank of Scotland Plc & National Westminster Bank Plc*[188] the claimants were required by the defendant banks to buy interest rate hedging products as a condition of loans taken out by the claimants. Through an agreement with the financial services regulator, the banks were required to carry out a review of their sales of such products and to provide appropriate redress where mis-selling was found to have occurred. The claimant customers sought to establish that the banks owed them a duty of care to carry out the review with reasonable skill and care. In framing their claim, the claimants relied upon *White v Jones*. The Court of Appeal rejected the duty, for reasons given by Beatson LJ. The statutory regime in that case meant that there was no 'lacuna' to be filled, and in any event, insofar as there could be thought to be a gap, it reflected 'the considered decision of Parliament'.[189]

the law of delict is the general law and has a much wider role than gap-filling. Were the law of delict, even in the field of economic loss, to be merely a gap-filler, that would be inconsistent with the existence of concurrent liability in contract and delict.'

[180] *JD v East Berkshire Community Health NHS Trust* [2005] UKHL 23, [2005] 2 AC 373 [100]; see further at [100]–[105]. Dissenting in that case, Lord Bingham, invoked the *White* 'impulse' ([36]) as supporting a duty of care on the facts.

[181] *White* (n 2) 277.

[182] *HR v JAPT* [1997] OPLR 123 [44] (Lindsay J).

[183] D Johnston, 'Appointments and Disappointments: *White v Jones* in Rome and Today' (2000) 53 *Current Legal Problems* 283, 295.

[184] See Goff (n 1) 183–84; Johnston (n 183) 295.

[185] *Sebry v Companies House* [2015] EWHC 115 (QB), [2016] 1 WLR 2499.

[186] ibid, heading before [116]. See also Lord Mance in *Customs and Excise Commissioners v Barclays Bank plc* [2006] UKHL 28, [2007] 1 AC 181, [91]–[92] 'Incrementalism operates as an important cross-check on any other approach.'

[187] *Sebry* (ibid) [112].

[188] *CGL Group Ltd v The Royal Bank of Scotland Plc & National Westminster Bank Plc* [2017] EWCA Civ 1073, [2018] 1 WLR 2137.

[189] ibid [96]. For similar reasoning, see *Hodge v Newport Borough Council* (2001) 33 HLR 18 [36] (Ferris J, speaking of the framework under the Housing Act 1985).

Similarly, any claims of a 'legal black hole' must be policed carefully,[190] as 'a lacuna is in the eye of the beholder'.[191] But the trend of decisions has shown a readiness to differentiate between categories of lacunae: as Lord Phillips MR said in *Reeman v Department of Transport*, '[o]nly in exceptional cases will the Court accept that the interests of justice justify such an extension of the law'.[192] The pattern of cases applying *White* illustrate that it is regarded as an exceptional case, even if it is subject to incremental development within cognate areas.[193] Citing Lord Goff's 'impulse to do practical justice' can be an appeal to a slogan or a *deus ex machina* to reach a desired result, and such an approach might occasionally lead to the indulgence of idiosyncratic judgements and judgments. Generally, however, the courts are mindful of the concerns adumbrated here.

C. Retrenchment: A Coda

This chapter has reviewed the story of the duty of care and argued that *White* is a high point in Lord Goff's approach to negligence. Before concluding, we should refer to the most recent jurisprudence from the UK Supreme Court, which has undergone a period of revolution with respect to liability in negligence.[194] However, in that same time, the Court has taken a more restrictive approach in the case of pure economic loss in two cases: *NRAM v Steel*[195] and *Banca Nazionale del Lavoro SPA v Playboy Club London*.[196]

In *Steel*, a solicitor acting on behalf of a borrower misrepresented the terms of a loan agreement to the commercial lender. The Supreme Court held that there was no duty owed by that solicitor towards the lender, on the basis that she had not assumed responsibility. The assumption device fit the case 'perfectly, and there is no need to consider whether there should be any incremental development of it'.[197] Lord Wilson cited *Ross*[198] (though not *White*)[199] as authority for the general rule that a solicitor owes no duty to those other than their own client. There was no liability on the facts in *Steel* because it was not reasonable for the commercial lender to rely on a careless misrepresentation 'about a fact wholly within the knowledge of the representee'.[200] Equally, since it was not reasonable for the claimant so to rely, it was reasonable for the representor not to foresee that he would do so: Ms Steel could therefore not be said to have assumed responsibility.[201] *Playboy Club* concerned the claimant casino, which had sought a reference as to the creditworthiness of a client. It approached the defendant bank, but did so via a third party, Burlington, which the casino used to protect its clients' privacy. The request did not state that it was on behalf

[190] *Sainsbury's Supermarkets Ltd v Condek Holdings Ltd & Ors* [2014] EWHC 2016 (TCC).

[191] Johnston (n 183) 299.

[192] *Reeman v Department of Transport* [1997] 2 Ll Rep 648, 677.

[193] *Farah & Ors v British Airways & Anor* [1999] EWCA Civ 305 [28] (Lord Woolf MR).

[194] J Lee, 'Trends in Tort Law: Bad Form and Addictive Substance?' in A Robertson and J Goudkamp (eds), *Form and Substance in the Law of Obligations* (Oxford, Hart Publishing, forthcoming 2019).

[195] *Steel & Anor v NRAM Ltd (formerly NRAM Plc) (Scotland)* [2018] UKSC 13, [2018] 1 WLR 1190.

[196] *Banca Nazionale del Lavoro SPA v Playboy Club London* [2018] UKSC 43, [2018] 1 WLR 4041.

[197] *Steel* (n 195) [25].

[198] ibid.

[199] The case was cited by Lady Smith in the (overruled) Inner House decision in the litigation: *NRAM PLC v Jane Steel* [2016] ScotCS CSIH 11.

[200] *Steel* (n 195) [38].

[201] ibid. See similarly *Deslauriers v Guardian Asset Management Ltd (Trinidad and Tobago)* [2017] UKPC 34, [2018] 2 All ER (Comm) 596 [21]–[22].

of any party other than Burlington itself.[202] The bank provided a careless reference and the casino suffered losses as a result. It sued the bank in negligence; however, since the bank had not known that the reference was for the Playboy Club, having only provided the reference to Burlington, it denied that it owed a duty. The Supreme Court agreed with the bank and held that there could be no liability in such circumstances to an undisclosed principal: as Lord Sumption put it, 'they had no reason to suppose that Burlington was acting for someone else, and they knew nothing of the Playboy Club. In those circumstances, it is plain that they did not voluntarily assume any responsibility to the Club.'[203]

These two decisions demonstrate that the Supreme Court continues to see the assumption of responsibility device as fundamental: Lord Wilson reiterated in *Steel* that although assumption of responsibility 'may require cautious incremental development in order to fit cases to which it does not readily apply, this concept remains the foundation of the liability'[204] in such cases. Taken together, *Steel* and *Playboy Club* indicate a reluctance to develop the principle to such a creative extent as was demonstrated in *White*; instead, caution is the watchword, and assumption of responsibility operates as a control mechanism. Nevertheless, the appeal of the concept endures.[205]

VI. CONCLUSION

In this chapter, we have examined the legacy of *White v Jones*, some 25 years after it was decided. Coming at the end of a period when the House of Lords was exploring and expanding liability for pure economic loss, *White* was the culmination of Lord Goff's trilogy, after *Spring* and *Henderson*. Our argument has been that the case can now be seen as a product of its time: *White* is as representative of thinking in the mid-1990s as Britpop or an episode of *Friends*.

It is therefore understandable that the immediate reaction to the decision was that it had the potential to lead to a major extension of liability, whether for solicitors or more generally. And yet, subsequent case law has not borne out those fears: what developments there have been can for the most part be regarded as relatively minor and incremental. We have suggested that there are a number of reasons for this: the courts have shown appropriate restraint when invited to extend the scope of *White*, while statutory reform addressed some of the possible wider implications.

We have argued that, just as *Ross v Caunters* could only have been reasoned in the way it was in the aftermath of *Anns*, so *White v Jones* could only be reasoned by the majority in the way it was at exactly that point in the mid-1990s. It is thus a salutary example of the temporal contingency of legal reasoning. *White* stands, if not quite as a landmark in the development of the tort of negligence, at least as a high-water mark in the pragmatic search for principle.[206]

[202] For the significance of this point, see Lord Mance (ibid) [24]–[25].

[203] *Playboy Club* (n 196) [16].

[204] *Steel* (n 195) [24]. See also Lord Lloyd-Jones in *James-Bowen v Commissioner of Police of the Metropolis* [2018] UKSC 40, [2018] 1 WLR 4021 [24].

[205] Compare JAW Grower and OF Sherman, 'Equivalent to Contract? Confronting the Nature of the Duty Arising under *Hedley Byrne v Heller*' (2019) 135 *LQR* 177.

[206] 'the essentially pragmatic approach … is perhaps the most fundamental of all the characteristics of the common law': Goff (n 11) 87.

8

Williams v Hensman (1861) and the Law of Severance: Janus Personified

MARTIN DIXON

I. INTRODUCTION

IT USED TO be a fundamental principle of English law that a testator or testatrix could dispose of their property by will in any manner they chose. Unlike some civil law jurisdictions, the common law had no concept of forced heirship.[1] Of course, there is now a reasonable and proportionate statutory jurisdiction to interfere with a will maker's intention, whether or not the prior exclusion of persons who might otherwise be expected to 'benefit' from a person's death is motivated by good reason or fickle choice.[2] Moreover, in recent years, there has been a more disruptive attack on testamentary freedom, albeit indirect. The modern approach to proprietary estoppel has generated many cases where a potential testator or testatrix has found themselves prevented from disposing of their property by will because of some assurance made during their lifetime, which cannot then be withdrawn.[3] Such cases are, perhaps, symptomatic of a twenty-first-century belief that those left behind have some sort of entitlement to the assets of those now gone, irrespective of the wishes of the deceased.

Of course, the common law, fortified by statute, has always embraced limited ways in which a person could control the destination of property on death – either to include or exclude particular people or an entire generic class. The once common strict settlement, with its emphasis on patriarchal and lineal succession, was such a device, and were it not constrained by perpetuity rules perhaps would have been more extensively used

[1] Forced heirship, with or without a reserved portion for a spouse, is a common feature of civil law systems, such as Spain, France and Belgium, although there are moves in some jurisdictions to limit its impact: see, eg the new Belgium law on inheritance, effective September 2018. See, generally, Walter Pintens's chapter in this volume.

[2] Inheritance (Provision for Family and Dependants) Act 1975. See Brian Sloan's chapter in this volume.

[3] *Thorner v Major* [2009] UKHL 18, [2009] 1 WLR 776 (on which see John Mee's chapter in this volume) and *Suggitt v Suggitt* [2012] EWCA Civ 1140, [2012] WTLR 1607 are striking examples of how estoppel can interfere with inheritance law and testamentary freedom, respectively. *Moore v Moore* [2018] EWCA Civ 2669, [2018] 11 WLUK 405 and *Thompson v Thompson* [2018] EWHC 1338 (Ch) are recent examples of the many cases which followed the dam-breaking decision in *Gillet v Holt* [2001] Ch 210. However, the claim is obviously heavily factually dependent. See *Shaw v Shaw* [2018] EWHC 3196 (Ch), [2018] 11 WLUK 630, where the claimant had not kept the commitment on which the promise to inherit had been made.

until socio-economic changes made it redundant. So, too, with the joint tenancy. The joint tenancy cuts across testamentary freedom. It forces a result as to the destination of property through the application of survivorship. It takes no regard of changing circumstance, but fixes the identity of the future owner by reference to wishes and intentions that were current when the property was acquired but which may no longer be relevant, fiscally efficient or reasonable. However, the law of severance, as epitomised by *Williams v Hensman*, is an antidote to the certainty and capriciousness of the joint tenancy.[4] It provides a fork in the road, diverting property away from its otherwise inevitable destination. The law of severance is a boon and a bane. It releases the unwilling from the chains of joint tenancy and it frustrates the once clear intention of the purchasers or donors of property. It is the Janus concept of the law of succession.

Williams v Hensman[5] was not the first case to consider the law of severance,[6] and that it is now generally regarded as defining the circumstances in which severance at common law might take place is, perhaps, a combination of chance, time and opportunity. Certainly, one suspects that there was nothing unusual about the trials and tribulations of the moderately comfortable Hensman family of Kimbolton, in the ancient County of Huntingdonshire. In 1828, the matriarch of the family, Mrs Hensman, was left a legacy in the will of Sarah Creak, who died one week after the will had been executed. Mrs Hensman was left a life interest, and the associated capital sum of some £4000[7] was destined for her eight children as joint tenants. In the years that followed, the residuary joint-tenant legatees dealt, or attempted to deal, with the fund in various ways, in various combinations of persons, including having to manage the consequences of breach of duty on the part of the executor of Sarah Creak's will.[8] Almost inevitably, given the number of persons comprised in the joint tenancy, a dispute arose on the death of the life tenant as to the proper distribution of the capital sum, especially as some of those joined in the joint tenancy of the remainder had previously died. Was the joint tenancy still in existence at the death of the life tenant, that being the moment to decide the destination of the capital sum? Did the capital sum accrue to the survivors entitled in remainder by reason of survivorship or had severance by some or all taken place during the lives of the original tenants so that their heirs could take a portion?

The fairly complex legal transactions entered into by Mrs Hensman and her children in the years following the death of the settlor are admirably dissected in Peter Luther's legal and historiographical analysis of the case.[9] These transactions, while painting a picture of Victorian England that would not be out of place in a Dickens serial, are for present purposes merely the scenery that stands as a backdrop to the analysis that was to follow when, with a certain inevitability, the matter came to court. Of more immediate

[4] Thus, while it may be prudent to complete Land Registry Form JO in respect of registered land (whereby the beneficial interests in co-owned land are expressly declared in writing), if a joint tenancy is chosen, this prevents reliance on a constructive trust to vary the shares (*Pankhania v Chandegra* [2012] EWCA Civ 1438, [2013] 3 FCR 16), leaving only severance to deal with changing circumstances.

[5] *Williams v Hensman* (1861) 1 Johnson and Hemming 546; 70 ER 862.

[6] *Jackson v Jackson* (1804) 9 Ves 591; *Wilson v Bell* (1843) 5 Ir Eq Rep 501.

[7] Roughly equal to £431,000 as at 2019.

[8] One Buswell Hensman, another member of this extensive family. This caused a loss of some £201 (£23,753).

[9] P Luther, '*Williams v Hensman* and the Uses of History' (1995) 15 *Legal Studies* 219. This is required reading for those wanting to understand how the case came to be and how it was received in the following years.

interest is the fact that eight people are playing on the stage and that the script will be rewritten to become a classic of property and succession law. In this vein, two preliminary points stand out. First, in seeking to determine the effect of the various and complex transactions of the Hensman children, Vice-Chancellor Sir W Page Wood was required to set out all possible known options for effecting a severance. This was not a story where one or two discrete events occurred. Given the complexity of the transactions, their possible contradictory effect and the number of persons involved, we should not be surprised that the learned judge wanted to spell it out. Who knows whether the Vice-Chancellor wanted to fashion a template for the future, but force of circumstance and the activities of the many limbs of the Hensman family meant that he did.

Secondly, today, at least where land is concerned,[10] a beneficial joint tenancy comprising more than two people is unusual,[11] and so the modern operation of the law of severance is (very often) in an entirely different context from that in which it was most clearly expounded. In the twenty-first century, severance occurs, or is alleged, most commonly following the breakdown of an intimate family relationship in respect of the shared home: *Hensman* was eight siblings disputing ownership of a fund of money. The transformation of the law of severance from a general property doctrine expounded in a case concerning personal property shared by many into a tool for deciding the destination of real property shared by few, and then only because of the mandatory statutory imposition of a trust, might help explain much about the development of common law severance after *Hensman*.[12]

II. THE RATIO

The judgment in *Hensman* was given at a time when law reporting was neither as systematic nor as clear as it is now. As Peter Luther points out, there are differences between the various versions of Page Wood's judgment,[13] and accuracy might have been compromised given that the judgment might have been given extempore, and certainly without much time for reflection.[14] Nevertheless, it is now established, irrespective of doubts expressed prior to the explanatory analysis of *Hensman* given in *Burgess v Rawnsley*,[15] that at

[10] Disputes as to the ownership of land, usually the most valuable property of the deceased, form the vast majority of disputes about the application of the law of severance.

[11] In *City of London BS v Flegg* [1988] AC 54 (HL), the four equitable co-owners of the entirely appropriately named Bleak House were tenants in common. In *Kaki v Kaki* [2015] EWHC 3692 (Ch), there were nine equitable tenants in common, each with an equal share.

[12] For example, two persons in a relationship might not think at all about severance until the relationship has broken down and then it could be too late if one has died. Then we are left with courts trying to find a written notice, or mutual agreement/conduct in their various dealings. Likewise, in these two-party cases, conscious unilateral severance by an act on one's share under *Hensman* is less common. Bankruptcy and forgery might cause it, but it is unlikely that either of the couple is going to specifically mortgage, sell or lease their interest while the relationship persists. Of course, joint tenancies and severance today are not only concerned with land; but that is there most common field of operation.

[13] Luther (n 9) fn 4.

[14] ibid 221. Luther notes that Page Wood often gave extempore judgments (the report of *Hensman* is silent) and that, in any event, there was little time for reflection between hearing and judgment.

[15] *Burgess v Rawnsley* [1975] Ch 429 (CA).

common law there are three distinct methods of severance.[16] To quote Page Wood's oft-cited passage, which, as Luther points out, 'has never been overruled, or even doubted':[17]

> [I]n the first place, an act of any one of the persons interested operating upon his own share may create a severance as to that share. The right of each joint-tenant is a right by survivorship only in the event of no severance having taken place of the share which is claimed under the *jus accrescendi*. Each one is at liberty to dispose of his own interest in such manner as to sever it from the joint fund – losing, of course, at the same time, his own right of survivorship. Secondly, a joint-tenancy may be severed by mutual agreement. And, in the third place, there may be a severance by any course of dealing sufficient to intimate that the interests of all were mutually treated as constituting a tenancy in common.[18]

Burgess, of course, settled the point that *Hensman* had identified three distinct methods of severance: a legally enforceable act operating on one's own share; mutual agreement (whether enforceable[19] or not); and mutual conduct (whether enforceable or not). The *Burgess* clarification settled an argument which suggested that there were but two methods of severance, both of which had to be enforceable beyond effecting a severance: a unilateral method (an act operating on one's own share) and a mutual one (being a mutually enforceable compact, evidenced by agreement or conduct). Indeed, on a simple reading, Page Wood's judgment does not appear to stipulate only two methods of severance, and so it turned out to be. In fact, the objection to mutual conduct as a separate method of severance after *Hensman* (which was the main point of contention) was due largely to objections to a wide principle of 'mutuality' (not any particular expression thereof) on the ground that to be effective, the mutuality had somehow to amount to a legally enforceable event.[20] Hence, so the argument ran, while it was possible that severance could occur by a mutual agreement, because a mutual agreement could be enforceable if it was in writing, clearly mutual conduct could not meet this criterion.[21] This led to the conclusion that severance by mutual conduct could not occur at all.[22] However, once it became clear, as was explained in *Burgess*, that 'mutuality' did not require enforceability,[23] objections to mutual conduct necessarily fell away. So, as well as unilateral severance by legally effective act, we are left with severance by mutual agreement and severance by mutual conduct,

[16] ibid; *Carr v Issard* [2006] 11 WLUK 578.

[17] Luther (n 9) 220.

[18] *Williams v Hensman* (n 5) 557.

[19] 'Enforceable' means having legal effect other than as an act of severance.

[20] The (now rejected) argument was based on a line in *In Re Wilks, Child v Bulmer* [1891] 3 Ch 59, 62, where Stirling J noted that it is 'contended on behalf of the infants that there is no other way in which a joint tenancy can be severed. Without going so far, I think that if the act of a joint tenant amounts to a severance it must be such as to preclude him from claiming by survivorship any interest in the subject-matter of the joint tenancy.' Despite the obvious qualification here ('without going so far'), some decisions, such as that of Walton J in *Nielson-Jones v Fedden* [1975] Ch 222, took the view that severance based on mutuality had to be legally enforceable in the same way as severance based on a unilateral act. That is no longer good law.

[21] Is it possible to argue that today mutual conduct actually could be legally enforceable due to the expansion of the law of constructive trusts in *Stack v Dowden* [2007] UKHL 17, [2007] 2 AC 432, or perhaps even because of proprietary estoppel?

[22] The essence of *Wilks* is lack of mutuality in any form, with one joint tenant forming an intention not agreed to, or acted on, by the other.

[23] *Burgess* (n 15) 439.

neither of the last two needing to be 'enforceable' in the sense of amounting to something whose performance the law would compel. In this sense, both forms of mutual severance are negative in operation: they stop survivorship happening. Severance by reason of an enforceable act operating on one's own share is both negative and positive: it stops survivorship, but it also disposes of property (or at least an interest in it) to a third party.

III. THE LEGACY

More importantly, perhaps, than the nuts and bolts of the ratio decidendi, or indeed the result itself in *Hensman* (which was that there had been acts of severance sufficient to prevent survivorship), the decision led to the identification of some key principles that still ripple through the law of severance. These go beyond the important point that the *Hensman* principles of severance are still in use today,[24] despite the introduction of a 'simple' method of severance by section 36(2) of the Law of Property Act 1925 (LPA 1925).[25]

First, *Hensman* confirms (even without the largely pointless argument about whether it comprises two or three methods of severance) that severance may be unilateral or mutual. Freedom to deal with one's property during life (as wanted by some of the Hensman children) and freedom to dispose of it as one chooses on death can result from individual choice or collective action. Necessarily, however, the consequences are different: unilateral severance leaves any remaining co-owners tied to the joint tenancy; mutual action destroys the joint tenancy for all. Indeed, although it is not spelt out in *Hensman* itself, it is clear that the unilateral and mutual routes (meaning both mutual agreement and mutual conduct) to severance are different in detail and effect, and for good reason. Unilateral severance, through an act operating on own's share, requires an act of alienation in some form or other.[26] It is critical that the act of alienation is legally enforceable, in the sense of being permitted (or caused) by an act valid under the general law, because it affects a person external to the joint tenancy – be that a mortgagee, transferee or creditor.[27] Of course, on a strict view, this method of severance is largely circular (and this might explain

[24] *Wall v Munday* [2018] EWHC 879 (Ch), [2018] 4 WLUK 536 (mutual conduct); *Davis v Smith* [2011] EWCA Civ 1603, [2012] 1 FLR 1177 (mutual agreement); *Barracks v Barracks* [2005] EWHC 3077 (Ch), [2005] 4 WLUK 627 (if in the alternative there had been a joint tenancy, a mortgage was an act operating on one's own share).

[25] Severance by written notice. Issues with this attempt to provide an easy route of a joint tenancy include: questions about what amounts to a written notice (*Quigley v Masterson* [2011] EWHC 2529 (Ch), [2012] 1 P & CR DG8); what amounts to 'written'; what amounts to delivery (*Kinch v Bullard* [1999] 1 WLR 423); and the largely ignored (because it is inconvenient) question arising from the words of s 36(2) as to whether it applies at all when the beneficial and legal owners are not the same people, eg because the statute says 'Provided that, where a legal estate (not being settled land) is vested in joint tenants *beneficially* …' (emphasis added).

[26] And what form is discussed below in section III.B.

[27] In *Hawkesley v May* [1956] 1 QB 304, 313, Havers J says that the first *Hensman* method 'obviously includes a declaration of intention to sever by one party', perhaps implying that a mere declaration (presumably in writing?) without alienation could have this effect. With respect, there is nothing obvious about this interpretation and it rather elides the important 'operating' part of the *Hensman* ratio. In *Hawkesley* itself, the severer both indicated an intention to sever and the 'share' was alienated. There is precious little support elsewhere for the idea that a mere unilateral statement of intent indicating an intention to be severed is sufficient to actually sever within *Hensman*. Why, then, would s 36 LPA 1925 have been necessary?

inconsistency of application), because logically the severer must already have a share in order to alienate a share and thereby cause severance! But recognition of this form of severance is a pragmatic response to a practical situation and validates acts of one of the joint tenants, which technically they had no power to make but on which others might have relied. This is also why the first *Hensman* method is avowedly unilateral – the third party cannot be expected to know that the alienator is a joint tenant and so should not be required to seek the concurrence of other joint tenants.[28] By contrast, mutual severance, whether by 'agreement' or 'conduct', is not an act of alienation and does not affect third parties. It operates only to explode the joint tenancy for the parties to it. In both types of mutual severance, the primary purpose of the joint tenancy (survivorship) is prioritised and cannot be disabled without a clear intention (as manifested either by agreement or conduct), shared by all joint tenants, to bring it to an end. There is no room, or need, for unilateral severance when it comes to agreement or conduct, for there is no risk that a third party will be comprised by the severance (or failure to achieve it). So, if the parties are to escape the ties of a joint tenancy where there is no risk to a third party, they must all intend to end it, and it will end for all of them simultaneously.

Secondly, following from the above, *Williams v Hensman* continues to remind us, in a manner undiminished by time, that the ties of a joint tenancy are not permanent, and that testamentary freedom is not permanently compromised because of the way property was held during life. The joint tenancy is not back-door forced heirship. Crucially, the ability to break the tie does not depend on whether the parties chose a joint tenancy when the property was conveyed to them, or whether (as in *Hensman*) the joint tenancy was imposed by the terms of a gift, devise or bequest. It is equally possible to break out of a joint tenancy through severance, whether the original intention was that of the joint tenants or of another person from whom the property came. This result, which may seem unremarkable, is in fact very remarkable indeed. While there are clear policy reasons for not subjecting those currently entitled to property to the wishes of those who gave them the property and who may be long since departed,[29] a case could be made (even now) that this should not be the position where the joint tenancy is the freely chosen path of the joint tenants themselves. Why should one of A and B, who have, as a result of a well-informed decision and conscious intention, taken property as joint tenants, be permitted to resile from their intention and destroy the agreed destination of property which they have freely entered into? Perhaps severance is understandable if the joint tenancy is the result of someone else's choice (as in *Hensman*), or not really 'chosen' because it arises as a result of a statutory fiction, as where co-owned land is held as joint tenants at law and this statutorily imposed trust leads to a joint tenancy in equity on the basis that 'equity follows the law'. But what if the joint tenancy of property, or of the equitable title of land, is chosen by the parties and effected by those parties in a written instrument? In such cases, in respect of land, the use of a constructive or resulting trust to vary the equitable

[28] Also, of course, the law's preference for facilitating alienation of property supports severance by an act of unilateral alienation.

[29] eg free alienability; perpetuity, distaste of the rule of 'dead hand' of the settlor. The policy is expressed in many ways in common law and statute, eg the rule in *Saunders v Vautier* (1841) Cr & Ph 240; Trusts of Land and Appointment of Trustees Act 1996 (TLATA), s 14.

joint tenancy is not permitted[30] but, incongruously, severance by unilateral act is permitted even though it necessarily deprives the other joint tenants of something very valuable and even though they have expressly agreed to that outcome. In other circumstances – for example, the use of constructive trusts to enforce mutual wills[31] – the parties are held to their intentions, and there is at least one case where one joint tenant was estopped from severing because of assurances that had been given to the other.[32] Indeed, the Janus quality of severance is illustrated by *Roy v Roy*.[33] In this case, land was conveyed to two brothers on a written express equitable joint tenancy. One lived there, the other did not and made very little contribution to its upkeep or running. A notice of severance[34] was given by the absent brother, who sought confirmation of his 50 per cent share.[35] The remaining brother argued that the written declaration did not represent the parties' true intentions and should be rectified. This got short shrift on the ground that the document meant what it said and the parties should be held to the joint tenancy as proven by the written declaration.[36] Then severance was allowed to destroy that intention. The legal reasoning is faultless: the inconsistency is blinding. In *Roy*, severance was effected by a written notice rather than a unilateral act operating on one's own share under *Hensman*. But the point here is powerful irrespective of the method of severance. A court will uphold the parties' intentions when creating an express joint tenancy and will not allow it to be undone by that very expression of equity, the constructive trust; but it will also allow the act of one of them to unilaterally destroy that joint tenancy immediately or at a later date. Far from arguing for the abolition of the joint tenancy,[37] might it not be appropriate to remove the ability to sever an expressly created joint tenancy?

Thirdly, and made explicit in *Hensman* in a way that has affected future cases and our perception of the joint tenancy,[38] there is the sentiment captured in the opening paragraph of Page Wood's judgment. The Vice-Chancellor opens his judgment with the observation that it is the

> unfortunate circumstance that the Legislature has not thought fit to interpose by introducing the rule that express words shall be required to create a joint-tenancy in place of the contrary rule which is established, that words pointing to severalty of interest are necessary to constitute a tenancy in common. Under certain circumstances, as in the case of mortgages of trust money, a joint-tenancy is a considerable convenience; but it would be very desirable that, in general, in the absence of any express direction, a tenancy in common should be the construction adopted.

[30] And proprietary estoppel would be rare, perhaps only where one party has specifically promised not to rely on the written declaration of trust, *Clarke v Meadus* [2010] EWHC 3117 (Ch), [2013] WTLR 199.

[31] *Legg v Burton* [2017] EWHC 2088 (Ch), [2017] 4 WLR 186. See, generally, Ying Liew's chapter in this volume.

[32] *Price v Hartwell* [1996] 6 WLUK 38. This is an interesting case in another respect. The joint tenant who had given the estoppel generating assurance had died, but the third (there were three originally) was held to this assurance even though they had not given it.

[33] *Roy v Roy* [1996] 1 FLR 541. In this case, one brother (of two) sought rectification of an express declaration of joint tenancy on the ground that it did not reflect his true intention.

[34] Under s 36(2) LPA 1925, rather than utilising *Williams v Hensman*.

[35] Because severance operates to give equal shares regardless of who did what and when, save perhaps where there is a clear (written?) agreement to sever to unequal shares.

[36] And *Stack v Dowden* (n 21) would not have helped, given that the declaration was in writing: see *Pankhania v Chandegra* (n 4).

[37] See text immediately below.

[38] See text accompanying n 43 below.

Or, to put it another way, the common law may prefer the certainty of the joint tenancy, but equity favours the tenancy in common: '[t]he thing to remember today is that equity leans against joint tenants and favours tenancies in common'.[39] This expression of policy leads inevitably to the conclusion that, if at all possible, the parties to a joint tenancy should be able to escape the handcuffs through severance, both when they all wish to or when just one of them desires it. Not only has this given rise to a pattern of generosity when it comes to interpreting both the common law[40] and statutory[41] methods of severance, it also led the Law Commission at one time to ask whether the ways to sever should be clarified and liberalised, and even that it be made possible by will.[42] It also encouraged some commentators to take the next logical step and argue, at least in relation to land, that the joint tenancy should be confined to the legal estate and have no role in beneficial interests at all.[43] The idea that the joint tenancy is unfit for purpose has some currency and it might lie behind the step change adopted in *Stack v Dowden*[44] whereby (in the absence of a written declaration) beneficial interests behind a trust of land can be varied through a constructive trust based on the whole course of dealings between the co-owners. The ambulatory constructive trust based on an inferred common intention appears to have many similarities with severance by mutual conduct, save that the result in these constructive trust cases is not usually a tenancy in common in equal shares. However, while it is self-evident that the joint tenancy can cause difficulties and unfairness, let us remember that this is always an ex post facto assessment in the light of events which have occurred, rather than those that must have occurred. The joint tenancy, with the right of survivorship, undoubtedly can distort testamentary freedom and succession, but only because it turned out like that. The marriage or relationship was not doomed to fail; the family arrangement between siblings was sensible at the time it was created; the testator actually meant the beneficiaries to benefit for life, with the survivor obtaining the whole. So, it is not that the joint tenancy is inherently objectionable; it just might look like that as things turned out. There are, in fact, many advantages to a joint tenancy, which is why it was chosen as the only way in which legal title to land could be co-owned.[45] The point is that, looking backwards, the joint tenancy can appear to be unfair for one party. But we should remember, first, that for every loser in survivorship, there is a winner who might reasonably be said to have got exactly what they deserved; and secondly, that retrospection is not a sound basis for law reform. We should be wary of dispensing with a concept simply because, as things turned out, it operated detrimentally.

[39] *Burgess v Rawnsley* (n 15) 438 (Lord Denning). Despite this criticism in *Hensman*, the legislature was not persuaded, for in 1925 it made joint tenancy the only way of holding the legal title to land – precisely because of the 'considerable convenience' it offered.

[40] As in *Burgess* itself and *Hunter v Babbage* (1995) 69 P & CR 548.

[41] *Quigley* (n 22); *Kinch* (n 25).

[42] Law Commission, *Trusts of Land* (Law Com No 94, 1985). To this author, the possibility of severance by will seems bizarre, not to say illogical. It would necessarily remove the very heart of the joint tenancy.

[43] M Thompson, 'Beneficial Joint Tenancies: A Case for Abolition?' [1987] *Conveyancer & Property Lawyer* 29. See also L Tee, 'Severance Revisited' [1995] *Conveyancer & Property Lawyer* 105.

[44] *Stack v Dowden* (n 21).

[45] LPA 1925, s 36(1). That said, given the now near universality of guaranteed registered title, would it be unwise to reintroduce the legal tenancy in common?

IV. SEVERANCE: LINGERING PROBLEMS

Williams v Hensman might represent the *locus classicus* of common law severance,[46] but obviously it did not and could not deal with all eventualities. Couched, as it was, in general and conceptual terms, it gives us a template, but not always an answer.[47] Necessarily, of course, not every problem is foreseeable and times change. What was common when *Hensman* was decided – for example, complex family settlements – is less common now, and different eras bring different challenges. Although this author regards the joint tenancy as offering a valuable alternative to the tenancy in common, it is right to ask whether it should be used only where it is expressly adopted. In relation to land, we should not forget that the incidence of land ownership is fundamentally different from that which obtained in 1925, let alone when *Hensman* was decided. Land ownership is no longer the preserve of the relative few and it is rarely tied up in complex trust relationships. Co-ownership of land is common, but it is not generally multi-party. Land – the home – is very likely to be the family's greatest financial asset and the question needs to be asked whether the joint tenancy is a suitable vehicle for dealing with it. This is particularly so if a joint tenancy in equity really is the default option in the absence of a written declaration of trust, which worry is only aggravated by the relative lack of such written declarations. How suitable is the joint tenancy in modern family relations, where the home-owning couple might have children or dependants from a previous relationship who themselves are expecting, needing or intended to be looked after from the estate of one of the co-owners? The joint tenancy is simple, convenient, efficient, dangerous, distorting and powerful. And some very modern problems remain.

A. A Failure of Advice

Much that is good about the joint tenancy, and which therefore reflects on the law of severance, presupposes that the parties know what a joint tenancy is and that they are entering into one. The value of the joint tenancy largely supposes that the parties have chosen to utilise it and welcome the right of survivorship that it brings. However, in respect of land, while legal title to co-owned land must be held under a joint tenancy, the parties are free to choose the nature of their co-ownership in equity. Yet they rarely do so deliberately, even though there is now a Land Registry form on which new owners can declare the nature and extent of their equitable ownership. This is why, in far too many cases, we are left with 'equity following the law'. In turn, this leads us to disputed cases of severance where we see the judiciary bending over backwards to find a severance so that the parties can escape from the unintended consequences of a joint tenancy. It also, perhaps, played a major part in the development of the ambulatory constrictive trust in *Stack v Dowden*: if the parties have not severed,[48] perhaps they never were joint

[46] Luther (n 9) 219. See also n 2 above.

[47] This was recognised with the enactment of s 36(2) LPA 1925, which was intended to provide a clean and simple route to severance. Of course, s 36(2) has its own problems.

[48] Assuming – a weak assumption – that the parties knew they could or should.

tenants in equity (or not for long) because of the redistributive effect of a post-acquisition common intention constructive trust that has the effect of varying the parties' equitable interests. Consequently, if the joint tenancy is to survive as an alternative to the tenancy in common (which this author would support), those giving advice on the acquisition of co-owned land and those advising on the drafting of testamentary trusts for the benefit of others must explain adequately what these two forms of co-ownership mean. This cannot be done properly by 'one-stop-shop', telephone only, supermarket conveyancers. Getting it right, rather than getting it cheap might prevent parties from drifting into a relationship of joint tenancy that they did not intend and then trying to force their way out of it through severance. Even then, those giving advice must be prepared to give it. If professionals cannot raise difficult personal issues with their clients about death and survivorship, inheritance and succession, then disputed severances will not diminish. Nor will professional indemnity claims. If we are to keep the joint tenancy and only allow severance in (relatively) clearly defined circumstances, our property professionals need to consider consciously what a joint tenancy or tenancy in common means for their clients and advise accordingly. Making presumptions about what they might or should want is not good enough.

B. An Act of Alienation On One's Own Share: What Act?

One of the significant achievements of *Williams v Hensman* is that it establishes a route to unilateral severance at common law. Despite some minority support for the contrary, which is now of historical interest only, the unilateral act which achieves severance has to be legally enforceable under the general law. As explained above, there are good policy reasons for this. But there are still doubts as to what might amount to an enforceable act sufficient to establish severance. We all know that an assignment,[49] a mortgage[50] and bankruptcy[51] will effect a severance. But what of a lease or the written declaration of a sub-trust? The former raises significant problems, not least because of an apparent conflict between partial alienation by the potentially severing owner[52] and exclusive possession.[53] The latter would create an entangled relationship whose practical manifestation would be complex to say the least.[54] Further, it is clear that not every act of one of the joint tenants is even potentially capable of effecting a partial alienation and thereby a severance: for example, one joint tenant cannot activate a break clause in a fixed-term lease.[55] And even with a mortgage (an apparently obvious example of an act operating

[49] As in *Williams* itself.

[50] *Ahmed v Kendrick* [1988] 2 FLR 22.

[51] *Re Dennis (A Bankrupt)* [1996] Ch 80.

[52] For a comprehensive analysis of severance by partial alienation see B Crown, 'Severance of Joint Tenancy of Land by Partial Alienation' (2001) 117 *LQR* 477.

[53] For an analysis of all possibilities see L Fox, 'Unilateral Demise by a Joint Tenant: Does It Effect a Severance?' [2008] *Conveyancer & Property Lawyer* 208.

[54] See, eg *Creasey v Sole* [2013] EWHC 1410 (Ch), [2013] 5 WLUK 645, where a person holding an interest under a co-ownership sub-trust was held not to have an interest in land sufficient to establish a right of occupation.

[55] *Hammersmith and Fulham LBC v Monk* [1992] 1 AC 478.

on one's share), there is now the complication of registered title. When one joint tenant forges the signature of the other on a mortgage deed,[56] the conventional analysis is that the potential legal mortgage is invalid for the lack of consent of one of the legal owners, but that it operates over the equitable share (if any[57]) of the co-owner actually consenting. This, in turn, is a severance by reason of a legally enforceable act operating on one's own share, being an equitable mortgage of their share by the co-owner who did genuinely consent.[58] What, however, is the effect of title guarantee on this result, for under *Swift 1st v Chief Land Registrar*[59] the mortgage is valid while registered, even if apparently void for lack of consent? Does it mean that no severance can take place until the register is rectified by removing the defective legal charge? And, if so, does the removal that causes the severance relate back to the time of the lack of consent or is it effective only when rectification is ordered?[60] This could well be critical if one of the parties has died.

C. Severance and Ambulatory Resulting and Constructive Trusts

It is now established that where land is acquired on the basis of a default joint tenancy in equity – that is, where the equitable interest is not expressly declared in writing and there is no reason to disapply the presumption that equity follows the law – then either party can deploy the resulting or (more usually) the constructive trust in order to cause a variation of the parties' entitlement. There might be some disagreement after *Stack v Dowden* as to the precise circumstances in which the ambulatory constructive trust can arise,[61] but we know it can, and that it can vary the shares of the equitable owners. However, what we do not know is the precise relationship of this post-acquisition constructive trust to the law of severance. For example, in *Jones v Kernott*[62] the end result was an uneven distribution of the equitable interest in the land because of the constructive trust, but there is obscurity about when a severance of the parties' joint tenancy took place, or even the course it took. Indeed, were the parties ever joint tenants in equity in *Kernott*? If they were, did the parties sever to create equal shares, which were then varied by the constructive trust, or was there a severance to inequality? Did severance occur (if needed) at the start of the parties' relationship, sometime during its course, at its end or when the court

[56] Or the consent of the co-owner is vitiated for some other reason, such as duress, misrepresentation or undue influence.

[57] *Abbey National v Stringer* [2006] 2 P & CR DG15.

[58] See *Ahmed* (n 50); *First National Bank v Achampong* [2004] 1 FCR 18.

[59] *Swift 1st v Chief Land Registrar* [2015] EWCA Civ 330, [2015] Ch 602.

[60] The present author takes the view that there cannot be severance until the defective mortgage is removed from the register because, up until then, there is no valid legal act operating on one's share. The removal from the register creates the equitable charge, which severs the joint tenancy. Logically, therefore, it should be the date of rectification that matters for severance, not the date of the defective charge. But nothing is certain in a court of equity, and rectification of the register can have a retrospective effect: *Gold Harp Properties v Macleod* [2014] EWCA Civ 1084, [2015] 1 WLR 1249.

[61] The present author takes the view that *Marr v Collie* [2017] UKPC 17, [2018] AC 631 establishes that a court must search for either a real intention as to a resulting trust or a real common intention as to a constructive trust from the evidence it has before it. More particularly, a court cannot presume either intention because they fit a preconceived type of case where such intention usually arises.

[62] *Jones v Kernott* [2011] UKSC 53, [2012] 1 AC 776.

made an order about the size of the shares? And, just for interest, which of the methods of severance was it? It could be mutual agreement or mutual conduct, as neither event is required to be externally enforceable, but could it even have been an act operating on one's share (a declaration of an equitable interest by constructive trust)? Of course, in both *Stack* and *Kernott* the issue of severance per se was irrelevant as both parties were still alive, there was no third-party interest and the court simply confirmed a tenancy in common when it identified the respective shares of the parties. But what if one had died before the decision of the court? Would it matter when they died? Would, say, Ms Jones's share have been less if she had died early? More radically, would there even have been severance if Mr Kernott had died? *Williams v Hensman* cannot answer these questions, but its application alongside the law of resulting and constructive trusts is going to generate a whole new set of problems.[63]

V. CONCLUSION

Williams v Hensman is not the only source of the law of severance. Although it is likely that the defects in the common law as expounded in *Hensman* played a role in prompting the legislature to enact section 36(2) LPA 1925, the statute and the common law do not overlap. Likewise, severance caused by unlawful killing[64] is neither unilateral or mutual, but the result of the application of clear public policy. Neither is *Hensman* the last word on common law severance, nor was it the first. Yet there is no denying that *Hensman* has left a vibrant legacy, with a judgment that has never been doubted or distinguished. It has been the purpose of this analysis to examine that legacy. We have seen that it is impossible to disentangle the legacy from the concept of the joint tenancy to which it relates. We have seen also that whether an act of severance produces a 'good' or a 'bad' result depends entirely on the context. Severance is a creature of its context and it takes its colour from that context. It is both a boon and a bane. It looks back to intentions existing at the time the joint tenancy was created and it looks forward to those that exist at the time of dispute. It can both support and destroy those intentions. It is a Janus concept. *Williams v Hensman* has left a legacy; but it is a chameleon.

[63] See, generally, M Pawlowski and J Brown, 'Co-ownership and Severance after *Stack*' (2013) 27 *Trust Law International* 59.

[64] *Dunbar v Plant* [1998] Ch 412 (CA).

9

Birmingham v Renfrew (1937): The Foundations of the Mutual Wills Doctrine

YING KHAI LIEW*

I. BACKGROUND

ALEXANDER RENFREW (ALEXANDER) was born in Lanarkshire, Scotland in 1858. On 27 June 1874 he embarked the ship *Cartvale*, along with his brother John and sister-in-law Christina, setting sail for Wellington, New Zealand. They arrived on 11 November.[1] After having worked on several sheep stations for five years, Alexander travelled to Melbourne, and lived in Fitzroy from 1879[2] until his death.

Alexander gained much societal standing in Melbourne. In 1894 he was elected to the Fitzroy Council for the East Ward, a position he held for 30 years. He served as mayor of the City of Fitzroy between 1895 and 1897. Among his numerous contributions, he was a member of the Metropolitan Board of Works for 20 years and a foundation member of the Fitzroy, Northcote and Preston Tramway Trust. So significant was he to the local community that a committee was formed to arrange for a recognition of his services when he retired in 1929.[3]

Between his retirement and his death, Alexander was a 'furniture warehouseman'[4] who 'owned a furniture business in Fitzroy and two-thirds interest in the Bon Stores'.[5] The last mentioned was presumably Miller's Bon Store Pty Ltd, a company set up in Melbourne

* I thank Michael Bryan and Brian Sloan for comments on an earlier draft. I am also grateful to Harrie Bantick and Robin Gardner at the MLS Academic Research Service, and Stefan Prelevic for research assistance.

[1] Hutt City, 'Petone Settlers Data' www.huttcity.govt.nz/Leisure--Culture/Museums-and-galleries/Our-museums/petone-settlers-data/DisplayPerson/?Id=36944&SearchString=renfrew&Page=1&searchYear=1874.

[2] 'Councillor's Retirement' *The Argus* (Melbourne, 20 August 1929) 7.

[3] 'The Local Tramway Trust' *Preston Leader* (Melbourne, 30 November 1918) 2; 'Councillor's Retirement' *The Argus* (Melbourne, 20 August 1929) 7; 'Appreciation of Mr A Renfrew' *The Herald* (Melbourne, 8 November 1929) 18.

[4] '£45,000 Will Contested: Claim by Family' *The Herald* (Melbourne, 8 February 1937) 3.

[5] '£45,000 Involved in Will Dispute: Breach of Agreement Alleged' *The Argus* (Melbourne, 6 February 1937) 21.

on 16 March 1927, bearing the description 'furniture dealers and manufacturers' and having a capital at that date of £100,000.[6]

Alexander died on 25 May 1931, aged 74,[7] with no record found of him having married or having any offspring. He did, however, have eight nephews and nieces, who were all children of John and Christina.

In his last will, probate of which was granted to The Trustees Executors and Agency Co Ltd on 15 December 1931,[8] Alexander left the residue of his estate to Grace Alexandra Russell (Grace),[9] one of his nieces. The residue was valued at around £60,000 at the time of his death.[10] This generous bequest was perhaps motivated by the fact that Grace was 'at one time his housekeeper'.[11]

After Alexander's death, a relative of Grace's, one Jack Miller, claimed that Alexander promised to leave him part of the Bon Store, valued at £25,000. Grace unthinkingly accepted the claim, but later sorely regretted doing so. She engaged Corr & Corr, the Renfrew family's solicitors, to deal with the potential legal consequences of her change of mind; but even then, it caused her a great deal of anxiety.

Grace was married to Joseph Garrett Russell (Jack, as he was known),[12] to whom she was 'very devoted'.[13] In order to ensure that no further trouble would arise in relation to her own will,[14] and believing also that it was Alexander's intention that his bequest should remain in the Renfrew family,[15] Grace entered into a mutual wills agreement with Jack. Grace and Jack had no children.

Pursuant to this agreement, on 1 April 1932 Grace executed a will and codicil prepared by Alan Manson Corr (Alan) of Corr & Corr. She named Jack as executor and trustee, and after directing payment of certain annuities and making certain bequests and devises, gave the residue of her estate to Jack if he survived her, and otherwise to Alexander Renfrew Jr (Alexander Jr),[16] Elsie Eliza Mabel Renfrew (Elsie), Catherine Fulton Johnston (Catherine) and William Alexander Johnston (William). Similar terms were contained in Jack's will, also prepared by Alan and executed on 31 March 1932: after providing for the payment of his debts, funeral and other expenses, the residue of Jack's estate was left to Grace, and if Grace predeceased him, to Alexander Jr, Elsie, Catherine

[6] 'New Companies' *Daily Commercial News and Shipping List* (Sydney, 21 March 1927) 4.

[7] 'Deaths' *The Argus* (Melbourne, 26 May 1931) 1.

[8] Public Record Office Victoria (PROV), VPRS 268/P0000 Transcripts of Appeal to the Privy Council (1901–1903), High Court of Australia (1903–?1950), Unit 20, File 737, *Birmingham v Renfrew*, 'Probate of Will of Alexander Renfrew (senior)', Transcript, 228.

[9] Or 'Gracie', perhaps a term of endearment, which appears in the advertisement of Alexander's death in 'Deaths' (n 7).

[10] '£45,000 Will Contested' (n 4).

[11] '£45,000 Involved in Will Dispute' (n 5).

[12] PROV, VPRS 267/P0002 Civil Case Files, Unit 296, 1935/830, *Renfrew v Birmingham*, 'Transcript of Evidence of Percival James Palmer', [90].

[13] PROV (ibid) 'Transcript of Evidence of Mrs Amy Louisa Ellen Palmer', [162].

[14] PROV (ibid) 'Transcript of Evidence of Percival James Palmer', [16]–[19]; see PROV (n 8) Transcript, 172.

[15] '£45,000 Involved in Will Dispute' (n 5); '£45,000 Will Contested' (n 4).

[16] PROV, VPRS 267/P0002 Civil Case Files, Unit 341, 1938/779, *Renfrew v Birmingham (No 2)*. While the judgments cite this individual as 'Alexander Renfrew', it is clear from the case files that he in fact identified himself as Alexander Renfrew Jr.

and William. Alexander Jr was Grace's brother, who was married to Elsie.[17] Catherine was Grace's sister[18] and the mother of William.[19]

Jack was, financially speaking, unsuccessful. As a 'fruiterer and confectioner', he was declared insolvent in 1902 due to 'insufficient capital, pressure of creditors, and dulness of trade', with an outstanding debt of £85/14s/1d.[20] At the time of Grace's death Jack was described as 'a leading bookmaker';[21] a witness had described him as 'an abstemious man [who] liked the good things in life';[22] and at his death he was described as 'penniless'.[23]

On 5 April 1932 Grace and Jack embarked on a 'pleasure trip' to the UK, even though neither of them was in good health,[24] because Grace wanted to get away from 'a great deal of upset' caused by the episode involving Jack Miller.[25] Having spent a month in London and then a week in Leeds, they eventually went to Wales, where Grace died of pneumonia in Llandudno on 26 July 1932.[26]

Grace left personal property valued at £62,296/11s/3d. Of this, £56,990 represented her interest as residuary beneficiary under Alexander's will. Alexander's will remained unadministered at the time of Grace's death,[27] but his estate included 'considerable real estate consisting principally of suburban properties producing rent and valued at £23,300 or thereabouts'.[28] Jack was granted probate of Grace's will and codicil on 10 November 1932.

Alexander's estate was subsequently administered, and on 30 June 1933 Jack received 13 properties from Alexander's executor in his capacity as executor of Grace's will.[29] These comprised the following:

In Fitzroy:

1. A modern one-storey brick factory;
2. A two-storey brick building and a four-room 'W.B.' (presumably 'winter barn'?) cottage;
3. A three-room brick dwelling and a two-storey brick shop and dwelling;
4. Two two-storey brick shop and dwellings;
5. A two-storey brick residence;
6. A brick garage and workshop;
7. A two-storey brick shop and factory;

[17] Australian Imperial Force, 'Attestation Paper of Persons Enlisted for Service Abroad' (5 July 1915) https://recordsearch.naa.gov.au/SearchNRetrieve/Interface/ViewImage.aspx?B=8027961&S=1.
[18] 'Deaths' *The Argus* (Melbourne, 29 July 1932) 1.
[19] *Renfrew v Birmingham* (1937) VLR 180 (VSC) 181. William was a minor at the time the action was brought; his next friend was William Johnston, his father.
[20] 'New Insolvents' *The Argus* (Melbourne, 20 February 1902) 4.
[21] 'Presbyterian Hotel' *The Argus* (Melbourne, 9 November 1932) 6.
[22] PROV (n 12) 'Transcript of Evidence of Percival James Palmer' [74].
[23] '£45,000 Involved in Will Dispute' (n 5).
[24] PROV (n 12) 'Transcript of Evidence of Mrs Amy Louisa Ellen Palmer' [154], [157]; 'Transcript of Evidence of Percival James Palmer' [31], [33].
[25] PROV (ibid) 'Transcript of Evidence of Mrs Amy Louisa Ellen Palmer' [156], [167]–[169].
[26] 'Deaths' (n 18); 'Presbyterian Hotel' (n 21).
[27] *Birmingham v Renfrew* (1937) 57 CLR 666 (HCA) 682. Which perhaps explains why she did not simply make Jack a tenant for life with remainder to her intended relatives.
[28] PROV (n 16) 'Affidavit of Alexander Renfrew Jr and Alan Manson Corr' [6].
[29] PROV (n 8) Transcript, 167.

In Footscray:

8. A two-storey brick warehouse and a single storey 'of wood and iron';
9. A two-storey building;
10. A two-storey building;
11. Three brick shops each with four-room dwellings; and

In Elwood:

12. A brick villa.

These properties also devolved to Jack in his personal capacity as residuary beneficiary under Grace's will.

The thirteenth property, used as a warehouse for many years and valued at £2,000, was given by Grace to the Presbyterian Church of Victoria to be used as a hostel or school in honour of Alexander.[30] (The Alexander Renfrew Presbyterian Girls' Hostel began operating on 29 June 1935 and in 1940 it was described as 'impressive', where 'the girls seemed happy and well cared for'.[31])

After Grace's death, Jack executed new wills on 13 October 1932, 29 March 1934 and 11 March 1935, each progressively departing from the mutual wills agreement.

On 20 March 1935 Jack died due to illness with his bowel and liver.[32] He had not fully administered Grace's estate. Jack's estate was valued at £45,461,[33] of which £43,172/7s represented the value of his interest as residuary beneficiary under Grace's will. His last will was admitted to probate on 31 May 1935, which appointed Alexander Jr and Alan as executors and trustees, with benefits going predominantly to seven of his own relatives, having almost completely written out Grace's relatives.

On 20 December 1935 Alexander Jr, Elsie, Catherine and William commenced an action against Jack's seven relatives, and Alan in his capacity as Jack's executor, in the Supreme Court of Victoria for the enforcement of what was argued to be a binding mutual wills agreement – that Jack had agreed not to revoke his will dated 31 March 1932 and therefore that Jack's executors were bound to distribute Jack's residuary estate to the beneficiaries originally so named.

II. IN THE SUPREME COURT

At first instance the plaintiffs argued, first, that Jack's will was made under a binding promise, consideration from Grace being provided in the form of her making her last will; and second, that Jack had accepted the benefits under Grace's will.[34] They claimed four remedies as alternatives: specific enforcement of the agreement between Joseph and Grace; a declaration that Jack's executors held Jack's estate on trust for them (presumably

[30] 'Hostel Gift to Church' *The Herald* (Melbourne, 4 July 1935) 10; PROV (n 8) Transcript, 243.
[31] 'Victorian Welfare Workers' *Advocate* (Tasmania, 22 February 1940) 7.
[32] PROV (n 8) Transcript, 237.
[33] PROV (n 16) 'Answers of the Abovenamed Defendant Alan Manson Corr to the Interrogatories for his Examination', [1](a).
[34] *Renfrew v Birmingham* (n 19) 184.

on the basis that Jack, during his lifetime, held the same on trust); payment out of Jack's estate for loss and damage they suffered; and a declaration that Jack (and hence his executors) held the residue under Grace's will on trust to leave whatever was left of the residue by will.[35]

The defendants' case was that such an agreement did not exist, and that even if it did it was unenforceable due to section 128 of the (now replaced) Instruments Act 1928 and section 53 of the Property Law Act 1928.[36] These respectively provided that a contract concerning an interest in land must be in signed writing, and that a declaration of trust concerning an interest in land must be manifested and proved by signed writing.

On 22 March 1937 Gavan Duffy J handed down a judgment in favour of the plaintiffs.[37] On the evidence, the judge found that Jack and Grace did enter into the relevant agreement, and therefore that there was an 'enforceable contract'.[38] He held that section 128 of the Instruments Act 1928 did not apply because, at the time the contract was entered into, all Grace had was a residuary interest under Alexander's will and not an interest in land.[39] Alternatively, relying on the doctrine of secret trusts, the judge considered that 'the equitable principle illustrated by such cases as *McCormick v Grogan*[40] applied', namely that Jack induced Grace to leave her residue to him by way of a clear undertaking but, having received the residue, then failed to carry out the promise which induced the disposition.[41] Holding further that Grace held the benefit of the contract on trust for the plaintiffs,[42] Gavan Duffy J ordered further submissions to be made as to whether the appropriate award ought to be one of damages, specific performance or an order for payment out of Jack's net estate.[43]

III. IN THE HIGH COURT

The appeal by the defendants to the High Court, based on substantially the same grounds as they had raised in the Supreme Court, was unanimously dismissed by Latham CJ, Dixon J and Evatt J. Each judge gave a reasoned judgment. From these, two substantive points of agreement and two crucial points of divergence emerge.

The points of agreement can be stated briefly. First, their Honours agreed that a mutual wills arrangement is binding only where there is clear and satisfactory evidence of a binding agreement, and any evidence should be treated with caution.[44] Secondly, they agreed that the statutory formality requirements were no bar to the outcome. In relation to the contractual formality requirement, both Latham CJ and Dixon J agreed with Gavan Duffy J's reasoning, namely that the contract was not one relating to land.[45]

[35] *Birmingham v Renfrew* (n 27) 668.
[36] *Renfrew v Birmingham* (n 19) 184.
[37] ibid.
[38] ibid 186.
[39] ibid 187–88.
[40] *McCormick v Grogan* (1867) 1 IR Eq 313.
[41] *Renfrew v Birmingham* (n 19) 188.
[42] ibid 189.
[43] ibid 190.
[44] *Birmingham v Renfrew* (n 27) 674–75, 681–82, 692.
[45] ibid 679–80, 690–91.

In relation to the formality requirement for the creation of a trust, Latham CJ (the only judge who explicitly dealt with this point) held that the trust enforced was not an express trust, but a constructive trust falling within the exception of section 53(2) of the Property Law Act 1928.

Significantly, however, Latham CJ and Dixon J differed in their views of the underlying rationale of the mutual wills doctrine and the appropriate remedy. These differences were left unresolved in Evatt J's judgment, due to its lack of engagement with these points.[46]

In Latham CJ's judgment, his Honour noted a number of 'obvious prima facie difficulties' in giving effect to a mutual wills agreement, namely that the plaintiffs were not parties to the contract, that the contract did not create a trust on its terms and that Jack was not prevented from dealing with the property received from Grace during his lifetime 'so that any trust which was created can only be a kind of floating trust which finally attaches to such property as he leaves upon his death'.[47] Yet, skirting these difficulties, his Honour went on to state that 'it is not necessary for any court at the present day to concern itself with the difficulties in legal theory which the simultaneous recognition of these principles may involve'.[48] Instead, relying purely on past authorities, chiefly *Dufour v Pereira*,[49] his Honour concluded that the order made by Gavan Duffy J was appropriate, namely a declaration that Grace had 'entered into the alleged agreement as trustee for and on behalf of the plaintiffs and that the agreement is binding upon and enforceable against the executors of [Jack]'.[50]

In stark contrast, Dixon J fully engaged with the rationale underlying mutual wills. His Honour held that there was a long-established rule 'that a contract between persons to make corresponding wills gives rise to equitable obligations when one acts on the faith of such an agreement and dies leaving his will unrevoked so that the other takes property under its dispositions'.[51] The doctrine came 'under the equitable jurisdiction for the prevention of fraud', and the secret trusts cases of *Blackwell v Blackwell*[52] and *McCormick v Grogan*[53] were cited as examples of this jurisdiction.[54]

In terms of remedy, Dixon J held that it was the survivor – Jack – who became 'a constructive trustee', on the terms of which were contained in 'the will which he undertook would be his last will'.[55] Despite referring to the agreement as a 'contract' throughout the judgment, his Honour held that '[i]t is the constructive trust and not the contract that [the plaintiffs] are entitled to enforce'.[56]

Dixon J also had much to say about the practical and theoretical effects of a binding mutual wills agreement. During Grace's lifetime, Jack was bound not to revoke his will without notice to her.[57] If Grace had died without altering her will (which she did),

[46] ibid 691–92.
[47] ibid 675.
[48] ibid 676.
[49] *Dufour v Pereira* (1769) 1 Dick 419; 21 ER 332.
[50] *Birmingham v Renfrew* (n 27) 677.
[51] ibid 683.
[52] *Blackwell v Blackwell* [1929] AC 318 (HL).
[53] *McCormick v Grogan* (n 40).
[54] *Birmingham v Renfrew* (n 27) 688.
[55] ibid 683.
[56] ibid 690.
[57] ibid 682.

then Jack would be bound not to revoke his will at all.[58] Jack's obligation after Grace's death was described as 'a floating obligation, suspended … during [his] lifetime … [and] descend[ing] upon the assets at his death and crystallis[ing] into a trust'.[59] While full enjoyment for his own benefit was allowed, he could not make any gifts which were 'calculated to defeat the intention of the compact'.[60]

In May 1938 the Judicial Committee of the Privy Council refused a petition for special leave to appeal by two of Jack's relatives.[61]

IV. IMPACT

At the time the case was decided, *Birmingham* did not have any immediate impact on the law. In Australia, it was not until 1979 that *Birmingham* was even cited in a mutual wills case,[62] with three previous citations having been made in completely different contexts.[63] Similarly, the first citation of *Birmingham* by an English court was made in the context of secret trusts,[64] and it was only in 1980 that it was cited in a mutual wills case.[65]

A survey of the relevant practitioners' texts existing at the time *Birmingham* was decided also reveals the lack of immediate impact of the case. For example, comparisons between the 7th (1930) and 8th (1951) editions of *Jarman on Wills*,[66] the 12th (1930) and 13th (1953) editions of *Williams on Executors*[67] and the 13th (1928) and 14th (1939) editions of *Lewin on Trusts*[68] reveal no significant change in the law, with a surprising lack of any citation of *Birmingham* in the latter editions of those texts.

Quantitatively, a significant difference emerges in relation to the citation count between England and Australia. As of 14 June 2019, *Birmingham* has been cited around 100 times by Australian courts, in contrast to a mere 10 times by English judges.

It would be tempting, but wrong, to surmise from the above that the decision in *Birmingham* has had a muted impact on the law, either in general or in English law. The lack of immediate impact of the case can be explained on the basis that it was only in

[58] ibid 682–83.

[59] ibid 689.

[60] ibid.

[61] 'Privy Council Decision: Leave to Appeal Refused' *The Argus* (Melbourne, 26 May 1938) 4.

[62] *Staib v Powell* [1979] Qd R 151.

[63] *Purves v Smith* [1944] VLR 186, in the context of floating charges; *Dixon v White* (NSWSC, unreported, 14 April 1982) BC8211705 and *Last v Rosenfeld* (1972) 2 NSWLR 923, both in the context of formality requirements.

[64] *Ottaway v Norman* [1972] 1 Ch 698 (Ch).

[65] *Re Cleaver* (deceased) [1981] 1 WLR 939 (Ch). Indeed, *Birmingham* was not even cited in a number of English mutual wills cases decided shortly after the High Court's decision: see, eg *Re Marsland* [1939] Ch 820 (CA); *Re Green* [1951] Ch 148 (Ch).

[66] T Jarman, *A Treatise on Wills*, 7th edn (London, Sweet & Maxwell, 1930); T Jarman, *A Treatise on Wills*, 8th edn (London, Sweet & Maxwell, 1951).

[67] DH Parry and J Cherry, *A Treatise on the Law of Executors and Administrators*, 12th edn (London, Stevens, 1930); DH Parry and DC Potter, *A Treatise on the Law of Executors and Administrators*, 13th edn (London, Stevens & Sons, 1953).

[68] W Banks, *Lewin's Practical Treatise on the Law of Trusts*, 13th edn (London, Sweet & Maxwell, 1928); RI Henty and JPL Redfern, *Lewin's Practical Treatise on the Law of Trusts*, 14th edn (London, Sweet & Maxwell, 1939).

1981 'that any major litigation occurred, either in the United Kingdom or Australia, on mutual wills'.[69] As for the lack of citation by English courts, this can be explained on the basis that the adoption of the principles in *Birmingham* by English judgments has dispensed with the necessity of citing the case directly – a case which is, after all, not immediately binding on English courts.

Upon closer inspection, *Birmingham* is not only a landmark case, but also a foundational case in relation to the mutual wills doctrine. This is not meant to suggest that it was the first case which established the doctrine. Rather, much like laying the secure foundations of a building, *Birmingham* has supplied three central 'pillars' upon which the doctrine has gradually been built upon, and upon which the future development of the doctrine can securely be based. The three 'pillars' are: the interaction between 'contract' and equity; the meaning of 'contract'; and the rationale of the mutual wills doctrine.

A. Contract and Equity

The very first mutual wills case decided in English law was *Dufour v Pereira*,[70] and even in that case a mutual wills agreement was described as a 'contract'. To quote Lord Camden:

> It is a contract between the parties, which cannot be rescinded, but by the consent of both. The first that dies, carries his part of the contract into execution. Will the Court afterwards permit the other to break the contract? Certainly not.[71]

The same language was employed by all the judges involved in the *Birmingham* litigation, with the plaintiffs having argued that the agreement between Grace and Jack constituted an enforceable contract.[72]

But it is also abundantly clear from the *Birmingham* judgments and other case law that the mutual wills doctrine is not simply a common law contractual doctrine: equity also plays a significant role. A relevant question, therefore, is how contract and equity interact; the resolution of this will have significant practical and theoretical implications on how the doctrine is understood and applied.

It is first useful to distinguish between equity's concurrent jurisdiction and its exclusive jurisdiction. The former relates to cases where one has a right at common law but nevertheless seeks a remedy in equity which the common law cannot provide; the latter describes cases where one's only right is equitable.[73] Although the origin of this distinction is found in the historical interaction between courts of common law and those of Chancery, it remains a helpful analytical tool.

[69] K Mackie, 'Recent Developments in the Law Relating to Mutual Wills' (1997) 5(2) *Australian Property Law Journal* 95.

[70] *Dufour v Pereira* (n 49).

[71] ibid 333.

[72] *Renfrew v Birmingham* (n 19) 184.

[73] See L Smith, 'Common Law and Equity in R3RUE' (2011) 68 *Washington and Lee Law Review* 1185, 1194–95. A third jurisdiction is the auxiliary jurisdiction, which refers to pretrial procedure. See also M Macnair, 'Equity and Conscience' (2007) 27 *OJLS* 659, 664–66.

As an example, compare constructive trusts which arise in the context of specifically enforceable contracts of sale and those which arise to enforce secret trusts. The former reflects equity's concurrent jurisdiction, while the latter reflects its exclusive jurisdiction.[74] Impliedly, it is a precondition of the former, and not the latter, that the parties must have entered into a valid contract for equity to intervene:[75] the reason is that the parties must first have a common law relationship in order to engage equity's concurrent jurisdiction. For the same reason, the contract in the former context must also be specifically enforceable:[76] only then can it be said that common law damages are an inadequate remedy, justifying the imposition of a constructive trust. And because in the former context the constructive trust has an ancillary role, courts must ensure that they do not overstep the common law jurisdiction, which explains why there are 'bars' which may prevent contracts from being specifically enforceable, which likewise prevent constructive trusts from arising.

In relation to mutual wills, the crucial question is: by virtue of which jurisdiction does the constructive trust arise? While Latham CJ's judgment reflects an understanding of the doctrine as falling within equity's concurrent jurisdiction, Dixon J's views reflect equity as operating within its exclusive jurisdiction. Dixon J's decision has proved to have contributed most significantly towards our modern understanding of the doctrine. This point can be made by exploring four areas of distinction between the 'concurrent jurisdiction' and 'exclusive jurisdiction' views, namely: (i) the nature of a mutual wills claim; (ii) formalities; (iii) the nature of the trust; and (iv) the timing of the trust.

(i) Nature of a Mutual Wills Claim

In judicial discourse, the discussion concerning whether a mutual wills agreement is enforceable is often couched in terms of whether the agreement satisfies the relevant contractual principles. For example, courts ask whether the agreement reflects certainty of terms,[77] whether consideration was provided[78] or whether the relevant statutory formality requirements affecting contracts concerning land apply and were discharged.[79] Moreover, in most cases the requirements for 'equitable fraud' – a promise by the survivor and reliance by the first-to-die – also naturally fulfil the contractual requirements of offer, acceptance and consideration.[80]

It is not surprising that judges employ contractual terminology, given that parties often rely on contractual principles in constructing their claims or responses. In employing a 'catch-all' tactic, however, plaintiffs also often claim an array of remedies which cut across both contract and equity. Take the plaintiffs in *Birmingham*, for example. Their statement of claim at first instance sought, among other things, a declaration that Jack's executors held his estate on trust for the plaintiffs, but basing their argument on

[74] Discussed more fully in YK Liew, *Rationalising Constructive Trusts* (Oxford, Hart Publishing, 2017) ch 8.
[75] *Lysaght v Edwards* (1875–76) LR 2 Ch D 499, 506.
[76] *Howard v Miller* [1915] AC 318 (PC) 326.
[77] *Renfrew v Birmingham* (n 19) 186.
[78] *Re Dale* [1994] Ch 31 (Ch) 38.
[79] *Birmingham v Renfrew* (n 27) 680; *cf Healey v Brown* [2002] EWHC 1405 (Ch).
[80] See, eg *Birmingham v Renfrew* (n 27) 682–83.

two alternative grounds, namely 'that the said agreement ought to be specifically enforced' and 'that [Jack] received and held the said residue upon trust to leave to the Plaintiffs by Will so much thereof as should not be disposed of by him during his lifetime'.[81]

While this sort of tactic may be advantageous in terms of achieving the outcome sought by plaintiffs, it obscures the true nature of a mutual wills claim. The two alternatives are mutually exclusive: one is a contractual claim for specific performance, the other is a claim that equity should recognise a constructive trust in its exclusive jurisdiction. Both views can be detected in the High Court judgments in *Birmingham*. While Latham CJ thought that the 'contract' between Grace and Jack could be enforced directly by the plaintiffs,[82] Dixon J held that '[i]t is the constructive trust and not the contract that they are entitled to enforce'.[83]

Dixon J's view has proven to be the basis upon which the doctrine has come to be understood. For example, in *Re Dale*, Morritt J said that:

> The principles on which the court acts in imposing the trust to give effect to the agreement to make and not revoke mutual wills must be found in the cases dealing with that topic, not with those dealing with the availability of the remedy of specific performance.[84]

Likewise, in *Borgese v Cater & Blumer Pty Ltd (No 2)* N Adams J found occasion to reaffirm Dixon J's view that a mutual wills case is brought 'on the constructive trust, rather than on the contract'.[85] The same is the case in the academic commentary: a cursory survey of trusts and contracts texts would reveal that the mutual wills doctrine is discussed alongside other constructive trust doctrines such as secret trusts, rather than as a specific example of a wider discussion concerning an exception to the contractual privity rule.[86]

(ii) Formalities

Closely related to the nature of the claim is the second area of distinction, which is whether fulfilling the statutory formality requirements for a contract concerning an interest in land[87] is a prerequisite. As we have seen, in *Birmingham* both Latham CJ and Dixon J dismissed the relevance of the formality statute on the basis that the contract between Grace and Jack did not concern an 'interest in land'.[88] They distinguished the

[81] PROV (n 12) 'Plaintiffs' Statement of Claim' [10].

[82] *Birmingham v Renfrew* (n 27) 677.

[83] ibid 690.

[84] *Re Dale* (n 78) 38.

[85] *Borgese v Cater & Blumer Pty Ltd (No 2)* [2017] NSWSC 79, [137]. See also *Olins v Walters* [2009] Ch 212 (Ch) [36].

[86] See, eg J McGhee (ed), *Snell's Equity*, 33rd edn (London, Sweet & Maxwell, 2016) [24-032]–[24-037]; D Hayton, P Matthews and C Mitchell, *Underhill and Hayton: Law Relating to Trusts and Trustees*, 19th edn (London, LexisNexis Butterworths, 2016) [30.54]–[30.73]; J Glister and J Lee, *Hanbury and Martin: Modern Equity*, 21st edn (London, Sweet & Maxwell, 2018) [12-012]–[12-018].

[87] In English law: Law of Property (Miscellaneous Provisions) Act 1989, s 2(1). In Australia: Civil Law (Property Act) 2006 (ACT), s 201; Conveyancing Act 1919 (NSW), s 54A; Law of Property Act (NT), s 9; Property Law Act 1974 (Qld), s 59; Law of Property Act 1936 (SA), s 26; Conveyancing and Law of Property Act 1884 (Tas), s 36; Instruments Act 1958 (Vic), s 126; Law Reform (Statute of Frauds) Act 1962 (WA), s 2.

[88] *Birmingham v Renfrew* (n 27) 678, 690–91.

previous High Court decision of *Horton v Jones*,[89] which decided that an oral contract to leave one's fortune in one's will was unenforceable for lack of writing, on the basis that the subject matter in *Horton* was specifically an interest in land. But what if the subject matter of a mutual wills agreement expressly concerns land: for instance, where each testator promises to leave a specific plot of land to the other in the case of predecease, and to a beneficiary otherwise?

In Australia, while a mere three cases have cited *Birmingham* for the proposition that the mutual wills doctrine requires compliance with the formality requirements for a contract concerning land,[90] a significant number of cases take the contrary view, both obiter[91] and as ratio decidendi.[92] The majority understanding is undoubtedly correct. It is a clear ratio of *Birmingham* that a mutual wills agreement is inherently non-specific because it is to leave whatever is left of the subject matter of the agreement at the time of the survivor's death, even if the subject matter is land.[93] Moreover, the cases also embrace Dixon J's 'fraud' rationale to make the point that the survivor (and those claiming through him or her) should not be allowed to use a formality statute as an instrument of fraud.[94]

In English law, only one case – *Healey v Brown*[95] – has cited *Birmingham* in relation to the formality point, and the conclusion reached was that writing was a prerequisite. But that decision is undoubtedly suspect.[96] Other English courts have said that the principles of the mutual wills doctrine are not precisely the same as those which apply to contractual disputes.[97] Since a mutual wills agreement can be made orally[98] or be inferred from the circumstances of a case,[99] then surely it is contemplated that formalities have no relevance to the mutual wills doctrine. Indeed, in *Olins v Walters*,[100] the English Court of Appeal applied the doctrine where the relevant agreement was held not to be certain enough to amount to a contract enforceable at common law. Support can also be found in New Zealand, where the Court of Appeal has expressly held that the constructive trust arises from the parties' course of conduct and not the contract itself, and therefore '[a] contract made without formality is enough'.[101]

[89] *Horton v Jones* [1935] HCA 7, 53 CLR 475.

[90] As ratio: *Salasoo v Korbe* (NSWSC, unreported, 8 March 1990) BC9002664, 9; *Flocas v Carlson* [2015] VSC 221, 15 ASTLR 192, [99]ff; as obiter: *Bridge Wholesale Acceptance Corporation (Australia) Ltd v Burnard* (1992) 27 NSWLR 415, [4].

[91] *Hendriks v McGeoch* [2008] NSWCA 53, [67]; *Last v Rosenfeld* (n 63) 935; *Osborne* v Osborne [2001] VSCA 228, [18]; *Radalj v Di Francesco* [2003] WASC 57, [40]; *Stoeve v Horowitz* (NSWSC, unreported, 18 June 1982) BC8211828, 15.

[92] *Hubbard v Mason* (NSWSC, unreported, 9 December 1997) BC9706574, 14; *Pridham v Pridham* [2010] SASC 204, [57]; *Staib v Powell* (n 62) 156.

[93] *Staib v Powell* (n 62) 56.

[94] *Last v Rosenfeld* (n 63) 934–35; *Hubbard v Mason* (n 92) [14].

[95] *Healey v Brown* (n 79) [19].

[96] See also *Legg v Burton* (n 143) [23]. *cf* the views of some commentators, eg C Davis, 'Mutual Wills; Formalities; Constructive Trusts' [2003] *Conveyancer and Property Lawyer* 238, 239; B McFarlane, 'Constructive Trusts Arising on a Receipt of Property *Sub Conditione*' (2004) 120 *LQR* 667, 688; A Braun, 'Revocability of Mutual Wills' in KGC Reid, MJ de Waal and R Zimmermann (eds), *Exploring the Law of Succession: Studies National, Historical and Comparative*, Edinburgh Studies in Law vol 5 (Edinburgh, Edinburgh University Press, 2007) 221.

[97] *Re Hobley (Deceased)* (*The Times*, 16 June 1997).

[98] *Charles v Fraser* [2010] EWHC 2154 (Ch), [2010] WTLR 1489, [59].

[99] *Fry v Densham-Smith* [2010] EWCA Civ 1410, [2011] WTLR 387, [33].

[100] *Olins v Walters* (n 85). See especially counsel's submission at [24], which the Court of Appeal rejected at [35].

[101] *Lewis v Cotton* [2001] 2 NZLR 21, [44], [55].

The prevailing position in both English and Australian law therefore supports the view that it is equity's exclusive jurisdiction which is in play: the doctrine is not conditional upon first establishing a contract enforceable at common law. This is wholly in line with what Dixon J contemplated in *Birmingham*.

(iii) Nature of the Trust

At first instance in *Birmingham*, counsel for the plaintiffs pleaded that Grace had 'entered into the said agreement as trustee for the Plaintiffs and/or constituted herself a trustee for the Plaintiffs of her rights thereunder'.[102] Gavan Duffy J dealt with this point in the course of discussing whether the plaintiffs could sue as third parties to the contract. Ruling in the affirmative, he found that Grace had entered into the agreement with Jack for the plaintiffs' benefit, and that the plaintiffs were therefore beneficiaries under a trust.[103] The judge appears to have thought that the mutual wills agreement created an express trust, finding that 'it is not necessary, in order that there should be a trust of [a] chose in action, that any specific words such as "trust" or "trustee" should be used'.[104] All that was necessary was that 'it was intended by [Grace] to enter into [the agreement] for the benefit of the plaintiffs'.[105]

In the High Court, both Latham CJ and Dixon J found that Jack's executors held the residue of the estate on constructive trust for the plaintiffs.[106] However, they differed in relation to the genesis of the constructive trust.

Latham CJ was content to adopt Gavan Duffy J's analysis – that Grace was trustee for the plaintiffs[107] – but thought that the trust was constructive in nature:

> The trust … is not an express trust which [Jack] created. The only trust alleged is a trust which is declared by the law to affect the conscience of his executor and of the volunteers who are devisees or legatees under his will.[108]

In contrast, Dixon J, speaking of the mutual wills doctrine generally, was firmly of the view that the constructive trust only arises upon 'the death of one of the parties leaving a will in the form agreed', with the result that there is 'a disposition of property made upon the faith of the survivor's carrying out the obligations of his contract'.[109] This brings the case 'under the equitable jurisdiction for the prevention of fraud', an example of which is the secret trusts doctrine, which his Honour went on to cite.

Dixon J's judgment has emerged as the 'landmark' analysis in the modern law.

First, it is clear that the mutual wills doctrine is understood as giving rise to constructive, as opposed to express, trusts.[110]

[102] PROV (n 12) 'Copy Pleadings' [2].
[103] *Renfrew v Birmingham* (n 19) 189.
[104] ibid.
[105] ibid 189.
[106] *Birmingham v Renfrew* (n 27) 680 (Latham CJ), 690 (Dixon J).
[107] ibid 677.
[108] ibid 680.
[109] ibid 688.
[110] See, eg *Re Cleaver* (n 65) 947; *Re Dale* (n 78) 46–47; *Healey v Brown* (n 79) [8]; *Osenton v Osenton* [2004] EWHC 1055 (Ch) [33]; *Olins v Walters* (n 85) [39]; *Charles v Fraser* (n 98) [59]; *Shovelar v Lane* [2011] EWCA Civ 802, [2012] 1 WLR 637, [37].

Secondly, even today, the trust device – whether express or constructive – cannot generally be used as a mechanism for circumventing contractual privity rules in the absence of clear evidence of an intention to create a trust of the benefit of the contract.[111]

Thirdly, Dixon J's decision has provided the foundation upon which the mutual wills doctrine has been understood in English law. Thus, in *Re Cleaver*,[112] the first English mutual wills case which cites *Birmingham* substantively, Nourse J quotes extensively from Dixon J's judgment, describing it as stating 'what I believe to be a correct analysis of the principles on which a case of enforceable mutual wills depends'.[113] In addition, Nourse J also expressed agreement with Dixon J that 'mutual wills are only one example of a wider category of cases, for example secret trusts, in which a court of equity will intervene to impose a constructive trust'.[114] Just as is the case with secret trusts, there need not be a contract at common law for the constructive trust to arise. Rather, the trust is triggered by other contract-independent events.[115]

(iv) Timing of the Trust

On Latham CJ's analysis, the constructive trust arises at the moment the mutual wills agreement is entered into. It also follows that, in principle, it is not possible to revoke the agreement from that point without consequence. On Dixon J's analysis, however, the constructive trust only arises on the death of the first-to-die, leaving room for the parties to revoke the agreement beforehand.

Before *Birmingham*, *Re Hagger* had held that a mutual wills agreement is binding 'on the death of the first testator'.[116] Arguably, however, this left open the possibility that it was only so binding because the first testator was a trustee while alive, in line with Latham CJ's analysis. Support for that sort of argument might have been thought to be found in Lord Camden's judgment in *Dufour v Pereira*, where his Lordship said that neither testator 'could, during their joint lives, [revoke] secretly'.[117] This was taken in *Bigg v Queensland Trustees Ltd* to indicate that '[w]hether the parties should be entitled to revoke during their joint lifetimes … depend[s] upon the contract which was made',[118] which appears to support the view that the mutual wills doctrine falls within equity's concurrent jurisdiction.

But an alternative take on Lord Camden's statement is possible, and has proven to be the prevailing view. On this view, whether a mutual wills agreement is revocable without consequence depends on the time at which the constructive trust arises, and (as will be

[111] See *Trident General Insurance Co Ltd v McNiece Bros Pty Ltd* (1998) 165 CLR 107; note also Leeming JA's recent comment in *Benson v Rational Entertainment Enterprises Ltd* [2018] NSWCA 111, [118]: '*Trident* … does not bind other Australian courts other than as to the relaxation of the doctrine of privity in insurance contracts.'

[112] *Re Cleaver* (n 110).

[113] ibid 945.

[114] *Re Cleaver* (n 110) 947.

[115] Namely, a promise by the survivor and reliance by the first-to-die: see Liew (n 74) ch 5; YK Liew, 'The Ambit of the Mutual Wills Doctrine' (2016) 132 *LQR* 664, especially s IV.

[116] *Re Hagger* [1930] 2 Ch 190 (Ch) 195.

[117] *Dufour v Pereira* (n 49) 1 Dick 421, 21 ER 333.

[118] *Bigg v Queensland Trustees Ltd* [1990] 2 Qd R 11, 15, citing *Atkinson's Law of Wills* (1980) 225 with approval.

discussed below) it is precisely the moment when one testator incurs substantial reliance on the other's promise to carry out the agreement. This mirrors Dixon J's conception of the mutual wills doctrine. His Honour suggested that the doctrine fell 'under the equitable jurisdiction for the prevention of fraud', alongside secret trusts, in a category of cases where 'equities [are fastened] upon property because of a testamentary disposition made in reliance upon an understanding or promise'.[119]

In the usual case, reliance on the agreement is fulfilled upon the death of the first-to-die, leaving his or her testamentary affairs as agreed. As Gummow and Hayne JJ held in *Barns v Barns*, citing Dixon J's judgment in *Birmingham* as authority:

> it is the disposition of the property by the first party under a will in the agreed form and upon the faith of the survivor carrying out the obligation of the contract which attracts the intervention of equity in favour of the survivor ...[120]

And as Buchanan JA held in *Osborne v Estate of Osborne*:[121] 'The fraud in equity lies in the departure by the survivor from the agreement or understanding that caused the first testator to act in reliance upon the survivor abiding by the agreement or understanding.'

But reliance on the agreement by the survivor may also be relevant where the first-to-die attempts to revoke the agreement. This is why no constructive trust arose in *Stone v Hoskins*, where the first-to-die departed from the mutual wills agreement but the survivor was 'not in any way prejudiced';[122] in contrast, a constructive trust arose in *Bigg*, where the first-to-die revoked her will secretly, leaving the survivor to make and continue to make investments in the former's name on the faith of the agreement.

In either case, it is clear that the constructive trust is not simply contingent upon the forming of a 'contract' between the testators, but at least on the fulfilment of the additional element of reliance. Such an analysis is entirely consistent with Dixon J's view, and reflects equity's operation within its exclusive jurisdiction.

B. Meaning of 'Contract'

It is undoubtedly clear that, in *Birmingham*, the agreement between Grace and Jack fulfilled the preconditions for the creation of a legally enforceable contract. As Gavan Duffy J had found as a matter of fact, there was an agreement which was certain and was meant to create a binding legal relationship between themselves;[123] and as Dixon J held, Grace 'afforded the consideration for [Jack's] promise by making her will'.[124]

As discussed above, however, a legally binding contract is not a precondition for the doctrine to operate, consistent with the view that the mutual wills doctrine reflects equity operating within its exclusive jurisdiction. Given that equity does not intervene in order to allow the plaintiffs to sue upon the contract, the better view is that it was simply a coincidence that the agreement in *Birmingham* also fulfilled the preconditions for a

[119] *Birmingham v Renfrew* (n 27) 688.
[120] *Barns v Barns* (2003) 214 CLR 169, 199.
[121] *Osborne v Osborne* (n 91) [24]. See also *Olins v Walters* (n 85) [38].
[122] *Stone v Hoskins* [1905] P 194 (Probate) 197.
[123] *Renfrew v Birmingham* (n 19) 186.
[124] *Birmingham v Renfrew* (n 27) 683.

legally binding contract, and that a binding contract is sufficient, but not necessary, to engage the mutual wills doctrine.

Yet, in a trend which appears contrary to the proposition just cited, judges still refer to binding mutual wills agreements as 'contracts'. What do courts really mean? The answer to this question also tells us something about the impact which *Birmingham* has had on the development of the mutual wills doctrine.

(i) What It Entails

It is necessary first to observe that, in this area of law, the term 'contract' is not always used in its technical sense to refer to a legally binding contract. Morritt LJ's judgment in *Re Goodchild* is a good example. In the course of explaining that the mutual wills doctrine requires 'a contract between the two testators', his Lordship drew an analogy with fully secret trusts, which also required 'the proof of a contract'.[125] By this his Lordship meant that proof was required of the 'essential elements' of intention, communication and acceptance.[126] These elements alone are, of course, insufficient to create a legally enforceable contract at law.

Bearing in mind the potentially loose use of the term 'contract', then, there are three good reasons why the language of 'contract' is employed in the mutual wills context.

First, courts have always required highly exacting evidence before being willing to find that a binding mutual wills agreement exists. This attitude is encapsulated well in the language of 'contract' because a legal contract requires an intention to create legally binding obligations. As Winneke P held in *Osborne v Estate of Osborne*:

> equity will not intervene unless the plaintiff can establish, upon clear evidence, that a testator has bound himself to an obligation (whether one calls it contract, agreement, promise or otherwise) not to revoke his will, and in such terms as to render it enforceable in equity.[127]

Secondly, and relatedly, because the mutual wills doctrine operates in the domestic as opposed to the commercial context, parties regularly enter into agreements, yet seldom intend to subject themselves to the sanction of a court of justice[128] and thus to be legally bound. Rather than requiring the precise threshold of intention to be spelt out, the language of 'contract' allows courts to adopt the different presumptions which operate in domestic and commercial contexts for establishing an 'intention to create legal relations' for the purposes of legal contracts.[129] In substance, this approach helps to preclude the mutual wills doctrine from operating where the arrangement simply reflects an honorary engagement,[130] merely mutual expectations or desires,[131] or purely coincidental testamentary intents.[132]

[125] *Re Goodchild (Deceased)* [1997] 1 WLR 1216 (CA) 1229.

[126] *Re Goodchild (Deceased)* (ibid) 1229, citing *Ottaway v Norman* (n 64) 711.

[127] *Osborne v Osborne* (n 91) [18].

[128] On the dichotomy of intending the sanction to be 'the authority of a Court of Justice' and 'the conscience of the devisee', see *McCormick v Grogan* (n 40) 328; *Re Snowden (Deceased)* [1979] Ch 528 (Ch) 537.

[129] See, eg *Edwards v Skyways Ltd* [1964] 1 WLR 349 (QB).

[130] *Dufour v Pereira*, as reported in F Hargrave, *Juridical Arguments and Collections*, vol 2 (London, GG and J Robinson, 1799) 276; *Lord Walpole v Lord Orford* (1797) 3 Ves Jun 402, 420; 30 ER 1076, 1085.

[131] *Re Goodchild (Deceased)* (n 125) 1225; *Re Dale* (n 78) 38; *Charles v Fraser* (n 98) [59]; *Osenton v Osenton* (n 110) [33].

[132] *Healey v Brown* (n 79) [9].

Thirdly, the mutual wills doctrine is clearly 'agreement-based':[133] the constructive trust gives effect to the express intentions of the relevant parties by imposing obligations which mirror the terms of the parties' agreement.[134] In this regard, the methodology by which courts deal with the incorporation and interpretation of contractual terms is also useful for determining whether 'the terms of the mutual engagement … are sufficiently certain that the court can see its way to enforce them'[135] and, if so, what the precise terms may be.

(ii) The Impact of Birmingham

It can be observed that the above-mentioned reasons reflect a common theme, namely that courts ought to be cautious in finding that a binding mutual wills agreement has been reached; and it is in relation to this very point that the impact of *Birmingham* can be detected.

In the High Court, all three judges expressed the need to treat the evidence cautiously. Thus, Latham CJ said that 'a heavy burden of proof' is required;[136] Dixon J held that 'clear and satisfactory evidence' was necessary;[137] and Evatt J spent a significant bulk of his concurring judgment commenting on the sufficiency of the evidence before the court.[138]

Certainly, *Birmingham* was not the first case to call for caution when dealing with the relevant evidence. In *Re Oldham*, Astbury J had refused to find that such an agreement was reached because he was not convinced that a binding agreement was the 'sole inference' that could be drawn from the evidence;[139] and in *Gray v Perpetual Trustee* the Privy Council had held that a binding agreement did not exist on the facts because the mere simultaneity of wills and their terms did not in themselves provide evidence of it.[140] However, *Birmingham* was the first case in Australian or English law in which caution was expressly advised and yet a binding agreement was nevertheless found to exist on the facts.

It may be for this reason that the earliest Australian cases which cite *Birmingham* did so in relation to this point, and it is also in relation to this point that *Birmingham* has come to be most frequently cited in Australia.[141] Similarly, *Birmingham* is also often taken

[133] See YK Liew, 'Explaining the Mutual Wills Doctrine' in B Häker and C Mitchell (eds), *Current Issues in Succession Law* (Oxford, Hart Publishing, 2016) 111.

[134] *Olins v Walters* (n 85) [40]; *Fazari v Cosentino* [2010] WASC 40, [31].

[135] *Lewis v Cotton* (n 101) [55], paraphrasing *Re Oldham* [1925] Ch 75 (Ch) 86.

[136] *Birmingham v Renfrew* (n 27) 674.

[137] ibid 681.

[138] ibid 692–94.

[139] *Re Oldham* (n 135) 89.

[140] *Gray v Perpetual Trustee Co Ltd* [1928] AC 391 (PC) 400.

[141] See, eg *Borgese v Cater* (n 85) [136]; *Masci v Masci* [2015] QCA 245, [33]; *Re Cobcroft* [2015] NSWSC 346, [72]; *Larkin v Borg* [2013] VSC 138, [20]; *Kennedy v Griffiths* [2014] QSC 43, [138]ff; *Bauer v Hussey* [2011] QCA 91, [22]–[23]; *Pridham v Pridham* (n 119) [27]; *Schmidt v Watkins* [2002] VSC 273, [20]–[21]; *Osborne v Osborne* (n 91) [7]; *Baird v Smee* [2000] NSWCA 253; *Hunt v Barlow* [2000] NSWSC 324, [7]; *Day v Couch* [2000] NSWSC 230, [9]; *Atsas v Gertsch* [1198] NSWSC 522, [28]; *Swain v Mewburn* (WASC, unreported, 3 March 1994) BC9401458, 13; *Hunt v Luengo* (VSC, unreported, 21 May 1992) BC9200682, 39; *Dunn v The Public Trustee* (NSWSC, unreported, 1 June 1989) BC8902109, 22; *Landman v Feil* (NSWSC, unreported,

as authority for this point in English law, as seen, for example, in both *Re Cleaver*[142] and *Legg v Burton*,[143] respectively the first and latest English mutual wills case which cites *Birmingham*.

It is unsurprising that *Birmingham* has played a crucial role in the development of the courts' attitude towards the relevant evidence. Not only was this a point which found concurrence between all three judges, the application of the point to the facts of the case also provides a helpfully guideline as to what that exacting standard might look like in practice. As Dixon J explained concerning the facts of *Birmingham*:[144]

> The circumstances of the present case … invest the story told on the part of the [Plaintiffs] with some probability. The testatrix had succeeded to a large amount of property in consequence of some predilection in her favour on the part of an uncle who might have spread his gifts more widely among the members of the family. Some difficulties had arisen in the administration of his estate which worried her and made it appear inexpedient to make her husband tenant for life under her will and bequeath her estate in remainder to the four respondents. The time had come when she considered that she ought to make a will. And it was natural that she should wish to be sure that the relatives of her late uncle and of herself would succeed to the estate which he had left to her. Witnesses deposed to a circumstantial account of discussions between the wife and one or other of the intended beneficiaries. They narrated how the wife definitely stated in his presence the terms of the arrangement made with the husband and how he assented to her statement. The evidence, if believed, could leave no doubt that the wife made her will upon the faith of assurances on the part of her husband that he would leave his will unrevoked should she die first and that he made his will as part of the arrangement under which she made hers. This evidence was corroborated by evidence, taken on commission, of statements made by the spouses while abroad … Gavan Duffy J found that an agreement had been made, and I do not think that his finding can be set aside. He found, too, that the arrangement was not of a character leaving legal relations unaffected. So far as this is a question of fact, I think he was fully justified in taking the view that the wife meant to obtain from her husband a promise and meant that it should be communicated to the intended beneficiaries in order the better to ensure its fulfilment.

C. The Rationale of the Doctrine

The final – and arguably most significant – impact of *Birmingham* relates to the rationalisation of the doctrine. The focus is almost exclusively on Dixon J's judgment in the High Court. This is not only because the other judges, in particular Latham CJ, refused to 'concern [themselves] with the difficulties in legal theory' raised by the doctrine,[145] but also because Dixon J's judgment appears to be the only substantive attempt to date by any judge in Australian or English law to explore the rationale of the mutual wills doctrine.

26 May 1989) BC8902133, 8; *Butler v Craine* [1986] VR 274, 281; *Thwaites v Ryan* [1984] 1 VR 63, 79; *Robb v Strain* (NSWSC, unreported, 13 February 1981) BC8111264, 13; *Staib v Powell* (n 62) 155.

142 *Re Cleaver* (n 110) 947.

143 *Legg v Burton* [2017] EWHC 2088 (Ch) [40].

144 *Birmingham v Renfrew* (n 27) 682.

145 *Birmingham v Renfrew* (n 27) 676.

Far from engaging in an 'unnecessary' or 'fanciful' explanation of the doctrine,[146] it will be seen that his Honour's judgment has had a significant impact on the development of the doctrine – the impact of which, it will also be suggested, has the potential for further development.

Two important points will be discussed: the 'floating' nature of the constructive trust and the 'fraud' justification of the mutual wills doctrine.

(i) The 'Floating' Trust

In *Birmingham*, Dixon J described the mechanics of the typical[147] mutual wills case in an often cited[148] passage. His Honour said:

> It is only by the special doctrines of equity that such a floating obligation, suspended, so to speak, during the lifetime of the survivor can descend upon the assets at his death and crystallize into a trust ... [The survivor is] allow[ed] full enjoyment for [his] own benefit and advantage upon condition that at his death the residue shall pass as arranged ... I do not see any difficulty in modern equity in attaching to the assets a constructive trust which allowed the survivor to enjoy the property subject to a fiduciary duty which, so to speak, crystallized on his death ...[149]

An obvious difficulty with adopting the 'floating' analysis of the constructive trust at face value is that nowhere else in the law do we find the notion of a 'floating trust'. Nevertheless, the *substance* of Dixon J's analysis provides fertile ground for understanding the mutual wills doctrine.

It is interesting to note that the first judicial citation of *Birmingham* was in the Australian High Court decision of *Purves v Smith*,[150] where Rich J cited *Birmingham* as authority to make a point concerning floating charges.[151] Certainly, trusts and charges are different devices, so perhaps the point is better made by Callinan J in the High Court in *Barns v Barns*, that the 'floating' nature of the trust 'invites *comparison*' with a floating charge, with both devices reflecting similar features.[152]

One of the common features is that a floating chargee's interest 'is in a *fund* of circulating capital, and unless and until the chargee intervenes (on crystallisation of the charge) it is for the trader, and not the bank, to decide how to run its business'.[153] So it is in relation

[146] HAJ Ford, 'Sir Owen Dixon: His Judgments in Private Law' (1986) 15 *Melbourne University Law Review* 584.

[147] 'Typical' because the quoted words describe the case where the agreement reflects a promise by the survivor to leave 'whatever is left' at his or her death to the agreed beneficiaries. It may well be the case that the agreement expressly provides that the survivor will obtain a mere life interest, with remainder to the agreed beneficiaries (as recognised by Dixon J: *Birmingham v Renfrew* (n 27) 690; see too *Re Hagger* (n 116)). In these cases the 'floating' analysis does not apply.

[148] See, eg *Barns v Barns* (n 120) [29]; *Re Cleaver* (n 110) 946–47; *Re Goodchild* (n 125) 700; *Jaeger v Bowden (No 2)* [2016] NSWSC 897, [634]; *Ottaway v Norman* (n 64) 713–14.

[149] *Birmingham v Renfrew* (n 27) 689–90.

[150] Purves v *Smith* (n 63).

[151] In Australia floating charges have now been abolished by the Personal Property Securities Act 2009 (Cth) and replaced by a statutory charge over circulating assets – but the substance of both are similar for the purposes of the present discussion.

[152] *Barns v Barns* (n 120) [152] (emphasis added).

[153] *Re Spectrum Plus* [2005] UKHL 41, [2005] 2 AC 680, [139] (emphasis in original). '[A] fund is considered to have an existence distinct from that of its components. The contents of the fund are constantly changing as assets are removed from the fund and new assets come into it, but the identity of the fund itself remains unchanged': L Gullifer (ed), *Goode on Legal Problems of Credit and Security*, 5th edn (London, Sweet & Maxwell, 2013) [4-04].

to the typical mutual wills agreement: the parties intend to treat the survivor's estate, at the point of the death of the first-to-die, as a single fund (which would usually include property left to the survivor), intending the survivor to deal freely during his or her lifetime, with the intended beneficiary's interest 'crystallising' only at the survivor's death.

Another common feature is that a floating chargee has an existing security interest, which enables him to apply to the court for the appointment of a receiver where necessary even before crystallisation.[154] The beneficiary's position under a mutual wills agreement after the death of the first-to-die is similar: he or she has standing to apply to court to remove the executor and trustee of the first-to-die, a position which 'does not depend upon crystallisation of a constructive trust' in the beneficiary's favour.[155]

There is no difficulty in accounting for these features of the mutual wills doctrine by way of orthodox trust principles while avoiding the notion of a 'floating trust'. The constructive trust provides the survivor with a life interest in his or her estate at the death of the first-to-die and the beneficiary obtains the remainder interest, with the survivor having a general, personal power by which he or she may appoint the capital assets in favour of anyone, including him- or herself.[156]

This sort of analysis also accounts for yet another feature in common between the constructive trust and a floating charge: A chargee's interest in the fund may crystallise automatically, for instance upon the occurrence of a defined event, without any further act on the part of the chargee.[157] The same is the case where a survivor breaches the mutual wills agreement. As Dixon J observed:

> No doubt gifts and settlements, inter vivos, if calculated to defeat the intention of the compact, could not be made by the survivor and his right of disposition, inter vivos, is, therefore, not unqualified … [The survivor] is disabled … only from voluntary dispositions inter vivos.[158]

By way of an orthodox analysis, the survivor must not exercise his power in such a way as would amount to a fraud on a power. A 'fraud' on a power means 'that the power has been exercised for a purpose, or with an intention, beyond the scope of or not justified by the instrument creating the power'.[159] Such a 'fraud' occurs where there is 'a deliberate defeating of what the donor of the power authorized and intended'[160] – an exercise of power with an 'ulterior object to be accomplished'.[161] This is why, in the mutual wills context, crystallisation would occur where the survivor transfers property out of his estate in a way which runs 'directly and fully counter to the *intention* of the mutual will compact'.[162]

[154] *Re London Pressed Hinge Co Ltd* [1905] 1 Ch 576 (Ch).

[155] *Russo v Russo* [2009] VSC 491, [18]–[33].

[156] This point is developed in greater detail in Liew (n 133) s 4. Charles Mitchell's contribution in this volume might suggest that an alternative analysis is possible, namely that it is not a logical necessity for the survivor to be subject to the relevant duties that in order for the beneficiaries to have proprietary interests during the survivor's lifetime. This argument would, however, run into the further difficulties of explaining why, precisely, it is that the beneficiaries have certain rights against the survivor and volunteer third parties during the survivor's lifetime and (stating the same from the survivor's point of view) how, precisely, the survivor's duties come into being. These difficulties do not arise on the analysis suggested in the text.

[157] *Evans v Rival Granite Quarries Ltd* [1910] 2 KB 979 (CA).

[158] *Birmingham v Renfrew* (n 27) 689–90.

[159] *Vatcher v Paull* [1915] AC 372 (PC) 378.

[160] *Re Dick, Knight v Dick* [1953] Ch 343 (CA) 360.

[161] *Duke of Portland v Topham* (1864) 11 HLC 32, 55; 11 ER 1242, 1251.

[162] *Healey v Brown* (n 79) [14] (emphasis added).

The orthodox analysis of Dixon J's judgment is capable of clarifying the Australian confusion as to what constitutes a breach by the survivor. In *Fazari v Cosentino* it was held that the survivor commits a breach only where he effectuates a transfer which is in substance a testamentary (as opposed to *inter vivos*) disposition.[163] But Dixon J's judgment suggests that the better view is found in *Russo v Russo*, that the survivor 'may only use the assets … bona fide without any intention to defeat the mutual wills agreement'.[164]

The orthodox analysis also reflects a less well-known aspect of the *Birmingham* litigation. On 29 November 1938, a year or so after the High Court's decision, Alexander Jr and Alan brought an action by way of originating summons as Jack's executors against Jack's six relatives, whereby the plaintiffs sought the court's guidance as to the validity of three deeds Jack had executed on 25 September 1933 which purported to appropriate or charge some of the 12 properties Jack had received with payment of annuities in fulfilment of Grace's will,[165] even though Grace's personal estate would have been sufficient to meet those annuities. On 16 December 1938 Macfarlan J handed down a judgment in the Supreme Court of Victoria holding that those deeds were void and of no effect. No reasoned judgment was provided.[166] However, that decision affirms that the plaintiffs' rights in Jack's estate arose from the time of Grace's death, and that in charging those properties Jack had perpetrated a fraud on a power. Because a fraudulent execution of a power is wholly void,[167] the charges were held to be void.

(ii) The 'Fraud' Justification

In *Birmingham*, Dixon J observed that equity's intervention in mutual wills cases:

> … is affected by … the … consideration [of] the death of one of the parties leaving a will in the form agreed. The result is a disposition of property made upon the faith of the survivor's carrying out the obligations of his contract. It is an element which brings such a case under the equitable jurisdiction for the prevention of fraud.[168]

Within this jurisdiction, 'equities [are fastened] upon property because of a testamentary disposition made in reliance upon an understanding or promise',[169] a jurisdiction which, according to Dixon J, also encompasses the secret trusts doctrine.[170]

This analysis has proven to be crucial for working out the ambit of the mutual wills doctrine.

It is well known that, in *Re Dale*,[171] Morritt J held that the doctrine was applicable where a mutual wills agreement contemplates that the testators will leave property directly to a beneficiary, with the survivor not taking any benefit under the first-to-die's will.

[163] *Fazari v Consentino* (n 134) [41]–[51].

[164] *Russo v Russo* (n 155) [32]. This view was applied in *Bauer v Hussey* [2010] QSC 269.

[165] PROV (n 16) 'Summons'.

[166] PROV (n 16) 'Order'.

[167] *Vatcher v Paull* (n 159) 378; *Pitt v Holt* [2013] UKSC 26, [2013] 2 AC 108, [97]–[98].

[168] *Birmingham v Renfrew* (n 27) 688.

[169] ibid.

[170] His Honour quoted from two well-known secret trusts cases, *Blackwell v Blackwell* (n 52) and *McCormick v Grogan* (n 40).

[171] *Re Dale* (n 78).

The same position was adopted in the Australian case of *Osborne v Estate of Osborne*,[172] where Morritt J's judgment was also cited with approval.

It can be seen from *Re Dale* that Dixon J's judgment in *Birmingham* played a central role in extending the ambit of the mutual wills doctrine. At first sight this would appear to be surprising, given that Dixon J had suggested that:

> The purpose of an arrangement for corresponding wills must often be … to enable the survivor during his life to deal as absolute owner with the property passing under the will of the party first dying. That is to say, the object of the transaction is to put the survivor in a position to enjoy for his own benefit the full ownership so that, for instance, he may convert it and expend the proceeds if he choose.[173]

But '[h]aving read and re-read the judgment of Dixon J', Morritt J held that this passage did not decide 'that mutual benefit is an essential condition'; rather, it 'was only a reference to what in fact must often be the purpose and is not a definition of when that purpose may be achieved'.[174] Whether the survivor obtains an interest under the first-to-die's will does not affect the fact that the case equally falls within the 'equitable jurisdiction for the prevention of fraud'.[175] In the same vein, Buchanan JA held in *Osborne* that the doctrine could apply in a *Re Dale*-type case because '[t]he essence of the fraud in equity is the betrayal of the basis upon which the parties reached an agreement or understanding and on the faith of which the first testator acted'.[176]

Certainly, this extension of the mutual wills doctrine based on Dixon J's judgment is to be applauded, for it avoids arbitrarily drawing a distinction between cases where the survivor receives and does not receive a benefit under the first-to-die's will. Yet, the present understanding of the distinction between these two categories of case remains ill-refined, and in this regard the full potential of Dixon J's judgment has not yet been realised.

As Dixon J highlighted, there is a clear similarity between secret trusts and the typical mutual wills case. That similarity is that the relying party contributes to the trust fund over which the constructive trust arises. Stated from the trustee's point of view, prior to obtaining the other party's property, he or she makes a promise (which induces the other's reliance) to the effect that he or she will only take a qualified interest in the trust fund.[177] The constructive trust is therefore invariably justified: it holds the trustee to the promise, colouring '[h]is possession of the [fund] … from the first by the trust and confidence by means of which he obtained it'.[178]

But the elements of promise and reliance may not necessarily arise in this way. As in *Re Dale*-type cases, the survivor's promise may relate to property he or she has always owned absolutely, and the first-to-die's reliance may not result in a contribution to the fund which is the subject matter of their agreement. In such a case, there is a strong

[172] *Osborne v Osborne* (n 91) [24]–[25]. See too *Hubbard v Mason* (NSWSC, unreported, 8 July 1998) BC9803106, 31.

[173] *Birmingham v Renfrew* (n 27) 689.

[174] *Re Dale* (n 78) 46.

[175] *Birmingham v Renfrew* (n 27) 688, cited by Morritt J in *Re Dale* (n 78) 46.

[176] *Osborne v Osborne* (n 91) [24], citing, among others, Dixon J in *Birmingham v Renfrew* (n 27).

[177] Liew (n 133) 106.

[178] *Paragon Finance Plc v DB Thakerar & Co* [1999] 1 All ER 400 (CA) 409.

argument for saying that a constructive trust cannot possibly be invariably justified, given that the promisor ought not to be deprived of his or her own property if the relying party's acts of reliance do not proportionally justify that outcome. That is to say, a proprietary estoppel-type analysis would be more appropriate:[179] the remedy imposed would have to be proportionate to the degree of detrimental reliance incurred by the relying party.

Although the analytical distinction between the two categories of case has not yet been explicitly recognised, hints of that distinction can be found in case law. For example, in *Re Dale*, one point which Morritt J relied upon in the course of reasoning was the fact that 'certain cases of proprietary estoppel may be regarded as a species of constructive trust, but in those cases the factor which gives rise to its imposition is not the receipt of property'.[180] This suggests that the facts of *Re Dale* can – and ought to – be understood as reflecting an application of proprietary estoppel.

It is easy to see why the courts have not drawn a distinction between the analyses between the two categories of case. In the few *Re Dale*-type cases which have come before the courts, the relying party had relied significantly by giving up the opportunity to make an alternative form of testamentary disposition which leaves property of substantial value to the beneficiary, and this would surely justify the imposition of a constructive trust. But drawing an analytical distinction between the two categories of case has two obvious advantages.

First, it allows courts to deny a constructive trust in *Re Dale*-type cases where the relying party acts in such a way that does not justify holding the promisor to his or her promise. Such may arguably be the case where, for example, a mutual wills agreement is reached by two young testators who then divorce, with the first-to-die becoming insolvent shortly before an early death, leaving no valuable asset to the beneficiary, while the survivor has amassed a great deal of wealth before dying at a ripe old age. A constructive trust may be a disproportionate response in such a case.

Secondly, it avoids the need to draw arbitrary distinctions in the law. Consider the pre-*Birmingham* decision of the Australian High Court in *Horton v Jones*.[181] The plaintiff promised to look after one Gordon Philip Jones, and to make a home for him and look after him for the rest of his life, in return for the latter's promise to leave to her certain properties by will. The plaintiff sued when, having performed her promise, Jones died without making a will in her favour. The plaintiff's case for damages for breach of an oral agreement failed on the basis that the contract could not be enforced for lack of writing, the agreement being caught by the Statute of Frauds. It is unclear why the case was pleaded in contract. It might have been thought that the mutual wills doctrine was inapplicable because the plaintiff's promise was not testamentary in nature, or that proprietary estoppel was inapplicable because Jones's promise did not relate to land.[182]

[179] See YK Liew, 'The "Prima Facie Expectation Relief" Approach in the Australian Law of Proprietary Estoppel' (2019) 39 *OJLS* 183.

[180] *Re Dale* (n 78) 47, citing *Re Basham* [1986] 1 WLR 1498 (Ch) 1504. More accurately, the constructive trust is one of a range of possible remedies a court may award to a claimant who successfully claims by way of proprietary estoppel: see Liew (n 74) 134.

[181] *Horton v Jones* (n 89).

[182] It may also be the case that the principles of proprietary estoppel were not as well established then as they are today.

Regardless, there is no reason why, if the case arose today, the facts of the case should fall between the cracks in this way. The overlap between the *Re Dale*-type case and proprietary estoppel would allow the plaintiff to argue that the degree of detrimental reliance she incurred justified a declaration that a constructive trust arose to bind Jones to his promise, a trust which would likewise bind his executors and trustees.[183]

V. CONCLUSION

It is unsurprising that, of all the judges involved in the *Birmingham* case, it is Dixon J's judgment which has been described as 'stat[ing], with all the clarity and learning for which the judgments of that most eminent judge are renowned, what I believe to be a correct analysis of the principles on which a case of enforceable mutual wills depends'.[184] Looking at the various judges' backgrounds, it can be seen that Dixon J was the only judge who could potentially be described as a Chancery 'expert'. Discussing his Honour's legal career, it has been written that '[i]n all fields of the Common Law Sir Owen also excelled and his grasp of the principles of equity was masterly'.[185] His Honour's background can be contrasted with those of Gavan Duffy J and Latham CJ, both of whom held lectureships at the University of Melbourne in the law of contracts and personal property.[186] Of Latham CJ, it has been written that, '[i]n the fields other than Constitutional Law Latham's contributions as a jurist were not, I suspect most would agree, of outstanding significance'.[187] As for Evatt J, he appears to have practised primarily in industrial and labour law.[188]

It is Dixon J's uniquely equitable take on the mutual wills doctrine which has contributed most significantly in elevating *Birmingham* to its 'landmark' status. And it will be Dixon J's judgment which will continue to provide the basis for further developing our understanding of the doctrine.

[183] *cf* S Hudson and B Sloan, 'Testamentary Freedom: Mutual Wills Might Let You Down' in W Barr (ed), *Modern Studies in Property Law*, vol 8 (Oxford, Hart Publishing, 2015) 169–70.

[184] *Re Cleaver* (n 110) 945.

[185] N Stephen, *Sir Owen Dixon: A Celebration* (Carlton, Melbourne University Press, 1986) 23.

[186] 'Personalia – Mr Justice Charles Gavan Duffy' (1933) 7 *Australian Law Journal* 91; Z Cowen, *Sir John Latham and Other Papers* (Oxford, Oxford University Press, 1965).

[187] 'Sir John Latham – a Tribute' (1964) 38 *Australian Law Journal* 188.

[188] K Tennant, *Evatt: Politics and Justice* (Sydney, Angus & Robertson, 1970) 36, 93.

10

Sugden v Lord St Leonards (1876): Probate of the Missing Will – Hamlet Without the Prince?

SIMON COOPER

I. INTRODUCTION

> 'it is not an ordinary case; it involves legal considerations of great importance, although of great rarity'[1]

KNOWN, WITH RATHER insipid humour, as the case of the Lord Chancellor who urged the public to look after their wills and then lost his own, *Sugden v Lord St Leonards* is a prominent decision on probate that has become a popular and memorable anchor for certain legal propositions concerning lost wills and an indicator of the furthest limits of proof by informal means. It deals with two points that arise in the context of a missing will: the approach to reconstructing its contents and the approach to inferring its revocation.

Matters of evidence are of paramount importance to the law of wills. There are several circumstantial factors which suggest that, without legal intervention, evidence as to wills would be at greater risk of error or fraud than evidence as to bilateral, lifetime arrangements. Wills, unlike lifetime arrangements, are not acted upon immediately or even by the parties during their lives; disputes over them almost never arise when the disponor is alive to give evidence of the dealing; antecedent contracts which would supply evidence are not customary; there is no passing of consideration to be recorded; and they control the entirety of one's property. Wills are high value, are often complex in content, run long into the future and are frequently prepared in circumstances of emotional stress. It is these factors which justify particular concern over the evidence of wills, manifested most strongly by the exclusion of certain types of high-risk evidence by requiring compliance with certain formalities. This is the topic that *Sugden v Lord St Leonards* explores.

[1] *Sugden v Lord St Leonards* (1876) 1 PD 154, 231 (Jessel MR) (*Sugden*).

II. THE CASE OF THE MISSING WILL

A. The Great Property Lawyer

Edward Burtenshaw Sugden's career in law and politics had been legendary. From a relatively lowly birth to a London hairdresser[2] in 1781, he was a conveyancer at Lincoln's Inn in his twenties, published the magisterial 'Sugden V and P'[3] aged 24, moved from transactional work to the Bar, where he took silk at 41, was elected as an MP at 47 and appointed Solicitor-General with a knighthood at 48, became Lord Chancellor of Ireland and a Privy Councillor at 53, then became Lord Chancellor of Britain at 71, joining the peerage in the style Baron St Leonards. With such a career – not quite rags to riches, but at least perukes to peerages – it is hardly surprising that he chose the motto '*Labore Vinces*'. He accumulated personal wealth and purchased landed estates. Ensconced in his residence of Boyle Farm,[4] a great villa on the Thames overlooking its own aits in the river and Hampton Court Palace beyond, he spent his later years dwelling on the division of his property amongst his many descendants, with a particular concern to ensure that the new peerage would be supported by suitable financial means, while wrestling with how to signify his displeasure with his grandson Edward, the heir apparent to the peerage and the heir-at-law of the real property.[5]

His internal fluctuations were abundantly clear from the eight codicils he left and from the testimony of a number of persons from different stations in life who had conversed or corresponded with Lord St Leonards in his later years during the 1870s. The unfortunate discovery at his death on 29 January 1875 was that the alleged will, of which he had spoken many times, was not to be found. Despite admonishing the lay readers of his 'Handy Book'[6] to deposit their wills in the central registry, the most eminent property lawyer had neglected to do so, with the result that his estate was drawn into contentious probate proceedings.

B. The Key Witness

The principal witness to the preparation and execution of the alleged will, and the only witness who was able to give evidence as to its contents, was the Hon Charlotte Sugden. She was the only unmarried daughter of the deceased and resided with him

> from childhood up to the time of his death and for many years prior to his death undertook the management of the House for him and was a great favourite of his and nursed him with the utmost unremitting attention during his declining years.[7]

[2] Variously described as a hairdresser, barber or wig maker in the many obituaries of Lord St Leonards.

[3] EB Sugden, *A Practical Treatise of the Law of Vendors and Purchasers of Estates* (London, Butterworth, 1805). The fourteenth and final edition was published in 1862, when the author was in his eighties.

[4] His legal acumen was not matched by his architectural taste: onto the handsome Georgian villa he added a jarring tripartite gabled storey in the Jacobean style with pinnacles. This was taken down, and the facades reworked in brick, as soon as the house was sold.

[5] Lord St Leonards' eldest son, Henry, had died in 1866; Edward was entitled as the eldest son of Henry.

[6] Lord St Leonards, *A Handy Book on Property Law*, 4th edn (London, Blackwood, 1858) 158.

[7] Taken from the affidavit of Frank Sugden: National Archives, J 121/2644, para 4.

She gave evidence that the will had been written in the deceased's own hand and that it was kept along with the codicils in a small black box, something like a dispatch box. The box was usually placed on the floor in the sitting room, it was usually kept locked and the key was on a bunch kept by the deceased. There was a duplicate key kept in an escritoire, and there were five keys in the house by which the escritoire could be opened, one of them lying in a wine cupboard under the charge of the butler.

The last time Charlotte saw the will was on 20 August 1873, when the final codicil was executed and the will replaced in the box. The deceased took ill in September 1873 and was confined to his room from that time until Christmas of the same year, during which time the box was kept by Charlotte in her own room; when he again rejoined the family downstairs, she replaced the box in the sitting room and it remained there until his last illness commenced in March 1874. At that point, the box was again taken by Charlotte, who kept it in her room until his death.

After his death, the three who believed themselves to have been appointed executors under the alleged will called their solicitor, who looked in the box. Although the codicils and some other testamentary papers (a list of assets and an aide-memoire listing the legacies) were found in the box, the will was not there. Every possible search was made for it. A reward of £5,000 was offered for its production,[8] although the family drew the line at the many offers from spiritualists to furnish tidings of it.[9] Undaunted, the alleged executors claimed that the substance of the will could be reconstructed from memory and they propounded for probate a written declaration embodying it.

The existence of the will, its due execution and attestation were all initially denied in the pleadings of the parties who sought to challenge the will. Once the various witnesses had come forward to give evidence of due execution, however, those parties admitted the will's creation and quondam existence.[10] Having made those admissions, there were no disputed primary facts, leaving only two broad matters as the basis for resisting probate: first, whether the evidence of the contents of the will was sufficient; and secondly, whether the evidence rebutted the presumption of revocation that arose from the disappearance of the will.

C. The Feat of Recollection

The first issue effectively raised the principal question of Charlotte's ability to recall the substance of the will. Immediately after the will was found to be missing from the box, Charlotte wrote out from memory a statement of the substance of the will. This was at the suggestion of her solicitor, perhaps remembering the old rule for oral wills under the Statute of Frauds, which required the will or the substance thereof to have been committed to writing by the witness within six days of the making of the will.[11]

[8] Advertisement in *The Times*, 4 March 1875. Perhaps the family did not check the furniture carefully enough for concealed recesses: a housemaid solemnly testified that the deceased was fond of humming a ditty which described how 'an old lady hid her will in the secret drawer of the cabinet' (*The Times*, 20 November 1875, 11).

[9] *The Times*, 20 November 1875, 11.

[10] *Sugden* (n 1) 175.

[11] Statute of Frauds 1677, s 19, applicable whenever six months or more had passed since the speaking of the pretended testamentary words.

The court accepted that she abstained from consulting any other person in order that what she wrote might be the result of her own unassisted recollection. The codicils and other testamentary papers were kept locked and sealed in the box in the presence of the principal party challenging the will, and were only taken out after Charlotte's written statement had been placed in the hands of the solicitor.

According to Charlotte herself, the original will was a large document, filling 19 pages. As counsel challenging the will pointed out,[12] it must have been complicated and replete with technical legal terms.[13] Charlotte's statement indicated devises of several estates and other lands to the executors on trust for Edward for life, followed by an entail to his heirs male, with contingent life estates and entails to the other male grandchildren in order, followed by similar dispositions to the deceased's other sons and their male descendants. Heirlooms were to follow the real estates. An estate in Kent went to the deceased's younger son Frank for life, with entails in tail male to his issue in order and remainder to the persons entitled under the other real estate trusts; it was subjected to a charge for the deceased's debts and a charge for certain expenses owed by a son-in-law. Charlotte received life estates in a nearby house and two tenanted cottages, a tenanted farm, two further tenanted houses and a legacy of £6,000. There were many pecuniary legacies in various specified amounts to other descendants. The residue of the personal estate was divided equally between Charlotte and two of her sisters (estimated at around £10,000 apiece in value[14]), with no share for Charlotte's other siblings, who took only fixed legacies. In the event of the real property devises and limitations failing, there were absolute devises as follows: the main residence at Boyle Farm to Edward, the Kent estate to Frank and the Peasemore estate to Charlotte absolutely. According to these arrangements, Charlotte, along with two of her sisters, did rather better out of the estate than they would have done on intestacy.

Charlotte acknowledged that her recollection of the will was only to the best of her belief, and in relation to some of the legacies she said 'I do not remember how the rest was left'.[15] Nevertheless, when it came to her own legacies, her recollection extended to such details as the gift to her of 'two cows to be selected by herself, out of my conservatory two dozen plants, also to be selected by herself, and two dozen bottles of my old sherry … two loads of hay and two loads of straw'.[16]

Charlotte's solicitor embodied her statement in a more detailed and technical declaration, which was then propounded as the substance of the will. Both her original statement and the refined declaration were admitted in evidence in the proceedings.

D. The Disappearance: Revocation, Foul Play, Misadventure?

The second issue was whether the will had been revoked. Its disappearance while in the possession of the testator led to a presumption of its revocation, so the question turned

[12] *Sugden* (n 1) 174.

[13] That is not to say that Charlotte recalled all 19 pages of drafting: it appears that she recalled the gist of the dispositions, but in the declaration prepared by the solicitor much of the detail was standard-form successive entails in remainder to junior branches and common Victorian boilerplate.

[14] *Sugden* (n 1) 201.

[15] ibid 163.

[16] *Sugden* (n 1) 156–57.

on whether this presumption was rebutted on the facts. That involved an inquiry into the state of mind of the testator, the probability that he changed his intention that the instrument should remain his will, and the opportunity to remove it from the box for destruction.

According to the testimony of several witnesses, the deceased had repeatedly indicated that he had a will, or at least affirmed that he would benefit certain family members in ways that tallied with the alleged will, right up to his conversation with the gardener in May 1874 and some oblique comments to one of his daughters in November 1874. These took place at a time when the deceased had ceased to have practical access to the box, which was in Charlotte's room (for good measure, it was made clear by Charlotte's testimony that others had the means to remove the will from the box, including the butler, who had a key to the escritoire in which the key to the box was kept). On top of that, the deceased had expressed satisfaction that he would die with his affairs in order: Charlotte relayed his comments from 1874 proclaiming that it was the first duty of every man to make a distribution of property in such a manner as to prevent dispute, and describing his pleasure at having settled his earthly affairs.[17]

On the other hand, there was one matter which might have led to a change of heart for the deceased's testamentary intentions: the deceased had ceased to entertain the same degree of affection for his grandson, Edward, that he presumably had at the time of writing the will. This, according to the second codicil, was on account of Edward's proposed matrimonial alliance, which the deceased had vetoed. Edward ceased visiting and the deceased used two codicils to reduce his inheritance significantly, providing a greater share for another son and a daughter-in-law instead. It led to discussion whether the disapproval of Edward's proposals might have prompted the deceased to destroy the will with the intention of writing another in which Edward was further disinherited.[18]

E. The Proceedings

The three individuals claiming to be appointed executors under the will propounded the will as represented by the solicitor's declaration of its substance and effect. The three

[17] 'Remarkable Trials – The St Leonards Will Case', *The Annual Register 1875*, vol 117 (London, Longman, 1876) 186 (reporting Charlotte's examination in chief). Sadly, there is nothing there to corroborate the charming tale that Charlotte was tongue-tied in the witness box until prompted by counsel sipping his water noisily, thus reminding her of the occasions when the deceased had sipped his bedtime nightcap as she read the will aloud to him: RE Megarry, *Miscellany-at-Law* (London, Stevens, 1955) 172.

[18] The testimony dwelt more on the relations with Edward than might be supposed from the judgment. Relations had soured to the extent that the deceased expressed regret at having accepted the peerage (Frank Sugden's testimony reported in *The Times*, 20 November 1875, 11). Charlotte testified to distressing tricks or hoaxes that had been played on the deceased, declining to name the object of her suspicions, although she admitted to holding 'some ideas' – undoubtedly hinting at Edward's hand in it. Certainly the perpetrator had been in a position to replicate the deceased's signature. Charlotte even moved the will box temporarily for fear that 'the perpetrators might carry their malevolence to the extent of abstracting his papers' (*The Times*, 19 November 1875, 11). The family never got to the bottom of the hoaxes. Scotland Yard were baffled. The deceased's anxiety was evident in his plaintive public letters to *The Times* (27 December 1869, 8; 31 December 1869, 9) and in his box of papers relating to the hoaxes (affidavits of Charlotte and Frank Sugden, National Archives, J 121/2644). Subsequent events did little to vouch for Edward's character: following his adultery, his wife obtained a judicial separation and custody of their daughter with costs (National Archives, J 77/274/8051); he descended to an impoverished life in the billiard halls of Richmond (internationally syndicated gossip column, eg *Perth Daily*

were Charlotte herself, the second son of the deceased and a son-in-law. The deceased's first son had died long before, and was survived by his own eldest son, Edward, who, as successor to the peerage, became the second Lord St Leonards. It was Edward who stood to gain most from a challenge to the will: as heir-at-law he would take the deceased's real estate absolutely and to the exclusion of all others. He was named as first defendant, with his siblings also joined as defendants. A daughter and several granddaughters supported the defendants' arguments as interveners.

Leave was granted to hear the cause before the court without a jury. The hearing to determine the issues of fact came before Sir James Hannen, President of the newly established Probate, Divorce and Admiralty Division of the High Court.[19] The plaintiffs, defendants and interveners were represented by two silks and a junior apiece, the teams including those learned in the civil law.[20] The decision was that the will had been duly executed and attested, and its contents were as set out in the declaration save for one minor amendment.

On the question of the will's contents, Hannen P accepted that secondary evidence of the contents was admissible and that it required no higher standard of evidence than for other instruments. In relation to Charlotte's reliability, he found that she was the deceased's daily companion, she had heard the deceased read the will aloud, she had read it herself on three occasions and on several occasions when he was dealing with his testamentary papers she had the will before her or in her hands for reference. She had, therefore, a 'special training' and ample opportunities of becoming acquainted with its contents.[21] Furthermore, her recollection was in so many particulars (although not perfectly) corroborated by the codicils and other papers in the box that her recollection could be regarded as reliable even where there was no other evidence, and that despite her great financial interest in the outcome as one of the residuary legatees.

On the question of revocation, Hannen P found that the deceased's disagreement with Edward was not of such a nature that it would have led the deceased to revoke his will. A revocation prompted by that motive was unlikely as it would have also taken away the testamentary gifts to Charlotte and Frank, who had grown in his affections.[22] In the light of his many subsequent statements about his testamentary gifts, the will's disappearance could be explained by a revocation only if he had either revoked it and forgotten that fact or had systematically lied to Charlotte and Frank and those around him. Neither was probable. Furthermore, it was not in keeping with the deceased's known character. It was:

> wholly impossible to believe that Lord St Leonards, with his knowledge upon such subjects, with the pride which he manifested in doing things as he thought in the right way, even to vanity,

News, 29 July 1884, 3); he indecently assaulted a housemaid and was convicted at the Old Bailey, where he was sentenced to six weeks in prison (*The Times*, 7 July 1884, 11); bankruptcy ensued, Boyle Farm was auctioned by his creditors and he removed to Ireland until his death in 1908, leaving an estate of a mere £4,817: *Calendar of the Grants of Probate* (London, Principal Probate Registry, 1908).

[19] The transfer of jurisdiction to the High Court from the Court of Probate had been effected by the Supreme Court of Judicature Act 1873, s 16. The Court of Probate, in turn, had obtained its jurisdiction in place of the ecclesiastical courts by the Court of Probate Act 1857, s 4.

[20] Drs Deane, Spinks and Tristram.

[21] *Sugden* (n 1) 177–78.

[22] Although not mentioned in the judgment, it was sworn that Charlotte had 'no property with the exception of £350 in the Turkish bonds and about £50 cash': affidavit of Frank Sugden (n 7).

> should have destroyed this will, knowing, as he must have done, the confusion he would throw his affairs into, and the certainty there would be of bringing about that litigation which he so frequently expressed a desire to avoid.[23]

Having made the findings of fact, a later hearing briskly pronounced in favour of the will as contained in the declaration, limited until the original or a more complete copy could be found,[24] and in favour of the eight codicils.

F. The Appeal

Edward and his siblings appealed. The hearing took place on 7 March 1876 and judgment was delivered by the Court of Appeal only six days later. The Court of Appeal referred to the judgment of Hannen P with approbation and dismissed the appeal. Full judgments were delivered by Sir Alexander Cockburn CJ and Sir George Jessel MR, who reached the same conclusions; short concurring judgments were added by James LJ, Mellish LJ and Bagallay JA.[25]

On the question of revocation, Cockburn CJ confirmed the presumption of revocation arising when a will missing at the testator's death is shown to have been in the custody of the testator, but added the rider that the presumption will be more or less strong according to the character of the custody which the testator had over the will. In the case, it was 'anything but a close custody',[26] the presence of the will in the strong box being well known, the location of the box being visible until removed to Charlotte's room and the keys being accessible to the household. There was, moreover, evidence against the deceased having revoked the will by the powerful combination of the deceased's attentiveness to his testamentary arrangements, his sense of duty in providing for his dependants, his methodical habits, his warmest affection for Charlotte, who would have been left unprovided for had the will be revoked, and his repeated statements to all and sundry expressing his satisfaction at what he had been able to do for Charlotte and Frank. In the light of those considerations, it was vastly improbable that the testator had revoked it.

What had happened to it was no part of the findings, but a little speculation could not be resisted:

> The only conclusion I can arrive at is, not that he destroyed it, but that it was clandestinely got at by somebody and surreptitiously taken away; who that somebody is, is one of those mysteries which time may possibly solve, but which at present it would defy human ingenuity to say.

Decidedly speculative in the absence of any motive offered – such as the butler's curiosity or the heir-at-law's greed – but no more so than the fantastically speculative observation

[23] *Sugden* (n 1) 203.
[24] The report of *Sugden* does not refer to this limit in its summary of the decree (207), but it was in the notice of application (National Archives, J 121/2644); it was proposed by counsel in *Sugden* (n 1) 205 and was acknowledged by Jessel MR (238).
[25] Sir Richard Bagallay retained his original title as Justice of Appeal pursuant to the Supreme Court of Judicature Act 1875, which, as Attorney-General, he had piloted through committee stage.
[26] *Sugden* (n 1) 218.

in another missing will case, stating that it was in no degree improbable that the deceased, being a great smoker, had taken the will out of his trunk and used it to light his pipe![27]

Despite its brief foray into hypothetical realms, the court showed considerable self-restraint in forbearing from any aspersions directed towards Edward. There had been considerable evidence raised at trial which could have been understood to blacken Edward's character and to insinuate in the audience's mind not just a motive for the revocation of the will, but a motive for Edward, spurred either by malice or greed, to steal and destroy it.[28] While the rules of evidence might have been liberal and inclusive, the court seems extremely careful to dismiss from consideration any such evidence which carries insubstantial probative force and which might, had a jury been sitting, have had a seriously prejudicial effect.

Having dispatched the revocation point, the next issue was the reconstruction of the contents of the will. There was in principle no difficulty in admitting parol evidence of the contents of a will in the same manner as for any other instrument. That had been established by authority[29] and was consistent with good policy: to refuse such evidence 'would enable any person who desired, from some sinister motive, to frustrate the testamentary disposition of a dead man, by merely getting possession of the will'.[30] Cockburn CJ did not explicitly consider whether the degree of cogency required of secondary evidence was the same for wills as for other instruments, but Jessel MR made the equation clear,[31] just as Hannen P had done in rejecting certain dicta to the effect that reconstructing the contents of a will demanded 'the strictest proof'.[32]

The Court of Appeal held Charlotte's parol evidence to be entirely sufficient to prove the contents. Her honesty was admitted on all sides, her deep interest in the residuary legacy had not tainted her evidence and the accuracy of her recollection was generally reliable for the reasons given in the High Court, despite it falling short of perfection. That much was corroborated by the codicils, along with the other testamentary documents and oral statements of the deceased, which, despite earlier conflicting judicial opinions,[33] were held to be admissible hearsay, though the court would have reached the same conclusion without relying on them.

Finally, the court dealt with the problem arising from the incompleteness of Charlotte's recollection. The issue was whether this was a ground for refusing probate. The court decided that its duty was to give probate to the will so far as it could be ascertained, though it might leave unfulfilled an intended legacy, this being a lesser evil than striking down all of the testator's wishes.

[27] *Davis v Davis* (1824) 162 ER 275, 277; 2 Add 223.

[28] Above n 18. This seems to have been the commonly held suspicion: eg 'Correspondence' (1884) 18 *American Law Review* 875, 879. The notable exception is JB Atlay, *The Victorian Chancellors* (London, Smith Elder, 1908) 50, who claimed to have it on good authority that it was taken by a household servant anxious to see what legacies it gave to domestics, only to find that the opportunity of replacing it evaporated when the will-box was removed to Charlotte's room.

[29] *Brown v Brown* (1858) 120 ER 327; 8 E & B 876.

[30] *Sugden* (n 1) 220.

[31] ibid 239.

[32] ibid 176 (Hannen P), rejecting the dicta in *Wharram v Wharram* (1864) 164 ER 1290, 1292; 3 Sw & Tr 301, 306 (Sir JP Wilde).

[33] *Doe d Shallcross v Palmer* (1851) 20 LJQB 367; *In the Goods of Ripley* (1858) 164 ER 632; 1 Sw & Tr 68, *Quick v Quick* (1864) 164 ER 1347; 3 Sw & Tr 442.

III. DOCTRINAL SIGNIFICANCE

The Court of Appeal's contribution to the development of legal doctrine is modest. No issues of substantive law were in dispute. The significance attributed to the case is in the field of procedural law, and even there its precedential status is not always entirely clear.[34] It offers a range of determinations which concern presumptions, evidentiary thresholds, and the admissibility and sufficiency of evidence. Within those elements, the case does not break new ground in all respects, but, rather, selects from amongst various competing traditions.

A. Presumption of Revocation

The decision establishes two points about the presumption of revocation arising from a missing will that had been in the testator's custody. First, the strength of the presumption varies with the closeness of the custody. Secondly, declarations by a testator of his adherence to the will are admissible in evidence to rebut the presumption, as an exception to the general rule excluding hearsay evidence.

B. Proof of Contents

The points relating to proof of the contents of a missing will were the occasion for the more intense argumentation. Five items can be extracted from the Court of Appeal's decision.

(i) The decision confirms that the contents of a will may be proved by secondary evidence. This is far from a novel point, many cases having been previously decided on that basis.[35] However, *Sugden* quelled the doubts raised a decade earlier in the Court of Probate by Sir JP Wilde, who questioned whether the legislative intent implicit in the Wills Act 1837 was that the will itself be produced to the court.[36] Even though *Sugden* confirms the earlier case law allowing secondary evidence of contents, the judgments in *Sugden* pass silently over the ancient case law of the King's Bench, which had refused to reconstruct a will that had been ceased to be physically in existence at the time of death. Regrettably, nobody cited[37] the whimsical seventeenth-century case, *Etheringham v Etheringham*,[38] in which a will was found 'gnawn all to pieces with rats'; there, in

[34] E Kahn, 'Trimestral Potpourri' (1995) 122 *South Africa Law Journal* 351, 356.

[35] eg *Trevelyan v Trevelyan* (1810) 1 Ph 149; 161 ER 944; *Foster v Foster* (1823) 1 Add 462; 162 ER 163; *Davis v Davis* (1824) 2 Add 223; 162 ER 275; *Martin v Laking* (1828) 1 Hagg Ecc 244; 161 ER 152; *Brown v Brown* (1858) 120 ER 327; 8 E & B 876. Lord St Leonards himself knew that 'destruction of the will by accident or mistake, if clearly proved, would not defeat the gifts if the contents of the will could be shown': Lord St Leonards (n 6) 146.

[36] *Wharram v Wharram* (1864) 3 Sw & Tr 301, 304–05; 164 ER 1290, 1292.

[37] Yet Jessel MR in *Sugden* (n 1) 237 seems to recall its memorable facts when he briefly alludes to an example of a will that had been eaten by rats.

[38] *Etheringham v Etheringham* (1670) Aleyn 2; 82 ER 883.

relation to devises of real property,[39] the King's Bench held that the jury could accept the secondary evidence of contents only if the gnawing had occurred after the testator's death.[40] *Sugden* holds that secondary evidence is admissible whenever the destruction or loss occurred and abandons all idea that the documentary record must enjoy a real physical existence at the time when it becomes effective.

(ii) The threshold for the cogency of evidence for establishing the content of the will is not pitched at some particular high level but is simply equated with the threshold for deeds and other instruments. This is not a novel point, but merely reasserts the long-standing approach in probate, which had recently been shaken by Sir JP Wilde in the Court of Probate stating that 'In the absence of the will itself this portion of the case requires clear, strong and irrefragable evidence, free from suspicion or doubt in its sources, exact and certain in its conclusions'.[41] The response in *Sugden* was that the court need not bind itself to some particular abstract threshold, but would weigh the evidence in the normal manner.[42]

(iii) Declarations by a testator made before or after execution of the will are admissible as evidence of the contents of the will.[43] In respect of post-execution declarations, this required the court to create a new exception[44] to the rule excluding hearsay and to overrule an earlier case to the contrary.[45] The point may, however, have been obiter dictum since it was concluded that Charlotte's direct evidence alone would have been sufficient without the hearsay.[46]

The decision to admit a testator's post-execution declarations is interesting because of its interaction with the principle that unattested alterations to the will made after its execution are void. The dictum in *Sugden* would allow the testator's unattested and unwritten statements to control what is probated, despite being made after execution. While that does not directly contradict the rule against unattested alterations, it does show that the court in *Sugden* refuses to take analogies that would restrict the evidence, and instead demonstrates the court's confidence in its ability to discern whether a declaration comprises a bona fide representation of the will as executed, a mistake of recollection or some disingenuous ploy to informally revise its content.

[39] Presumably the Ecclesiastical Court applied no such rule requiring existence at death, since the will had already been proved there in relation to personal property.

[40] See also *Lawrence v Kete* (1648) Aleyn 54; 82 ER 912 (not cited in *Sugden*): 'If a will continue in writing at the time of the death of the testator, although it be lost or burnt afterwards, it stands good; but if it be burnt at the time of his death, the devise is void.'

[41] *Podmore v Whatton* (1864) 3 Sw & Tr 449, 451; 164 ER 1349, 1350 (not cited in *Sugden*). See also *Wharram v Wharram* (1864) 164 ER 1290, 1293; 3 Sw & Tr 301, 307.

[42] This part of the decision was in turn shaken by Lord Herschell's obiter comments that parol evidence of contents must be of 'extreme cogency' and convincing 'beyond reasonable doubt': *Woodward v Goulstone* (1886) 11 App Cas 469, 475.

[43] This was the only point for dissent: Mellish LJ (251) argued that to allow the testator's post-execution statements would subvert the rule against hearsay by allowing too broad an exception, and that even pre-execution statements should be limited to those which corroborate other evidence of contents. The House of Lords felt that there was much in favour of entirely excluding the testator's post-execution statements: *Woodward v Goulstone* (1886) 11 App Cas 469, 480, 484.

[44] For a penetrating analysis of the hearsay issue, including a critique of Cockburn CJ's equation of pre- and post-execution declarations, see C Tapper, 'Hillmon Rediscovered and Lord St Leonards Resurrected' (1990) 106 *LQR* 441. The proposition that *Sugden* restricts admissible post-execution declarations to those which corroborate other evidence seems to be incorrect: S Alward, 'Chief Justice Cockburn' (1915) 35 *Canadian Law Times* 655, 663.

[45] *Quick v Quick* (1864) 164 ER 1347; 3 Sw & Tr 442.

[46] *Sugden* (n 1) 224.

(iv) Incomplete evidence of the will's contents does not preclude it from probate. In this regard, the court took a view entirely opposed to the Real Property Commissioners, whose work led to the Wills Act 1837. Their view – not put before the court – was that 'the most serious evil'[47] lay in disrupting the balance set by the testator's will if only part were probated. In particular, the testator might in one clause bequeath all his leaseholds and personal estate to his eldest son, the heir-at-law, and in a later clause might devise all his freeholds to his younger son. If the part of the will containing the first clause were admitted to probate but not the second, then the eldest son would take the entire estate and the younger son nothing. Such a result would not only deprive the younger son of what he was intended to receive under the missing part of the will, but would also take away that which he would otherwise have received on intestacy. That was thought to be too much of a risk. It motivated some of the commissioners' proposals, such as the rule that the testator must sign at the foot in order to signify that the testator's record of testamentary intentions was not incomplete.[48] The Court of Appeal nonetheless dismissed concerns of that nature and allowed probate, even though it was aware that Charlotte could not precisely remember all the legacies and had erred in some particulars.

In relation to Charlotte's errors, the court corrected the declaration on the basis of circumstantial rather than direct evidence of the will's content. The court was influenced by evidence that the errors were minor: so where Charlotte could not recall which items had been struck through, the court acted upon the testator's own declaration in a codicil that his 'principal alteration'[49] had been the substitution of one trustee for another. Rather than failing the entirety, the court took an approach of weighing the evidence and making inferences about the extent of the possible errors and omissions in Charlotte's reconstruction.

(v) In determining the contents of a will, it is open to the court to rely on the testimony of a sole witness who takes a substantial interest under the will. This is a matter that was clearly raised by counsel, but it is easily overlooked since the appeal judgments do not tackle it expressly and do not refer to the authority counsel cited in support. The court did acknowledge the corroboration to Charlotte's testimony which was afforded by the codicils, the testamentary papers and the deceased's declarations, but all that was held not to be essential to the decision. The court forcibly asserted that Charlotte's evidence would have been accepted 'if there were not one tittle of confirmatory evidence'.[50]

A sole interested witness might therefore prove the contents – a decisive break from the ecclesiastical court's rule in probate proceedings, which had required the evidence of two witnesses.[51] The two-witness rule was not merely based on some inference from, or

[47] 'Fourth Report of the Commissioners Appointed to Inquire into the Law of England Respecting Real Property' (1833, HCP) 13.

[48] ibid 16. The abolition of the foot rule of the Wills Act 1837, s 9 by the Wills Act Amendment Act 1852, s 1 was an achievement for which Lord St Leonards himself took the credit.

[49] *Sugden* (n 1) 182.

[50] ibid 224.

[51] JH Wigmore, 'Required Numbers of Witnesses: A Brief History of the Numerical System in England' (1901) 15 *Harvard Law Review* 83; 'Fourth Report of the Commissioners' (n 47) 62. Not every particular fact or every part of the testamentary transaction need be proved by two witnesses, provided that the circumstances showed that a testamentary act was in progress and tended to corroborate the act itself: EV Williams, A *Treatise on the Law of Executors and Administrators*, 5th edn, vol 1 (London, Stevens & Norton, 1856) 306.

analogy to, the formality rule concerning the execution of a will, as it pre-dated both the Wills Act 1837 and the Statute of Frauds 1677. In relation to evidence of contents, the rule was acknowledged by the first published source of probate law written in English, citing the continental authorities of the Renaissance:

> What if a Testament being made in Writing, and afterwards lost by some Casualty … whether may this Will written and lost be proved by Witnesses, yea or nay? Whereunto my Answer is, that albeit the very original Testament be lost, yet if there be two Witnesses, which did see and read the Testament written, and do remember the Contents thereof, these two Witnesses, so deposing the Tenor of the Will, are sufficient for the Proof thereof …[52]

From 1857, the rules of evidence in contentious probate were aligned with those of common law,[53] so that two witnesses were no longer insisted upon. Yet there were 'great lawyers'[54] at the time of the *Sugden* litigation who advised that a court would still not go as far as granting probate to a will where the contents were proved by secondary evidence from only one witness who had a financial interest in the outcome. They had even begun preparing heads of compromise to be embodied in a private Act of Parliament.[55] But the great lawyers were wrong. *Sugden* shows the court's inclination to resist any predetermined rule of evidence based on numerical minima and instead assess for itself the credibility of the particular speaker and her testimony.

C. Overall Impression

Taking collectively all the above points resolved by the Court of Appeal in respect of proof, it is apparent that the court has entered an era in which it has an unwavering belief in its ability to sift evidence. This should be no surprise when the King's Bench practice of the time is compared to the old ecclesiastical courts' custom of trying issues on written depositions taken in private through the medium of an examiner,[56] without face-to-face cross-examination by the other side in front of the tribunal of fact.[57] In *Sugden*, various

[52] H Swinburn, *A Brief Treatise of Testaments and Last Wills* (London, Company of Stationers, 1611) 265b (pt 6, s 14, pl 4).

[53] Court of Probate Act 1857, s 33: 'The rules of evidence observed in the superior courts of common law at Westminster shall be applicable to and observed in the trial of all questions of fact'; Rules of HM Court of Probate in Respect of Contentious Business 1857, r 32.

[54] WS Holdsworth, *History of English Law*, vol 16 (London, Methuen, 1936) 46. The great lawyers included 'some of the ablest members of the Common Law bar and that great real property lawyer, the late Mr Joshua Williams': JB Atlay, *The Victorian Chancellors* (London, Smith Elder, 1908) 50.

[55] Atlay (n 54) 50. Atlay also reports, perhaps surprisingly, that the suggestion to pursue proceedings came from an old member of Doctors' Commons.

[56] See generally 'Report of the Commissioners Appointed to Inquire into the Practice and Jurisdiction of the Ecclesiastical Courts' (1831–2 PP 199, xxiv) 18–19; BG Hutton, 'The Reform of the Testamentary Jurisdiction of the Ecclesiastical Courts 1830–1857', PhD Thesis (Brunel University, 2002).

[57] These shortcomings had been one motivation for the establishment of a temporal probate court: 'Fourth Report of the Commissioners' (n 47) 62–65. Viva voce testimony and cross-examination before the tribunal were introduced for contentious probate regarding personal property by the Court of Probate Act 1857, s 31, and specifically confirmed on the transfer of jurisdiction to the High Court under the Supreme Court of Judicature Act 1875, Schedule, O 37, r 1, along with the general preservation of other probate rules under the Supreme Court of Judicature Act 1875, s 18 and the broad adoption of the practice and procedure of the predecessor court under the Supreme Court of Judicature Act 1873, s 21.

rigid constraints on admissibility are consigned to history: no blanket prohibition on secondary evidence, no minimum threshold for its cogency, no restriction of evidence to account for the loss of the will before death, no two-witness rule, no ban on interested witnesses, no rejection of testator's post-execution hearsay and no preclusion of evidence which shows that the incompletely reconstituted parts of the will were insubstantial. The court dismissed the opportunity presented by Sir JP Wilde[58] to tighten the rules of evidence in probate and even to suppress altogether secondary evidence of the contents. There are consequential questions about whether similarly bold approaches would be taken in relation to other doctrines reliant on external evidence, such as rules concerning interpretation and rectification of wills or additions and deletions to documentary wills.[59]

The decision in *Sugden* reveals a rational spirit of factual inquiry that dismisses prophylactic evidential rules which would deny the courts access to evidence for fear of being swayed by deception or flawed memory. It betokens a supreme confidence in the forensic process and its capacity to test the evidence and arrive at the truth. This liberality in the rules of evidence stands in contrast to the stark formality rules of statute law. There appears at first glance a certain tension between the statutory rule requiring that a will must be in writing, executed and attested on the one hand, and on the other hand the judicial rule that a single interested witness may establish the contents (and due execution) by oral testimony. Does this application of the procedural law of evidence undercut the substantive law of formalities? The answer requires a consideration of the functions of formalities.

IV. FUNCTIONAL ANALYSIS OF FORMALITIES

A. A Catalogue of Formality Functions

The idea behind the functional analysis of formality requirements is that they are underpinned by considerations of policy. They are not ends in themselves, but are capable of being justified as a means to attain objectives concerning the law relating to property transfers. The classic reference point for analysis is an article by Fuller concerned primarily with contract formalities.[60]

Fuller advanced three functions.[61] The first is the Evidentiary Function, which recognises the effect of formalities in ensuring a record of the existence and contents of the disposition. The second is the Cautionary Function. This recognises the paternalistic role of formalities in hindering legal effect until some rite has been carried out, which allows a pause for deliberation and an opportunity for circumspection, perhaps even to consider taking legal advice. It acts as a check against impulsive or inconsiderate action,

[58] *Wharram v Wharram* (1864) 164 ER 1290, 1292; 3 Sw & Tr 301, 304–6; *Podmore v Whatton* (1864) 3 Sw & Tr 449; 164 ER 1349.

[59] See B Häcker, 'What's in a Will?' in B Häcker and C Mitchell (eds), *Current Issues in Succession Law* (Oxford, Hart Publishing, 2016) 158–64.

[60] LL Fuller, 'Consideration and Form' (1941) 41 *Columbia Law Review* 799.

[61] ibid 800–03.

and potentially a moment away from external pressures.[62] The third is the Channelling Function. Fuller argued that a legal formality requirement may serve to encourage owners to implement their wishes through a particular medium, thereby making it easier for others to determine whether the owner intended to alter legal rights and, if so, what type of alteration.

Fuller appreciated the intimate connection between the three functions:[63] whatever tends to accomplish one often also tends to accomplish the others. A requirement to furnish a record of intention will encourage the author to deliberate. Devices which induce deliberation are also likely to aid in generating evidence of the intention. Whenever deliberation is induced and a record generated, it is more likely that the party will channel his or her intention through a recognised legal category. Any channelling which effects a division between legally effective and ineffective outcomes, or between types of legal transactions, tends also to support the deliberation as to the legal consequences. Despite these close interrelationships, Fuller counselled against confusing the functions because the determination of a marginal case may hinge upon assumptions about what is the primary function of a particular formality requirement. That certainly rings true for the analysis of an outlier such as *Sugden*.

Fuller's analysis does not exhaust the scholarship on formalities. Writing at the same time, Gulliver and Tilson created their own tripartite functional analysis of formalities which covers similar but not identical ground.[64] First, they recognised the same Evidentiary Function that formalities may enhance the reliability of the evidence of the testator's wishes, particularly through the requirement of writing to preserve a record that is free from the risks of misunderstanding or unconscious bias in recollecting its terms and which may be available long after the witnesses have died. Secondly, a Ritual Function recognises that a formality may impress the testator with the significance of his actions and will therefore both encourage the testator not to act ill-advisedly, and also assist the court to infer that the expressed intention was meant to be legally operative and not merely a tentative, unconfirmed draft. This function possesses two limbs, which correspond to aspects of Fuller's Cautionary Function and Channelling Function. Thirdly, a Protective Function is alleged to safeguard a testator from undue influence and other forms of imposition at the time of execution. This corresponds to another aspect of Fuller's Cautionary Function.

Another contributor, Langbein, approached the subject specifically with regard to wills and distilled four functions.[65] He accepted the Evidentiary Function and Cautionary Function. A Protective Function recognised the effectiveness of formalities in protecting a testator from external impositions or documentary substitutions. Langbein's fourth function was labelled a Channelling Function, but was a novel concept that differed

[62] The obvious example springing to Hannen P's mind was the 'young man caught in the toils of a harlot, who makes use of her influence to induce him to make a will in her favour': *Wingrove v Wingrove* (1885) 11 PD 81, 82.

[63] Fuller (n 60) 803–04.

[64] A Gulliver and C Tilson, 'Classification of Gratuitous Transfers' (1941) 51 *Yale Law Journal* 1, especially 3–15.

[65] JH Langbein, 'Substantial Compliance with the Wills Act' (1975) 88 *Harvard Law Review* 489, 492–27. See also JH Langbein, 'Excusing Harmless Error in the Execution of Wills' (1987) 87 *Columbia Law Review* 1, 3.

from Fuller's analysis under the same name. Langbein understood formalities to have the potential to encourage such a degree of uniformity in the organisation, language and content of wills that their validity could be routinely and efficiently determined by bureaucratic probate processes that are more administrative than adjudicative in nature.

Further purposes attributable to formalities have been raised by Perillo.[66] He identified a Clarifying Function which acknowledges that formality requirements may tend to focus the testator's attention on drafting the formal document and consequently serve to refine the terms of the transaction as he contemplates his intentions in depth. Perillo also identified a Regulatory and Taxation Function on the ground that directing a transaction into a particular formal channel may make it easier for the state to pursue its interest in regulating, policing and taxing certain transactions.[67] To that might also be added the state's interest in collecting data.[68]

The functions outlined above have been widely accepted as the catalogue of purposes capable of being served by formalities in respect of wills. But it has been argued that only one subset of them truly justifies the imposition of statutory formalities, and that all the other functions are matters that could be perfectly well (and more efficiently) achieved by other means. Eric Posner[69] has proposed arguments which, translated to the case of wills, suggest that the testator rather than the state should be permitted to decide whether it is worth running the risks against which the formalities typically protect – the risk of recording a will in a form possessing lower evidential reliability, the risk of making a will via a less clear channel and the risk of hastiness when preparing the will. After all, the costs of doing so would be borne by the intended beneficiaries, not inflicted more widely on society, so the testator should be permitted to opt out. But optional formalities would not protect against a fraudster who simply gave false testimony that the testator had opted out of the formalities and made an oral will. Posner contends that the only function which justifies mandatory formalities is to hinder fraudsters from making such false claims. In view of its special attributes, Posner seeks to isolate it from the Evidentiary Function of which it is a subset under Fuller's account. A suitable label might be the Anti-fraud Function.

B. *Sugden* and the Formality Functions

This section turns to what the decision in *Sugden* implies for the formality functions canvassed above. The Wills Act requires a will to satisfy formality requirements of writing, signature and attestation,[70] to which the full catalogue of formality functions

[66] JM Perillo, 'The Statute of Frauds in the Light of the Functions and Dysfunctions of Form' (1974) 43 *Fordham Law Review* 39, 56–58.

[67] ibid 62–64.

[68] P Critchley, 'Taking Formalities Seriously' in S Bright and J Dewar (eds), *Land Law: Themes and Perspectives* (Oxford, Oxford University Press, 1998) 518.

[69] E Posner, 'Norms, Formalities and the Statute of Frauds' (1996) 144 *University of Pennsylvania Law Review* 1971, 1976–77, 1984–86.

[70] Wills Act 1837, s 9: 'No Will shall be valid unless it shall be in Writing and executed in manner herein-after mentioned; (that is to say,) it shall be signed at the Foot or End thereof by the Testator, or by some other Person in his Presence and by his Direction; and such Signature shall be made or acknowledged by the Testator in the Presence of Two or more Witnesses present at the same Time; and such Witnesses shall attest and shall subscribe the Will in the Presence of the Testator, but no Form of Attestation shall be necessary.'

outlined above can be attributed. *Sugden* allowed the reconstruction of the contents of a will through highly informal evidence, principally Charlotte's oral testimony, supplemented by various hearsay statements found to be unnecessary for the decision. Yet doing so would not prevent the fulfilment of many of the formality functions associated with the Wills Act.

In particular, the Cautionary Function is preserved intact because of the need for evidence of due execution (which, by the time of trial, had been conceded). If duly executed, the testator must have committed the will to writing and sought out witnesses for its attestation, the very processes which bring an opportunity for the testator to reflect and deliberate. The same process would engage the Clarifying Function. The testator's signature and attestation may also be taken as convenient signals that the testator intended to make the document operative as a testamentary instrument and that it represented his settled wishes, in which case *Sugden* is also fully consistent with the implementation of the Channelling and Ritual Functions. And it does nothing to impair the Regulatory, Taxation or Information Functions. But all those functions rank low in the list of priorities. The main issue emanating from *Sugden* is its impact on the Anti-fraud Function.

C. *Sugden* and the Anti-fraud Function

The Evidentiary Function is the most obvious and prominent function of statutory formalities for private instruments. To the extent that the formalities deter fraudsters, they pursue the Anti-fraud Function. Take the example of the requirements imposed by the Wills Act formalities: writing, signature and attestation. They exclude any non-conforming putative wills from admission in evidence and thus discourage all but the most dedicated fraudster who is prepared to go beyond mere perjured testimony and forge a documentary will.

If the Wills Act was understood to require that a will could be proved in the probate court by no method other than producing the conforming physical embodiment of the will, then a strong Anti-fraud Function could be attributed to the statutory formalities. But the decision in *Sugden* clearly derogates from that potential function by reconstructing the contents of a will on the oral evidence of a sole interested witness. *Sugden* asserts that there are no rules that would automatically filter out evidence of contents simply because the evidence is of a class that is generally perceived to be unreliable. Perhaps this is unsurprising given that *Sugden* was, in a sense, a hard case. On the facts, there were very powerful circumstances to lend credibility to Charlotte's story.[71] Her testimony was consistently corroborated by the deceased's written notes and declarations by multiple witnesses. Moreover, Charlotte had her reputation to protect, for if the will were later to emerge and differ from her testimony, it would be very difficult for her to claim that such a complex and intricate content as she claimed to have memorised was all an innocent mistake. In circumstances where her credibility was universally commended, these factors

[71] Highly credible secondary evidence in the form of lawyer's drafts had long been accepted: see *Podmore v Whatton* (1864) 3 Sw & Tr 449; 164 ER 1349. Lord St Leonards had missed such an opportunity by doing his own 'home-made' will!

could only have encouraged the court to seek substantive justice and avoid restrictions on admissibility.

Doubtlessly the court in *Sugden* regarded itself as competent to determine the truth of the oral testimony on each of these matters through the normal processes of requiring oaths, observing the demeanour during viva voce testimony, live cross-examination and self-administered judicial cautions in relation to hearsay evidence and interested witnesses. Nevertheless, the effect of *Sugden* is that the Wills Act is perceived not to exclude evidence of contents on the ground that such evidence is unwritten, unsigned or unattested; instead, the decision shows a notable willingness to admit the high-risk class of informal evidence. The decision therefore prevents the Wills Act formalities from pursuing any Anti-fraud Function in relation to the will contents. This does not sit very comfortably with the general understanding of the Wills Act that may be deduced from its attestation rules or from its antecedents.

D. The Wills Act and Attestation

The tension between *Sugden* and the Wills Act is brought into stark relief by considering two elements of attesting the execution of a will. First, Charlotte alone could not have validly attested the testator's execution of the will because a second attesting witness would have been required. Secondly, Charlotte could not have taken her legacy under the will and also proved due execution as an attesting witness, not even alongside a second witness; before the Wills Act, her legacy would have led to disqualification, whereas after the Wills Act the incompatibility between legacy and attestation would have been manifested by her forfeiting the legacy.[72] So Charlotte's competence to testify as attesting witness to the execution of the will in either of these circumstances would have been impaired. In direct contrast to proof of execution, *Sugden* confirms that Charlotte was fully competent to give proof of contents – without a second witness and without forfeiting her legacy.

The statutory rules for proof of execution could have been used as the basis for arguing that similar restrictions ought to apply to proof of contents. It is submitted that they are more than merely analogous to proof of contents; rather, they are integral to the idea of authenticity which underlies the Wills Act formalities. Prior to the Wills Act, when oral wills could still be made, the witnesses had to give evidence not only that the testator had bidden them to attest his declaration, but also of the contents declared. There was no separation between the proof of attested publication and the proof of content. Once the Wills Act imposed a written form, the signature and attesting subscriptions served to authenticate the preceding record of contents. If the signature and attesting subscriptions are divorced from the record of the content, as *Sugden* necessarily implies, they lose their capacity to authenticate the terms of the will. The outcome was that the execution ceremony was devoid of any power to authenticate Charlotte's evidence as to contents.

The argument that proof of contents should not be divorced from the proof of attested execution which authenticates the contents was one which found favour with the former

[72] Wills Act 1837, s 15.

probate judge, Sir JP Wilde, who, after mentioning some recent cases of reconstructing missing wills, launched this attack:

> Now, in all this I venture to doubt if the operation of the statute relating to wills has been sufficiently considered. To what end, it may be asked, does the Wills Act of 1857 declare that 'no will shall be valid' unless it be in writing and signed by the testator in the presence of witnesses, and signed by them in the presence of the testator, if a parol oath and the fiction of a loss can make a will valid without any writing at all? … Was not this writing itself, and the triple signatures with the detailed requirements as to position on the paper, intended also, as living witnesses, to bear visible testimony to the reality of the act and the exact disposition of the property which they were designed to attest? And if so, can the Court dispense with the paper and writing altogether?[73]

The powerful logic against separating proof contents from proof of execution, coupled with the stiffly worded remonstration of the Court of Probate, presented the court in *Sugden* with an opportunity to reject Charlotte's non-compliant proof of content. In deciding the opposing way, the court in *Sugden* selected to remove an Anti-fraud Function that could have been attributed to the statute, leaving only a rump of miscellaneous and considerably less important functions.

E. The Wills Act and Its Antecedents

The Wills Act 1837 may not have explicitly ordered the courts to reject oral evidence of contents, but could that have been the assumption of those who prepared the Act? The Act was substantially driven by the Fourth Report of the Real Property Commissioners,[74] who never confronted the issue of secondary evidence. One of the immense written submissions to the Commissioners briefly mentioned an old case in which it was held that devises in a will were good even though the will be lost or burnt after the testator's death,[75] from which the Commissioners ought to have appreciated the necessary implication that secondary evidence was admissible. On the other hand, the only relevant comment by the Commissioners themselves was to record the common law practice that in a title contest depending on the validity of the will, 'the Will must be produced before the Judge and Jury'.[76] Bearing in mind that the Commissioners had felt constrained not to suggest alterations in the general rules of evidence,[77] the common law rule might have been an assumption on which their proposed reforms were founded. The inference is not strong, but if the Commissioners perceived the necessity for actual production of the documentary will as an integral part of their scheme, then it is another ground for arguing that *Sugden*'s admission of secondary evidence of contents was a significant step away from the legislative policy.

The thrust of the Commissioners' report was to rationalise and unify the law of wills, in particular the form of execution, and this was achieved by a single solution for all

[73] *Wharram v Wharram* (1864) 164 ER 1290, 1292; 3 Sw & Tr 301, 304–05.
[74] 'Fourth Report of the Commissioners' (n 47).
[75] ibid 'Appendix, Evidence of Samuel Gale', [267], citing *Lawrence v Kete* (1648) Aleyn 54; 82 ER 912.
[76] ibid 34.
[77] ibid 20.

wills based on the writing, signature and attestation requirements applicable to wills of real property under the Statute of Frauds 1677.[78] It is therefore also worth considering the motivations for the Statute of Frauds as the direct ancestor of the Wills Act. Without any doubt, the Statute of Frauds was not merely aimed at fulfilling various Cautionary or Channelling functions: its preamble recites that it exists 'For prevention of many fraudulent Practices which are commonly endeavoured to be upheld by Perjury and Subornation of Perjury'. Although historical investigations have shown that its early sections were designed with a channelling goal in mind, namely to force title documents into a form that could voluntarily be enrolled or registered,[79] the immediate objective was to ensure that documents affecting real property were authenticated to reduce fraud.[80] This was how the bench understood it.[81] The primacy of this Anti-fraud Function is evident from the explanation that the will formality rules in the Statute of Frauds were a specific response to a case involving oral testimony to the effect that one will had been orally revoked and replaced by another oral will – all of which evidence was later found to be perjured.[82] Tracking its descent into the Wills Act suggests that the same anti-fraud objective should have been the primary concern in *Sugden*.

In fact, the Court of Appeal in *Sugden* passed over the risk of fraud and instead focused on the reasons for admitting secondary evidence of contents. Cockburn CJ adhered to an earlier decision on wills[83] without addressing any tensions with the Statute of Frauds or the Wills Act, but rather presenting the converse argument that without secondary evidence valid wills might occasionally be excluded from probate – a view which the Commissioners had seen as a necessary sacrifice.[84] Jessel MR justified the admission of secondary evidence by reference to case law on deeds which had accepted it. But deeds in those days had not been regulated by any statutory formalities, so the matter of legislative anti-fraud policy was absent from discussion.

In summary, *Sugden* deprives the Wills Act formality requirements of any role in excluding informal evidence of contents so as to secure an Anti-fraud Function. There is no filter by way of fixed rules of inadmissibility; instead, all goes to the judicial forum for ad hoc assessment of credibility. In this way it repeats the approach taken in relation to hearsay evidence pertaining to the testator's declarations. It does not transgress any particular rule of the Wills Act 1837, but it does frustrate the Act's general ambitions as

[78] ibid 14; Wills Act 1837, s 9. The exceptions relate to soldiers' and sailors' wills.

[79] P Hamburger, 'The Conveyancing Purposes of the Statute of Frauds' (1983) 27 *American Journal of Legal History* 354.

[80] JB Baron, 'Gifts, Bargains and Form' (1989) 64 *Indiana Law Journal* 155, 166; CI Nelson and JM Stark, 'Formalities and Formalism: A Critical Look at the Execution of Wills' (1978) 6 *Pepperdine Law Review* 331, 339. E Rabel, 'The Statute of Frauds and Comparative Legal History' (1947) 63 *LQR* 174 points to the anti-fraud function, but also suggests broader evidential and cautionary functions.

[81] eg *Chetwynd v Wyndham* (1757) 1 Bl Rep 95, 100; 96 ER 53, 55 (Lord Mansfield CJ): the Statute of Frauds exists 'to guard against fraud'.

[82] *Cole v Mordaunt* (unreported, 22 May 1676), discussed in *Mathews v Warner* (1798) 4 Ves Jun 186; 31 ER 96, 107, fn 2. See CD Hening, 'The Original Drafts of the Statute of Frauds and Their Authors' (1913) 61 *University of Pennsylvania Law Review* 283; Nelson and Stark (n 80) 338; AJ Hirsch, 'Formalizing Gratuitous and Contractual Transfers' (2014) 91 *Washington University Law Journal* 797, 853.

[83] *Brown v Brown* (1858) 8 El & Bl 876; 120 ER 327.

[84] 'Fourth Report of the Commissioners' (n 47) 22.

inferred from the attestation requirement, the Commissioners' report and ultimately the original motivations behind the Statute of Frauds.

V. CONCLUSION

Succession to property on death depends on the deceased's intention, but statute law regulates the expression of that intention by requiring it to be mediated through a particular form. *Sugden v Lord St Leonards* fixes the judicial approach to regulating the evidence of that formal expression. The decision came at an important moment. First, the two great streams of probate jurisdiction (ecclesiastical and common law) had merged 17 years earlier, then transferred to the High Court in the previous year, and the conflicting case law from those streams had not been brought into full alignment. Secondly, the procedure in probate had at the same time ceased to follow that of the ecclesiastical courts and turned exclusively to that of common law, with its far superior fact-finding capacity. Thirdly, the Real Property Commissioners had reviewed will formalities, and their reinvigorated scheme of formalities had been implemented in the Wills Act 1837. Fourthly, recent probate cases had asserted that will reconstructions required the highest threshold of proof and had also suggested that the enactment of the Wills Act 1837 justified a re-evaluation of the earlier authorities.

Sugden responded with a decision that eroded the significance of the formal written instrument. The will, having once been captured in writing, was held to survive the loss of its corporeal manifestation, so that its contents could be supplied by external evidence. That signifies that it is the act of publishing the testamentary intention which has normative force as the reason for changing the private legal order and not the continued existence of some physical object in which it is embodied. It implies an enlightened jurisprudential approach which accepts substantive law as being separate from evidence so that the legal efficacy of the testator's expressed intention does not depend on the great mystical object being flourished in court. Having established a judicial willingness in principle to admit secondary evidence, the decision goes on to regulate other rules of evidence relevant to adherence and reconstruction. In every respect it liberalises the rules, admitting hearsay evidence, accepting the testimony of interested witnesses, dispensing with corroboration, tolerating incomplete recollection and so on. The downplaying of the physical document is therefore coupled with an emphatic assertion of the court's ability to assess the credibility of informal evidence under the common law process of proof.

In dispensing with the need for the documentary will to be produced at trial, it may be argued that *Sugden* went too far and disrupted the integrity of attestation as authentication of content. The reconstruction of a will's contents necessarily relies on sources of evidence that lack the legislature's hallmarks of authenticity as mandated in the Wills Act 1837. This causes a possible tension with the functions or objectives of the statutory formalities. *Sugden*'s approach does not automatically exclude claims based on informal evidence, but rather directs them into proceedings where credibility is decided ad hoc: anyone can challenge the putative beneficiaries expecting to take under a will or intestacy by alleging the existence of another will supported by merely oral evidence of its execution and contents. *Sugden* therefore deprives the Wills Act of automatic preventative effect in relation to fraudulent evidence of a will's contents. Any suppression of fraud is to be achieved after *Sugden* only by individual assessment at trial and not by the peremptory rejection of claims. This point has been neglected in the literature, which generally perseveres in extolling the anti-fraud function of statutory will formalities.[85] It shows how judge-made procedural law can discreetly effectuate a radical reshaping of the formality functions achieved by the law in action. It should prompt critics to query whether modern fact-finding procedures are so effective that they have quite overtaken the surrogate for authenticity that is afforded by the formal expression of intention in a written, signed and attested will.

[85] The exception is A Gulliver and C Tilson, 'Classification of Gratuitous Transfers' (1941) 51 *Yale Law Journal* 1, 7, which notes the point but does not elaborate on its significance.

11

Thorner v Major (2009): Proprietary Estoppel and Inheritance

JOHN MEE*

I. INTRODUCTION

IN FRANZ KAFKA'S novel, *The Castle*, the protagonist struggles to be admitted to a mysterious castle with an impenetrable bureaucracy. At one point he meets an official named Bürgel, who explains that if, by some improbable coincidence, a party manages to surprise at night the one official who is authorised to deal with his case, his plea will be granted:

> You just have to picture the situation correctly. Sitting there is the party whom one has never seen, always awaited, awaited with genuine thirst … Through his silent presence alone, he invites one to invade his poor life … On a quiet night an invitation like that is enchanting. One accepts it and has then actually ceased to be an official. The situation then is such that it soon becomes impossible to turn down a request. Strictly speaking, one is desperate, and speaking even more strictly, quite happy. Desperate, for the vulnerability with which one sits there waiting for the party's plea, knowing that one must grant it as soon as it is uttered, even if it should … literally tear apart the official system[.][1]

In respect of challenges to a testator's decisions about his or her property, it also seems to make a considerable difference how the claim is put. It is rather difficult, for example, to challenge a will on the basis of undue influence[2] or on the basis that the testator lacked

* I am grateful for the comments of Professor Mary Donnelly and Professor Ben McFarlane, as well of the participants in the workshop associated with this volume. An earlier version of this chapter was given at 'Wealth, Families and Death: Socio-Legal Perspectives on Wills and Inheritance', a workshop held in the International Institute for the Sociology of Law, Oñati, Spain, 25–26 April 2013. The usual caveats apply.

[1] *The Castle* (first published 1926; tr M Harman, Schocken Books, New York, 1998) 269.

[2] The equitable doctrine of undue influence (which governs challenges to transactions between living people) does not apply and instead the courts apply a 'probate' version of the doctrine, the requirements of which 'are more onerous and are not well known': P Ridge, 'Equitable Undue Influence and Wills' (2004) 120 LQR 617, 621. On another potential invalidating feature, see B Sloan, 'Burdens, Presumptions and Confusion in the Law on Want of Knowledge and Approval' [2017] *Conveyancer & Property Lawyer* 440. For further discussion of testamentary undue influence and the requirement of knowledge and approval, see Law Commission *Making a Will* (Law Com No 231, 2017) 130–62.

the requisite mental capacity.[3] It is also far from easy for an adult child (or other adult who is not the spouse or cohabitant) of the deceased to make a successful claim under the Inheritance (Provision for Family and Dependants) Act 1975, the legislation that allows family members and dependants to seek increased provision from a deceased person's estate.[4] If, however, the claimant is able to take the alternative route of relying on an expectation of inheritance created by the deceased, allowing him or her to rely on the equitable doctrine of proprietary estoppel, he or she may be able to free himself or herself of the inconvenient limits that restrict other types of claim. As will emerge in the course of this chapter, although the case is not quite a decade old at the time of writing, *Thorner v Major* seems clearly to represent a landmark in this area of the law, having consolidated the role of proprietary estoppel as a potential restraint on freedom of testation.[5] The chapter focuses primarily on the law of England and Wales, but – as an illustration of the landmark status of the case in other jurisdictions – it also makes some reference to its impact in Irish law.

In exploring the relevant issues, this chapter emphasises the role played by narrative in this area of the law.[6] Storytelling is relevant, in the first instance, in terms of the stories constructed by the courts (and, indeed, by the media in reporting the cases), from the narrative provided by claimants and their lawyers. While an adult child claiming under the Inheritance (Provision for Family and Dependants) Act 1975 will most likely have to rehearse the unglamorous part of 'lame duck',[7] rather more archetypal roles and stories are available in the estoppel context. Of course, these stories are immanent in the facts underlying these real-life disputes, but there is particular scope for them to shape the ultimate result where one is dealing with the application of a very open-ended equitable doctrine.

[3] Note *Banks v Goodfellow* (1870) LR 5 QB 549, where a will was upheld although the testator suffered from 'certain fixed delusions' involving evil spirits. This landmark case is discussed in Juliet Brook's chapter in this volume. See also Law Commission (n 2) 18–48; text to nn 117–21 below.

[4] Note the recent Supreme Court decision in *Ilott v The Blue Cross* [2017] UKSC 17, [2017] 2 WLR 979, discussed in Brian Sloan's chapter in this volume. The claimant in the case, who was the daughter of the testatrix, obtained an award of £50,000 out of a net estate valued at £486,000. Some indication of the greater prospects offered by proprietary estoppel is provided by the fact that the claimant in *Thorner v Major* [2009] UKHL 18, [2009] 1 WLR 776 was awarded a farm worth over £2 million (representing 75% of the intestate's estate), although he was only the first cousin once removed of the intestate. Note also the New Zealand's Law Reform (Testamentary Promises) Act 1949, discussed by Nicola Peart in her chapter in this volume.

[5] See generally the thoughtful discussion in B McFarlane, 'Proprietary Estoppel: Undermining the Law of Succession?' in B Häcker and C Mitchell (eds), *Current Issues in Succession Law* (Oxford, Hart Publishing, 2016). McFarlane suggests (ibid 77–78) that, rather than 'undermin[ing] the law of succession', the law of proprietary estoppel 'supports the continued existence of [the strict rules of succession law] by ensuring that they do not become a source of palpable injustice'. Note, however, that McFarlane emphasises that, in order for it to play the role he envisages for it, 'the doctrine must be carefully limited' (ibid 77).

[6] See generally RM Cover, 'Nomos and Narrative' (1983) 97 *Harvard Law Review* 4; JB Baron, 'The Many Promises of Storytelling in Law' (1991) 23 *Rutgers Law Journal* 79; DA Farber and S Sherry, 'Telling Stories Out of School: An Essay on Legal Narratives' (1993) 45 *Stanford Law Review* 807. For more recent examples focusing on specific areas of the law, see HW Tang, 'Storytelling in the Law of Unjust Enrichment' in A Robertson and HW Tang (eds), *The Goals of Private Law* (Oxford, Hart Publishing, 2009); J Benjamin, 'The Narratives of Financial Law' (2010) 20 *OJLS* 787; E Porter 'Gendered Narratives: Stories and Silences in Transitional Justice' (2016) 17 *Human Rights Review* 35.

[7] R Kerridge with AHR Brierley, *Parry and Kerridge: The Law of Succession*, 13th edn (London, Sweet & Maxwell 2016) [8.62].

Another aspect of the role of narrative in the area under discussion relates to the stories that equity tells about itself and the narratives by reference to which equitable intervention is justified in the specific context of proprietary estoppel. All legal systems, including the large number that do not recognise a separate body of law known as 'equity', must address the danger that the universality of legal norms may lead to injustice in individual cases. What is special about common law systems is that the impulse towards particularised justice is reified as a distinct set of rules called 'equity'. When applying 'equity', judges may feel that they have a special permission and obligation to put aside the generally applicable rules and resolve the dispute before them on a more intuitive and non-technical basis. As Lord Denning, who did a fair deal of violence to the law in the name of equity, commented in a proprietary estoppel case, 'Equity comes in, true to form, to mitigate the rigours of strict law'.[8]

In *Thorner v Major*, the House of Lords gave approval, at the highest level of the judicial system, to the vision of proprietary estoppel that had been developed in a series of lower court cases. This vision involves, to an extent, the celebration of the rejection of principled analysis and the fetishising of 'flexibility'. The justificatory narrative here draws upon the Greek myth of Procrustes, son of Poseiden, who invited passing travellers to stay with him. If the guest was too short for his iron bed, Procrustes stretched him to fit; if he was too tall, Procrustes chopped off his feet. In a highly influential modern statement of the theoretical basis of proprietary estoppel, Oliver J rejected the idea of forcing proprietary estoppel 'into a Procrustean bed constructed from some unalterable criteria'.[9] In fact, the label 'proprietary estoppel' subsumes a number of distinct principles – acquiescence in another's mistake, resiling from a promise and denying the truth of one's previous representation of fact.[10] Oliver J's unfortunate method of side-stepping this complexity was to state a unifying principle of 'unconscionability', pitched at a sufficiently high level of generality that it could cover all three distinct principles.[11] Reliance on this shapeless concept has created much confusion in the law of proprietary estoppel,[12] but it also leaves a wide scope for claimants to weave attractive narratives to support their attempt to override the testator's exercise of his testamentary freedom. While highlighting the importance of narrative in this area of the law, this chapter's sympathies are with the idea of a more cautious and rigorous approach to equitable intervention in cases fitting within the fact pattern of *Thorner v Major*.

The structure of the chapter is as follows. The next section will explain the facts of *Thorner v Major*. The section after that attempts to set *Thorner* in its wider context, discussing the requirements of proprietary estoppel and the role of that doctrine in the

[8] *Crabb v Arun UDC* [1976] Ch 179 (CA), 187. Contrast PBH Birks 'Equity in the Modern Law: An Exercise in Taxonomy' (1996) 26 *University of Western Australia Law Review* 1, 22: 'One large-scale danger to the rationality of our law lies in the exaggeration of the historical mission of equity to do justice, as though it had some special licence to ignore the requirements of legal certainty.'

[9] *Taylors Fashions v London Victoria Trustees Ltd* [1982] 1 QB 133n, 154.

[10] See text to nn 38–39 below.

[11] [1982] QB 133n, 151–52: 'a very much broader approach which is directed rather at ascertaining whether, in particular individual circumstances, it would be unconscionable for a party to be permitted to deny that which, knowingly, or unknowingly, he has allowed or encouraged another to assume to his detriment'.

[12] Note, eg the failure of the House of Lords in *Yeoman's Row Management Ltd v Cobbe* [2008] UKHL 55, [2008] 1 WLR 1752 to grasp the basics of the doctrine. See the text to nn 59–61 below.

context of succession law. This is followed by a discussion of a leading Irish case that was heavily influenced by *Thorner*, *Naylor v Maher*,[13] the facts of which raise interesting issues concerning the proprietary estoppel jurisdiction as shaped by *Thorner*. Next, consideration is given to the significance of *Thorner*, including an examination of the potential impact of the case on freedom of testation. Finally, some concluding observations are offered, reflecting in general terms on the impact of *Thorner* as a landmark decision in this area of the law of succession.

II. THE STORY OF *THORNER v MAJOR*[14]

The main characters in *Thorner* were two Somerset farmers. They were 'taciturn and undemonstrative men committed to a life of hard and unrelenting physical work … largely unrelieved by recreation or female company'.[15] Since 1976, David Thorner had worked long hours without pay on the farm of Peter Thorner, his father's first cousin. Peter was 'a man of few words … who hardly ever spoke in direct terms'[16] and the representations relied upon by David were very oblique. In 1990, Peter handed David a document related to two insurance policies, saying 'That's for my death duties'. David interpreted this as an indication that he would inherit the farm. He had been considering various other opportunities at around this time, but decided that his future lay with Peter's farm. Later remarks by Peter confirmed David in his expectation of inheritance. As the first instance judge explained:

> Peter would point out to him little things about the farm which would only be of relevance to someone … who would be there after Peter had gone, and the undocumented knowledge in his head was no longer available … One such remark was when Peter made a point of drawing to David's attention a cattle trough which, he explained to him, never froze up in winter.[17]

Some of these indications were given in front of other people.[18] Peter made a will in 1997, leaving David the farm and his residuary estate. However, apparently after a falling-out with another beneficiary, Peter revoked the will and, despite having been warned by his solicitor of the importance of making a new will, died intestate in 2005. David would have received nothing under the intestacy rules, and Peter's property would instead have gone to blood relations (sisters and nieces) to whom he was not close. David relied on the doctrine of proprietary estoppel. He was successful at first instance, and was awarded the farm and the other assets of the farming business.

This decision was overturned by the Court of Appeal.[19] Lloyd LJ felt that:

> there are dangers unless the established requirements of proprietary estoppel are applied with a certain degree of rigour of analysis. Otherwise not only the strict requirements of the Wills Act

[13] *Naylor v Maher* [2012] IEHC 408, [2018] IECA 32.

[14] For a doctrinal analysis of the case, see J Mee, 'The Limits of Proprietary Estoppel: *Thorner v Major*' [2009] *Child & Family Law Quarterly* 367.

[15] [2009] UKHL 18, [59] (Lord Walker).

[16] [2007] EWHC 2422 (Ch), [94] (Judge Randall QC).

[17] ibid [98] (Judge Randall QC), quoted by Lord Walker [2009] UKHL 18, [43].

[18] [2007] EWHC 2422 (Ch), [128] (Judge Randall QC).

[19] [2008] EWCA Civ 732.

as to how to give effect to testamentary intentions, but also the basic proposition of freedom of testamentary disposition, might be subverted.[20]

While he acknowledged that 'David had a strong moral claim to inherit Peter's farm', Lloyd LJ concluded that if David's claim were permitted to succeed, 'the ingredients of proprietary estoppel in such cases would have been diluted in such a way as to create a dangerous precedent'.[21] However, the first instance decision was unanimously reinstated on appeal to the House of Lords.

The main doctrinal obstacle to David's argument was that there had been no clear-cut promise that he would inherit the farm. However, the first instance judge, and ultimately the House of Lords, emphasised the personality of the parties and the indirect way in which they, and other farmers in the area, were wont to communicate with each other. This reticence seems to be prevalent in other rural areas, since an Irish judge has also commented on 'that natural courtesy (which John Millington Synge[22] associated with the west of Ireland) which often results in an unwillingness to pursue discussion to a logical and perhaps harshly expressed commercial conclusion'.[23] The trial judge in *Thorner* was, according to Lord Walker, 'sensitive to the complexities of human nature'.[24] Lord Neuberger felt that:

[I]t would be quite wrong to be unrealistically rigorous when applying the 'clear and unambiguous' test [in respect of the requirement of a representation]. The court should not search for ambiguity or uncertainty, but should assess the question of clarity and certainty practically and sensibly, as well as contextually.[25]

A related problem was that any promise that had been (obliquely) made was likely to have been intended to be conditional to some extent. However, Lord Walker noted the observation of Hoffmann LJ in *Walton v Walton*[26] that proprietary estoppel 'looks backwards from the moment when the promise falls due to be performed and asks whether, in the circumstances which have actually happened, it would be unconscionable for the promise not to be kept'.[27] As Lord Hoffmann (as he had then become) commented enigmatically, in a somewhat different context, in *Thorner*: 'The owl of Minerva spreads its wings only with the falling of the dusk.'[28] The effect of this reasoning is that liability can attach to the breach of promises that, because they are subject to complex unspoken qualifications and conditions, would be too uncertain to attract contractual liability.[29]

[20] ibid [69].

[21] ibid [75].

[22] Irish dramatist, author of 'The Playboy of the Western World' (first performed, causing a riot, in 1907).

[23] *McCarron v McCarron* (unreported, Irish Supreme Court, 13 February 1997) transcript, 9 (Murphy J). Finding, on facts somewhat similar to those in *Thorner v Major*, that an enforceable contract had been created, Murphy J noted (ibid) that 'in some, particularly rural areas, a meeting of minds can be achieved without as detailed discussion as might be necessary elsewhere'.

[24] [2009] UKHL 18, [32].

[25] ibid [85].

[26] *Walton v Walton* (unreported, Court of Appeal, 14 April 1994).

[27] ibid [19]–[21], quoted by Lord Walker in *Thorner v Major* [2009] UKHL 18, [56].

[28] [2009] UKHL 18, [8], using this phrase from the preface to GWF Hegel's *The Philosophy of Right* (1820) to make the point that: 'Past events provide context and background for the interpretation of subsequent events and subsequent events throw retrospective light upon the meaning of past events.'

[29] See B McFarlane, 'Proprietary Estoppel: The Importance of Looking Back' in PS Davies and J Pila (eds), *The Jurisprudence of Lord Hoffmann* (Oxford, Hart Publishing, 2015).

The trial judge exercised his discretion in relation to the remedial question to grant David the farm and associated assets, and this was not seriously challenged in the House of Lords. Although the speeches in the House of Lords did not put a precise value on the award, in the Court of Appeal it was described as having a net value of 'some £2.1 million'.[30] A newspaper report of the House of Lords decision put the value of the assets obtained by David at £2.3 million, subject to an inheritance tax bill of around £300,000.[31] Taking its value as £2 million after tax, the remedy amounted to a generous £133,333 after tax for each year of work on the farm since the key 1990 representation. David was clearly extremely hard-working and 'thoroughly decent',[32] but it seems speculative to suggest that, if he had devoted his efforts to the other business opportunities which were available to him around 1990, he would have amassed anything like £2 million by 2005.

David came across as a 'painfully honest witness', impressing the trial judge 'very favourably'.[33] He had worked for over 30 years without payment on Peter's farm (although roughly half of this period pre-dated any promise of inheritance). In addition to his work on Peter's farm, he also worked on his father's farm. The trial judge refers a stage when was working 18 hours a day, 7 days a week. Yet '[d]espite working such punishing hours, David lived off what he was not embarrassed to call "pocket money" given to him by his parents'.[34] One witness mentioned that he had 'never met a more trustworthy man or a harder worker'.[35] Even if there had been no promise of inheritance by the deceased, many would regard it as a desirable result if the succession law rules could somehow be overturned so as to favour David. Therefore, it is not surprising that the qualms of the Court of Appeal were swept aside and the House of Lords brought the story to a happy conclusion by granting the farm to the decent and guileless claimant.[36]

III. SETTING *THORNER* IN CONTEXT

A. The Requirements of Proprietary Estoppel

The doctrine of proprietary estoppel, the application of which is not limited to the succession context, can be traced back to the decision of the House of Lords in

[30] [2008] EWCA Civ 732, [27].

[31] L Salkeld, 'Labourer is handed £2.3 million farm where he worked unpaid for 25 years', *Daily Mail* (25 March 2009). On the question of whether proprietary estoppel awards attract inheritance tax, see B McFarlane, *The Law of Proprietary Estoppel* (Oxford, Oxford University Press, 2014) 598–601.

[32] [2009] UKHL 18, [53] (Lord Walker), reporting the description of him by counsel for the other side.

[33] [2007] EWHC 2422 (Ch), [20] (Judge Randall QC).

[34] ibid [68].

[35] ibid [63].

[36] Note that counsel for the claimant in the recent case of *Gee v Gee* [2018] EWHC 1393 (Ch), [28] sought to fit his client into the mould of David Thorner, portraying that client as 'a countryman without guile or sophistication', who had answered certain questions 'in an entirely artless manner'. A postscript to the story of *Thorner v Major*, which does not reflect badly on David's character but which does seem to disrupt the expected flow of the narrative, is that he sold the farm to Sainsbury's, which in May 2014 obtained planning permission to build a supermarket with a sales area of 23,000 square feet: McFarlane (n 31) 2. In October 2015, Sainsbury's

Ramsden v Dyson.[37] As the current author has suggested elsewhere,[38] it is possible to identify three distinct principles that have been (somewhat arbitrarily) grouped together under the heading of proprietary estoppel. This line of argument has been further developed by Ben McFarlane in *The Law of Proprietary Estoppel*.[39] The principle that is likely to be relevant in the type of case under discussion has been described by McFarlane as the 'promise-detriment' principle (and has also been called the 'expectation limb' of proprietary estoppel). In order to be successful under this principle, the claimant must show that:

1. The defendant made a promise (or an 'assurance' or 'representation') that the claimant would become entitled to an interest in land, or other identified property, belonging to the defendant;[40] and
2. the claimant has changed his position in reliance on the promise
3. in a way that would be to his detriment if the promise were not fulfilled.

An 'equity' is then said to arise in favour of the claimant which the court must decide how best to satisfy.

Unlike in relation to promissory estoppel,[41] it is not the case that proprietary estoppel is 'a shield not a sword'.[42] Therefore, a wide range of remedies are possible, including, for example, obtaining the ownership of the disputed property, being granted a monetary remedy or being allowed an indefinite licence to occupy land. The obligation of the court has traditionally been seen as to grant the minimum remedy necessary to satisfy the equity. In practice, however, the courts have tended to require the defendant to fulfil his promise or, in other words, to give effect to the claimant's expectation as reasonably derived from the defendant's promise. Following *Jennings v Rice*,[43] it has been accepted that the expectation remedy is the starting point but that, if such a remedy would be disproportionate to the detriment incurred by the claimant, the court will choose an alternative remedy.[44]

announced that they were abandoning the plan: http://cheddarvillage.co.uk/sainsburys-statement-regarding-steart-farm/. Instead, in June 2018 they sought outline planning permission to build 60 houses on the site: www.thewestonmercury.co.uk/news/sainsbury-s-hopes-to-build-60-houses-in-cheddar-1-5554375.

[37] *Ramsden v Dyson* (1866) LR 1 HL, 129.

[38] J Mee, 'Proprietary Estoppel, Promises, and Mistaken Belief' in S Bright (ed), *Modern Studies in Property Law, vol 6* (Oxford, Hart Publishing, 2011) 181–83.

[39] B McFarlane, *The Law of Proprietary Estoppel* (Oxford, Hart Publishing, 2014) ch 1. See also B McFarlane, 'Understanding Equitable Estoppel: From Metaphors to Better Laws' (2013) 66 *Current Legal Problems* 267; B McFarlane and P Sales, 'Promises, Liability, and Detriment: Lessons from Proprietary Estoppel' (2015) 131 *LQR* 610.

[40] On balance, it can be concluded that the House of Lords in *Thorner* confirmed the need for a promise, rather than a representation that did not amount to a commitment: see Mee (n 14) 370–72.

[41] This doctrine, often seen as part of the law of contract, grew from the decision of Lord Denning (then Denning J) in *Central London Property Trust v High Trees House Ltd* [1947] KB 130.

[42] This frequently invoked metaphor is intended to convey the fact that the doctrine can only be used in a defensive manner and cannot, of itself, constitute a cause of action.

[43] *Jennings v Rice* [2002] EWCA Civ 159, [2003] 1 FCR 501.

[44] For more detailed discussion of the remedial issue, see J Mee, 'The Role of Expectation in the Determination of Proprietary Estoppel Remedies' in M Dixon (ed), *Modern Studies in Property Law, vol 5* (Oxford, Hart Publishing, 2009).

B. Proprietary Estoppel and Inheritance[45]

It was not until comparatively recently that the promise-detriment principle was applied in the context of promises of succession. In *Taylor v Dickens*,[46] judicial concern was expressed on the basis that a will is, of its nature, revocable,[47] so that potential claimants should be aware that the testator might change his or her mind. In *Taylor*, the claimant's wife 'gave evidence that on no less than three occasions she told him not to count his chickens before they were hatched' in respect of his expectation of inheriting from a woman for whom he worked as a gardener and handyman.[48] Rejecting the claim, HHJ Judge Weeks warned of the dangers if one were to 'forget the law of contract and issue every civil judge with a portable palm tree'[49] (to facilitate the dispensing of discretionary 'palm tree' justice). However, this cautious approach was not accepted in later judgments.[50] Claimants were successful on the basis of promises of inheritance in a series of cases, including *Re Basham*,[51] *Wayling v Jones*[52] and *Gillett v Holt*.[53] This trend was consolidated in *Thorner v Major*. There have been parallel developments in the law of proprietary estoppel in Ireland, exemplified by *Naylor v Maher*[54] (which is discussed further below), as well as in other common law jurisdictions, such as Australia.[55]

IV. THE SIGNIFICANCE OF *THORNER*

A. *Thorner* as Landmark

There are at least two senses in which *Thorner v Major* counts as a landmark case. First, it is the only decision of the House of Lords/Supreme Court to uphold a claim on the basis of the promise-detriment principle. In the nineteenth century case generally cited as the origin of proprietary estoppel, *Ramsden v Dyson*,[56] the majority of the House of Lords did not recognise the promise-detriment principle. Instead, the principle considered was what has later been described as 'the mistake limb' of proprietary estoppel, which is triggered when the defendant sees that the claimant is improving the defendant's

[45] See generally A Braun, 'Formal and Informal Testamentary Promises: A Historical and Comparative Perspective' (2012) 76 *Rabels Zeitschrift fur Auslandisches und Internationales Privatrecht* 994.

[46] *Taylor v Dickens* [1998] 1 FLR 806 (Ch).

[47] See *Vynior's Case* (1609) 8 Co Rep 81b, 82a.

[48] [1998] 1 FLR 806 (Ch), 822. Compare the comment of Carnwath J at first instance in *Gillett v Holt* that it would be odd if 'the plaintiff's proprietary rights should be diminished merely because he was unfortunate enough to have a wife who (as in *Taylor v Dickens)* regularly reminded him "not to count his chickens before they were hatched"': [1998] 3 All ER 917 (Ch), 929.

[49] [1998] 1 FLR 806 (Ch), 820. Note also D Hayton, 'By-passing Testamentary Formalities' [1987] CLJ 215.

[50] As noted by Robert Walker LJ in *Gillet v Holt* [2001] Ch 210 (CA), 227, *Taylor v Dickens* was compromised on appeal.

[51] *Re Basham* [1986] 1 WLR 1498 (Ch).

[52] *Wayling v Jones* [1995] 2 FLR 1029 (CA).

[53] *Gillett v Holt* [2001] Ch 210 (CA).

[54] *Naylor v Maher* [2012] IEHC 408, [2018] IECA 32.

[55] See, eg *Delaforce v Simpson-Cook* [2010] NSWCA 84.

[56] (1866) LR 1 HL 129.

land, in the mistaken belief that it belongs to the claimant, and the defendant fails to intervene.[57] The only mention in *Ramsden* of a principle that might correspond to the promise-detriment principle occurs in the brief dissenting speech of Lord Kingsdown. As the current author has pointed out elsewhere, there is an element of rewriting history in the conventional account of the development of proprietary estoppel which suggests that Lord Kingsdown dissented only on the facts, so that it can be assumed that the rest of the House of Lords regarded the promise-detriment principle as part of the law.[58] On a fair view, *Thorner* represents the first acceptance by the House of Lords of that principle.

Secondly, *Thorner* is significant because it followed closely upon another House of Lords case, *Yeoman's Row Management Ltd v Cobbe*,[59] which – in the context of a commercial dispute not involving any promise of inheritance – took a very restrictive view of the scope of the promise-detriment principle. The factual basis of the claim in *Cobbe* was weak and it was justifiably rejected. Unfortunately, however, the speeches in the case were unsatisfactory, with both Lord Scott and Lord Walker stating the law in confused and restrictive terms.[60] This led some commentators to question whether *Cobbe* signalled the 'death of proprietary estoppel'.[61] In *Thorner*, however, the House of Lords essentially ignored the restrictive aspects of *Cobbe*, with Lord Walker referring dismissively to the 'rather apocalyptic view that has been suggested by some commentators' to the effect that *Cobbe* had 'severely curtailed, or even virtually extinguished, the doctrine of proprietary estoppel'.[62] Despite the tone of Lord Walker's remarks, it is difficult to deny that *Cobbe* had departed from the approach that had been developed by the lower courts in the preceding case law, so that *Thorner* takes on added importance as an authority at the highest level which discounts the restrictive approach of *Cobbe*.

B. *Thorner* as High-Water Mark

In a rather different sense, *Thorner* is significant in the development of the expectation limb of proprietary estoppel because the case seems to represent a high-water mark in terms of generosity in relation to the key requirement of a promise or assurance by the defendant. It will be recalled that Peter Thorner never made an explicit promise to David that he would inherit the farm. Instead, the requirement of a promise or assurance was held to be satisfied on the basis of oblique statements. The first instance judge, whose view was upheld by the House of Lords, relied strongly on the fact that the parties were taciturn and undemonstrative. The argument was essentially that, if Peter had wanted to make a promise to David, he would not have made it in express terms but would have conveyed his meaning indirectly. Peter's lack of directness was illustrated in evidence by

[57] For discussion of this doctrine, see K Low, 'Nonfeasance in Equity' (2012) 128 *LQR* 63. Note that the claim based on this principle was unsuccessful in *Ramsden*.

[58] Mee (n 38) 184–86.

[59] [2008] UKHL 55, [2008] 1 WLR 1752.

[60] For detailed discussion, see Mee (n 58) 177–88.

[61] See B McFarlane and A Robertson, 'The Death of Proprietary Estoppel' [2008] *Lloyd's Maritime and Commercial Law Quarterly* 449; T Etherton, 'Constructive Trusts and Proprietary Estoppel: The Search for Clarity and Principle' [2009] *Conveyancer & Property Lawyer* 104, 116–20.

[62] [2009] UKHL 18 [31].

the example that 'when Peter said "What are you doing tomorrow?" he generally meant "Would you come and help me tomorrow?"'[63]

However, it is arguable that there was more to the matter than the fact that Peter was 'a man of few words'.[64] Why assume that Peter's cautious mode of expression was a purely verbal phenomenon and did not reflect a more general reluctance to commit himself, making it unlikely that he would promise to leave the farm to David with no possibility of changing his mind? It seems significant that the example of Peter's obliqueness mentioned earlier in the previous paragraph is also an illustration of his expectation that others would accommodate themselves to his requirements. The first instance judge referred to 'Peter's apparent ability to secure unpaid help on Steart Farm from quite a number of people' (although he did not regard Peter's conduct as cynical),[65] and one witness commented that 'as long as Peter was breathing he would always be in charge'.[66] It is quite possible to interpret Peter's words and actions to have meant, in effect: 'I am currently planning to leave the farm to you and, in light of this, I expect you to work without pay to help me. But, of course, I'll change my mind if I choose. It's my farm.' On this view, it would not have been reasonable for David, in light of his knowledge of Peter's character, to interpret Peter's words and conduct as amounting to a promise that would put it out of Peter's power to exert any more control over the situation. If Peter had really done no more than convey his current (revocable) intention to leave the farm to David and to demand that David continue to work for him for free, no remedy under the promise-detriment principle should have arisen in David's favour.

It may be true that the appellate courts in *Thorner* had limited scope to interfere with the holding in favour of David because the first instance judge had found as a fact (or at least as an inference from the basic facts) both that Peter had indirectly promised that he would leave the farm to David and that it was reasonable for David to have relied on that promise.[67] However, in terms of the future impact of the case, it probably does not greatly matter if its result is explicable on the basis of the first instance judge's interpretation of the unusual facts of the case. The message likely to be taken by lower court judges in future cases is that a claim can succeed even if the evidence of a promise is uncertain or indirect. This was a concern for Lloyd LJ in the Court of Appeal, but the House of Lords was dismissive of his argument that the requirements of proprietary estoppel had to be applied with 'a certain degree of rigour of analysis'.[68] Lord Walker commented that:

> I do not share the Court of Appeal's apparent apprehension that floodgates might be opened, because cases like this are fairly rare, and trial judges realise the need to subject the evidence (whether as to assurances, as to reliance or as to detriment) to careful, and sometimes sceptical, scrutiny.[69]

[63] [2007] EWHC 2422 (Ch) [32].
[64] ibid [31].
[65] ibid [33].
[66] ibid [40].
[67] See [2009] UKHL 18 [6] (Lord Hoffmann), [17] (Lord Scott), [27] (Lord Rodger), [60] (Lord Walker), [76]–[83] (Lord Neuberger).
[68] [2008] EWCA Civ 732 [69].
[69] [2009] UKHL 18 [60].

However, it is arguable that Lord Walker's remarks betray a naivety about the practical effect of the decision in *Thorner* on the likelihood that a disappointed (non-)beneficiary in a broadly analogous fact-situation will bring a claim based on proprietary estoppel. There have been at least 25 cases since *Thorner* involving proprietary estoppel claims based on promises of inheritance, with eight of these being decided in 2018 alone.[70] In terms of a snowballing effect, it is interesting to note that the claimant in the recent case of *Habberfield v Habberfield*[71] explained that she had been 'unaware that a claim of this kind could be brought until … she heard about a newspaper article concerning the *Davies v Davies* case'.[72]

This kind of case typically involves a change of mind (a point that will be explored further later in this chapter), so that there will usually have been a long period in which it was envisaged that the claimant would be the one to inherit. In light of this, it is arguable that it will nearly always be possible for a claimant to cobble together some remarks, or alleged remarks, made over the years by the deceased defendant which a sympathetic court can construe as amounting to the necessary promise. An example is provided by another 2018 case, *Gee v Gee*,[73] where the claimant pleaded 'six particular representations',[74] none of which was very impressive.[75] In response to counsel's argument that these representations were 'a thin basis for a proprietary estoppel claim',[76] Birss J responded that:

> Counsel is right to emphasise that this is only a very few instances spread over a long period of time. However the claimant explained that these were not the only instances which he thought had occurred, rather he was sure his father had given him the assurance he contended for and these were the particular incidents he could now remember.[77]

The fact that a claimant has convinced himself that he has received an assurance, even if he cannot remember the details, does not seem to be a secure basis for interfering with a testator's intended disposition of his property.

The effect of overly generous treatment of claims would be to subvert the wishes of the deceased by depriving his or her intended beneficiaries of their inheritance,

[70] See *Moore v Moore* [2018] EWCA Civ 2669; *Gee v Gee* [2018] EWHC 1393 (Ch); *Thompson v Thompson* [2018] EWHC 1338 (Ch); *Dobson v Griffey* [2018] EWHC 1117 (Ch); *McDonald v Rose* [2018] EWHC 445 (Ch) (on appeal: [2019] EWCA Civ 4); *Culliford v Thorpe* [2018] EWHC 426 (Ch); *Habberfield v Habberfield* [2018] EWHC 317 (Ch) (on appeal: [2019] EWCA Civ 890); *James v James* [2018] EWHC 43 (Ch). Note also *Guest v Guest* [2019] EWHC 869 (Ch). The older cases are: *Ritchie v Joshlin* [2009] EWHC 709 (Ch); *Gill v Woodall* [2009] EWHC 3778 (Ch) (aff'd on different grounds: [2010] EWCA Civ 1430); *Macdonald v Frost* [2009] EWHC 2276 (Ch); *Clarke v Meadus* [2010] EWHC 3117 (Ch); *Cook v Thomas* [2010] EWCA Civ 227; *Shirt v Shirt* [2010] EWHC 3820 (Ch); *Murphy v Rayner* [2011] EWHC 1 (Ch); *Webster v Ashcroft* [2011] EWHC 3848 (Ch); *Suggitt v Suggitt* [2012] EWCA Civ 1140; *Bradbury v Taylor* [2012] EWCA Civ 1208; *Turner v Phythian* [2013] EWHC 499 (Ch); *Creasey v Sole* [2013] EWHC 1410 (Ch); *Wright v Waters* [2014] EWHC 3614 (Ch); *Rawlings v Chapman* [2015] EWHC 3160 (Ch); *Davies v Davies* [2014] EWCA Civ 568, [2016] EWCA Civ 463; *McGuinness v Preece* [2016] EWHC 1518 (Ch).

[71] *Habberfield v Habberfield* [2018] EWCH 317 (Ch).

[72] ibid [81], referring to *Davies v Davies* [2016] EWCA Civ 463 (see also [2014] EWCA Civ 568).

[73] [2018] EWHC 1393 (Ch).

[74] ibid [21].

[75] For example, on one occasion (ibid) 'there was a discussion between various farmers about the inheritance of their farms and [D] agreed, within [C]'s hearing, that such farms should pass to the son who stayed on the farm and worked and farmed there'.

[76] ibid [111].

[77] ibid.

as well as to increase the likelihood of divisive litigation whenever a family member feels aggrieved at his or her treatment by the deceased.[78] An example of a case which suggests that the law may indeed have gone too far is provided by *Suggitt v Suggitt*[79] ('Prodigal son wins £3m in battle over farmer's will').[80] John Suggitt, the successful claimant in this case, was 29 years old when his father died. His claim 'depended almost entirely on oral statements made by Frank [the father]', who was dead and not in a position to contradict his assertions (although those assertions were contradicted by what Frank had told third parties). John was not 'a very reliable witness' and 'he frequently did not answer the questions asked, tended to exaggerate, be argumentative, self-serving and evasive in his answers'.[81] John's evidence as to the promises made was 'opaque to say the least'.[82] In relation to the issue of reliance, the trial judge regarded 'John's case and evidence in support as weak'.[83] On the question of detriment, the work John claimed to have done was 'barely, vaguely and weakly particularised';[84] John was 'a disappointment to his father'[85] and was apparently regarded by him as 'lazy'.[86] He failed to finish a course paid for by his father at an agricultural college. Later, he had 'effectively run away to York and spent his inheritance'[87] of £38,000 from a great aunt before returning to the farm after nine months when 'the money had run out'.[88] The work he did on the farm was limited by the fact that the father, having no faith in him to run the farm, had leased most of it to third parties. He 'did not work for nothing, but he did not work for as much as he might have expected had he been an agricultural worker. On the other hand as an agricultural worker he would have had his own living expenses.'[89] His father provided a house for John and his family, as well as paying the utility bills and doing the basic weekly shop for John and his wife and children.[90] Frank had promised Caroline, John's sister, that he would make her a rich woman on his death; 'she had lived all her life with him after his divorce, save for the two years that she was in Holland and in University'.[91] She had to make do with what was left after John's award of £3.3 million, which was confirmed by the Court of Appeal; this left her with an entitlement valued at around £0.66 million, one-fifth of what her brother obtained.

[78] Compare D Hacker, 'Disappointed "Heirs" as a Socio-Legal Phenomenon' (2014) 4(2) *Oñati Socio-legal Series* 243.

[79] *Suggitt v Suggitt* [2012] EWCA Civ 1140, [2012] WTLR 1607.

[80] See C Brooke, 'Prodigal Son Wins £3m in Battle over Farmer's Will: Sister Loses Appeal to Her "Lazy" Brother', *Daily Mail* (21 June 2012). For a detailed critique of the case (on which this paragraph draws), see J Mee, 'Proprietary Estoppel and Inheritance: Enough Is Enough?' [2013] *Conveyancer & Property Lawyer* 280, 281–86.

[81] [2011] EWHC 903 (Ch), [38].

[82] ibid [45].

[83] ibid [57].

[84] ibid [59].

[85] ibid [55].

[86] ibid [46].

[87] ibid [55].

[88] ibid [21].

[89] ibid [57].

[90] [2012] EWCA Civ 1140, [36].

[91] ibid [25].

V. SPREADING THE STORY – *NAYLOR v MAHER*: 'STEPSON WINS FATHER AND A FARM'[92]

This section looks at *Thorner*'s impact in the neighbouring jurisdiction of Ireland, where *Thorner* was applied in the leading case of *Naylor v Maher*.[93] As well as being instructive in respect of the role of narrative in these cases, *Naylor* raises some wider issues concerning the post-*Thorner* law of proprietary estoppel, to which the discussion will return later. The claimant in the case, Willie Naylor, had worked for 'minimal remuneration' for close to 40 years on a farm in County Tipperary that belonged to the testator. The claimant believed the testator to be his stepfather, and it was only after the testator's death that the claimant learned that the testator was, in fact, his biological father. Ultimately, the testator left the 120 acre farm (as well as a house and the residue of the estate after various legacies) to the claimant's sister, Jean, and the claimant received only a legacy of €150,000. He successfully relied upon proprietary estoppel to claim the farm.

The claimant had left school at the age of 14, unable to read or write, and went to work full-time on the disputed farm. Conditions were primitive on the farm at this stage. As O'Keeffe J put it: 'The water did not come until the 1970s' (referring to the absence until then of running water).[94] When he was 17, the claimant went to Dublin for six months to facilitate 'professional consultations and assistance in relation to his learning difficulties'.[95] While the claimant was in Dublin he 'worked diligently and was most resourceful in the jobs he obtained'.[96] At that point, according to O'Keeffe J at first instance, the claimant was 'likely to have had an open mind' about pursuing a career away from the family farm.[97] However, the claimant's brother then decided to move to England and the claimant was recalled by the testator to work on the farm in his place. It seemed that the testator had health difficulties throughout his life and he left the physical work on the farm to the claimant, who 'had a natural aptitude at farming'.[98] The claimant had a close relationship with the testator, although the latter was 'a gruff man with whom one would not win an argument' and who 'was not a man one would tell what to do'.[99] Upon his return to work on the farm, the claimant questioned the low wages he was receiving, given that in Dublin he had been 'getting the big money'[100] (a reference to the £25 to £30 per week he had been earning in his three jobs in the city).[101] In response, the testator indicated that 'you will be farming for yourself' and the promise that the claimant would inherit the farm was repeated, in more explicit terms, on numerous subsequent occasions.[102] The claimant continued to work on the farm over the decades.

[92] A O'Faolain and B Duggan, *Irish Independent* (18 September 2012).

[93] [2012] IEHC 408, [2018] IECA 32. Other Irish cases involving proprietary estoppel claims in the context of farm inheritance include *Coyle v Finnegan* [2013] IEHC 463; *Finnegan v Hand* [2016] IEHC 255; *K v K* [2018] IEHC 615.

[94] [2012] IEHC 408 [178].

[95] ibid [16].

[96] ibid [404].

[97] ibid.

[98] ibid.

[99] ibid [52].

[100] ibid [41].

[101] ibid [16].

[102] ibid [40]–[51].

The claimant's sister, the defendant, lived nearby. She learned during the testator's lifetime that she was the natural child of the testator but believed that it was 'not her place' to tell her siblings but rather that this was up to her parents.[103] O'Keeffe J described as 'unimpressive' her evidence as to why she had not informed the claimant, noting that doing so would have allowed the claimant to discuss the issue of his own parentage with the testator.[104] Overall, he 'found her evidence and demeanour to the court as a whole uncooperative and calculated to confuse the court'.[105] This contrasted with the claimant, whose evidence was 'not exaggerated, but controlled' and 'truthful'.[106] While a negative picture of the defendant's character emerges from the judgment, it can also be seen that she did a great deal for her parents. When their mother contracted cancer in the 'mid-1990s', the defendant cared for her until her death in 2001.[107] She also cared for the testator in the final years of his life. From 2000 to 2005, 'she would have the dinner ready for him in the evening and at night time he would go to the pub' and she would bring him home 'at midnight'.[108] In 2005, the testator fell and cracked three ribs. The defendant would visit him in hospital for six hours a day, lived with him for some months upon his discharge and 'would be on call for him'. Her routine

> as a carer for him in late 2005 and through 2006, was to go up to his house in the morning, get his breakfast, bring up the oxygen machine from his room, take his blood, put him on a nebuliser, take out the ashes, light the fire and bring in turf.[109]

A will that the testator had made in 2005 left the farm to the claimant. However, in 2006, five months before his death, the testator changed his will so that the farm went to the defendant and, as has been mentioned, the claimant would take only a gift of €150,000. One witness for the claimant had been a friend of the defendant and stated that she had 'had many discussions about the deceased where the defendant did the talking and she did the listening'.[110] According to this witness, the defendant had said that she wanted the testator to change his will. The defendant was reported as having said that 'the deceased had asked her what she would do with a farm and that she had replied that she wouldn't mind putting on a pair of wellies'.[111] Following the making of the new will, the defendant, who was 'absolutely ecstatic', had announced to her friend that she 'had got the lot'. The friend asked about the defendant's brother and, according to her evidence, the defendant replied: 'F*** Willie, I am the one looking after'.[112]

[103] ibid [231].
[104] ibid [428].
[105] ibid.
[106] ibid [403].
[107] ibid [188].
[108] ibid [194].
[109] ibid.
[110] ibid [142].
[111] ibid.
[112] ibid [147] (original bowdlerisation). The former friend also reported the defendant as having remarked that, if the testator did not change his will, 'that f***** would see himself in the [nursing] home' (ibid [145]). Note that proprietary estoppel is capable of providing a remedy for a carer seeking an increased share in the estate of the person who was being cared for, but it would be necessary for the claimant to establish the making of an appropriate representation. See generally B Sloan, *Informal Carers and Private Law* (Oxford, Hart Publishing, 2013) ch 2.

In terms of the proprietary estoppel issue, there were many similarities with the facts of *Thorner v Major*. In this case, however, the representations were more clear-cut than in *Thorner* and it is not surprising that the claimant was successful in his claim. The most striking aspect of O'Keeffe J's resolution of the case is that he did not believe that there was any basis on which the court could deprive the claimant of his bequest of €150,000. He reasoned that 'The unfulfilled commitment and obligation of the deceased to the plaintiff pursuant to the various commitments made by him, is a matter and entitlement that is separate from the bequest'.[113] Thus, O'Keeffe J was willing to give the claimant (the hero of the tale) a bonus of €150,000 in addition to the farm, at the expense of the defendant (clearly its villain). This aspect of the judgment was overturned on appeal as 'unduly severe'.[114]

In narrative terms, the story of Willie Naylor is rather similar to that of David Thorner. One difference is that the story in the judgment in *Naylor* is enriched by the casting of Jean in the role of 'ugly sister' to Willie's Cinderella. The story in *Naylor* is also distinguished by the curious twist whereby the man who had promised to leave Willie the farm turned out to be his father rather than his stepfather. Thus, as picked up in the newspaper reporting of the case,[115] the story had the classic dimension of the son seeking his lost father, like Telemachus in search of wandering Ulysses.

VI. *THORNER*, FREEDOM OF TESTATION AND THE ARC OF A LIFE

Cases like *Thorner* generally involve a change of mind on the part of the defendant, a decision to end the story differently. To others, who do not share the defendant's subjective experience of his or her life, such a change of mind may be difficult to understand. It has long been argued, at a more general level, that freedom of testation is a chimera and that courts use a variety of doctrinal devices to strike down wills of which they do not approve:

> [M]any courts are as committed to ensuring that testators devise their estates in accordance with prevailing normative views as they are to effectuating testamentary intent. Those courts impose upon testators a duty to provide for those … whom the court views as having a superior moral claim to the testator's assets, usually a financially dependent spouse or persons related by blood to the testator. Wills that fail to provide for those individuals typically are upheld only if the will's proponent can convince the fact-finder that the testator's deviation from normative values is morally justifiable. This unspoken rule, seeping quietly but fervently from the case law, directly conflicts with the oft-repeated axiom that testamentary freedom is the polestar of wills law.[116]

The law may be equally reluctant to give effect to a change of mind on the part of a testator that offends assumptions about the appropriate narrative of a person's life. One possible example is provided by *Sharp v Adam*,[117] a case which did not involve estoppel

[113] ibid [426].
[114] [2018] IECA 32, [21] (Peart J).
[115] See text to n 92 above.
[116] See M Leslie, 'The Myth of Freedom of Testation' (1996) 38 *Arizona Law Review* 235, 236 (footnotes omitted). Her discussion, in the context of US law, assumes the absence of the kind of statutory restriction on testamentary freedom represented by the Inheritance (Provision for Family and Dependants) Act 1975.
[117] *Sharp v Adam* [2006] EWCA Civ 449, [2006] WTLR 1059.

but which has factual similarities to *Thorner* and related estoppel cases. The testator in *Sharp*, who suffered from secondary progressive multiple sclerosis, changed his will so as to leave nothing to his two daughters, instead leaving his stud farm to two trusted employees who had been involved in its operation for a number of years and giving smaller gifts to one of his carers and to an old friend. While the testator's illness had progressed so far that he was only able to communicate by means of nods and shakes of his head, those around him had no doubt that he was mentally competent. The execution of his will was conducted 'in a quite exemplary fashion' and the so-called 'golden rule'[118] was observed 'in every particular and beyond'.[119] Nonetheless, the decision to leave nothing to his daughters, with whom he did not appear to have quarrelled, was regarded as irrational. The Court of Appeal took the view, in reliance on 'the tenuous thread'[120] of one passage in the evidence of a medical expert, that the testator's disease had damaged his brain so as, in the words of the classic test for mental capacity, to 'poison his affections, pervert his sense of right or prevent the exercise of his natural faculties'.[121]

It may be that it is difficult for an outside observer, or a court, to accept that a will accurately reflects the current preferences of the testator where those preferences do not fit with what the testator, for most of his or her life, would have wanted. A person might, in the years of his or her prime, have intended to pass on their farm to their eldest son but might, in their declining years, come to focus more on the immediate present and (along the lines of the facts of *Naylor v Maher*) decide to prefer the daughter who is providing them with day-to-day care. In his novel *Immortality*,[122] Milan Kundera writes about the final period of life, 'the shortest and most mysterious, about which little is known and little is said'.[123] He continues:

> Strength is ebbing, and a person is seized by disarming fatigue. Fatigue: a silent bridge leading from the shore of life to the shore of death. At that stage death is so close that looking at it has already become boring … Not everyone reaches this furthest limit, but whoever does reach it knows that there, and only there, can true freedom be found.[124]

The freedom that Kundera has in mind is the freedom to act inconsistently with what we had previously thought was important, to suddenly cease to care how we are judged by others.

As the philosopher Derek Parfit emphasised,[125] we are inclined to overestimate the identity between current and future selves, so that we may, in an important sense, be different people at 30 and at 75. In thinking about other people's lives, we may be too inclined to look for unbroken continuity of preference and to assume that what they decide to do in their will should reflect what they wanted for the greatest length of time in their lives, not what they want at the time when they make their will, when their horizons may

[118] '[T]hat the making of a will by an old and infirm testator ought to be witnessed and approved by a medical practitioner who satisfies himself as to the capacity and understanding of the testator and makes a record of his examination and findings': ibid [27].

[119] ibid.

[120] ibid [93].

[121] ibid. The relevant test is stated in *Banks v Goodfellow* (1870) LR 5 QB 549, 565. See also n 3 above.

[122] (London, Faber and Faber, 1992).

[123] ibid 80.

[124] ibid 80–81.

[125] *Persons and Identity* (Oxford, Clarendon Press, 1984).

have narrowed and, in a perhaps unappealing way, their priorities may have completely changed. The desire to create a consistent narrative in respect of a person's life may lead the courts to defeat what were, at the end of their lives, the person's true preferences by finding a past commitment where none was really made.

VII. CONCLUDING OBSERVATIONS

This chapter has suggested that proprietary estoppel, as applied in the landmark case of *Thorner v Major*, has particular advantages for a claimant, so that (as suggested in the introduction to this chapter) it does indeed make a real difference how a succession claim is presented to the court. The nature of proprietary estoppel as a non-statutory doctrine of private law means that it tends to be concerned with what private law theorists refer to as 'corrective' as opposed to 'distributive' justice.[126] The focus is on the relationship between the claimant and the testator, reflecting a concern with the 'special morality' linking 'the doer and the sufferer'. The sufferer, the claimant, hogs the spotlight in these dramas. The other half of the 'bipolar relationship of liability' envisaged by private law – the testator – is generally dead by the time the matter comes to court.[127] As a result, the testator usually cannot speak for himself or herself, and his or her character is revealed only through the testimony of others.

The testator is often portrayed as wielding power, as the person making representations that manipulate the conduct of the claimant. Thus, Robert Walker LJ commented that 'it is notorious that some elderly persons of means derive enjoyment from the possession of testamentary power'.[128] In *Bradbury v Taylor*,[129] the elderly testator was twice described as having 'enticed' the claimants into moving from another part of the country to live in his house. However, his motivations show him as more vulnerable since he seems to 'have felt a need for someone else to be living at the property after a lawnmower which he prized, and a chainsaw, were stolen from outbuildings' at his house.[130] Similarly, the testatrix in *Jennings v Rice*,[131] who was around 90, had 'had a burglary, which must have been a shocking and upsetting experience for her' and, 'determined to go on living in her own house', persuaded the claimant to sleep downstairs in the house.[132] Comparatively rarely do the courts show real sympathy for the testator, as when (in a much criticised judgment) HHJ Weeks explained in *Taylor v Dickens* that:

> [O]ne has to bear in mind that Mrs Parker was 85, in acute pain, lonely, frightened of a confrontation with a younger man, desperate to die in her house, and anxious to have the house preserved after her death in the way in which she would wish.[133]

[126] See generally E Weinrib, *The Idea of Private Law* (Oxford, Oxford University Press, 1995; revised edn 2012).

[127] Though sometimes a dispute arises where the testator attempts to resile from his promises during his lifetime: see, eg *Gillett v Holt* [2001] Ch 210.

[128] ibid 228.

[129] *Bradbury v Taylor* [2012] EWCA Civ 1208, [2013] WTLR 29, [25] and [27] (Lloyd LJ, quoting from the first instance judgment).

[130] ibid [10].

[131] [2002] EWCA Civ 159.

[132] ibid [6].

[133] [1998] 1 FLR 806 (Ch), 822.

While, of course, testators (not all of whom are elderly) may engage in manipulation and unconscionable dealing, the power apparently given to them by their wealth may be balanced by other frailties.

The other characters marginalised in these estoppel stories are the other family members who may have claims on the testator's generosity, claims which may be reflected in the will actually made by the testator. The stories that are suppressed as a result might seem as compelling as those of the claimant, if more attention were given to them. In *Naylor v Maher*, despite the unattractive aspects of her behaviour revealed in the judgment, the defendant could have told a convincing story about her years of caring for the testator and of their closeness at the end of the testator's life. However, this is not how proprietary estoppel works. Under the Inheritance (Provision for Family and Dependants) Act 1975, the court must consider the actual and potential financial needs and resources of the beneficiaries under the will and any responsibilities and obligations owed to them by the testator, as well as any physical or mental disability of theirs.[134] There is no obvious scope within the doctrine of proprietary estoppel to weigh up the competing merits of the claims of those who would otherwise be entitled under the claimant's will. Academic commentators have reacted negatively to the circumscribed suggestion by Robert Walker LJ in *Jennings v Rice* that it might be appropriate, only in those cases where it was necessary to devise a lesser remedy for proprietary estoppel because an expectation remedy would be disproportionate, to consider '(to a limited degree) the other claims (legal or moral) on the benefactor or his or her estate'.[135] This reaction is consistent with the vision of proprietary estoppel as an instrument of corrective justice. It is also significant that the application of the proprietary estoppel doctrine is by no means limited to the succession law context; it is unlikely that it would be doctrinally defensible to argue for a special version of the doctrine in that context which would be sensitive to its impact on other possible beneficiaries in a way which would not apply in other contexts.

With the testator generally out of the way and the actual beneficiaries under the will at a remove from the main narrative, the spotlight is firmly on the claimant. Once the matter is presented to the court in the form of the claimant's story, it quite quickly comes to seem plausible to disregard the result dictated by the law of succession. In the complex context of a story, the simple succession law idea of a single testamentary intention, expressed formally in a will, is rather limiting. It takes comparatively little to justify the conclusion that, as in *Thorner*, the court should take account of the testator's actual intention, even though it was not expressed in a valid will. When they are applying equity, the rhetoric of centuries encourages judges, like God in the old proverb, to 'temper the harsh wind to the shorn lamb'.[136] From the point of view of a judge, it must be more fulfilling to dispense discretionary justice to the parties before the court than to feel obliged to apply, in a more mechanical way, the strict rules of succession law. However, there is a cost. Stories are inherently unpredictable. The trial judge in *Suggitt v Suggitt*, remarked that '[o]ne of

[134] Section 3(1)(c), (d) and (f).

[135] [2002] EWCA Civ 159, [52]. See, eg S Gardner, 'The Remedial Discretion in Proprietary Estoppel – Again' (2006) 122 *LQR* 492, 501: 'Relief is about giving concrete effect to a well-founded claim, so the factors determining its scale must be those upon which the claim itself rests.'

[136] See *Murad v Al-Saraj* [2005] EWCA Civ 959, [81] (Arden LJ). See also *Pennington v Waine* [2002] 1 WLR 2075 (CA), 2087, 2088, 2089 (Arden LJ).

the unfortunate features of this case has been the inability of the parties to compromise an obviously compromisable case'.[137] This, however, seems to overstate the predictability of proprietary estoppel. The 'flexibility' of proprietary estoppel makes it difficult for the parties to bargain in the shadow of the law, generating a great deal of litigation that is 'bitterly fought and ruinously expensive'.[138]

A final thought is that it may not be possible to sustain in practice the judicial conceit that proprietary estoppel applies only after the event, with equity coming to the aid of trusting parties who acted with no foreknowledge of its rules. The assumption is that proprietary estoppel is a decision rule (directed to judges), rather than a conduct rule (directed to citizens). In Meir Dan-Cohen's terms, a state of acoustic separation is thought to prevail, whereby potential claimants are unaware of the content of the decision rule of proprietary estoppel.[139] If that assumption is true, there is no danger that the doctrine will interfere with the development of trust in human relationships by making it impossible to make a promise which is not to be the source of potential legal liability.[140] Also, claimants will not deliberately act so as to build up an estoppel claim, but will only think of the legal consequences of their actions after their trust has been betrayed in an unconscionable manner. In 1994, one judge dismissed the possibility that the claimants had fabricated their claim, noting that 'The doctrine of proprietary estoppel is a closed book to many lawyers, let alone a builder and a housewife'.[141] However, the doctrine of proprietary estoppel has become much more prominent over the last 20 years, partly as a result of *Thorner v Major*. As McFarlane points out, the case featured in a permanent exhibition at the Supreme Court which is designed to illustrate 'The relevance of the Supreme Court to everyday life'.[142] *Thorner*, and some of the cases that have followed it, were featured in national newspapers, with an emphasis on the generosity of the remedies. These stories make engaging reading. Potential claimants, working on the basis of a hope rather than a promise of inheritance, may decide to make up their own stories, long before the owl of judicial wisdom spreads its wings.

[137] [2011] EWHC 903 (Ch), [66].

[138] *Gillett v Holt* [2001] Ch 210 (CA), 228 (Robert Walker). See also, eg *Moore v Moore* [2018] EWCA Civ 2669, [1] (Henderson LJ): 'the dispute has already been ruinous in both human and financial terms'; the legal costs were estimated at £2.5 million. This point is also made in Mee (n 80) 296–97.

[139] 'Decision Rules and Conduct Rules: On Acoustic Separation in Criminal Law' (1984) 97 *Harvard Law Review* 625.

[140] For discussion of the issue of trust, and the importance of the distinction between promise and contract, see Mee (n 38) 195–97.

[141] *Durant v Heritage* (unreported, Chancery Division, 20 July 1994) (Lexis) (Judge Park QC).

[142] McFarlane (n 31) 1.

12

Re Welch (1990): Enforcing Testamentary Promises

NICOLA PEART*

I. INTRODUCTION

RE WELCH IS a decision of the Privy Council dealing with New Zealand's Law Reform (Testamentary Promises) Act 1949 (hereafter TPA), a statute apparently unique to New Zealand.[1] The purpose of this Act is to enforce unfulfilled promises to make testamentary provision as a reward for services provided to the deceased during the deceased's lifetime. The TPA was introduced because it was thought that a promise to pay for services by making testamentary provision was not contractually enforceable under the common law.[2] The TPA was intended to reform contract law to remedy that injustice. As a result of increasingly liberal construction of its jurisdictional elements, the TPA became an avenue for enforcing a deceased's moral obligations, sometimes with little to distinguish it from family provision enforceable through the Family Protection Act 1955.

Re Welch is a turning point in New Zealand's testamentary promises jurisprudence and in succession law generally, and hence is a landmark case. It concerned a claim by a stepson against his stepfather's estate to enforce his stepfather's promise to leave him most of his estate. It dealt with the difficult question of whether services, in particular intangible services, provided within a family relationship could support a testamentary promises claim and, if so, how quantum was to be assessed. The claim largely failed because the intangible services the stepson relied on to support his claim did not go beyond what would normally be expected in a family relationship and the promise of testamentary provision was made out of love and affection, not as a reward for services. This case redefined the basis upon which testamentary promises claims should be considered, thus distinguishing it from family provision. More broadly, the case addresses constraints on testamentary freedom, which subsequently became the subject of a Law

* I am indebted to Kyla Mullen LLB Hons for her invaluable research and editorial assistance.

[1] *Re Welch* [1990] 3 NZLR 1 (PC).

[2] B Coote, 'Testamentary Promises Jurisdiction in New Zealand' in JF Northey (ed), *The AG Davis Essays in Law* (London, Butterworths, 1965) 4–8.

Commission review.[3] *Re Welch* has the further distinction of being the only testamentary promises case in the TPA's 75-year history to reach New Zealand's top appellate court, then the Privy Council, now the New Zealand Supreme Court.

This chapter begins by setting out the history that led to the introduction of the testamentary promises jurisdiction in 1944 and eventually the Law Reform (Testamentary Promises) Act in 1949. The chapter then analyses *Re Welch* and concludes by addressing *Re Welch's* influence on subsequent testamentary promises claims and the relationship between TPA claims and those based on the general law.

II. THE LEGISLATIVE HISTORY

A. The Perceived Inequity of the Common Law

Testamentary promises legislation was introduced to remedy a perceived inequity in contract law. Property owners are free to enter into a contract to leave some or all of their estate by will,[4] but they are enforceable only if they meet the requirements for a valid contract: offer and acceptance, consideration (or a deed), certainty of terms, intention to create legal relations and compliance with any required formalities (or part performance).[5] Establishing each of these requirements has proven to be difficult. A promise by a family member may not be intended to create binding legal relations;[6] or the promise may be an acknowledgement for past services and fail for lack of consideration;[7] or the terms of the arrangement may be too vague.[8] If the promise related to land, it could fail for lack of compliance with the writing requirement, unless the contract was partly performed.[9] Even if the promise was fulfilled, it could fail by operation of law or for reasons beyond the testator's control.[10] Promises of testamentary provision were therefore often contractually unenforceable.

A misunderstanding about two old English cases and a passage in *Halsbury's Laws of England* gave rise to New Zealand's testamentary promises legislation. The first case was *Osborn v The Governors of Guy's Hospital*, decided in 1726, in which Mr Osborn made

[3] Law Commission, *Succession Law: A Succession (Adjustment) Act*, NZLC R39 (Wellington, 1997). Its proposals have not been implemented. For a discussion of the proposed reforms to the testamentary promises legislation, see B Sloan, *Informal Carers and Private Law* (Oxford, Hart Publishing, 2013) 3.3.

[4] B Sloan, *Borkowski's Law of Succession*, 3rd edn (Oxford, Oxford University Press, 2017) 3.1.2; A Alston, *Garrow and Alston Law of Wills and Administration*, 5th edn (Wellington, Butterworths, 1984) 1.48.

[5] *Hammersley v de Biel* (1845) 12 Cl & F 45; 8 ER 1312; *Synge v Synge* [1894] 1 QB 466 (CA); *Schaefer v Schuhmann* [1972] AC 572 (PC); *Fleming v Beevers* [1994] 1 NZLR 385 (CA).

[6] The law would not imply a promise to reward services provided by near relatives: J Macdonnell, *The Law of Master and Servant* (London, Stevens, 1838) 144; *Walton v Walton* [1994] EWCA Civ J0414-1; *Taylor v Dickens* [1998] 1 FLR 806.

[7] *Bennett v Kirk* [1946] NZLR 580.

[8] *Horton v Jones* (1935) 53 CLR 475.

[9] For example, *Young v Anderson* [1940] NZLR 239. Statute of Frauds 1667, s 4; Contracts Enforcement Act 1956 (NZ), s 2, now Property Law Act 2007 (NZ), s 24.

[10] For example, revocation of the will by subsequent marriage or lapse or an order under the Family Protection Act 1955 (NZ): *Dillon v Public Trustee* [1941] NZLR 557 (PC); *Bristow v French* (unreported, HC Christchurch CIV-2011-409-2181, 17 August 2012). See further Coote (n 2) 2–4; M Davey, 'Testamentary Promises' (1988) 8 *Legal Studies* 92, 94–96.

a quantum meruit claim against the estate of Mr Guy for transacting Guy's stock affairs. Osborn was Guy's friend, not a broker, and had provided the services in the expectation of testamentary provision.[11] Osborn failed to recover payment for his services because he provided the services gratuitously, albeit in the expectation that Guy would leave him a legacy in his will. The central question was the parties' understanding at the time of providing the services. As Osborn had not then expected to be paid for his services, he could not later recover payment from the estate.

The second case was *Baxter v Gray*, decided in 1842, in which the plaintiff was successful.[12] Baxter was a surgeon and apothecary who had provided medicines and attended upon Mrs Bostock for about 11 years. Like Mr Osborn, Baxter was a friend of Mrs Bostock and had never sent her a bill because he expected a legacy. He successfully recovered payment for his services against the estate executors. The Court held that services are normally provided in the expectation of payment. The onus was on the executors to rebut this presumption by proving that the parties had an understanding that the plaintiff was not to be paid for his services. The executors failed to satisfy that onus.

In reliance on these authorities, *Halsbury's Laws of England* stated the common law on testamentary promises in the following passage:

> A man who does work for a testator on the understanding that he is to be remunerated by a legacy has no claim against his estate if the testator fails to provide for the legacy, and the executors are not entitled to satisfy such a claim. It rests, however, upon the executors to show that the work was done upon such an understanding; the mere forbearance to send in a claim for work done in the expectation of a legacy is no bar to a claim against the executors for the services rendered if the party is disappointed in his expectation.[13]

The New Zealand courts understood this passage to mean that a promise of testamentary provision as a reward for services was unenforceable. That was the reason the claimant in *Te Ira Roa v Materi Omipi* failed in 1912.[14] He was a cousin of the deceased, Mary Grey, who had hired him to work as a labourer on her farm, which he did until her death 13 years later. She treated him like an adopted son, providing him only with board and lodging. He never asked for wages, because she often told him that she would provide for him in her will. She died intestate. Citing the two English cases and *Halsbury*, the court found that the plaintiff's work deserved remuneration, but that he did the work on the understanding that he would not be paid and instead would receive a legacy. As he had trusted her generosity to provide for him by will, he could not recover payment for his services after her death.

Sutherland v Towle brought matters to a head in 1937.[15] Mrs Sutherland had provided domestic and nursing services to Mr and Mrs Hastings for many years at Mr Hastings's request. He told her he was unable to pay her until his assets were realised on death, but that he had remunerated her in his will. She continued working for him on that understanding, but received nothing under the will. As the evidence clearly established an

[11] *Osborn v The Governors of Guy's Hospital* 2 Strange 728; 93 ER 812.

[12] *Baxter v Gray* 3 Manning and Grainger 771; 133 ER 1349.

[13] Lord Hailsham (ed), *Halsbury's Laws of England*, 2nd edn (London, Butterworths, 1934) vol 14: Executors and Administrators, [712].

[14] *Te Ira Roa v Materi Omipi* [1919] GLR 492.

[15] *Sutherland v Towle* (1937) GLR 509.

understanding that Mrs Sutherland would be remunerated by will, Ostler J concluded that he had no option but to non-suit her claim. Although there was a contract, he could find no way of getting around the law, as stated in *Halsbury* and New Zealand cases, that a contract to pay for services by making testamentary provision was unenforceable. Ostler J greatly regretted this conclusion, commenting: 'I do not think that the law is equitable, and in this case I feel that it will work an injustice. But it is clearly the law, and my duty as a Judge is to follow the law.'[16] He expressed the hope that the beneficiaries would recognise Mrs Sutherland's moral claim by giving her some allowance. The executors were reportedly glad to convey that recommendation to the beneficiaries![17]

As one commentator observed, Ostler J's decision was arguably wrong on the law.[18] The question in *Osborn* and *Baxter* was not how or when payment for services was to be made, but whether the parties understood that those services were to be remunerated. If the services were to be provided gratuitously, but in the hope or expectation of a legacy, then testamentary provision was at the testator's discretion. On the other hand, if there was an express or implied contract to provide services for payment, it was enforceable even if the expected payment was to be made by a legacy. Failure to claim payment during the deceased's lifetime or uncertainty as to quantum was no bar to recovery of a reasonable sum if no testamentary provision was made. As Mrs Sutherland provided her services on the understanding that she would be paid for those services, albeit by means of a legacy, she should have been entitled to damages for her loss.

B. The Law Reform Act 1944

Sutherland was the impetus for reform of the law. Ostler J's judgment and his criticism of the common law were reported in newspapers across the country.[19] The issue was placed on the next agenda of the newly formed New Zealand Law Revision Committee,[20] with a suggestion that the common law be modified by statute to remedy the inequity.[21] EP Hay, a legal expert in estates and administration,[22] was asked to provide a report on the desirability of legislative reform.[23] He concluded, with some hesitation, that the law should be amended. While claims of testamentary promises were generally viewed with suspicion, as one of the principal parties to the alleged bargain was unable to speak, the existing law caused hardship to claimants such as Mrs Sutherland. Hay recommended that claimants who showed that they had provided services to the deceased on the understanding that

[16] ibid 511.

[17] 'Claim Fails – "Law Inequitable"' *The New Zealand Herald* (Auckland, 10 September 1937).

[18] Coote (n 2) 6.

[19] 'Claim Fails' (n 17); 'Work Done before Death – Plaintiff Non-suited' *The Press* (Christchurch, 10 September 1937); 'Law Inequitable' *Evening Post* (Wellington, 10 September 1937).

[20] The New Zealand Law Revision Committee was New Zealand's first law reform committee, established in 1937 to replace the English Law Revision Committee: Hon HGR Mason, Attorney-General, Chair of the Committee, at the commencement of the first meeting of the Committee on 26 August 1937.

[21] 'Report of the New Zealand Law Revision Committee Meeting of 29 October 1937' (1937) 13 *New Zealand Law Journal* 307.

[22] 'The New Judge' (1949) *New Zealand Law Journal* 41.

[23] EP Hay, *Memorandum re Contracts of Service; Work done on Agreement to Make Testamentary Provision as Remuneration* (Wellington, 1937) 6.

they would be remunerated by testamentary provision should be in no worse position than claimants who could establish a true contractual basis for their claim.

The Law Revision Committee adopted Hay's report in February 1938 and referred it to the Law Draftsman, who promptly inserted a clause in a Law Reform Bill. The war delayed its adoption until 1944.[24] Section 3 of that Act established the testamentary promises jurisdiction:

> Where in the administration of the estate of any deceased person a claim is made against the estate founded upon the rendering of services to or the performance of work for the deceased in his lifetime and the claimant proves an express or implied promise by the deceased to reward him for the services or work by making some testamentary provision for the claimant, the claim shall, to the extent to which the deceased has failed to make that testamentary provision or otherwise remunerate the claimant (whether or not a claim for such remuneration could have been enforced in the lifetime of the deceased), be enforceable against the personal representatives of the deceased in the same manner and to the same extent as if the promise of the deceased were a promise for payment by the deceased in his lifetime of the amount specified in the promise or, if no amount is specified, of such amount as may be reasonable, having regard to all the circumstances of the case, including in particular the circumstances in which the promise was made and the services were rendered or the work was performed, the value of the services or work, the amount of the estate, and the nature and amounts of the claims of other persons against the estate, whether as creditors, beneficiaries, wife, husband, children, next-of-kin, or otherwise.

Most parliamentarians supported the reform.[25] Such debate as there was focused on an amendment that an award under the section be classified as a legacy, rather than satisfaction of a debt, despite the contractual foundation of the claim.[26] The Attorney-General justified this apparent inconsistency by pointing out that if the promise had been fulfilled, it would have been a legacy.[27] An award under the Act put promisees in the position they expected to be in. If awards were treated as payments of debt, then performance of the promise should similarly be classified and be exempted from the dutiable estate. This was the first acknowledgement of the complex status of testamentary promises claims, which still haunts this jurisdiction.[28] Were they contractual in nature, as the wording of section 3 suggested, or were they a claim on the deceased's bounty and thus part of succession law?

The judicial response to the new jurisdiction was to proceed with caution and adhere closely to established contract law principles to prevent unscrupulous claims. The wording of section 3 invited a contractual approach to the jurisdictional requirements, which restricted its remedial effect.[29] In *Bennett v Kirk*, the first reported decision on the section,

[24] 'The Law Reform Act, 1944' (1945) 21 *New Zealand Law Journal* 1.

[25] (23 November 1944) 267 New Zealand Parliamentary Debates 299, 301, where Mr Oram (Manawatu) objected to enforcing a contract on death that was not enforceable during the deceased's lifetime.

[26] This clause was added in response to *Dillon v PT* (n 10), where the Privy Council overruled the New Zealand Court of Appeal by deciding that a contract to make testamentary provision, whether it had been fulfilled or not, was subject to any provision the court might order under the Family Protection Act 1955.

[27] (23 November 1944) 267 New Zealand Parliamentary Debates 299, 302.

[28] *Bristow v Smith* [2013] NZHC 2866. See also W Lee, 'Contracts to Make Wills' (1971) 87 *LQR* 858, where the issue in other common law jurisdictions is discussed.

[29] *Jones v Public Trustee* [1962] NZLR 363 (CA), 372.

the court insisted on satisfactory evidence that the deceased had promised to make testamentary provision in favour of the plaintiff, that the plaintiff had relied on the promise and that the plaintiff's services resulted in benefit to the deceased or detriment to the plaintiff.[30] Past consideration would therefore not support a claim under section 3. Other judges thought the section could extend to promises made in appreciation for past services, but the promise had to be an actual agreement, not a mere statement of intent.[31] Section 3 also did not override the writing requirement in the Statute of Frauds 1677 (Eng), creating uncertainty about the enforceability of a verbal promise to devise land by will.[32] Furthermore, jurisdiction was founded on a promise to pay a sum of money and hence an award could only sound in money, not any other kind of property, even if the promise was to leave a specific item of property.[33]

C. The Law Reform (Testamentary Promises) Act 1949

The Law Revision Committee had kept section 3 under review and anticipated the concerns raised by the courts. By 1948 it had proposed amendments to address those concerns and the adoption of a separate statute.[34] The TPA was adopted in 1949. Section 3(1) re-enacted the 1944 provision, retaining its contractual analogy, but clarified that the promise could relate to specific property, including land. New sections were added to give better effect to the Act's remedial purpose. A 'promise' was defined to include 'any statement or representation of fact or intention'.[35] It was enforceable notwithstanding anything to the contrary in section 4 of the Statute of Frauds 1677.[36] Furthermore, the section applied whether the services or work were performed before or after the promise of testamentary provision was made.[37] The courts were given the power to vest all or any part of promised real or personal property in the claimant and could make a monetary award in the form of a lump sum or periodic payments.[38] The incidence of such payments would fall rateably upon the whole estate, unless the court determined otherwise.[39]

In 1961 the TPA was further amended to remove constraints on assessing quantum. The court was given the power in all cases to award such amount as was reasonable, even where a specific amount had been promised, and to determine priorities between awards under the Act and the beneficial interests of any other person in the estate.[40] As before,

[30] *Bennett v Kirk* [1946] NZLR 580, 583.

[31] *McAllister v Public Trustee* [1947] NZLR 334, 340. But opinions remained divided: see *Ace v Guardian Trust* [1948] NZLR 103, 106; *Jennings v Harper* [1949] GLR 280, 281; *Nealon v Public Trustee* [1949] NZLR 148 (CA), 160.

[32] *Nealon v PT* (ibid) overruled the Supreme Court decision that a promise to leave land by will was not enforceable in the absence of writing.

[33] *McAllister v PT* (n 31) 340–41; *Nealon v PT* (n 31).

[34] 'The Work of the New Zealand Law Revision Committee, 1948' (1949) 25 *New Zealand Law Journal* 49.

[35] TPA, s 2.

[36] TPA, s 3(2), now the Property Law Act 2007.

[37] TPA, s 3(2).

[38] TPA, ss 3(3) and (4).

[39] TPA, ss 3(5) and (6).

[40] TPA, s 3(6).

any award was part of the dutiable estate.[41] The jurisdiction was thus a matter of estate administration, not succession law. The 1961 amendment also clarified that claimants had the option of pursuing other remedies instead of the statutory claim.[42]

Section 3(1) has not been substantively amended since and now states:

> Where in the administration of the estate of any deceased person a claim is made against the estate founded upon the rendering of services to or the performance of work for the deceased in his lifetime, and the claimant proves an express or implied promise by the deceased to reward him for the services or work by making some testamentary provision for the claimant, whether or not the provision was to be of a specified amount or was to relate to specified real or personal property, then, subject to the provisions of this Act, the claim shall, to the extent to which the deceased has failed to make that testamentary provision or otherwise remunerate the claimant (whether or not a claim for such remuneration could have been enforced in the lifetime of the deceased), be enforceable against the personal representatives of the deceased in the same manner and to the same extent as if the promise of the deceased were a promise for payment by the deceased in his lifetime of such amount as may be reasonable, having regard to all the circumstances of the case, including in particular the circumstances in which the promise was made and the services were rendered or the work was performed, the value of the services or work, the value of the testamentary provision promised, the amount of the estate, and the nature and amounts of the claims of other persons in respect of the estate, whether as creditors, beneficiaries, wife, husband, civil union partner, children, next-of kin, or otherwise.

The amendments made in 1949 and 1961 liberated the jurisdiction from its contractual shackles. By the time *Re Welch* came before the courts in 1989 there was little sign of the TPA's contractual origins.[43] There was no need for an offer and acceptance, or an intention to create legal relations. A unilateral declaration of intent to make testamentary provision as a reward for past or future services sufficed to found jurisdiction.[44] The promisee's motive in providing the services was irrelevant. They could have been provided out of generosity or kindness, without any expectation of a reward.[45] What mattered was that the deceased valued the services and promised to reward them either out of gratitude for past services or to encourage future services. The award was a matter of discretion, in which the promise of a specified amount was merely one factor to take into consideration along with other factors, some of which were more relevant to a moral claim on the deceased's bounty than the recovery of a debt. As Coote observed in 1965 in a notable essay on the TPA:

> Instead of being a mere reform of the law of contract the testamentary promises legislation seems to have become, like the Family Protection Act, a more general means by which the Courts can repair the failure of deceased persons to provide adequately for those with merely moral claims upon them.[46]

[41] TPA, s 4. Following repeal of estate duty in 1999, s 4 was amended to deem an award under the Act to be a bequest or devise: Estate Duty Repeal Act 1999, s 15(1).

[42] TPA, s 3(8).

[43] Coote (n 2) 10–12.

[44] *Jones v PT* (n 29) 374.

[45] *Smith v Malley* [1950] NZLR 145; *Jones v PT* (n 29) 375.

[46] Coote (n 2) 13. For a discussion of the TPA, see WM Patterson, *Law of Family Protection and Testamentary Promises*, 4th edn (Wellington, LexisNexis, 2013); Sloan (n 3) ch 3; see also the detailed analysis of R Wells, 'Testamentary Promises: A New Approach' (PhD thesis, King's College London, 2007).

Re Welch reversed this trend by reinjecting some rigour into the analysis of the jurisdictional elements to distinguish the TPA from the moral duty enforceable through the Family Protection Act. In doing so, it laid the foundation for a new approach to testamentary promises claims, based on principles of unjust enrichment.

III. *RE WELCH*

A. The Facts[47]

The plaintiff in *Re Welch*, Albyn Stewart, was the stepson of the deceased Mr Welch. Albyn's mother had been married to the deceased for 32 years. Mr Welch had promised Albyn that he would leave him most of his estate, but he died intestate in April 1982, seven weeks after his wife died.

Albyn was very young when his parents separated, after which he had little to do with his father. He was 10 years old when his mother met Mr Welch in 1947. They married in 1949. They had no children together, but Albyn was like a son to his stepfather. He called him Dad and his stepfather was in all respects a father to him. The family initially lived in Dunedin in a house owned by Mrs Welch. In 1953 Mr and Mrs Welch moved to Alexandra, a country town in the South Island. Mr Welch was penniless at the time, having been unwell for several years, but with his wife's financial support he was able to buy a carrying business. The couple worked hard to establish a home and build up the business, with Mrs Welch making significant contributions to the physical work and management of the business.

Albyn married in 1954, when he was 17 years old. He and his wife moved to Alexandra in 1956. Mr Welch gave Albyn considerable assistance, arranging employment for him and gifting him for his twenty-first birthday a block of land on which to build a home. Albyn contributed to his parents' business in his spare time and often accompanied his stepfather to social occasions. Albyn and his wife had five children, and the family had frequent contact with Mr and Mrs Welch. In 1959 Mr Welch sold his business to a large construction company, accepting shares in the company and a role as manager. From then on he often mentioned to Albyn that the shares and the family home would eventually be Albyn's. In 1981 Mrs Welch was diagnosed with terminal cancer. During discussions about her will, Mr Welch repeatedly referred to Albyn as his only son and that everything he owned would ultimately go to Albyn except for three specific items. He asked Albyn to hold on to the shares and pass them on to his own children. Those statements were made to Albyn and to others, who later corroborated Albyn's testamentary promises claim.

Mrs Welch had executed a will in which she left specific gifts to her grandchildren, a life interest to her husband and the remainder capital to Albyn. Her estate had a residue of only $25,000. Mr Welch owned most of the couple's assets or took them by survivorship. When he died his estate, valued at $308,799, passed on intestacy to his eight siblings in the United Kingdom with whom he had maintained friendly but infrequent contact.[48]

[47] *Re Welch* [1989] 2 NZLR 1 (HC), 2–4.
[48] Administration Act 1969 (NZ), s 77.

B. Claims

Albyn made two claims against his stepfather's estate. In his capacity as executor of his mother's estate he made a claim under the Matrimonial Property Act 1963 (NZ) to recover property for her estate. That Act gave the court the power to redistribute a couple's assets on separation and on death based on the claimant's direct and indirect contributions to those assets.[49] Given Mrs Welch's substantial financial and non-financial contributions to the home and the business, the Court awarded her estate 50 per cent of the value of the home and the company shares.[50] That increased her estate by $133,000, which Albyn inherited under her will.

Albyn's TPA claim was brought in his personal capacity, seeking to enforce Mr Welch's promise to leave Albyn most of his estate. Albyn lacked eligibility to claim under the Family Protection Act 1955 (NZ), because he was not financially dependent on his stepfather.[51]

C. High Court Decision on the TPA

Williamson J was satisfied that Albyn met the requirements for an award under the TPA. He had worked in his stepfather's business and been like a son to his stepfather. Relying on precedent in which intangible services had founded jurisdiction, his Honour held that the benefits of companionship and enrichment that Albyn and his family had provided to Mr Welch were of particular significance to the deceased, as he had no children of his own.[52] The evidence also showed that Mr Welch had made an express promise to leave Albyn his shares and his interest in the home. While Albyn's services were carried out for reasons of affection and filial duty, such motives did not defeat a relationship between those services and the promise.[53] Having regard to the specific promise made, the value of Albyn's services to Mr Welch, the value of the provision promised, the size of the estate and the absence of competing moral claims on the deceased's bounty, the court awarded Albyn the remainder of Mr Welch's company shares and interest in the family home with a total value of $133,000.

The combined effect of the orders under the Matrimonial Property Act and the TPA was that Albyn received all but $40,000 of his stepfather's estate. The administrator of Mr Welch's estate appealed both orders.

[49] Matrimonial Property Act 1963 (NZ), ss 5 and 6. The 1963 Act was replaced by the Matrimonial Property Act 1976 (NZ) for marriages ending on separation or divorce, which introduced a presumption of equal sharing of matrimonial property. The 1963 Act continued to apply to marriages ending on death until 2002, when the 1976 Act was amended to include de facto relationships and relationships ending on death. The 1976 Act was then renamed the Property (Relationships) Act 1976 (NZ).

[50] Mrs Welch's award constituted 43% of the couple's total assets.

[51] Family Protection Act 1955 (NZ), s 3(1)(d).

[52] *Hawkins v Public Trustee* [1960] NZLR 305 (SC). The Supreme Court was renamed the High Court in 1980.

[53] *Re Welch* (n 47) 6.

D. Court of Appeal Decision

The appeal against the matrimonial property award had no merit and was quickly dismissed.[54] The appeal against the testamentary promises award succeeded. The appellant conceded that Albyn had provided services and that there was evidence of a promise to reward those services. Only quantum was challenged. That constrained the court's consideration of the jurisdictional elements. It is nonetheless evident from the judgment that the court was not satisfied that there was jurisdiction to make an order. It did not agree with the High Court that Albyn's relationship with his stepfather qualified as a service or that the deceased's promise was intended to reward Albyn for services he had provided. Mr Welch made the promise out of love and affection for his stepson.

> The evidence points to nothing more than a normal family relationship between a stepfather and stepson, who had the good fortune to get on well with each other. There was a reasonable balance of benefits and personal satisfaction on each side, and in earlier years Mr Welch helped his stepson with job opportunities and the gift of a section, as well as providing the general support of a father, and this carried on into the mutual companionship and family association of later times … We think that in making such a large award the Judge must have overlooked the reciprocal advantages Mr Stewart received from his stepfather, and paid too little regard to the latter's motive in saying he would leave him the estate, which in all probability must have been due simply to the natural love and affection he felt for him.[55]

The court pointed out that the TPA was not concerned with the moral duty of a deceased to make proper provision for children and other dependants. That was the purpose of the Family Protection Act.[56] But, given that the appellant did not dispute jurisdiction, an award that recognised those aspects of Albyn's conduct that went beyond the normal incidents of his family relationship with the deceased was appropriate. The sum had to be modest, which the Court of Appeal fixed at $20,000. Albyn appealed to the Privy Council, seeking reinstatement of the High Court award.

E. Privy Council Decision[57]

The Judicial Committee that heard Albyn's appeal comprised four members of the House of Lords and Sir Robin Cooke, then President of New Zealand's Court of Appeal, who delivered the judgment, upholding the Court of Appeal's decision and reasoning. Their Lordships commented that the estate's concession on jurisdiction was 'generous'.[58] They regarded much of the evidence of services as 'tenuous', stating: 'Some straining of the scope of the Act is required to bring within the concept of services the natural incidents and consequences of life within a close family group, such as existed in this case.'[59]

[54] *Welch v Stewart* [1989] 2 NZLR 6 (CA) 7.
[55] ibid 8.
[56] ibid 8.
[57] *Re Welch* [1990] 3 NZLR 1 (PC).
[58] ibid 3.
[59] ibid 7.

They also rejected Albyn's argument that Mr Welch had made his own assessment of the value of his stepson's services by promising to leave him the main assets in his estate and that his assessment should not be disturbed. There was no evidence that either party saw the promises as an assessment of a reward for services rendered.[60] Quite the contrary:

> The discrepancy between the value of the deceased's assets and the value of anything that can pass muster as 'services or work' underlines that the predominant motive of the deceased in making the representations was affection for his stepson and the latter's family, and the natural tendency to give effect to ordinary family expectations.[61]

The Privy Council felt some sympathy for Albyn not receiving his full expectations, but concluded:

> It is of the essence of the jurisdiction under the Law Reform (Testamentary Promises) Act 1949 that an award must be not more than reasonable recompense for services or work for the deceased. While a liberal approach to the question is fitting, and especially so when there are no competing moral claims, the conclusion that the initial award here went beyond the true scope of the Act is inescapable.[62]

F. Analysis

While the appeals were only against quantum, the value and importance of the appellate decisions lie in the analysis of the TPA's jurisdictional requirements. Comments in the judgments of both the Court of Appeal and the Privy Council indicate that, but for the administrator's concession on jurisdiction, they would have dismissed Albyn's TPA claim for lack of qualifying services and causal connection to the promise.

Albyn's claim must be seen in the context of an increasingly expansive approach to testamentary promises claims. From the late 1940s onwards the courts consistently advocated for a 'large and liberal construction and interpretation so as to attain the remedial objects of the enactment'.[63] Each of the jurisdictional elements has been broadly construed.

Mr Welch's frequently expressed statements about making testamentary provision for Albyn clearly met the TPA's wide definition of a 'promise'. Any uncertainty about what precise testamentary provision had been promised did not invalidate the promise. Nor did the form of the promise matter,[64] or the manner in which it was conveyed. A promise can be inferred from broad statements or conduct, as reasonably understood by the claimant.[65] The promise can be made long after the qualifying services were performed, but it must relate to services, which Mr Welch's promise was not.

There is no statutory definition or guidance on the meaning of 'services' or 'work'. The early cases were concerned with services of a tangible nature, capable of monetary

[60] ibid 7.
[61] ibid 7–8.
[62] ibid 8.
[63] *Nealon v PT* (n 31) 155. See also *Tucker v Guardian Trust Executors Co of NZ* [1961] NZLR 773 (SC) 776.
[64] *Jones v PT* (n 29); *Heathwaite v NZ Insurance Co Ltd* [1951] NZLR 6.
[65] *Heathwaite v NZI* (ibid); *Re Greenfield* [1985] 2 NZLR 662; *Busch v Ireland* [2016] NZCA 391.

assessment, such as domestic services, personal care, labour and financial support.[66] There was initially some doubt as to whether housekeeping and personal care qualified as services if they were provided by a close family member. In 1958, in *Hall v Public Trustee*, the High Court dismissed a daughter's testamentary promises claim against her father's estate because looking after a father in a daughterly way, even for a prolonged time, was not sufficient to prosecute a TPA claim.[67]

Two years later, the court accepted that 'services' could be intangible, such as companionship, emotional support and affection.[68] *Hawkins v Public Trustee*, which the High Court relied on in *Re Welch*, paved the way for this wider meaning of services.[69] The late Mr Hawkins was proud of his name and wanted his work to continue under his name after his death. His son was a disappointment and a waster, but Hawkins saw in his daughter's eldest son the qualities of a worthy successor. While his grandson was still a child, Hawkins proposed legally adopting him. His daughter and son-in-law refused consent, believing it was up to their son to make that decision when he was an adult. Hawkins did gradually annex his grandson, and when he turned 21 Hawkins promised him that if he changed his name to Hawkins and stuck by the deceased, managing his properties, he would inherit his grandfather's estate. In reliance on that promise, the grandson changed his surname by deed poll to Hawkins and from then on associated with his grandfather as a son, working on his farms for little pay. Some years later, his grandfather told his grandson that he would leave him only a quarter of his estate, which his grandson accepted. When Hawkins revised his promise to an annuity, his grandson ceased working his grandfather's farms.

The court held that the grandson met the jurisdictional requirements for a testamentary promises award. Taking on his grandfather's name at his grandfather's request, having a relationship akin to an adopted son and, as such, working for his grandfather were qualifying services.

> Superimposed upon the mutual rights and duties of master and servant were the filial rights and duties of an adopted adult son in respect of his father. In this framework of filial respect, loyalty, and goodwill, the plaintiff rendered the services of providing the deceased with an accepted substitute for a good son and a worker and farm manager in whom the deceased appears to have found no fault.[70]

The intangible services were 'the principal services' that Hawkins sought to secure from his grandson in return for his promise of testamentary provision.[71] They were the services the deceased valued. That they were intangible and incapable of precise monetary valuation was immaterial.

[66] Housekeeping and personal care of the deceased: *Nealon v PT* (n 31); *Allender v Gordon* [1959] NZLR 1026 (CA); *Byrne v Bishop* [2001] 2 NZLR 780 (CA); *Samuels v Atkinson* [2009] NZCA 556; unpaid or underpaid labour: *Hawkins v PT* (n 52); *Sullivan v Brett* [1981] 2 NZLR 202 (CA); *Re Townley* [1982] 2 NZLR 87 (CA); surrendering an inheritance in favour of the deceased: *Tucker v GT* (n 63); financial assistance: *Re Oliver (decd)* [1968] NZLR 113; *Edwards v NZ Insurance Co Ltd* [1971] NZLR 113; *Re Webster* [1976] 2 NZLR 304; *Ireland v Grant* [2014] NZHC 1523.

[67] Noted in 'Testamentary Promises: Some Recent Cases' (1959) 35 *New Zealand Law Journal* 193, 195.

[68] *Tucker v GT* (n 63) 776, where the claimant surrendered his right to an equal share of his mother's house so that his brother could continue to reside there on the promise that his brother would leave him the house.

[69] *Hawkins v PT* (n 52).

[70] ibid 313.

[71] ibid 313.

In subsequent cases the intangible benefits of companionship, support and affection provided by a de facto partner (cohabitant) have also founded jurisdiction where the deceased had promised to reward such services by will.[72] Like Albyn, de facto partners were not then eligible claimants under the Family Protection Act.[73]

Most of Albyn's services were intangible, but by comparison were less extensive than the grandson's services in *Hawkins*. While Albyn was a son to his stepfather, which his stepfather evidently valued and which enriched his life, this was not out of the ordinary. Even the work that Albyn did in Mr Welch's business was limited and occasional, and only occurred between 1954 and 1959. Such assistance could be expected in a family relationship, especially where it was offset by reciprocal benefits. There was nothing extra or unusual that took Albyn's services beyond the norm of a family relationship.

Fatal to Albyn's claim was the court's finding that his stepfather's promise was made out of love and affection for his stepson, not as a reward for services. The promise acknowledged the close relationship they enjoyed, not services that Albyn had provided either to the business or to Mr Welch personally. There was no nexus between the promise and qualifying services. The promise in *Hawkins v Public Trustee*, by contrast, was clearly intended to reward the grandson for the services his grandfather had asked him to perform. They had struck a bargain, which Mr Hawkins later reneged on.

The judicial observations on jurisdiction call into question the basis for Albyn's award. The comments on assessing quantum indicate that the primary focus is on the value of the qualifying services, rather than the value of the promise. It is only to the extent that services have not been rewarded that there is jurisdiction to make an award. Reciprocal benefits may reduce or remove the need for an award. These comments suggest that unjust enrichment is the conceptual basis for this jurisdiction. That is how *Re Welch* has been understood in subsequent cases.

G. The Family Provision Context

There was considerable sympathy for Albyn, both from his stepfather's siblings and from the courts. He had been a son to his stepfather in every meaningful sense of the word. There was a common view that Mr Welch had breached his moral duty to Albyn by not executing a will in his favour. In New Zealand a breach of moral duty to make provision for a family member is normally actioned through the Family Protection Act 1955.[74] This jurisdiction was introduced in 1900 to prevent spouses and children from becoming dependent on the state for support.[75] It gave the court the power to override a will if the deceased had failed to make 'adequate provision for the proper maintenance

[72] *Wright v Slane* (unreported, High Court A936/75, 4 September 1978), where Chilwell J held: 'The fact that the services and/or work equate that which would normally form part of the concept of consortium ought not to bar the claim'; *Chambers v Weston* (1982) 1 NZFLR 377 (HC).

[73] The Family Protection Act was amended in 2001 to include de facto partners who were living with the deceased as a couple for at least three years immediately preceding the deceased's death: Family Protection Act 1955 (NZ), ss 3 and 4A.

[74] Patterson (n 46) is the leading text on this jurisdiction.

[75] See R Atherton, 'New Zealand's Testator's Family Maintenance Act 1900 – The Stouts, the Women's Movement and Political Compromise' (1990) *Otago Law Review* 202.

and support' of his or her surviving spouse or child.[76] The Act was characterised as an extension of the Destitute Person's Act, but over time the courts adopted an increasingly broader view of a deceased's moral duty to provide for their family. 'Proper' maintenance and support meant more than the basic necessities of life. It included social, moral and ethical considerations.[77] In 1962 financial need ceased to be a prerequisite for adult children's claims.[78] The nature of their relationship with their deceased parent, the size of the estate and competing moral claims determined a parent's moral duty to provide for his or her children.

When *Re Welch* came before the courts in the late 1980s, the most common Family Protection Act claim was from adult children, many of whom were not in any financial need. They sought recognition as a valued member of their parent's family.[79] The courts were open to such claims because the relationship between parent and child had, and still has, primacy in New Zealand society.[80] The Act's reference to 'maintenance and support' invited a broader construction, as outlined by the Court of Appeal in 2000:

> Support is an additional and wider term than maintenance. In using the composite expression, and requiring 'proper' maintenance and support, the legislation recognises that a broader approach is required … Support is used in its wider dictionary sense of 'sustaining, providing comfort'. A child's path through life is supported not simply by financial provision to meet economic needs and contingencies but also by recognition of belonging to the family and of having been an important part of the overall life of the deceased. Just what provision will constitute proper support … is a matter of judgment in all the circumstances of the particular case. It may take the form of lifetime gifts or a bequest of family possessions precious to its members and often part of the family history. And where there is no economic need it may also be met by a legacy of a moderate amount. On the other hand where the estate comprises the accumulation of the family assets and is more than sufficient to meet other needs, provision so small as to leave a justifiable sense of exclusion from participation in the family estate might not amount to proper support for a family member.[81]

At the time of *Re Welch* family protection awards were generous, particularly if the deceased left only one child and no competing moral claims.[82] Had Albyn been Mr Welch's son, he might have been awarded as much as two-thirds of the estate. As a stepchild he was ineligible, because he was not being maintained wholly or partly by Mr Welch when he died.[83] Albyn's testamentary promises claim was in reality a claim for family provision,

[76] Testator's Family Maintenance Act 1900 (NZ), s 2.

[77] *Welsh v Mulcock* [1924] NZLR 673 (CA); *Bosch v Perpetual Trustee Co Ltd* [1938] AC 463. N Peart, 'The Direction of the Family Protection Act 1955' [1994] *New Zealand Recent Law Review* 193.

[78] *Re Harrison* [1962] NZLR 6 (CA).

[79] This approach was criticised in the *Report of the Working Group on Matrimonial Property and Family Protection* (Wellington, 1988) 50 and by the Law Commission in *Succession Law: Testamentary Claims*, NZLC PP24 (Wellington, 1996) paras 203–09. The Commission's proposed restrictions on family provision in NZLC R39 (n 3) have not been implemented.

[80] *Flathaug v Weaver* [2003] NZFLR 730 (CA) [32].

[81] *Williams v Aucutt* [2000] 2 NZLR 479 (CA) [52]. *Ilott v The Blue Cross* [2017] UKSC 17, [2018] AC 545 provides a stark contrast to New Zealand. See further Brian Sloan's contribution to this volume (chapter 17).

[82] N Peart, 'Awards for Children under the Family Protection Act' (1995) *Butterworths Family Law Journal* 224. In *Williams v Aucutt* (n 81) [45] and [68] the Court of Appeal accepted extra-judicial criticism that some awards may have been out of line with current social attitudes to testamentary freedom.

[83] Stepchildren were included as eligible claimants in 1955: Family Protection Act 1955 (NZ), s 3(1)(d).

seeking to enforce his stepfather's moral duty to recognise their relationship. But that was not the purpose of the TPA. While a liberal approach to the TPA was appropriate, it was not to be used to cure perceived deficiencies in the Family Protection Act.[84]

H. Alternative Causes of Action for Albyn

The TPA preserved the right to bring alternative causes of action, but none would have assisted Albyn. Mr Welch's promise did not meet any of the requirements for an enforceable contract. Nor were Albyn's services sufficient to support a quantum meruit claim.[85] By 1989, the equitable doctrines of estoppel and constructive trust had evolved to provide redress for claimants whose legitimate expectations of acquiring a property interest had not been met. Unlike England, New Zealand has unified the various forms of estoppel into one doctrine of equitable estoppel, requiring detrimental reliance on a belief or expectation encouraged by the defendant that makes the defendant's denial unconscionable.[86] While the requirements for estoppel are more flexible than they were in the past, Albyn did not perform his services in reliance on his stepfather's promise of testamentary provision. Nor would he have succeeded in a constructive trust claim, because he did not make significant contributions to his stepfather's property that would have given rise to a common intention or reasonable expectation of a beneficial interest in the property.[87] Aside from the matrimonial property award, which would not have been available in other common law jurisdictions, there was no legitimate reason to intervene in the intestate distribution of Mr Welch's estate. Albyn had provided no unreciprocated benefits to Mr Welch.

IV. THE ENDURING INFLUENCE OF *RE WELCH*

Re Welch has had a profound effect on the TPA jurisdiction. The reasoning of the Privy Council has been applied in several cases, not only when services were provided within family relationships, but also in relationships which are functionally similar to a family relationship. In *Byrne v Bishop* and *Samuels v Atkinson* the deceased men were not related to the claimants, but had been treated as a member of their family, enjoying their support, companionship, family life and affection over the course of many years.[88] In both cases the deceased had promised to make testamentary provision for the children of the family and the court accepted that those promises were made to reward the tangible and intangible services the families had provided. They went beyond what might be expected in such a family relationship. That the services were mostly provided by the parents, rather than

[84] *Humphrey v NZ Guardian Trust* (2003) 23 FRNZ 239 (HC) [65].
[85] *Daly v Gilbert* [1993] 3 NZLR 731 (HC); *Buysers v Dean* [2002] NZFLR 1 (HC).
[86] *Gillies v Keogh* [1989] 2 NZLR 327 (CA); *Gold Star Insurance Co Ltd v Gaunt* [1998] 3 NZLR 80 (CA). J Every-Palmer, 'Equitable Estoppel' in A Butler (ed), *Equity and Trusts in New Zealand* (Wellington, Thomson Reuters, 2009) 19.1. Contrast England, where proprietary and promissory estoppel remain separate causes of action: Sloan (n 3) ch 2. See further John Mee's contribution to this volume (chapter 11).
[87] *Hayward v Giordani* [1983] NZLR 140 (CA); *Gillies v Keogh* (n 86). Sloan (n 3) 2.5.
[88] *Byrne v Bishop* (n 66); *Samuels v Atkinson* (n 66).

the children, was no obstacle to the children's claims.[89] Provision for the children was seen as a benefit to the parents and an acknowledgement of their services.

Samuels v Atkinson is of particular interest, because it further developed the reasoning in *Re Welch* by articulating the conceptual basis for the jurisdiction in unjust enrichment terms. The late Mr Samuels was a Scot who emigrated to New Zealand in 1930 at the age of 20. He became a good friend of Mr Atkinson Sr. They served in the same battalion in World War II and were both wounded. Those experiences created a special bond between them. After returning to New Zealand, Mr Samuels settled in Auckland and Mr Atkinson acquired a farm on the east coast of the North Island. They both married and their wives became close friends. Mr and Mrs Samuels regularly visited the Atkinsons on their farm and spent their summer holidays there. The Atkinsons' three children played a special role in the lives of Mr and Mrs Samuels, as they could not have children. When Mrs Samuels developed cancer, Mrs Atkinson nursed her until she died in 1964. Thereafter, the friendship with the Atkinsons became all the more important to Mr Samuels. The Atkinson farm was a home from home for him and his relationship with the children grew into a real friendship on both sides. In 1966 Mr Atkinson approached Mr Samuels for a loan to expand his farm for economic reasons. Mr Samuels agreed on the basis that he became a shareholder in the farming company with a financial stake in the farm. He received nearly 13 per cent of the shares and was a director. He took an active interest in the farm, visiting regularly and staying with the Atkinsons. He assisted the children financially, but always on business terms, and all loans were repaid with interest before his death in 2006. When he developed Alzheimer's, the Atkinsons' daughter, Jennifer, provided him with personal care and practical assistance. Sometime in the 1970s Mr Samuels told Mr and Mrs Atkinson that he would leave his farm shares to their two sons and do something else for Jennifer. But by 1990, when he made his will, he had developed a close relationship with his nephew and niece in Scotland, and left them his substantial estate. He never disclosed to the Atkinsons his reservations about the value of the return he was receiving for his investment in the farm and the family.

The three Atkinson children sought to enforce his testamentary promise, arguing that it was made as a reward for the services that Mr Samuels had received from the Atkinson family. The High Court upheld their claim, awarding them the farm shares as tenants in common in equal shares.[90] Although this award exceeded the value of the services provided by each claimant, the court concluded that it fairly reflected the extensive services rendered collectively by the Atkinson family to Mr and Mrs Samuels for nearly 60 years.[91]

The Court of Appeal agreed that there was jurisdiction to make a testamentary promises award, but overruled the High Court on quantum. The Court of Appeal identified two difficulties arising from *Re Welch*. The first was that services lovingly provided should be worth less than services contractually given.[92] That was a logical downstream consequence of the ruling in *Re Welch*. The second difficulty was drawing a line between

[89] *Byrne v Bishop* (n 66) [9].
[90] *Atkinson v Samuels* (unreported, High Court Auckland CIV 2006-404-7878, 30 May 2008).
[91] ibid [91].
[92] *Samuels v Atkinson* (n 66) [50].

services that might be expected in a normal family relationship and those going beyond that threshold.[93] In response to this difficulty, the court held that 'something extra' had to be identified that took the facts of the particular case beyond the norm expected in the particular relationship.[94] That approach would have the added benefit of making quantification of claims more straightforward. The burden of providing 'something extra' had to be 'netted off' against benefits received, because 'a claim could succeed only to the extent of the unremunerated balance'.[95] In other words, a claimant has to show that the deceased was enriched at the claimant's expense. The injustice of that enrichment arises from the unfulfilled promise of testamentary provision.

In this case, the Court of Appeal was satisfied that the benefits Mr Samuels received exceeded the benefits received by the Atkinson children. While there were reciprocal benefits in the form of friendship and loans, the Atkinsons provided Mr Samuels with a surrogate family and emotional support when he was in need. Those services went beyond ordinary love and affection within an extended family. Jennifer also provided personal care and practical assistance to Mr Samuels whenever he was unwell and increasingly as his Alzheimer's progressed. Those services avoided the need for home help and delayed his admission into residential care.

In assessing a reasonable amount as remuneration for those services, the court separated Jennifer's tangible services from the children's intangible services. Her tangible services were objectively measurable and assessed at $12,000 per year for four years, rounded up to $50,000. Valuing the three children's unremunerated intangible services was more difficult. Mr Samuels did not rate their economic value highly, but on an objective assessment the solidarity and humanity of a surrogate family were very important to him and had real worth that should not be downgraded.[96] They could only be measured 'in the round' at $50,000 for each claimant.[97]

While quantification of the value of intangible services remains an imprecise exercise, *Samuels v Atkinson* furthers the analysis initiated in *Re Welch* by netting off the benefits and burdens of the services and rewarding services only to the extent that they are unremunerated, thus, in effect, redressing the deceased's enrichment at the expense of the claimant.[98]

V. RELATIONSHIP BETWEEN THE TPA AND OTHER CAUSES OF ACTION

The TPA has provided relief in many cases where other jurisdictions have been hamstrung by the constraints of the common law and equity.[99] Recent developments in estoppel and

[93] *Samuels v Atkinson* (n 66) [50], citing *Thwaites v Keruse* [1993] 11 FRNZ 19 (CA) and *Re Fagan* [1999] NZFLR 222 (HC).

[94] *Samuels v Atkinson* (n 66) [53].

[95] *Powell v Public Trustee* [2003] 1 NZLR 381, [31], cited in *Samuels v Atkinson* (n 66) [77].

[96] *Samuels v Atkinson* (n 66) [86].

[97] *Samuels v Atkinson* (n 66) [98].

[98] See also *McCormack v Foley* [1983] NZLR 57 (CA), 68, where Richardson refers to 'the flavour of unjust enrichment' inherent in the jurisdiction.

[99] S Nield, '"If You Look After Me, I Will Leave You My Estate": The Enforcement of Testamentary Promises in England and New Zealand' (2000) 20(1) *Legal Studies* 85; Wells (n 46).

constructive trusts provide hope for testamentary promise claimants in other jurisdictions, but they do not cover the full range of circumstances that the TPA can address.[100] As *Thorner v Major* shows, estoppel does not cover services provided before the representation on which the detrimental reliance is based.[101] And constructive trusts require contributions to property as well as a justification for sharing its beneficial ownership.[102] Unjust enrichment, as an independent cause of action, is still in its infancy in common law jurisdictions other than Canada.[103]

Despite the broad reach of the TPA, it does not cover every deserving claimant, leaving scope for other causes of action, including constructive trusts, estoppel and unjust enrichment.[104] There have even been cases in which a contract to leave property by will has been enforced.[105] Sometimes these causes of action are preferred over the TPA, in an attempt to achieve a more predictable outcome than the TPA's broad discretion provides, or to secure priority over other claims against the estate.[106] Where there are competing claims, such attempts may be thwarted. Fulfilled and unfulfilled promises of testamentary provision are vulnerable to each other and to family provision claims.[107] Even a binding contract to leave property by will is not immune to competing testamentary promises or family provision claims, particularly not if the person seeking to enforce the contract is a family member rather than a genuine creditor.[108] Only a claim for division of relationship property under the Property (Relationships) Act 1976 takes priority over testamentary promises and family provision claims.[109] In relation to all other claims against the estate, there are no clear priorities, which is a weakness.[110]

VI. CONCLUSION

The TPA has provided a useful remedy for enforcing unfulfilled testamentary promises to reward services. Despite the more rigorous approach introduced by *Re Welch*, the broad reach of the TPA remains a significant constraint on testamentary freedom, alongside the

[100] Sloan (n 3); Wells (n 46) ch 6.

[101] *Thorner v Major* [2009] UKHL 18, [2009] 1 WLR 776.

[102] *Stack v Dowden* [2007] UKHL 17, [2007] 2 AC 432; *Jones v Kernott* [2011] UKSC 53, [2011] 3 WLR 1121; *Baumgartner v Baumgartner* [1987] HCA 59, (1987) 164 CLR 137; *Giumelli v Giumelli* [1999] HCA 10, (1999) 196 CLR 101.

[103] *Peter v Beblow* [1993] 1 SCR 980; *Kerr v Baranow* 2011 SCC 10, [2011] 1 RCS 269; see also Wells (n 46) ch 7. Contrast Australia: *Equus Pty Ltd v Haxton* [2012] HCA 7, (2012) 246 CLR 498; and New Zealand: *Commonwealth Reserves I v Chodar* [2001] 2 NZLR 374 (HC).

[104] *Hayward v Giordani* [1983] NZLR 140 (CA) (common intention constructive trust); *Wischnewsky v Public Trustee* [1995] NZFLR 166 (FC) (unjust enrichment); *Carroll v Bates* [2018] NZHC 2463 (estoppel).

[105] *Reynolds v Marshall and Von Sturmer* [1952] NZLR 384 (SC); *Fleming v Beevers* (n 5), specific performance of an oral contract to leave property by will in reliance on the doctrine of part performance. *Johnston v Hattaway* (unreported, HC Christchurch A 106/81, 8 March 1984); *Bristow v French* (unreported, HC Christchurch CIV-2011-409-2181, 17 August 2012), damages for breach of contract to leave property by will.

[106] *Bristow v French* (n 10). Patterson (n 46) 13.3–13.7.

[107] *Dillon v PT* (n 10); *Hamilton v Hamilton* [2003] NZFLR 883 (HC). Australia now adopts a similar approach to New Zealand, having rejected *Schaefer v Schuhmann* (n 5) in *Barns v Barns* (2003) 214 CLR 169 (HCA).

[108] *McCormack v Foley* (n 98); *Bristow v Smith* (n 28).

[109] Property (Relationships) Act 1976, s 78.

[110] Wells (n 46) identifies priorities as a significant problem for creditors, family provision claimants and the volunteer beneficiaries, and has addressed that in her proposed legislation.

very liberal treatment of Family Protection Act claims. A broad discretion and an absence of clear priorities create great uncertainty in the distribution of an estate and erode testamentary freedom. While New Zealand adheres to the principle of testamentary freedom, it does not enjoy the respect that it does in other common law jurisdictions, particularly when compared to England.

Re Welch developed a fresh conceptual approach to a jurisdiction that had lost direction. By articulating the jurisdiction in what are essentially unjust enrichment terms, it distinguished a deceased's duties under the TPA from the purely moral duty of the Family Protection Act. *Samuels v Atkinson* took this approach a stage further in assessing quantum. Only qualifying services for which no reciprocal benefits or other remuneration has been provided can be the subject of a testamentary promises award.

Re Welch is a landmark case in both a positive and a negative sense. Services lovingly provided by friends or family members will often be beyond the scope of the TPA, which may be seen as creating an injustice. On the positive side, it has clearly defined the jurisdictional scope of the Act, thus removing some of the uncertainty that prevailed before *Re Welch* was decided and providing greater clarity on the constraints of testamentary freedom. That is why it is a landmark case in succession law.

13

Strong v Bird (1874): Reassessing the Rule

ELIZABETH DRUMMOND*

'Feelings of jealousy often arise in relations when property is left to strangers in blood …'[1]

I. INTRODUCTION

WILLIAM BIRD, THE defendant in *Strong v Bird*, was born in Hammersmith in 1832. He was privately educated and although initially destined for the army, decided to pursue a career in the medical profession. After training at St George's Hospital, he became the first surgeon on staff at the Fulham and Hammersmith General Dispensary, founded by his father in 1856[2] – perhaps, according to an article in *The Lancet* on the hospital's centenary, because Bird had failed to gain a surgical post at St George's.[3] Bird's involvement with the dispensary, later renamed the West London Hospital, was lifelong. After 16 years on staff as Senior Surgeon he resigned in 1872, and was appointed Chairman and Consulting Surgeon, an office he held to his death on 4 October 1902. His obituary in the *British Medical Journal* also records as his 'hobby' (which most would find 'too exacting for pleasure') his magisterial duties, as presiding justice at Harlesden Police Court and Chairman of the Kensington Bench of Magistrates.[4]

This chapter examines a rather different contribution to the law: 'the rule in *Strong v Bird*', established by the case brought against Bird concerning the estate of his stepmother Frances Bird. Under this rule, as developed through subsequent cases, an imperfect gift made during a person's lifetime can be perfected on death if the intended donee is appointed as the would-be donor's personal representative. The rule has been attractively presented as achieving justice through a mere omission to intervene and take the property

* I am grateful to those conference participants who commented on this chapter, and in particular to Brian Sloan, John Mee and Jamie Glister; any errors are my responsibility.

[1] Letter from Thomas Strong to Henry Mason (1 March 1871), as quoted in the Answer of William Bird to the Bill of Complaint in *Strong v Bird* (filed 1 June 1871) [18].

[2] 'Obituary, William Bird, FRCSEdin, MRCSEng, JP, DL' [1902] 2 *British Medical Journal* 1190.

[3] 'The West London's Centenary' (1956) 268 *The Lancet* 30.

[4] William Bird Obituary (n 2).

away from a deserving personal representative, and is appealing in individual cases on the basis that it honours a clear intention to make a lifetime gift. However, this chapter will conclude that the rule must be assessed in terms of the impact it has on the distribution of estates, and that it is difficult to justify either retaining it in its current form or extending it.

II. FRANCES BIRD'S FAMILY, HER WILL AND HER ESTATE

A. Family Background

Frances Bird was William Bird's stepmother. In 1835, when Bird was about three years old, she had married his father, William Bird senior, who was a widower following the death of his first wife. The couple lived together at Bute House, Hammersmith, until William Bird senior's death on 16 July 1864. Frances Bird outlived him by six and a half years. She appears to have been on affectionate terms with her stepson and his wife Mary, who was her niece, the daughter of one of her sisters. They invited her to live with them at Bute House during her widowhood, and it was arranged that Frances would pay her stepson £212 10s per quarter for her board and lodging. The three also shared the expenses of visits together to Brighton, Margate and other places; and it was during a visit to Brighton that Frances Bird died, on 1 December 1870.[5]

Frances Bird was survived by 11 blood relatives who would have been entitled under the Statute of Distributions 1670 had she died intestate. They were her three surviving sisters, Jane Emerson, Sarah Stone and Catherine Mander, and eight nieces and nephews, children of her deceased sister Mary Strong – including Thomas Strong, the plaintiff in *Strong v Bird*.[6]

B. Frances Bird's Will

Frances Bird's will, dated 23 July 1864, appointed Bird as her executor and left to him:

> all money which shall be in my dwellinghouse at the time of my decease and all money which shall then be in my banker's hands. And also all my carriages horses and harness. And all the furniture plate linen china books pictures wines provisions and all other effects whatsoever which shall be in or about my dwellinghouse at the time of my decease for his own use and benefit …

Bird proved the will on 20 December 1870, about three weeks after her death. Thomas Strong, however, was not happy with the situation. His aunt had been a wealthy woman, receiving a substantial income from her father's estate. Now it appeared that all of her money was being claimed by her stepson, at the expense of her blood relatives – under a will made just seven days into her widowhood. According to Bird, Strong approached Bird's solicitor Henry Mason and 'expressed himself in strong

[5] Affidavit of Mary Hannah Bird in *Strong v Bird* (20 March 1872) [4].
[6] Bill of Complaint of Thomas Strong in *Strong v Bird* (filed 30 March 1871) [2].

terms about the impropriety of … having … got the testatrix to make a will in my favour on the day of her husband's funeral'.[7]

The new will was in fact drawn in the same terms as Frances's previous will, dated 8 July 1864 and made with the consent of her husband William Bird senior. As a woman married prior to the Married Women's Property Act 1882, she had no independent power to dispose by will of personalty which did not form part of her separate estate, and as to which she had not been given an appropriate power of appointment.[8] During her marriage, the effectiveness of the 8 July will depended on her husband's consent. After his death, it could not govern the disposition of the personalty to which it referred.[9] Hence, Frances Bird needed to make a new will urgently, even though she did not want to change its terms. Her signature was witnessed by Mason and her brother-in-law Samuel Strong, Thomas Strong's father.[10]

Having learned these facts, Strong appears to have accepted that the will Bird had proved was beyond reproach. However, on 30 March 1871 he filed a Bill of Complaint arguing that the next of kin had some entitlement to Frances Bird's estate.

C. The Distribution of Frances Bird's Estate

Strong's first argument was that Bird had managed his stepmother's affairs and, in defiance of her instructions to invest her money and knowing the wording of her will, manipulated matters so that over £5,000 should stand to her account at the Bank of England at her death and pass to him under the will. He prayed that Bird might be declared a trustee of this sum for the next of kin.[11] Bird vigorously denied this allegation,[12] and in July 1871 the Bill of Complaint was amended to strike it out.

Secondly, Strong argued that the estate included personalty which did not pass to Bird under the terms of the will, but to the testatrix's next of kin, there being no general residuary legacy.[13] Under section 1 of the Executors Act 1830, Bird as executor was:

> deemed … to be a Trustee … for the Person or Persons (if any) who would be entitled to the Estate under the Statute of Distributions, in respect of any Residue not expressly disposed of, unless it shall appear by the Will, or any Codicil thereto, the Person or Persons so appointed Executor or Executors was or were intended to take such Residue beneficially.

There was no such indication in Frances Bird's will, so Bird would be a trustee of any residue for her next of kin, and Strong's Bill of Complaint alleged that there was residuary personalty in the testatrix's estate. In Bird's Answer to the Bill of Complaint, dated 1 June 1871, he responded that he had no such personal estate in his hands. He had received the balances held in two bank accounts, some cash in the house and a sum from the trustees of the testatrix's father's estate in respect of income accrued to her date of death: a total of £6,109 19s 3d.

[7] Answer of William Bird to the Bill of Complaint in *Strong v Bird* (filed 1 June 1871) [17].
[8] This principle was not affected by the Wills Act 1837; see s 8.
[9] *Noble v Willock* (1874–75) LR 7 HL 580, 591 (Lord Cairns LC).
[10] Answer of William Bird to the Bill of Complaint in *Strong v Bird* (filed 1 June 1871) [2].
[11] Bill of Complaint of Thomas Strong in *Strong v Bird* (filed 30 March 1871) [5] and Prayer [3].
[12] Answer of William Bird to the Bill of Complaint in *Strong v Bird* (filed 1 June 1871) [8]–[14].
[13] Bill of Complaint of Thomas Strong in *Strong v Bird* (filed 30 March 1871) [6], [7].

He acknowledged that the bequest to him did not cover all of her personal estate, but noted that funeral expenses, testamentary expenses and debts must also be paid.[14]

Bird also provided a schedule of cheques drawn by the testatrix in favour of Bird and his wife in the period from 6 September 1864 to 29 September 1870.[15] In June and July 1866 three payments have the note 'originally a loan': £400 on 16 June, £300 on 27 June and £400 on 16 July. Against this third payment appears a note explaining that all three were loans which were to be paid off by a deduction of £100 from Frances Bird's payment, each quarter, for board and lodging. After two such deductions, 'she refused to make any further deduction and expressly forgave me the debt'.[16] Strong responded to this additional information by amending the Bill of Complaint to allege that the balance of the £1,100 loan remained outstanding at Frances Bird's death, and to pray that in taking an account of the testatrix's personal estate, Bird should be charged with that balance.[17]

Was Bird required to distribute £900, as the amount of the debt outstanding at Christmas 1866, to Frances Bird's next of kin as part of her estate? That was the question on which Sir George Jessel MR gave judgment on 12 June 1874.[18] He found for Bird on two grounds, the first of which has become known as the rule in *Strong v Bird*.

III. THE DECISION IN *STRONG v BIRD*

A. Arguments Concerning the Debt

According to Bird and his wife Mary, Frances Bird expressly purported to release the debt in her lifetime. In accordance with the arrangement for repayment, Frances Bird did deduct £100 from her payments for board and lodging at the June and September quarter-days in 1866. However, Mary Bird's affidavit describes the following conversation between Bird and his stepmother when she wrote a cheque for the full £212 10s at the Christmas quarter-day:

> Some discussion … took place between her and the Defendant in my presence and at length she said she should write a cheque for the full amount. She said she did not want the 100*l*. and indeed did not want to have any more of the money lent returned adding that it would only lie in her bankers hands and she should not do anything with it. The said Defendant accepted the gift with many expressions of gratitude … and added jokingly 'I ought to pay you interest' to which … Frances Bird replied 'I don't want interest or the money either you foolish boy' and so the matter ended and to the best of my recollection and belief … Frances Bird never mentioned it again and in accordance with such gift she then and always afterwards paid her board in full.[19]

As Jessel MR stated, however, a mere statement of forgiving a debt (however sincere) does not effect a release at law.[20] That requires either consideration or the use of a deed.

[14] Answer of William Bird to the Bill of Complaint in *Strong v Bird* (filed 1 June 1871) [12]–[16].
[15] ibid sch 2.
[16] ibid note against 16 July 1866 entry.
[17] Bill of Complaint of Thomas Strong in *Strong v Bird* (filed 30 March 1871, as amended 18 July 1871) [7].
[18] *Strong v Bird* (1874) LR 18 Eq 315.
[19] Affidavit of Mary Hannah Bird in *Strong v Bird* (20 March 1872) [8].
[20] *Strong* (n 18) 317.

Since Frances Bird was owed a certain sum of money, accepting a lesser sum was not good consideration;[21] and the arrangement was not recorded in a deed.

Given that the debt was still owing at Christmas 1866, had things changed by Frances Bird's death four years later? Jessel MR found in *Strong*, as a second ground of decision, that the debt had by then been repaid because of Frances Bird's continuing quarterly payments of the full £212 10s originally agreed for board and lodging. Jessel MR analysed the Christmas 1866 and following eight payments as amounting to the repayment of the debt accompanied by nine gifts of £100 each.[22] On 6 January 1869, when Frances Bird paid £212 10s in respect of board to the 1868 Christmas quarter-day, the debt was cleared and William Bird had received gifts amounting to £900. That second ground was sufficient for a decision in Bird's favour.

The first ground proceeded on the basis that £900 was still outstanding at Frances Bird's death, and depended on Bird's appointment as her executor. At law, that appointment released the debt on Frances Bird's death. Strong argued that equity would nevertheless require Bird to account to the estate. Jessel MR decided that in this case, it did not. Even though Frances Bird was not aware of the effect of the appointment at law, it perfected the attempted release in her lifetime; and since at her death she had a 'continuing intention to give', there was 'no equity against [Bird] to take the property away from him'.[23] In order to understand the significance of this ruling, we must look in more detail at the stages of the reasoning.

B. Release of a Debtor-Executor's Debt at Law

It has long been held that the appointment of a debtor as executor releases the debt at law. The principle is clearly stated in *Sir John Nedham's Case* in 1610 – 'if the obligee makes the obligor his executor, it is a release in law of the debt, for it is the act of the obligee himself'[24] – and referenced back to the fifteenth-century year books. Where the executor is one of two or more debtors who are jointly liable, both are discharged.[25] It does not matter that the will was made before the debt was incurred, as the executor is only appointed on the testator's death.[26]

The release occurs due to a combination of two points. First, the 'artificially logical principle'[27] that, as Salter J stated in *Jenkins v Jenkins*, 'a debt is a right to sue and the executor cannot sue himself'.[28] Secondly, the fact that the appointment of the debtor as executor on the creditor's death occurred by the creditor's voluntary act. As Eyre CJ stated

[21] *Foakes v Beer* (1884) 9 App Cas 605; *Re Selectmove Ltd* [1995] 1 WLR 474. Had Frances Bird accepted some other thing in satisfaction, that could have been good consideration: *Pinnel's Case* (1602) 5 Co Rep 117a; 77 ER 237.

[22] *Strong* (n 18) 319.

[23] *Strong* (n 18) 319.

[24] *Sir John Nedham's Case* (1610) 8 Co Rep 135, 136a; 77 ER 678, 680.

[25] *Cheetham v Ward* (1797) 1 Bos & P 630, 633; 126 ER 1102, 1104 (Eyre CJ); *Jenkins v Jenkins* [1928] 2 KB 501.

[26] *Jenkins v Jenkins* [1928] 2 KB 501.

[27] CA Wright, 'Imperfect Gift – Donee Appointed Administrator of Donor – Rule in *Strong v Bird*' (1936) 14 *Canadian Bar Review* 57.

[28] *Jenkins* (n 26) 506.

in *Cheetham v Ward*, 'where a personal action is once suspended by the voluntary act of the party entitled to it, it is for ever gone and discharged'.[29] An appointment as administrator, on the other hand, is an 'act of law' rather than of the testator,[30] so originally occasioned 'not an extinction of the debt, but a suspension of the remedy'[31] while the administration was ongoing. However, this distinction was removed on the recommendation of the Law Reform Committee.[32] Section 10 of the Limitation Amendment Act 1980 inserted section 21A of the Administration of Estates Act 1925, under which the administrator's debt is extinguished, but he or she is accountable for the amount of the debt in the same way as if appointed as executor by the will.

The debtor is so accountable by reason of equity's intervention, which ensures that he or she does not escape liability simply by virtue of having been appointed executor. In *Flud v Rumcey*, the testator appointed his debtor and another as his executors, and provided that the debtor should pay to the defendant £101 out of the £301 which he owed to the testator. It was held that although 'by the law the … debt is extinguished', 'yet the debt is not extinguished, but remains as assets'.[33] We find a similar statement in *Askwith v Chamberlain*: 'a Debtor made Executor shall not extinguish his Debt, but the same to be taken as Part of the Testator's Personal Estate'.[34] The same message is reflected in other cases.[35] As Lord Thurlow said in *Carey v Goodinge*, in the court of equity 'the appointment of the debtor executor, was no more than parting with the action'.[36] This liability in equity will now be further examined.

C. The Debtor-Executor's Liability in Equity

Wankford v Wankford[37] concerned a will made by a testator, Shelly, who appointed his debtor Robert Wankford as his executor. Robert Wankford did not prove the will, but did act as executor and administered some of the assets of the estate before his death a few years later. His own will was proved by the executrix appointed in it, who also became Shelly's administrator. She claimed against Robert Wankford's son for payment of his father's debt to Shelly. The question was whether the debt was released even though the debtor had not proved the will. The Court of King's Bench agreed that it was; Robert Wankford had not refused to act, and had carried out acts of administration before his death. Two judges put forward different analyses of the circumstances in which a debtor-executor would be liable to the estate.

Powell J said that the debt was extinguished 'by way of legacy or gift of the debt by the will'.[38] He suggested that the debt would not be extinguished if the debtor actually

[29] *Cheetham v Ward* (1797) 1 Bos & P 630, 633; 126 ER 1102, 1104.

[30] *Wankford v Wankford* (1701) 1 Salk 299, 306; 91 ER 265, 269–70 (Holt CJ).

[31] *Seagram v Knight* (1866–67) LR 2 Ch App 628, 633 (Lord Chelmsford LC).

[32] Law Reform Committee, 21st Report, *Final Report on Limitation of Actions* (Cmnd 6923, 1977) 3.85–3.93.

[33] *Flud v Rumcey* (1609) Yel 160; 80 ER 107.

[34] *Askwith v Chamberlain* (1640) 1 Rep Ch 138; 21 ER 530.

[35] *Phillips v Phillips* (1676) 2 Freem Ch 11, 12; 22 ER 1024 (Lord Nottingham LC); *Woodward v Lord Darcy* (1557) 1 Plow 184, 186; 75 ER 282, 286; *Dorchester v Webb* (1633) Cro Car 372, 373; 79 ER 924; *Errington v Evans* (1772) Dick 456, 457; 21 ER 347 (Lord Bathurst LC).

[36] *Carey v Goodinge* (1790) 3 Bro CC 110, 111; 29 ER 439.

[37] *Wankford v Wankford* (1701) 1 Salk 299; 91 ER 265.

[38] ibid 268.

refused the executorship, as he would then 'lose the benefit of what he would have had by being executor'.[39] However, Robert Wankford had accepted the executorship by conduct. Powell J also excepted cases such as *Flud v Rumcey*,[40] where the will stated that a legacy was to be paid out of a debt, 'because the testator did not intend to extinguish the whole debt'.[41]

A similar analysis is adopted by Toller, writing in 1800, who attributes the deemed legacy in the debtor-executor's favour to an inference, from the fact of the appointment, 'that such was [the testator's] meaning'.[42] He states that the testator's intention is not prioritised over the interests of creditors, and so (like a genuine legacy) the deemed legacy does not take effect if the estate is insolvent. Furthermore, he says, equity would not allow a release if such an inference of intention to discharge the debt was 'contradicted by the express terms of the will; or by strong inference from its contents'.[43] A direction for a legacy to be paid out of the debt (as in *Flud*) or an express legacy to the executor would give rise to such a contradiction.[44]

This explanation rests on a fiction of intention to release the debt which seems unrealistic. Few testators would be likely even to realise that appointing a debtor as executor would have the effect at law of releasing the debt. The basis and scope of the exceptions in equity are artificial and unclear, particularly when we consider that the debt is released at law.

A better explanation was put forward by Holt CJ in *Wankford*. He said:

> the making him executor does not amount to a legacy, but to a payment and a release … [The debtor] has actually received so much money, and is answerable for it, and if he does not administer so much, it is a devastavit.[45]

This view treats the debt as paid, and the deemed payment as assets of the estate for which the executor is accountable.[46] It still rests on a fiction, but one which fits more easily with the release of the debt at law. That release would not occur, Holt CJ said, if the debtor positively refused to act as executor: no one can be forced to accept a release unwillingly, and 'if the obligor were never executor, then was he never the person entitled to receive the money, and consequently not within the reason of the rule of extinguishment'.[47]

On this analysis, if the debtor-executor does act, the release occurs at law but the debtor-executor is liable in equity to account as a matter of course, whether in the interest of creditors or legatees. That approach fits with Lord Erskine's decision in *Simmons v Gutteridge* that a legatee can request an account and ask whether the executor was indebted to the testator. He drew no distinction between legatees and creditors in stating the principle that '[a] debt, due by an executor to the estate of the testator, is assets'.[48]

[39] ibid 269.

[40] *Flud* (n 33).

[41] *Wankford* (n 37) 268.

[42] S Toller, *The Law of Executors and Administrators* (London, J Exshaw, 1800) 272.

[43] ibid 274.

[44] *Carey v Goodinge* (1790) 3 Bro CC 110, 29 ER 439; *Brown v Selwin* (1734) Cas t Talb 240, 25 ER 756 (affd (1735) 3 Bro PC 607, 1 ER 1527).

[45] *Wankford* (n 37) 270.

[46] See Lord Tenterden CJ in *Freakley v Fox* (1829) 9 B & C 130, 133–34; 109 ER 49, 50.

[47] *Wankford* (n 37) 270.

[48] *Re Bourne* (1806) 13 Ves Jr 262, 264; 33 ER 292, 293. See also Sir William Grant's summary rejection of an argument that the debtor-executor would have no liability except against creditors in *Berry v Usher* (1805) 11 Ves Jr 87, 90; 32 ER 1021, 1022. In the third edition of his book, Toller explained this case as illustrating a

Re Bourne also supports Holt CJ's analysis.[49] The testator appointed as his executors his nephew Bourne and one Davey, and left all his property to a third party legatee. Bourne had owed his uncle over £21,000 and Davey sought to recover that sum from him. Unable to sue at law, he turned to an action in equity and secured a declaration that Bourne was accountable for a sum equivalent to the debt. Bourne did not comply, and Davey sought a writ of attachment, available under section 4 of the Debtors Act 1869 for a case of 'default by a trustee or person acting in a fiduciary capacity and ordered to pay by a court of equity any sum in his possession or under his control'.[50] The reasoning of the Court of Appeal, upholding the order for attachment made at first instance, shows that the executor's liability in equity rests on a deemed payment of the debt. The amount of the debt was treated as a 'sum in [Bourne's] possession or under his control' on the basis that he was 'deemed as debtor to have paid himself in a fiduciary capacity as executor, and he is deemed to be in possession of the sum which he owed to the estate'.[51] This possession is fictional, as recognised by the court's acceptance that an order might be refused as a matter of discretion if the executor had never had the means of paying.[52]

The reasoning of Lord Russell, giving the opinion of the Privy Council in the Australian case of *Commissioner of Stamp Duties v Bone*,[53] is also consistent with Holt CJ's analysis. The testatrix appointed as her executors her three children, to each of whom she had lent money. Her will included clauses expressly forgiving and releasing each child's debt, and dividing the residue of the estate equally between them. The children claimed that death duty was not chargeable on the amount of the loans outstanding at the death under the description of 'property of the deceased which is situate in New South Wales at his death … to which any person becomes entitled under the will … of the deceased' in section 102(1)(a) of the Stamp Duties Act 1920. One of their arguments[54] was that, as they had been appointed as executors, the debts had been released at law on the testatrix's death; and that the obligation in equity replacing each debt was not 'property of the deceased' at her death within section 102(1)(a).

Lord Russell rejected that argument. Although 'the liability of the debtor as such is extinguished':

> Equity will at once fasten upon the executor an exactly equivalent obligation to account to those interested in the estate (whether creditors, legatees, residuary legatees, or next of kin) for the amount of the debt. The obligation of the debtor to the testator which existed at the moment of death is converted by the combined operation of law and equity into exactly the same obligation with a different technical character or label or method of enforcement.[55]

These authorities show that the equitable rule requiring the debtor-executor to account was applied systematically in response to the extinguishment of the debt

further exception where the will shows that the testator considered the executor as 'a mere trustee': S Toller, *The Law of Executors and Administrators*, 3rd edn (London, Butterworth, 1814) 350.

[49] *Re Bourne* [1906] 1 Ch 697. See further *Jenkins* (n 26) 506 (Salter J), 509 (Talbot J).

[50] Debtors Act 1869, s 4(3).

[51] *Re Bourne* (n 49) 707 (Collins MR).

[52] ibid 709 (Romer LJ, distinguishing between possession 'as a matter of law' and possession 'in fact and in substance').

[53] *Commissioner of Stamp Duties v Bone* [1977] AC 511.

[54] Another line of argument was based on the clauses of the will expressly releasing the debts.

[55] *Bone* (n 53) 518. The enforcement would be 'an order declaring that the executor was accountable … for the amount of the debt … followed by appropriate consequential order and execution, theoretically based on a devastavit'.

at law. The question then is why, in *Strong v Bird*, no such equitable obligation was applied to Bird.

D. Why Was Bird Not Liable in Equity?

Jessel MR stated that Bird, who was not liable at law due to his appointment as executor, would be liable in the Court of Equity – 'unless he could shew some reason for not being liable'.[56] He went on to reason that, since there was a 'continuing intention to give' and 'a legal act which … released the obligation', 'the transaction is perfected … and there is no equity against [Bird] to take the property away from him'.[57]

Jessel MR's reasoning relates the release of the debt on Frances Bird's death to the attempted release at Christmas 1866. He stated: 'The law requires nothing more than this, that in a case where the thing which is the subject of donation is transferable or releasable at law, the legal transfer or release shall take place.' Although the testatrix did not anticipate the release of the debt on her death, it was nevertheless a release at law which, in the circumstances, perfected the earlier transaction: 'It is not necessary that the legal change shall knowingly be made by the donor with a view to carry out the gift.'[58] In Bird's case, his appointment as executor on Frances Bird's death completed the imperfect lifetime gift at Christmas 1866, and equity did not impose liability on him.

Jessel MR drew a comparison with a hypothetical case in which, as he considered,[59] a presumed resulting trust could have arisen.[60] He described the following scenario. X has ineffectually attempted to give Blackacre to Y by endorsing a memorandum of the gift on the title deeds.[61] Later on, X makes a conveyance to Y of lands 'by a general description' which is apt to encompass Blackacre,[62] not intending to change the gift he thinks he has made. Jessel MR envisaged an argument that on this voluntary conveyance a resulting trust arises in favour of X, because X – believing that Y already had title to the property – did not intend to convey Blackacre to Y on this occasion at all. He stated that 'there is no resulting trust; that is rebutted by shewing that [X] did not intend [Y] to be a trustee', and that even though X thought that he had already made a gift of Blackacre, 'still the estate would pass at law … and there being no intention to revoke the gift, surely it would get rid of any resulting trust'.[63]

Jessel MR's approach here is consistent with the view that the presumption at work in a presumed resulting trust is of an intention to make the recipient a trustee, rebuttable by evidence that there was no such intention on the transfer.[64] Other judges have taken the

[56] *Strong* (n 18) 319.
[57] ibid.
[58] ibid,318.
[59] Jessel MR assumes that a presumed resulting trust can arise on a voluntary conveyance of land; but see J Mee, 'Resulting Trusts and Voluntary Conveyances of Land, 1674–1925' (2011) 32 *The Journal of Legal History* 215, in particular 236–38. In *Re Pink*, Farwell LJ reinterpreted Jessel MR's example as referring to 'the conveyance on purchase by the owner to AB by C's direction, in which case the resulting trust for C, who finds the money, does arise' ([1912] 2 Ch 528, 536); but this does not seem to be what Jessel MR meant to say in *Strong v Bird*, as it would make little sense of the comparison he was drawing.
[60] I am grateful to John Mee for his helpful comments on these issues.
[61] As in *Richards v Delbridge* (1874) LR 18 Eq 11.
[62] Mee (n 59) 237, fn 152.
[63] *Strong* (n 18) 318.
[64] See generally J Mee, 'Presumed Resulting Trusts, Intention and Declaration' (2014) 73 *CLJ* 86.

comparison he drew as suggesting that *Strong* involves a similar rebuttal. Cozens-Hardy MR in *Re Pink*, for example, refers to 'a presumption of accountability negatived by the circumstances of the case',[65] with the result that a 'presumption of law [is] given effect'.[66] In *Re Applebee*, Stirling J stated that in *Strong* 'any claim in Equity was rebutted by the evidence of a continuing intention on the part of the testatrix to forgive the debt'.[67] These explanations suggest that the rule in *Strong v Bird* is about rebutting a presumption that, the debtor-executor's liability being extinguished at law on the appointment, the testator intends the debtor-executor to be accountable in equity. But such a presumption would be artificial and unnecessary. As shown above, equity developed a simple rule that the extinguished liability of a debtor-executor should always be replaced by a requirement to account in equity, rationalised as a fiction of payment.

Jessel MR does not use the language of presumption in this context. Instead, he restates equity's rule with a new exception: the debtor-executor 'would be liable in this Court ... *unless he could shew some reason for not being made liable*'.[68] He goes on to say that a 'continuing intention to give' coupled with the appointment as executor (which actually releases the obligation) has the effect that 'the transaction is perfected', and that 'there is no equity against [the executor] to take the property away from him'.[69] That differs from Jessel MR's approach to the Blackacre case, where he reasons that the established presumption of resulting trust is rebutted because it is falsified by X's lack of intention to make the recipient a trustee.

Wright argues that in *Strong* 'Equity merely withdrew her presumption of payment' of the debt by the debtor-executor into the estate, leaving the release to take effect at law, and that in a case such as *Strong v Bird* 'There is no completing of an incomplete gift'.[70] However, Jessel MR does not say that the debtor-executor can escape liability on the basis of withdrawing a presumption of payment. Rather, he says that where 'the gift is clear, and there is to be no recall of the gift, and no intention to recall it',[71] on the appointment as executor 'the transaction is perfected' – that is, the incomplete gift is completed – and equity exceptionally does not impose any liability to account.

IV. THE RULE IN *STRONG v BIRD*

A. The Extent of the Rule

From the start, the rule in *Strong v Bird* represented a new principle about the completion of incomplete lifetime gifts on death. In *Strong* itself, the rule created an exception to an

[65] *Re Pink* (n 59) 532.

[66] ibid 535. See also Farwell LJ (536), stating that in a case within *Strong v Bird*, 'if there is an immediate gift, then the resulting trust for the benefit of the beneficiaries [under the will] is rebutted'. It is difficult to understand the reference to a resulting trust in favour of beneficiaries; the executor is accountable for the amount of the debt but does not hold it on trust.

[67] *Re Applebee* [1891] 3 Ch 422, 429. See also 429–30, Stirling J stating that Jessel MR used evidence of Frances Bird's intention 'to rebut an equity'.

[68] *Strong* (n 18) 319 (emphasis added).

[69] ibid.

[70] Wright (n 27) 58.

[71] *Strong* (n 18) 318.

equitable principle which would have imposed liability on the debtor-executor. However, Jessel MR stated the rule in general terms, as applicable to all cases where a requisite legal transfer or release is not made immediately but does take place on death.

Consistently with that approach, in *Re Stewart*,[72] Neville J held that the transfer of legal title to an executor on death perfected an imperfect lifetime gift. The deceased instructed his brokers to buy bonds which he intended to give to his wife. The brokers wrote a letter to inform him that they had made the purchase, enclosing a bought note. He gave this letter and the enclosure to his wife, saying 'I have bought these bonds for you', but died shortly afterwards without completing the gift. The wife was appointed as his executrix. Neville J held that she was entitled to the bonds. He found that the testator's intention to make the gift was proved, and that when the property vested in the wife as his executrix, the gift was completed.

In *Re James*,[73] the rule in *Strong v Bird* was further extended to administrators. The deceased, John James, had inherited a property called Green Vale from his father James James, who had died intestate in 1924. James James had employed the defendant, Sarah James, as an unpaid housekeeper, and had stated his intention that Green Vale and his furniture should go to her on his death, but failed to make a will. On his father's death, John James handed over to Sarah James the furniture and the title deeds to Green Vale, and she lived there with her husband. John James died intestate, and letters of administration were granted to Sarah James and the plaintiff, who claimed that Green Vale formed part of John James's estate. Farwell J found for the defendant under *Strong v Bird*. He found the requisite continuing intention, and reasoned that, since the legal title to the property was vested in Sarah James as administrator,[74] she did not need equity's assistance and could rely on that title as against the intestacy beneficiaries.

The rule in *Strong v Bird* has thus developed into a general principle about the completion of incomplete lifetime gifts on death by virtue of the intended donee becoming the would-be donor's personal representative. The deceased must originally have intended to make an immediate lifetime gift, as shown by *Re Innes*.[75] Elizabeth Innes kept house for her father, John Innes, for over 20 years. She argued that he should make her an allowance, and he wrote a letter agreeing to pay one, but did not make the promised payments. He appointed Elizabeth and his son as his executors. After his death, Parker J found that there was no contract between Elizabeth and John Innes, and that the principle in *Strong v Bird* did not apply. He insisted that there must be 'certain definite property which a donor has attempted to give' and 'in every case a present intention of giving'.[76] *Strong v Bird* did not apply beyond 'a gift in the present which though failing on technical considerations may be subsequently perfected', and certainly not to 'an announcement of what a man intends to do in the future'.[77]

The requirements for definite current property and an immediate intention of giving distinguish the effect of the rule in *Strong v Bird* from testamentary dispositions. A legacy,

[72] *Re Stewart* [1908] 2 Ch 251.
[73] *Re James* [1935] Ch 449.
[74] John James died on 17 June 1933, so the title to Green Vale devolved on his administrators under s 1 of the Administration of Estates Act 1925.
[75] *Re Innes* [1910] 1 Ch 188.
[76] ibid 193.
[77] ibid 194.

in contrast, can operate on property acquired after the date of the will, to a sum of money with no specified source or to the residue of an estate; and the testator's intention is to give on death, not immediately. In *Re Hyslop*,[78] the testator's brother-in-law, Chamberlain, owed him £100. The testator appointed Chamberlain as one of his two executors, and gave him a legacy of £500 in consideration of acting. He also left an informal document stating, 'The hundred pounds I lent you does not form part of the money I left you; it is cancelled'. The executor remained liable in equity. North J held that

> the letter was intended to be instructions to the executor as to the mode of winding up the estate – that is, it was intended to operate as a testamentary document, and was not executed in the way it ought to have been for that purpose.[79]

The point is further illustrated by *Re Gonin*.[80] The deceased had three daughters who were born illegitimate, and mistakenly believed that any will drawn in their favour would be invalid. Two of her daughters married and left home; the third, Lucy, remained single and looked after her mother and father for 24 years on the basis that she would have their house in return. The father died first; on the mother's death intestate, Lucy took out letters of administration to her estate. Walton J did not apply *Strong v Bird* because he found no immediate intention to give the property, only an intention that Lucy should take the property on her mother's death – that is, a testamentary intention.

Testamentary intention must be carefully distinguished from the idea of a 'continuing intention' in relation to the rule in *Strong v Bird*. The term is somewhat misleading,[81] as in a true *Strong v Bird* case the deceased will have been under the impression that a lifetime gift had already been made, which is inconsistent with a continued positive intention for a gift. The sense of the phrase is rather that the deceased does not demonstrate an intention which is inconsistent with the completion of the gift on death.

In *Re Wale*,[82] the testatrix had in 1939 executed a settlement in favour of her daughter, with her two sons as trustees. On the same day, she also executed a will which divided her estate equally between the sons, excluding her daughter as being already provided for by the settlement. One of the recitals to the settlement stated that investments registered in the testatrix's name – the 'A' investments – had been transferred to the trustees. However, this transfer did not take place. From 1946 onwards, as the proceeds of the 'A' investments were paid to the testatrix, she received them and dealt with them as she pleased, including making gifts to her sons. Furthermore, subsequent wills signed by her in 1942, 1945 and 1950 divided the estate equally between her sons and daughter, and on her death in 1953 they were appointed her executors. Upjohn J did not apply the rule in *Strong v Bird* to the 'A' investments because the testatrix did not have a 'continuing intention'. She had forgotten the existence of the settlement and thought that the proceeds of those investments belonged to her. Therefore, they were not treated as comprised in the settlement.

[78] *Re Hyslop* [1894] 3 Ch 522.

[79] ibid 523. See also the pre-*Strong* case of *Brown v Selwin* (1734) Cas t Talb 240, 25 ER 756 (affd (1735) 3 Bro PC 607, 1 ER 1527. The testator instructed his attorney that a debt was to be released by his will, but no such provision was included in the will as drawn and signed. The instructions could not be given effect without contradicting the Statute of Frauds. See *Re Applebee* [1891] 3 Ch 422, 429–30 (Stirling J, emphasising that in *Strong* the evidence was of a lifetime intention to forgive the debt).

[80] *Re Gonin* [1979] Ch 16.

[81] See *Re Pink* (n 59) 538–39 (Kennedy LJ).

[82] *Re Wale* [1956] 1 WLR 1346.

B. The Impact of the Rule

The rule in *Strong v Bird* concerns the completion of an incomplete lifetime gift on death, justified by a 'continuing intention' in the testator or intestate concerning that lifetime gift. The beneficiaries who would usually take under the will or the intestacy rules benefit to a lesser extent than they would if the attempted lifetime gift remained uncompleted.

In *Re Stewart*, Neville J reasoned that 'the intention of the testator to give the beneficial interest to the executor is sufficient to countervail the equity of beneficiaries under the will, the testator having vested the legal estate in the executor'.[83] However, it is not merely the intention to give which affects the rights the beneficiaries would otherwise have, but the law's decision that the earlier intended gift can be connected with, and completed by, the vesting on death. The same point applies to *Strong v Bird* itself. Jessel MR decided that Frances Bird's forgiveness of the debt at Christmas 1866 could be connected with the automatic release of that debt on her death. That excluded rights which her next of kin would otherwise have had, because equity would have obliged Bird to account to the estate in the sum of £900, in respect of which he would have been a trustee for the next of kin.[84] The principle has now been applied beyond the original case to complete imperfect gifts of personalty and land in favour of executors and administrators, excluding the rights of beneficiaries under wills and the intestacy rules.

Strong v Bird itself may appear less controversial than those cases, because the next of kin would have had no entitlement to the £900 if equity had never developed a rule of requiring the executor to account where a debt was released at law. However, equity did develop such a rule, and *Strong* represents a decision to prevent it from applying: a significant choice, with important effects on the estate and how it is to be distributed after the death. That significance is amplified by *Re Stewart* and *Re James*, but while those cases could have been distinguished from *Strong*, they are not inconsistent with it and in fact accurately apply Jessel MR's reasoning.

We need to ask whether the rule can now be justified. While in individual cases its application is less objectionable than might at first appear, when set in its wider context the rule proves to be incoherent.

C. The Application of the Rule in Individual Cases

The rule in *Strong v Bird* might seem to invite fraud or imposition: it can operate on a lifetime gift attempted many years ago, and *ex hypothesi* in a way which did not comply with requirements such as writing or delivery.[85] However, in individual cases fraud is in fact unlikely, because the claimant must undertake the burden of proving the elements of the rule.

Judges insist on strong evidence. In *Re Pink* Cozens-Hardy MR stated that 'one cannot be too careful in dealing with the estate of a deceased man to remember that an affidavit

[83] *Re Stewart* (n 72) 254.
[84] See text to n 13 above.
[85] See eg Walton J's comments in *Re Gonin* (n 80) 32.

in support of a claim or a release must be very carefully scrutinized'.[86] In *Re Freeland*, Evershed MR emphasised that the claimant personal representative 'has a heavy onus to discharge; he or she must prove the case against his or her own estate, clearly and convincingly'.[87] Furthermore, the claimant must prove both initial intention to make an immediate gift, and 'continuing' intention. As Walton J pointed out in *Re Gonin*, the more significant the gift, the more difficult it is to believe that the deceased intended to be deprived of it during his or her lifetime.[88] And positive evidence against 'continuing intention' is likely to build up over time as the deceased acts inconsistently with what he or she is asserted to have attempted – as occurred in *Re Wale*.[89] In *Strong v Bird* itself, by contrast, both the oral forgiveness of the debt and Frances Bird's lack of intention to renege on it were strongly supported by positive evidence. She had continued to pay the full amount agreed for board and lodging until her death, as shown by her memoranda on the counterfoils of the cheques she wrote for that purpose.[90]

The rule does operate to perfect imperfect gifts which the deceased would have been free to resile from during his or her lifetime, bypassing any protection offered by requirements such as delivery or a written conveyance or release. The would-be donor need not have handed over indicia of title, as for a *donatio mortis causa*,[91] or have had time before death for second thoughts about the intended gift. However, the existence of the rule has no effect on the donor's position during his or her lifetime – the transfer of property is only triggered on death. Furthermore, the decided cases show the rule being applied where circumstances such as the passage of time, recording the gift in writing and handing over indicia of title strongly suggest a genuine, considered and voluntary intention to give. In *Strong v Bird* itself, although the conversation was oral, four years passed before Frances Bird's death and there was other evidence that she really had meant to release the debt once and for all, and of her own free will. *Re James*[92] is even stronger, since the deceased not only purported to make the gift about nine years before his death, but also handed over the title deeds to the property to the intended donee.

In *Re Stewart*,[93] in contrast, only days intervened before the death – but the testator had been planning the gift for some months. He had previously presented over £16,000-worth of bonds to his wife, listing them in a notebook under the heading 'Mrs Stewart's capital account'. In 1905 he noted his intention to add £1,000 next year, and the bonds he purchased in May 1906 were consistent with replacing one previously paid off and adding a further £1,000.[94] In *Day v Royal College of Music*[95] the deceased's intention to make a gift of manuscripts was set out in a signed document prepared by his adviser and sent to the intended donee. The gift was ineffective during his lifetime because of the lack of

[86] *Re Pink* (n 59) 533–34.
[87] *Re Freeland* [1952] Ch 110, 117. See also at 540 (Kennedy LJ).
[88] *Re Gonin* (n 80) 33.
[89] *Re Wale* (n 82).
[90] *Strong* (n 18) 316.
[91] See *Sen v Headley* [1991] Ch 425 (CA).
[92] *Re James* (n 73).
[93] *Re Stewart* (n 72).
[94] ibid 254 (Neville J). See also *Re Pink* (n 59) (memorandum in testator's ledger stating that the debt was cancelled as to £4,800 and interest from that date, a full year before his death).
[95] *Day v Royal College of Music* [2013] EWCA Civ 191, [2014] Ch 211.

delivery, but completed under the rule in *Strong v Bird* when the intended donee became one of his executors.

The rule has worked well in individual cases: its application is infrequent and, when it is invoked, claims are scrutinised carefully. Future cases could resolve uncertainties about the circumstances in which it applies, such as its effect on the claims of creditors,[96] or whether the would-be donee must actually prove the will or be ready and willing to prove it.[97] But when considered more widely, the rule can be shown to be incoherent.

D. Reassessing the Rule

The rule in *Strong v Bird* is difficult to support when looked at in the wider context of the law of succession. As a rule about the completion of an attempted lifetime gift on death, it represents an exception to the general scheme of the distribution of estates by will and by the intestacy rules – but not a coherent one.

The rule does not contradict the Wills Act 1837, since it does not purport to give effect to an informal legacy or other testamentary disposition. It is, however, arguably inconsistent with the statutory intestacy rules. According to section 33 of the Administration of Estates Act 1925, if a person dies intestate as to any real or personal estate, 'that estate shall be held in trust by his personal representatives with the power to sell it', and is to be applied to 'funeral, testamentary and administration expenses, debts and other liabilities' before making provision for any pecuniary legacies. The remainder is 'the residuary estate of the intestate', and is to be distributed to family members as set out in section 46. 'Real and personal estate' is defined as 'every beneficial interest … of the intestate in real and personal estate which … he could, if of full age and capacity, have disposed of by his will'.[98]

The rule in *Strong v Bird* does not remove the would-be donor's ability to dispose of the subject matter of the gift by will, so it is arguable that the personal representative cannot retain the subject matter of an incomplete lifetime gift but must hold it as part of the residuary estate and distribute it according to the intestacy rules. Certainly, the statutory intestacy scheme does nothing to accommodate an exception.

The scope of the exception is also difficult to defend. The inclusion of administrators has been criticised as making the application of the rule particularly haphazard. In *Re Gonin*, Walton J said that it is 'often a matter of pure chance which of many persons equally entitled to a grant of letters of administration finally takes them out' – making the application of the rule 'something in the nature of a lottery'.[99] Jaconelli rightly points out that the *Strong v Bird* rule could complicate decisions about who, of those entitled to a grant of administration, is to administer the estate, including whether to pass over someone who would otherwise be entitled to a grant.[100]

[96] See J Jaconelli, 'Problems in the Rule in *Strong v Bird*' [2006] *Conveyancer & Property Lawyer* 432, 447.
[97] See G Kodilinye, 'A Fresh Look at the Rule in *Strong v Bird*' [1982] *Conveyancer & Property Lawyer* 14, 18–19.
[98] Administration of Estates Act 1925, s 52.
[99] *Re Gonin* (n 80) 35.
[100] Jaconelli (n 96) 448.

Even where the rule operates in favour of an executor, it is not clear why the imperfect gift should be perfected by that appointment. It is true that the testator deliberately appoints the would-be donee as executor, but it is unclear why this circumstance should be relevant to the perfection of an imperfect lifetime gift. The testator is unlikely to realise that it is, and certainly need not form an intention along those lines – indeed, he or she believes that the gift was already effective and requires no further act, and the will can even precede the gift, as occurred in *Strong v Bird* itself.

The rule could be reformed by removing the requirement that the intended donee is appointed as a personal representative. This reform would represent a shift to a principle of completing imperfect gifts on death provided that the intending donor had not changed his or her mind in the meantime, subject to the claims of creditors. Such a principle could be defended as consistently – rather than by 'lottery' – upholding the would-be donor's original intention while protecting his or her freedom to resile from the gift during lifetime.

Such an extension would, however, squarely contradict the principle that equity will not perfect an imperfect gift. It would involve raising a constructive trust on the death in order to require the personal representatives to perfect the imperfect gift, justified by the would-be donor's original intention. The nearest precedent can be found in a constructive trust arising to effectuate a *donatio mortis causa* of a chose in action or land.[101] This doctrine is, however, regarded as anomalous.[102] The constructive trust is imposed to enable *donationes mortis causa* of these kinds to be treated similarly to those of chattels, where the delivery has already taken place, and the conditional gift is therefore perfected on death. On the other hand, the rule in *Strong v Bird* does not involve a conditional gift or require the delivery of indicia of title. It seems unlikely that the courts would at this stage be willing to extend the newer rule in such a way as to impose a constructive trust when this has never previously been required – and it is questionable whether such a reform would be desirable.

Extending the rule in *Strong v Bird* would increase the burden on personal representatives and the courts, and the disruption to the general rules applicable to the distribution of every deceased person's estate, especially the statutory scheme in the Administration of Estates Act 1925. It is not clear that rectifying a would-be donor's mistake about the requirements for lifetime transfers justifies the disadvantages of maintaining a broad exception to those general rules.

The other option is to abolish the doctrine. A would-be donee would still be able to make other claims. In particular, if he or she has relied on the gift, that reliance might form part of a claim in proprietary estoppel[103] or found an argument that, on account of the reliance, it had become unconscionable for the donor to change his or her mind.[104] But that takes the matter one stage further than a mistake about the requirements for a lifetime gift and the coincidental appointment of the would-be donee as executor.

Removing the rule in *Strong v Bird* would be more consistent with the general rule that the personal representative holds an office in relation to the estate, title being transferred

[101] See *Sen v Headley* (n 91).

[102] ibid 440 (Nourse LJ).

[103] *Thorner v Major* [2009] UKHL 18, [2009] 1 WLR 776 (see John Mee's chapter in this volume). The facts in eg *Re Gonin* (n 80) might have supported such a claim; see text to n 80 above.

[104] *Pennington v Waine* [2002] EWCA Civ 227, [2002] 1 WLR 2075; *Curtis v Pulbrook* [2011] EWHC 167 (Ch), [2011] 1 BCLC 638.

to him or her for those purposes only. As Viscount Radcliffe stated in *Commissioner of Stamp Duties (Queensland) v Livingston*, while the executor does hold the property of the estate 'in full ownership', he or she holds it 'for the purpose of carrying out the functions and duties of administration, not for his own benefit'.[105] In particular, there is no merger between a personal representative's interest in the estate by virtue of his or her office and any interest he or she may personally have in the assets of the estate.[106] If the personal representative is a legatee, or set to benefit on intestacy, he or she does take beneficially – but only after the period of administration is complete, and only to the appropriate extent according to the will or the intestacy rules as applicable to the estate in question.

The legislation abolishing the rule should also enact that a debt owed to the deceased by a personal representative is unaffected by the appointment. Section 21A of the Administration of Estates Act 1925 ensures that administrators are treated similarly to executors on this point, in that the debt is released but they may be accountable for the amount of it in equity.[107] It would be better to establish that the debt is not released at all, and consistently treat personal representatives as taking on a role of administering an estate which is distinct from their personal affairs.

V. CONCLUSION

> Notwithstanding the arguments … and the cases … I think I can do justice in this case …[108]

As shown by the above quotation, Jessel MR was concerned to reach a fair result in *Strong v Bird*. There was strong evidence that Frances Bird genuinely intended to release the debt, stated that intention in clear terms and until her death remained happy in the belief that she had done so. The release failed only because – quite understandably – she did not know of the law's insistence on consideration or the use of a deed. Jessel MR was no friend to that requirement, stating in *Couldery v Bartrum* that it was 'a most extraordinary peculiarity of the English Common Law' that a creditor might accept in satisfaction of the debt another thing, such as a canary, but not a lesser sum.[109]

In order to 'do justice' in *Strong v Bird*, Jessel MR invented a principle that equity would not intervene to require a debtor-executor to account in respect of a debt released by virtue of the appointment if the creditor had ineffectually forgiven it and had not resiled from that position. That principle was later applied to allow incomplete *inter vivos* gifts to be perfected on death, such that executors and even administrators might retain property coming to them by virtue of their office. The rule appears to do little harm in individual cases, but its scope is incoherent, and this contribution has argued for its abolition. The law would be improved by dispensing with the complication of the rule in *Strong v Bird* and making a clearer commitment to the view that personal representatives take charge of the estate for the purposes of administration only.

[105] *Commissioner of Stamp Duties (Queensland) v Livingston* [1965] AC 694, 707 (see Charles Mitchell's chapter in this volume).

[106] *Chambers v Kingham* (1878) 10 Ch D 743; *Re Radcliffe* [1892] 1 Ch 227; Law of Property Act 1925, s 185.

[107] See text to n 32 above.

[108] *Strong* (n 18) 317 (Jessel MR).

[109] *Couldery v Bartrum* (1881) 19 Ch D 394, 399.

14

Williams v Williams (1882): Succession Law Rules and the Fate of the Dead

HEATHER CONWAY*

I. INTRODUCTION

At first glance, the decision in *Williams v Williams*[1] might not seem like an obvious choice for a collection of landmark cases in succession law. There were no disappointed beneficiaries or disinherited relatives pleading unjust treatment; the judgment does not discuss the technicalities of will making, nor does it establish or malign any formal rules for passing property on death. Like every succession law case, the deceased's own wants and desires played a central role, and financial entitlements were at stake – though not in the conventional sense. The narrative in *Williams* is deceptively simple. Henry Crookenden had wanted to be cremated, and instructed his unmarried sister-in-law and good friend Eliza Williams to carry out his wishes; having done so, she brought an action against the executors of his estate for expenses sustained in fulfilling this request.

It is trite but true that succession law only activates when someone dies,[2] yet the death of any one individual triggers other legal obligations beyond administering the estate and distributing the deceased's worldly goods. More pressing is the need to dispose of the body, a basic social-cultural obligation which exists as a legal duty and is predicated on the core precepts of public health and respect for the dead. The decision in *Williams* shows

* I am grateful to all the participants at the Landmark Cases in Succession Law Conference for their comments on an earlier version of this paper, and to Dr Brian Sloan and Professor Prue Vines for summarising those comments. A special word of thanks to Prue, for presenting the paper on my behalf when I was unable to attend.

[1] *Williams v Williams* (1882) 20 Ch D 659. While the case was reported elsewhere, eg at (1882) 30 WR 348, the discussion below refers to this particular report. For an excellent analysis of the decision in its legal and historical contexts, see S White, 'A Burial Ahead of Its Time: The Crookendon Burial Case and the Sanctioning of Cremation in England and Wales' (2002) 7 *Mortality* 171.

[2] Or is presumed dead because they have been missing for seven years, allowing their estate to be administered on the grant of a declaration of death: see, eg the Presumption of Death Act 2013 in England and Wales. For reasons which will become apparent, this paper is only concerned with the scenario in which someone has died, leaving a corpse or bodily remains of some sort to deal with.

how the deceased's personal representatives – under a will or intestacy – can discover that their legal responsibilities extend beyond allocating property under a fixed or selectively distributive scheme. Core elements of succession law apply to the other fundamentals of death, resulting in the same individuals assuming a pivotal legal role when it comes to the arrangements for the deceased's funeral. In contrast, *Williams* also shows how the dead person's own wishes can be completely disregarded, again by drawing on succession law fundamentals. These themes form a major part of the analysis below – an analysis which is 'bookended' by the legality (or otherwise) of cremation as something which pervades the case and its factual narrative, and the implications of *Williams* for the recovery of funeral costs (since recovering costs was the reason why the case ended up in court in the first place).

II. THE LITIGATION IN *WILLIAMS v WILLIAMS*

Henry Crookenden died in December 1875, survived by his wife and two adult sons. An advocate for cremation, which was – at the time – slowly emerging as an alternative means of corpse disposal in England, Henry wanted his remains to be burnt instead of buried. By a fourth codicil to his will, he directed that his body should be given to Eliza Williams within three days of his death,[3] to be dealt with as he had directed in a private letter to her. Eliza was also given an earthenware Wedgewood vase, to be used as stipulated in the same letter. Any expenses incurred by her in carrying out these instructions were to be paid by Henry's executors within three months of his decease. The letter in question was dated 28 March 1875 and had been sent to Eliza along with a copy of the codicil. In the letter, Henry stated that he would like his body to be burnt on or under a pile of wood, and the ashes placed in the Wedgewood vase; the ultimate disposal of the vase and its contents was down to Eliza.[4]

Eliza had promised Henry that she would carry out his wishes, but things did not transpire as planned. Two days after Henry's death, his remains were buried in an unconsecrated part of Brompton Cemetery, as arranged by his wife and one of his sons (and with the assent of the executors). The case report states that Eliza made some sort of 'protest' at the funeral or 'claim as to the disposal of the body',[5] but did not apparently have the codicil or letter with her. However, what happened next is not in doubt.[6] In March 1876, Eliza – without consulting Henry's family or executors – sought a licence from the Home Secretary to exhume his body 'for the purpose of carrying out [Henry's] wishes …, either by having [the body] burnt in this country or elsewhere; or if there

[3] Or as soon as might be convenient thereafter.

[4] Contrast this with the growing number of disputes today around who 'owns' ashes post-cremation and the lack of a definitive legal answer (something this author is currently researching).

[5] *Williams* (n 1) 660.

[6] There is a detailed account of this in White (n 1) 173–75. It notes that Eliza was assisted in her efforts by the Cremation Society of Great Britain, which was founded in 1874 to pioneer (and subsequently promote) cremation in the jurisdiction – see generally www.cremation.org.uk/. The author is a current Council Member and trustee of the Society.

is any legal impediment or objection to that, for the purpose of having it placed in consecrated ground'.[7]

A written reply indicated that permission to exhume would be refused for cremation but could be granted for reburial, and asked Eliza which burial ground she proposed to move the body to. Her response was simple: she was to reinter the remains in a churchyard in Manafon, some 200 miles away. Towards the end of 1877, Eliza notified the managers of Brompton Cemetery about the proposed exhumation, and that December they informed Henry's widow and sons about the licence. Having discovered that the family was unaware of and actively opposed the exhumation,[8] the Home Secretary revoked the licence on 20 March 1878 – six days after Eliza had disinterred the body and had it shipped to Milan, where it was cremated in April 1878.[9]

Whether or not Eliza's misrepresentation to the Home Secretary was a criminal offence is certainly debatable,[10] though Henry's ashes were eventually buried in the Manafon churchyard in August 1878. Eliza then claimed her expenses of £321, and brought an action against the executors of Henry's estate. The case came before Kay J, who dismissed her claim. Eliza's duplicity in obtaining the licence, alongside the fact that – on a literal interpretation of the letter – Henry wished to be cremated before being buried were noted in the judgment. More importantly, Henry's wishes as to the disposal of his body were not legally binding; the duty of burial and consequent right to possession of the remains lay with the executors, and had been discharged by the initial interment in Brompton Cemetery.

III. THE LEGALITY OF CREMATION: HISTORICAL SUBPLOT WITH MODERN RESONANCE

The litigation in *Williams* is an interesting snapshot of attitudes towards cremation in Britain in the latter half of the nineteenth century. Until that time, burial had been the prevailing method of bodily disposal; the dominance of Christianity and its core belief of bodily resurrection, alongside the societal repugnance towards burning human corpses (seen as a pagan ritual, and as a means of concealing infanticides),[11] demanded that the

[7] *Williams* (n 1) 660. Exhuming human remains still requires some form of licence or authorisation, and in England and Wales this extends to ashes as well. The type of permission sought will depend on whether the deceased was interred in ground which was consecrated according to the rites of the Church of England (in which case, a faculty is required under ecclesiastical law) or unconsecrated ground (in which case, a licence is sought from the Ministry of Justice under s 25 of the Burial Act 1857). For a detailed account, see H Conway, *The Law and the Dead* (Abingdon, Routledge, 2016) ch 7.

[8] This would not occur today, since the deceased's next-of-kin are automatically consulted and asked to consent to any proposed exhumation.

[9] Henry's family only discovered this from reading a report in an Italian newspaper – *Williams* (n 1) 661. The lapse in time between the initial burial and the subsequent exhumation and cremation is attributable to a number of things, including the time for letters to be sent and received (considerably longer than today's methods of instantaneous communication) and the logistical arrangements for shipping the remains abroad.

[10] It is a common law offence to exhume remains without lawful authority, regardless of the underlying motivation (*R v Lynn* (1788) 2 Term Rep 73), while s 25 of the Burial Act 1857 makes it a criminal offence to exhume or disturb remains in contravention of the licensing requirements under that Act. Technically, Eliza had authority to exhume here, but whether her misrepresentations to the Home Secretary invalidated that permission is an obvious question. The criminal law aspect was not raised in the case, and does not seem to have been actioned elsewhere.

[11] White (n 1) 173 notes that cremation was also tainted by its punitive legacy as an execution method for 'heretics, witches and female traitors'.

dead be buried. However, cremation was slowly asserting itself as a credible alternative in late 1800s, prompted by growing urban populations, overcrowded burial grounds and a demand for more sanitary methods of bodily disposal at lower costs than the typically elaborate Victorian funeral.[12] From a legal perspective, the question was whether or not cremation was lawful, given that it was not actively prohibited and English law did not prescribe burial as the only means of dealing with the dead.

Against this contextual backdrop, it is surprising that the legality issue did not assume a more central role in either the legal arguments or the ruling in the case. It was certainly the proverbial 'elephant in the room', but was only dealt with briefly by Kay J, who remarked that having a body burnt raises a 'very considerable question whether that is or is not a lawful purpose according to the law of this country', and one 'which I am not going to decide'.[13] However, a definitive answer would emerge some two years later in *R v Price*,[14] when Dr William Price – a neo-druid who was opposed to burying the dead – burnt the remains of his five-month-old son[15] in a field nearby his house, two days after the child's demise. Having been indicted for burning rather than burying the body, the case came before Stephen J, who held that cremation was lawful so long as it did not constitute a public nuisance and there was no attempt to prevent a coroner's inquest where one was needed.[16] Any lingering doubts on legality were finally removed by the enactment of the Cremation Act 1902.

It is easy to forget that cremation was not always as popular as it is today, when statistics indicate that it accounts for almost 77% of corpse disposals in the UK.[17] Kay J's comments in *Williams*, and the overall tenor of the judgment, suggest that he was not supportive of cremation – an attitude that probably reflects wider societal sentiments in the nineteenth century, when the practice was viewed as heretical and profane. While this aspect of the case might seem like little more than an interesting historical footnote, the same debate is likely to emerge in the near future as new bodily disposal methods are introduced as alternatives to burial and cremation. One example is alkaline hydrolysis,[18] which uses a combination of water and potassium hydroxide to dissolve the body's organic matter inside a metal chamber, and at much lower temperatures than flame cremation; the final result is a sterile liquid which can be discharged into the water system, and white bone ash which can be given to the deceased's family.[19] Marketed as

[12] For a detailed analysis of the reasons surrounding cremation's renaissance and subsequent dominance of the bodily disposal landscape here, see PC Jupp, *From Dust to Ashes: Cremation and the British Way of Death* (Basingstoke, Palgrave Macmillan, 2006).

[13] *Williams* (n 1) 665–66. However, White (n 1) 177–78 states that the various law reports on the case are not consistent on this point, and that one of them records Kay J (in what was an ex tempore judgment) concluding these particular remarks with his opinion that cremation was not lawful.

[14] (1884) 12 QBD 247.

[15] The child's name was Iesu Grist, which is Welsh for Jesus Christ.

[16] For an analysis of the case, see White (n 1) 179–84.

[17] 'International Statistics' (2017) 83 *Pharos International*, though there are regional variations within the UK (the lowest rates are in Northern Ireland – around 21%). It seems ironic that Henry Crookenden's remains were cremated in Milan, given that current cremation rates in Italy are around 23% (ibid).

[18] Known variously as resomation, biocremation and aquamation – see respectively Resomation Ltd (www.resomation.com), BioCremation (biocremationinfo.com) and Aquamation International (www.aquamationindustries.com).

[19] For a brief overview of this and promession (another alternative disposal method which effectively 'freeze dries' corpses and shatters the remains, leaving an odourless, organic residue), see Conway (n 7) 47–50.

a form of water cremation which is more environmentally friendly than burning bodies, the process is available in parts of the USA but not in the UK – at least, not yet.[20] When this happens, two discussions are virtually guaranteed: whether the process is culturally acceptable (is it a dignified means of bodily disposal?) and whether it is legal. This has shades of cremation in the nineteenth century, and the issues that were brought to a head through the respective decisions in *Williams* and *Price*. Of course, societal attitudes are hard to predict, and the populist narrative of protecting the environment through sustainable end-of-life choices[21] may result in this new technology being widely embraced in the longer term. Any new stage in the evolution of bodily disposal practices can trigger public hostility; rhetorical descriptions of 'dissolving' corpses are hugely evocative and will be seen, by some, as offending basic standards of human dignity and fundamental religious beliefs about treatment of the dead.[22] Like conventional cremation, how the general public perceives alkaline hydrolysis (and correcting any popular misconceptions) will be integral to its success. Meanwhile, the answer to the legality point is broadly the same as it was back in the 1880s: as long as there are no public health or environmental issues, the process does not cause an actionable nuisance and it is conducted in such a way that it does not infringe public decency, alkaline hydrolysis is legal under English law, even if it is currently unregulated (in the same way as cremation was pre-1902).[23] Whether these assurances are enough to prevent legal challenges once the process is operational here remains to be seen.

IV. FALLACIES, FICTIONS AND CHANGING TIMES: UPHOLDING FUNERAL INSTRUCTIONS

Eliza's actions in the *Williams* case were driven by her determination to do what the deceased had asked her to do. But did this entitle her to the sum claimed as expenses, and which the executors were refusing to pay?

At the crux of this issue was the enforceability of Henry's clearly articulated funeral instructions, set out in the codicil to his will and in the private letter to Eliza. In dealing with the legal issues, Kay J began with an emphatic statement: '[i]t is quite clearly the law of this country that there can be no property in the dead body of a human being'.[24] Eliza had physical possession of the remains when she exhumed the body; however, the legal right to possession lay with the executors of his will since it was a basic principle of

[20] In the UK, the process is being actively developed and promoted by a Glasgow-based company, Resomation Ltd – see http://resomation.com/. The environmental credentials are showcased on both the company website and in an industry presentation given by Sandy Sullivan, the founder and director of Resomation Ltd, which is reproduced as 'Resomation Has the Least Impact on the Environment' (2017) 83 *Pharos International* 18.

[21] See H Knight, 'Depart This World with a Clean Conscience' (2010) 206 *New Scientist* 8; H Rumble et al, 'Disposal or Dispersal: Environmentalism and the Final Treatment of the British Dead' (2014) 19 *Mortality* 243, 251–52.

[22] See, eg KJ Lasnoski, 'Are Cremation and Alkaline Hydrolysis Morally Distinct' (2016) 16 *National Catholic Bioethics Quarterly* 233; PR Olsen, 'Basic Cremation' (2018) 8 *Wake Forest Journal of Law and Policy* 149.

[23] Rumble et al (n 21) 251–52; Conway (n 7) 50.

[24] *Williams* (n 1) 661–62, citing *R v Sharpe* (1857) Dea & Bell CC 160 (and in particular the statement of Erle J that '[o]ur law recognises no property in a corpse' – ibid 163).

English law that the executor (or estate administrator) was under a legal duty to bury the deceased and had possessory rights in the body for this purpose.[25] This did not infringe the 'no property rule', because Henry's executors were simply entitled to 'custody and possession of his body (although they have no property in it) until it [was] properly buried'.[26] More importantly, applying the rule meant that 'a man cannot by will dispose of his dead body. If there be no property in a dead body it is impossible that by will or any other instrument the body can be disposed of.'[27]

As a result, the codicil direction that Henry's executors should deliver his body to Eliza 'could not be enforced, and was void'[28] – and even if the letter had required Eliza to bury his remains in a particular cemetery (instead of the legally dubious request to cremate the body), this would not have made 'the direction to deliver the body to someone who was not an executor any more legal or enforceable'.[29] This would have been enough to dismiss Eliza's claim on its own, though two other points were also noted. First, the wording in the codicil suggested that Henry had wanted to be cremated before being buried (hence the stipulation for the body to be delivered to Eliza within three days of his death and expenses paid to her within three months);[30] and secondly, Eliza's claim for expenses was founded on what was 'clearly a fraudulent act',[31] given her misrepresentations to the Home Secretary when securing the exhumation licence.

A. Flawed Premises and Shifting Narratives

Kay J's ruling in *Williams* stands as authority for the basic proposition that an individual's funeral instructions are not legally binding: a will is an instrument for disposing of property on death, but if a corpse is not property it cannot be 'bequeathed' in this manner. While ostensibly correct as a piece of deductive reasoning, the problem with this particular legal syllogism is that one of its formative principles is fundamentally flawed. The 'no property rule' apparently dates back to the seventeenth-century decision in *Haynes Case*,[32] which said nothing of the sort; a judicial statement that a dead person could not own property was misinterpreted as holding that a dead body was not property in any legal sense. This spawned a line of similar authority,[33] some of which was cited by Kay J in *Williams*.

[25] Citing statements to this effect in *Williams on Executors* (EV Williams, *A Treatise on the Law of Executors and Administrators*, 6th edn (London, Stevens & sons, 1867) 906) and 2 Bl Com 508, as well as the decisions in *R v Fox* (1841) 2 QB 246 and *R v Scott* (1842) 2 QB 248n.

[26] *Williams* (n 1) 665.

[27] ibid 665.

[28] ibid 665.

[29] ibid 665.

[30] Though it is worth noting that the obvious delay in Eliza claiming the expenses (well beyond the contemplated three months) was not mentioned as a reason for dismissing the claim.

[31] *Williams* (n 1) 667.

[32] *Haynes Case* (1614) 12 Co Rep 113.

[33] Most notably *Exelby v Handyside* (1749) 2 East PC 652; *R v Lynn* (1788) 2 Term Rep 733; *R v Scott* (n 27); *Re Sharpe* (1857) Dears and Bell 160.

The origins of the no property rule have been rightly criticised.[34] However, unlike the biblical parable about the wise and foolish builders,[35] this particular rule has not been washed away over the centuries, despite such intrinsically weak foundations.[36] Instead, it has been widely applied as a means of denying property in corpses, and (by extension) in living body parts as well.[37] In some ways, the rule is a convenient one; it avoids the debate around the potential commodification of bodies and body parts, and the morality of treating ourselves as 'mere' items of property[38] – though certain exceptions to the rule have developed over time.[39] Focusing on the matter in hand, the application of the no property rule in *Williams* created the scenario whereby funeral instructions are not legally binding. The case still stands as authority for this in English law,[40] and its ruling has permeated other common law jurisdictions with derivative legal systems.[41]

When we pause to think about it, *Williams* produces a fairly radical result. As a competent adult, I can dictate what happens to my financial estate on death (the core succession law value of testamentary freedom prevails, at least in common law legal systems), but not what happens to my corpse.[42] Any instructions that I set out in a will, pre-paid funeral contract or anywhere else[43] about whether I want to be buried or cremated, the type of

[34] For an excellent critique, see P Matthews, 'Whose Body? People as Property' (1983) 36 *Current Legal Problems* 193, 196–221. See also M Pawlowski, 'Property in Body Parts and Products of the Human Body' (2009) 30 *Liverpool Law Review* 35.

[35] The wise man who built his house on the rock and the foolish man who built his on the sand – Matthew 7: 24–27.

[36] Despite misgivings over its origins, the English Court of Appeal endorsed the rule in *Dobson v North Tyneside Area Health Authority* [1996] 4 All ER 474 and *R v Kelly* [1998] 3 All ER 741, the latter case suggesting that it could only be undone by Parliament. See also the discussion in *Yearworth v North Bristol NHS Trust* [2009] EWCA Civ 37, [2010] QB 1.

[37] See the discussion in Pawlowski (n 34).

[38] For an effective critique of this particular argument, see K Greasley, 'Property Rights in the Human Body: Commodification and Objectification' in I Goold et al (eds), *Persons, Parts and Property: How Should We Regulate Human Tissue in the 21st Century* (Oxford, Hart Publishing, 2014) ch 6. See also M Quigley, *Self-Ownership, Property Rights and the Human Body* (Cambridge, Cambridge University Press, 2018).

[39] With living body parts, courts have negotiated the problems of a blanket ban by embracing a quasi-property approach, which applies some of the sticks in the property law bundle where this is needed to achieve a particular result in specific cases. For a perfect illustration, see *Yearworth* (n 36) (property rights in frozen sperm samples). With corpses, there are two recognised exceptions to the rule, one of which was fundamental to the ruling in *Williams* and is discussed immediately below (the other is mentioned briefly at n 78).

[40] See, eg *Burrows v HM Coroner for Preston* [2008] EWHC 1387 (Admin), [2008] 2 FLR 1225; *University Hospital Lewisham Trust v Hamuth* [2006] EWHC 1609 (Ch), [2007] WTLR 309; *Re JS (Disposal of Body)* [2016] EWHC 2859 (Fam), [2017] 4 WLR 1.

[41] For Canadian illustrations, see *Hunter v Hunter* (1930) 65 OLR 586; *Saleh v Reichert* (1993) 104 DLR (4th) 384; *Sopinka v Sopinka* (2001) 55 OR (3d) 529. In New Zealand, see *Murdoch v Rind* [1945] NZLR 425; *Awa v Independent News Auckland Ltd* [1995] 3 NZLR 701 (affirmed on other grounds at [1997] 3 NZLR 590); see also the first instance decision in *Clarke v Takamore* [2009] NZHC 901 (though note the concerns expressed by the Supreme Court in *Takamore v Clarke* [2012] NZSC 116). There is a wealth of Australian case law on this topic; for a flavour, see *Robinson v Pinegrove Memorial Park* (1986) 7 BPR 15,097; *Smith v Tamworth City Council* (1997) 41 NSWLR 680; *Jones v Dodd* [1999] SASC 125; *Keller v Keller* [2007] VSC 118; *Tufala v Marsden* [2011] QSC 222. One notable exception is the United States, where courts (and subsequently individual state legislatures) have typically allowed individuals to dictate the posthumous fate of their remains: see Conway (n 7) 130–34 and the sources cited therein.

[42] However, it would be misleading to say that the law disregards any ante-mortem preferences around the treatment of one's mortal remains; obvious examples include organ donation and posthumous reproduction, though any rights which a deceased person enjoys in these scenarios are not unfettered rights: see Conway (n 7) ch 6.

[43] Since, according to Kay J in *Williams*, disposal of the body cannot be directed 'by will or any other instrument': (1882) 20 ChD 659, 665.

ceremony and where I would like my remains or ashes to be laid to rest can be completely disregarded: these directions may impart some sort of moral obligation, but are not legally enforceable if the person deciding the funeral arrangements elects not to follow them. And taking the succession law analogy one step further, it seems ironic that, on the facts of *Williams* itself, the reference in Henry's codicil to Eliza carrying out certain instructions which he had communicated to her in a letter might have been effective under the rules of half secret trusts (depending on the timing of the communication)[44] if these directions had dealt with specific items of property as opposed to Henry's mortal remains.

Unfavourable comparisons with succession law and transferring property on death are not the only reasons to question the ruling in *Williams* and its legacy. Nwabueze has criticised the decision on the basis that the 'critical question' of whether funeral directions are legally binding and enforceable 'was left almost completely unanswered';[45] Kay J simply reached his conclusion on a strict application of the no property rule.[46] The fallacy of this rule as an underpinning principle has already been noted and, in any event, funeral instructions could be made legally binding without corpses being classed as property. All that would be needed is a discrete statutory provision that allows an individual to direct the posthumous fate of their mortal remains.[47] For example, section 5 of the Cremation, Interment and Funeral Services Act 2004 (British Columbia) prioritises 'any reasonable[48] directions given by the deceased respecting the disposition of his or her … remains or cremated remains' in the event of a dispute over funeral arrangements, while section 6 makes these preferences binding if they are set out in a will or pre-paid funeral plan.[49] Similar legislation could be introduced elsewhere, to counter this specific aspect of the ruling in *Williams*.

Yet, there are signs that its legacy is diminishing and that judges will not simply ignore the deceased's wishes because of the strict stance adopted in an old nineteenth-century case. In the English context, the best example is *Burrows v HM Coroner for Preston*,[50] when the court released the remains of a teenage boy to his paternal uncle, who was intent on cremation as the boy had requested, instead of the teenager's estranged mother, who wanted to bury her son. The deceased's wishes were a powerful factor in the case and, according to Cranston J, assumed a prominent role under Article 8(1) of the European Convention on Human Rights:

> One thing is clear, that in as much as our domestic law says that the views of a deceased person can be ignored it is no longer good law … It is quite clear from the jurisprudence of

[44] See G Virgo, *Principles of Equity and Trusts*, 3rd edn (Oxford, Oxford University Press, 2018) 111–23.

[45] RM Nwabueze, 'Legal Control of Burial Rights' (2013) 2 *Cambridge Journal of International and Comparative Law* 196, 209–10.

[46] And, according to Matthews (n 34) 210–12, failed to distinguish between alleged proprietary rights in buried and unburied corpses.

[47] Something that the current author and others have argued for: see Conway (n 7) ch 5; Nwabueze (n 45). See also the various sources cited immediately below.

[48] This particular theme is addressed in the text to nn 69–72 below.

[49] Of course, there is always the danger that a will is not consulted until after the funeral takes place, by which time it is too late for the deceased's wishes to be implemented. This places an even greater onus on the deceased – while alive – to make his or her wishes known, and to make a copy of the document available (or leave it in an accessible place for those who will take charge of the funeral arrangements).

[50] *Burrows* (n 40).

> the European Courts [*sic*] of Human Rights that the views of a deceased person as to funeral arrangements and the disposal of his or her body must be taken into account.[51]

This basic sentiment has been echoed in other cases, both here and elsewhere, though the respective courts did not find it necessary to adopt a rights-based analysis to focus on what the deceased had requested when faced with contested funeral arrangements.[52] For example, in *Hartshorne v Gardner*[53] the court indicated that 'the deceased's wishes are one of the relevant factors to be taken into consideration',[54] and in *Anstey v Mundle*[55] these were deemed to be a 'particularly weighty factor'.[56] Antipodean courts have expressed similar sentiments. For example, McKechnie J in *Ugle v Bowra & O'Dea*[57] suggested that '[t]he views of the deceased, though not decisive, should nevertheless be accorded considerable weight',[58] while Elias CJ in the Supreme Court of New Zealand in *Takamore v Clarke*[59] was highly critical of the existing legal position, because in 'modern conditions' it was 'unacceptable to say that the views of the deceased are views that can be ignored'. Yet, while the deceased's wishes are an increasingly important reference point in these cases, they are nothing more than that – for the time being, at least. Several law reform bodies have entered the debate, proposing that funeral instructions are legally effective in New Zealand[60] and in the Australian states of Queensland[61] and Victoria,[62] and similar changes may be put forward in England and Wales in the (hopefully) not too distant future.[63] Meanwhile, Scotland has gone a step further by passing legislation which allows anyone aged 16 or over to make an 'arrangements on death declaration', specifying the person that they want to organise their burial

[51] ibid [20], citing *X v Federal Republic of Germany* (1981) 24 D & R 137 and *Dödsbo v Sweden* (2007) 45 EHRR 22. Though note the criticisms in *Ibuna v Arroyo* [2012] EWHC 428 (Ch), [2012] WTLR 827 [55] (personal representatives ought to take account of the deceased's wishes, but these 'should not … have the paramountcy' suggested in *Burrows*).

[52] This is not to disregard human rights arguments as a basis for upholding funeral instructions; the current author has argued that they strengthen the case for this: see Conway (n 7) 139–44.

[53] *Hartshorne v Gardner* [2008] EWHC B3 (Ch), [2008] 2 FLR 1681.

[54] ibid [7], citing *Grandison v Nembhard* [1989] 4 BMLR 140.

[55] *Anstey v Mundle* [2016] EWHC 1073 (Ch), [2016] WTLR 931 [45].

[56] See also *Re JS* (n 40) (these are 'relevant, perhaps highly so, but … not determinative').

[57] *Ugle v Bowra & O'Dea* [2007] WASC 82 [16].

[58] See also the comments of Nicholson J in *State of South Australia v Smith* [2014] SASC 64 [61] ('the wishes of a deceased person, where they can be ascertained with some confidence, should be given significant weight'), though note the somewhat more lukewarm observations of North J in *Johnson v George* [2018] QSC 140 [28] (the deceased 'cannot dictate' these things, but such wishes 'deserve some respect').

[59] *Takamore v Clarke* (n 41) [82]. See also the comments of Tipping, McGrath and Blanchard JJ: 'Consideration must also be given to the [deceased's] wishes … since the law has moved on from its early rejection of the significance of this factor' (ibid [168]).

[60] New Zealand Law Commission, *Death, Burial and Cremation: A New Law for Contemporary New Zealand* (Report 134, 2015) pt 4.

[61] Queensland Law Reform Commission, *A Review of the Law in Relation to the Final Disposal of a Dead Body* (Report No 69, 2011) ch 5.

[62] Victorian Law Reform Commission, *Funeral and Burial Instructions* (2016).

[63] In announcing its Thirteenth Programme of Law Reform in December 2017, the Law Commission for England and Wales listed 'A Modern Framework for Disposing of the Dead' as one of its projects. In setting the context to the project it noted that the current law 'does not ensure that a person's own wishes as to the disposal of their remains are carried out, leading to disputes where family members disagree': Law Commission for England and Wales, *Thirteenth Programme of Law Reform* (Law Com No 337, 2017) 13. Unfortunately, there is (as of yet) no scheduled start date for the project.

or cremation.[64] Presumably, a key factor in making such a declaration will be to ensure that the funeral conforms – as far as possible – to what the nominator wanted.

The reasons behind this shift in attitudes are not solely linked to the jurisprudential flaws in *Williams* itself; they are more pervasive than that. From a basic socio-cultural perspective, funerals have changed significantly in the last 20–30 years; they are less ritualistic and much more personalised, often celebrating the life of the deceased instead of focusing solely on the transition into the afterlife.[65] The decline of established religions and emergence of multi-faith, multi-ethnic societies, alongside more complex family arrangements and an increased emphasis on personal choice, are also reasons why many people include specific funeral directions in their will or pre-paid funeral plan. From a legal perspective, succession law analogies and upholding the core values of autonomy and personhood are the two key arguments which are often cited in favour of making an individual's funeral preferences legally binding.[66] For example, Sperling has argued that:

> If by enforcing a will what we care deeply about is respecting the decedent's prior wishes and autonomy, then it is not clear why this principle should be defeated in situations where the decedent's wishes are concerned with the disposal of her own body. On the contrary, it seems unambiguous that a person's body is one of the most precious things about which she cares, certainly more than her real property.[67]

In recent years, there has also been a resurgence in academic literature around the rights of the dead.[68] While some might argue that funeral instructions should not prevail, because the person in question is deceased, this misses the point: it is not about the rights of the dead, but enforcing and upholding the ante-mortem preferences of the individual about the fate of their mortal remains (in the same way that succession law upholds and respects lifetime choices around the post-mortem disposal of property).

Of course, this is not to suggest that the deceased's every whim can, or should, be catered for. Funeral instructions could only be upheld where they were legal, practical and not contrary to public policy, and any legislation which allowed an individual to dictate how their remains should be disposed of would have to include some sort of provision to this effect.[69] The legality and practicality tests are relatively straightforward: current burial and cremation laws dictate the former, and specific funeral directions would have to be incapable of being carried out (for example, if a chosen cemetery was full) to fall foul

[64] Burial and Cremation (Scotland) Act 2016, s 65 which came into effect in April 2019.

[65] See, eg B Parsons, *The Evolution of the British Funeral Industry in the 20th Century: From Undertaker to Funeral Director* (Bingley, Emerald Publishing, 2018).

[66] These themes and the various academic commentaries which analyse them at length are considered in Conway (n 7) 136–39. See also the report of the Victorian Law Reform Commission (n 62) and its emphasis on respect for autonomy in upholding an individual's funeral instructions.

[67] D Sperling, *Posthumous Interests: Legal and Ethical Perspectives* (Cambridge, Cambridge University Press, 2008) 152–53.

[68] See, eg KR Smolensky, 'Rights of the Dead' (2009) 37 *Hofstra Law Review* 763; see also the collection of articles in the special edition of (2016) 3 *Savannah Law Review*.

[69] For example, the British Columbia legislation only mandates compliance with the deceased's wishes where this 'would not be unreasonable or impracticable or cause hardship': Cremation, Interment and Funeral Services Act 2004 (British Columbia), s 6(c).

of the latter.[70] Meanwhile, basic constructs of public decency and social mores around the 'proper' treatment of the dead would bring the third limitation into play, preventing funerals which were deemed offensive or indecent – regardless of what the deceased wanted. And the decision in *Oldham Metropolitan Borough Council v Makin*[71] shows how English courts are willing to intervene directly here, the judge ruling that the funeral of Moors murderer, Ian Brady, should take place with no music and no ceremony. Brady's apparent request to have the fifth movement of Berlioz's *Symphony Fantastique*, with its satanic themes, played at his cremation was something that would cause legitimate offence to the families of the serial killer's victims.[72]

Legality and other issues aside, upholding funeral instructions might also be problematic where the deceased's preferences conflict with those of surviving family members. Tensions between the individual and the collective are nothing new, and have been played out in other scenarios where the wishes of the dead conflict with the desires of the living. Post-mortem treatment of the body is one example, when surviving relatives have a de facto right of veto over the deceased's decision to be an organ donor;[73] what happens to the deceased's financial estate is another, given that validly executed wills can sometimes be 'undone' because of financial obligations to certain family members and dependants.[74] Both examples might suggest that funeral directions would be equally susceptible if family members objected to what the deceased had stipulated. However, the fact that many people assume they can decide what happens to their mortal remains suggests some sort of normative preference for upholding funeral instructions, while the increased emphasis on self-determination and associated ideas such as personhood, human dignity and the rights of the individual are powerful arguments for prioritising the deceased's intent.[75] A family power of veto would be a significant encroachment on these core ideals.

Returning to the factual narrative in *Williams*, it seems safe to assume that Henry's wish to be cremated was contrary to that of his wife and sons, who opted for burial (hence the reason for entrusting cremation to Eliza in the first place). The question of whose preferences should prevail here was not something that Kay J had to decide. Instead, Kay J confirmed – in what has become another core aspect of the ruling in *Williams* – that

[70] Funeral expenses act as another limitation here: specified funeral arrangements could not be carried out if there were insufficient funds in the deceased's estate to pay for this. The rules around recovery of funeral expenses, and their significance on the facts of *Williams*, are discussed in section V.

[71] *Oldham Metropolitan Borough Council v Makin* [2017] EWHC 2064 (Ch), [2018] Ch 543.

[72] There was also speculation that Brady had wanted his ashes to be scattered on Saddleworth Moor, where his victims were buried; and in using s 116 of the Senior Courts Act 1981 (the provision is discussed in the text to n 82) to give control of the funeral arrangements to the local council authority instead of Brady's solicitor as executor under his will, the court was determined to prevent this from happening given the inevitable public outcry. Brady's ashes were eventually buried at sea in a weighted urn, somewhere off the coast of Liverpool.

[73] Despite, for example, both the Human Tissue Act 2004 and accompanying codes of practice in England and Wales clearly prioritising the wishes of the deceased.

[74] In England and Wales, this is under the Inheritance (Provision for Family and Dependants) Act 1975, though equivalent legislative mechanisms exist in both Australia and New Zealand (and in Canada, where it is known as 'dependants' relief').

[75] This also resonates with the emphasis that mental capacity legislation places on respecting an individual's right to make their own decisions and, where possible, upholding someone's last-expressed wishes. See, eg the Mental Capacity Act 2005 in England and Wales; see also Barbara Rich's chapter in this volume.

the final decision on disposal of the body and consequent funeral arrangements lay with the executors of Henry's will.

B. The Executor Rule: Diminished, But Not Discarded

The common law position has always been clear. For testate deaths, the executors of the deceased's will are under a legal duty to bury or cremate the body, and have a right to possession of the remains for this purpose; where the deceased died intestate, the same obligation and associated possessory entitlements fall on the highest ranking next-of-kin, who would qualify as the estate administrator under intestacy legislation.[76] Herein lies another irony: since a dead body is not property, the deceased's funeral instructions are not legally binding, yet the legal right to dispose of it is governed by the same succession law rules that govern property transfers on death. And to facilitate this principle, the law recognises time-limited and purposive proprietary rights in corpses (possessory entitlements are for disposal purposes only),[77] as an exception to the no property rule.[78]

This places quite an obligation on the personal representatives, and one which goes far beyond the purely administrative and fiscal remits of their role. In carrying out this task, the executor or presumptive administrator can ignore the deceased's wishes – as occurred in *Williams* itself, though there are various examples of this in other cases decided since then.[79] It is also worth pointing out that the executors in *Williams* were 'independent', in the sense that they were not members of Henry's family.[80] And while they acceded to the wishes of Henry's wife and sons when it came to the decision to bury the body, this was simply a happy coincidence on the facts. Should they choose to do so, executors are free to ignore the wishes of the deceased's family when making funeral arrangements, though this tends to be more common where the executors are non-relatives or professionals (for example, lawyers) who are intent on following the deceased's wishes and were selected for this reason.[81]

We might assume, then, that the outcome in *Williams* would have been different if Henry had appointed Eliza as executor under his will. As such, she would have been entitled to take possession of Henry's remains and to cremate them as instructed, though, had this transpired, Kay J might just have ruled that cremation was illegal, given his own opposition to the practice and, more importantly, the spectre of a dead person's family being unable to stop their remains from being burnt because the final decision lies with the executor. However, the common law position is no longer as unassailable as it once seemed. First, section 116 of the Senior Courts Act 1981 in England and Wales allows the High Court to appoint a different administrator or executor if 'special circumstances' make it 'necessary or expedient' to do so, and has been used to contest

[76] For a more detailed discussion, see Conway (n 7) 61–67.

[77] With burial, these would cease on interment; however, with cremation, the right extends until the ashes have been interred, scattered or otherwise dispersed.

[78] The second exception relates to the application of labour and skill to corpses or body parts, and derives from the Australian case of *Doodeward v Spence* (1908) 6 CLR 406.

[79] See *Hunter v Hunter* (1930) 65 OLR 586; *Holtham v Arnold* [1986] 2 BMLR 123.

[80] This will not be the case with estate administrators on intestacy – though whether the definition of 'next-of-kin' for these purposes accords with modern-day notions of family and kinship is another matter entirely.

[81] See, eg *Grandison* (n 54); *Abeziz v Harris Estate* [1992] OJ No 127.

specific funeral arrangements.[82] Secondly, the executor rule has been downgraded in at least two recent cases, both of which involved bitter family disputes over where to bury the deceased. In the Scottish case of *C v M*,[83] where the court ruled for the deceased's widow despite his mother being executor under her son's will, it was suggested that an executor does not have priority over close family members in Scotland.[84] The deceased's wife also had the legal right to decide where her husband should be buried in *Takamore v Clarke*,[85] a decision of the Supreme Court of New Zealand and one of the few recent appellate judgments on bodily disposal issues.[86] The widow's position as executor of her husband's will was a major factor here,[87] though not one that was universally endorsed by the court. Both Elias CJ and William Young J suggested that supporting authority[88] for the executor rule was limited and more concerned with payment of funeral debts than the fate of the dead; as such, there was 'no clear basis'[89] for an executor being entitled to possession of the deceased's remains above everyone else (including the deceased's family, where the executor was a non-relative). The presumptive administrator's role was also open to question, given its origins in estate distribution[90] and the fact that the executor rule was simply extrapolated onto intestate deaths.[91]

V. THE COST OF A 'GOOD SEND-OFF': RECOVERY OF FUNERAL EXPENSES

With all the focus on the legalities of cremation and upholding funeral directions, what was at stake in *Williams* – in real terms – is easy to overlook. Eliza Williams was seeking £321 in expenses – a substantial sum of money which, according to the Bank of England inflation calculator, is just over £37,930[92] and nearly nine times the average cost of a basic funeral in the UK today.[93] Funerals are one of the UK's fastest rising costs, outstripping inflation by some distance.[94] Who bears these costs when someone dies is as pressing an issue now as it was when Kay J was deciding the outcome in *Williams*.

[82] See, eg *Buchanan v Milton* [1999] 2 FLR 844; *Burrows* (n 40); *Re JS* (n 40). Other English cases, eg *Anstey* (n 55), and those decided elsewhere have achieved the same result using the court's inherent jurisdiction as a procedural alternative.

[83] *C v M* 2014 SLT (Sh Ct) 109.

[84] The Burial and Cremation Act (Scotland) 2016, s 65 (which came into effect in April 2019) confirms this. The provision gives decision-making powers to specified family members where the deceased has failed to make an 'arrangements on death' declaration, and the executor is not mentioned.

[85] *Takamore* (n 41).

[86] The case is more significant in reflecting the tension between English common law and Maori customary law, the deceased's family insisting that he be buried in the traditional urula (burial ground) of his family.

[87] As was the fact that she intended to bury her husband in Christchurch, where he wanted to be buried.

[88] Including *Williams* (n 1).

[89] *Takamore v Clarke* (n 41) [53] (Elias CJ). The Chief Justice even went so far as to suggest that the executor rule may not apply in New Zealand (ibid [90]).

[90] ibid [206] (William Young J).

[91] ibid [55] (Elias CJ). However, the other members of the Supreme Court (Tipping, McGrath and Blanchard JJ) did not share these concerns, accepting that the duty of disposal falls on the deceased's personal representative: ibid [152].

[92] www.bankofengland.co.uk/monetary-policy/inflation/inflation-calculator. This calculation is based on equivalent expenditure in 1882 – when *Williams* was decided.

[93] Which is £4,271, according to the latest available figures: *Sunlife Cost of Dying Report* (2018).

[94] ibid. In November 2018, concerns over soaring costs prompted the Competitions and Markets Authority to announce an investigation into the UK funeral industry: 'UK Funerals Industry Under Investigation for High Prices' *The Guardian* (29 November 2018) www.theguardian.com/business/2018/nov/29/uk-funerals-industry-under-investigation-high-prices-cma.

The basic rule is that funeral expenses are recoverable from the deceased's estate.[95] Where the personal representatives organise the funeral, they are reimbursed accordingly;[96] where someone else has taken care of the arrangements, they can recover expenses from the deceased's estate via the personal representatives.[97] This is what Eliza was attempting to do in *Williams*, though the case imposes an important qualification on recovery of funeral expenses in the latter scenario: payment is extremely unlikely where alternative funeral arrangements have been made that were not sanctioned by the personal representatives and/or the deceased's immediate family. In this respect, the decision serves as a salutary warning for those who are considering putting other plans in place.

The issue in *Williams* was whether Eliza was legally entitled to recoup the costs of exhuming Henry's remains and having them cremated; the question of whether or not the estate could actually afford to pay that amount, had her claim been a legitimate one, did not arise. However, this speaks to another core theme: if the rule is that recovery from the deceased's estate is limited to 'reasonable' expenses only,[98] at what point does the amount spent on a funeral exceed this particular threshold? Certain guidelines apply; for example, costs are not restricted to a percentage value of the net estate,[99] and what is appropriate depends on the deceased's 'position in life',[100] as well as their religious and cultural beliefs (if, for example, these mandate more elaborate funeral requirements and mourning rituals).[101] Of course, there is a distinction to be drawn here between the costs incurred where the deceased's own views on the matter are unknown and where the funeral has been organised as per the deceased's instructions with all attendant costs. *Williams* is an example of the latter, insofar as Eliza's actions were concerned; and the costs incurred were high, given the need to ship the remains to Milan for cremation. Drawing on this particular aspect of the case, someone who is planning their final send-off, and wants

[95] See generally R Kerridge and AHR Brierly, *Parry and Kerridge: The Law of Succession*, 13th edn (London, Sweet & Maxwell, 2016) 535–36; Conway (n 7) 75–79 and the cases cited therein. Of course, the legal rules around recovery of costs assume that the estate contains sufficient funds to cover the funeral; where it does not, the costs will usually be shared by the deceased's family, causing problems for the poorest and most vulnerable in society, who cannot afford to bury or cremate their dead. The growing issue of 'funeral poverty' is well documented: see, eg L Foster and K Woodthorpe, 'What Cost the Price of a Good Send Off? The Challenges for British State Funeral Policy' (2013) 21 *Journal of Poverty and Social Justice* 77.

[96] Personal representatives can recover the costs incurred as a first charge on the estate: *Rees v Hughes* [1946] 1 KB 517

[97] *Green v Salmon* (1838) 8 Ad & E 348. In this and similar 'old' cases, such as *Jenkins v Tucker* (1788) 126 ER 25 and *Ambrose v Kerrison* (1851) 138 ER 307, the legal issue arose because the person with the duty of disposal was absent at the time and responsibility for the deceased's burial had been assumed by someone else.

[98] See *Hancock v Podmore* (1830) 1 B & Adol 260; *Edwards v Edwards* (1834) 2 C & M 613; *Green v Salmon* (ibid). For more recent confirmation, see the comments in *Smith v Tamworth City Council* (n 41) 694; *Chernichan v Chernichan (Estate)* [2001] ABQB 913, [11] ('[t]he responsibility at law for funeral expenses is not unlimited, and only extends to "reasonable" expenses').

[99] It is a 'question of fact to be decided having regard to the circumstances of the particular case': Kerridge and Brierly (n 95) 536, citing various authorities.

[100] *Re Walter (Deceased)* [1929] 1 Ch 647, 655. This presumably includes an individual's social standing, successes and achievements; and while we might regard it as an anachronism, the test still applies – see *Chernichan* (n 98) [24]. In *Zannetides v Spence* [2013] NSWSC 2032 a son claimed almost AUS$18,000 for his father's funeral expenses (out of an estate worth almost AUS$282,000); the court held that this sum was reasonable, the son having arranged a funeral and memorial which he felt were 'worthy' of his father. There are strong parallels here with the Roman law *actio funeraria*, under which funeral expenses were assessed according to the wealth or rank of the deceased: see P du Plessis, *Borkowski's Textbook on Roman Law*, 4th edn (Oxford, Oxford University Press, 2010) 313.

[101] *Gammell v Wilson* [1982] AC 27, 43; *Chernichan* (n 98).

this to be a particularly lavish or grandiose affair, must ensure that they leave enough money behind to cover the costs. Yet, therein lies a bigger policy issue. It is trite but true that the sums paid out of the estate as funeral expenses will impact on the amount that is left to distribute to the designated or presumptive beneficiaries of the deceased. Should individuals be in a position to 'insist' that significant sums of money are spent on their own funerals, at the expense of those they leave behind?

The ultimate marker here will be the overall value of the deceased's estate – and while the £37,930 incurred in *Williams* might seem excessive if the estate in question was worth £60,000, the position might be different if the deceased left an estate worth several hundred thousand or millions of pounds. The test is what is reasonable in the circumstances, and the question posed here is one which highlights once again the perennial tension between the deceased's own wants and desires, and the obligation that is owed to surviving close relatives and dependants.[102] One suspects, though, that if the latter were in need of financial support, those tasked with organising the funeral may opt for something a little more basic (just as they could do if money was not an issue, but an extravagant send-off was seen as wasteful).

VI. CONCLUSION

On first reading, *Williams* seems to be a fairly unremarkable case – and, if anything did catch the reader's interest, it would probably be the fact that one of the deceased's close friends was able to exhume his body and ship it to Milan for cremation without the dead man's family knowing anything about this. This is not something that would happen today, yet *Williams* is about much more than improved exhumation protocols. The case creates its own distinct legacy, and on issues which will probably be more pressing, at least initially, for the deceased's family and loved ones than administering the estate: namely, what happens to the body itself and who has the legal right to decide this. Like several other cases which make up this collection, it is a first instance ruling (and a short one at that) which establishes core principles. And the significance of the case, in the context of the collection, is that it maps succession law rules onto entitlements to dispose of the dead, so that decision-making rights lie with those individuals whose task is to administer the deceased's estate.

Succession law is all about how the law treats the interests of the dead when it comes to property. Yet questions about how the dead are treated arise at much earlier stage – and it seems both unsatisfactory and ironic that succession law rules are applied to the disposal of the deceased's remains, despite them not being property, and that *Williams* still exerts such a strong influence across the common law world, while other issues around the post-mortem fate of body parts have their own distinctive legal framework.[103] There are signs that this is changing, and that we now have some sort of legal 'halfway house' in which courts might look at what the deceased wanted if the living cannot agree on the appropriate funeral arrangements. However, the legal position remains that funeral instructions

[102] Naturally, if the deceased left no family or dependants, the issue would not arise.

[103] Organ donation and posthumous reproduction do not fall within the succession paradigm, but are dealt with under their own specific statutes.

are mere precatory statements which may generate some sort of moral compulsion but do not impose any legal obligation on those tasked with the funeral.

It is perhaps questionable how long this particular aspect of the ruling in *Williams* can survive, given changing social expectations, the emergence of more individualised funerals and the frailties in the legal logic of the ruling itself. Also, moving to a position whereby a person had the legal right to control the disposal of their remains could be achieved without undoing the no property rule and its well-established place in legal folklore. So, if England and Wales introduced legislation which upheld funeral instructions, would *Williams* be decided any differently if the same factual scenario arose today? On the one hand, Eliza would have a strong legal basis for cremating Henry's body, despite not being the executor of his estate – in applying the new legislative framework, the court would have to give custody of the remains to the person intent on carrying out the deceased's wishes. Of course, whether it would be willing to do so where the deceased's family objected raises its own issues. But, if funeral instructions were to be legally binding, an essential part of this would be to favour the wishes of the deceased over the desires of surviving relatives, and the legal presumption would have to be that the person intent on carrying out the deceased's wishes would have the strongest legal claim to the deceased's remains, despite any protestations. Eliza would also have to intervene immediately, to prevent the body from being buried, rather than trying to exhume the body afterwards, since this might not be an option.

However, and herein lies the final irony, the prospects of Henry's wishes being met in full would still be slim if the law was changed in this manner. Upholding funeral instructions is not a carte blanche for doing whatever the deceased requested. Funeral expenses act as natural limitation; more pressingly, the specific instructions would have to be legal, practical and conform to basic standards of public decency – and Henry's wishes would fail on the first of these grounds. Henry had asked to be burnt on or under a pile of wood, yet English law only allows cremation in a licensed crematorium,[104] and these are all gas powered in the UK. So Eliza would have to compromise here, and opt for an indoor cremation using gas flames in this country or ship the body to India with the intent of burning it outside on a funeral pyre constructed of wood,[105] depending on whether Henry's instructions were to be followed to the letter (no pun intended).[106] Legally binding funeral instructions might allow an individual to have the final say, but not to get everything their own way.

[104] *Ghai v Newcastle City Council* [2009] EWHC 978 (Admin).

[105] Logistics aside, it should be pointed out that open-air cremation in India depends on caste and is a community event, and that the extent to which it still happens is not straightforward: see D Arnold, 'Burning Issues: Cremation and Incineration in Modern India' (2017) www.ncbi.nlm.nih.gov/pmc/articles/PMC5357291/. Traditional Hindu cremation practices are also being adapted to deal with environmental challenges, and in particular the river and air pollution (and deforestation) attributed to open-air pyres: see H Hadders, 'Establishment of Electric Crematorium in Nepal: Continuity, Charges and Challenges' (2018) 23 *Mortality* 19.

[106] Again, assuming that the funds were available to pay for this – though whether a court would uphold Eliza's perceived entitlement to implement these wishes by moving the remains (Henry did not apparently stipulate that he should be cremated in England) despite familial objections might be harder to call here.

15

Commissioner of Stamp Duties (Queensland) v Livingston (1964): Rights of Estate Beneficiaries and Trust Beneficiaries Compared

CHARLES MITCHELL

I. INTRODUCTION

Commissioner of Stamp Duties (Queensland) v Livingston[1] reaffirmed the proposition, established by earlier cases, that residuary legatees have no 'beneficial interest' in the assets which make up a testator's estate during administration.[2] They can, however, prevent the executors from disposing of these assets in an unauthorised transaction and they can demand the return of such assets from third parties to whom they have been improperly transferred. Residuary legatees have these rights although nothing may remain in the estate for them once administration is complete because by then the assets have all been paid to the creditors. *Livingston* therefore establishes that duties can be imposed on an owner of property respecting her stewardship of the property, and that another person can be given corresponding rights against her, and rights against third parties with whom she has improperly dealt, although this other person has no right to beneficial enjoyment of the property and may never acquire one. This idea has been generalised within the law governing the administration of estates, which gives the same rights to general and specific legatees (where a testator has made general and specific legacies), next of kin (in cases of intestacy) and estate creditors (whether or not there is a will).

In recent times, the same idea has acquired some significance in the law of trusts. Particularly in offshore jurisdictions, family settlements are now often drafted as discretionary trusts with very wide classes of objects. Most strikingly, the beneficiaries

[1] [1965] AC 694 (PC).

[2] HMRC considers that the question of when an administration period ends 'is essentially one of fact and will depend on individual circumstances' but that it 'may in some cases coincide with the date when the residue of the estate can be identified': HMRC, *Trusts, Settlements and Estates Manual* (28 March 2018 version) www.gov.uk/hmrc-internal-manuals/trusts-settlements-and-estates-manual/tsem7360.

of a 'Red Cross trust' are defined as the Red Cross (or some other named charity) and any other person who may later be added to the class of beneficiaries out of a very widely drawn class of people, following the exercise of a power to do this that is typically (though not always) vested in the trustees. These drafting practices are controversial. Some scholars have argued that the duties ostensibly owed by the trustees of such trusts are effectively unenforceable because the named charity has no practical interest in enforcing them (since it knows that it will never receive any trust assets) and the objects of the power can have no enforcement rights because they have no present beneficial interest in the trust fund. Other scholars have argued that the law does not require enforcement rights to be vested in people with a present beneficial interest in the trust property, and they have drawn on *Livingston* to support this view.[3]

An associated debate concerns the legislation enacted by certain offshore jurisdictions to authorise the creation of private purpose trusts, the trustees of which owe duties to people (who might be named 'protectors' or 'enforcers') who have corresponding enforcement rights against the trustees but who have no beneficial interest in the trust property. An example is the Cayman Islands 'STAR trust'.[4] Those who support the validity of such arrangements argue that enforcement rights need not be vested in a person with a right to beneficial enjoyment of the trust property; their opponents variously deny that such arrangements count as 'trusts' (because no one has an equitable beneficial interest) and deny that they are conceptually and practically workable because enforcers without beneficial enjoyment lack sufficient incentive to act on their rights, in which respect they can be distinguished from residuary legatees who may well be entitled to property out of the testator's estate once administration is complete.[5]

This all suggests that it may be a fruitful exercise to compare the rules which establish the rights and duties of estate beneficiaries and personal representatives with analogous rules which establish the rights and duties of trust beneficiaries and trustees. Considering these rules side by side may help us to understand them all more clearly. After the facts and reasoning in *Livingston* have been described and the scope of the decision examined, the discussion will therefore turn to the similarities and differences between these two sets of rules. It will be asked if these are well justified and whether it is possible to sustain the

[3] Discussion in P Matthews, 'The Black Hole Trust – Uses, Abuses and Possible Reforms' [2002] *Private Client Business* 42 and 103; LD Smith, 'Massively Discretionary Trusts' (2017) 70 *Current Legal Problems* 17; RC Nolan, 'Invoking the Administrative Jurisdiction: The Enforcement of Modern Trust Structures' in PS Davies and J Penner (eds), *Equity, Trusts and Commerce* (Oxford, Hart Publishing, 2017). See also P Parkinson, 'Reconceptualising the Express Trust' [2002] *CLJ* 657, 663, relying on *Livingston* to support an obligational characterisation of discretionary trusts because the case shows that equitable obligations in relation to property need not be owed to people with equitable property rights. *cf* J Palmer and C Rickett, 'The Revolution and Legacy of the Discretionary Trust' (2017) 11 *Journal of Equity* 157, who make the associated but rather different point that by validating and enforcing discretionary trusts with very wide classes of objects the courts have transformed the general understanding of what trusts are, perhaps to the point that traditional rules of trusts law cannot successfully be applied to trusts of the present day.

[4] Named for the Special Trusts Alternative Regime currently contained in the Cayman Islands Trust Law (2017 Revision), pt VIII. See also Trusts (Special Provisions) Act 1989 (Bermuda), pt II; Purpose Trusts Act (Bahamas) 2004; Trusts Law 2007 (Guernsey), s 12; Trusts Law 1984 (2007 revised edition) (Jersey), ss 12 and 13.

[5] Parkinson (n 3) 680–82. Other contributions to this debate include: D Hayton, 'Developing the Obligation Characteristic of the Trust' (2001) 117 *LQR* 96; P Matthews, 'From Obligation to Property, and Back Again? The Future of the Non-charitable Purpose Trust' in D Hayton (ed), *Extending the Boundaries of Trusts and Similar Ring-Fenced Funds* (The Hague, Kluwer, 2002); A Duckworth, 'Star Trusts' (2013) 19 *Trusts & Trustees* 215.

contrast drawn by Viscount Radcliffe in *Livingston* between a residuary legatee's rights respecting the assets that make up an unadministered estate and the 'beneficial interest' of a trust beneficiary in the trust property.

II. THE *LIVINGSTON* CASE

Hugh Livingston died in 1948. By his will he left one-third of his residuary estate to his widow, Jocelyn Livingston. She remarried after his death and became Jocelyn Coulson. However, she died intestate in 1950, before the administration of Livingston's estate had been completed, and before any residue had been ascertained and any final balance payable or attributable to the residuary legatees had been determined. Livingston had been domiciled and resident in New South Wales at the time of his death and his will had been proved there. Coulson had also been domiciled and resident in New South Wales at the time of her death. However, Livingston's estate included property in Queensland, and the question was whether Queensland succession duty was payable by Coulson's executors in respect of her share of the Queensland property. The duty was payable under the relevant legislation only if Coulson had died possessed of a 'beneficial interest' in the property, language which was understood by the court to signify an interest akin to the 'beneficial interest' which a trust beneficiary has in the trust fund. The Privy Council held that Coulson had not had such an interest. She had only had a personal right against Livingston's executors which had been 'capable of being invoked for any purpose connected with the proper administration of his estate'.[6] It might have been said in a 'loose and general way' that this right amounted to an 'interest' in the assets which made up the unadministered estate, but not that this was a 'beneficial interest' of the requisite kind.[7] So the duty was not payable.

The Privy Council's advice was given by Viscount Radcliffe. He found that a residuary legatee's interest in the testator's unadministered estate had been 'conclusively defined by decisions of long-established authority'.[8] He had in mind *Lord Sudeley v Attorney General*,[9] where the House of Lords had held that a residuary legatee can have no beneficial interest in the estate until the creditors, specific and general legatees and testamentary expenses have all been paid, because until then the residue of the estate does not exist. Applying this principle, the court in *Sudeley* had concluded that no probate duty was payable on mortgages on foreign property which formed part of an unadministered estate at the time when the residuary legatee died. A second House of Lords authority to the same effect was *Dr Barnardo's Homes National Inc Assoc v Special Commissioners of Income Tax*.[10] There, Viscount Cave had followed *Sudeley* to hold that a residuary legatee has 'no property in any specific investment forming part of the estate' prior to

[6] *Livingston* (n 1) 717.

[7] *Livingston* (n 1) 717, quoting *Lord Sudeley v Attorney General* [1897] AC 11, 15 (Lord Herschell). *cf Gartside v IRC* [1968] AC 553 (HL) 617 (Lord Wilberforce), accepting that the word 'interest' is 'capable of a very wide and general meaning', but emphasising that 'the wide spectrum that it covers makes it all the more necessary, if precise conclusions are to be founded upon its use, to place it in a setting'; he also endorsed Viscount Radcliffe's dictum in *Livingston* at 719 that the word 'has to do duty in several quite different legal contexts to express rights of very different characters and that to transfer a meaning from one context to another may breed confusion'.

[8] *Livingston* (n 1) 707.

[9] *Sudeley* (n 7) 11, 15.

[10] [1921] 2 AC 1, 10.

the completion of administration and that, until then, 'both corpus and income are the property of the executors and are applicable by them as a mixed fund for the purposes of administration'. To this Viscount Finlay had added that a residuary legatee has nothing more than a 'right to have the estate properly administered and applied for his benefit when the administration is complete'.[11] Applying these rules, the court had concluded that a payment of income tax by executors had not been made on behalf of charities which were the residuary legatees of an unadministered estate, and so the charities could not make a claim for repayment.

In *Livingston*, Viscount Radcliffe held on the strength of these authorities that property received by an executor by virtue of his office comes to him 'in full ownership, without distinction between legal and equitable interests', but he holds this property 'for the purpose of carrying out the functions and duties of administration, not for his own benefit'; hence he holds the property, subject to duties which can be enforced by a residuary legatee,

> to preserve the assets, to deal properly with them, and to apply them in a due course of administration for the benefit of those interested according to that course, creditors, the death duty authorities, legatees of various sorts, and the residuary beneficiaries.[12]

It followed that residuary legatees have a corresponding (and 'transmissible') set of personal rights against the executor.[13] However, what equity does not do is:[14]

> to recognise or create for residuary legatees a beneficial interest in the assets in the executor's hands during the course of administration. Conceivably, this could have been done, in the sense that the assets, whatever they might be from time to time, could have been treated as a present, though fluctuating, trust fund held for the benefit of all those interested in the estate according to the measure of their respective interests. But it never was done.

Since the executor cannot take the estate for himself, and since neither the estate creditors nor any of the estate beneficiaries has an equitable beneficial interest in the estate assets during administration, it followed that nobody has such an interest in these assets. However, there was nothing wrong with this conclusion, for equity brings such interests into being only in situations where there is a need for them, and there was no need for them in *Livingston* because

> the court will control the executor in the use of his rights over assets that come to him in that capacity … [by enforcing] remedies which do not involve the admission or recognition of equitable rights of property in those assets.[15]

III. THE SCOPE OF THE *LIVINGSTON* DECISION

Livingston was an appeal from the High Court of Australia to the Privy Council, but Viscount Radcliffe's findings rested on previous House of Lords authorities, and they have

[11] *Barnado's* (ibid) 8.
[12] *Livingston* (n 1) 707.
[13] ibid 710.
[14] ibid 707–08.
[15] ibid 712.

all been affirmed by the English courts in subsequent decisions. They were summarised in the following terms by Buckley J in *Re Leigh's WT*:[16]

1. The entire ownership of the property comprised in the estate of a deceased person which remains unadministered is in the deceased's legal personal representative for the purposes of administration without any differentiation between legal and equitable interests.[17]
2. No legatee or person entitled upon the intestacy of the deceased has any proprietary interest in any particular asset comprised in the unadministered estate of the deceased.[18]
3. Each such legatee or person so entitled is entitled to a chose in action, viz a right to require the deceased's estate to be duly administered, whereby he can protect those rights to which he hopes to become entitled in possession in the course of the administration of the deceased's estate.[19]
4. Each such legatee or person so entitled has a transmissible interest in the estate, notwithstanding that it remains unadministered … If a person entitled to such a chose in action can transmit or assign it, such transmission or assignment must carry with it the right to receive the fruits of the chose in action when they mature.[20]

These propositions are stated rather more broadly than a strict reading of *Livingston*, *Barnado's* and *Sudeley* would permit, since these cases concerned the interests of residuary legatees and were not concerned with the interests of general or specific legatees, or of a person entitled to a share in the estate of a deceased who has died intestate. So far as intestate estates are concerned, the position was formerly governed by an 1874 decision of the House of Lords – *Cooper v Cooper* – in which Lord Cairns LC said that the next of kin had a 'clear and tangible interest in specie' in the assets of an unadministered estate.[21] In *Livingston*, however, Viscount Radcliffe disavowed this finding, holding that it could not stand with the House of Lords' decision in *Sudeley*: 'Lord Cairns's words cannot be treated as an accurate statement of the law in the light of the later decision.'[22] Since then, several cases have accordingly held that the rules governing the position of residuary legatees apply with equal force to the position of the next of kin on intestacy. For example, Buckley J held in *Lall v Lall* that:[23]

> if a residuary legatee who has some sort of interest in the totality of the assets cannot be said to have a particular interest in a particular asset, I think it must be equally true that a surviving spouse who has a particular sort of interest in the matrimonial home, conferred by the Intestates' Estates Act 1952, by parity of reasoning has not got any equitable interest in that asset of the deceased's estate recognisable by law.

[16] [1970] Ch 277, 281–82.
[17] Affirmed in *Passant v Jackson* [1986] STC 164 (CA); *Westdeutsche Landesbank Girozentrale v Islington LBC* [1996] AC 669 (HL) 706.
[18] Affirmed in *Marshall (Inspector of Taxes) v Kerr* [1995] 1 AC 148 (HL) 165.
[19] Affirmed in *Crowden v Aldridge* [1993] 1 WLR 433 (Ch) 439.
[20] Affirmed in *Marshall* (n 18) 158.
[21] (1874) LR 7 HL 53, 65.
[22] *Livingston* (n 1) 710–11.
[23] [1965] 1 WLR 1249 (Ch) 1251. See also *Eastbourne Mutual BS v Hastings Corp* [1965] 1 WLR 861 (Ch) 870; *Re Hayes' WT* [1971] 1 WLR 758 (Ch) 764.

For specific legatees, there is some contrary authority. For example, in *IRC v Hawley*,[24] Rowlatt J held that a specific legatee acquires an equitable beneficial interest in the gift property from the moment when the testator dies with the result that legal ownership of his estate vests in the executors. In principle, however, this finding cannot stand with Viscount Radcliffe's reasoning either, given that in such a case the gift property, like all the other assets in the estate, may be needed to pay the creditors.[25] Where there are a large estate and few debts, it might seem pernickety to insist on this as a reason to deny that a specific legatee acquires an immediate beneficial interest, but the problem of borderline cases makes it undesirable to allow the creation of beneficial interests for specific legatees in some cases but not others, ie where the estate is large and the debts small, but not where the estate is smaller and the debts larger. Doing this would prompt the obvious questions: how much smaller and how much larger? Hence, it would be best to say that a specific legatee never has a proprietary interest in the gift property that could defeat a creditor's claims.

Of course, one could say that a specific legatee has a defeasible beneficial interest, but then one might as well say the same thing about the interests of general and residuary legatees, and the next of kin in an intestacy, and that course seems to have been decisively closed off by *Livingston* and the House of Lords authorities which it followed. As Julie Maxton has observed, it would also significantly complicate the personal representative's responsibilities if any legatee or next of kin were given a defeasible interest from the date of death, for cases might then arise in which this interest was 'mortgaged … prior to the completion of administration … with subsequent contests over priorities' between mortgagees and creditors; the recognition of such interests would therefore 'hinder [personal representatives] in carrying out their duties and increase unnecessarily the scope for fraud'.[26]

IV. PERSONAL REPRESENTATIVES AS 'TRUSTEES'

Viscount Radcliffe observed that an executor is 'in a fiduciary position with regard to the assets' which come to her by virtue of her office, and that 'for certain purposes and in some aspects' she is 'treated by the court as a trustee'.[27] The language of 'trusteeship' has often been used to describe the office of executorship[28] since the seventeenth century, when the Chancery courts appropriated the ecclesiastical courts' jurisdiction over contentious succession matters and at the same time began to develop rules about the

[24] [1928] 1 KB 578, 583: 'The shares were left to the respondent as a specific legacy, and from the date of the death … they were his property, subject to the right of the executors to keep control of them for the purpose, if necessary, of paying the testator's debts.' See also *Re Neeld* [1962] Ch 643, 687–88, 691; *Williams v Holland* [1965] 1 WLR 739 (CA) 743–44; *Re K* [1986] Ch 180 (CA) 188.

[25] For the same conclusion, see R Kerridge and AHR Brierley, *Parry and Kerridge: The Law of Succession*, 12th edn (London, Sweet & Maxwell, 2009) [24.34]; JG Ross Martyn et al, *Theobald on Wills*, 18th edn (London, Sweet & Maxwell, 2016) para 8.007. Relying on the cases cited in the previous note, the editors of *Snell* have taken the opposite view: J McGhee (gen ed), *Snell's Equity*, 32nd edn (London, Sweet & Maxwell, 2010) [33.003].

[26] J Maxton, 'The Nature of a Beneficiary's Interest Pending the Administration of an Estate' [2002] *Conveyancer* 92, 95–96.

[27] *Livingston* (n 1) 707.

[28] The definition section of the Trustee Act 1925, s 68(1)(17), provides that 'the expressions "trust" and "trustee" extend to … the duties incident to the office of a personal representative'. See also Trustee Act 2000, s 35: 'this Act applies in relation to a personal representative administering an estate according to the law as it applies to a trustee carrying out a trust for beneficiaries'.

administration of trust funds by trustees. However, this terminology is notoriously misleading, since it can mean nothing more than that the court will enforce the executors' duty to obey the testator's instructions.[29] As Viscount Radcliffe said, such obligations 'might just as well have been termed "duties in respect of the assets" as trusts'.[30] And as he also said, it did not follow from the fact that one could meaningfully have described Livingston's executors as Coulson's 'trustees' in this sense that the executors held the assets in the unadministered estate on trust for her.[31]

In cases of intestacy, the question of what it means to say that a personal representative is a 'trustee' must be answered by reference to the Administration of Estates Act 1925, section 33, which imposes a statutory trust for sale on the intestate's assets and requires the administrators to pay expenses and debts out of the property before distributing the residue, a duty which they must then perform in their capacity as the trustees of a statutory trust of the residue for the benefit of the next of kin under section 46. In cases of testamentary succession, while it follows from *Livingston*, *Barnado's* and *Sudeley* that there is no trust of the estate assets during administration, it is often said that the executors start holding these assets on trust for the legatees once administration is complete.[32] To understand this, however, some different situations must be distinguished. If the will requires the executors to hold property on trust for someone, then her rights will crystallise into those of a trust beneficiary when administration is complete,[33] as they will in cases where executors are directed to convey legal title to someone who is not *sui juris* and for whose benefit they must therefore hold the property on trust.[34] Matters are different where executors are directed to convey legal title to property to somebody who is *sui juris*, but in this situation, too, once administration is complete but before the executors convey legal title, they owe an enforceable duty to convey the legal title, the existence of which turns the legatee into the beneficiary of a bare trust.[35]

V. CERTAINTY OF SUBJECT MATTER

Viscount Radcliffe explained the rule that the assets which make up an unadministered estate are not held on trust for the legatees on the basis that this:[36]

[29] eg *Re Marsden* (1884) 26 Ch D 783, 789 (Kay J): 'An executor is personally liable in equity for all breaches of the ordinary trusts which in Courts of Equity are considered to arise from his office.'

[30] *Livingston* (n 1) 707.

[31] See also *Best v Curtis (administrator of the estate of Curtis)* [2016] EWLandRA 2015_0130 [23]: personal representatives 'are not trustees in any usual sense of an unadministered estate'.

[32] eg *Re Ponder* [1921] 2 Ch 59, 61. Many cases turn on the consequences of this change of status because the powers and duties of personal representatives and trustees differ in various respects. For examples besides *Ponder*, see *Attenborough v Solomon* [1913] AC 76 (HL); *Harvell v Foster* [1954] 2 QB 367 (CA); *Re Aldhous* [1955] 1 WLR 459 (Ch). There is further discussion in DJ Hayton et al, *Underhill and Hayton: Law Relating to Trusts and Trustees*, 19th edn (London, LexisNexis Butterworths, 2016) paras 1.49–1.51. The practice of appointing the same people as executors and trustees dates back a long way: N Jones, 'Wills, Trusts and Trusting from the Statute of Uses to Lord Nottingham' (2010) 31 *Journal of Legal History* 273, 283–94.

[33] See also *Dix v Burford* (1854) 19 Beav 409, 52 ER 408 (Ch); *Re Timmis* [1902] 1 Ch 176, 183; *Solomon v Attenborough* [1912] 1 Ch 451 (CA) 458; affirmed [1913] AC 76 (HL); *Re Cockburn's WT* [1957] Ch 438, 439–40.

[34] *Harvell* (n 32) esp 383–84.

[35] As in eg *Re Richardson* [1920] 1 Ch 423 (CA).

[36] *Livingston* (n 1) 707–08, also stating that 'until administration was complete no one was in a position to say what items of property would need to be realised for the purposes of that administration or of what the residue, when ascertained, would consist or what its value would be'.

> would have been a clumsy and unsatisfactory device from a practical point of view; and … would have been in plain conflict with the basic conception of equity that to impose the fetters of a trust upon property, with the resulting creation of equitable interests in that property, there had to be specific subjects identifiable as the trust fund. An unadministered estate was incapable of satisfying this requirement. The assets as a whole were in the hands of the executor, his property; and until administration was complete no one was in a position to say what items of property would need to be realised for the purposes of that administration or of what the residue, when ascertained, would consist or what its value would be.

Lionel Smith has objected to this explanation that the interests of trust beneficiaries, like the interests of estate beneficiaries, are defeasible by the exercise of the trustees' powers to pay debts incurred in the course of pursuing trust business and to appoint property out of the trust fund to other people.[37] If this does not prevent trust beneficiaries from acquiring a beneficial interest in the trust fund, he asks, then why should it prevent estate beneficiaries from acquiring a beneficial interest in the unadministered estate? However, this criticism does not hit the mark. Smith's examples are of situations where a trust has been successfully created, and the trust fund is then depleted by (authorised) disposals of trust property. But Viscount Radcliffe's point is that a trust cannot be validly created in the first place if the property to which it is meant to attach cannot be certainly identified because some or all of it must first be used to pay liabilities to third parties, the extent of which is unknown at the time of the declaration.[38]

As a general proposition of trusts law, it is uncontroversial that property cannot be made the subject matter of a trust unless it has been clearly identified and allocated to the intended trustees. It is possible to create a trust of after-acquired property if this is described in certain terms and if the settlor clearly intends that it will be caught by the trust once it is acquired.[39] However, these conditions are not satisfied where there is only an intention that the trust property will be identified later on, so that there is no way to tell at the time of the declaration exactly what property that will be. This is why there was no trust in *Re Goldcorp Exchange Ltd*, where the rule was said by Lord Mustill to be no 'arid legal technicality' but to follow from 'the very nature of things'.[40] There a company promised to sell a particular quantity of gold bullion to each of its customers. However, its promises did not relate to any specific bullion, and so no customer could acquire legal title to specific bullion even if she paid for it in advance. On the company's insolvency, customers in this position claimed that the bullion remaining in the company's ownership was held on trust for them, but their claim failed because it could also not be said that any specific bullion had been allocated to a trust for the benefit of any particular customer.

[37] L Smith, 'Scottish Trusts in the Common Law' (2013) 17 *Edinburgh Law Review* 283, 289–90.

[38] In the case of intestacy, this rule is circumvented by the statutory magic of the Administration of Estates Act 1925, s 36(2), which provides that an assent of an interest in real property relates back to the time of the testator's death.

[39] eg *Tailby v Official Receiver* (1888) 13 App Cas 523 (HL) (equitable assignment by way of security of all the present and future book debts of the assignor), followed in *Re Lehman Brothers International (Europe) (In Administration)* [2010] EWHC 2914 (Ch) [235].

[40] [1995] 1 AC 74 (PC) 90.

VI. DUTIES OF PERSONAL REPRESENTATIVES AND TRUSTEES

At the heart of Viscount Radcliffe's analysis is the proposition that a personal representative owes a duty to the estate beneficiaries 'to preserve the assets' of an unadministered estate, 'to deal properly with them, and to apply them in a due course of administration'.[41] This rule is an old one: there are cases stretching back for many years which say that proving a will connotes acceptance of the testator's instructions and that it follows from such acceptance that the executors can only exercise their powers in a manner authorised by the testator.[42] In this respect their duty is the same as that owed by trustees, who must comply with the terms of the trust deed and cannot validly exercise their powers in an unauthorised way.[43] Since personal representatives and trustees are both the owners of property vested in them on the agreed basis that they will hold and apply it for the benefit of other people who are vulnerable to abuses of their power, it is no surprise to find that they are also generally required to avoid conflicts of interest and to prioritise the interests of the estate or trust beneficiaries over their own interests and those of other people.[44] Out of this requirement flows the further rule that they must disgorge any unauthorised profits which they make from their position.[45]

For these duties to be meaningful, the persons to whom they are owed must be afforded a realistic opportunity to enforce them. This means that they must be told that their rights exist and they must be given access to the information which they need to determine whether any breach of duty is contemplated or has been committed. This is why trustees owe additional duties to take reasonable steps to inform the beneficiaries that they are beneficiaries, to keep an accurate record of their dealings with the trust property[46] and to supply the beneficiaries with information relating to the trust affairs when they are requested to do so.[47] These principles were restated in *Schmidt v Rosewood Trust Ltd*, where Lord Walker said that ownership of an 'equitable proprietary right' in trust assets is 'neither [a] sufficient nor [a] necessary' basis for requiring disclosure of trust documents.[48] The reason why persons interested in the proper administration of a

[41] *Livingston* (n 1) 707.

[42] *Stiles v Guy* (1832) 4 Y & C Ex 571, 575; 160 ER 1137 (KB) 1139: 'The executors, by proving the will, took upon themselves, and accepted the trust, and were bound, therefore, to discharge the duties they voluntarily imposed upon themselves.' See also *Mucklow v Fuller* (1821) Jac 198, 37 ER 824 (Ch); *Booth v Booth* (1838) 1 Beav 125, 128; 48 ER 886 (Ch) 888.

[43] *Youyang Pty Ltd v Minter Ellison Morris Fletcher* [2003] HCA 15, (2003) 212 CLR 484 [32].

[44] *Re Thomson* [1930] 1 Ch 203. Personal representatives and trustees must always act in good faith, but there is no absolute rule requiring them to exercising their powers in a self-denying way; thus it is possible for an executor to be a legatee and for a trustee to be a beneficiary: C Mitchell, 'Good Faith, Self-Denial and Mandatory Trustee Duties' (2018) 32 *Trust Law International* 92.

[45] *Vyse v Foster* (1874) LR 7 HL 318, 329 (Lord Cairns LC): 'a trustee or an executor who uses trust-money in trade must account for the profits which he makes by that use of it'. See also *Piety v Stace* (1799) 4 Ves Jun 620; 31 ER 319 (Ch) (executor); *Docker v Somes* (1834) 2 My & K 655, 39 ER 1095 (Ch).

[46] *Pearse v Green* (1819) 1 J & W 135, 37 ER 327 (KB); *Springett v Dashwood* (1860) 2 Giff 521, 66 ER 218 (Ch).

[47] For this principle in the context of testamentary trusts, see *Burrows v Walls* (1855) 5 De G M & G 233, 43 ER 859 (QB); *Brittlebank v Goodwin* (1868) LR 5 Eq 545, 550. More generally, see also *Talbot v Marshfield* (1868) 3 Ch App 622; *Re Tillott* [1892] 1 Ch 86. But note that the reasons for confidential discretionary decision making need not be disclosed, following *Re Londonderry's Settlement* [1965] Ch 918 (CA).

[48] [2003] UKPC 26, [2003] 2 AC 709 [54].

trust are entitled to the information contained in the trust deeds and trust accounts is a different one, namely that this will enable them to monitor the trustees and prevent them from committing unauthorised actions. It followed, in Lord Walker's view, that there is 'no reason to draw any bright dividing line either between [the interests of beneficiaries under fixed and discretionary trusts] … or between the rights of an object of a discretionary trust and those of the object of a mere power (of a fiduciary character)'.[49]

In the same way, and for the same reason, personal representatives must keep accurate records and produce these for inspection by estate beneficiaries.[50] A statutory provision also entitles estate beneficiaries to apply for an order that the personal representatives should supply them with information relating to the administration of the estate.[51] It has been said, however, that unless the will expressly requires them to do so, executors have no duty to inform legatees of the terms of a legacy or explain the consequences of them.[52] Two reasons have been given: that a will is a public document available for inspection by everyone once it has been formally proved; and that it would be too burdensome to expect an executor to discover the whereabouts of a legatee whom he does not know and cannot discover by making reasonable efforts. These reasons are unconvincing in a post-*Schmidt* world, where the provision of information to those with a legitimate interest in the proper administration of funds is understood to be a key part of the process by which stewards of the property are held to account. Hence there is much to be said for the different view expressed by John Sunnucks that personal representatives should be placed under a duty to take reasonable steps to locate legatees and inform them of the terms of the will.[53] What counted as 'reasonable steps' would vary with the circumstances of the case, as it does in the law of trusts.[54]

VII. TRANSMISSIBILITY OF RIGHTS

In *Livingston*, Viscount Radcliffe held that a residuary legatee's right to require the executors to administer the estate in accordance with the testator's instructions is a 'transmissible' right,[55] and the case establishes that this right can itself pass to the next of kin on an intestacy. Other cases show that it is also a right that can pass by will,[56] be settled on trust,[57]

[49] ibid [66].

[50] Executors: *Freeman v Fairlie* (1812) 3 Mer 29, 43; 36 ER 12 (Ch) 17; *Ottley v Gilby* (1845) 8 Beav 602, 50 ER 237 (Ch); *Wroe v Seed* (1863) 4 Giff 425, 428–29; 66 ER 773 (QB) 774–75; *Re Bosworth* (1889) 58 LJ Ch 432. Administrators: Administration of Estates Act 1925, s 21.

[51] Administration of Estates Act 1925, s 25(b).

[52] *Re Lewis* [1904] 2 Ch 656 (CA); *Re Mackay* [1906] 1 Ch 25.

[53] J Sunnucks, 'The Executor's Duty to Inform' (1995) 145 *New Law Journal* 1408. In *Hawkesley v May* [1956] 1 QB 304, 322, Havers J refused to extend the rule for executors to trustees as it had 'no attraction for [him] on the merits'.

[54] See eg *McPhail v Doulton* [1971] AC 424 (HL) 457 (Lord Wilberforce): to carry out the settlor's intentions in a reasonable way the trustees of a discretionary trust with many beneficiaries need not communicate with every beneficiary; they only have to 'make such a survey of the range of objects or possible beneficiaries as [will] enable them to carry out their fiduciary duty'.

[55] *Livingston* (n 1) 710.

[56] *Re Leigh's WT* (n 16).

[57] *Marshall (Inspector of Taxes) v Kerr* (n 18) 158.

pass to a trustee in bankruptcy,[58] be caught by a confiscation order[59] or be assigned by way of gift,[60] by way of sale[61] or as a security.[62] The reason why the residuary legatee's right is worth having is, of course, that if property remains after the creditors and other legatees have been paid, this will fall into the residue and go to the residuary legatee in line with the testator's instructions. It can thus be seen that there are different aspects to a residuary legatee's right to require the executors to act in accordance with the terms of the will – during administration, she can prevent them from transferring assets to people who are not entitled to them and, if necessary, recover wrongfully distributed assets from third party recipients; once administration is complete and the residue has been identified, she can require the executors to transfer this to her.

The residuary legatee's right to insist that the executor obeys the testator's instructions during administration resembles the right of a discretionary trust beneficiary, and the right of an object of a fiduciary power of appointment, to insist that the settlor's instructions are obeyed, because it cannot immediately be known in any of these cases what property will be distributed when the executors or trustees carry out their orders. However, the residuary legatee's position differs from the position of the others because the executors have no discretion to decide what property she will receive once administration is complete. This is decided in advance by the testator when he orders that the legatee must be given the residue, and in this respect the legatee's position more closely resembles that of a fixed trust beneficiary whose share of the trust fund is fixed in advance by the settlor.

Contrast the position of discretionary trust beneficiaries and objects of a fiduciary power of appointment: what property they receive is not fixed in advance by the settlor and turns on the exercise of a dispositive discretion in their favour by the trustees. As Peter Turner has argued,[63] this difference explains why the beneficiary of a discretionary trust – unlike the beneficiary of a fixed trust or an estate beneficiary – does not have any right to receive property which can be assigned to other people: because the trustees of discretionary trusts can only exercise a dispositive discretionary power in their favour after taking account of their personal characteristics and circumstances. This is why the beneficiary of a discretionary trust (unlike the beneficiary of a fixed trust) has no rights in the trust fund to which her trustee in bankruptcy can succeed.[64] It is also why Lord Walker held in *Schmidt* that the rights of a beneficiary under a fixed trust are 'transmissible', but that 'the object of a discretionary trust has no more of an assignable or transmissible interest than the object of a mere power'.[65] He was thinking here of their rights to receive property out of the trust fund rather than their more general rights to insist that the trustees act in accordance with the terms of the trust.

[58] *Official Receiver in Bankruptcy v Schultz* [1990] HCA 45, (1990) 170 CLR 306, esp 313–14; *Re Hemming (deceased)* [2008] EWHC 2731 (Ch), [2009] Ch 313.

[59] *Re Maye* [2008] UKHL 9, [2008] 1 WLR 315.

[60] *Re Robson, deceased* [2014] EWHC 295 (Ch), [2014] Ch 470 [35].

[61] *Wu Koon Tai v Wu Yau Loi* [1997] AC 179 (PC).

[62] *Maye* (n 59) [13].

[63] PG Turner, 'The Entitlements of Objects as Defining Features of Discretionary Trusts' in RC Nolan, KFK Low and Tang HW (eds), *Trusts and Modern Wealth Management* (Cambridge, Cambridge University Press, 2018) 263–64.

[64] *Re Smith* [1928] Ch 915, 919; *Re Malcolm* [2004] EWHC 339 (Ch), [2004] 1 WLR 1803 [16]; *Agarwal v Canara Bank* [2017] BPIR 842 (Ch) [98]–[100].

[65] *Schmidt* (n 48) [40].

It follows that if we wish to compare the 'transmissibility' of estate beneficiaries' rights and trust beneficiaries' rights, we must distinguish between their respective rights to require executors and trustees to follow instructions and their respective rights to receive property out of the estate or trust fund. Rights of the first kind are vested in all estate beneficiaries and all trust beneficiaries because they all possess a sufficient interest in the proper administration of the estate or trust fund to make them appropriate people to monitor the personal representatives or trustees and hold them to account. Rights of the second kind are vested in estate beneficiaries and fixed trust beneficiaries on the basis that the executors and trustees have no discretion in the matter, but they are vested in discretionary trust beneficiaries on the basis that they depend on the exercise of a dispositive discretionary power in their favour. For the reason which has been given, rights of the second kind are therefore transmissible by estate beneficiaries and fixed trust beneficiaries, but not by discretionary trust beneficiaries.

VIII. VARIATION OF RIGHTS

Even if they were all *sui juris* and in agreement and acted unanimously, estate beneficiaries could not require the personal representatives to transfer legal title to the assets to them, or to some third party, before administration was complete, because this would prevent the executors from performing their prior duty to the creditors. However, given that expectant heirs can bind themselves during the testator's lifetime to assign whatever they receive under the will after the testator's death,[66] one would expect them to be able to do the same thing after the testator has died, and in fact it often happens that estate beneficiaries wish to vary their entitlements under the will in order to mitigate the tax liabilities incurred on the estate. This can be done by instruments of variation under which the estate beneficiaries transfer their rights to a third party, either by way of assignment or by a declaration of trust.

The editors of *Lewin* express some doubts about the effectiveness of this and recommend that the personal representatives make an assent in respect of the relevant assets before the variation is made, to ensure that the assets themselves are caught by the varying instrument.[67] Their reason is presumably that the instrument cannot otherwise take effect as an immediate trust or assignment of the assets but can only take effect as a promise to do all that is necessary to ensure that the third party is benefited in due course. Such a promise would be enforceable if it were supported by consideration, but in order for the relevant tax advantages to be obtained it is generally essential that no extraneous consideration is given.[68] However, it would also be enforceable if done by deed, and this is the usual practice.[69]

[66] There are many 18th- and 19th-century cases concerning expectant heirs who charged their expectancies to moneylenders; there are also some cases where expectant heirs agreed among themselves to share whatever legacies they received in a particular way, eg *Beckley v Newland* (1723) 2 P Wms 182, 24 ER 691 (Ch); *Harwood v Tooke* (1828) 2 Sim 192, 57 ER 761 (Ch).

[67] L Tucker et al, *Lewin on Trusts*, 19th edn (London, Sweet & Maxwell, 2015) [2.040].

[68] See, eg Inheritance Act 1984, s 142(3); see generally E Chamberlain and C Whitehouse, *Trust Taxation and Estate Planning*, 4th edn (London, Sweet & Maxwell, 2014) ch 45.

[69] *cf Crowden v Aldridge* [1993] 1 WLR 433 (Ch), although the wording of the deed signed by the legatees in this case unfortunately did not make it clear that the variation was intended to take effect by an assignment as

The rule in *Saunders v Vautier* permits trust beneficiaries to terminate the trusts and call for the transfer of legal title to the trust property if they are all *sui juris* and in agreement and owners of the entire beneficial interest.[70] However, the rule does not enable beneficiaries to vary the terms of trusts without the trustees' consent.[71] The reason is that the trustees only agree to take office on the basis that they will have a particular set of powers and duties owed to a particular set of beneficiaries, and so it would be unfair to them if the beneficiaries could unilaterally rewrite the terms of the 'deal' which the trustees made with the settlor. This was brought out by Walton J in *Stephenson v Barclays Bank Trust Co Ltd*, where he said that:[72]

> once the beneficial interest holders have determined to end the trust they are not entitled, unless by agreement, to the further services of the trustees. Those trustees can of course be compelled to hand over the entire trust assets to any person or persons selected by the beneficiaries against a proper discharge, but they cannot be compelled, unless they are in fact willing to comply with the directions, to do anything else with the trust fund which they are not in fact willing to do.

Personal representatives also take on their duties voluntarily, suggesting that their consent may also be required if estate beneficiaries wish them to remain in office but to carry out their duties for the benefit of other people.

IX. BANKRUPTCY OF PERSONAL REPRESENTATIVES AND TRUSTEES

The personal creditors of a personal representative cannot attach the assets of an unadministered estate even though he is the legal owner of the property. This was decided over 200 years ago, in *Farr v Newman*, where Grose J explained that the estate assets are not available to meet an executor's personal debts because he is 'only the distributor and dispenser of them for the benefit of the creditors, the legatees, and the next of kin of the testator'.[73] This principle has also been held to apply to the personal creditors of a trustee, and finds its modern expression in the Insolvency Act 1986, section 283(3),

it was phrased as a direction to the testators: JG Ross Martyn, 'Variation of Wills: Some Thoughts on *Crowden v Aldridge*' [1994] *Conveyancer* 446.

[70] The rule is named for *Saunders v Vautier* (1841) 4 Beav 115, 49 ER 282 (Ch), but the principle is older: P Matthews, 'The Comparative Importance of the Rule in *Saunders v Vautier*' (2006) 112 *LQR* 266. The conditions for operation of the rule will not be satisfied where there is a discretionary trust with an open-ended class of objects, and although it can be satisfied where there is a discretionary trust with a closed class of objects and no power to accumulate income (as in eg *Sir Moses Montefiore Jewish Home v Howell & Co (No 7) Pty Ltd* [1984] 2 NSWLR 406), the conditions are unlikely to be satisfied where there are many beneficiaries.

[71] D Waters, 'Does the Rule in *Saunders v Vautier* Include the Power of Beneficiaries to Vary the Terms of the Trust?' (2014) 33 *Estates, Trusts & Pensions Journal* 78; *Lewin* (n 67) [24.024]–[24.026]; *Underhill and Hayton* (n 32) [66.27]–[66.30]; YK Liew and C Mitchell, 'Beneficiaries' Consent to Trustees' Unauthorised Acts' in P Davies et al (eds), *Defences in Equity* (Oxford, Hart Publishing, 2018). A contrary view is taken in J Nitikman, 'Variation under the Rule in *Saunders v Vautier*: Yes or No?' (2015) 21 *Trusts & Trustees* 923.

[72] [1975] 1 All ER 625 (Ch) 637. See also *Tempest v Lord Camoys* (1882) 21 Ch D 571 (CA) 578.

[73] (1792) 4 TR 620, 629; 100 ER 1209 (KB) 1213. See also *Howard v Jemmet* (1768) 3 Burr 1368, 1369; 97 ER 878 (KB); *Kinderley v Jervis* (1856) 22 Beav 1, 23; 52 ER 1007 (Ch) 1016; *Re Morgan* (1881) 18 Ch D 93 (CA) 101.

which excludes from the statute's definition of a bankrupt's estate 'property held by the bankrupt on trust for any other person'. For trust lawyers, it is tempting to rationalise this rule on the basis that a person other than the trustee has a 'beneficial interest' in the trust property – and we can find Roxburgh J giving exactly this explanation of the rule in *Re a Solicitor*.[74] However, there is cause to doubt that this is the true reason for the rule, given that it also protects the beneficiaries of an unadministered estate and the beneficiaries of a discretionary trust, neither of whom has a present right to beneficial enjoyment of any particular asset in the estate or trust fund.

X. RIGHTS AGAINST THIRD PARTY RECIPIENTS OF MISAPPLIED ESTATE OR TRUST ASSETS

The same can also be said of the rights which estate beneficiaries and estate creditors have to pursue the third party recipients of misapplied estate or trust assets and recover the property. In *Livingston*, Viscount Radcliffe denied that the question whether a residuary legatee has a beneficial interest in an unadministered estate can be answered by 'referring to those cases in Equity Courts in which a creditor or a pecuniary or residuary legatee has been allowed to follow and recover assets which have been improperly abstracted from an estate'.[75] He did not identify any relevant cases, but the proposition that legatees can do this is supported by *Hill v Simpson*,[76] where an executor owed a debt to his bankers and used stock which formed part of the estate to pay off the debt. The bankers knew that the executor was acting in that capacity, and although he was also the residuary legatee, the specific legatees were able to recover the stock from the bank. There are also many cases which say that estate creditors can reclaim misapplied assets from third party recipients,[77] although bona fide purchasers for value without notice are protected.[78]

Viscount Radcliffe's reason for denying that these cases were relevant to the issue in *Livingston* was that:[79]

> The basis of such proceedings is that they are taken on behalf of the estate and, if they are successful, they can only result in the lost property being restored to the estate for use in the due course of administration. Thus, while they assert the beneficiary's right of remedy, they assert the estate's right of property, not the property right of creditor or legatee; indeed, the usual situation in which such an action has to be launched is that in which the executor himself, the proper guardian of the estate, is in default, and thus his rights have to be put in motion by some other person on behalf of the estate.

[74] [1952] Ch 328, 332, speaking of the similarly worded Bankruptcy Act 1914, s 38.

[75] *Livingston* (n 1) 713–14.

[76] (1802) 7 Ves Jun 152, 32 ER 63 (Ch); approvingly noted by Lord Brougham in *Wilson v Moore* (1834) 1 My & K 337, 357; 39 ER 709 (Ch) 716. See also *M'Leod v Drummond* (1810) 17 Ves Jun 152, 169–70; 34 ER 59 (Ch) 65–66; and note the Administration of Estates Act 1925, s 38.

[77] *Noble v Brett* (1858) 24 Beav 499, 510; 53 ER 450 (Ch) 455; *Hooper v Smart* (1875) 1 Ch D 90, 98; *cf Haynes v Forshaw* (1853) 11 Hare 93, 105; 68 ER 1201 (Ch) 1206.

[78] *Nugent v Gifford* (1738) 1 Atk 463, 26 ER 294 (Ch); *Dilkes v Broadmead* (1860) 2 Giff 113, 66 ER 48 (QB); *Graham v Drummond* [1896] 1 Ch 968.

[79] *Livingston* (n 1) 714.

This passage requires some unpacking because an estate is not a legal person with the capacity to own rights and so it is meaningless to speak of an 'estate's right to property'.[80] Some legal scholars have concluded that the cases allowing legatees to follow misapplied estate assets and assert a proprietary claim to them must therefore be founded on an equitable proprietary right vested in the legatees, contrary to Viscount Radcliffe's assertion that legatees have no such beneficial interest in the assets of an unadministered estate and only have a personal right against the executors. For example, Christine Davies has argued that legatee's ability to follow, trace and assert an equitable proprietary claim against traceable proceeds in the hands of third parties is 'inconsistent with the proposition that full ownership is in the personal representative', and that 'for a claim based on tracing [by the legatee] to be possible … the equitable interest [must be in the legatees as a whole], either from the outset or as a result of any misappropriation'.[81] Similarly, the editors of *Snell's Equity* have commented that the legatees' right to follow and make a proprietary claim to assets wrongfully distributed out of an unadministered estate means that their 'interest in the estate has an external aspect that gives it some force as a proprietary interest'.[82] However, this analysis is inconsistent with Viscount Radcliffe's reasoning, and with the reasoning in *Sudeley* and *Barnado's*. As Lionel Smith has observed, it also proves too much, since it leads to the indefensible conclusion that estate creditors must also have a proprietary interest in the assets of the estate.[83]

The question therefore arises whether there is any other way to explain the rights which estate beneficiaries and creditors have to make claims *in specie* against third party recipients of misdirected estate assets. Viscount Radcliffe evidently thought that although they can do this, they cannot do it with a view to taking the recovered property for themselves but can only do it on behalf of everyone with an interest in the proper administration of the estate. A possible difficulty with this is that one would have thought that it was therefore a job for the personal representatives – and, indeed, that they would owe a duty – to pursue third parties and recover the assets. *Brooksbank v Smith*[84] shows us that they can: the executors there brought a proprietary claim against the recipient of funds paid out of the estate under a mistake of fact, and they would have succeeded but for the fact that their claim was out of time. However, it does not follow from the fact that personal representatives can and must sue third parties to reverse wrongful transfers that the legatees and next of kin cannot also do this, and circumstances can be imagined where

[80] *cf Piggott v Aulton* [2003] EWCA Civ 24, [2003] RTR 540 [21], where Arden LJ referred to a deceased person's estate as a 'person without legal personality'. This is quoted by Smith (2013) (n 37) 296, who adds that it is 'not a bad description of a separate patrimony, coming from a legal tradition that lacks the concept'. The argument of Smith's article is that *Livingston* would be easier to understand if it were recognised that a personal representative has two separate patrimonies: one made up of her own property and the other made up of the estate assets. Estates would then resemble the conceptualisation of Scottish trusts which has been advocated by George Gretton and Kenneth Reid, for which see, eg G Gretton, 'Trusts without Equity' (2000) 49 *ICLQ* 599; KGC Reid, 'Patrimony not Equity: The Trust in Scotland' (2000) 8 *European Review of Property Law* 427. All of these articles are reprinted as chapters in R Valsan (ed), *Trusts and Patrimonies* (Edinburgh, Edinburgh University Press, 2015), which also contains a sceptical response to Smith's paper by Paul Matthews entitled 'Square Peg, Round Hole? Patrimony and the Common Law Trust'.

[81] CJ Davies, 'Floating Rights' [2002] *CLJ* 423, 425; see also her comments at 456–57.

[82] *Snell* (n 25) [2.012].

[83] Smith (2013) (n 37) 293–94.

[84] (1836) 2 Y & C Ex 58, 160 ER 311 (KB).

it is desirable to let them: for example, where the personal representative has become insolvent or unreasonably refuses to act, or where she colluded with the third party and cannot now be relied upon to bring proceedings.

In fact, there are cases where legatees and next of kin have been allowed to do this for precisely these reasons. In *Travis v Milne*, for example, Turner V-C said that parties interested in the estate of a deceased partner could sue the surviving partners in special circumstances:[85] 'where the relation between the executors and the surviving partners [was] such as to present a substantial impediment to the prosecution by the executors of the rights of the parties interested in the estate against the surviving partners'.

Again, in *Beningfield v Baxter* Lord Selborne said that:[86]

> When an executor cannot sue, because his own acts and conduct, with reference to the testator's estate, are impeached, relief, which (as against a stranger) could be sought by the executor alone, may be obtained at the suit of a party beneficially interested in the proper performance of his duty.

It is important to understand, however, that in cases of this kind the estate beneficiaries do not sue in their own right: instead, they bring 'derivative proceedings' which entail 'stepping into the shoes' of the personal representative and bringing the claim that she would have brought if she had initiated the proceedings herself. Proceedings of this kind were discussed by the Supreme Court in *Roberts v Gill & Co*,[87] where a residuary legatee unsuccessfully sought to bring a 'derivative action' in negligence against two firms of solicitors which had advised the administrator of the estate. Several points of note emerge from the court's discussion. First, a personal representative who brings proceedings against a recipient of wrongfully misapplied funds makes the claim in a representative capacity and must state this in her claim form.[88] Where the deceased's estate has not been fully administered, the personal representative necessarily conducts the proceedings for the benefit of all those interested in the estate, whether as creditors or as beneficiaries. And it follows that a legatee or next of kin who brings derivative proceedings in these circumstances can herself only bring them in a representative capacity.[89] Secondly, such derivative claims are only permissible where there are 'special circumstances', such as those outlined above.[90] Thirdly, the personal representative through whom the legatee claims must be joined as a defendant to the proceedings – a procedural requirement inherited from the old rule that if a personal representative would not take action against a third party then the legatee or next of kin could sue her in a court of equity to compel her to lend her name for an action at law. Fourthly, the legatee or next of kin can be in no better position than the personal representative, and so any bar to her proceedings, such as the expiry of a limitation period, will also bar the derivative proceedings.

Looking across to trusts law, we find an identical set of rules which say that trust beneficiaries can bring derivative proceedings on behalf of all those interested in the trust fund

[85] (1851) 9 Hare 141 (Ch) 150. See also *Bickley v Dorrington* (1737) West t Hard 169, 171; 25 ER 877 (Ch) 879.
[86] (1886) 12 App Cas 167 (PC) 178–79.
[87] *Roberts v Gill & Co* [2010] UKSC 22, [2011] 1 AC 240.
[88] CPR, r 16.2(3).
[89] *Roberts* (n 87) [102] (Lord Walker).
[90] See also *Davies v Davies* (1837) 2 Keen 534, 48 ER 733 (Ch); *Yeatman v Yeatman* (1877) 7 Ch D 210.

> in special circumstances which embrace a failure, excusable or inexcusable, by the trustees in the performance of the duty owed by the trustees to the beneficiary to protect the trust estate or to protect the interests of the beneficiary in the trust estate.[91]

It follows that in cases where trustees have improperly transferred trust property to third parties it should sometimes be possible for the beneficiaries to bring derivative proceedings against the recipients with a view to obtaining an order that the misapplied property must be restored to the trust fund. Such proceedings would be materially identical to derivative proceedings brought by estate beneficiaries to recover misapplied estate assets, suggesting that we do not need to explain the right of trust beneficiaries to bring such actions by pointing to their beneficial ownership of the trust property. Turning the Davies/*Snell* argument on its head, we can argue instead that they have the right to do this as an incident of their rights to enforce compliance with the trust terms.

Having said this, however, we also know at least some trust beneficiaries have a right to recover misapplied trust assets and their traceable proceeds not by bringing derivative proceedings on behalf of everyone interested in the trust fund, but by bringing an action on their own behalf, and that their right to do this follows from the fact that they had an equitable 'beneficial interest' in the original assets. The best-known statement of this principle appears in *Foskett v McKeown*, where Lord Millett said that:[92]

> A beneficiary of a trust is entitled to a continuing beneficial interest not merely in the trust property but in its traceable proceeds also, and his interest binds everyone who takes the property or its traceable proceeds except a bona fide purchaser for value without notice.

It should be recalled, however, that *Foskett* was a claim by the beneficiaries of a fixed trust to recover the traceable proceeds of trust property, and the question arises whether the beneficiaries of a discretionary trust are given the same rights for the same reason.

The problem with this, of course, is that the beneficiary of a discretionary trust only has the hope of a distribution following the exercise of a discretionary distributive power in her favour, and until then she has no specific right to any part of the fund or even to a share in the whole fund. Several cases have held for this reason that individual discretionary trust beneficiaries (unlike fixed trust beneficiaries) have no proprietary 'interest' in the trust assets for the purposes of tax legislation where this language has been used.[93] Since these cases turned on points of statutory construction, however, it can be said that they establish no general principle; and it can be argued that even if individual beneficiaries of discretionary trusts lack a beneficial interest in the trust property, all the beneficiaries collectively are nevertheless its owners in equity. In turn, this might form the basis of

[91] *Hayim v Citibank NA* [1987] AC 730 (PC) 748. See *Sharpe v San Paulo Rly Co* (1873) LR 8 Ch App 597, 609–10; *Re Forest of Dean Coal Mining Co* (1878) 10 Ch D 450, 453–54; *Parker-Tweedale v Dunbar Bank plc (No 1)* [1991] Ch 12 (CA) 19–20; *Young v Murphy* [1996] 1 VLR 279, esp 281–82; *Alexander v Perpetual Trustees WA Ltd* [2004] HCA 4, (2004) 216 CLR 109 [55]–[56]; *Lewis v Condon* [2013] NSWCA 204, (2013) 85 NSWLR 99 [107]–[110]; *El Sayed v El Hawach* [2015] NSWCA 26, (2015) 88 NSWLR 214 [47]–[56]. On the question whether trust beneficiaries who bring a derivative action should have their costs borne out of the trust fund, see *In the Matter of X (Trust)* [2012] JRC 171, discussed in Tang HW, 'Derivative Actions on Behalf of the Trust: Beddoe Orders for Beneficiaries' in RC Nolan, KFK Low and Tang HW (eds), *Trusts and Modern Wealth Management* (Cambridge, Cambridge University Press, 2018).

[92] [2001] 1 AC 102 (HL) 127.

[93] *Gartside* (n 7) 617. See also *Re Munro's ST* [1963] 1 WLR 145 (Ch) 148; *Sainsbury v IRC* [1970] Ch 712, 724–25. And see Dominic de Cogan's chapter (chapter 16) in the present volume.

an argument that, at least collectively, their position is sufficiently analogous to that of a fixed trust beneficiary for the *Foskett* reasoning to apply to them as well. This seems rather strained, however, and in this context at least it seems more plausible to say that the position of a discretionary trust beneficiary more closely resembles that of an estate beneficiary during administration – suggesting that she should only have the right to bring derivative proceedings.[94]

XI. SUMMARY AND FINAL COMMENTS

Trust beneficiaries and estate beneficiaries have many similar rights, but different types of trust beneficiaries have different rights, and this affects the extent to which their position resembles the position of estate beneficiaries during administration. It also affects the extent to which the courts feel confident in describing the rights of trust beneficiaries as 'proprietary'. This language is often used to describe the rights of trust beneficiaries,[95] but its dangers are well known: it begs the question of what is meant by 'proprietary right' and it encourages the false perception that the owners of such rights always enjoy the same set of advantages.[96] In *Livingston*, Viscount Radcliffe was aware of these problems,[97] and sought to avoid using the terms 'proprietary interest' and 'beneficial interest' in his exposition of the law, although he did not quite succeed in doing so.

The discussion in this chapter suggests that resort to these terms is not particularly helpful even when it is sought to explain the rights of a beneficiary under a fixed trust. Following *Foskett*, English law is committed to an explanation of a fixed trust beneficiary's right to recover misapplied trust funds and their traceable proceeds for herself, which depends on her ownership of an equitable proprietary interest. But there is no need to rely on this idea to explain why she is entitled to prevent the trustee's personal creditors from attaching the trust property, to prevent the trustee from committing unauthorised and/or self-interested acts and to obtain information from the trustee. These rights are also given to the estate beneficiaries during administration of a deceased person's estate, although they have no 'proprietary' interest in the estate assets. This suggests that they may all be given these rights for a different reason, namely to ensure that the settlors' and testators' instructions are properly carried out by the trustees and executors who have promised to perform them.

The same is true of the rights given to the beneficiaries of discretionary trusts, whose position resembles the position of estate beneficiaries for the purposes of many of the rules considered here, although for the purposes of the rules on transmissibility, the position of estate beneficiaries is closer to that of the beneficiaries of a fixed trust.

[94] *cf* His Honour Judge Paul Matthews's rather ambiguous comments about this in *Lewis v Tamplin* [2018] EWHC 777 (Ch), [2018] WTLR 215 [39].

[95] eg *Westdeutsche Landesbank Girozentrale v Islington LBC* (n 17) 705; *Foskett v McKeown* (n 92) 108–09; *Akers v Samba Financial Group* [2017] UKSC 6, [2017] AC 424 [17].

[96] For a general critique of judicial reasoning founded on this false premise, see B McFarlane and S Douglas, 'Property, Value and Analogy' (2019) 39 *OJLS* forthcoming.

[97] Consider his discussion of Lord Russell's speech in *Skinner v A-G* [1940] AC 350 (HL): *Livingston* (n 1) 714–17.

16

Gartside v IRC (1967): 'This decision involved a small point'[1]

DOMINIC DE COGAN*

I. INTRODUCTION

A CASE BEST known as authority for the simple resolution of a difficult point of equity law turns out to invite a much deeper exploration of tax avoidance and succession planning. This more sophisticated landmark status of *Gartside v IRC*[2] has previously been overlooked, probably because the outcome of the case was reversed by Parliament within months of the decision. This reversal itself, however, is significant as marking the outset of the process by which successive governments have removed the tax advantages of onshore trusts, to the extent that it is now often quite tax disadvantageous to establish them. The differences in opinion between the Court of Appeal and the House of Lords also present the problem of tax avoidance in an interesting light, transcending simple ideas of purposive and literal readings of tax legislation.

This argument is expanded as follows. The textbook coverage of *Gartside v IRC* emphasises the dicta of Lords Reid and Wilberforce on the existence and nature of a discretionary object's interests in trust property. This is reviewed in section II. In section III, it is pointed out that the dispute concerned a very particular set of statutory provisions relating to estate duty that underwent fundamental reform shortly afterwards. Although the judgments of Lords Reid and Wilberforce rely upon and advance general principles of property law, the case could easily have been confined to its facts and was in no sense predestined to become a leading case in trusts law. In section IV, the most standard types of estate duty mitigation at the time are set out, and in section V, some peculiarities of the *Gartside* scheme are unpacked in more detail. It is shown that

* I am very grateful to members of the Private Law Centre at the University of Cambridge, to attendees of the 'Landmarks' workshop for invaluable comments on earlier drafts, and in particular to Ruth Hughes, Brian Sloan and Glen Loutzenhiser, who provided written comments. I am also grateful to Stanley Challenger Graham for providing fascinating biographical details on the Gartsides and for pointing me to *The Shiloh Story 1874–1974* (Royton, Shiloh Spinners Ltd, 1974). All errors, omissions and controversial opinions remain my own responsibility.

[1] BW Harvey, 'Tax Avoidance – Illegal, Immoral or Fattening' (1970) 21 *Northern Ireland Legal Quarterly* 235, 251.

[2] *Gartside v IRC* [1968] AC 553 (HL).

the behaviour of the Gartsides fell outside the most ordinary and widely accepted forms of estate planning, but would not easily have been described as an extreme form of tax avoidance according to the standards of the time. In section VI, it is observed that the operative statutory provision, section 43 of the Finance Act (FA) 1940 was known by the Inland Revenue to be targeted at a different set of circumstances than obtained on the facts of *Gartside v IRC*. Indeed, the failure of the Revenue's arguments in the House of Lords is consistent with their own contemporaneous Notes on Clauses to the Finance Bill in 1940. In section VII, the diverging approaches of the House of Lords and the Court of Appeal are examined in the light of differing attitudes towards the interpretation of tax legislation. It is concluded that the common distinction made by tax specialists between literal and purposive interpretation is unsuited to this task, given that both courts demonstrated a keen awareness of the purposes underlying the legislation, the difficulty in reconciling those purposes on the facts and the structural weaknesses in the law revealed thereby. The difference between the courts was more about whether a court could interpret section 43 in a way that lent overall coherence to the law as a whole, even if it contradicted the apparent purpose of the provision when taken on its own. The Court of Appeal, led by Lord Denning, was sympathetic to this exercise, whereas the closer fidelity of the House of Lords to the purpose of section 43 had the effect of passing responsibility for legal coherence back to the legislature. As section VIII relates, this point was not lost on Parliament, which reversed the decision in *Gartside* on a narrow basis in the Finance Act 1968 and on a broad basis in the Finance Act 1969. In section IX, this reform process is identified as perhaps the most important consequence of the case, contributing to the long-term decline in the attractiveness of onshore trusts for estate planning purposes.

In short, *Gartside v IRC* is at the same time less important for trusts law than is usually admitted, and is of central historical importance in the tax and estate planning context. This chapter seeks to redress the balance.

II. THE TEXTBOOKS

The decision of the House of Lords was that John Travis Gartside, the object of a discretionary trust established on his father's death, did not enjoy an 'interest in possession' and therefore that estate duty was not exigible under section 43 of the FA 1940 on his own death. The point of law that is usually distilled from the cases is accordingly that the object of a discretionary trust lacks an interest in possession in the underlying property. In *Pearce & Stevens' Trusts and Equitable Obligations*, it is explained that 'the potential beneficiary of a discretionary trust has no actual proprietary interest in the fund unless a selection in their favour has been made'.[3] Likewise, Davies and Virgo state that 'the objects of such trusts do not have a proprietary right to trust property' and that 'nobody knows whether an object will benefit under the trust until the trustees have exercised their discretion to distribute the trust property to members of the class'.[4]

[3] R Pearce and W Barr, *Pearce & Stevens' Trusts and Equitable Obligations*, 7th edn (Oxford, Oxford University Press, 2018) 464. See, however, the comments on taxing provisions on page 517, which are consistent with the thesis of this chapter.

[4] PS Davies and G Virgo, *Equity & Trusts: Text, Cases and Materials*, 2nd edn (Oxford, Oxford University Press, 2016) 493.

As is to be expected, the precise boundaries of this point of law are disputable. Hudson, citing *Thomas on Powers*, explores circumstances in which the entire class of objects might have collective property rights in the trust fund even before the trustees' discretion is exercised.[5] Some authors describe the position of individual objects in terms of a mere hope that the trustees' discretion will be exercised in their favour,[6] whereas others emphasise the range of rights short of a conventional property interest that may be enjoyed by an object.[7] The commonality in the views presented so far is that they focus on the property law analysis of the potential objects of a discretionary trust. The fact that the dispute in the *Gartside* case concerned liability to estate duty is recognised, but is ultimately treated as background context to the property point.

A different perspective is suggested by *Snell's Equity*:

> The relevant conception of ownership may also depend on the purpose of the question ... The terms of tax legislation, rather than any abstract conception of ownership, may determine whether a beneficiary is to be treated as having a sufficient interest in the trust to be liable to tax.[8]

This subverts the usual understanding of *Gartside* by reminding us of the obvious point that tax legislation has prime importance in the resolution of tax disputes. Property theory may be relevant, but only to the extent that it assists with the interpretation or application of this legislation. A similar destination is reached by Garton, who outlines various rights that may be enjoyed by the objects of discretionary trust, but then adds that this 'is not sufficient to establish a basis for assessing tax on the footing that the beneficiary has an interest'.[9]

If *Gartside v IRC* was at heart a dispute about tax liabilities on succession, an intriguing possibility arises. This is that the more general comments of the House of Lords could have been confined by courts and commentators to the particular statutory context rather than being cited as authority for a more general point of property law. Indeed, given that the Inland Revenue persuaded Parliament to neutralise the outcome of the case in the FA 1968,[10] *Gartside* could have been treated as a decision on a narrow point of a law relating to repealed legislation. The fact that it has nevertheless been cited ever since says something rather interesting about its landmark status, a matter that is explored further in section IX of this chapter.

III. THE STATUTORY CONTEXT

The key piece of legislation at issue in *Gartside v IRC* was section 43 of the FA 1940. The effect of this provision was to bring within the main charges to estate duty situations

[5] A Hudson, *Equity and Trusts*, 9th edn (Abingdon, Routledge, 2017) 161–64.

[6] J Glister and J Lee, *Hanbury and Martin: Modern Equity* (London, Sweet & Maxwell, 2018) 210; B McFarlane and C Mitchell, *Hayton and Mitchell: Text, Cases and Materials on the Law of Trusts and Equitable Remedies*, 14th edn (London, Sweet & Maxwell, 2015) 34.

[7] J Garton, *Moffatt's Trusts Law: Text and Materials*, 6th edn (Cambridge, Cambridge University Press, 2015) 274.

[8] J McGhee QC, *Snell's Equity*, 33rd edn (London: Sweet & Maxwell, 2014) [21-016].

[9] Garton (n 7) 274.

[10] Inland Revenue, *Notes on the Finance Bill 1968*, 248–49, 280–83. A copy of these notes on clauses is held by the Centre for Tax Law, University of Cambridge.

where 'an interest limited to cease on death has been disposed of or has determined … after becoming an interest in possession'. The most obvious application of this was where a person came into possession of a life interest, but then disposed of this interest shortly before his death.

The application of this section is more limited than it seems, though, as many arrangements would be caught straightforwardly by the main charging provisions of section 1 and 2 of the FA 1894. Section 1 imposed duty on 'the principal value … of all property, real or personal, settled or not settled, which passes on the death of [a] person'.[11] It was decided in *Earl Cowley v IRC*[12] that this applied on the death of a life tenant, and that the property passing in these circumstances was the principal value of the entire fund. The provision imagined above, where the life tenant disposes of his interest shortly before death, seems therefore to be caught by section 1. The property still passes on the death of the former life tenant even if he is no longer in possession of the interest.[13]

If, for some reason, section 1 of the FA 1894 did not apply, the estate would have to contend with section 2(1)(b), which provided that

> Property passing on the death of the deceased shall be deemed to include … property in which the deceased or any other person had an interest ceasing on the death of the deceased, to the extent to which a benefit accrues or arises by the cesser of such interest.

On its terms this would clearly encompass a case where a life tenant disposed of his interest and then died. There was a long-lasting controversy as to whether sections 1 and 2 were mutually exclusive, with Lord Macnaghten in *Earl Cowley v IRC*[14] stating that they were and that section 1 took priority and the House of Lords in *Public Trustee v IRC*[15] deciding to the contrary. Either way, it is clear that section 43 of the FA 1940 was redundant in the factual context to which it appears, on its face, to have been targeted.

This impression is confirmed by the Inland Revenue's notes on the draft clauses of the Finance Bill 1940. The intended targets of section 43, according to these notes, were more complicated schemes whereby the life tenant did not merely dispose of his interest but ensured that there was no passing on death for the purposes of section 1 of the FA 1894. The most straightforward of these schemes was to dispose of the life interest to the remainderman so that the interests merged before death, and this was countered by section 11 of the FA 1900. A slightly more complicated scheme was for the life and remainder interests to be transferred into a company in such a way that the life tenant continued to receive income during his life in the form of directors' fees or dividends. This was countered by section 35 of the FA 1930.[16]

After experiencing a number of even more technical devices by which taxpayers sought to circumvent section 35, the Inland Revenue sponsored section 43 as a broader way of

[11] This would, of course, include any death relevant to a royal lives clause.

[12] *Earl Cowley v IRC* [1899] AC 198 (HL). See also SR Richardson, 'The Nature and Taxation of Discretionary Trusts' (1973) 31 *University of Toronto Faculty of Law Review* 1, 4.

[13] Inland Revenue, *Notes on the Finance Bill 1940*, 38.

[14] *Earl Cowley* (n 12) 211–12.

[15] *Public Trustee v IRC* [1960] AC 398.

[16] Inland Revenue, *Notes on the Finance Bill 1940*, 41c.

sweeping away all of these types of schemes in one go. The Revenue's note on the relevant budget resolution explains this clearly:[17]

> The remedy now proposed is simple and comprehensive. Briefly, it is to the effect that where there is a life tenancy the property shall be deemed to pass on the life-tenant's death notwithstanding that he may have surrendered, etc., his interest and without regard to whom the surrender, etc., may have been made. The only exception from this general provision is where the life interest surrendered more than three years before the life-tenant's death and thereafter he had no interest whatsoever in the property transferred …

As we shall see in sections V and VI of this chapter, the Revenue's attempted use of section 43 in the *Gartside* litigation was a very long way away from its own statement of the section's purpose.

IV. BOILERPLATE ESTATE DUTY MITIGATION

The discussion so far has centred around life interests, but an easier way of avoiding estate duty was to ensure that no such interest ever arose in the first place. In his contemporary case note on the *Gartside* case, Tiley described the 'basic estate duty advantage of the discretionary trust' as follows:

> If property is settled for successive life interests for A, B, C and D, duty will be paid on the capital value of the property settled on each of the four deaths, assuming that they die in alphabetical order. If, however, the property is held by trustees on discretionary trust for A, B, C and D, duty will be paid on the death of the last of the four to die but not usually on the three previous deaths.[18]

This was the case even if the deceased object of the discretionary trust 'received some, or indeed all the income'.[19] This very generous position was not entirely without its pitfalls. If a discretionary trust was set up in such a way that the death of an object triggered a change in the class of objects, then in Hawkins's words, 'The beneficial interests in the property change hands under section 1, notwithstanding that one or more of the objects fulfil both sets of qualifications'.[20] Another potential pitfall was when the settlor included himself within the class of objects of a discretionary trust. In this case, the estate could be subjected to duty on the basis that the settlor had reserved a benefit in the settled property.[21] A third and even more obvious risk was that the settlor died within a short

[17] ibid 39.

[18] J Tiley, 'Trusts: Discretionary Interests Not Interests' (1968) 26(2) *CLJ* 209, 209. To similar effect see AJ Hawkins, 'A Discretionary Object's Interest' [1968] *British Tax Review* 351, 361; Richardson (n 12) 4; J Tiley, 'Estate Duty (1965–75): The Making of a Modern Tax' in J Tiley (ed), *Studies in the History of Tax Law, vol 6* (Oxford, Hart Publishing, 2013) 336, referring to *Re Weir's Settlement* [1968] 2 All ER 124; GSA Wheatcroft, *The Taxation of Gifts and Settlements* (London, Pitman, 1953) 17.

[19] Hawkins (ibid) 361.

[20] ibid 354; see also Richardson (n 12) 5. Attempts to avoid or delay this outcome by varying the terms of the trust were known pejoratively as 'grafting' and gave rise to a significant amount of litigation: ibid 355.

[21] For the purposes of s 2(1)(c) of the FA 1894 and, by reference, s 38 of the Customs and Inland Revenue Act 1881: *AG v Farrell* [1931] 1 KB 81 (CA); Wheatcroft (n 18) 127; Hawkins (n 18) 372. In *Farrell* the settlor had in fact received a benefit, but the same principle might apply even if he had not: see Richardson (n 12) 8.

period of transferring property into the trust.[22] In this case, section 2(1)(c) of the FA 1894 treated as passing on death a gift 'which shall not have been bona fide made three months before the death of the deceased', a period which had been extended to five years by the time of the *Gartside* litigation.[23] A fourth limitation on tax planning through discretionary trusts was posed by the normal operation of the perpetuity rules, which were typically managed by royal lives clauses until the enactment of the Perpetuities and Accumulations Act 1964, which allowed a period of up to 80 years to be specified by the settlor.

A more controversial question was whether a different analysis might apply to a closed-ended class like Tiley's example (A, B, C and D) and to an open-ended class such as the staff, relatives and dependants in *McPhail v Doulton*.[24] A particular dispute concerned the case of a discretionary trust with a closed class and no provision for accumulation. Might it be said, on the death of the penultimate member of the class (X), that the surviving member (Y) was put in a position so analogous to a life tenant that duty ought to be paid on X's death? Hawkins adopted this logic, despite the contrary decision in *Re Weir's Settlement*[25] and the 'coy' approach of textbook writers.[26] He went further than this and argued that objects of a closed class had 'interests … closely analogous to interests that are vested but defeasible'. This meant, in his view, that 'not only will the death of the penultimate beneficiary of a "closed class" trust give rise to a charge for duty, but so also will the earlier deaths of the other beneficiaries'.

This is rather strong stuff for an article written after the decision of the House of Lords in *Gartside*. It ought to warn us from any overly simplistic assumptions as to what that case decided, either on the tax side or on the correct understanding of the interest held by the object of a discretionary trust.[27]

V. THE GARTSIDE PLAN

The difficulty with the facts in *Gartside v IRC* was that they did not fit neatly into the category either of the death of an object of a discretionary trust or of a life interest disposed of before the death of the life tenant. As we already know, the former was usually not dutiable, but the latter would be caught by section 43 of the FA 1940 if not by section 1 or 2(1)(b) of the FA 1894.

The basic fact pattern in *Gartside* was as follows. On the death of the testator in 1941, a discretionary trust took effect in favour of his son and his son's wife and children. On the future death of the son, this was to be replaced by a fixed trust in favour of the son's children. During the operation of the discretionary trust, the trustees had a power to accumulate any surplus income and conversely to distribute income accumulated in previous years. At all points the trustees had a further power to advance to any grandchild up to one-half of the presumptive share of that grandchild.

[22] Wheatcroft (n 18) 127.
[23] Tiley, 'Estate Duty (1965–75)' (n 18) 341.
[24] *McPhail v Doulton* [1971] AC 424 (HL).
[25] *Re Weir's Settlement* (n 18).
[26] Hawkins (n 18) 364, 367.
[27] Having said this, the question of trusts with closed classes was explicitly left open by Lord Wilberforce: *Gartside* (n 2) 621.

It is obvious and was never disputed that the fund was dutiable on the death of the son. We saw in section IV of this chapter that changes in the class of objects of a discretionary trust might be treated as a passing of property under section 1 of the FA 1894. All the more, then, should a conversion of a discretionary trust into a fixed trust count as a passing of property. The complication was that the trustees had used their power of advancement to pay £23,500 to each of the son's two children in January 1962, shortly before the son's death in May 1963. The Inland Revenue claimed that this was subject to duty. The trustees of the testator's will disagreed and initiated the instant litigation.

The problem for the Revenue was that there was no easy route to applying duty. A straightforward application of section 1 of the FA 1894 imposed duty on 'all property ... which passes on the death of [a] person'. The amounts of £23,500 did not pass on the son's death, because they had been advanced to the grandchildren more than a year previously. Section 2(1)(b) of the FA 1894 deemed property to pass where a benefit arose on account of an interest ceasing on the death of the deceased, but this simply does not describe the benefits received by the grandchildren.[28] The Revenue might then have looked to section 2(1)(c), which imposed duty on certain transactions in an analogous manner to potentially exempt transfers in the modern inheritance tax. This subsection deemed property to pass when it matched the descriptions in section 38 of the Customs and Inland Revenue Act 1881, the relevant one of which was 'property ... taken under a ... disposition, made by any person so dying, purporting to operate as an immediate gift inter vivos ... which shall not have been bona fide made [five years] before the death of the deceased'. The transfer of the amounts of £23,500 was made by the trustees, not by the son, and could not possibly be described as a gift of property belonging to the son. So section 2(1)(c) did not help either.

The Revenue were therefore pushed back onto the provisions of section 43 of the FA 1940. The logic was as follows. The discretionary trust ceased on the death of the son, and it was uncontroversial that duty could be exacted on the entire fund at this date. A part of the funds comprising the discretionary trust had been disposed of within five years of death. Therefore an 'interest limited to case on a death' had 'been disposed of'; 'apart from the disposition ... the property in which the interest subsisted would have passed on the death under section one of the Finance Act, 1894' or 'would have been deemed by virtue of paragraph (b) of subsection (1) of section two of the said Act to be included ... in the property passing on death'; and 'the relevant disposition' had not been 'bona fide effected [five] years before the death'. In other words, the Revenue claimed, the provisions of section 43 had been satisfied and the transfers of £23,500 could be included within property passing on death for estate duty purposes.

On closer inspection, though, the Revenue's argument can be seen to contain a sleight of hand. Section 43 does not refer in general terms to any property that would have passed on death under section 1 or 2(1)(b) of the FA 1894; rather, it refers to the disposition or determination of an 'interest'. This begs the question of what interest must be in point before the Revenue can apply section 43. Does this term refer to the interests of the objects of the trust, of the son in particular or of the objects as a group? There is also the

[28] This is because the benefit to the grandchildren in respect of the payments of £23,500 arose on the date of advancement and was unaffected by the death.

inconvenient further phrase in section 43(1), that before the section applies, the interest in question must be an 'interest in possession'. What precisely does this mean? Furthermore, does the interest depend on general principles of trusts law or simply on the interpretation of section 43 itself?

VI. DIFFERING INTERPRETATIONS

A wide range of answers to these questions were canvassed as the litigation progressed. The starting point in examining the Revenue's position is that it focused on the death of the son. The argument was not that the death of any discretionary object would dispose of or determine an interest so as to bring section 43 into play; rather, it was that there would have been a liability to estate duty on the son's death, but this had been avoided by making advancements to the grandchildren shortly beforehand.

The Revenue's position can be seen as making an analogy with life interests. An arrangement was in place during the son's life and terminated on his death. This is analogous to a life interest, and hence dispositions made shortly before the son's death should be treated analogously to a life interest. This is not as fanciful an argument as it might immediately seem. As we have already seen in section III of this chapter, in straightforward situations the fund would be subjected to duty on the death of a life tenant. Section 43 was targeted at more complicated situations where taxpayers had avoided the normal consequences of this death by making transfers shortly beforehand. The Revenue could be forgiven for thinking that the Gartsides had done something very similar. The son had not enjoyed a formal life interest, but, as an object of the discretionary trust, could certainly have been looked after during his lifetime – and, indeed, did receive a small payment for his own purposes. The normal consequences of his death (ie the exaction of duty on the entire fund following its conversion to a fixed trust under the terms of the settlement) had been avoided by making transfers shortly beforehand. In other words, the Revenue were attempting to treat him in line with the position for actual life tenants, using a piece of legislation that had specifically been designed to sweep away fine distinctions.[29]

Things would have looked very different from the perspective of the trustees. It was a well-known and structurally important feature of the taxation of discretionary trusts that duty would not be exacted on the death of each object, even if they had received money from the trust.[30] This was exactly the position in which the grandchildren found themselves. They had received property as objects of a discretionary trust and ought not to be subject to duty simply because one of the objects had died. The payments of £23,500 had not been made out of funds in which the deceased son had held a life interest, or, indeed, any other interest in possession. If they had been, then section 43 would admittedly have been applicable. What the Revenue was not permitted to do was to cancel a long-established and widely relied-upon advantage of discretionary trusts by taking an irrelevant statutory provision and applying it out of context. In other words, the trustees

[29] Inland Revenue, *Notes on the Finance Bill 1940*, 38–39.
[30] *Gartside* (n 2) 618–19 (Lord Wilberforce).

saw an analogy not between the facts of the case and a life interest, but with an ordinary case of an object of a discretionary trust dying.

The key thing to notice here is that the trustees were not relying on literalism against the purposive interpretation of the Revenue. Both sides were appealing to what they considered to be the structure of the legislation. It is true that the trustees' position was closer than the Revenue's to the words of the legislation, but this should not obscure the underlying arguments, which were undeniably substantive in nature. A comparison of the decisions in the Court of Appeal and the House of Lords brings out this point very clearly, despite the variability in the decisions in the lower court.

Lord Denning MR's view was that each object had an 'interest' in the fund, although not to any defined part. It was difficult to say that an object who received nothing had an interest 'in possession'. The class of objects as a whole, however, had an interest in the entire fund. This was not an expectancy and therefore had to be in possession, with the outcome that section 43 applied.[31] In line with the Revenue's position as presented above, he remarked that 'If the interest had not been so determined, the advanced sums (of £47,000) would have passed or be deemed to pass on the son's death under section 1 or section 2 (1) (b) of the Act of 1894'.[32] He noted the rule that the death of an object of a discretionary trust is not dutiable, but expressed doubts on its rationale. He added that he was 'not prepared to extend the special rule … to cover this case'.[33]

Salmon LJ decided on rather different grounds. He considered that the rights of each object to proper consideration by the trustees was both an 'interest' and 'in possession' within the meaning of section 43. To the objection that this interest could not be measured,[34] he replied that courts were frequently able to measure chances. Even if this problem could not be surmounted, the entire class of beneficiaries clearly had a measurable interest consisting of the entire fund. He disagreed with Lord Denning MR's view that individual interests in expectancy could be combined into a group interest in possession, although this was obiter in view of his decision that individual objects had interests in possession. Despite these detailed disagreements, Salmon LJ took essentially the same attitude as Lord Denning MR to the Revenue's central arguments. He stated the counterfactual as follows: 'But for the advancement, the £47,000, like the rest of the trust fund, would have passed or be deemed to have passed on the son's death under section 1 or section 2 (1) (*b*) of the Finance Act, 1894.'[35] He found the rule on the death of an object 'difficult to understand … but so well established that it is now impossible to question it'.[36]

The most unfathomable judgment in the Court of Appeal, against some strong competition, was that of Harman LJ. He considered it obvious that an object of a discretionary trust was an 'interest' but that it was not 'in possession'. Unlike Lord Denning, the existence of a power of accumulation prevented him from agreeing that the class of objects was collectively in possession, but equally he considered that 'somebody

[31] See also the analysis in JC Brady, 'The Demise of the Discretionary Trust' (1967) 18 *Northern Ireland Legal Quarterly* 343, 344–45.

[32] *Gartside* (n 2) 566.

[33] ibid 569.

[34] And therefore not a 'passing' under ss 2(1)(b) and 7(7) of the FA 1894.

[35] *Gartside* (n 2) 574.

[36] ibid 576.

must have an interest in possession'.[37] He held that this could be spelt out from the entire 'bundle of rights' consisting of 'both the discretionary rights and the right to accumulations'.[38] It is not surprising that Harman LJ was alone in this highly abstract conception of possession,[39] yet once again he agreed with his colleagues and the Revenue on the broad underlying arguments. The transfer of the £47,000 was of the same character as the 'admitted passing of the unadvanced' funds on death, albeit a little earlier.[40] As to the usual rule on the death of a discretionary object, Harman LJ said simply that on 'well-known principles no duty is payable'.[41]

The problem with this Revenue position, as endorsed by the Court of Appeal, is that it contradicts the Revenue's own explanations of the purpose of section 43. As noted above, the notes on clauses clearly indicate that the provision was targeted against avoidance schemes involving actual life interests.[42] It is also quite reasonable to suppose that the counsel for the Revenue in *Gartside v IRC* had direct or indirect access to these notes. As neither the son nor anyone else in the *Gartside* case had a life interest despite the possible attractiveness of an analogy, the implication is that the Revenue were seeking to apply a provision outside the context that they had themselves explained to Parliament in 1940. This is, of course, not so far from the behaviour for which tax authorities routinely censure tax avoiders.

The House of Lords, as is well known, overruled the decision of the Court of Appeal, and in the course of doing so preferred the analogy drawn by the trustees. The facts of the case resembled not the death of a life tenant, but the general rule that funds could be transferred to the objects of a discretionary trust without attracting duty.

This reversal of the priorities of the Court of Appeal is clearly reflected in the judgment of Lord Reid. He treated the word 'interest' in section 43 as falling into an established statutory scheme consisting of section 2(1)(b) and 7(7) of the FA 1894. In this context the word clearly referred to an entitlement to income that extended to the whole or a defined part of the fund. This meant that, in contrast to the Court of Appeal, he considered that the rights of objects to be properly consulted and to restrain misapplication of the fund were not sufficient to amount to an interest within the meaning of the Act. In a famous passage he denied that the class of objects as a whole held a single 'interest' jointly or in common; on the contrary, the objects held individual rights and were in competition with each other.[43] On the question of the term 'in possession', this indicated that a person was able to claim, now, whatever might be the subject of his interest. This was clearly not the position of the objects of the Gartside trust.

[37] ibid 573.

[38] ibid.

[39] Described as a 'quite extraordinary view' in Brady (n 31) 345.

[40] *Gartside* (n 2) 573. Harman LJ reached this view by means of the bundle of rights argument already discussed: 'on the making of the advancements, the whole bundle of rights in the advanced funds changed hands … and this change of hands caused a new interest in possession to arise'. His next comment is a little alarming: 'this must, in my view, have arisen from the interest in possession existing immediately before the deeds were executed'. It is not entirely clear at this point whether he was reasoning from the existence of an interest in possession to the applicability of s 43 or the other way around.

[41] ibid.

[42] See the text at n 17.

[43] *Gartside* (n 2) 605–06.

As to the competing analogies drawn by the parties, Lord Reid took a similar approach to the members of the Court of Appeal, but in reverse. He acknowledged, curtly, the Revenue's observation about the consequences of the son's death: 'It is admitted that estate duty was payable on John's death on the whole of these trust funds, including the accumulations, with the exception of the £47,000 which had been advanced to his twin sons.' By contrast, he explained with force the rationale for treating the death of an object of a discretionary trust differently from that of a life tenant:[44]

> In the course of a few years estate duty would have to be paid on the whole trust fund as many times as there were deaths of objects of the discretionary trust, even if those objects who had died had never in fact received anything, the trustees having throughout exercised their discretion in favour of other objects of the trust who had survived. That would be a monstrous result which could never have been intended.

He admitted that the Revenue did not in fact administer estate duty in this manner, but thought that it was the logical implication of counsel's arguments. He was unwilling to interpret the legislation in the Revenue's favour simply on the basis that 'the Revenue authorities have chosen to refrain from collecting tax which, if their view of the law is right, they are entitled to exact'.[45]

A similar pattern can be seen in the particularly lucid judgment of Lord Wilberforce. In line with Lord Reid, he interpreted the word 'interest' in the context of sections 2(1)(b) and 7(7) of the FA 1894, reading from the latter provision that the right in question must extend to the whole income or to a definite part of the income. The rights of the objects in the present case evidently did not meet this criterion individually, and in the light of the accumulation provision did not do so collectively either.[46] In response to the willingness of Lord Denning MR and Salmon LJ to identify an interest in the chance of selection by the trustees,[47] Lord Wilberforce remarked that this

> may be a right, with some degree of concreteness or solidity, one which attracts the protection of a court of equity, yet it may still lack the necessary quality of definable interest which must exist before it can be taxed.

This reminds us, in case we had forgotten, that the House of Lords was deciding a point of statutory interpretation in relation to a tax dispute, and that, however much the judgments of Lord Reid and Lord Wilberforce may enlighten wider debates of property law, they did not actually decide more than was necessary on the facts. Hence, having decided the case on the basis that there was no 'interest' for the purposes of section 43, Lord Wilberforce considered it unnecessary to dwell on 'in possession'.[48] He did, however, indicate disagreement with the ideas that there always had to be someone in

[44] ibid 605.
[45] ibid.
[46] Lord Wilberforce explicitly left open the question of a '"closed class", that is, a class of discretionary objects, no one of whom is entitled to any income, but who between them can claim to be entitled, in each year, to the whole': ibid 621.
[47] Lord Denning used the now rather uncomfortable analogy of the chances of 'a girl who goes in for a beauty competition': ibid 566.
[48] ibid 616.

possession, and that 'in possession' and 'in expectancy' were not only mutually exclusive but exhaustive.[49]

On the underlying analogies, Lord Wilberforce's approach was in line with that of Lord Reid. He acknowledged that section 43 of the FA 1940 employed the counterfactual of the property that would have passed on death, but did not labour the point. By contrast, he offered a substantive defence of the usual rule on the death of an object. This was 'a matter of long-established acceptance, and also of authoritative decision'.[50] He noted the disapproval of Lord Denning MR and Salmon LJ, but thought that it was an 'inevitable and necessary and, I am tempted to add, reasonable, consequence of the method of taxation laid down by section 2(1)(b) and section 7(7) of the Finance Act, 1894'.[51] His next comments strike at the heat of the analogy drawn by the Revenue and all members of the Court of Appeal:

> if, as seems indisputable, the exemption from duty which arises in such cases as these arises directly from the legislative scheme, it becomes a task of great difficulty for the Crown to suggest a definition of interest which … will cover the present situation. No formulation suggested in argument was in fact able to achieve this.[52]

These strong words are firmly on the mark. The Revenue's own notes to the FA 1940 would have told them that the section 43 was targeted against life interests. In attempting to apply the provision against the Gartside trustees, the Revenue was not seeking to advocate a purposive interpretation but was instead adapting the statutory wording to a factual context that was outside the purpose as explained by the Revenue's own briefings. In a layperson's sense, it might indeed be said that the son in *Gartside* enjoyed a status not too unlike that of a life tenant. It might even be said that the same treatment ought to have been applicable to the two situations, with the usual rules on the death of objects being qualified if necessary. This point is revisited in section VIII of the chapter, below. However, it was quite a different matter to apply section 43 to a case that was neither within its words nor the Revenue's own explanation of its purpose, and the short shrift given to this technique by the House of Lords is a welcome relief.

VII. RESPONSIBILITY FOR COHERENCE

In line with the analysis above, it is not especially helpful to analyse the *Gartside* case in terms of whether the settlor or trustees could be described as 'tax avoiders'. The contemporary literature, like the Court of Appeal and House of Lords, focused on the structural integrity of the legislation rather than on the particular behaviour of the Gartsides. Brian Harvey, despite holding that *Gartside* 'involved a small point', explained that the approach of the House of Lords 'left the widely exploited gap involving exemption from duty in the ordinary case of the death of one of a number of discretionary beneficiaries wide open'.[53] Likewise, Richardson reported that the 'onerous tax burden

[49] ibid 616–17, 622.
[50] ibid 618.
[51] ibid 619.
[52] ibid.
[53] Harvey (n 1) 251.

which the English system places on the life tenant could ... be avoided by use of discretionary trusts'.[54] Maudsley[55] and Brady[56] also described discretionary trusts as a means of avoiding taxation. Monroe contrasted the 'highly beneficial' treatment on the death of an object with the taxation of the entire fund in cases where a discretionary trust was limited to terminate on a death, which might 'cause grave hardship'. From this perspective, he thought that 'the effect of the decision' of the House of Lords in *Gartside* 'was to mitigate the hardship of the existing law where it was unjust'.[57] It is curious, but not ultimately surprising, that *Gartside* provoked a great deal of general commentary on tax avoidance but not a great deal on whether the Gartsides in particular were tax avoiders.

A good way out of this conundrum is to look at the *Gartside* litigation in terms of who is responsible for ensuring coherence in the legislation. The rules allowing families to place assets in discretionary trusts and thereby avoid duty for the perpetuity period regardless of a series of intervening deaths[58] were clearly difficult to defend on a principled basis, especially in view of the harsh consequences following from certain other circumstances, such as the death of a life tenant. Nevertheless, every commentator and judge reviewed so far in this chapter admitted that this favourable treatment was in fact available on any reasonable understanding of the authorities. In other words, there was an apparent conflict between the principled tax treatment of trusts and statutory authority. Through this lens, the problem in *Gartside* was not really about avoidance versus not-avoidance, or literal interpretation versus purposive interpretation, but rather the extent to which courts may impose order on statutory provisions that produce perversely different outcomes in similar factual circumstances.

The complicating factor is that the judiciary has tended to be especially sensitive, in the tax field, to the limited nature of parliamentary authorisation of executive power. This is typically explained by reference to Article 4 of the Bill of Rights 1689, which prohibits the levying of taxation 'by pretence of Prerogative without Grant of Parlyament'.[59] It follows, according to the usual understanding, that a person cannot be taxed unless there is a convincing basis for the liability in primary legislation.[60] It is now accepted, after a lengthy period of uncertainty, that literal interpretation is not a helpful method of demonstrating this sensitivity or discovering whether the legislation does contain a convincing basis for liability.[61] However, the recognition of purposive interpretation as the normal judicial approach to tax statutes has not solved all problems, and there are

[54] Richardson (n 12) 4.

[55] R Maudsley, 'Tax Planning in England' (1972) 9 *San Diego Law Review* 264, 281.

[56] Brady (n 31) 343.

[57] JG Monroe, 'The Estate Duty Provisions of the Finance Act 1968' [1968] *British Tax Review* 238, 241.

[58] This position was subject to certain additional complications, eg with regard to 'grafting' operations that were designed to extend the duration of a trust and therefore postpone the imposition of duty. These are not relevant for present purposes, but further detail is provided in Hawkins (n 18).

[59] This position was both modified and reinforced by the Parliament Act 1911, which heavily restricted the influence of the House of Lords over tax legislation and correspondingly confirmed the dominance of the Commons.

[60] Some of the detailed procedures may be contained in secondary legislation, the most famous example being the rules of the Pay As You Earn system for collecting income tax and National Insurance contributions on employment income.

[61] See especially *Ramsay v IRC* [1982] AC 300 (HL); *Pepper v Hart* [1993] AC 593 (HL).

awkward cases in which the identification of a purpose either remains impossible[62] or does not prevent the provisions in question from producing a perverse outcome. In the recent case of *UBS v HMRC*,[63] for example, bankers' bonuses were provided in a manner that was designed to attract the favourable tax treatment of the 'restricted securities' regime. In broad terms, the restrictions placed on the securities were artificial and did not realistically fall within the purpose of the restricted securities regime. The problem facing the court was that the legislation defined the term 'restricted' in detail and the definition did appear to be satisfied on the facts. For the court to ignore this but nevertheless to treat the securities as unrestricted would have crossed the line from purposive interpretation into law reform and might well have been contrary to Article 4 of the Bill of Rights.[64] The dilemma facing the Supreme Court was therefore not between literal and purposive interpretation, but between finding some means of applying the legislation in a coherent way despite the definition of 'restricted' and accepting that the taxpayers escaped charge on this occasion and recommending that the matter be reconsidered by Parliament. As I have related in critical terms elsewhere,[65] the Supreme Court chose the first option and imported a notion of commercial reality into the apparently innocuous statutory requirement that there be a 'provision' of the restricted securities.

The judgments in *Gartside* were handed down long before a judicial consensus emerged in favour of purposive interpretation, and without the conceptual apparatus that has been developed in the tax avoidance field since *Ramsay v IRC*.[66] Nevertheless, the central problem facing the courts in the earlier case is reminiscent of *UBS*. To what extent could the courts use their interpretative ingenuity to overcome an apparent inconsistency in tax treatment between life tenants and similarly placed discretionary objects? Unlike *UBS*, Lords Reid and Wilberforce refused to come to the rescue of the tax authorities, emphasising that the term 'interest' in section 43 of the FA 1940, in the context of sections 2(1)(b) and 7(7) of the FA 1894, referred to a right that extended 'to the whole income or to a definite part of the income'.[67] The Revenue's argument that the term 'interest' could be stretched to encompass the rights of the discretionary objects prior to the two payments of £23,500 was too tenuous. Indeed, it was much weaker than HMRC's argument in *UBS*, given that the Revenue's interpretation was contradicted by its own advice to Parliament in 1940.[68]

If the House of Lords decision allowed the trustee to escape duty and left it to Parliament to address any unfair advantage enjoyed by the Gartsides relative to life tenants, the Court of Appeal judges were much readier to resolve problems with the legislation using their own interpretative powers. The purpose of section 43 was to prevent estate duty avoidance relating to the disposal of life interests before the death of the life tenant. Although the son in the *Gartside* case was not strictly a life tenant, his position

[62] *Mayes v HMRC* [2011] STC 1269 is sometimes cited as the central example of a case in which the court could not identify a purpose in the legislation that was relevant to the facts and was therefore forced back upon literal interpretation.

[63] *UBS v HMRC; Deutsche Bank v HMRC* [2016] UKSC 13, [2016] 1 WLR 1005.

[64] Refer to text at n 59.

[65] D de Cogan, 'Defining Tax Avoidance: Flirting with Chaos, Again' [2016] *CLJ* 474.

[66] *Ramsay* (n 61).

[67] *Gartside* (n 2) 603–06, 615–16.

[68] See text following n 15.

in relation to family wealth was not sufficiently different to justify a radically more generous tax treatment. The statutory wording was not ideally positioned to impose duty in relation to the payments of £23,500, but there was some precedent for wide readings of the words 'interest' and 'in possession', which in some lights are almost more natural than the wide reading of 'provision' in *UBS*. As to the risk that the Court of Appeal's experimental approaches to statutory interpretation might distort a proper understanding of the nature of an interest in trusts law, it could easily be answered that the decision was restricted to the particular meaning of section 43 in the context of the facts of the case. On this point, at least, there is a certain common ground with the decisions of Lords Reid and Wilberforce.

Ultimately both *Gartside* and *UBS* were marginal cases, in which differing views can be (and have been) held on the propriety of judicial interventionism in relation to structural problems in tax legislation. There is certainly an argument that, despite having at least one annual opportunity to use the Budget and Finance Bill process to improve the coherence of the tax system, Parliament shows far too little interest in doing so. In cases where this leads to egregious examples of unequal treatment of similarly situated taxpayers, it is hard not to have some sympathy with the view that courts should have some backstop powers to ensure minimum standards of fairness.[69] Nevertheless, in a UK setting this seems difficult to square with Article 4 of the Bill of Rights, and is particularly dubious in a succession context, where there are often extreme delays between the establishment of an arrangement and the emergence of a dispute in a courtroom. In the *Gartside* case, for example, section 43 of the Finance Act 1940 was followed by the testator's death in 1941, the Revenue's claim for duty in 1963 and the House of Lords decision in 1967. If statutory words are to be stretched by judges in pursuit of greater coherence in the law, 27 years is a long time for taxpayers to wait before finding this out, especially if their tax liability increases as a consequence of the stretching. The decision of the House of Lords in *Gartside* to leave to Parliament the task of repairing structural problems in the legislation seems especially appropriate in this succession context.

VIII. THE ATTACK ON DISCRETIONARY TRUSTS

This leads us to an aspect of *Gartside v IRC* that has long lain dormant: its historic significance for tax and succession law. The reason for this neglect is probably that the outcome of the case was reversed by Parliament within months. The House of Lords decision was handed down on 13 December 1967 and Royal Assent to the FA 1968 was given on 26 July 1968. This leaving little to discuss on the tax side, it is natural that the property law issues discussed in the case have been abstracted from the details of a long-vanished method of avoiding a long-vanished tax. The irony of this is that by provoking the Revenue into sponsoring amending legislation in 1968 and, more significantly, in 1969, the *Gartside* litigation made a key contribution to the removal of the

[69] Perhaps along the lines of the principle of equality that applies to some European tax system: see, eg H Gribnau, 'Equality, Legal Certainty and Tax Legislation in the Netherlands' (2013) 9(2) *Utrecht Law Review* 52.

central tax advantage of discretionary trusts and, in turn, to the long-term decline of onshore trusts as an attractive method of family wealth management.

The reversal of *Gartside v IRC* by section 39 of FA 1968 was effected on a narrow basis. The operative subsection was 39(2), which provided that

> if a discretionary trust is limited to determine on a death then, for the purposes of estate duty leviable on that death, the persons eligible under the discretionary trust to receive the whole or any part of the income of any property shall together be treated as having an interest in the property limited to cease on the death, and as having an interest in the property which is different from any interest which those persons or any of them may have otherwise than under the discretionary trust.

Subsection (3) clarified that this applies even where there is a 'discretion or power to accumulate all or any part of the income' and subsection (5) confirmed that persons with an interest under 39(2) were to be treating as having an 'interest in possession … if income … was or could have been distributed to them or any of them'.

This reversed the conclusion of the House of Lords on the questions of 'interest' and 'interest in possession', and would have engaged section 43 of the FA 1940 on facts identical to those in *Gartside*. Apart from raising further doubts as to how far subsequent equity lawyers ought to have relied on Lord Wilberforce's and Lord Reid's interpretations of statutory terms that were overturned by Parliament within 8 months, FA 1968 did not introduce any fundamental changes in the law.

Part III and Schedule 17 of FA 1969 were a different matter altogether. In language that is complex and verbose even by modern standards, fundamental changes were made to the basic charging provisions in sections 1 and 2 of the FA 1894. The key provision for present purposes was the new section 2(1)(b)(iii) of the FA 1894, inserted by section 36(2) of the FA 1969. Tiley explains that this involved 'taxing the benefit from discretionary trusts by looking at the proportion of trust income spent on the now deceased beneficiary over the period relevant for gifts and taking the same proportion of the trust capital'.[70] In other words, discretionary objects were brought into line with the long-standing treatment of life tenants, but in a modified and softened way so that only a proportion of the fund was brought into charge.

It can be seen that this reform achieved the reconciliation of principle and parliamentary control of taxation that eluded both the Court of Appeal and the House of Lords in *Gartside v IRC*. By removing the key estate planning advantage of discretionary trusts, it also heralded a long-term process of reducing the tax incentives to transfer property into onshore trusts. Under rules introduced in the Finance Act 2006, even transfers into fixed trusts are treated as 'chargeable lifetime transfers' and subject to an immediate charge to inheritance tax at a rate of 20%.[71] This is one of the reasons why many equity cases can seem old-fashioned; they describe family arrangements that would have deeply unattractive tax consequences if established in the present day.

[70] Tiley, 'Estate Duty (1965–75)' (n 18) 360.

[71] Subject to a nil-rate band and limited exceptions, such as certain trusts for disabled persons. Inheritance tax is the modern equivalent of the estate duty, although it differs in various respects from the older tax. A helpful review of the period following *Gartside* can be found in C Hood, 'British Tax Structure Development as Administrative Adaptation' (1985) 18(1) *Policy Sciences* 3, 12–14.

IX. *GARTSIDE* AS A LANDMARK

The significance of the discussion throughout this chapter is that the landmark status of the *Gartside* case is more complicated than it might perhaps have seemed. It is most commonly cited as authority for the proposition that the objects of a discretionary trust do not have an interest in possession in the underlying fund. When we look closer at the judgments of the House of Lords, however, we find that the comments of Lords Reid and Wilberforce on general points of property law were closely intertwined with the interpretation of a particular set of tax provisions, with Parliament enacting amending legislation within months clarifying that objects do, after all, have an interest in possession.

If the direct consequences of *Gartside* for property law have been exaggerated, the significance of the case for tax and succession law has been consistently overlooked, probably exactly because it was so quickly reversed by the Finance Acts 1968 and 1969. In what sense, then, is it meaningful to describe the case as a landmark? If, by 'landmark', we mean a single case that decides a cardinally important point of law one way or another – and is for many years cited as authority for that point – then *Gartside* is not a landmark case. It had precedential value as the correct interpretation of section 43 of FA 1940 between December 1967 and July 1968, which seems rather specialised even for tax historians.

As John Snape and I have argued, however, this is to take too restricted an attitude towards the nature of a landmark case.[72] In our view, what demarks a case as a landmark is not its strict precedential value, but the fact that people keep on talking about it. Quite often, this quality arises not because of the clarity with which a case decides a certain point, but conversely because the views of the judges are discursive enough to be helpful to future generations of lawyers and commentators considering problems outside the narrow scope of the decision itself. In this manner, *Gartside v IRC* is better seen not as simple authority for the legal status of discretionary objects, but rather as helpful support for scholars or practitioners seeking to promote particular understandings of discretionary trusts.[73]

This aspect of the case can be seen even more clearly from its influence on tax law and estate practices. It may have been decided on a rather narrow point, but it nevertheless highlighted to the Revenue the problems with the advantageous treatment of objects of discretionary trusts.[74] It therefore acted as a prompt to start removing those advantages, a process which continued in subsequent decades and has significantly reduced the attractiveness of onshore trusts to testators.

The final word should go to succession law. There is a huge literature on 'tax exceptionalism', which considers whether ordinary principles of private or public law ought

[72] J Snape and D de Cogan, 'Introduction: On the Significance of Revenue Cases' in J Snape and D de Cogan, *Landmark Cases in Revenue Law* (Oxford, Hart Publishing, 2019) 10–15.

[73] Some commentators do not unequivocally approve of the influence of *Gartside* on property law debates: see, eg P Turner, 'The Entitlements of Objects as Defining Features of Discretionary Trusts' in R Nolan, K Low and Tang Hang Wu (eds), *Trusts and Modern Wealth Management* (Cambridge, Cambridge University Press, 2018).

[74] Inland Revenue, *Notes on the Finance Bill 1968*, 280–81.

to be modified in order to take account of the special characteristics of taxation.[75] It is worth considering whether *Gartside v IRC* lends some support to 'succession law exceptionalism'. Several decades elapsed between the writing of TE Gartside's will, his death, the termination of the trust, the Revenue decision and ultimately the House of Lords litigation. In this particular context, the decision of the House of Lords to adhere to the statutory scheme despite its structural problems seems more civilised than Lord Denning MR's adventurism; even more so than in other tax contexts.

[75] A good starting point is K Hickman, 'Administering the Tax System We Have' (2014) *Duke Law Journal* 1717.

17

Ilott v The Blue Cross (2017): Testing the Limits of Testamentary Freedom

BRIAN SLOAN*

I. INTRODUCTION

WHILE THE DEFAULT position is that 'an Englishman still remains at liberty at his death to dispose of his own property in whatever way he pleases',[1] the Inheritance (Provision for Family and Dependants) Act 1975 allows certain categories of claimant, including adult children, to seek discretionary provision from an estate in a manner that overrides a will and/or the intestacy rules. This chapter considers a case ultimately called *Ilott v The Blue Cross*,[2] the first case under the 1975 Act to reach the highest judicial level. The case involved an estranged but needy daughter who had been 'disinherited' by her mother in favour of various animal charities. As Lady Hale was eventually to put it, the case raised

> some profound questions about the nature of family obligations, the relationship between family obligations and the state, and the relationship between the freedom of property owners to dispose of their property as they see fit and their duty to fulfil their family obligations.[3]

This chapter begins with a brief history of family provision legislation, including its application by courts in cases involving adult children before *Ilott*. It then examines the factual background of the *Ilott* case in some depth, making more use of an interview that the claimant gave to the *Daily Mail* than the author might ideally have liked.[4] It then considers the long history of the litigation (caused in part by the traditional two-stage

* I am indebted to Penelope Reed QC and Hugh Cumber for making Judge Million's judgment available to me, and to the conference participants for their comments.

[1] *Re Coventry (decd)* [1980] Ch 461, 474 (Oliver J).

[2] *Ilott v The Blue Cross* [2017] UKSC 17, [2017] 2 WLR 979. At lower levels, the case was known variously as *Ilott v Mitson*, *H v Mitson* or *H v J's Personal Representatives*.

[3] ibid [49].

[4] H Weathers, 'All I Ever Wanted Was My Mum's Love: Daughter Left None of Her Mother's Estate Tells of the Bitter Family Rift behind Legal Case Which Saw Judges Overturn the Will' *Daily Mail* (London, 1 August 2015) www.dailymail.co.uk/news/article-3181900/All-wanted-mum-s-love-Daughter-left-none-mother-s-estate-tells-bitter-family-rift-legal-case-saw-judges-overturn-will.html.

approach to claims under the Act)[5] leading up to the Supreme Court's decision, including the first instance decision of District Judge Million that has not been published in full.[6] The Supreme Court's judgments themselves are then analysed, including with reference to *Ilott*'s early impact on academic writing and subsequent case law. By way of conclusion, the chapter makes the argument for *Ilott* as a 'landmark case'.

II. A BRIEF HISTORY OF FAMILY PROVISION

It has been seen that the predominant principle of English succession law is that of testamentary freedom. While Nield claims that the principle has existed since feudal times,[7] Borkowski argues that 'testamentary freedom was severely limited for much of English legal history' and that testators were substantially unencumbered for only about a century.[8] The testamentary freedom principle contrasts with the position in many civil law jurisdictions, where testamentary freedom is limited by compulsory portions of the estate being reserved for particular family members.[9] The English Law Commission considered the introduction of compulsory portions for family members in 1971,[10] but subsequently rejected the idea.[11] Family provision is therefore an important exception to the general rule of testamentary freedom.

The concept of family provision did not originate in England. The New Zealand Testator's Family Maintenance Act 1900 was the first statute in a common law jurisdiction to place testators under a legal duty to provide for their family and dependants.[12] The Act was an attempt to prevent men from leaving their wives and children destitute by bequeathing their entire estate to persons outside the immediate family circle. It has been described as a 'highly significant landmark in the way in which common law jurisdictions dealt with succession to property on death', since its principles were adopted by all the Australian states and most of the Canadian provinces.[13]

The New Zealand statute was also influential in England, where considerable public and press support for reform to qualify testamentary freedom was claimed in the 1920s.[14] The scope of family provision statutes in England and Wales, Australia and New Zealand has widened significantly compared to their original forms.[15] An applicant under the original English Inheritance (Family Provision) Act 1938 had to be a spouse, an unmarried

[5] See, eg B Sloan, *Borkowski's Law of Succession*, 3rd edn (Oxford, Oxford University Press, 2017) 264 figure 9.1.

[6] *Ilott v Mitson* (HC, 7 August 2007).

[7] S Nield, '"If You Look After Me, I Will Leave You My Estate": The Enforcement of Testamentary Promises in England and New Zealand' (2000) 20 *Legal Studies* 86.

[8] A Borkowski, *Textbook on Succession*, 2nd edn (Oxford, Oxford University Press, 2002) 258.

[9] See, eg C Castelein, R Foqué and A Verbeke (eds), *Imperative Inheritance Law in a Late-Modern Society* (Antwerp, Intersentia, 2009); see also the chapters by Walter Pintens and Daniel Carr (chapters 18 and 19) in this volume.

[10] Law Commission, *Family Property Law* (Law Com No 42, 1971) pt 4.

[11] Law Commission, *First Report on Family Property: A New Approach* (Law Com No 52, 1973).

[12] Nield (n 7) 86 fn 6.

[13] N Peart and A Borkowski, 'Provision for Adult Children on Death – The Lesson from New Zealand' (2000) 12 *Child & Family Law Quarterly* 333, 333.

[14] SM Cretney, *Family Law in the Twentieth Century: A History* (Oxford, Oxford University Press, 2003) 486.

[15] Peart and Borkowski (n 13) 333.

or disabled daughter, or a son who was under 21 or disabled.[16] Relief was limited to maintenance and subject to a maximum award of two-thirds of the net estate, the Act applied only to testate succession and there were restrictions on an adult child's ability to apply based on the proportion of the estate left to a spouse. Significantly, Probert has emphasised that 'the 1938 Act was the first legislative interference with freedom of testation as regards *children*',[17] but both the provisions and the application of the Act were cautious.[18]

The 1938 Act was then the subject of piecemeal reforms. These included the extension of its application to intestacy,[19] the inclusion of the former spouse who had not remarried as an eligible applicant[20] and the removal of the restrictions on the proportion of the estate that a claim could exhaust.[21]

The Inheritance (Provision for Family and Dependants) Act 1975 removed the 'maintenance' restriction for spouses. Most significantly for present purposes, the 1975 Act extended the potential class of applicants to include all legal children of the deceased, in addition to those whom the deceased treated as a child of the family, and those who were factually dependent on the deceased irrespective of whether they had a familial relationship with her (cohabitants later being included through the Law Reform (Succession) Act 1995). Probert alleges that when the Law Commission recommended the removal of age limits for adult children,[22] 'it provided no principled reasons for doing so and did not seem to envisage that many claims by adult children would be regarded as meritorious'.[23] In his 2003 *Family Law in the Twentieth Century: A History*, however, Cretney opined that the distinction between the maintenance standard and the spousal standard 'might come to be seen as an anomaly'.[24]

A. Claims by Adult Children

It is now necessary to outline the courts' approach to claims by adult children before *Ilott*. Under the 1975 Act, the court must ascertain whether the will and/or the intestacy rules 'make reasonable financial provision'[25] for the applicant's maintenance.[26] The term 'maintenance', in turn, has been defined as in *Re Dennis* as encompassing 'payments which, directly or indirectly, enable the applicant in the future to discharge the cost of his daily living at whatever standard of living is appropriate to him'.[27] If the court concludes that reasonable financial provision has not been made, it must then decide which of its powers to exercise in order to remedy that insufficiency.[28] Section 3 of the Act contains a list of factors to which the court should have regard in making its determinations,

[16] For a detailed discussion of the 1938 Act, see Cretney (n 14) 485–98.
[17] R Probert, 'Family and Other Animals' (2017) 133 *LQR* 550, 553 (original emphasis).
[18] Cretney (n 14) 496–97.
[19] Intestates' Estates Act 1952.
[20] Matrimonial Causes (Property and Maintenance) Act 1958.
[21] Family Provision Act 1966.
[22] Law Commission, *Second Report on Family Property: Family Provision on Death* (Law Com No 61, 1974) [79].
[23] Probert (n 17) 553.
[24] Cretney (n 14) 511.
[25] Inheritance (Provision for Family and Dependants) Act 1975 (hereafter 1975 Act), s 1(1).
[26] 1975 Act, s 1(2)(b). Spouses and civil partners are not subject to this limitation: s 1(2)(a–aa).
[27] *Re Dennis (decd)* [1981] 2 All ER 140, 145 (Browne-Wilkinson J).
[28] 1975 Act, s 2.

some of which apply to all applicants[29] and some of which are aimed specifically at claims by children of the deceased.[30]

The focus of the award of relief is very much on the future needs of the applicant considered at the date of the hearing, due to the 'maintenance' limitation.[31] For example, the Act specifies 'the manner in which the applicant was being or in which he might expect to be educated or trained' in applications by adult children, a distinctly forward-looking and potentially limiting factor.[32] Indeed, although the award is not necessarily limited to providing 'bare necessities',[33] it was suggested by Peart and Borkowski that the English judiciary adopted a 'parsimonious' approach to claims by adult children.[34] This is encapsulated in Browne-Wilkinson J's remark in *Re Dennis* that:

> A person who is physically capable of earning his own living faces a difficult task in getting provision made for him, because the court is inclined to ask: 'Why should anybody else make provision for you if you are capable of maintaining yourself?'[35]

It seemed that a claim by an adult child in employment and/or with future earning capacity was unlikely to succeed in England unless the applicant could show that the deceased owed a moral obligation to him, or that some other special circumstances justify the order,[36] although the size of the estate was a pertinent consideration.[37] In *Re Coventry*,[38] 'regarded as the leading authority',[39] no provision was made for an adult son who had lived with his now-deceased father for a significant period and was earning only modestly, in circumstances where his needy mother would have been prejudiced by an award to him. It was suggested that a moral obligation could be generated by an applicant's forgoing of an adequate living to look after a disabled parent. However, neither the first instance judge nor the Court of Appeal could find sufficient evidence of such a sacrifice on the facts.

The tendency to emphasise a need to show moral obligations owed by the deceased in the English case law involving adult children[40] has been criticised as a value-laden relic of earlier legislation.[41] In *Espinosa v Bourke*, Butler-Sloss LJ denied that the Court of Appeal had placed a 'gloss' on the language of the present legislation,[42] under which

[29] 1975 Act, s 3(1).

[30] 1975 Act, s 3(3).

[31] See generally G Miller, 'Provision for Adult Children under the Inheritance (Provision for Family and Dependants) Act 1975' [1995] *Conveyancer & Property Lawyer* 22.

[32] 1975 Act, s 3(3).

[33] N Lowe and G Douglas, *Bromley's Family Law*, 11th edn (Oxford, Oxford University Press, 2015) 983.

[34] Peart and Borkowski (n 13) 333.

[35] *Re Dennis* (n 27) 145.

[36] *Re Hancock (decd)* [1998] 2 FLR 346, 351. The idea of moral duty receives some attention in Nicola Peart's contribution (chapter 12) to this volume.

[37] *Myers v Myers* [2004] EWHC 1944 (Fam), [2005] WTLR 851.

[38] *Re Coventry* (n 1).

[39] H Conway, 'Do Parents Always Know Best? Posthumous Provision and Adult Children' in W Barr (ed), *Modern Studies in Property Law* (Oxford, Hart Publishing, 2015) 118.

[40] This has been caused mainly by the 'misinterpretation' of *Re Coventry*, which prevailed for some time: A Borkowski, 'Moral Obligation and Family Provision: *Re Hancock (Deceased)* and *Espinosa v Bourke*' (1999) 11 *Child & Family Law Quarterly* 305.

[41] J Wilson and R Bailey-Harris, 'Family Provision: The Adult Child and Moral Obligation' (2005) 35 *Family Law* 555.

[42] *Espinosa v Bourke* [1999] 1 FLR 747, 755.

the court is directed to have regard, inter alia, to 'any obligations and responsibilities which the deceased had towards any applicant'.[43] All of the judges in that case expressed misgivings about the use of the word 'moral', emphasising that it was intended simply to avoid restricting relevant obligations to legal ones. In *Re Hancock*, moreover, it had previously been confirmed that a moral obligation was not a precondition of a successful application.[44] The concept of a moral obligation remained in evidence, however, and Borkowski noted that the courts were often reluctant to clarify its meaning.[45] There is some suggestion that care could be a relevant 'moral obligation', even though it is not necessary to demonstrate one. In *Re Jennings*, Henry LJ considered a hypothetical scenario in which an adult child gave up a university place 'to nurse the deceased through his long last illness'.[46] Henry LJ suggested that there would be a 'clear' moral obligation on the deceased to enable the applicant to take up that place.[47]

In *Espinosa v Bourke*, it was accepted that the applicant was owed a moral obligation by her deceased father because of the care that she provided for him (as well as because of a promise that he would leave certain property to her).[48] The first instance judge found that any obligation had been discharged by the deceased during his life through direct transfers and benefits in kind. On appeal, however, it was held that the judge had focused too heavily on the obligation question at the expense of considering the applicant's financial position. The Court of Appeal concentrated instead on the applicant's lack of earning capacity and the promise of provision that the father had made in allowing the applicant's appeal and making an order. The first instance judge was influenced by the fact that the applicant's commitment to her father dwindled, implying that a failure to care for a deceased parent may have a negative effect on a claim under the Act. Although the Court of Appeal made an order on the basis of her need and the promise made to her, Butler-Sloss LJ admitted that the daughter's eventual neglect of her father could have counted against any obligation owed to her because of her care.[49] Provision was nevertheless made despite the neglect and the fact that she found herself in necessitous circumstances due at least in part to a lifestyle of which the deceased clearly disapproved.

If disapproval was not fatal to claims under the Act, nor was estrangement. In *Gold v Curtis*, provision was made for an estranged daughter with mental health issues.[50] A need for maintenance was key, however: on the facts of *Re Jennings*, no obligation was found on the part of the deceased father in spite of the fact that he had failed to maintain the applicant (a 45-year-old successful businessman at the time of the father's death) during his minority.

As for the relationship between family provision and state benefits, courts were generally reluctant to attach a great deal of significance to the availability of state support for a family provision applicant, particularly in cases involving large estates.[51] In summarising

[43] 1975 Act, s 3(1)(d).
[44] *Re Hancock* (n 36).
[45] Borkowski (n 40).
[46] *Re Jennings (decd)* [1994] Ch 286 (CA) 300.
[47] ibid 300.
[48] *Espinosa v Bourke* (n 42).
[49] ibid 757.
[50] *Gold v Curtis* [2005] WTLR 673.
[51] See, eg *Re E, E v E* [1966] 1 WLR 709 (Ch); *Re Collins (decd)* [1990] Fam 56, 61–62 (Hollings J).

the courts' approach to claims by adult children before *Ilott*, Conway wrote that '[s]ince *Re Coventry*, much judicial time and effort has been expended on trying to formulate a workable and coherent set of universal principles to supplement the statutory framework for determining family provision claims by independent adult children', but '[t]he extent to which courts have succeeded in this objective is questionable'.[52] She was also of the view that 'there are no discernible trends in the value of any award relative to the value of the deceased's estate, and few attempts to rationalise the sum given to the claimant by the court'.[53]

III. THE FACTUAL BACKGROUND TO THE *ILOTT* CASE

Melita Jackson was born in 1934.[54] At 21, she married Thomas, who was killed in an industrial accident at the BBC (falling 600 feet from a broadcasting mast while not wearing a helmet)[55] just four years later while Melita was pregnant with their daughter, Heather. In 1978, at the age of 17, Heather left home to go and live with her boyfriend Nick Ilott at his parents' home. Heather did so without telling Melita, who disapproved of Nick because she thought that he would not make much of his life (apparently because of his parents' circumstances)[56] and that Heather was thus wasting her future. Melita was shocked and called the police. Heather was found at the Ilotts' home and refused to return to Melita.

Heather married Nick in 1983, again without telling Melita. She gave birth to A the following year, and set up home with Nick and A in a cottage in Ware[57] in Hertfordshire rented from a housing association. She subsequently gave birth to B in 1987, L in 1988, M in 1991 and E in 1996. At the time of Judge Million's decision, she and Nick lived in the same Hertfordshire house with the youngest four children. She had not done any paid work since A's birth, she and Nick having decided that she would be a stay-at-home mother. Having worked as a delivery driver, he developed a back problem and worked part-time as a non-speaking supporting actor in television and films at the time of the judgment. By the time of the 2014 High Court judgment, evidence (by way of anonymous letter) had emerged that Nick was offering 'spiritualist services', but he claimed not to profit from these and Parker J discounted the evidence.[58]

At the time of Judge Million's judgment, A was a care worker living away from home, B was living at home and working as a plumber's apprentice, and the younger three lived at home and were either in or seeking education. Heather and Nick's joint net annual income was put at around £15,000, over half of which came from tax credits, plus £5,000 in housing and council tax benefits. They were left with just over £14,000 after payment of rent and council tax, and 'lived modestly and within their means'.[59]

[52] Conway (n 39) 130.
[53] ibid 131.
[54] This summary is derived from Judge Million's judgment (n 6) unless otherwise stated.
[55] Weathers (n 4).
[56] ibid.
[57] ibid.
[58] *Ilott v Mitson* [2014] EWHC 542 (Fam), [2015] 1 FLR 291 [51].
[59] *Ilott v Mitson* (n 6) [48].

Heather and Melita attempted to reconcile over the years: first when Heather was pregnant with A until a few months after his birth, then between April and June 1994, and finally for six months between 1999 and 2000. Significantly, Melita made a will in 1984 (while she and Heather were on speaking terms) that excluded Heather. The ending of each short-lived reconciliation was characterised by bitterness and aggression.

In 2002, Melita made her last will. In it, she left a £5,000 legacy to the BBC Benevolent Fund[60] (which had apparently provided for her following Thomas's death)[61] and divided the residue between the Blue Cross, the Royal Society for the Protection of Birds and the Royal Society for the Prevention of Cruelty to Animals. She wrote a letter of wishes explaining her decision to exclude Heather from the will, referring to the 1978 separation and claiming that she had seen her daughter only twice since then, that Heather had made no effort to reconcile with her and that Heather had used 'lies and deceit'. Judge Million found that the letter contained 'many inaccuracies' and was 'unfairly critical' of Heather.[62] He also found that

> the overwhelming and longstanding reason why Mrs Jackson made no provision to her daughter was that she had left the home of her mother at the age of 17 … to go to and remain with a man of whom the mother disapproved.[63]

While Melita had asked for an apology and received one in both oral and written form, Judge Million was of the view that 'the only apology which would have satisfied Mrs Jackson is one in which Mrs Ilott in effect rejected her own husband'.[64]

Melita had no particular connection with the animal charities between which she had divided her residuary estate, or animal welfare or birdlife more generally, with Heather recalling having only a single pet dog while she was growing up and suspecting that Melita had benefited the charities 'to hurt [Heather] even more'.[65]

Melita died in 2004 at the age of 70, having lived alone since the death of her long-term companion in 1996. Her body was not discovered until several days after her death. Judge Million described her as 'lonely, isolated and reclusive' by the end of her life,[66] and the only mourners at her funeral were Heather, Nick, their five children, Melita's solicitor and one other person. Melita's net estate was valued at £486,000 in cash or liquid assets, described as 'significant … but not unusually large'.[67]

Heather claimed that at least some of the money represented by Melita's estate was inherited by Melita following Thomas's death, notwithstanding the fact that Melita claimed to have been left 'penniless'.[68] Heather described her motivation in bringing the 1975 Act claim as not being about the money per se, but about 'the principle' of accomplishing what '[her] late father would have wanted for the child he never lived to see'.[69]

[60] *Ilott v Mitson* [2015] EWCA Civ 797, [2016] 1 All ER 932 [2].
[61] Weathers (n 4).
[62] *Ilott v Mitson* (n 6) [41].
[63] ibid [42].
[64] ibid [43].
[65] Weathers (n 4).
[66] *Ilott v Mitson* (n 6) [45].
[67] ibid [56].
[68] Weathers (n 4).
[69] ibid.

The charities, meanwhile, accepted that their resources and needs were 'irrelevant',[70] a concession that was to be significant as the case proceeded through the courts.

IV. THE ROAD TO THE SUPREME COURT

A. Judge Million's Decision

Judge Million granted Heather's application and awarded her £50,000 out of the estate. Judge Million described Melita as owing Heather 'the ordinary family obligations towards her only child who was an independent adult',[71] albeit that Melita had 'gone out of her way' to tell Heather that 'she felt no responsibility towards her as a daughter'.[72] The judge rejected the suggestion that Heather could not complain about a lack of provision because she had 'thrown her lot' in with a man against her mother's wishes. On his analysis, '[a] daughter is entitled (indeed would be expected) to make a life with a partner of her choice and a family of her own', and 'would reasonably hope that a parent would accept such a choice and not blame her for it'.[73] While he accepted that Heather and Nick 'contributed to some of the later difficulties in effecting a sustained reconciliation',[74] he described Melita's reasoning and decision as 'capricious and unfair'[75] and 'harsh and unreasonable'.[76]

Following his application of the statutory factors in light of *Re Coventry* and *Espinosa v Bourke*, Judge Million held that an 'unreasonable result' had been produced by the will in that no provision was made in circumstances of 'some financial need'.[77] Judge Million accepted that Heather had 'some possibility in the future of obtaining part-time work', but was conscious that she lived in an 'isolated' village and had no driving licence.[78] At the same time, he was clear that Heather and Nick had no expectation of provision, which did not mean 'that the result is a reasonable one in the straightened [sic] financial circumstances of the family', but did mean 'that any provision now must be limited'.[79]

On the second stage, concerning what provision should be made for Heather, all parties were agreed that any award should take the form of a capitalised sum, albeit that Judge Million was conscious that such a sum 'must be based on income need'.[80] In response to inevitably conflicting submissions on the size, including some that would have involved an award exceeding the size of the estate and had not adequately taken account of the effect on benefits, Judge Million undertook a more 'rough and ready' approach.[81] Having taken account of the tax credits position, he regarded around £4,000

[70] *Ilott v Mitson* (n 6) [50].
[71] ibid [51].
[72] ibid [55].
[73] ibid [58].
[74] ibid [59].
[75] ibid.
[76] ibid [60].
[77] ibid [67].
[78] ibid [48].
[79] ibid [67].
[80] ibid [68].
[81] ibid [75].

as an 'indicated amount of maintenance that the government accepts as being needed currently to provide [Heather] with a reasonable, but basic, standard of living'.[82] With reference to the *Duxbury* tables used on divorce,[83] he then deduced that the amount needed to produce such an income would be around £69,000, and reduced it in light of the expectation that Heather should find some work to produce a sum of £50,000.

It is easy to see why the judge's conclusion and its relationship with Heather's benefits position was to become such an issue in subsequent proceedings. It is not immediately clear why he took account of the approximately £4,000 figure. On its own, this might suggest that he was intending to replace the relevant portion of Heather's income, yet it seems clear that he was intending not to affect her entitlements. That, however, leaves the question why he thought she should have double the government's 'indicated amount', though it may be that his objective was to ensure that the Act independently provided an accepted standard of living which the state could supplement, but without the need for the court to take into account the supplement.

B. The High Court in 2009

Heather appealed as to quantum (ie the second stage), prompting the charities to cross-appeal the finding that Melita's will had not made reasonable financial provision for her (the first stage).[84] The charities successfully convinced Eleanor King J that Judge Million had erred in law by asking the wrong question, because he had focused on whether Melita had acted unreasonably (which was the explicit judicial approach under the 1938 Act[85] but not the 1975 Act) rather than whether the result produced by the will was objectively unreasonable. Heather and Nick had not expected any provision, and Heather had apparently accepted that situation. Moreover, 'the single most relevant fact which determined the deceased's decision to exclude the daughter from her will was a breach of the most profound and enduring nature … from a time when the daughter was only 17 years old'.[86] Heather's circumstances were due to 'lifestyle choices', and there was no basis on which the family could look forward to a windfall.[87] A 'weighty factor' was required before an applicant with earning capacity could succeed and there was nothing in the ordinary obligations of a mother or the conduct of the parties that could constitute one.[88]

Eleanor King J held that in any event, Judge Million had erred in his balancing of the section 3 factors. He had overemphasised subjective reasons, failed to take a holistic approach to the factors and come 'perilously close to allowing necessitous circumstances to be determinative'.[89] In her view, 'the court was left with a filial relationship and necessitous circumstances with nothing more of sufficient cogency to drive a court to conclude

[82] ibid [79].
[83] Family Law Bar Association, *At A Glance 2007–08: Essential Tables for Financial Remedies* (London, Family Law Bar Association) Table 20.
[84] *H v Mitson* [2009] EWHC 3114 (Fam), [2010] 1 FLR 1613.
[85] Cretney (n 14) 497.
[86] *H v Mitson* (n 84) [61].
[87] ibid.
[88] ibid.
[89] ibid [64].

that, in all the circumstances of the case, no provision for the daughter was unreasonable provision'.[90] The charities' cross-appeal was allowed and Heather's appeal dismissed (without her submissions on quantum having been heard).

C. The Court of Appeal in 2011

Heather successfully appealed against Eleanor King J's decision.[91] In the Court of Appeal, Sir Nicholas Wall asserted that he did not base his decision 'on the ground that a claim under the Act can properly be used to relieve the State of the obligation to support an applicant'.[92] Similarly, on Arden LJ's analysis, '[t]he fact that the State makes provision for financial hardship does not mean that it is reasonable for a testatrix to make no provision for an adult child'.[93]

Sir Nicholas Wall held that he could not sustain Eleanor King J's criticism of the District Judge because Judge Million had explicitly asked whether the result was unreasonable. Black LJ agreed, although she acknowledged that he had also evaluated Melita's conduct earlier in his judgment. Moreover, Judge Million was not required to '"balance" the section 3 factors or to explain why the combination of factors under section 3 led him to the conclusion that no provision was unreasonable'.[94]

Sir Nicholas Wall directed that 'the appellant's appeal against the quantum of the district judge's decision be heard by a judge other than Eleanor King J'.[95] The Supreme Court then refused permission to appeal the Court of Appeal's conclusion.[96] Given the subsequent emphasis on testamentary freedom and the suggestion that Heather was somewhat fortunate in the Supreme Court's eventual judgment on quantum, one can perhaps detect a tinge of regret that permission to appeal on the first stage was refused.

Writing after the 2011 Court of Appeal decision, Conway opined that

> There is little doubt that the ... decision strengthens the idea of adult children being able to make a successful financial provision claim despite not having been financially dependent on their parent (even for many years), and raises questions as to what steps a testator can actually take to disinherit an adult child.[97]

She accused the court of 'merely pa[ying] lip service to the notion of testamentary freedom',[98] an issue that would rear its head again when the Court of Appeal was next to give judgment in the case. That said, it must also be borne in mind that, throughout the life of the 1975 Act, it has been a calculated risk to 'disinherit' children who might need maintenance in the future, and that the deceased's views and intentions have

[90] ibid [67].
[91] *Ilott v Mitson* [2011] EWCA Civ 346, [2012] 2 FLR 170.
[92] ibid [14].
[93] ibid [75].
[94] ibid [52].
[95] ibid [60].
[96] Supreme Court, 'Applications for Permission to Appeal Results June 2011' www.supremecourt.uk/docs/PTA-1106.pdf.
[97] Conway (n 39) 126.
[98] ibid.

always been somewhat relevant to, but obviously not conclusive of, the appropriate level of provision. *Ilott*, moreover, was by no means the most dramatic case in which provision has been made for an adult child. In *Re Land (decd)*,[99] for example, an adult son successfully claimed provision from his mother's estate notwithstanding his conviction for her gross negligent manslaughter and the resulting application of the forfeiture rule[100] to his share under her will (albeit that the case can be explained in part by the court's inability to modify the rule's application due to delay). Moreover, it has been seen that neither disapproval of lifestyle[101] nor estrangement[102] has inevitably prevented awards in previous cases.

D. The High Court in 2014

Despite the Court of Appeal's hope that a further hearing could in fact be avoided, Parker J gave judgment upholding Judge Million's conclusion in 2014.[103] Parker J rejected the argument that the sum paid to Melita on Thomas's death should be paid to Heather because it derived from Thomas, since there was 'no evidence to suggest that this sum was anything other than a payment to the deceased as widow'.[104] Judge Million's award was 'intended to provide the claimant with a windfall for her to spend as she liked in improving her circumstances'.[105] He had not been given the material with which to ascertain the precise effect on benefits, but Parker J had not been given it even then. It could not be said that the judge was wrong 'in taking the view that notwithstanding that the claimant and her husband and family lived in straightened circumstances, the fact they had done so for so many years did not justify an award which improved their circumstances',[106] which appears to accept that the award had no substantive effect. Nevertheless, Parker J opined that it could not be correct that 'because there will be no benefit to the claimant unless her housing need is met, the award must achieve that result', since that would render 'meaningless' Judge Million's conclusion that the lack of expectation tempered the award.[107]

E. The Court of Appeal in 2015

Heather then appealed Parker J's conclusion on quantum. Giving judgment on the case for the second time in the Court of Appeal, Arden LJ identified two 'fundamental errors' in Judge Million's approach.[108] The first was the fact that the judge stated that

[99] *Re Land (decd)* [2006] EWHC 2069 (Ch), [2007] 1 WLR 1009.
[100] Forfeiture Act 1982, s 1.
[101] *Espinosa v Bourke* (n 42).
[102] *Gold v Curtis* (n 50).
[103] *Ilott v Mitson* (n 58).
[104] ibid [41].
[105] ibid [51].
[106] ibid [52].
[107] ibid.
[108] *Ilott v Mitson* (n 60) [35].

the award should be 'limited' because of the applicant's lack of expectation of provision and her ability to live within her current means, but wrongly omitted to explain 'what the award might otherwise have been and to what extent it was limited by the matters in question'.[109] The second error was the judge's failure to verify what effect his award would have on the applicant's entitlement to state benefits, simply assuming that a large capital payment (even including the one he made) would disentitle the family to most, if not all, of their benefits.

In light of those perceived errors, the Court of Appeal proceeded to exercise the discretion afresh, considering the section 3 factors in relation to the facts as they stood at the time of its own judgment. In doing so, Arden LJ noted that the charities did not have any relevant resources or needs, and that anything they received from the estate was a windfall. In addition, they were not held to have any expectation of such a benefit, since Melita had had no involvement with them during her lifetime.

While Arden LJ accepted that Heather was an adult child living independently – a relevant factor meaning 'at a minimum' that the court was 'not concerned to provide her with an income that would fully support her needs'[110] – Arden LJ also agreed that Heather's current standard of living was not conclusive regarding the appropriate level of maintenance, and reaffirmed that an adult child did not need to show a moral obligation or other special circumstance in order to succeed. The absence of an expectation of inheritance on her part was not to be given 'much weight', since Arden LJ upheld Judge Million's finding that Heather 'was deprived of any expectation primarily because Melita had acted in an unreasonable, capricious and harsh way towards her only child'.[111]

In response to conflicting submissions from Heather and the charities on the weight that should be attached to Melita's testamentary intentions, Arden LJ concluded that Parliament had 'entrusted the courts with the power to ensure, in the case of even an adult child, that reasonable financial provision is made for maintenance only', and that this limitation itself gave appropriate weight to testamentary freedom at least in cases where the other claimants on the estate have no demonstrated need or expectation.[112] She later accepted, however, the need to balance claims on the estate 'fairly',[113] albeit surprisingly suggesting that the charities were 'not prejudiced' by a higher award.[114] Arden LJ refused to hold that the estrangement should eliminate or substantially diminish an appropriate award. There was no suggestion that Heather had wanted to be estranged from Melita, Heather's disapproved lifestyle choices had nevertheless allowed her to become a successful mother and homemaker, and fault for the estrangement was difficult to apportion and might even have been absent.

In evaluating Heather's needs and resources, Arden LJ noted the absence of any savings and her limited income and earning capacity, the latter being something that

[109] ibid.
[110] ibid [49].
[111] ibid [51](iii).
[112] ibid [51](v).
[113] ibid [60].
[114] ibid [61].

could only have diminished since Judge Million's original decision. Even including her state benefits, it was held that Heather's resources were 'at such a basic level that they outweigh the importance that would normally be attached to the fact that [she] is an adult child who had been living independently for so many years'.[115] Having earlier recognised that the size of the estate did not 'impinge' on the award sought,[116] and aiming to preserve the family's state benefits, Arden LJ ultimately concluded that Heather should receive £143,000 to enable her to purchase the housing association property, in addition to the reasonable costs of the purchase. Heather was also given an option to claim up to £20,000 as a capital sum from the estate, in order to provide 'a very small additional income to supplement her state benefits'.[117]

The Court of Appeal's judgment caused a stir in some quarters, not least to the Comment Editor of the *Daily Telegraph*, who wrote the day after the judgment that '[a]ll of a sudden, the judges are trampling on the deepest and darkest fabric of family life'.[118] Moreover, despite its interview with Heather considered earlier in this chapter (which may have saved her from some abuse), the *Daily Mail* also published a comment piece by Max Hastings, under the headline 'Who are judges to tell us who we can leave our money to in our wills!', in which he acknowledged the 'compassion' of the decision but intemperately attacked it as 'as yet another example of the mounting alienation between [lawyers] and the rest of humanity'.[119] Both the *Daily Telegraph* and *Daily Mail* columns conveniently omitted to mention the fact that, while one can legitimately query its exercise on particular facts, the judiciary's power was expressly conferred by Parliament via the 1975 Act. While it might reasonably be construed as an attack on the core principle of testamentary freedom, particularly if it limits the extent to which testamentary intentions should be specifically evaluated against reasonable financial provision, the 2015 decision stopped very far short of introducing the kind of 'forced heirship' associated with civil law jurisdictions.

While *Ilott* at this stage did not therefore represent a sea change in the law, the portion of the estate awarded to Heather was considerable (albeit that her need was relatively high) and the judgment provided pause for thought to solicitors advising clients wishing to exclude adult children from their wills, particularly in favour of non-natural persons such as charities. Whatever the complaints, the Law Commission's most recent report to consider the 1975 Act recommended no change in the approach to adult children and appeared to assume that any reform would be in the direction of facilitating increased rather than decreased provision for adult children in any event.[120] The charities, meanwhile, appealed to the Supreme Court.

[115] ibid [57].
[116] ibid [50].
[117] ibid [63].
[118] H de Quetteville, 'Belt Up Judges, I'll Disinherit the Kids if I Want' *The Telegraph* (London, 28 July 2015) www.telegraph.co.uk/lifestyle/11768612/Belt-up-judges-Ill-disinherit-the-kids-if-I-want.html.
[119] M Hastings, 'Who Are Judges to Tell Us Who We Can Leave Our Money to in Our Wills!' *Daily Mail* (London, 29 July 2015) www.dailymail.co.uk/debate/article-3178080/MAX-HASTINGS-judges-tell-leave-money-wills.html.
[120] Law Commission, *Intestacy and Family Provision Claims on Death* (Law Com No 331, 2011) [6.2]–[6.26].

V. THE SUPREME COURT'S DECISION

A. Lord Hughes's Main Judgment

The Supreme Court unanimously allowed the charities' appeal, restoring Judge Million's original £50,000 order. Lord Hughes (with whose main judgment all six other Justices agreed) accepted that '[s]ome of the factors inevitably dealt with in [the Supreme Court's] judgment may apply also to types of case other than those of adult children living separately from the deceased', but he was clear that 'there is no occasion for this court to attempt to meet every difficulty to which claims for family provision may give rise'.[121]

Lord Hughes reasserted the centrality of testamentary freedom in English law. He emphasised the importance of the 1975 Act's limitation to 'reasonable financial provision' for maintenance for non-spouse/civil partner applicants, reflecting what was described as a 'deliberate legislative decision' that was 'important'.[122] He also held that a need for maintenance was a necessary but not sufficient condition for a successful claim.

The Supreme Court considered the maintenance standard at some length. Lord Hughes approved previous case law in holding that maintenance could not 'extend to any or every thing which it would be desirable for the claimant to have',[123] but was not limited to 'subsistence' either.[124] Needs would not necessarily be the measure of what is provided by the court if it has been concluded that reasonable financial provision has not been made by the will and/or the intestacy rules: the claims of others, and importantly the relationship between the claimant and the deceased, could justifiably limit the size of the award.

Lord Hughes also confirmed that the focus of the correct test under the 1975 Act is not on the behaviour of the testatrix, but opined the reasonableness of her decision (not always easily distinguishable from that of a result) may still be a significant consideration. This is also true of the extent of any 'moral claim', which will often be at the centre of the decision under the 1975 Act, particularly in claims by adult children capable of living independently, even if that is not a 'sine qua non'.[125] While Lord Hughes did not reject the traditional two-stage approach to the Act, he did say that in many cases 'exactly the same conclusions will both answer the question whether reasonable financial provision has been made for the claimant and identify what that financial provision should be'.[126]

The Supreme Court unanimously held that Judge Million had not made either error alleged by the Court of Appeal. On the first (that he did not explain what the award would have been had it not been 'limited'), the Act required 'a single assessment … of what reasonable financial provision should be made in all the circumstances of the case'.[127] It did not require the judge 'to fix some hypothetical standard of reasonable

[121] *Ilott v The Blue Cross* (n 2) [3].
[122] ibid [13].
[123] ibid [14].
[124] ibid [15].
[125] ibid [20].
[126] ibid [24].
[127] ibid [34].

provision and then either add to it, or discount from it … for variable factors'.[128] The two dominant factors in the case were the estrangement and Heather's straitened circumstances, and Lord Hughes even suggested that it would have been legitimate for the judge to have concluded that it was entirely reasonable for no provision to be made at all in the will because of the estrangement (a matter on which leave to appeal had of course been refused by the Supreme Court in 2011). The judge was therefore definitely able to say that 'what reasonable provision would be was coloured by the nature of the relationship between mother and daughter'.[129] The Court of Appeal's order, by contrast, had given 'little if any weight' to the length of the estrangement between the protagonists.[130]

The Supreme Court was also concerned that again 'little if any weight' had been given by the Court of Appeal's order to Melita's very clear wishes.[131] It was incorrect to say that the charities' lack of any expectation of benefit was on a par with Heather's lack of any similar expectation. They were the beneficiaries under Melita's will, and were not required to justify their claim to the estate with reference to needs in the same way that Heather did. The Court of Appeal had erred in suggesting that they were not prejudiced by a higher award to Heather because they could not plead human needs, which is significant in light of their concession at trial that their needs and resources were irrelevant. Clearly the benefit to an estate beneficiary is inherently reduced by an order under the 1975 Act. The Supreme Court was sympathetic to the general position of charities in this context, emphasising that they 'depend heavily on testamentary bequests for their work, which is by definition of public benefit and in many cases will be for demonstrably humanitarian purposes'.[132] One study indeed suggests that over 25 per cent of charitable donations come from wills.[133] The Supreme Court also considered it erroneous to suggest that the court had no need to give specific consideration to Melita's wishes because Parliament had limited claims under the 1975 Act to particular circumstances. Those wishes were relevant factors and fell to be considered alongside the others.

On the second alleged error, that Judge Million had been unaware of the effect of his order on Heather's entitlement to benefits, the Supreme Court held that Judge Million had in fact addressed the impact on benefits. Lord Hughes regarded the essence of the Court of Appeal's criticism to be that the judge's order would have little or no value to Heather because of the impact on her benefits. He, however, held that if Heather spent the £50,000 in a particular way, that impact would be minimised. In fact, Lord Hughes suggested that the Court of Appeal had somewhat ironically given insufficient attention to the impact of its own order on Heather's benefits position. That said, Lady Hale was prepared to accept that the Court of Appeal's order was 'benefits-efficient' from both Heather and the public's point of view.[134]

The conclusion that Judge Million had made neither alleged error was sufficient to dispose of the case: the £50,000 award met many of Heather's needs for maintenance,

[128] ibid.
[129] ibid [35].
[130] ibid [46].
[131] ibid.
[132] ibid [46].
[133] nfpSynergy, 'Facts and Figures: Legacies for Charities' (London, nfpSynergy, 2017).
[134] *Ilott v The Blue Cross* (n 2) [65].

allowing her to 'buy much needed household goods and have a family holiday',[135] and should be restored. These suggested uses for the money may not obviously be consistent with Judge Million's calculations, which were based on a comprehensive (albeit basic) standard of living. On Lord Hughes's analysis, however, it was 'a central feature of Mrs Ilott's financial position that although the family could manage – just – on its income, this was at the cost of being unable to maintain the ordinary domestic equipment on which every household depends'.[136] He also held that, although Judge Million had taken into account what the government regarded as a minimum level of income, 'he did not make his award on this basis',[137] and produced an approximated award reflecting the fact that Heather's needs exceeded driving lessons and a small amount of capital.

Even if housing provision had been appropriate, Lord Hughes held that a life interest would have been preferable to capital, even though the parties had agreed at trial that any award should take the form of capitalised maintenance. While there is no reason why housing cannot be maintenance in some cases, Lord Hughes emphasised that the overall power is to provide for maintenance and that housing is more likely to be provided by way of a life interest rather than a capital sum.

Lord Hughes appeared to approve the relevance of care to 1975 Act cases. He considered a hypothetical contrasting case to *Ilott* involving a

> claimant [who was] a child of the deceased who had remained exceptionally and confidentially close to her mother throughout, had supported and nurtured her in her old age at some cost in time and money to herself, and … had been promised many times that she would be looked after in the will.

While 'adhering to the concept of maintenance', he held that 'a judge ought in such circumstances to attach importance to the closeness of the relationship in arriving at his assessment of what reasonable financial provision requires'.[138] That said, he was also anxious that 'care must be taken to avoid making awards under the 1975 Act primarily rewards for good behaviour on the part of the claimant or penalties for bad on the part of the deceased'.[139]

B. Lady Hale's Powerful Supplement

Lady Hale then gave a striking supplementary judgment, with which Lords Wilson and Kerr agreed. As has been seen, she observed that *Ilott* raised 'some profound questions about the nature of family obligations, the relationship between family obligations and the state, and the relationship between the freedom of property owners to dispose of their property as they see fit and their duty to fulfil their family obligations', claiming that 'none [of those questions are] answered by the legislation which [the Supreme Court] had to apply'.[140] It may be true that the questions are not conclusively resolved

[135] ibid [66] (Lady Hale).
[136] ibid [40].
[137] ibid [43].
[138] ibid [35].
[139] ibid [47].
[140] ibid [49].

on the face of the 1975 Act, but the Supreme Court did manage to resolve the case. In any event, Lady Hale criticised 'the unsatisfactory state of the present law' for 'giving … no guidance as to the factors to be taken into account in deciding whether an adult child is deserving or undeserving of reasonable maintenance', particularly in light of the range of public views on the point.[141] She took the unusual step of expressing 'regret that the Law Commission did not reconsider the fundamental principles underlying such claims when last they dealt with this topic in 2011'.[142] It is somewhat ironic that, with her family law background, Lady Hale is entirely accustomed to applying, and, indeed, giving authoritative guidance on,[143] section 25 of the Matrimonial Causes Act 1973, whose only remotely clear 'answer' is that the welfare of minor children of the family should be given first consideration in relief on divorce.[144] It is clear from her judgment, however, that she regarded the question of maintaining spouses and that of maintaining children as significantly different.

C. Implications

The end result will be a relief for the charities, who took a financial and reputational risk in fighting the case all the way to the Supreme Court, which gave judgment well over 12 years after Melita's death. The charities did so largely on principle because of the possible wide impact of the Court of Appeal's approach. The decision will also be welcomed by many private client practitioners and those who support the idea that property rights extend to control on death and that able-bodied adult children should not be able to disrupt testamentary intentions.

Some of the clearly contestable elements of the Court of Appeal's judgment, such as the suggestion that the charities were not prejudiced by a higher award to Heather, have been satisfactorily resolved. But the Supreme Court's decision may itself be questioned in some respects. There would arguably be little point in the 1975 Act's application to non-spouse/civil partnership cases if it were not able to raise a claimant's standard of living reasonably significantly beyond what is available from state benefits. Otherwise, the Act would simply become a means for the state to save money rather than genuinely assisting those expressly listed as potential applicants, the money-saving potential of the Family Protection Act 1955 having been expressly recognised by the legislature in New Zealand.[145] On the basis that the English Act is aimed at improving living standards beyond benefits, Heather had a need for maintenance by the standards of many people, and since the courts are often reluctant to consider the conduct regarding the relationships of the protagonists in intra-family disputes, as Lord Hughes recognised, it could

[141] ibid [66].

[142] ibid.

[143] See, in particular, *Miller v Miller; McFarlane v McFarlane* [2006] UKHL 24, [2006] 2 AC 618.

[144] Matrimonial Causes Act 1973, s 25(1).

[145] Under the Social Security Act 2018, s 203, where an applicant for a benefit 'has a tenable claim under the Family Protection Act 1955 for a share of or provision out of the estate of a deceased relative' and 'has failed to take reasonable steps to advance that claim', the relevant body 'may refuse to grant the benefit, grant it at a reduced rate, or cancel a benefit already granted'. *cf*, eg, the more general (English) Housing Benefit Regulations SI 2006/213 r 49(2).

be seen as surprising for the Supreme Court to accept that her claim should be quite so limited with reference to the relationship between mother and daughter. That said, if it is arguable that positive contributions and conduct should be given some recognition within the limitations of maintenance,[146] a general idea that Lord Hughes appeared cautiously to approve, that is consistent with his reasoning on the converse case, where parent and child have not been close at all.

The debate over the proper balance between testamentary freedom and provision for family members will inevitably continue. For now, it seems as though the 'testamentary freedom' camp are in a stronger position than they were before the Supreme Court's decision. But it should be remembered that Heather Ilott still went away with something despite being left out of her mother's will (even if similar future claimants may not be so lucky and the details of an arrangement between her and the charities are not public), and it will be interesting to see whether Lady Hale's plea for reform is heeded.

D. Academic Reaction

On Douglas's analysis, the Supreme Court's decision 'will surely give pause to those who might be planning a challenge to wills of this kind; one may expect them now to face a harder task in satisfying the court that the deceased's wishes should be overridden'.[147] Conway describes the case as one where 'the right outcome … [was] more or less reached on the facts', but asserts that 'important issues remain'.[148] In her view, '[f]or all the attention it attracted, *Ilott* was an atypical case, [such] that few other applications will replicate this particular scenario'.[149] She finds it 'hard to disagree with the Supreme Court's assessment of the judgment below and the reasons for overturning it', since both estrangement and benefits were part of the factual matrix that the District Judge supportably took into account.[150]

Conway regards the Supreme Court's extensive analysis of the 1975 Act as 'the more pertinent aspects of the judgment … likely to influence future claims under the Act'.[151] On her analysis, while 'the Court of Appeal judgments … were seen as turning points, signifying that adult children who had been disinherited (whether wholly or partly) could succeed and be given a significant award, despite not having been financially reliant on their dead parent', 'the Supreme Court ruling suggests otherwise, and that independent adult children who lack "reasonable financial provision" will probably receive much less generous awards than the Court of Appeal gave Heather Ilott'.[152] In doing so, she considers that the Supreme Court 'probably return[ed] the law to its pre-*Ilott* position'.[153]

[146] See, eg B Sloan, *Informal Carers and Private Law* (Oxford, Hart Publishing, 2013) ch 5.
[147] G Douglas, 'Inheritance: Provision for Family and Dependants' [2017] *Family Law* 494, 496.
[148] H Conway, 'Rights versus Responsibilities: Adult Children, Parental Wealth and Contested Wills' (2017) 39 *Journal of Social Welfare and Family Law* 494, 494.
[149] H Conway, 'Testamentary Freedom, Family Obligation and the *Ilott* Legacy' [2017] *Conveyancer and Property Lawyer* 372, 377.
[150] ibid 375.
[151] ibid.
[152] Conway (n 148) 496.
[153] Conway (n 149) 378.

It 'reassures will-makers that, while their wishes may not always be respected, they now have much more prominence in family provision claims'.[154] Conversely, 'independent adult children who have been disinherited by their parents will take little comfort from the Supreme Court ruling, and lawyers advising them should downgrade the chances of success or caution about more modest awards'.[155] As Probert puts it 'assessing what was said – and what was not said – reveals a very strong preference for individuals being able to exercise their economic power beyond the grave'.[156] She opines, however, that 'the case offers little by way of specific guidance for future litigants, even where the facts are substantially similar', and (perhaps more surprisingly) that '[i]t also makes it very difficult even to identify the crucial factors in *Ilott* itself'.[157]

Despite broadly supporting the result, Conway admits that:

> One might question whether, in an era of reduced public spending and ongoing welfare reforms, Melita Jackson should have been able to leave an estate worth almost half a million pounds to three animal welfare charities while her daughter and her family survived almost exclusively on benefits and a small sum of savings.

She does, however, also say that '[r]eplacing state provision with estate provision in cases such as these would be extremely controversial, raising complex issues of law and social policy', and it is unclear whether a debate on the matter will be had.[158]

E. The Influence of *Ilott* on Subsequent Cases

The Supreme Court's decision in *Ilott* has already been cited by the Court of Appeal in *Lewis v Warner*,[159] by the High Court in *Re Wynford Hodge*,[160] *Ball v Ball*,[161] *Banfield v Campbell*,[162] *Ubbi v Ubbi*[163] and *Wellesley v Earl Cowley*,[164] by County Courts in *Re Nahajec*[165] and *Miles v Miles*,[166] and by the Family Court in *M v M*.[167] The last decision did not concern the 1975 Act at all: *M* was an ancillary relief on a divorce case in which *Ilott* was cited to highlight the difference between an 'evaluative' and a 'discretionary' determination.[168]

Lewis v Warner involved a claim by a former cohabitant who was wealthy but sought the ability via the 1975 Act to buy the property that he had shared with the deceased for full valuable consideration, arguing that he needed to remain there because of his

[154] ibid 379.
[155] ibid.
[156] Probert (n 17) 551.
[157] ibid 552.
[158] Conway (n 148) 496.
[159] *Lewis v Warner* [2017] EWCA Civ 2182, [2018] 2 WLR 1205.
[160] *Re Wynford Hodge* [2018] EWHC 688 (Ch).
[161] *Ball v Ball* [2017] EWHC 1750 (Ch), [2017] WTLR 891.
[162] *Banfield v Campbell* [2018] EWHC 1943 (Ch).
[163] *Ubbi v Ubbi* [2018] EWHC 1396 (Ch).
[164] *Wellesley v Earl Cowley* [2019] EWHC 11 (Ch).
[165] *Re Nahajec* [2017] EW Misc 11 (CC).
[166] *Miles v Miles* [2018] WTLR 1347 (CC).
[167] *M v M* [2017] EWFC 25, [2018] 1 FLR 313.
[168] ibid [12] (Mostyn J).

age and disability. Counsel for the deceased's daughter relied on *Ilott* to submit that the applicant 'had failed to advance a case that he *needed* any financial provision for his maintenance out of the deceased's estate (being significantly financially better off than the deceased, and able to afford alternative accommodation)'.[169] Significantly for present purposes, Sir Geoffrey Vos said that '[i]t is not actually necessary to look behind *Ilott*' in elucidating the relevant case law, 'because the relevant preceding cases are all referred to within Lord Hughes's seminal judgment'.[170] Similarly, in *Ball v Ball* it was said that *Espinosa* does not add anything to *Ilott*.[171] In *Lewis*, lengthy passages were said to '[be] directly relevant to what this court has to decide' and 'provide the legal background without the need to trawl through the pre-existing authorities'.[172] There were said to be 'clear indications' in Lord Hughes's judgment that 'the broad concept of "maintenance" … can extend to the provision of a house in which the applicant can live, albeit that it might most often be provided by way of a life interest'.[173] Mindful of *Ilott*'s approach to needs, moral obligations and the appellate jurisdiction, the Court of Appeal upheld the first instance decision that the applicant should be allowed to purchase the property. Sir Geoffrey's remarks were themselves cited in *Banfield v Campbell* in the course of granting the claimant a life interest in half the sale proceeds of his former partner's home for the purposes of providing alternative accommodation (with only a limited lump sum kept available in case adaptation was required). In *Re Wynford Hodge* it was said that *Ilott* 'emphasised that the statutory power is to provide maintenance, not to confer capital',[174] albeit that on the facts of the case the care needs of the applicant made capital provision reasonable. In *Re Nahajec* the facts were said to be very similar to *Ilott* and extensive reference was made to it.[175] In allowing the claim, the judge was adamant that he had done so not simply because *Ilott* had done so, but did note that 'in *Ilott* the claimant could meet her outgoings from her own resources but nevertheless it was considered that that did not disqualify her from an award'.[176] The judge noted that he was awarding the claimant in *Re Nahajec* 11.3 per cent of the net estate, which was within 1 per cent of the 10.3 per cent awarded to Heather.[177] In *Ubbi v Ubbi*, Master Shuman recognised *Ilott*'s emphasis on testamentary freedom and the limitations of maintenance, but also that maintenance was not limited to subsistence in making provision for minor children born after their father's last will was made. *Ball v Ball*, by contrast, is an example of a claim by estranged adult children failing following *Ilott* because the estate was small, the applicants' needs were not significantly different from those of the will beneficiaries and neither the deceased's conduct nor her husband's sexual abuse of the claimants created a moral obligation. Somewhat similarly, a £20,000 legacy was said to be reasonable in the context of 35-year estrangement despite a large estate and reliance on benefits in

[169] *Lewis v Warner* (n 159) [3].
[170] ibid [5].
[171] *Ball v Ball* (n 161).
[172] ibid [22].
[173] ibid [25].
[174] *Re Wynford Hodge* (n 160) [36].
[175] *Re Nahajec* (n 165).
[176] ibid [100].
[177] ibid [107].

Wellesley v Earl Cowley, with the judge adopting a single determination approach to the Act. In *Miles v Miles*, moreover, Judge Farquhar invoked *Ilott* in holding that the District Judge below had given insufficient weight to the testator's wishes, and reduced the quantum for his separated widow.

Aside from case law per se, the Law Commission cited *Ilott* in discussing the relationship between mutual wills and the 1975 Act in its Consultation Paper on wills, noting that Lady Hale 'was critical of the lack of guidance provided in the statute as to how the court should deal with claims for financial provision'.[178] Internationally, *Ilott* was widely cited in the South Australian Law Reform Institute's recent report on family provision.[179]

It is arguable that in none of these instances did *Ilott* make a fundamental difference to the matter under discussion. But it is plausible to argue that *Ilott* has become the 'go-to' authority under the 1975 Act (even in cases not involving children), and that its influence has already extended beyond that Act.

VI. CONCLUSION

On what basis might *Ilott* be described as a 'landmark' case, particularly given the short time between the Supreme Court handing down its judgment and this chapter being written? The fact that it received quite so much judicial consideration over so many years is surely a key factor. There is also the fact that it was the first substantive consideration at the highest judicial level of the 1975 Act (more than 40 years after its enactment), and it may remain the only such example for some time. This is surely significant, even if *Ilott*'s importance might have been greater still had the Supreme Court granted the charities permission to appeal the threshold stage in 2011.

More substantively, *Ilott* may not have broken entirely new ground, but it does confirm some vitally important principles both in respect of claims by adult children and under the 1975 Act generally. Conway has argued explicitly that '[t]he Supreme Court ruling in *Ilott* is not a landmark one in the sense of fundamentally altering the law on family provision', but that 'it is an important one in terms of analysing the 1975 Act and its operation, and emphasising some core principles'.[180] These include: that 'maintenance' can be provided even where it is literally possible for an applicant to live without it, and that it can improve an applicant's situation beyond what is available from state benefits (even if the latter issue is crying out for further clarification); that a moral obligation or claim is not a required feature of a claim by an adult child; that testamentary freedom is an important value that should be given specific consideration by a judge deciding a 1975 Act claim; that non-human entities are not to be prejudiced by the Act merely because they do not have needs that are comparable to those of humans; that care on the one hand and estrangement on the other are both relevant but not decisive; that the absence of any

[178] Law Commission, *Making A Will* (Law Com 231, 2017) [12.42] fn 54.

[179] South Australian Law Reform Institute, '"Distinguishing between the Deserving and the Undeserving": Family Provision Laws in South Australia' (Report 9 Adelaide, South Australian Law Reform Institute, 2017).

[180] Conway (n 149) 379.

expectation of provision is not necessarily fatal; and that a life interest is generally to be preferred to capital housing provision under the Act.

Moreover, if the true test is that people keep on talking about *Ilott*,[181] the level of media coverage and the likely impact of *Ilott* on relevant textbook chapters[182] might be sufficient in themselves to qualify it as a 'landmark' case. There is also a possibility that Lady Hale's plea for reform will be heeded and that *Ilott* will herald the beginning of a new phase in the life of the 1975 Act. Whether or not this is a realistic prospect, it seems highly likely that *Ilott* will be cited and discussed for decades to come.

[181] J Snape and D de Cogan, 'Introduction: On the Significance of Revenue Cases' in J Snape and D de Cogan (eds), *Landmark Cases in Revenue Law* (Oxford, Hart Publishing, 2019) 10–15.

[182] See already A Learmonth et al, *Williams, Mortimer & Sunnucks – Executors, Administrators and Probate*, 21st edn (London, Sweet & Maxwell, 2018) pt 8.

18

S and S (2005): Compulsory Portion and Solidarity between Generations in Civil Law[1]

WALTER PINTENS

I. THE CIVIL LAW APPROACH

ALTHOUGH, BEING UNDER the influence of Roman law, testamentary freedom is highly valued in civil law, this liberal approach is limited in almost all civil law jurisdictions by a child's compulsory portion.[2] This portion is a part of the statutory portion and is calculated on the basis of a fictive mass composed by the assets the deceased left at his or her death, and by the donations during his or her lifetime.[3] In most of these systems, such as those in Austria (Article 765 of the ABGB), Belgium (Article 915, paragraph 1 of the Civil Code (CC)), the Czech Republic (Article 479 CC), Germany (§ 2303, paragraph 1 of the BGB), Greece (Article 1825 CC), Hungary (Article 665 CC), Sweden (Chapter 7, § 1 of the Inheritance Code) and Switzerland (Article 471 of the ZGB), the children's compulsory portion is fixed at one-half of their statutory portion. This latter portion applies where a person dies without leaving a will or leaving only a partial will. In Norway the compulsory portion is fixed at two-thirds (but with a limit) (§ 29 of the Inheritance Act). In Spain the compulsory portion (*legítima*)

[1] This chapter is largely inspired by my following publications: W Pintens, 'Die Europäisierung des Erbrechts' [2001] *Zeitschrift für Europäisches Privatrecht* 628ff; W Pintens and S Seyns, 'Compulsory Portion and Solidarity between Generations in German Law' in C Castelein, R Foqué and A Verbeke (eds), *Imperative Inheritance Law in a Late-Modern Society* (Antwerp, Intersentia, 2009) 167ff; W Pintens, 'Need and Opportunity of Convergence in European Succession Laws' in M Anderson and E Arroyo i Amayuelas (eds), *The Law of Succession: Testamentary Freedom. European Perspective* (Groningen, Europa Law Publishing, 2011) 3ff; W Pintens, 'Tendencies in European Succession Law' in T Frantzen (ed), *Inheritance Law – Challenges and Reform* (Berlin, Wissenschafts-Verlag, 2013); W Pintens, 'Public Policy in Succession Matters' in B Hess, E Jayme and H-P Mansel (eds), *Europa als Rechts- und Lebensraum. Liber Amicorum für Christian Kohler zum 75. Geburtstag* (Bielefeld, Gieseking, 2018) 393ff.

[2] Some of the very few exceptions can be found in the law of Navarre and the Fuero of Ayala applicable to a part of the province of Alava in the Basque Country. See S Camara Lapuente, 'Freedom of Testation, Legal Inheritance Rights and Public Order under Spanish Law' in Anderson and Arroyo i Amayuelas (n 1) 271ff. In several legal systems holders of the compulsory portion are not only the descendants but also the parents, the surviving spouse and the registered partner of the testator.

[3] Some legal systems exclude the donations to a certain extent (Germany) or completely (Denmark, Norway).

is also fixed at two-thirds of the estate, but the testator can differentiate between his children.[4] The children are entitled to one-third in equal shares (*legítima estricta*), but the testator can freely dispose of the other third in favour of some of his or her children (*mejora*) (art 806). In Catalonia (Article 451-5 CC) and Denmark (with a limit) (§ 5, paragraph 1 of the Inheritance Act), where more emphasis is put on private autonomy and freedom of testation, the portion is only one-quarter of the estate (Article 451-5). In other legal systems the portion depends upon the number of children: in France it is fixed at one-half if the deceased has left one child, at two-thirds if he or she has left two children and at three-quarters if he or she has left three or more children (Article 913); in Portugal, the portion is fixed at one-half when there is one child, and at two-thirds when there are two or more children (Article 2159). In both models, however, the compulsory portion is independent of the size of the estate. Only in Norway and Denmark has a limitation been introduced. As early as 1918 the Norwegian *Lex Michelsen* restricted the compulsory portion, which is two-thirds of the estate, to 1,000,000 crowns per child (§ 29 of the Inheritance Act).[5] In Denmark, where the compulsory portion is only one-quarter of the estate, the testator can restrict it to 1,000,000 crowns per child (§ 5 of the Inheritance Act).[6]

The compulsory portion traditionally found its roots in the notion of solidarity between generations.[7] This solidarity implied that specific heirs had the right not to be left uncared for. The compulsory portion performed a maintenance function. It provided the heir with a certain standard of living. Increases in life expectancy have vitiated these rationales. Today children inherit at a later age, at a time when they have often achieved an elevated standard of living and have often accumulated assets through their own labour.[8] However, we must not overlook the fact that in bad economic times children may also be in a difficult position; they may face a reduction in purchasing power, high social dues and taxes, or even unemployment. That said, viewed in general, the law of succession no longer provides a standard of living, but rather mostly improves the standard at a time when it is no longer necessary. The compulsory portion therefore no longer has a maintenance function and can thus no longer be viewed as an extension of the parental obligation to provide for their children. Parents accomplish their obligations to provide for their children through the financing of their education. The wealth of these children therefore no longer lies in their future inheritance, but rather in their academic or other achievements. Increasing wealth has stimulated discussions about the compulsory portion even more.[9]

In view of these sociological developments, the question of whether or not a testator, who was able to deal freely with his estate during his lifetime, should face restrictions in

[4] See E Arroyo i Amayuelas, 'Pflichtteilsrecht in Spanien' in A Röthel (ed), *Reformfragen des Pflichtteilsrechts* (Cologne, Carl Heymanns Verlag, 2007) 262ff; Camara Lapuente (n 2) 273ff.

[5] See P Lødrup, 'Pflichtteilsrecht in Norwegen und in den nordischen Staaten' in Röthel (n 4) 237ff; P Hambro, 'The Norwegian Approach to Forced Share, the Surviving Spouse's Position and Irrevocable Wills' in Anderson and Arroyo i Amayuelas (n 1) 232ff.

[6] See G Ring and L Olsen-Ring, 'Dänemark' in R Süβ (ed), *Erbrecht in Europa*, 3rd edn (Bonn, *Zeitschrift für die Steuer- und Erbrechtspraxis* Verlag, 2015) 451.

[7] Pintens, 'Tendencies in European Succession Law' (n 1) 15ff.

[8] See J Beckert, 'Familiäre Solidarität und die Pluralität moderner Lebensformen Eine gesellschaftstheoretische Perspektive auf das Pflichtteilsrecht'in Röthel (n 4) 4ff; R Nave-Herz, 'Erbengenerationen in Zahlen' in Röthel (n 4) 23ff.

[9] T Pikety, *Le capital au XXIe siècle* (Paris, Ed Du Seuil, 2013) 599ff.

his freedom to make a will has been debated in many European legal systems.[10] If there are dependent heirs at the time of the testator's death who have to rely on the inheritance for support, then a compulsory portion is not necessary to solve this problem; a maintenance claim could provide a remedy. Only in some civil law jurisdictions need plays a role, and then only to a certain extent. In Lithuania, the compulsory portion is only attributed in case of need (Article 5.20 CC). In Polish law, where the compulsory portion is fixed at one-half of the statutory portion, the compulsory portion increases to two-thirds of the statutory portion if the children are minors or permanently unable to work (Article 999, § 1 CC). However, in general, the debates have been in vain: the compulsory portion has been maintained, as will be explained with the example of Germany.

II. *S AND S*: THE COMPULSORY PORTION UNDER CONSTITUTIONAL REVIEW

A. A Constitutional Debate

Germany is an example of a legal system with a very strong protection of the compulsory portion.[11]

The German constitution, the Grundgesetz (GG) of 1949, has exercised a huge influence on inheritance law. Article 14, paragraph 1 GG safeguards the law and the right of succession, together with the right of ownership. By doing so, this article emphasises the ties between those two rights and underlines that the right of ownership and the right of succession are two fundamental basic elements of the social and economic order.

Besides the subjective right to inherit, the constitution also safeguards the law of succession as a legal institution (*Institutsgarantie*).[12] This means that the legislator needs to respect the fundamental content of the law of succession, as it is incorporated in the BGB (Article 19, paragraph 2 GG). According to the prevailing view, the constitution protects both testamentary freedom (*Testierfreiheit*) and the family character of succession (*Verwandtenerbrecht*) as fundamental elements of the law of succession. The former characteristic is the result of the right of ownership guaranteed by the constitution; the latter is the result of the protection of marriage and family (Article 6, paragraph 1 GG), from which it is derived that the children are entitled to claim an inviolable right upon a part of the estate of their parents.[13] Consequently, the legal order needs to observe this constitutional compromise between testamentary freedom and family succession. The family character of the law of succession implies more than a claim to maintenance of the heir in need. It means that the freedom to dispose by will needs to be restricted

[10] See, eg the Netherlands: M Van Mourik, 'De legitieme portie: weg ermee' (1991) 6018 *Weekblad voor privaatrecht, notariaat en registratie* 621.

[11] See Pintens and Seyns (n 1) 169ff.

[12] K Lange in *Münchener Kommentar zum Bürgerlichen Gesetzbuch*, 7th edn (Munich, Beck, 2017) § 2303, no 3ff.

[13] Minority legal doctrine advocates that the compulsory portion is only protected by Art 14, para 1 GG, whereby Art 6, para 1 GG exercises a certain influence on the interpretation of Art 14. Another doctrine favours Art 6 as the only applicable article because implementing Art 14 would mean that the same article protects both the testamentary freedom and the compulsory portion. See P Badura, 'Erbrecht, Testierfreiheit und Schutz der Familie' in Röthel (n 4); H Lange and K Kuchinke, *Erbrecht*, 5th edn (Munich, Beck, 2001) 25ff and 872ff.

by a compulsory portion allocated to the descendants, the parents, the spouse and the registered partner. The way the legislator needs to organise the compulsory portion cannot be derived from the constitution. It is open to the legislator to grant the forced heir a compulsory portion in kind or only one in value.[14] The extent of the compulsory portion has not been laid down by the constitution either. Nevertheless, the legislator's general duty to warrant forced heirs an appropriate share in the estate can be derived from the constitution.

Even so, German legal scholars started a debate on the compulsory portion.[15] However, the questions were mostly formulated from a social policy perspective. The constitutionality of the compulsory portion as such was not doubted.[16] Despite all sociological changes, the argument of the solidarity between generations remained decisive in defending the compulsory portion.[17]

In an earlier case the Bundesverfassungsgericht, the German Constitutional Court, had to decide on a constitutional complaint (*Verfassungsbeschwerde*) seeking a judgment that the entire law governing the compulsory portion was unconstitutional. In the claimant's opinion, limitations of testamentary freedom would no longer be justifiable since the maintenance function of the compulsory portion had become out of date due to demographic developments. In view of the previous case law from the Bundesverfassungsgericht, it was hardly to be expected that the complaint would succeed completely. As it turned out, the complaint was not accepted for judgment as the requirements of § 93a, paragraph 2 BVerfGG were not met, since the complaint was not of fundamental importance, nor had the complaint any prospect of succeeding.[18]

The judgment is nevertheless of importance. It affirms the freedom to make a will as a guaranteed individual right and as a definitive element of the law of succession, as established by Article 14, paragraph 1, section 1 GG. In addition to this fundamental content of the law of succession, its family character imposed by Article 6, paragraph 1 GG was underlined as well. According to article 14, paragraph 1, section 2 GG it is the duty of the legislator to prescribe the content and boundaries of the law of succession, for which he has a discretionary power. However, the compulsory portion limits the testamentary freedom. Overall, this judgment affirms the majority opinion in case law and legal doctrine.

But the Bundesverfassungsgericht pointed out that the Constitutional Court's judgments have not settled the problem of the extent to which testamentary freedom and

[14] U Haas, 'Ist das Pflichtteilsrecht verfassungswidrig?' (2000) *Zeitschrift für Erbrecht und Vermögensnachfolge* 249, 255.

[15] D Henrich, *Testierfreiheit vs. Pflichtteilsrecht* (Munich, Beck, 2000) 20. See also B Dauner-Lieb, 'Das Pflichtteilsrecht: ketzerische Fragen an ein altehrwürdiges Institut' [2000] *Forum Familienrecht* 110; D Martiny, 'Zur Reform des Pflichtteilsrechts' in Röthel (n 4) 21.

[16] Haas (n 14) 249ff; G Otte, 'Das Pflichtteilsrecht – Verfassungsrechtsprechnung und Rechtspolitik' [2002] *Archiv für die civilistische Praxis* 317; H Strätz, 'Rechtspolitische Gesichtspunkte des gesetzlichen Erbrechts und Pflichtteilsrechts nach 100 Jahren BGB' [1998] *Zeitschrift für das gesamte Familienrecht* 1553, 1566. Contra: K Petri, 'Die Pflicht zum Pflichtteil' [1993] *Zeitschrift für Rechtspolitik* 205.

[17] V Lipp, 'Finanzielle Solidarität zwischen Verwandten im Privat- und im Sozialrecht' [2002] *Neue Juristische Wochenschrift* 2206; G Otte (n 16) 351ff; H Zacher, 'Pflichtteil und intergenerationelle Solidarität' in Röthel (n 4) 135.

[18] BVerfG 30 August 2000, [2000] *Zeitschrift für das gesamte Familienrecht* 1563, [2001] *Neue Juristische Wochenschrift* 141, [2000] *Zeitschrift für Erbrecht und Vermögensnachfolge* 339, note J Mayer. See also G Otte (n 16) 326ff; Pintens, 'Die Europäisierung des Erbrechts' (n 1) 640.

the compulsory portion are compatible with one another, or whether or not the constitution always requires close family members to be granted a minimum portion of the estate, even if this is against the will of the testator. However, these questions were not relevant for the case. Nevertheless, the Bundesverfassungsgericht seized the opportunity to emphasize that this relationship might be reviewed on the basis of the last will of the testator in cases where he or she firmly expressed his wish to exclude the holder of a compulsory portion (eg due to the estrangement of the two parties) or in situations where the statutory provisions of the compulsory portion would lead to a disproportionate limitation of the freedom to dispose of the assets in a particular case. Consequently, a large part of the legal academic community had the impression that an absolute right to a compulsory portion would not survive, but that it would be necessary to review whether the compulsory portion and the limitations that it brings about were still adequate and compatible with the doctrine of proportionality.[19]

When new complaints on the constitution were pending a few years later, the expectations were that the Constitutional Court would stay on the same path. However, the outcome was rather surprising.[20]

B. The Facts

Two complaints were decided together.

The first complaint dealt with the following facts: the testator lived with her son, who was suffering from a schizophrenic psychosis. Due to his illness, the son physically attacked his mother several times. For those reasons the mother deprived her son of the compulsory portion on the basis of § 2333, no 2 BGB, which allows a testator to withdraw the compulsory portion from a descendant who is guilty of intentional physical mistreatment of the testator. The mother appointed her other son as the sole heir. One month later the first son killed his mother out of fear and anger for a confinement in an asylum. He divided the body into several parts and buried it in a wood. The Landgericht, the lower regional court in civil and criminal matters, decided that the son was not guilty due to his illness and ordered his confinement. The son claimed his compulsory portion. The Oberlandesgericht, the regional court of appeal, accepted the claim since the son was found incapable of guilt (*schuldunfähig*) and for this reason a deprivation of the compulsory portion could not have any effect since the condition of guilt was not fulfilled. The other son filed a complaint on the constitution for violation of his fundamental rights under Article 14 GG.

The facts of the second case were quite different. A very ill testator and his son quarrelled about the father's visiting rights vis-à-vis his grandson. Ultimately, the father deprived his son of the compulsory portion with the justification that his son had refused him his visiting rights, despite his illness. The testator appointed his wife as preliminary

[19] See the legal doctrine cited in n 18.

[20] BVerfG 19 April 2005, BVerfGE 112, 332, [2005] *Zeitschrift für das gesamte Familienrecht*, 872, 1441, note J Mayer, [2005] *JuristenZeitung* 1007, note G Otte, [2005] *Neue Juristische Wochenschrift* 1561, [2005] *Zeitschrift für die Steuer- und Erbrechtspraxis* 169, [2005] *Zeitschrift für Erbrecht und Vermögensnachfolge*, 301. English translation: www.bundesverfassungsgericht.de/SharedDocs/Entscheidungen/EN/2005/04/rs20050419_1bvr164400en.html.

heir and his other children as reversionary heirs. The son challenged his deprivation and the lower courts upheld his claim to the compulsory portion because there were no legal grounds for this deprivation. However, the other heirs challenged this decision and filed a complaint on the constitution for violation of Article 14 GG.

C. The Judgment

The Constitutional Court elaborated on the constitutional principles governing the testamentary freedom and the compulsory portion. Concerning the latter, the court clearly adhered to the majority opinion of the legal doctrine and invoked both Articles 14 and 6 GG. The guarantee of Article 14 safeguards the rights of the children to an irrevocable participation in the inheritance from their parents, independent of need. The compulsory portion is part of the right of inheritance guaranteed by Article 14 GG as a principle passed down through the ages. The court strongly emphasized the historical argument. Moreover, the compulsory portion is the expression of family solidarity. Article 6 GG guarantees the relationship between the testator and his children as a lifelong community, with the right and the obligation to take responsibility for each other. This obligation justifies guaranteeing the children an economic base with the compulsory portion. Especially in cases of estrangement between the parent and children, the compulsory portion sets forth limitations to the testamentary freedom and to the possibility of punishing a child through deprivation.

The rules of the BGB on the compulsory portion of children (§ 2303, paragraph 1 BGB) were declared to be compatible with the constitution. On the one hand, they guarantee children an appropriate participation in the inheritance from their parents; on the other hand, they leave the testator enough freedom to realise his ideas on the devolution and division of his estate.

The rules on the deprivation of the forced portion in case of an attempt to kill the testator and in case of guilty intentional physical mistreatment of the testator (§ 2333, nos 1 and 2 BGB) are also constitutional. They limit the deprivation to cases involving extraordinarily weighty shortcomings. Only in those cases would it be unacceptable for the testator that the heir would participate in the inheritance. The court underlined that only shortcomings that are more than a disturbance of the family relations can be taken into account. If one would accept any estrangement as a valid reason for exclusion, then the rules on the compulsory portion would lose their significance.[21] Therefore, the second complaint was rejected.

The Constitutional Court underlines that very clear rules are necessary and objects to a general clause of deprivation.[22] The Constitutional Court did, however, criticise the judgment in the first case with the argument that the testamentary freedom was not sufficiently taken into account. In an opinion for the penal procedure, an expert concluded that the son had to be found incapable in a penal sense but that he was still capable of understanding the injustice and unlawfulness of his act. The courts should

[21] R Gaier, 'Pflichtteil und grundrechtliche Freiheit' in Röthel (n 4) 164.

[22] ibid. See also M Schöpflin, 'Verfassungsmäßigkeit des Pflichtteilsrechts und Pflichtteilsentziehung' [2005] *Zeitschrift für das gesamte Familienrecht* 2028, 2030.

have considered this in ascertaining whether the conditions for deprivation of § 2333, no 2 BGB were fulfilled. A *natürlicher Vorsatz* (*dolus naturalis*) suffices.[23] The first complaint was accepted.

D. The Impact of the 2005 Judgment on Substantive Law

From this case we can conclude that the Bundesverfassungsgericht clearly declared the law on the *Pflichtteil* to be constitutional and gave a crushing reply to the compulsory portion's critics.[24] The judgment was criticised by a part of the legal doctrine since the historical argumentation was rather weak and the court did not discuss the argument that the compulsory portion was a product of its time and was now outdated.[25] It was also deplored that the court rejected a general deprivation clause.

The judgment largely closed the door on the possibility of abolishing the compulsory portion or of a reform prescribing need as a preliminary condition.[26] The main principles governing the compulsory portion have been declared part of the *Institutsgarantie*, making reform impossible without a revision of the constitution, which is rather exceptional because a two-thirds majority in both chambers of Parliament is necessary (Article 79 GG). However, the door was not completely closed. The court clearly left a margin of appreciation to the legislator by admitting that certain elements of the compulsory portion are not part of the *Institutsgarantie*.[27] The legislator would therefore have been able to decide on, for example, the proportion between testamentary freedom and the compulsory portion, and to diminish this portion or vary it in relation to the value of the estate.[28]

The Minister of Justice made a reform proposal, but immediately declared that the amount of the portion as such would not be touched.[29]

The main part of the Act of 24 September 2009 concerns the deprivation grounds.[30] Dishonourable and indecent conduct was abolished as a ground because it was out of date. The other depreciation grounds were enlarged. An intentional criminal offence for which one may be sentenced to one year's imprisonment without suspension might lead to deprivation, where a participation of the heir in the inheritance would be unbearable for the testator. Following the 2005 judgment of the Bundesverfassungsgericht, comparable premeditated acts committed by an heir who is incapable of being found guilty of an offence might lead to deprivation if they have led to placement in a psychiatric institution

[23] Gaier (n 21) 166.

[24] ibid 164; Pintens and Seyns (n 1) 173ff.

[25] J Mayer, [2005] *Zeitschrift für das gesamte Familienrecht*, 1442; C Münch, 'Rechtsprechungsübersicht Erbrecht' [2006] *Zeitschrift für das gesamte Familienrecht* 234.

[26] Further complaints on the constitution were not accepted for judgment. See, eg BVerfG 11 May 2005, [2005] *Zeitschrift für das gesamte Familienrecht* 873, [2005] *Zeitschrift für Erbrecht und Vermögensnachfolge* 388.

[27] Badura (n 13) 155.

[28] Gaier (n 21) 163. Compare D Leipold, 'Wandlungen in den Grundlagen des Erbrechts' [1980] *Archiv für die civilistische Praxis* 197.

[29] See L Diwell, 'Reformen im Erb- und Pflichtteilsrecht – Spielräume aus Sicht des Bundesministeriums der Justiz' in Röthel (n 4) 192ff; Martiny (n 15) 195ff.

[30] Gesetz zur Änderung des Erb- und Verjährungsrecht, BGbl 2009, I, 3142. The act came into force on 1 January 2010.

and the participation of the heir in the inheritance would be unbearable for the testator (§ 2333, no 4 BGB).

The compulsory portion as such was not touched, and is still fixed at half of the statutory portion independent of need and the value of the estate. The right to a supplement to the compulsory portion was modified. Under the previous law, gifts could only be taken into account for the calculation of the compulsory portion if they were made within 10 years preceding the death of the testator. Gifts were always counted for the full amount, even if the testator died just one day before the expiration of the term. This all or nothing rule was replaced by a pro rata rule taking into account 10 per cent every year, such that if the death of the testator occurs eight years after the gift, only 20 per cent of the amount of the gift is taken into account (§ 2325, paragraph 3 BGB).

E. The Impact of the 2005 Judgment on Cross-Border Cases

The question arises whether the 2005 judgment also has implications in cross-border cases. Can public policy exclude the application of a foreign applicable law if this law does not provide a compulsory portion identical to or comparable with German law? Can the enforcement of a foreign judgment be refused on public policy grounds?

(i) Before the Succession Regulation

Traditionally, German law denied that in cross-border cases foreign law could violate public policy, when the compulsory share was not existent or led to a smaller amount, unless social security had to intervene.[31] After the 2005 judgment, the dominant opinion in legal doctrine considers it a violation of German public policy when foreign law exceeds the limits set by the judgment.[32]

Before the entry into force of the Succession Regulation,[33] most of the European legal systems did not have a specific public policy clause in their international succession laws, but applied their general public policy clause, which is a part of each jurisdiction's private international law. The clause is often seen as an impediment to the smooth functioning of the conflict rules and is therefore only used in exceptional cases where the fundamental principles of national law and universal human rights are violated.[34]

Not all the European legal systems had the same approach concerning the public policy character of the compulsory share in cross-border cases.[35] In some legal systems, the supreme courts have explicitly stated that the lack of compulsory share does not violate public policy. The Spanish Tribunal Supremo decided as much when considering

[31] See H Dörner in *J. von Staudingers Kommentar zum Bürgerlichen Gesetzbuch mit Einführungsgesetz und Nebengesetzen* (Berlin, Sellier, 2000) Art 25, No 695.

[32] See A Dutta, in *Münchener Kommentar zum Bürgerlichen Gesetzbuch*, 7th edn (Munich, Beck, 2017) Art 25 EGBGB, No 113, with further references.

[33] Regulation (EU) No 650/2012 of the European Parliament and of the Council of 4 July 2012 on jurisdiction, applicable law, recognition and enforcement of decisions and acceptance and enforcement of authentic instruments in matters of succession and on the creation of a European Certificate of Succession [2012] OJ L201/107.

[34] Pintens, 'Public Policy in Succession Matters' (n 1) 393.

[35] ibid 393ff.

the succession of an American citizen and was followed by several lower courts.[36] The Italian Corte di Cassazione came to the same conclusion. However, the case concerned a deceased person with a foreign nationality. The protection of the children of an Italian deceased person was never a question of public policy since a choice of law could not violate the compulsory share.[37] Until recently, French case law was scarce, because until 2011 it was not necessary to invoke the *ordre public international* to protect the compulsory share. In most cases, the *droit de prélèvement* was sufficient. This institute was only declared unconstitutional in 2011.[38] Recently the Cour de cassation had to decide two cases concerning the succession of a French citizen with habitual residence in the United States.[39] The court decided that a foreign law designated by the conflict rules which does not know the compulsory portion is not as such contrary to international public policy. This foreign law can only be disregarded if its application in a specific case leads to a situation that would be incompatible with the essential principles of French law.[40] The Supreme Court does not appreciate the violation of the *ordre public international* in a general manner but verifies if the lower court has focused on the facts of the case and decides *in concreto*, taking into account all the circumstances of the case. Foreign law is not as such contrary to public policy; only the result in a specific case is at stake. Although the French children of the first marriage who were living in France were completely deprived in favour of the second spouse by the creation of a trust, public policy was not applied since those children were not in an unstable economic situation or in need.[41] The court noted that the deceased had lived in California for more than 30 years and that most of his assets were located there. There was no strong connection with the forum.

Since the Succession Regulation has universal application and any law shall be applied whether or not it is the law of a Member State, all those rules have become obsolete.[42] However, they can still serve as a tool of interpretation of the Regulation because domestic public policy still plays a role.[43]

(ii) Succession Regulation

The Succession Regulation (SR) contains the classic public policy clause that was also introduced in other international instruments, such as the Rome I, II and III Regulations

[36] Trib Supr 15 November 1996. See Cámara Lapuente (n 2) 299ff.

[37] Art 46, para 2 PIL. Belgian private international law had the same rule (Art 79 PIL).

[38] C const 5 August 2011 (No 2011-159 QPC), AJ Famille 2011, 440, note B Haftel and A Boiché, [2012] *Dalloz* 1228, Anm V Gaudemet-Tallon and F Jault-Seseke; (2013) RCDIP 457, note B Ancel.

[39] Cass 27 September 2017 (No 16-13.151 and 16-17.198), [2017] *Dalloz* 2185, Anm Guillaumé, [2017] *Zeitschrift für das gesamte Familienrecht*, 294, note W Pintens, [2017] *Juris-Classeur Périodique* 1236, Anm C Nourissat and M Révillard. See A Boiché, 'La réserve héréditaire n'est pas d'ordre public international' [2017] *AJ Famille* 595; L Usunier, 'La reserve héréditaire n'est pas d'ordre public international' [2017] *Revue Trimestrielle de Droit Civil* 833.

[40] 'Une loi étrangère désignée par la règle de conflit qui ignore la réserve héréditaire n'est pas en soi contraire à l'ordre public international français et ne peut être écartée que si son application concrète, au cas d'espèce, conduit à une situation incompatible avec les principes du droit français considérés comme essentiels.'

[41] On those notions see H Fulchiron, 'Ordre public successoral et reserve héréditaire: réflexions sur les notions de précarité et de besoin' [2017] *Dalloz* 2310.

[42] Art 20 SR. The Regulation is applicable in all EU member states with the exception of Denmark, Ireland and the United Kingdom.

[43] Pintens, 'Public Policy in Succession Matters' (n 1) 395.

and the Hague Conventions: 'The application of a provision of the law of any State specified by this Regulation may be refused only if such application is manifestly incompatible with the public policy (*ordre public*) of the forum' (Article 35 SR).

The public policy clause will seldom be applied, since the application of foreign law will be exceptional: in most cases the court of the last habitual residence of the deceased will have jurisdiction, and will have to apply the law of this last habitual residence (Article 4 and Article 21, paragraph 1 SR). The application of the *Gleichlauf* theory means that in general the judge will apply his own law.

However, there are some exceptions. The courts of a Member State will have to apply foreign law in three cases: (i) where the deceased has his or her habitual residence in a Member State but has made a choice of law for his or her national law (Article 22 SR); (ii) where the last habitual residence is not located in a Member State, but the court of a Member State has subsidiary jurisdiction to rule on the succession as a whole insofar as the deceased had the nationality of that Member State at the time of death; or, failing that, the deceased had his previous habitual residence in that Member State, provided that, at the time the court is seized, a period of not more than five years has elapsed since that habitual residence changed. Where no court in a Member State has jurisdiction pursuant to those rules, the courts of the Member State in which assets of the estate are located shall nevertheless have jurisdiction to rule on those assets (Article 10 SR); and (iii) where no court of a Member State has jurisdiction pursuant to other provisions of the Regulation, the courts of a Member State may, on an exceptional basis, rule on the succession if proceedings cannot reasonably be brought or conducted, or would be impossible in a third state with which the case is closely connected (*forum necessitatis*) (Article 11 SR).

The question arises if public policy only refers to fundamental principles of law of the forum or to European principles, or to a combination of both. The legal doctrine mostly takes a middle position and refers equally to fundamental principles of the forum as to principles of European law such as the EU Charter and the ECHR.[44]

The EU Regulations do not define public policy, but their main function is to protect the fundamental values of the forum state against unacceptable results deriving either from the application of foreign law or from the recognition of foreign judgments.[45] The application of the public policy clause in cases between Member States should be exceptional because European law assumes that foreign decisions have the same value as domestic ones. Otherwise, a uniform area of law would be a fiction.[46]

The notion of public policy has to be interpreted in a strict sense. The limited scope of the public policy exception implies that only basic values and fundamental rights can be invoked. Normally, the courts refer to their constitutional principles.[47] However, several judgments of the European Court of Justice have underlined that public policy can be invoked to protect the national identity of the forum state.[48] Nevertheless, public

[44] See B Hess and T Pfeiffer, *Interpretation of the Public Policy Exception as Referred to in EU Instruments of Private International and Procedural Law* (Strasbourg, European Parliament, 2011) 28.

[45] ibid 27.

[46] Pintens, 'Public Policy in Succession Matters' (n 1) 396.

[47] Hess and Pfeiffer (n 44) 29.

[48] C-391/09 *Malgožata Runevič-Vardyn und Łukasz Paweł Wardyn/Vilniaus miesto savivaldybės administracija u.a.* ECJ, 12 May 2011, § 86 and 91; C-208/09 *Ilonka Sayn-Wittgenstein c/ Landeshauptmann von Wien* ECJ, 22 December 2010, § 95. See U Spellenberg, 'Der EuGH und das internationale Namensrecht' in A Verbeke et al (eds), *Liber amicorum Pintens* (Cambridge, Intersentia, 2012) 1352ff and 1358ff.

policy cannot be used to undermine the basic principle of the Succession Regulation: the application of the law of the last habitual residence or the law of the nationality of the deceased. The use of the public policy clause would ignore the spirit and the *effet utile* of the Succession Regulation. The phrasing of Article 35 clarifies this since public policy can only be invoked if the application of foreign law is manifestly incompatible with the public policy of the forum. This is underlined by Recital 58, which clarifies that the public policy clause may only be invoked in 'exceptional circumstances'. In addition, the case law of the Court of Justice indicates that public policy is an exceptional remedy and is restricted by European law.[49] The public policy clause cannot be applied in general, but only on a case-by-case basis. It is necessary that the concrete outcome of a case be against public policy.[50]

Since the applicable law governs the compulsory share (Article 23, paragraph 2h), one of the major questions concerns the applicability of the public policy clause against a foreign law depriving an heir in whole or in part from his compulsory share. The compulsory share was explicitly addressed in the original proposal for the Succession Regulation. The first paragraph of Article 27 contained the classical public policy clause. The second paragraph stated in particular that the application of a rule determined by the Regulation might not be considered to be contrary to the public policy of the forum on the sole ground that its clauses regarding the compulsory share differ from those in force in the forum. From this formulation, it was clear that the state of the forum could protect the compulsory share by means of the public policy clause, but that only major differences between the applicable law and the law of the state of the forum could justify the use of public policy. Article 27 was often misunderstood. Some authors thought in an extensive reading that there was no protection at all,[51] whereas the article was only restricting this protection to the core of the compulsory share. The only meaning of this article was that public policy could not be invoked against the modalities of the compulsory share.[52] The final version of the Succession Regulation has omitted the second paragraph. Article 35 is restricted to the general public policy clause.

What does this modification mean and what will be the influence of domestic law on the application of the public policy clause in the Succession Regulation? Since domestic public policy plays a role in the interpretation of the Regulation's public policy clause, the notion can be invoked as a counterpart to the liberal spirit of the Succession Regulation. It favours party autonomy, with the habitual residence as a connecting factor in combination with the possibility of a choice of law. However, this does not mean that the compulsory share may be protected with an excessive application of the public policy clause. Even if the national parliaments of certain Member States, such as Belgium, France and Romania, were opposed to the formulation of the original Article 27 and have underlined the public policy character of the compulsory share, the public policy clause cannot be used to undermine the *effet utile* of the main rules of

[49] C-7/98 *Krombach/Bambersky* ECJ, 28 March 2000, § 23. See A Bonomi and P Wautelet, *Le droit européen des successions*, 2nd edn (Brussels, Larcier, 2016) 577.

[50] F Bauer, in A Dutta and J Weber, *Internationales Erbrecht* (Munich, Beck, 2016) Art 35 EuErbVO, Nos 2 and 10.

[51] H Dörner, 'Der Entwurf einer Europäischen Verordnung zum Internationalen Erb- und Verfahrensrecht' [2010] *Zeitschrift für Erbrecht und Vermögensnachfolge* 227.

[52] Pintens, 'Public Policy in Succession Matters' (n 1) 399.

Succession Regulation. The application of a rule of the law determined by the Regulation may not be considered to be contrary to the public policy of the forum on the sole ground that its clauses regarding the compulsory share of a state differ from those in force in the forum. The new formulation of the public policy clause does not mean that the protection of the compulsory protection has been extended. Given that the public policy clause only applies in exceptional cases, the violation of the compulsory share has to be very invasive and should deprive the heirs completely or to a large extent of their compulsory share without any other compensation.[53] Minor differences between the applicable law and the law of the forum cannot justify the application of the public policy clause. Examples of those minor differences are a smaller, albeit not very significantly smaller, amount; usufruct instead of full property; a share in value instead of in kind; and differences in the statute of limitation.[54] On the contrary, the non-existence or the pure formal existence without any economic content and a significantly smaller amount may violate public policy. The same result can be achieved through the calculation of the compulsory share and the available share. Minor differences have to be disregarded; major differences should be treated in the same way as a significant lesser amount and may violate public policy.

If a legal system does not provide a compulsory share but provides adequate provision in another form, the application of the public policy clause should be excluded. An example is the statutory elective share in several states of the United States, which allows the surviving spouse to choose between the provisions in the will of the deceased spouse or a statutorily prescribed share of the estate. Such election may apply if the will leaves the surviving spouse less than he or she would otherwise receive by statute. This election may also be taken if the spouse seeks to set aside a will that contains a provision to the effect that an attempt to contest the will defeats the rights of one to take under the will. Other examples are the usufruct or the use of the family home insofar as this property is the major asset of the inheritance.[55] The same solution applies if the spouses have provided for the surviving spouse in their marital agreement by attributing the community or through an *institution contractuelle*, or if the deceased has provided sufficient dispositions in his will.[56]

Some legal systems only attribute a compulsory share in case of need, as in some Eastern European legal systems, or allow family provisions only in case of need, as in common law countries.[57] In practice, this means that adult children who can provide for an adequate standard of living cannot participate in the succession. This result is only acceptable if the child really gets adequate provision. We do not have to value the foreign law, but we should verify that the result complies with the basic principles of the state of the forum. When this is not realised, public policy applies.[58]

[53] Compare Bonomi and Wautelet (n 49) 593ff; W Pintens, 'Einführung in die Grundprinzipien der Erbrechtsverordnung' in M Löhnig et al (eds), *Erbfälle unter Geltung der Europäischen Erbrechtsverordnung* (Bielefeld, Gieseking, 2014) 29.

[54] Pintens, 'Public Policy in Succession Matters' (n 1) 399.

[55] Bonomi and Wautelet (n 49) 597.

[56] Pintens, 'Public Policy in Succession Matters' (n 1) 400.

[57] For Lithuania, see Art 5.20 CC; for England, see Inheritance (Provision for Family and Dependants) Act 1975 (see Brian Sloan's chapter in this volume).

[58] M Andrae, 'Wertungswidersprüche und internationals Erbrecht', in H Kronke and T Karsten (eds), *Festschrift von Hoffman* (Bielefeld, Gieseking, 2011) 19.

In practice, the national case law from the period before the entering into force of the Succession Regulation will play a role when national courts will have to apply Article 35. This may lead to different approaches. Since the 2005 judgment of the German Constitutional Court the dominant legal doctrine takes the position that the participation of a child in the succession of the parent, independent of need, is a rule of public policy also in cross-border cases.[59]

III. CONCLUSIONS

The starting points, especially between common and Continental law, remain very different. It is clear that the compulsory portion will remain a part of Continental succession law for a long time, but reform attempts will aim to restructure the compulsory portion through a compulsory portion in value instead of *in natura* and an extension of the deprivation grounds. Both reforms seem to be sufficient to relax the relationship between testamentary freedom and the family's right to succession. The German case indicates very clearly that the compulsory portion is deeply rooted in Continental legal culture and that the time is not ripe for a profound reform. Therefore, this case is a landmark case.

The Succession Regulation offers possibilities to avoid the compulsory share by moving to another country where a lesser compulsory share than the one in the former state of habitual residence exists or where a compulsory share does not exist at all. In addition, a choice of the law of the nationality can lead to the same result. However, as explained in Recital 38, the Regulation should enable citizens to organise their succession in advance by choosing the law applicable to their succession. As a compromise, that choice was limited to the law of a state of their nationality in order to ensure a connection between the deceased and the law chosen, and to avoid a law being chosen with the intention of frustrating the legitimate expectations of persons entitled to a compulsory share. But, although, in accordance with Recital 26, nothing in the Regulation should prevent a court from applying mechanisms designed to tackle the evasion of the law, such as *fraude à la loi* in the context of private international law, there is no room for the application of *fraude à la loi* if the choice of the habitual residence is not fictitious, or even if a regular choice of law has been made with the only aim being to frustrate the compulsory share.[60] This is an essential component of the political equilibrium of the Regulation. Therefore, the protection of the compulsory share by the public policy clause should also be limited to exceptional cases of gross violation of public policy.

[59] Bauer (n 50) Art 35 EUErbVO, No 11; S Lorenz, 'Internationaler Pflichtteilsschutz und Reaktionen des Erbstatuts auf lebzeitige Zuwendungen' in A Dutta and S Herrler (eds), *Die Europäische Erbrechtsverordnung* (Munich, Beck, 2014). Compare A Dutta in *Münchener Kommentar zum Bürgerlichen Gesetzbuch*, 7th edn (Munich, Beck, 2017) Art 35 EuErbVO, No 2.

[60] Lorenz (n 59) s 123.

19

Lashley v Hog (1804): Forced Heirship, and Succession across Borders

DANIEL J CARR

I. INTRODUCTION

LASHLEY V HOGG is something of a cheat when it comes to picking a landmark case – the case has been called so many times at various courts in various jurisdictions that it is poly-locutory.[1] Over two decades, in multiple hearings and various courts, the dispute between two children of the deceased Scots-born merchant Roger Hog provided succession law in Scotland with a landmark decision on the international private law of succession, as well as developing a number of discrete legal principles that have been further absorbed into the fabric of the law. In many respects, the crucial issue at the heart of the case concerned the law applicable to the administration and distribution of the estate of Roger Hog, who had left property in Scotland, England and France. The issue faced by the courts was to ascertain the domicile of Roger Hog, who had spent time in Scotland and England, and to further determine if the law of that domicile should determine the distribution of his estate. Piquancy was added to the dispute by the ancient forced heirship rights claimed by Hog's daughter, which would overcome the deceased's apparent wishes, and would amount to a considerable sum, if the law of domicile was found to apply to the estate of Roger Hog as a domiciled Scotsman. The courts' ultimate conclusion that the law of the domicile ought to apply, thereby allowing Hog's daughter a substantial claim, is reached by way of an interesting assessment of how an erroneous doctrinal rule could develop within the law at the time, and shows how the courts intervened to bring the case law into order.

There are a number of interesting subplots to the domicile question, including the motivations of the various judges in reaching their conclusions and the authorities considered by the courts: there is a true mixture of common law and civilian sources

[1] The case is reported in various stages in the following traditional locations for Scottish reporting: R Bell, *Cases Decided in the Court of Session, from November 1790 to July 1792* (Edinburgh, J Dickson, P Hill, and J Watson & Co, 1794) 491 (the fullest, though not entirely complete, report of the initial stages of the case in the Court of Session); *Hog v Hog* (1791) Mor 4619; *Hog v Lashley* (1792) 3 Paton 247 (HL); *Lashley v Hog* (1804) 4 Paton 581 (HL). The significance of the case also meant that it was reported in various guises in English reports: eg *Lashley v Hogg* (1804) 2 Coop T Cott 449; 47 ER 1243. References to *Lashley v Hog* (1804) (n 1) are to the report in (1804) 4 Paton 581.

cited. It is also an instructive instance of how the commercial actors, the law and those working within it were developing in Scotland to take account of the still reasonably new Union state. While the international private law of domicile is the central and most important dimension of the case, there are a number of distinct supplementary principles of law which have gone on to be influential. The law of legitim,[2] particularly the means of renouncing such legitim, was reviewed and clarified in the case so that it continued to be cited for these principles in later years. Furthermore, related to this question and the law of the domicile was a separate assessment of the right of a child to succeed to a mother's *jus relictae* as understood as part of a communion of goods. Although this area of law was substantially altered by legislation in later years, the case shows clearly the distinctive matrimonial property regime which applied in Scotland, and the rights which a wife was said to have in the communion of goods upon marriage. Undoubtedly a weak form of property right to modern eyes, the case demonstrates that the Scottish wife did have some kind of independent property interest within the matrimonial property in a way that was unlike the position in England at the time. Finally, the case also developed a test for when a father's attempt to defeat legitim claims by *inter vivos* actions would be unsuccessful. While it could be fairly argued that this limb of the case has not often been invoked in the years since the decision, it has been applied,[3] and it certainly has never been overruled or departed from, and therefore retains the potential to be applied by a future court in a way that would be consistent with modern doctrines of sham.

II. THE FACTUAL BACKGROUND

Roger Hog[4] was in many ways an example of his age: a Scotsman who moved to Hanoverian London to make his fortune as a merchant. Born 22 November 1715, Hog moved to London and married Miss Rachel Missing in 1737. Rachel Missing was an Englishwoman from Shebbington in the County of Southampton. Hog was evidently a successful merchant and made 'a considerable fortune' in London during his time in London. In 1752 he purchased Newliston, a considerable estate outside Edinburgh. When Roger Hog married Rachel Missing in 1737 she had a substantial[5] personal estate. A contract of marriage was concluded whereby Hog undertook to use £2,500 of that sum to purchase lands 'in any county within that part of Great Britain called England', and to immediately thereafter place those lands into the hands of trustees (also parties to the marriage contract), who would administer the lands in favour of Roger Hog and Rachel Missing during their lifetimes. After the death of both Roger and Rachel the benefits of the marriage contract estate would be equally divided, share and share alike, between each of the children.[6] In 1760, Mrs Hog died at Newliston, survived by Roger Hog and their three sons and three daughters. Roger Hog died in 1789.

[2] See section IV below.

[3] See n 104 below.

[4] The spelling of the surname 'Hog' is given as 'Hogg' in some reports, but 'Hog' is used here as the most common variant in the reported cases.

[5] The amount varies from report to report: £3,000 in *Hog v Lashley* (1792) (n 1) 248 and £3,500 in *Lashley v Hog* (1804) (n 1) 582.

[6] See the terms of the marriage contract as set out in a later report of the case: *Lashley v Hogg* (1804) 2 Coop T Cott 449, 449–50; 47 ER 1243, 1243.

Following Roger's death, a dispute arose between Thomas Hog of Newliston, the eldest son and heir of Roger Hog, and Rebecca Lashley (née Hog) and her husband[7] Thomas Lashley. It seems that Rebecca Lashley knew clearly what her life choices were, and in the understated language of court reporting her marriage with Lashley in 1766 was described thus: 'the marriage, having been gone into without the knowledge and consent of the father [Roger], created displeasure, and induced them to retire to Barbadoes'. It may be inferred that the father of the groom was similarly displeased with the match: he had disinherited Mr Thomas Lashley and left his whole estate to another son.[8] In correspondence with Mr Lashley's father, Roger Hog proposed to give Rebecca her 'portion'[9] of £2,000 if he was prepared to give the same amount to his son, Mr Lashley.[10] No answer to this proposal ever came, however, as Lashley's father was dead by the time the letter containing it reached Barbados;[11] though given the prior disinheritance, it is not clear it would have been acted upon in any event. Following this turn of events, the Lashleys were advanced £700 in 1767 by Roger Hog upon their departure for Barbados, but that advance was made upon Mr Lashley's bond. Around 1771[12] Roger Hog made arrangements for Rebecca Lashley to receive an annual payment of £65, apparently as the equivalent to the interest on £1,300, the balance of Roger Hog's considered provision of £2,000 following payment of the £700 in 1767.[13] These facts are set out in some detail because they are important context generally, and have particular relevance for the question of whether or not these payments could in some way discharge Roger Hog's estate of liability to provide legitim to Rebecca Lashley.[14] There was, fairly unusually, no contract of marriage in this case, which could be interpreted as discharging such liability.

Rebecca Lashley raised her action against her brother Thomas Hog, the eldest son of Roger Hog, who was both heir and the object of a general settlement[15] executed by Roger Hog.[16] The settlement essentially left all of Roger Hog's heritable and moveable estate to Thomas Hog. Yet, the settlement was not an unconditional windfall – Roger Hog's

[7] The reports refer variously to Mr Lashley ((1804) 4 Paton 581) and Dr Lashley ((1792) 3 Paton 247 (HL)) in a sometimes confusing and erroneous way.

[8] *Answers for Rebecca Hog, eldest daughter of the late Roger Hog Esq. of Newliston, and spouse of Mr Thomas Lashley, Esq. of London, and the said Thomas Lashley for his interest, to the ADDITIONAL PETITION of Thomas Hog, Esq. of Newliston*, 13 October 1791, 2.

[9] 'Portion' is one of the names given to the right of children to claim from the moveable estate of a parent,[9] which is also known more commonly today as legitim, and sometimes by the older term 'the bairns' part of gear', being derived from the Latin *legitima portio*. A standard term of contracts of marriage in 18th-century Scotland was that the wife made over her 'portion' to the husband: see, eg A Macdouall, Lord Bankton, *An Institute of the Laws of Scotland*, (Edinburgh, R Fleming, A Kincaid, and A Donaldson, 1751) I.5.5. Unusually, perhaps as a result of the apparently unconventional (and disapproved) circumstances around the Lashleys' marriage, no contract of marriage was entered into.

[10] *Answers* (n 8) 2.

[11] *Answers* (n 8) 2.

[12] Perhaps unsurprisingly, the Lashleys' *Answers* in the action before the Court of Session suggest they did not start to receive the payments until 'from about the year 1772': *Answers* (n 8) 2.

[13] *Hog v Lashley* (1792) (n 1) 248.

[14] See section IV below.

[15] On the nature of general settlements, and how they differ from a testament, see KGC Reid, 'Testamentary Formalities in Scotland' in KGC Reid, M J de Waal and R Zimmermann (eds), *Comparative Succession Law, Volume 1: Testamentary Formalities* (Oxford, Oxford University Press, 2011) 410–11.

[16] Many of the terms of Roger Hog's settlement are reproduced in an English report of the English probate proceedings associated with the case, which are themselves noted in another case: *Stanley v Bernes* (1830) 3 Hagg Ecc 373, 415ff; 162 ER 1190, 1207ff.

settlement required Thomas Hog, as universal legatee and sole executor, to use the personal property to purchase lands, and then, together with the estates held by Roger Hog upon his death, entail them in the same entail as that already set up the Newliston estate. Finally, for the sake of completeness, although there were other siblings, they did not join the case,[17] presumably on the basis that the reports' explanation they had barred themselves from claiming legitim was true.[18]

III. *LEX DOMICILII* OR *LEX SITUS*?

A. Unsettled Authority

The most fundamental legal proposition for which the case now stands is a question of international private law: should moveable property be governed by the law of a person's domicile (*lex domicilii*) or should the applicable law be that of the place where they are situated (*lex situs*)? Until the decision in *Hog v Lashley*, the law in Scotland, and to a lesser extent in England,[19] had been rather uncertain, or at least prone to instability.[20] At his death Roger Hog was a wealthy man with moveable (or personal) property located in Scotland, England and France. What law would apply to these assets? At first instance the Lord Ordinary held that the moveable estate, wherever situated, should be distributed[21] according to Scots law, and pronounced the following interlocutor:

> [T]here is no ground for distinguishing between Scots and English effects; because the succession to a defunct's effects ought to be regulated, not by the different laws of the many different countries in which these may happen to be locally situated at the time of the death, but by the law of the domicil, and because it has been in several cases so determined in England.[22]

The law represented by the Lord Ordinary's interlocutor would eventually be confirmed as the law of Scotland, as it remains the law today,[23] but when he delivered his judgment the Scottish law was far from settled. This becomes apparent from the judgment handed down on 2 December 1790, when the case was called before the Whole Court

[17] At least in this limb of the case. Later, one of the other siblings, no doubt inspired by Rebecca's considerable victory, attempted to claim legitim but was soundly rebuffed.

[18] See section IV below.

[19] The train of decisions in English cases seem to have been more settled upon the rule of the law of the domicile.

[20] See, eg Lord Kames, who noted that '[a]bout this question writers have differed widely': H Home, Lord Kames, *Principles of Equity*, 3rd edn (Edinburgh, J Bell & W Creech, 1778) vol 2, 333.

[21] While the actual administration of that process might well involve seeking to invoke foreign judicatories' authority, the rights to receive the property and the amounts to which claimants would be entitled should be in accordance with the law of Scotland.

[22] *Hog v Hog* (1791) (n 1) 4623.

[23] So far as the claim for legitim is concerned – Scottish international private law is to the effect that the law of the deceased's domicile governs the distribution of moveable property; however, what property is considered to be moveable property for that purpose and what is to be considered as heritable property is a matter properly for the law where the property in question is located: see *Macdonald v Macdonald* 1932 SC (HL) 79; P Beaumont and P McEleavy (eds), *Anton's Private International Law*, 3rd edn (Edinburgh, Thomson/W Green, 2011) [24.22].

following a reclaiming petition brought by Thomas Lashley.[24] The Court reached the opposite conclusion from the Lord Ordinary, noting in its interlocutor that Rebecca Lashley's 'claim of *legitim*, can in no degree affect the moveables not situated in Scotland, at the time of her father's death'.[25] This disagreement reflected what nowadays might be described as a 'wrong turn'[26] which the law had taken, and one could do worse than quote Lord Kames's view on the subject matter as a good basis for the next part of the discussion: 'Opinions so different are an incitement to trace this subject to its fountain-head, if it can be traced.'[27] Our search for this fountainhead will alight on a rather more mundane location than Kames's abstract reasoning, and instead highlights the misunderstandings in case law (to which Kames contributed, as it happens) which developed a doctrinal life of their own.

It seems – the provenance of the rule seems anecdotal[28] from the reports – that tensions in the case law began to emerge in the eighteenth century with the interpretation of a decision involving the estate of Alexander Ogilvie, Lord Banff, a naval officer who died in Lisbon in September 1746. Often at sea, Lord Banff had personal property in England, including his effects which had been brought from Lisbon, which were not disposed of by his testament.[29] The question arose whether the moveable estate located in England should be administered and distributed according to the law of Scotland, 'the place of his nativity and *domicile*',[30] or according to the law of England, where the personal property was located. An opinion was procured from Sir Dudley Ryder,[31] who indicated that the estate should be administered and distributed according to English law.[32] It seems this opinion, or at least the gist of it, circulated amongst the Scottish judges and formed the basis of further opinions[33] in which, taking their lead from this decision, the court held that the law where moveables were situated was the governing law for their distribution.[34] Yet, it is fair to say, and was argued by Thomas Lashley's counsel, that almost all earlier Scottish authority had also pointed towards the *lex situs*.[35] Of the later eighteenth-century

[24] First-time readers of 18th-century Scottish cases should brace themselves for an often confusing series of petitions, whereby the Court of Session reviews, and reviews, and reviews its own decisions, sometimes reversing itself multiple times.

[25] Bell (n 1) 492.

[26] *R v Jogee* [2016] UKSC 8, [2017] AC 387 [87].

[27] Lord Kames (n 20) vol 2, 333.

[28] D Robertson, *A Treatise on the Rules of the Law of Personal Succession* (Edinburgh, Thomas Clark, 1836) 55.

[29] Bell (n 1) 513.

[30] ibid 513.

[31] Then the Attorney-General, later (briefly) the Lord Chief Justice. Dudley also attended the University of Edinburgh (and Leiden): see D Lemmings, 'Ryder, Sir Dudley (1691–1756)' in *Oxford Dictionary of National Biography* (Oxford University Press, 21 May 2009) https://doi-org.ezproxy.is.ed.ac.uk/10.1093/ref:odnb/24394.

[32] Dudley's opinion is reproduced in Bell's report: Bell (n 1) 513.

[33] See the footnote in Bell's report: Bell (n 1) 518 n.

[34] *Davidson v Elcherson* (1778) Mor 4613; *Henderson v McLean* (1778) Mor 4615; There is an earlier decision, from 1744, in which the Court of Session upheld the Commissaries' application of the law of domicile on the basis of the 'the law of nations': *Brown v Brown* (1744) Mor 4604. A further decision in favour of the *lex situs*, *Lorimer v Mortimer* (1770), is only reported in a note to one of the editions of the institutional writer Erskine's authoritative work: J Erskine, *An Institute of the Law of Scotland* (Edinburgh, J Bell, 1773) vol II, 601 fn.

[35] See, eg J Dalrymple, Viscount Stair, *Institutions of the Law of Scotland* (ed DM Walker, Edinburgh and Yale University Press, 1981) 1.1.16; Bankton (n 9) I.1.82–83; *Purves v Chisholm* (1611) Mor 4494; *Henderson v Murray* (1623) Mor 4481; *Melvil v Drummond* (1634) Mor 4483; *Craig v Lord Traquair* (1656) in *The Decisions*

cases adopting the *lex situs*, the high-water mark comes with the decision in *Morris v Wright*,[36] where the court is reported to have observed, when applying the *lex situs*:

> Such was the decision in Duncan, in 1738, ... and in the competition for the moveable estate of Lord Daire, in 1744., as well as in the more recent cases of Davidson *contra* Elcherson ... and Henderson *contra* M'Lean ... The determination in the case of Brown of Braid[37], the only one which could be adduced in support of a contrary doctrine, was given by a thin Bench, upon a verbal report; and though not altered, because never brought under review, was exploded by the most eminent lawyers of the time.[38]

The language of this passage makes quite clear that the court seems to have entertained a pretty robust view of the applicable rule, and one might have expected the law to have been settled as suggested by the passage. Not so. In *Bruce v Bruce*[39] the law of domicile made something of a comeback, though, once again, the doctrinal effect of the decision occurred in a somewhat roundabout manner as it took some time for Lord Thurlow's reasoning in the House of Lords, adopting an approach consistent with the law of domicile, to be formally noted in case reports[40] (though it is said to have been in general circulation and 'known' to the Court of Session when deciding *Lashley v Hog*)[41]. Lord Thurlow's partially reported speech,[42] albeit technically obiter, was as trenchantly in favour of the law of the domicile as the Court of Session had been in favour of the *lex loci* in *Morris v Wright*.[43]

B. Early Victory for the *Lex Situs*

It was against this backdrop of conflicting authorities concerning the law of domicile and the *lex situs*, regarding moveable property, that *Lashley v Hog* came before the Court of Session. We have already seen that the Court initially allowed the initial reclaiming motion against the Lord Ordinary's interlocutor applying the law of domicile.[44] Their Lordships were not unanimous, with those for recalling the interlocutor, the majority at this stage of the case, reasoning that Roger Hog had the power to bequeath his personal

of the English Judges, During the Usurpation, From the Year 1655, to his Majesty's Restoration (Edinburgh, G Hamilton and J Balfour, 1762) 33; *Shaw v Lewis* (1665) Mor 4494; *Brown and Duff v Bizet* (1666) Mor 4498; *Davidson v Elcherson* (n 34); *Henderson v McLean* (n 34). Note, however, that a number of these cases were concerned with heritable property.

[36] *Morris v Wright* (1785) Mor 4616.

[37] This is *Brown v Brown* (n 34).

[38] *Morris v Wright* (n 36) 4616.

[39] *Bruce v Bruce* (1790) 2 Coop t Cott 510; 47 ER 1277.

[40] Lord Thurlow's remarks in the case are reproduced in a note to Bell's report of *Lashley*: Bell (n 1) 519–20 fn. They are also reproduced in *Marsh v Hutchison* (1800) 2 Bos & Pul 229, 229; 126 ER 1249. For details of the arguments in the case, collected some years after the decision itself, and Lord Thurlow's remarks see *Bruce v Bruce* (1790) 2 Coop t Cott 510, 516ff; 47 ER 1277, 1280ff. A further note of the arguments in the House of Lords can be found in an appendix to *Balfour v Scott* (1793) 6 Bro PC 556 (HL); 2 ER 1259, 1271.

[41] *Bruce v Bruce* (1790) 2 Coop t Cott 510, 520–21; 47 ER 1277, 1281.

[42] *Marsh v Hutchison* (1800) 2 Bos & Pul 229, 230 fn; 126 ER 1249, 1253 fn.

[43] *Morris v Wright* (n 36).

[44] See text to n 25.

property in England free from any claim for legitim.[45] Such a finding could only be made if the *lex situs*, the law of England, was being applied to the moveable estate. A further important part of the Court's reasoning discloses an awareness of Scottish law's forced heirship rules, and their compatibility with the will of the testator, and proceeds on the basis that the forced heirship rules rest upon the presumed will of the deceased, which will be displaced by the express will of the testator in questions involving moveables beyond Scotland. Indeed, there is a strong suggestion that they consider the *lex domicilii* to be concerned with intestacy only.[46] With that in mind, several judges were concerned about the extent to which judicial comity under the law of nations ought to allow the Scottish law of legitim to be seen as

> a branch of public law which ought to be extended to countries where it is unknown? *Extra territorium impune non paretur*. Our law is limited to our own country, and I see no ground for extending its influence to effects in England … I know of no *comitas* which can extend our law on this head to foreign countries.[47]

Nothing daunted, a further reclaiming motion was entered by Lashley with respect to the moveable property in England (the Scottish moveables had been determined to be subject to legitim)[48] and the case was heard in presence, with a number of luminaries of the bar appearing to plead the case.[49]

C. Domicile Prevails

The written pleadings prepared by counsel[50] for the second reclaiming motion, dated 14 December 1790, runs to 17 printed pages of argument in favour of a domiciliary approach to allow the legitim claim to be prestable in relation to the English moveables.[51] Relying heavily on the law of nations, the pleadings invoke the domicile approach taken by the House of Lords in *Bruce v Bruce*, a recent English decision,[52] and reason from first principles that the normative basis of legitim cannot properly be said to be the presumed will of deceased.[53] Furthermore, the Court of Session was also favoured with liberal citation of leading civilian writers on the law of nations,[54] and submissions on English law which are not disclosed in the written pleadings. On 7 June 1791, the Court altered its previous interlocutor applying the *lex situs*, and reverted to the Lord Ordinary's view that

[45] Bell (n 1) 492, per the Lord Justice-Clerk (Braxfield).

[46] See, eg the opinion of the Lord President (Sir Ilay Campbell) in Bell (n 1) 494.

[47] Bell (n 1) 492–93 (Lord Henderland); see also the remarks from Lord Eskgrove at 493–94.

[48] See section IV below.

[49] Counsel appearing before the Court of Session were John Clerk (later Lord Eldin) and the Solicitor-General (Robert Blair, later Lord President Blair) for Lashley, and George Fergusson (later Lord Hermand) and the Dean of Faculty (Henry Erskine) for Thomas Hog.

[50] It is signed by John Clerk.

[51] *The Petition of Mrs Rebecca Hog, eldest Daughter of the late Roger Hog, Esq; of New Liston, and Spouse of Thomas Lashley, Esq; of London, and the said Thomas Lashley for his interest*, 14 December 1790.

[52] *Kirkpatrick v Kirkpatrick* (note might be *Kilpatrick v Kilpatrick*).

[53] *The Petition of Mrs Rebecca Hog* (n 51) 11. See also Bell (n 1) 500ff.

[54] Argentraeus, Burlamaqui, Denisart, Eujacius, Grotius, Huber, Pickens, Puffendorff, Rodenburgh, de Vattel, Vinnius, Voet, Zachary and Zoesius are cited in Bell's report: Bell (n 1).

the law of the domicile was the proper law to be applied. The judges' reasoning included the fact that the English courts were clearly following an approach based upon the law of the domicile, which was itself 'the universal custom of nations'.[55] A further important consideration was the efficacy of following the law of domicile – following the law of where moveable property is situated would cause needlessly complex administration of estates. The Lord President and, to a lesser extent, the Lord Justice Clerk face squarely the difficulties posed by the state of the authorities, identifying Sir Dudley Ryder's opinion as the cause of the mischief.[56]

The Court of Session's decision was not unanimous, and Thomas Hog petitioned the Court against the decision in favour of the law of domicile, but this was rejected, and many of the judges who had been in favour of the *lex situs* changed their position in favour of the law of the domicile.[57] Thomas Hog then appealed to the House of Lords, on various grounds. There the case was pleaded by eminent counsel from the Scottish and English Bars.[58] The appellant's counsel conceded that the law of domicile must apply to cases of intestacy, but the presence of the settlement in the present case was a very different situation and should be given effect to in relation to the moveable estate located in England.[59] The argument seems not to have moved the House, and the appeal was dismissed on 7 May 1792, thereby clarifying that the applicable law was the law of the domicile.[60]

IV. LEGITIM

A. Clarification, Elaboration and Affinity

Scots law has long[61] accorded the children of the deceased a claim to part of the estate which overcomes any testamentary wishes of the deceased.[62] The right vests in the children at the moment of the deceased's death, and is known in the modern law[63] as legitim. When *Lashley v Hog* was decided the right arose solely with respect to the demise of the

[55] Bell (n 1) 521 (Lord Swinton).

[56] ibid 527.

[57] ibid 530ff.

[58] The stellar cast included Thomas Erskine (later Lord Chancellor) for Thomas Hog, while Rebecca Lashley was represented by the Lord Advocate (Dundas, later Chief Baron of the Court of Exchequer) and the (English) Solicitor-General (Sir John Scott, later Lord Chancellor Eldon).

[59] *Hog v Lashley* (1792) (n 1) 255–56.

[60] *Hog v Lashley* (1792) (n 1) 264. Following the decision in 1792, it was subsequently determined, as a matter of fact, that Roger Hog was domiciled in Scotland at the time of his wife's death, as well as at his own death: see *Lashley v Hog* (1804) (n 1) 620–21.

[61] See generally JC Gardner, *The Origin and Nature of the Legal Rights of Spouses and Children in the Scottish Law of Succession* (Edinburgh, W Green, 1928). At one time the law seems to have been similar in England, and, indeed, beyond; such customary law for testate succession endured in some areas of England (notably London) until the early 18th century: see, eg M Bateson (ed), *Borough Customs* (Selden Society, 1906) vol II, 136–37 and xcvi et seq; JP Cooper, 'Patterns of Inheritance and Settlement by Great Landowners from the Fifteenth to the Eighteenth Centuries' in J Goody, J Thirsk and EP Thompson (eds), *Family and Inheritance: Rural Society in Western Europe, 1200–1800* (Cambridge, Cambridge University Press, 1976) 225–26; R Helmholz, '*Legitim* in English Legal History' [1984] *University of Illinois Law Review* 659.

[62] Erskine (n 34) III.9.5.

[63] See n 9 for other terms which can be used to refer to the same right.

child's father; it was not until later that legitim could be claimed against both parents.[64] The earlier part of this chapter showed how the initial stages of the case settled the law in favour of distributing moveable property according to the law of the domicile of the deceased,[65] but the following points concerning legitim were also clarified and elaborated upon: elements of the renunciation of legitim by a child, and the extent to which a father[66] might frustrate a claim to legitim.

B. Renunciation of Legitim

Much of the case for Thomas Hog relied upon demonstrating that Rebecca Lashley had renounced her right to claim legitim. There was evidence that Roger Hog had made a number of payments to Rebecca Lashley,[67] and it was argued by Thomas Hog that these payments constituted a renunciation of the right to legitim.[68] Perhaps the most important sum argued to constitute a renunciation was the notional £2,000 which had been offered to Lashley, which had been partially paid and was apparently referred to in calculating other payments.[69] It was a matter of agreement between the parties that Roger Hog's other children had expressly renounced their claim to legitim.[70] But, as noted earlier, perhaps owing to Roger Hog's apparent disapproval of the Lashleys' marriage, there was no marriage contract to bear an express renunciation. Instead, it was argued that the Lashleys' correspondence with Roger Hog implied that they themselves understood payments received and promised to have been in discharge of any entitlement to legitim.[71] The Court of Session and the House of Lords were unmoved by the implied renunciation argument at all stages of the case, and were likely impressed by the contrary arguments[72] that inferring such a 'virtual renunciation' was against authority generally,[73] and that the particular facts of this case were inconclusive in any event.[74]

Furthermore, a related question was what effect the accepted renunciations of legitim, which had been made by Rebecca Lashley's siblings, would have on the division of the legitim fund. The answer to this question had been the subject of authoritative discussion

[64] The Married Women's Property (Scotland) Act 1881, s 7 extended the right to claim legitim from the moveable estate by a deceased woman's children.

[65] See section III.C above.

[66] Bearing mind that the legitim only arose with respect to a father's estate at this time.

[67] See text to n 14 above for the facts.

[68] *Hog v Lashley* (1792) (n 1) 253–54.

[69] See text to nn 10–14.

[70] See, eg *Answers* (n 8) 2.

[71] *Hog v Lashley* (1792) (n 1) 256–57. For details of that correspondence, see *Answers for Mrs Rebecca Hog, eldest Daughter of the late Roger Hog, Esq; of Newliston, and Spouse of Thomas Lashley, Esq; of London, and the said Thomas Lashley for his interest, to the PETITION of Thomas Hog, Esq; of Newliston*, 17 June 1790, 8–11.

[72] *Hog v Lashley* (1792) (n 1) 257.

[73] *Countess Dowager of Kintore v Earl of Kintore* (1886) 11 App Cas 394 (HL), which affirms that legitim cannot be excluded by implication or inference.

[74] Counsel made the telling point that Roger Hog had required Mr Lashley to give his bond in exchange for the payment of £700 upon departure to Barbados, which did not have the look of satisfying a future claim to legitim. Though it seems the bond was ultimately discharged by Roger Hog, he did this by a private deed which was not communicated to the Lashleys: *Answers for Mrs Rebecca Hog* (n 71) 9.

before, and the Court of Session was conscious to adhere to its previous jurisprudence[75] when deciding that Rebecca Lashley was entitled to the entire share of the legitim fund,[76] that is to say, one-half of the moveable estate. The Lord President noted that the argument that 'renunciation of their claims by the younger children of the deceased Mr. Hog operates in favour of Mrs Lashley, his surviving daughter' was 'unanswerable', and that 'even if there was any doubt upon the principle, the point is now so fixed by uniform authority, that it would be a dangerous precedent to throw it loose'.[77] While the Lord President's account of the state of the authorities before the case might be open to question,[78] the Court's decision in this case, and its affirmation by the House of Lords, settled the authorities and remains the law today. The result in the case was striking, because it showed that Rebecca Lashley was entitled to the full legitim fund, a not inconsiderable sum of money, and all this in apparent defiance of the deceased's wishes. So runs the logic of forced heirship provisions.

C. Property Subject to Legitim: The Dispositive Powers of the Deceased

Having failed to persuade the various judicatures that there had been conduct amounting to a renunciation of the legitim, and having failed to persuade the courts that the law of domicile should not apply to the moveable estate of Roger Hog, one might have expected that with the decision of the House of Lords in 1792 the substantive dispute between Thomas Hog and Rebecca Lashley might be at an end. However, the case was still rumbling on in 1804, and it returned to the House of Lords for further determination of elements of the legitim claim and new claims arising from the marriage (contract) between Roger Hog and his wife, Rachel Hog (née Missing).[79] The most interesting[80] for present purposes relate to the questions concerning the deceased's ability to defeat legitim claims by *inter vivos* transfer and the claim which Rebecca Lashley had to goods in communion in place of her deceased mother.[81]

The key question pertaining to *inter vivos* transfer for the purposes of legitim related to the status of 120 shares of stock of the Bank of Scotland. The circumstances in which the shares had been obtained were slightly different. Twenty years before he died, Roger Hog had acquired 39 shares 'in his son's [Thomas Hog] name, and with

[75] Eg *McGill v Earl of Oxenfoord* (1671) Mor 8179.

[76] In other words, she was solely entitled to what would have been divided between the siblings in equal shares had they not renounced their entitlements, because the renounced shares accresce to the entitlement of those who have not renounced their legitim.

[77] *Hog v Lashley* (1792) (n 1) 264.

[78] Indeed, the Lord Ordinary reached the opposite conclusion on this limb of the case: *Hog v Hog* (1791) Mor 8193, 8196.

[79] See section II above.

[80] There were five points of law taken to the House of Lords in the summer of 1804, the other three being: (i) confirmation that Roger Hog was domiciled in Scotland; (ii) some questions of accounting related to the moveable estate; and (iii) confirmation of the rule that a legitim claimant cannot take voluntary provisions in addition to any legitim claimed. See *Lashley v Hog* (1804) (n 1) 581.

[81] See section V below.

the special view of making him a bank director, the son giving the father a back letter, stating that these were held in trust'.[82] However, the back letter was (apparently) subsequently destroyed by Roger Hog, with the intention of removing any encumbrance or restriction upon Thomas Hog's ownership, upon the latter becoming a director of the bank with an obligation to take an oath that the shares of the stock belonged to him.[83] A further 81 shares were purchased shortly before Roger Hog's death, again, it would seem, in the name of Thomas Hog. However, while the shares of stock had been taken in Thomas's name, there was evidence of Roger's interactions with the shares – particularly the receipt of dividends and the use of those shares 'in making up states of his affairs in his books'[84] – which suggested a more complex picture. The status of the shares, and in particular the extent to which they were truly beneficially owned by Thomas, was directly linked to the question about their availability for the legitim fund. The significance of this point is that it leads to the deeper question about the powers of deceased persons to defeat legitim claims by their actions in life (and to some extent in death, though by this time few would argue that a deceased person might prejudice the legitim claim by action *mortis causa*). The ostensible reason for the transfer of the shares by Roger to Thomas appears to have been a deliberate (*inter vivos*) attempt to defeat legitim claims.[85]

At first instance the Lord Ordinary held that the shares were 'transferred to and vested in [Thomas Hog]' before Roger's death, thereby placing them outwith the legitim fund.[86] The Whole Court adhered to the Lord Ordinary's interlocutor, considering the question to be governed by clear authority[87] that *inter vivos* conveyances of property could frustrate legitim claims, even where that was the design of such a transfer.[88] Upon appeal to the House of Lords, two speeches were delivered in the case: the main speech was delivered by the Lord Chancellor (Eldon),[89] to which was added a much shorter concurring speech delivered by the Earl of Rosslyn. It is apparent from the speech of Lord Eldon that he was perfectly aware that the state of the Scottish authorities pointed to the validity of an *inter vivos* act of transfer to frustrate legitim claims.[90] Yet, he was not content to take the formalistic approach which had been taken in the Court of Session, which seems to have involved a straightforward assessment of the location of formal ownership of the shares. Lord Eldon was interested in assessing what we might today call the reality of the situation, with particular examination of the true state of affairs in terms of benefit

[82] *Lashley v Hog* (1804) (n 1) 590.

[83] ibid.

[84] ibid 591.

[85] This comes out more clearly from the report of the Court of Session decision than Paton's report of the case in the House of Lords: see *Hog v Hog* (1800) FC, 14 May 1800. Though note the evidence from Roger Hog's banker, recounted at *Lashley v Hog* (1804) (n 1) 639, that Hog had received 'anonymous letters of a very scurrilous nature' which he assumed were from Mr Lashley, and seem to have prompted him to transfer the shares to avoid legitim.

[86] *Lashley v Hog* (1804) (n 1) 591.

[87] *Agnew v Agnew* (1775) Mor 8210.

[88] *Hog v Hog* (1800) FC, 14 May 1800. See also *Lashley v Hog* (1804) (n 1) 593, where an extract of the Lord President's opinion is reproduced.

[89] As noted above, Lord Eldon had been involved in the earlier stages of the case as counsel.

[90] *Lashley v Hog* (1804) (n 1) 610.

derived from the stocks and shares.[91] Hints about the likely direction of his reasoning can be seen in the way that he framed that discussion by posing the following question:

> Whether the property in the stock of the Bank of Scotland was, at the death of Mr. Roger Hog, to be considered (for the purposes with reference to which his children can claim [legitim]) as the property of Mr. Roger Hog, whoever might be in the apparent ownership of it?[92]

His Lordship further developed this approach to valuing the legitim entitlement by reference to a more realistic or functional assessment of the true situation, by acknowledging a concept of 'fraud' which operates as a condition or control upon the generally accepted rule that legitim attaches only to property owned by the deceased at the moment of death.[93]

Applying this abstract idea of preventing a species of 'fraud', it is unsurprising that Lord Eldon should draw upon the English law with which he was more familiar. Drawing an analogy with the restrictions that English law would place upon an Englishman who purported to transfer property to frustrate an undertaking to one of his children, the ability of the Englishman to so dispose of that property was similarly uncontroversial. However, what was not permitted by English law was to have one's cake and eat it:

> [A]n interest of this sort would hardly be worth having, if the law did not impose, for the protection of that interest, this guard upon the parent, that he shall not enjoy his property as beneficially himself, having given it away, or nearly as beneficially as he would enjoy it if he had not given it away; and it would be competent for him at any moment to defeat the obligation he meant to enter into, to make an equal distribution among his children, if he could before his death say, I will give the whole of my property to one child, and that child shall give me the whole produce of that property during my life, and he may contend, after my death, that because I had given it on a day antecedent to my death, that it was given in such a way as to prevent the operation of my covenant with respect to that property. I take it to have been decided in our courts of justice repeatedly that *that* cannot be done.[94]

In light of the exposition of the relevant English law, and its focus upon the true position as regards the enjoyment of the property (in some ways akin to the modern doctrines of 'sham'), the particular facts relating to Hog's shareholding required close examination. With respect to the 39 shares that were ostensibly imprinted with a trust, as regards the quality of that trust and the back letter creating it, Thomas Hog's deposition was notably vague[95] – a fact that was remarked upon with a degree of politeness, which itself almost arouses suspicion![96] Light was shone upon the reality of the situation by

[91] This idea might be encapsulated by the term beneficial ownership, though that is a term with a chequered (and controversial) history in Scots law. See *Lashley v Hog* (1804) (n 1) 624–25, where Lord Eldon comes close to this when discussing the separation of ownership and beneficial enjoyment.

[92] *Lashley v Hog* (1804) (n 1) 610.

[93] 'The children can claim only against that which was the property of the father at his death, subject always to the consideration of what acts can be said to have put an end to the property of the father previous to his death, regard being had to the principles of the law as these respect fraud upon fair claims, and attending to the nature of those claims': *Lashley v Hog* (1804) (n 1) 610.

[94] *Lashley v Hog* (1804) (n 1) 624–25.

[95] See ibid 627.

[96] '[T]he son in his deposition might, without blame, be somewhat inaccurate, and the father might, without being exposed, I think, to the imputation of being an extraordinary inaccurate man, be also in some degree inaccurate': *Lashley v Hog* (1804) (n 1) 627–28.

the evidence that Roger Hog had been paying further subscription calls on the shares, and, more importantly, the dividends on the shares had been received by Roger Hog's bankers. In other words, Roger Hog was exercising 'every act of ownership (independent of the circumstances of the apparent ownership created by the property standing in the name of [Thomas Hog])'.[97] In such a situation, the law in England would reach the conclusion that:

> [I]f you could show that there was the appearance of an absolute gift, but that, at a time subsequent, the son had permitted the father, and particularly for a long course of years, to act with respect to the principal or of the interest, as if he was the owner of the principal; then the mere circumstance of the property standing in the son's name would not determine that the property was not the property of the father.[98]

Turning to Scots law and its authorities, the decision reached in *Agnew v Agnew*,[99] which the Court of Session had relied upon, was doubted (and distinguished, for good measure) by both speeches. Despite expressly reserving opinion about the correctness of the decision in *Agnew*, it was sufficiently distinguished from the present case by the fact that in *Agnew* the benefits which continued to be derived by the transferring father could be identified in express terms as arising from a liferent created by the deed of conveyance, which in turn spoke to doubts about the reality of the situation as regards the beneficial enjoyment of the property; no such agreement creating a discernible limited interest from which to derive benefit could be shown in *Lashley*.[100] Furthermore, a subsequent decision of the Court of Session had determined that where a purported transfer of property was made to frustrate legitim, but in fact the reality of the situation was that the transferor retained substantive rights to the benefits of ownership, the property remained amenable to a legitim claim.[101]

A further complication related to the 81 shares which were transferred shortly before Roger Hog's death: it seems clear that Roger and Thomas Hog shared a design to convert them into heritable estate (with entails). The same test was applicable for the amenability of those shares to the legitim entitlement – if Roger Hog continued to exercise control over the property, or enjoy its benefits, was that degree of ongoing interaction with the content of ownership sufficient to keep the property within the reach of a legitim claim? It seems that Lord Eldon considered it as at least relevant to answering that question to recall that the transfer to Thomas Hog appeared attended by specific instructions from Roger Hog and appeared to involve the possibility of other potential trustees.[102]

The House of Lords did not finally determine whether Roger Hog had indeed retained or exercised a sufficient degree of ongoing interest in those shares, partly as a result of the shared design and the suggestion that the transfer to Thomas Hog was for a very specific

[97] *Lashley v Hog* (1804) (n 1) 631.
[98] ibid.
[99] *Agnew v Agnew* (n 87).
[100] *Lashley v Hog* (1804) (n 1) 633.
[101] *Millie v Millie* (1803) Mor 8215; FC, 7 June 1803. The decision in *Millie* was affirmed by the House of Lords, after the decision in *Lashley*, in 1807: *Millie v Millie* (1807) 5 Paton 160; it is notable that *Lashley* was itself cited as authority by the successful side in the 1807 appeal.
[102] The evidence on this point was considered by Lord Eldon to be poorly recorded, with the result that the facts were opaque: see *Lashley v Hog* (1804) (n 1) 639–41.

purpose, and reached the same conclusion as regards the 39 shares ostensibly held on trust originally – the Court of Session would be required to make findings of fact about what exactly had happened.[103] Nevertheless, the decision did provide an authoritative basis upon which to assess whether an *inter vivos* transfer with the purpose of frustrating legitim was effective by considering the degree to which benefits and control associated with ownership remained in the hands of the transferor. That test would be applied in subsequent cases,[104] though it would prove to be unusual for it to be successfully invoked to bring property transferred in this way under a legitim claim.[105]

V. COMMUNION OF GOODS AND *JUS RELICTAE*

A. The Nature of the Widow's *Jus Relictae*

The final element of the decision in *Lashley* which is considered here is the Scottish law relating to the communion of goods in marriage. Rebecca Lashley brought part of her claim to her father's estate in the place of her mother, a claim which rested upon the nature of the widow's *jus relictae*. Although in the modern law there is a tendency to treat the 'legal rights' of the children (the legitim) and those of surviving spouses (relict's rights) together, not least because the proportions of estate available to each class are mutually defining,[106] the historical development of the principle behind the rights has different rationales. While legitim has generally been considered to be a right of succession, the understanding of the widow's *jus relictae* rested upon the idea of the communion of goods between husband and wife, as Baron Hume explained:

> It [the *jus relictae*] is in no wise a right of succession or representation of the deceased. It is a claim of partition rather, which belongs to her in her own proper and original (native and immediate) right. The goods in communion (so the term indicates) were the common property of her and her husband, during her marriage; and the change which takes place on his death is to this effect only, that her interest, which had formerly lain dormant (suspended) under the powers of the husband as administrator, now revives, – and applies, – assumes a more active phase – and produces a partition of their common fund and estate.[107]

The result of such an understanding was that the *jus relictae* was transmissible to heirs and next of kin, sometimes meaning that a claim could be brought with respect to the husband's estate at a period of some years after the predecease of the wife.[108]

[103] See also the terms of the interlocutor of the House of Lords: *Lashley v Hog* (1804) (n 1) 647.

[104] *Allan v Stark* (1901) 8 SLT 468 (OH); *Rowley v Rowley* 1917 1 SLT 16; *Scott v Scott* 1930 SC 903, 927–28 (Lord Blackburn); *Fann v McDonald* 1913 SC 937.

[105] See, eg *Buchanan v Buchanan* (1876) 3 R 556 (IH) 559 (the Lord Justice-Clerk (Moncrieff).

[106] If there is a surviving spouse (or civil partner) and surviving issue, then the spouse is entitled to one-third or the moveable estate by way of the *jus relictae*, the issue together are entitled to one-third of the moveable estate and the remaining one-third is said to be the 'dead's part', upon which the deceased is free to test without restriction. If there is only a surviving spouse, or there is no surviving spouse but there are issue, then they are entitled to one-half of the moveable estate, with the remaining half falling within the 'dead's part'.

[107] GCH Paton (ed), *Baron David Hume's Lectures 1786–1822, Volume V* (Edinburgh, Stair Society 18, 1957) 163–64.

[108] See *Lawson v Lawson* (1777) Mor 8190; and Appendix, 'Legitim' 1, 2.

B. Domicile and the *Jus Relictae*

In *Lashley* the claim brought in right of Rebecca Lashley was based upon her mother's death in 1760, and, in turn, its success was contingent upon matters of domicile and the effect of the antenuptial contract between Roger Hog and Rachael Hog (née Missing). The antenuptial contract's terms were held not to preclude the *jus relictae*,[109] therefore the central question became that of the domicile of Rachael Hog – if she was the wife of the domiciled Scotsman, Roger Hog, then she would have an entitlement to the *jus relictae*, of the character described by Hume above,[110] and such a right would have passed to Rebecca Lashley. In examining that question, the fact that Roger Hog's advances to his other children had contained an express renunciation of both their claim to legitim in their own right and any claim they might have by virtue of their mother.[111] Of course, as we have already seen above, Rebecca Lashley had never acceded to any such renunciation in a deed,[112] but the presence of such a clause by Roger Hog's design suggested his awareness of his Scottish domicile, and consequently of the potential for claims to be made in right of his deceased wife by his children, even at a distance of time after her death. The question of what to make of a change of a husband's domicile following the conclusion of a marriage contract, and the marriage itself, while domiciled elsewhere was one which had 'been hitherto unprejudiced by any direct decision …' so far as it related to the effects upon status of the wife's domicile, and the administration of any rights to which she might be entitled.[113]

The argument that the *locus contractus matrimonii* ought to be determinative was rejected by way of examples drawn from English law, the differences between the proportions given by the customs of York and Canterbury in the distribution of personal estate upon intestacy, and hypothetical cases involving the movements of husbands.[114] Deciding that the domicile of Roger Hog had already been determined to be Scotland for the purpose of the legitim claim in the earlier case, it was, said Lord Eldon, 'next to impossible to say that there is any distinction to be made between the legitim of the children as taking by such succession, and the *jus relictae* of the widow as taking by the same'.[115] Therefore, the relevant domicile for determining a wife's claim was that of her husband at his death,[116] which might be different from the place of the marriage, and therefore the House of Lords held that Rebecca Lashley was entitled to the *jus relictae* in place of her mother due to Roger Hog's domicile in Scotland upon her death in 1760.[117]

[109] See *Lashley v Hog* (1804) (n 1) 605.
[110] See also ibid 611–12 (Lord Eldon).
[111] *Lashley v Hog* (1804) (n 1) 608.
[112] Though such a clause was included in a bond which Roger Hog had left in the hands of his law agent with a view to being offered to, and accepted by, Rebecca Lashley; her rejection of that bond in order to claim legitim was the basis of the entire case.
[113] *Lashley v Hog* (1804) (n 1) 610–12.
[114] ibid 612–13.
[115] ibid 615.
[116] ibid 617. It would be open to the parties to the marriage contract to agree otherwise expressly, but there was no suggestion of that here.
[117] *Lashley v Hog* (1804) (n 1) 620–21.

C. Development of the Law

Legislative reforms in the mid- to late nineteenth century altered the law with respect to the *jus relictae* and the legal status of married women to a considerable degree. The right by which Rebecca Lashley claimed her predeceasing mother's *jus relictae* was abolished by statute in 1855,[118] apparently on account of the 'great hardship' which this right 'inflicted upon surviving husbands'.[119] The communion of goods recognised by Scottish law would come to be superseded by the Married Women's Property Act (Scotland) 1881, which provided that within marriage a woman would have a separate estate distinct from the *jus mariti*.[120] Therefore the rationale of the *jus relictae* as protecting, and reviving upon the husband's death, the woman's property interest in the communal moveable property of the marriage was altered. However, the decision in *Lashley v Hog* retained its influence as a determination of domicile for the purpose of ascertaining the rights of spouses as well as children. Furthermore, the decision clarified the classificatory decision taken by Scottish law to treat legal rights – both the relict's rights and those of children claiming legitim – as rights of succession and not, say, as matrimonial property.[121]

VI. CONCLUSION

The protracted litigation in *Lashley v Hog* laid down a number of distinct legal rules in relation to the law of succession which have been followed in Scotland since. While there have inevitably been legislative developments that have altered elements of the substantive law of legal rights, particularly that relating to the *jus relictae*, the cases were undoubtedly hugely influential. Probably the most significant dimension of the case was the settlement of questions around international private law and the application of such rules to legal rights. This is reflected by the statement in the leading text on international private law in Scotland that:

> In the cases since *Lashley v Hog* the courts have regarded it as beyond question that entitlement to the *jus relictae* and legitim is dependent upon the Scottish domicile of the husband or father after his death. The principle was extended by the legislature to the statutory rights to *jus relicti* and legitim from the estate of a deceased wife or mother.[122]

The legacy of the case is, therefore, predominantly one of having settled the vexed question of how Scottish law's forced heirship rights should be applied as a matter of international private law, a matter of some importance, particularly in a state such as the UK, where the law differs considerably between Scotland and England while property is often held in both jurisdictions. On the other hand, the influence of the decision with respect to the law of communion of goods in marital property has faded with the

[118] Intestate Moveable Succession (Scotland) Act 1855, s 6. However, the Act did not have retrospective effect, and therefore *Lashley* was followed in cases where the wife had died before its enactment: *Kennedy v Bell* (1864) 2 M 587 (IH) (reversed on a different ground at (1868) 6 M (HL) 69).

[119] W Alexander, *The Practice of the Commissary Courts in Scotland* (Edinburgh, A and C Black, 1859), 24.

[120] Section 1.

[121] DR Macdonald, *Succession*, 3rd edn (Edinburgh, W Green, 2001) [14.14].

[122] Beaumont and McEleavy (n 23) [24.21].

changing understanding of the nature of the *jus relictae* in the context of the development of what is meant by marriage, an evolution which itself would be an interesting assessment.

Furthermore, a subsidiary vein of authority was also substantially developed for the modern law, if not created entirely, as regards the examination of sham or simulated transfers from a husband in order to frustrate the legitim claims of his children. While it would be fair to say that there have not been a great many cases applying that principle, particularly in the modern law from the mid-twentieth century onwards, it nevertheless endures as a principle in the law books. Indeed, the relative paucity of references to it in case law is not particularly instructive, for there are very few cases pertaining to legal rights in that same era, and nobody would doubt their continued validity (despite questions about the incidence of their invocation in cases of testate and intestate succession). That principle, developed with intriguing reference to the spirit and principles of English law, which calls for an examination of the extent to which control and benefit is retained by the transferor, will likely prove fertile should a case be taken in such circumstances.

When taken together, it can be stated with confidence that the various principles established and clarified by the Court of Session and the House of Lords in the reports of the action brought by Rebecca Lashley against her brother, Thomas Hog, left an enduring and substantial mark on the law of succession and international private law in Scotland.

20

Re Estate Wilson, Deceased (2017): The Last Frontier for Aboriginal Intestacy in Australia?

PRUE VINES*

I. INTRODUCTION

IN JANUARY 2017 the first case in New South Wales was decided using a provision allowing the recognition of Aboriginal traditions and customary law in intestacy which had been inserted into the Succession Act in 2009. Such slow take-up of a provision might suggest that it was not important. Not so. This simply reflected something of the disruption between the common law in relation to inheritance in Australia and the inheritance needs of its Indigenous people. It is no secret that when the British landed in Australia they struck a blow to its Indigenous people from which, despite extraordinary resilience, they have suffered greatly. The idea that Aboriginal people might need any sort of provision for civil law needs simply did not strike the colonists at all and succession law was ignored for a long time.

Re Estate Wilson, deceased[1] concerned an Aboriginal man who died intestate after having been adopted by a non-Indigenous family from whom he became estranged. After adoption files became open his natural sisters, who regarded him as one of the 'stolen generations',[2] found him and he spent the next 20 years close to them. When he died intestate, his adopted status would have meant that only his estranged family would have inherited, but for the use of the new provision. The case is simple enough in some ways, but it raises and explores important issues about the impact of law on obligations,

* This project was carried out with the research assistance of Lachlan McFarlane. Ethics Approval UNSW HC 17117.

[1] *Re Estate Wilson, deceased* [2017] NSWSC 1, (2017) 93 NSWLR 119.

[2] 'Stolen generations' refers to the Aboriginal and Torres Strait Islander children who were removed from their families from 1910 to 1970 pursuant to state and Commonwealth government policy. This was part of the assimilationist policy. The removal of children not only traumatised children and families; it also disrupted the transmission of traditional cultural knowledge and laws, with consequential loss of community and native title rights. In 2008 Prime Minister Kevin Rudd made a historic apology to the stolen generations. Compensation for stolen generation people has been given in limited ways, and in only one case has a person been compensated in a tortious action for having been removed: *South Australia v Lampard-Trevorrow* [2010] SASCFC 56.

the stolen generations and the complexity of that status, the need for these claimants to represent themselves in a superior court because of cost and so on. In Australia, civil law needs in many ways are the last frontier for Aboriginal people. This case shows that the barriers may finally be dropping.

Normally one thinks of the landmark cases in succession law as being the old ones. We look back at them and know they are significant because we have seen them continue to make their mark over time – so, for example, *Banks v Goodfellow*[3] continues to clearly be a landmark case. *Estate of Wilson* is a recent case and has yet to make the kind of mark that *Banks v Goodfellow* has, but, because of its significance to the people whose legal system was so comprehensively ignored in the aftermath of British dispossession of the first nations of Australia, it is clearly a turning point in succession law.

The case is deceptively simple. It concerned an Aboriginal[4] man who died intestate. He had been adopted into a non-Indigenous family, but after the death of his adoptive mother, that family did not operate as a family to him and rarely saw him over the next 30 years. His original family had never stopped looking for him, and when it became possible, his Aboriginal sister found him when he was an adult. For the next 20 years he was integrated into his original family and when he died, they became the first applicants under the new New South Wales legislation which allowed the relatives of an Aboriginal person who died intestate to ask for the estate to be distributed according to Aboriginal customary law. The application was successful.

The background to the case is complex because this is also the story of a new law in the form of a provision inserted in 2009 into the Succession Act 2006 (NSW). Although slightly similar legislation had been tried in the Northern Territory, it had been rarely used. *Re Estate Wilson* has been followed by two other cases since it was decided, and more are likely to follow. *Re Estate of Wilson* also concerns a remarkable woman, the sister of Howard Wilson, Jill Bott. Not only did she find her brother, but she also investigated and found the new legislation and realised she could use it.

Many Aboriginal people have taboos about referring to the name or showing photographs of deceased people. This does not apply in this case, and I have the plaintiff Jill Bott's permission to write this. To investigate the background of the case I interviewed the judge, the judge's secretary, the judge's associate, Jill Bott and her sister Michelle Gardner. All were extremely generous with their time and very helpful.

II. THE LEGAL BACKGROUND

As is well known, when the British arrived in Australia in 1788 they brought British law with them. On the basis of the fiction that Australia was terra nullius,[5] and assuming that the Aboriginal people had no law of their own, they applied their law to the Aboriginal people. For a long time, succession law was regarded as something which

[3] See Juliet Brook's contribution to this volume (chapter 4) on *Banks v Goodfellow* (1870) 5 QB 549.

[4] The word 'Aboriginal' in Australia is capitalised to refer to the fact that the Australian Aboriginal people are designated and as a mark of respect. If it is not capitalised it might refer to aboriginal people of some other place. The same rule applies to 'Indigenous' in Australia. Indigenous people in Australia include both Aboriginal people and Torres Strait Islanders. See n 6 below.

[5] Only overturned in 1992 in *Mabo v Qld (No 2)* (1992) 175 CLR 1.

was irrelevant to Aboriginal people. Traditional Aboriginal people did not need it, non-traditional Aboriginal people were poor and therefore regarded as not needing wills, and when Aboriginal people died their communities just dealt with it on an ad hoc basis. This situation continued well into the twentieth century. Some jurisdictions made special provisions for Aboriginal and Torres Strait Islander people.[6] Intestacy laws specifically for Indigenous people were set up in Queensland and Western Australia.[7] These have been heavily criticised[8] because they effectively passed the estate to the public administration. The Northern Territory tried to accommodate customary law in 1979 in Part IV of the Administration and Probate Act. This has been little used,[9] possibly, in part, because it cannot apply to anyone who was married under the Marriage Act 1961 (Cth).[10] Unfortunately the prevalence of missions to which Aboriginal people were moved in the Northern Territory meant that many people who lived otherwise traditional lives were married under the Marriage Act and therefore unable to use the provision.

A very small number of Aboriginal people in Australia, between two and six per cent, make a will.[11] This compares with approximately 59 per cent of the non-Indigenous population.[12] The low rate of will making in the Aboriginal community creates a situation where the vast majority of Aboriginal people are left with the general rules of

[6] Australia has two groups of Indigenous people: Aboriginal people and Torres Strait Islander people. The Torres Strait Islander people are regarded as part of Queensland, Northern Territory and possibly Western Australia. In this chapter, because I am discussing New South Wales for the most part, I will refer to Aboriginal rather than Torres Strait Islander people.

[7] Aboriginal Affairs Planning Authority Act 1972 (WA), Pt IV, repealed in 2013; Aboriginal and Torres Strait Islander Communities (Justice, Land and Other Matters) Act 1984 (Qld), ss 56–60.

[8] Australian Law Reform Commission, *Report 31: Recognition of Aboriginal Customary Laws*, vol 1 (1986) 228; P Vines, 'Wills as Shields and Spears' (2001) 5(13) *Indigenous Law Bulletin* 16, 17; Law Reform Commission of Western Australia, *Aboriginal Customary Laws: Project 94, Discussion Paper* (2005) 287.

[9] There is only one recorded case: *Application by the Public Trustee of the Northern Territory* [2000] NTSC 52.

[10] Marriage Act 1961 (Cth), s 79. This remains a requirement.

[11] A study designed to determine the needs of Indigenous people in relation to civil law showed in New South Wales that 6.1% of the participants (nine out of 148) in focus groups had completed wills, twice as many women as men, and this was true irrespective of the age of the women. A desire for legal assistance to complete wills was felt by most participants. In addition, 9.5% of participants had been involved in a dispute over a deceased estate: C Cunneen and M Schwartz, 'The Family and Civil Law Needs of Aboriginal People in New South Wales: Final Report' (Sydney, Legal Aid NSW, 2008) 102. F Allison et al, 'Indigenous Legal Needs Project: NT Report' (Cairns, Indigenous Legal Needs Project, 2012) found that 10.1% of their focus groups had wills – since this was a project concerning legal needs, it is likely that the number of people with wills in both these studies would be higher than a random sample. In Queensland, a study of Indigenous peoples noted that very few of their randomly sought participants had wills: J Wilson and C Tilse, 'Will-Making in Queensland' (Report to the Office of the Public Trustee of Queensland, Brisbane, 2012).

[12] Most studies of rates of will making in Australia suggest a rate of 54–55% of adults over the age of 18 and this may be increasing. The 2013 survey by Newspoll for the NSW Trustee and Guardian showed a rate of 59%. In 2012, 79% of Queenslanders over the age of 35 and 98% of those over 70 had a current will: Wilson and Tilse (n 11). Intestacy rates considered as the rates of grants of letters of administration on intestacy were 6% in New South Wales in 2003 and 13% in Tasmania in 2005: NSW Law Reform Commission, *Uniform Succession Laws: Intestacy*, Report 116 (2007) [1.13]–[1.14]. This leaves a significant number of deaths for which no grant of any kind is made. More recently the Victorian Law Reform Commission reported 7.75% of grants involved total intestacy in 2010–11: *Succession Laws: Intestacy*, Consultation Paper 13 (2013) [2.23]. The rate of will making in Australia is, however, a great deal higher than that in either the United Kingdom (37%: A Humphrey et al, 'Inheritance and the Family: Attitudes to Will-Making and Intestacy', Working Paper (National Centre for Social Research, 2010) or the United States (31%: AA DiRusso, 'Testacy and Intestacy: The Dynamics of Wills and Demographic Status' (2009) 23(1) *Quinnipiac Probate Law Journal* 36).

intestacy or informal or traditional ways of dealing with the issues arising after death. The general intestacy law is not appropriate for Indigenous people in Australia for two major reasons:[13] a mismatch of ideas about kinship and problems concerning burial.[14] The latter is best dealt with by making a will.

A mismatch of kinship ideas between the common law of succession and Aboriginal views of kinship means that there may be a problem in identifying the correct beneficiaries and the correct children and guardians for guardianship. This could lead to chaos, since the wrong people could benefit from the estate. This is a problem that does not go away with modernisation or a move to urban residence of Aboriginal people, as kinship ideas and the sense of obligation that goes with them remain. The conception of family used by the common law of succession, and the intestacy laws in particular, is based on a nuclear family – mother, father, children – and a lineal view of time, beginning with the ancestor and moving in one direction towards descendants. Because there are some 300 nations in Australia and therefore multiple legal systems, kinship ideas are not the same in every group. However, some patterns are common. These include a circular idea of time and relationships so that people in different generations may all bear the same kinship name, for example 'husband', 'child' etc. Adoption is often very common and is easily accepted. It is also common in some groups for the children of same-sex siblings to be regarded as children rather than nephews and nieces, with the associated obligations being parent–child obligations rather than aunt–niece or aunt–nephew.[15] This means, for example, that if the general New South Wales intestacy rules were applied to an Aboriginal person, it is likely that a person whom the Aboriginal deceased regarded as their child (and therefore owed them that level of care) would be regarded as a niece or nephew and would not inherit. Similar problems arise for guardianship.

As a federation, Australia has some particular legal difficulties. In relation to most private law, the law is that of the state. The High Court, as the highest court in the nation, is simultaneously the highest court of the state, territory[16] and Commonwealth jurisdictions. This means that each state has different common law as well as

[13] P Vines, 'Consequences of Intestacy for Indigenous People in Australia: The Passing of Property and Burial Rights' (2004) 8(4) *Australian Indigenous Law Reporter* 1.

[14] A disproportionate number (approximately 70%) of burial disputes in Australian courts concern Aboriginal people. Given that the Indigenous population is approximately 2.5–3% of the national population, this is massively disproportionate. When I visited Aboriginal communities to interview them for my research (see P Vines, 'The NSW Project on the Inheritance Needs of Aboriginal People: Solving the Problems by Making Culturally Appropriate Wills' (2013) 16 (2) *Australian Indigenous Law Review* 18–32), all of them had had at least one major burial dispute which had split the community. A major reason that persuades Aboriginal people to make wills is the idea that appointing an executor means that there is a person that the law recognises as the person who has the right to deal with the body. See Heather Conway's chapter (chapter 14) in this volume.

[15] Aboriginal kinship rules are extremely complex, but are different from the common law rules in that they are less blood-focused, and kinship names such as 'child', 'mother', 'grandfather' etc may apply to more than one person or generation of people, or may be defined in different terms from those in the common law. See I Keen, 'Kinship' in RM Berndt and R Tonkinson (eds), *Social Anthropology and Australian Aboriginal Studies: A Contemporary Overview* (Aboriginal Studies Press, 1988) 77, 80. Having spent a long time in a particular community might also be regarded as establishing kinship, as the Northern Territory Law Reform Committee has observed: *Aboriginal Communities and Aboriginal Law in the Northern Territory*, Background Paper 1 (2003) 21.

[16] Australia has six states (New South Wales, Queensland, South Australia, Tasmania, Victoria and Western Australia) and two major territories (Northern Territory and Australian Capital Territory). There are also several other territories including the Antarctic Territory, Jervis Bay and others which are of less significance for succession purposes.

different legislation. The High Court may harmonise common law, but it cannot harmonise state legislation. Succession law in each state is different largely because the legislation for wills and intestacy is different in each jurisdiction. Since people move, this can cause difficulties. In recognition of these difficulties, the Standing Committee of Attorneys-General of Australia set in train a Uniform Succession Laws project in 1995 which has had mixed success, but which included the development of legislation allowing for the use of customary law for Aboriginal and Torres Strait Islanders dying intestate. The Report on Intestacy Law was submitted to the Attorneys-General in April 2007. The Report recognised the problems intestacy created for Indigenous people across Australia. So far, only NSW and Tasmania[17] have incorporated the uniform intestacy provision concerning Aboriginal people.

In introducing the legislation to the parliament in NSW, Mr Barry Collier, for the government, said:

> The new provisions provide that the personal representative of an indigenous estate, or a person claiming to be entitled to share in the intestate estate under the laws, customs, traditions and practices of the community or group to which the intestate belonged, can apply to the court for a distribution order that takes into account entitlement under those laws, customs, traditions and practices. If no such application is made, the estate will be distributed according to the general rules.[18]

Mr Greg Smith, for the opposition, endorsed the bill and noted:

> [I]t is worth mentioning that the purpose of the reforms … is to depart from the paternalistic approach previously in place in Western Australia and Queensland. This is achieved by drawing on the Northern Territory system, where kinship structures are governed by customary law, which is recognised by the courts in probate proceedings. The added benefit of the system is that instances of bona vacantia, where the property is declared vacant without an owner and passes to the State, may also be avoided.[19]

The Bill gained the Royal Assent on Tuesday 9 June 2009. No case was heard until late 2017. Since then two more cases have been decided and at least one more is in train.

III. THE BACKGROUND TO THE CASE ACCORDING TO THE PLAINTIFF

The road to the case was a long one. It began when a 17-year-old Gunditjmara woman from Western Victoria gave birth to a son in 1956. 'She had a pillow birth [meaning her face was covered] and she never saw her son,'[20] Jill said. Her mother didn't talk to her about it much:

> She did, but it was too painful so she didn't talk much about it … she'd just say, 'I had no choice', stuff like that … Get upset about his birthday every year … We kind of talked a bit [when it was] his birthday … She never stopped thinking about it. She always looked for him.[21]

[17] Succession Amendment (Intestacy) Act 2009 (NSW), Pt 4; Intestacy Act 2010 (Tas), Pt 4.
[18] Legislative Assembly (NSW) Hansard 01 April 2009.
[19] Legislative Assembly (NSW) Hansard 05 May 2009.
[20] C Overington, 'How One Family's Fight Turned Adoption Law Thinking on its Head', *The Australian* (Melbourne, 20 January 2017) 1.
[21] Unattributed quotations from Jill Bott are from the author's interview with her.

The adoption laws at the time meant that no information about where the baby had gone was available. Jill's mother died before the adoption laws were changed to allow mother and child to find each other. Jill said:

> When she died it wasn't changed … I think there'd been a couple of talks on the radio about maybe changing it. That's about all. But they didn't do it. But she was sick before she died, so …
>
> [Interviewer:] You knew what she would want. So when the legislation changed, you knew that she would want you to look for him.
>
> [J]: Oh yeah. For sure. Yeah …

The adoption laws were changed in 1990.[22] An organisation called 'Linkup' helped people to find each other. Jill said: 'I got involved in Linkup when I was trying to find him after they changed the adoption law. Because Linkup couldn't help me actually …'

Jill was not the parent and she did not have the Adoption Certificate. She challenged the view that siblings could not get access. According to Jill, she:

> [D]rove over to the government printers, got a copy of the law and I thought, what are they talking about? Section 91A, so I was reading it. And I went, nup, they're wrong, because it says here and it says here this is the stuff that you're entitled to so if it's got entitlements … They're telling me I'm not entitled to it. They're wrong. So I went to the ALS [Aboriginal Legal Service] and I said 'They're wrong. They are telling me I'm not entitled to it and I am.' And they're going, 'but you're not'. And I said 'But I am.' And she's going, scratch, scratch, scratch her head. 'I'm going to have to consult a barrister.' And a week later she comes back and she goes: 'Yeah we'll represent you. Because the barrister said yes.' And I said, 'Yes I know, I was right' so I won that one too!

Jill then said 'and in the end the solicitor didn't come for that and I stood up and represented myself … I know. I've done it twice. That's what I mean. It's like all this stuff in my head, reliving my mother's pain, affects you.'

When Jill and her sisters Michelle and Susan eventually made contact with their brother he was 38. Howard spent the rest of his life living with Jill or close by, as a proud Aboriginal man, accepted by the Aboriginal community. He died at the age of 56, without having made a will.

Howard was adopted by a white husband and wife. The facts as stated in the case by Lindsay J are that he was the only child of that marriage. His parents separated in 1965 and divorced in 1967. He remained with his mother until she died in 1980. He had little contact with his adoptive father, who went on to marry twice more and have two more children, daughters by the second marriage. These daughters were born in 1970 and 1971, when Howard was 16 and 17. They were the defendants in the case. Howard's adoptive father died in 1987. The judge held that the defendants had no contact with the deceased from about 1982 and made no efforts to contact him before he died in 2013. They only learned of his death when a genealogist contacted them in 2016.

This is consistent with Jill Bott's view that the defendants had had nothing to do with her brother. She gives a stronger picture of the separation between Howard's adoptive parents, however. According to her,

[22] Adoption Information Act 1990 (NSW); now replaced by the Adoption Act 2000 (NSW).

> So he got taken away for a better life and he didn't [get one] ... The family he was in, the father was ... I think the mother was nice. He had good words to say about her, she was lovely ... And she protected him because she ... Okay so the mother came home one day and found him in bed with a barmaid. And she protected him because the barmaid and the father started hitting her, and he kicked her out on the street. Yeah. And then she went and stayed at her sister's for a while, then she went back there. And he said no you can't stay here. He kicked her out on the street. He kicked her out on the street. A mother and her child ... That's why Howard hated him. Howard hated him! Howard would roll over in his grave if he knew his kids got something. That's what irks me about it.

This evidence was not given to the court. Of the defendants she said, 'But the first we heard of them was March 2016, which was right at the end, nearly three years after we'd started [the court case].'

How did Jill know that it might be possible to use the legislation?

> I knew what the adoption law was. That it said that we couldn't inherit ... And um, I dunno. I just was reading the law to make sure that, 'cause I knew it. Just from other times. I dunno how I knew that but I knew it. So I looked it up and then I found this section ... I saw the legislation and I thought, 'Well there's a way we can claim this' And I didn't have a conversation with Linda [Burney[23]] or anything. I didn't even. I haven't seen her for years.

IV. THE PROCEEDINGS

The first plaintiff, Jill Bott on behalf of herself and her two sisters, filed a Summons for Administration of the deceased's estate on 16 May 2016. The defendants filed a caveat against any grant of representation being made on 8 June 2016 and again on 21 October 2016. Both groups of parties were represented by solicitors initially, but this had changed to self-representation by the time the case reached the judge. The first and third plaintiffs appeared in person, the first and second defendants (the adoptive half-sisters) appeared by telephone. There were a number of hearings and formal notations, and orders were made after the directions hearing on 25 November 2016. Facts were agreed in that notation, and a note was made that the Registrar would attempt to find the relevant adoption and divorce files and any material probate files. The latter could not be found, but the others were. The matter had a final hearing on 20 December 2016 and judgment was handed down on 18 January 2017. Justice Lindsay said, 'The hearing was conducted, in effect, by me allowing each side of the record to tell their story afresh, to put questions to the other side through me, and to make submissions generally.'[24]

In my interview with Justice Lindsay he was at pains to explain that he saw the directions hearing as an important 'getting to know you' event. His practice is to create a

[23] Linda Burney, an Aboriginal woman who was a Member of Parliament in NSW and later for the Commonwealth Parliament, wrote a letter to the judge. She had been part of the NSW government when the legislation was passed.

[24] *Re Estate Wilson* (n 1) [42].

record of proceedings as in the notation above to give to the parties. He decided that it did not matter if some procedural corners were cut – for example, he said that one of the adoptive sisters was involved largely on the say-so of another, and he allowed them to appear by telephone. He was clearly attempting to ensure that with self-represented parties (as they all were once the case came before him), everyone got the maximum opportunity to put their story.

V. DETERMINATION OF THE CASE

A. The Requirements of the Legislation

Justice Lindsay set out Part 4.4 of the Succession Act 2006 (NSW) in his judgment with his own italicisation added as follows:

> **133 APPLICATION FOR DISTRIBUTION ORDER**
>
> (1) The personal representative of an Indigenous intestate, or *a person claiming to be entitled to share in an intestate estate under the laws, customs, traditions and practices of the Indigenous community or group to which an Indigenous intestate belonged*, may apply to the Court for an order for distribution of the intestate estate under this Part.
>
> (2) An application under this section must be accompanied by a scheme for distribution of the estate in accordance with the laws, customs, traditions and practices of the community or group to which the intestate belonged.
>
> (3) An application under this section must be made within 12 months of the grant of administration or a longer period allowed by the Court but no application may be made after the intestate estate has been fully distributed.
>
> (4) After a personal representative makes, or receives notice of, an application under this section, the personal representative must not distribute (or continue with the distribution of) property comprised in the estate until:
>
> (a) the application has been determined, or
> (b) the Court authorises the distribution.
>
> **134 DISTRIBUTION ORDERS**
>
> (1) The Court *may*, on an application under this Part, order that *the intestate estate, or part of the intestate estate*, be distributed *in accordance with the terms of the order.*
>
> (2) An order under this Part may require a person to whom property was distributed before the date of the application to return the property to the personal representative for distribution in accordance with the terms of the order (but *no distribution that has been, or is to be, used for the maintenance, education or advancement in life of a person who was totally or partially dependent on the intestate immediately before the intestate's death can be disturbed.)*
>
> (3) *In formulating an order under this Part, the Court must have regard to:*
>
> (a) the scheme for distribution submitted by the applicant, and
> (b) the laws, customs, traditions and practices of the Indigenous community or group to which the intestate belonged.
>
> (4) *The Court may not, however, make an order under this Part unless satisfied that the terms of the order are, in all the circumstances, just and equitable.*

135 EFFECT OF DISTRIBUTION ORDER UNDER THIS PART

A distribution order under this Part operates (*subject to its terms*) to the exclusion of all other provisions of this Act governing the distribution of the intestate estate.[25]

In order to obtain an order under this provision it must be shown that three requirements of the legislation are met. Lindsay J held that this was so – he held that the deceased was an intestate Aboriginal person; that his adoption and then reuniting with his Aboriginal family for the last 20 years of his life made the disconnection which meant that Part 4.4 was engaged; and that in the circumstances it was just and equitable for him to make such an order.

Section 101 of the Act provides the usual definition of Indigenous or Aboriginal person in Australia:

An "**Indigenous person**" is a person who:

(a) is of Aboriginal or Torres Strait Islander descent, and
(b) identifies as an Aboriginal person or Torres Strait Islander, and
(c) is accepted as an Aboriginal person by an Aboriginal community or as a Torres Strait Islander by a Torres Strait Islander community.

It was clear that Howard Wilson met this requirement.

As discussed above, there was dispute between the parties about whether Howard had known his adoptive half-sisters. The affidavits of Jill Bott and her sister Michelle Gardner both claimed that 'Howard never had any relationship or knowledge of these "adoptive sisters" and was not in contact with them in his lifetime'.[26] Jill Bott even disputed that the adoptive sisters' father was the correctly identified adoptive father of Howard because the father's death certificate does not mention Howard, nor does it appear to have the correct date of marriage to Howard's adoptive mother.[27] The adoptive sisters said that they had seen him before they were 12. However, Lindsay J accepted that he had seen his adoptive sisters more than once and that their father was Howard's adoptive father.

B. Laws, Customs, Traditions and Practices

No party put forward expert evidence of 'laws, customs, traditions and practices'.[28] The first plaintiff gave evidence that an elder had said that decision-making precedence

[25] *Re Estate Wilson* (n 1) [5].

[26] Affidavit of Jill Bott [13].

[27] In a reply to an email from Esther Khoo, the judge's tipstaff, who had notified Jill Bott that the judgment was available, Jill said 'How could my brother have visited their father in 1982 when the adoptive father was already deceased in 1980?' Her affidavit also makes this point.

[28] Michelle Gardner, in an interview with the author, said that they did put forward evidence of the law, but the judge did not accept it. On p 8 of transcript 20/2/16, Michelle Gardner, as third plaintiff, said '[The legislation] provided for a situation frankly when you are dealing with traditional community that does operate on a customary law basis and with a very clear set of customary laws. That is not our family clearly in that sense … We live in the community, we are accepted as Aboriginal people within our community and have always been and … we operate culturally within our own traditions and I think for the purposes of this we do reflect the customs, traditions and laws and practice of our community.'

was given to the deceased's family.[29] There was also a letter from Ms Linda Burney (the first Aboriginal person elected to the New South Wales parliament), who had been a member of the Legislative Assembly for Canterbury at the time the legislation was passed by parliament, and later a member of the Commonwealth House of Representatives.[30] Ms Burney's letter supported the claim of the plaintiffs, saying that in her view the application satisfied the requirements of Part 4.4. The judge noted that Ms Burney had been part of the parliament that had enacted Part 4.4.

Justice Lindsay noted[31] that the expression 'laws, customs, traditions and practices' is not defined in the legislation and does not appear in the Northern Territory legislation, the Uniform Intestacy Bill or the South Australian Bill on which it was modelled, or in any other NSW legislation. The only place it could be found is in the pleadings in *Mabo v Queensland*.[32] As Lindsay J noted, the Native Title Act uses 'traditional laws and customs'; the Australian Law Reform Commission model legislation, in *Recognition of Aboriginal Customary Laws*,[33] refers to 'the customary laws'; and the Northern Territory legislation uses 'laws and traditions'. For this reason, he did not see the differences in the references to 'Aboriginal and Torres Strait Islander customary law' in section 60(2)(o) and the idea of 'laws etc ...' as material. He regarded 'laws, customs, traditions and practices' in Part 4.4 as 'practically equivalent' to 'customary law' in section 60(2)(o). In my view, when one considers the history of the various law reform commissions considering the issue, what is notable is that various forms of these words have been used in a range of different ways and how often they have said that the configuration of these words should not be used to derogate from the recognition that Aboriginal customary law is law.

He considered the Report of the New South Wales Law Reform Commission on Family Provision[34] for the National Uniform Laws Project in 2005, which said that it did not consider it appropriate to specify 'what customary practices and customary laws should be taken into account ... especially bearing in mind that customary practices and laws will vary within and between communities'. However, it should be noted that despite this unwillingness to specify precisely what the laws were in the family provision legislation, the intestacy legislation does specify that where a distribution plan has made that clear, the court may put it into effect. In my opinion, it was entirely correct of Justice Lindsay to say that the differences between the different phrasing of the various words 'laws', 'customs' traditions' etc are not material. They are all practically equivalent to 'customary law'.

However, Justice Lindsay said 'laws, customs, traditions and practices' is a phrase to be read in its context as relating to the distribution of an intestate estate: 'Neither expression is intended necessarily to refer to a complete *system* of law with a field of operation beyond the particular subject-matter at hand.'[35] Lindsay J then argued that they are both

[29] *Re Estate Wilson* (n 1) [52]. In her interview, Jill Bott said that initially their solicitor contacted the Land Council of Gunditjmara and that led to a large number of cousins making claims.'I fought off a lot of people ... [we stopped them] by telling them we were sisters ... [so] They agreed that we should get it.' The sisters met with small groups of elders in their family group: 'And they said, nup, it should go to you.'

[30] Ms Burney was a friend of the family and Michelle Gardener asked her to provide the letter.

[31] *Re Estate Wilson* (n 1) [139]–[159].

[32] *Mabo v Queensland* (1988) 166 CLR 195, 209, 220 [15].

[33] Australian Law Reform Commission (n 8).

[34] New South Wales Law Reform Commission, *Report 110: Uniform Succession Laws: Family Provision* (2005) [2.61].

[35] *Re Estate Wilson* (n 1) [140].

is arguably not treating customary law as law but, rather, treating it at a much higher level of generality, as a general idea about community, which he held was manifest in the intestacy legislation within its context of the Succession Act. When Lindsay J considered the purposive interpretation of the Act required under section 33 of the Interpretation Act 1987 (NSW), he noted that the purpose is to be considered in the context of the Act. This need not be express, and he considered that the underlying themes of the legislation relate to people living and dying in community, that the intestacy legislation has often been changed to accommodate changing social views and that these threads run throughout the legislation.

He said the concept was 'too large an expression to be defined exhaustively'.[37] There is also the fact that, as in every succession case, the deceased is not present to give evidence and the court must always guard against the ease with which customs, habits and intentions can be attributed to the deceased. Here there was corroborating evidence of the relationship between the deceased and the plaintiffs in the form of the letter from Ms Burney. There were also letters from elders and the Gunditjmara Aboriginal Land Council all confirming that under customary law the three sisters would be entitled to inherit from their half-brother.

The legislation requires a 'scheme of distribution' showing the laws, customs, traditions and practices of the group. Again, Lindsay J emphasised the notion of substance over form, holding that this was satisfied by the claim that the three natural half-sisters were entitled in accordance with the laws, customs, traditions and practices of the family who came from the Gunditjmara nation of Western Victoria and the corroboration by Ms Burney. He did not require a detailed chart or other submission to establish this. It is notable that Lindsay J referred to Aboriginal views of family rather than to Aboriginal customary law about inheritance generally.

Extrajudicially, Lindsay J has said:

> For the reasons explained in *Re Estate Wilson*, in my opinion the expression 'laws, customs, traditions and practices' should be viewed *not* as *referring to a set of positivist rules* (such as found in Part 4.2 and Part 4.3 of the *Succession Act*) but as referring to a *general understanding, within a community, of rights and obligations of an individual living, and dying, in the community*. The expression should be read, in context, as 'laws, customs, traditions and practices' *relating to distribution of an intestate estate*, not as a reference to a complete *system* of law with a field of operation beyond that subject matter.[38]

Whether this view of the meaning of the provision ultimately prevails only time will tell. What is notable about it is that it does not recognise the 'laws, customs, traditions and practices' as part of 'a complete system of law with a field of operation beyond that subject matter'. As a practical remedial matter, this may be the best way to give the majority of applicants under this provision what they need – relatively quick, relatively accessible provision of the probable desire of the Aboriginal deceased without expensive

[36] ibid [141].
[37] ibid [151].
[38] Justice Lindsay, 'Indigenous Estate Distribution Orders', paper given at 'Sorry Business and Wills' seminar (Ngara Yura Program, Judicial Commission of NSW, 1 March 2018) [8] (italics in original).

recourse to experts or the need to hear long narratives of the oral law or the dreaming. However, some will be unhappy about the lack of recognition of Aboriginal customary law as law, so that the treatment of it would be the same as if we were determining the intestacy on the law of Italy or the law of the Netherlands, for example. There is a burgeoning literature recognising not only that Indigenous law is law, but also that it involves international legal recognition in the form of the First Nations in Australia recognising each other's law as well as the existence of the laws of their colonisers.[39] In correspondence with the author, Lindsay J has noted that because

> the meaning of the statutory concept of 'customary law' is a legal issue, the legislation ultimately depends for its efficacy on a finding of fact as to the existence and content of 'customary law' … [U]nder the general law, 'foreign law' must be proved by evidence because it too is regarded as 'fact'.[40]

C. The Stolen Generation Issue

In her submission to the court, plaintiff Jill Bott addressed this issue:

> [I]t is now indisputable that Aboriginal children throughout Australia, including in NSW have historically been stolen, forcibly adopted, and otherwise removed by the Aboriginal Welfare Board from their families. The Aboriginal Protection Act 1940 operated in NSW until the mid-1960s.
>
> Our family, as with all Aboriginal families in NSW, are affected still to this present day by these historical laws and policies.
>
> Whilst we acknowledge that Eunice Clark signed the papers that made the adoption of her son Robert James Clark, legal, it is important to place that event within the legal, social and moral regime that existed at that time in 1956.
>
> At 17 years old, Aboriginal and pregnant, in 1956, my mum, Eunice Valmai Clark was clearly in the scope of these laws and policies, particularly the Aboriginal Protection Act NSW. And she knew it. As a 17 year old, pregnant, Aboriginal woman, who at that time, was under the auspice and control of the Aboriginal Welfare Board, she knew that she was never going to be able to keep her son.
>
> The plaintiffs submit that the legal social and moral regime that existed at that time meant that the separation of Eunice Clark from her son Robert James Clark was inevitable – whether by consent or by force.
>
> Our family has sought to reconnect our family and deal with the impacts of the historical legal and social regime on our family at every available opportunity.

Justice Lindsay did not accept that Howard was a member of the stolen generations. This was not a legal issue which it was necessary for him to decide to determine the case, but he said, 'At the risk of courting controversy, but with an aspiration for clarity of thought,

[39] See, eg I Watson, *Aboriginal Peoples, Colonialism and International Law: Raw Law* (Abingdon, Routledge, 2014); A Kwaymullina, 'Aboriginal Nations, the Australian Nation State and International Indigenous Legal Traditions' in I Watson (ed), *Indigenous Peoples as Subjects of International Law* (Abingdon, Routledge, 2017).
[40] Email, 6 September 2018.

I note that I attribute little, if any, *legal* significance to Ms Burney's characterisation of the deceased's adoption as "a *forced* adoption".'[41] He noted that the consent given by the mother was clear:

> I do not doubt as an historical fact, that an Aboriginal woman who was single and pregnant in the mid-1950s would have likely either to have had her child removed from her care by or on behalf of the NSW Minister for Child Welfare and social Welfare or to be placed under social pressure to consent to an adoption. The same fate can reasonably be supposed to have awaited a single mother of non-Aboriginal descent at that time.[42]

And again:

> I do not doubt that characterisation of the deceased's adoption as 'forced' by his birth mother; and within his Aboriginal community, may have added a strong impetus to the plaintiff's search for their brother; and reinforced their perception of injustice arising from their family's separation from him in earlier days ...[43]

Jill Bott disagreed vehemently about the judge's treatment of her brother as not stolen:

> [After they found him] ... They [the Department of Community Services] sent him a letter saying 'Your mother's dead, you've got three sisters' all in a letter. All in a letter. Like I would've thought they'd have a social worker meet him ... They could've blown the whole thing. Could've blown the whole thing. Told him he was Aboriginal in the letter. 'Aboriginal, adopted, three sisters, mother's dead'
>
> [I:] Did he not know he was Aboriginal?
>
> [J:] Nup ... He didn't know. Because they changed his nationality and told him he was Maori ... He was told his whole life he was Maori. I know ... You tell me he wasn't stolen ... [After he found out] he was quite proud of his Aboriginality. And he used to get in a few fights after that with people at work, you know, staying stuff. If they said racist stuff he'd jump down their neck, and, yeah, he didn't like it. He was very proud ... it gave him something to live for. And an identity. And he was part of a family.

Ms Burney had also referred to Howard's adoption as a 'forced adoption'. Justice Lindsay attributed little legal significance to this, noting, as stated above, that in the 1950s both Indigenous and non-Indigenous women finding themselves in this situation might well have had their baby removed in a way which raised issues about the genuineness of consent. This is, of course, true, but an Indigenous child's removal was far more likely to create a huge cultural loss and a common teaching that their Indigeneity was a problem which would not apply to a non-Indigenous child. The fact that Howard was told he was Maori is significant to this consideration. It is very similar to the statement by Joy Williams in her stolen generations case in 1999: 'She believed herself to be a white orphan and was led to look down upon Aborigines.'[44] But Lindsay J thought that there were 'larger facts' – primarily that, for 20 years after Howard was reunited with his Aboriginal family, he was 'an integral part of that family (practically to the exclusion of his adopted

[41] *Re Estate Wilson* (n 1) [62] (original emphasis).
[42] ibid [64].
[43] ibid [70].
[44] *Kingsford Legal Centre Newsletter*, October 1999 (ISSN 1329-0177) 1; *Williams v the Minister, Aboriginal Land Rights Act 1983 & Anor* [1999] NSWSC 843.

family) by the free and voluntary choice of all concerned'.[45] One of the reasons Lindsay J was reluctant to treat Howard as a member of the stolen generations was that if he did, the plaintiffs would be put to proof of their mother's lack of consent and that would be very difficult. They would have been less likely to succeed and, if they did, the decision would have been more vulnerable to appeal.

D. Justice Lindsay's Approach: '... in Community'

Aboriginal people living in urban environments are still different from their non-Indigenous neighbours. Customary law may still be law for them.[46] Living away from traditional country does not mean that one loses all aspects of traditional culture – ideas about kinship remain strong, and many continue to visit and maintain connections with traditional country and customary law requirements. Lindsay J raised this issue when he noted:

> Part 4.4 is full of conundrums insofar as it turns upon an elusive concept of Indigenous 'customary law' and identification of an Indigenous 'community or group' to which the deceased 'belonged', resident in an urban area geographically removed from the land of his traditional Aboriginal heritage.[47]

Lindsay J argued that his judgment

> locates meaning in ideas that inform the law of succession generally: the concept of an individual living, and dying, in community; a perceived need for recognition of just or moral claims on a deceased estate (including, but not limited to, the claims of dependants); and an associated perceived need to provide for those whom an intestate person might reasonably be expected to have provision if required to make a will. These ideas are adaptable to Indigenous estates no less than to non-Indigenous ones.[48]

Thus he very much emphasised the idea that the community was fundamental to the application of Part 4.4. His construction was very much a matter of situating Part 4.4 into the whole of the Succession Act. This meant that the existence of chapter 2, the Wills section, implied that testamentary freedom will apply wherever the individual has capacity.[49] He argued that this recognition of testamentary freedom and testamentary capacity

> both generally require an individual to consult the interests of those who form part of the community in which he or she lives ... What emerges from an examination of the law of wills

[45] *Re Estate Wilson* (n 1) [71].

[46] There is a burgeoning Aboriginal middle class in Australia. In 2006 there were 14,000 Aboriginal professionals, making up 13% of the Indigenous workforce: Julie Lahn, 'Aboriginal Professional: Work, Class and Culture', Working Paper 89 (Centre for Aboriginal Economic Policy Research, ANU, 2013); see also M Langton, *Boyer Lectures 2012: The Quiet Revolution: Indigenous People and the Resources Boom*, (Sydney, Harper Collins, 2013).

[47] *Re Estate Wilson* (n 1) [4].

[48] ibid [15].

[49] ibid [80].

> (as an integral part of the law of succession) is that the paradigm for analysis of the law is generally the concept of an autonomous individual living, and dying, in community. The starting point for analysis is generally the perspective of the individual.[50]

Similarly, the family provision part of the Act meant 'We begin to see, here, not only a broad, flexible view of "family" but also an express accommodation of Indigenous concepts of "community" in dealing with the paradigm individual living, and dying, in community'.[51]

This is a view of the Succession Act as a whole which is substantive rather than formalistic, based on his view that it is about the 'individual living and dying in community'. He recognised that intestacy provisions have often changed to accommodate social change, and emphasised that the legislation has substantive themes of community running through it – he referred to the existence of a just or moral claim on the intestate and a reasonable expectation of provision. In his view, these ideas are universal and 'there is no reason to suppose that Indigenous concepts of family are less informed by such ideas than non-Indigenous ideas of family'.[52]

This is an analysis of the context of the provisions at a very high level of abstraction. It is submitted that the analysis is designed to avoid the difficulties of dealing with an idea of customary law which has been stated as 'laws, customs, traditions and practices' but is not defined. Again, it is submitted that this approach seeks to avoid confronting the view that Aboriginal customary law is law; law which is enforceable and which creates obligations. The highly discretionary approach Lindsay J has taken may be the most practical approach to a remedial jurisdiction, but some people will be concerned that it does not amount to full recognition of customary law.

The requirement that the distribution made by the judge be 'just and equitable' means that the judge can go beyond the strict customary law. That was the case in *Estate of Wilson*. The majority of the estate (approximately $100,000) was awarded to the three plaintiffs, but Lindsay J also held that it was just and equitable to include a small provision of $4000 each to the adoptive half-sisters in recognition of their relationship, although it was remote.

VI. THE FOLLOWING CASES

The Estate of Mark Edward Tighe[53] came to court soon after *Wilson* had been decided. It concerned a claim by a 'kinship brother' – that is, a foster brother within the Indigenous community – where there were no other kin so that the estate would pass to the Crown as bona vacantia if the claim were not successful. Justice Kunc took the opportunity to make some observations which drew on and clarified some of the remarks in *Estate of Wilson*. He emphasised the need to determine which group the intestate had belonged to in order to determine which customary law was relevant. He also noted that the requirement for

[50] ibid [83]–[84].
[51] ibid [93].
[52] ibid [104].
[53] *The Estate of Mark Edward Tighe* [2018] NSWSC 163.

a scheme for distribution in the legislation should be read as a matter of 'substance not form'.[54] He said the equitable and just jurisdiction is to be:

> exercised rationally in accordance with legal principles, including those which the Act itself lays down, and for the purpose for which it was intended. In the present case the court should, therefore, not start with the assumption that the Estate should be dealt with differently from how it would be dealt with under the general provisions of the Act to the extent that apply … nor should the court start with the proposition that the applicant has a right to the distribution order insofar as it has been established that the order is in accordance with the relevant Customary Law.[55]

Justice Kunc also noted that the Evidence Act 1995 (NSW) exempts evidence of representations about the existence or content of Aboriginal and Torres Strait Islander traditional laws and customs from the hearsay rule. With these clarifications on how to approach this legislation, Kunc J held that the claim by the 'kinship brother' could be upheld.

The case of *Re Estate Jerrard, deceased*,[56] which appeared soon after *Tighe*, required the court to consider competing demands within the same Aboriginal community. It was therefore necessary for the plaintiff to prove the 'laws, customs, traditions and practices of the Indigenous community or group to which the deceased belonged', as required by section 133(1); although, in the end, only the plaintiff gave evidence as to this. In this case it was the traditional laws and customs of the Nucoorilmaa Clan of the Gomeroi People from Tingha in Northern New South Wales which were in issue. The deceased was a young man, and there was a dispute between the mother and the father, who had never been married and only lived together briefly, about the deceased's estate. The mother had raised her son as a single parent within the Aboriginal community of which they were a part. The father had lived in the same community, but had three other sons with another woman. The mother claimed the whole of the deceased's estate, which, if the non-Indigenous intestacy laws applied, would be shared equally between the parents.

Lindsay J said:

> The necessity for Part 4.4 arises from the fact that, in an Indigenous community, the concept of 'family' relationships may differ radically from the general concept of 'family' relationships on which Parts 4.2 and 4.3 are predicated: GE Dal Pont and KF Mackie, *Law of Succession* (LexisNexis Butterworths, Australia, 2nd ed, 2017), para [9.76] citing (as does *Re Estate Wilson* at [106–107]) the writings of Professor Prue Vines.[57]

I would prefer to say that the necessity for Part 4.4 partly arises from this fact, which is the most obvious, but not the only, disadvantage of the application of the general laws of intestacy to Aboriginal people.

In proving the content of the Aboriginal law, customs, traditions and practices, the following were produced by the plaintiff mother:

- Affidavit from her mother claiming expertise in the traditional lore
- Letter from Chief Executive Officer of the Local Aboriginal Land council

[54] ibid [25].
[55] ibid [59].
[56] *Re Estate Jerrard, deceased* [2018] NSWSC 781.
[57] ibid [20].

- Letter from the Executive Committee Treasurer of the group applying for the Gomeroi Native title Claim
- Letter signed by 'The Aboriginal Elders of Tingha and Inverell'
- Letter from 'the community of Tingha and Inverell'
- Extracts from publications
- Affidavit from non-Indigenous friend who deposed to the matrilineal character of the Nucoorilma Clan.[58]

All these were given in evidence to prove that under that law the next of kin of a deceased should receive the full benefit of the estate and where the deceased dies without a spouse or children, that next of kin is 'the person who has borne responsibility for, cared for, and provided for the deceased person throughout his life'.[59]

The defendant argued that nothing in the traditional law would exclude him from participating in the estate, but that if there were, it would not be 'just and equitable' within the terms of the Act to exclude him.

It was common ground that the deceased lived with his mother and grandmother and had very little contact with his father, although he had a close personal relationship with his paternal grandmother and half-siblings. The defendant father argued that the mother had excluded him. It was common ground that there was no evidence that would amount to 'disentitling conduct'.

Admitting evidence of Indigenous laws, customs etc is governed by the Evidence Act 1995 (NSW),[60] which provides that the hearsay rule and the opinion rule do not apply to such evidence. Lindsay J observed that the aim of the various enquiries leading to this change was to give a broad meaning to traditional rules and customs, and that it is not appropriate to apply the hearsay rule to material which was traditionally and properly passed on orally. Thus, the practical effect is to focus on the relevance and probative effect of the material rather than the admissibility,[61] creating a situation where:

> The Court must necessarily depend in large measure on the integrity of witnesses and legal practitioners who supervise preparation of their evidence, as well as upon the sufficiency of publication of notice of the proceedings to ensure that potential contradictors are identified and given an opportunity to test evidence as to traditional laws and customs.[62]

This statement refers to the fact that the relaxation of the usual rules means that the court may need to use its discretion to exclude unfairly prejudicial or misleading evidence as provided in section 135 of the Evidence Act.

In *Jerrard*, the basic test set out in *Wilson* and affirmed in *Tighe* was confirmed:

> Had the deceased … been required to make a will disposing of his estate, what are the terms of the will he would have made having regard to the interests of any person who had a just or

[58] Adapted from ibid [11].
[59] ibid [10].
[60] Introduced into the Act in 2007.
[61] *Jerrard* (n 55) [76].
[62] ibid [79], drawing on *Re Estate Wilson* (n 1) [173].

> moral claim on him, and the interests of those for whom he might reasonably be expected to have made provision, paying due regard, in all the circumstances, to what would be just and equitable?[63]

And:

> The utility of such a question is that it focuses attention on a deceased person's testamentary freedom; the possibility that there are people who might be thought to have had a just or moral claim upon him or her; and the possibility that there are also people for whom he or she might have been expected to make provision, as factors bearing upon what might, in all the circumstances, be just and equitable, weighing everything in the context of the traditional customary law of the deceased's Indigenous community.[64]

VII. CONCLUSION

Australia has not treated its Indigenous people well. The gap in health and welfare remains enormous, and their treatment by the law has contributed to this gap. The failure to recognise the existence of the legal system of the longest continuous culture in the world, whose longevity makes the common law look new, has extended to the civil law for far too long. The recognition of Indigenous customary law which the Succession Act 2006 (NSW), Part 4 provides is a small, but significant, step in redressing this imbalance. *Estate of Wilson* embodies some of the tension between the mainstream law and customary law in its dealing with the first case concerning the new legislation. Because this is an example of the common law attempting to bring the customary law 'into the tent', it may not satisfy the purists in every aspect, but it stands as a powerful beginning to a new jurisdiction – clearly a benchmark succession law case for Australia.

[63] *Jerrard* (n 55) [124].
[64] ibid [126].

Index

Introductory Note

References such as '178–79' indicate (not necessarily continuous) discussion of a topic across a range of pages. Wherever possible in the case of topics with many references, these have either been divided into sub-topics or only the most significant discussions of the topic are listed. Because the entire work is about 'succession', the use of this term (and certain others which occur constantly throughout the book) as an entry point has been minimised. Information will be found under the corresponding detailed topics.

www.ingramcontent.com/pod-product-compliance
Lightning Source LLC
Chambersburg PA
CBHW051149180926
51611CB00001B/6